BMW R1200 Twins
Service and Repair Manual

by Phil Mather

Models covered

(4598-336-6AI1)

R1200 GS. 1170cc. 2004 to 2009
R1200 GS Adventure. 1170cc. 2006 to 2009
R1200 ST. 1170cc. 2005 to 2007
R1200 RT. 1170cc. 2005 to 2009
R1200 S. 1170cc. 2006 to 2008
R1200 R. 1170cc. 2007 to 2009

© Haynes Publishing 2009

A book in the **Haynes Service and Repair Manual Series**

ISBN 978 1 84425 801 7

British Library Cataloguing in Publication Data
A catalogue record for this book is available from the British Library

Library of Congress Control Number 2008938313

Printed in the USA

Haynes Publishing
Sparkford, Yeovil, Somerset BA22 7JJ, England

Haynes North America, Inc
861 Lawrence Drive, Newbury Park, California 91320, USA

Haynes Publishing Nordiska AB
Box 1504, 751 45 UPPSALA, Sweden

ABCDE
FGHIJ
KLMNO
PQR

Contents

LIVING WITH YOUR BMW R1200

Introduction

Pre-ride checks

MAINTENANCE

Routine maintenance and servicing

Contents

REPAIRS AND OVERHAUL

BMW – They did it their way

by Julian Ryder

BMW - Bayerische Motoren Werke

If you were looking for a theme tune for BMW's engineering philosophy you'd have to look no further than Francis Albert Sinatra's best known ditty: 'I did it my way.' The Bayerische Motoren Werke, like their countrymen at Porsche, takes precious little notice of the way anyone else does it, point this out to a factory representative and you will get a reply starting: 'We at BMW... '. The implication is clear.

It was always like that. The first BMW motorcycle, the R32, was, according to motoring sage L J K Setright: 'the first really outstanding post-War design, argued from first principles and uncorrupted by established practice. It founded a new German school of design, it established a BMW tradition destined to survive unbroken from 1923 to the present day.' That tradition was, of course, the boxer twin. The nickname 'boxer' for an opposed twin is thought to derive from the fact that the pistons travel horizontally towards and away from each other like the fists of boxers.

Before this first complete motorcycle, BMW had built a horizontally-opposed fore-and-aft

The roots of the GS range go back to the 2-valve Boxer engine, seen here fitted to the second generation R80GS

boxer engine for the Victoria company of Nuremburg. It was a close copy of the British Douglas motor which the company's chief engineer Max Friz admired, a fact the company's official history confirms despite what some current devotees of the marque will claim. In fact BMW didn't really want to make motorcycles at all, originally it was an aero-engine company - a fact celebrated in the blue-and-white tank badge that is symbolic of a propeller. But in Germany after the Treaty of Versailles such potentially warlike work was forbidden to domestic companies and BMW had to diversify, albeit reluctantly.

Friz was known to have a very low opinion of motorcycles and chose the Douglas to copy simply because he saw it as fundamentally a good solution to the engineering problem of powering a two-wheeler. In the R32 the engine was arranged with the crankshaft in-line with the axis of the bike and the cylinders sticking out into the cooling airflow, giving a very low centre-of-gravity and perfect vibration-free primary balance. It wasn't just the motor's layout that departed from normal practice, the clutch was a single-plate type as used in cars, final drive was by shaft and the rear wheel could be removed quickly. The frame and suspension were equally sophisticated, but the bike was quite heavy. Most of that description could be equally well applied to any of the boxer-engined bikes BMW made in the next 70-plus years.

With the introduction of the 4-valve engine, the R1100GS and R1150GS models followed . . .

Development within the surprisingly flexible confines of the boxer concept was quick. The second BMW, the R37 of 1925, retained the 68 x 68 mm Douglas bore and stroke but had overhead valves in place of the side valves. In 1928 two major milestones were passed. First, BMW acquired the car manufacturer Dixi and started manufacturing a left-hand-drive version of the Austin 7 under license. Secondly, the larger engined R62 and R63 appeared, the latter being an OHV sportster that would be the basis of BMW's sporting and record-breaking exploits before the Second World War.

The 1930s was the era of speed records on land, on sea and in the air, and the name of Ernst Henne is in the record books no fewer than ten times: eight for two-wheeled exploits, twice for wheel-on-a-stick 'sidecar' world records. At first he was on the R63 with supercharging, but in 1936 he switched to the 500 cc R5, high-pushrod design reminiscent of the latest generation of BMW twins. Chain-driven camshafts operated short pushrods which opened valves with hairpin - not coil - springs. A pure racing version of this motor also appeared, this time with shaft and bevel-gear driven overhead camshafts, but with short rockers operating the valves so the engine can't be called a true DOHC design. Again with the aid

. . . and were superseded by the R1200GS in late 2003

of a blower, this was the motor that powered the GP 500s of the late '30s to many wins including the 1939 Senior TT. After the War, this layout would re-emerge in the immortal Rennsport.

From 1939 to 1945 BMW were fully occupied making military machinery, notably the R75 sidecar for the army. The factory didn't restart production until 1948, and then only with a lightweight single. There was a false start in 1950 and a slump in sales in 1953 that endangered the whole company, before the situation was rescued by one of the truly classic boxers. Their first post-War twin had been the R51/2, and naturally it was very close to the pre-War model although simplified to a single-camshaft layout. Nevertheless, it was still a relatively advanced OHV design not a sidevalve sidecar tug which enabled a face-lift for the 1955 models to do the marketing trick.

The 1955 models got a swinging arm - at both ends. The old plunger rear suspension was replaced by a swinging arm while leading-link Earles forks adorned the front. Thus were born the R50, the R60 and the R69. The European market found these new bikes far too expensive compared to British twins but America saved the day, buying most of the company's output. The car side of the company also found a product the market wanted, a small sports-car powered by a modified bike engine, thus BMW's last crisis was averted

In 1960 the Earles fork models were updated and the R69S was launched with more power, closer transmission ratios and those funny little indicators on the ends of the handlebars. Very little changed during the '60s, apart from US export models getting telescopic forks, but in 1970 everything changed...

The R1200GS Adventure is established as one of the best long distance enduro bikes

The move to Spandau and a new line of Boxers

BMW's bike side had outgrown its site in Munich at the company's head-quarters, so, taking advantage of government subsidies for enterprises that located to what was then West Berlin, surrounded by the still Communist DDR, BMW built a new motorcycle assembly plant at Spandau in Berlin. It opened in 1969, producing a completely new range of boxers, the 5-series, which begat the 6-series, which begat the 7-series.

In 1976, at the same time as the launch of the 7-series the first RS boxer appeared. It's hard to believe now, but it was the only fully faired motorcycle, and it set the pattern for all BMWs, not just boxers, to come. The RS suffix came to mean a wonderfully efficient fairing that didn't spoil a sporty riding position. More sedate types could buy the RT version with a massive but no less efficient fairing that protected a more upright rider. Both bikes could carry luggage in a civilised fashion, too, thanks to purpose-built Krauser panniers. Both the RT and RS were uncommonly civilised motorcycles for their time.

When the boxer got its next major makeover in late 1980 BMW did something no-one thought possible, they made a boxer trail bike, the R80G/S. This wasn't without precedent as various supermen had wrestled 750 cc boxers to honours in the ISDT and in '81 Hubert Auriol won the Paris-Dakar on a factory boxer. Some heretics even dared to suggest the roadgoing G/S was the best boxer ever.

The K-series

By the end of the '70s the boxer was looking more and more dated alongside the opposition, and when the motorcycle division's management was shaken up at the beginning of 1979 the

The R1200ST fills the sport tourer sector of the range

team working on the boxer replacement was doubled in size. The first new bike wasn't launched until late '83, but when it was it was clear that BMW had got as far away from the boxer concept as possible.

The powerplant was an in-line water-cooled DOHC four just like all the Japanese opposition, but typically BMW did it their way by aligning the motor so its crank was parallel to the axis of the bike and lying the motor on it side. In line with their normal practice, there was a car-type clutch, shaft drive and a single-sided swinging arm. It was totally novel yet oddly familiar. And when RT and RS version were introduced to supplement the basic naked bike, the new K-series 'flying bricks' felt even more familiar.

It was clear that BMW wanted the new four, and the three-cylinder 750 that followed it, to be the mainstay of the company's production - but in a further analogy with Porsche the customers simply wouldn't let go of the old boxer. Just as Porsche were forced to keep the 911 in production so BMW had to keep the old air-cooled boxer going by pressure from their customers. It kept going until 1995, during which time the K-bikes had debuted four-valve heads and ABS. And when the latest generation of BMWs appeared in 1993 what were they? Boxers. Granted they were four-valve, air/ oil-cooled and equipped with non-telescopic fork front ends, but they were still boxers. And that high camshaft, short pushrod layout looked remarkably similar to something that had gone before...

The New 4-valve Boxers

Even by BMW's standards, the new-generation Boxers were a shock. Maybe we shouldn't have been surprised after the lateral thinking that gave us the K-series, but the way in which the men from Munich took the old opposed-twin Boxer concept that launched the company and projected it into the 21st-Century was nothing short of breath-taking in its audacity. About the only design features the old and new Boxers had in common was that they both had two wheels and two cylinders. The 4-valve engine was produced in 850 and 1100 cc version, with the later eventually being upgraded to 1150 cc for GS, R, RS and RT versions, and stretched further to 1200 cc for the C model made famous in the 007 film Golden Eye.

The new bikes mixed old and new technology in a very clever way. Fuel injection and four-valve heads were very cutting

Overall luxury is provided by the fully loaded R1200RT

The R1200S benefits from uprated suspension, considerable weight saving and a more highly tuned engine

edge, high camshafts operating pushrods (for ground clearance) and air cooling (albeit with some substantial help from oil) was not. The really revolutionary stuff was in the chassis department: Telelever at the front and Paralever at the rear bolted to the motor via tubular steel sub-frames and nothing in the way of a conventional frame in the middle. The Telelever front fork is carried on a couple of wishbones with anti-dive built into the linkage. Rear Paralever suspension uses a single-sided swingingarm with a shaft drive running inside it which forms not quite a parallelogram shaped system with a tie-arm running from just below to the swinging arm pivot to the rear hub. It ensures the rear axle moves in an (almost) straight line and suppresses the old BMW habit of the rear end rising when the throttle is opened. The styling was also anything but safe; the old cliché of the boring BMW was blown out of the water.

The R1200 Models

Ten years after the first four-valve Boxers appeared, the third generation was ready to roll. As usual with BMW, things progressed in an orderly fashion from 1994 when the first R1100GS appeared, then the R1150GS in 2002 and ultimately to the R1200GS in 2004. However, the new 1200cc bike is so different from its predecessors it should be considered a new model. The fact the 1200GS is 30kg lighter than the 1150 should give you an idea just how much changed. The motor is lighter and uses a balance shaft for the first time, the chassis is new with the linkarm of the Paralever rear suspension above the swinging arm not below it. Among a host of improvements, perhaps the most revolutionary is the Single Wire System using technology borrowed from the car world. This is basically a CAN-bus wiring circuit rather than a wiring loom connecting all control units and power-consuming components. No fuses, no relays (except for the starter motor) and built-in diagnostics make this a contender for the first motorcycle electrical system that looks like it was actually designed in the 21st-Century.

The GS gets first mention as it has become BMW's most popular model and was the first of the new generation models to get into the showrooms. No other manufacturer has had anywhere near this sort of success for a model that can trace its origins back to the Paris-Dakar bikes of the late 1970s and before that semi-official specials used in the International Six days Trial in the days when that event carried a lot of prestige and competitors had to ride bikes built in their own countries. Of course you'd have to be one of those Paris-Dakar heroes to contemplate taking one of today's GSs off road, but they have become favourites of riders who want to do big distances in comfort without riding a full-on tourer. Perhaps the best publicity a motorcycle has ever had came from Ewan McGregor and Charlie Boorman's TV programme 'The Long Way Round' in which the film star and his friend rode two 1150GS BMWs on their long-distance odyssey. The result was waiting lists at BMW dealers and GS-models also have the benefit of stronger residual values than just about anything else on the roads.

BMW define the GS as an 'Adventure Sports' motorcycle, which sums it up nicely. A GS is a bike that will take you just about anywhere and is equally at home on motorways, mountain hairpins and dusty tracks in the middle of nowhere.

Once BMW had got the GS launched, the R1200 ST and RT appeared in 2005. These models carried on BMW's tradition of cleverly differentiated sports tourer and full-house tourer, two motorcycles that look quite similar on paper but exhibit very different characters on the road.

The model that skipped the 1150cc phase of development was the S, the true sports bike with which BMW openly looked to take sales away from the Japanese and Italians. The R1200S that appeared in 2006 was the most powerful Boxer ever made with a 122hp engine, and with a whopping 18kg weight saving over the old 1100cc model was more than handy on the race track – not historically the Boxer's natural habitat. BMW gave it the best possible shop window by running a race series at MotoGP meetings. A highly competitive series well supported by national importers provided some startlingly fast and cut-throat racing as well as putting a few old heroes like Randy Mamola back on track.

A naked style model was added to the range in late 2006 in the form of the R1200R. It was much more agile than the R1150R classic roadster it replaced, being both lighter and more powerful.

The 1200 Boxer range covers all the bases from super sports to two-up tourer but it is the GS that has come to be the flagship and the big seller. Just in case the standard model isn't quite hardcore enough, 2006 saw the launch of the GS Adventure with giant 33-litre fuel tank, wire-spoked wheels, engine guards and a tough stainless-steel luggage rack for those who really do want to go The Long Way Round. The GS range doesn't stop there, for serious enduro riders, there's the HP2, that's HP for high performance. BMW have inserted a tuned Boxer engine into a completely new chassis to produce the ultimate competition machine.

The R1200 R naked roadster

Acknowledgements

Our thanks are due to CW Motorcycles of Dorchester who supplied the machines featured in the illustrations throughout this manual. We would also like to thank NGK Spark Plugs (UK) Ltd for supplying the colour spark plug condition photographs, the Avon Rubber Company for supplying information on tyre fitting and Draper Tools Ltd for some of the workshop tools shown.

Thanks are also due to Julian Ryder who wrote the introduction 'BMW – They did it their way' and to BMW (GB) Ltd. who supplied model photographs.

About this Manual

The aim of this manual is to help you get the best value from your motorcycle. It can do so in several ways. It can help you decide what work must be done, even if you choose to have it done by a dealer; it provides information and procedures for routine maintenance and servicing; and it offers diagnostic and repair procedures to follow when trouble occurs.

We hope you use the manual to tackle the work yourself. For many simpler jobs, doing it yourself may be quicker than arranging an appointment to get the motorcycle into a dealer and making the trips to leave it and pick it up. More importantly, a lot of money can be saved by avoiding the expense the shop must pass on to you to cover its labour and overhead costs. An added benefit is the sense of satisfaction and accomplishment that you feel after doing the job yourself.

References to the left or right side of the motorcycle assume you are sitting on the seat, facing forward.

We take great pride in the accuracy of information given in this manual, but motorcycle manufacturers make alterations and design changes during the production run of a particular motorcycle of which they do not inform us. No liability can be accepted by the authors or publishers for loss, damage or injury caused by any errors in, or omissions from, the information given.

Illegal Copying

It is the policy of Haynes Publishing to actively protect its Copyrights and Trade Marks. Legal action will be taken against anyone who unlawfully copies the cover or contents of this Manual. This includes all forms of unauthorised copying including digital, mechanical, and electronic in any form. Authorisation from Haynes Publishing will only be provided expressly and in writing. Illegal copying will also be reported to the appropriate statutory authorities.

Other titles of interest from Haynes Publishing

BMW Boxer Twins
Haynes Great Bike Series
ISBN
978 1 85960 963 7
Book No. H963

The BMW Story
Racing and production motorcycles from 1923 to the present day
ISBN
978 1 85960 854 8
Book No. H854

Buying spare parts

When ordering replacement parts, it is essential to identify exactly the machine for which the parts are required. While in some cases it is sufficient to identify the machine by its title e.g. 'R1200 GS', any modifications made to components mean that it is usually essential to identify the machine by its BMW **production** or model year e.g. '2004 R1200 GS', and sometimes by its engine and/or frame number as well. The BMW production year starts in September of the previous calendar year, after the annual holiday, and continues until the following August. Therefore a 2005 R1200 GS was **produced** at some time between September 2004 and August 2005; it may have been **sold** (to its first owner) at any time from September 2004 onwards.

To identify your own machine, record its full engine and frame numbers and take them to any BMW dealer who should have the necessary information to identify it exactly. Finally, in some cases modifications can be identified only by reference to the machine's engine or frame number; these should be noted and taken with you whenever replacement parts are required.

To be absolutely certain of receiving the correct part, not only is it essential to have the machine's identifying title and engine and frame numbers, but it is also useful to take the old part for comparison (where possible). Note that where a modified component has superseded the original, a careful check must be made that there are no related parts which have also been modified and must be used to enable the replacement to be correctly refitted; where such a situation is found, purchase all the necessary parts and fit them, even if this means replacing apparently unworn items.

Always purchase replacement parts from an authorised BMW dealer who will either have the parts in stock or can order them quickly from the importer, and always use genuine parts to ensure the machine's performance and reliability. Pattern parts are available for certain components (i.e. disc brake pads, oil and air filters); if used, ensure these are of recognised quality brands which will perform as well as the original.

Expendable items such as lubricants, spark plugs, some electrical components, bearings, bulbs and tyres can usually be obtained at lower prices from accessory shops, motor factors or from specialists advertising in the national motorcycle press.

Frame and engine numbers

The frame serial number is stamped into the frame behind the steering head. The engine number is stamped into the crankcase below the right-hand cylinder. Both of these numbers should be recorded and kept in a safe place so they can be furnished to law enforcement officials in the event of a theft.

The manufacturer's vehicle identification plate is located on the left-hand side of the rear sub-frame, the gearbox number is stamped into the case on the left-hand side below the gearchange shaft and the colour code label is on the rear sub-frame under the rider's seat.

The frame serial number, engine and gearbox serial numbers and colour code should also be kept in a handy place (such as with your driving licence) so they are always available when purchasing or ordering parts for your machine. The procedures in this manual identify the bikes by model code and, if necessary, also by production year. The model code (e.g. R1200 GS) is used by itself if the information applies to all bikes produced over the life of the model. The production year is added where the information applies only to bikes produced in certain years of the model's life, usually when a component has been changed or upgraded.

The frame number is stamped into the frame behind the steering head

The colour code label can be found after removing the rider's seat

The engine number is stamped into the crankcase below the right-hand cylinder

The gearbox number is stamped into the case below the gearchange shaft

The manufacturer's VIN plate is located on the rear sub-frame

Professional mechanics are trained in safe working procedures. However enthusiastic you may be about getting on with the job at hand, take the time to ensure that your safety is not put at risk. A moment's lack of attention can result in an accident, as can failure to observe simple precautions.

There will always be new ways of having accidents, and the following is not a comprehensive list of all dangers; it is intended rather to make you aware of the risks and to encourage a safe approach to all work you carry out on your bike.

Asbestos

● Certain friction, insulating, sealing and other products - such as brake pads, clutch linings, gaskets, etc. - contain asbestos. Extreme care must be taken to avoid inhalation of dust from such products since it is hazardous to health. If in doubt, assume that they do contain asbestos.

Fire

● Remember at all times that petrol is highly flammable. Never smoke or have any kind of naked flame around, when working on the vehicle. But the risk does not end there - a spark caused by an electrical short-circuit, by two metal surfaces contacting each other, by careless use of tools, or even by static electricity built up in your body under certain conditions, can ignite petrol vapour, which in a confined space is highly explosive. Never use petrol as a cleaning solvent. Use an approved safety solvent.

● Always disconnect the battery earth terminal before working on any part of the fuel or electrical system, and never risk spilling fuel on to a hot engine or exhaust.

● It is recommended that a fire extinguisher of a type suitable for fuel and electrical fires is kept handy in the garage or workplace at all times. Never try to extinguish a fuel or electrical fire with water.

Fumes

● Certain fumes are highly toxic and can quickly cause unconsciousness and even death if inhaled to any extent. Petrol vapour comes into this category, as do the vapours from certain solvents such as trichloro-ethylene. Any draining or pouring of such volatile fluids should be done in a well ventilated area.

● When using cleaning fluids and solvents, read the instructions carefully. Never use materials from unmarked containers - they may give off poisonous vapours.

● Never run the engine of a motor vehicle in an enclosed space such as a garage. Exhaust fumes contain carbon monoxide which is extremely poisonous; if you need to run the engine, always do so in the open air or at least have the rear of the vehicle outside the workplace.

The battery

● Never cause a spark, or allow a naked light near the vehicle's battery. It will normally be giving off a certain amount of hydrogen gas, which is highly explosive.

● Always disconnect the battery ground (earth) terminal before working on the fuel or electrical systems (except where noted).

● If possible, loosen the filler plugs or cover when charging the battery from an external source. Do not charge at an excessive rate or the battery may burst.

● Take care when topping up, cleaning or carrying the battery. The acid electrolyte, evenwhen diluted, is very corrosive and should not be allowed to contact the eyes or skin. Always wear rubber gloves and goggles or a face shield. If you ever need to prepare electrolyte yourself, always add the acid slowly to the water; never add the water to the acid.

Electricity

● When using an electric power tool, inspection light etc., always ensure that the appliance is correctly connected to its plug and that, where necessary, it is properly grounded (earthed). Do not use such appliances in damp conditions and, again, beware of creating a spark or applying excessive heat in the vicinity of fuel or fuel vapour. Also ensure that the appliances meet national safety standards.

● A severe electric shock can result from touching certain parts of the electrical system, such as the spark plug wires (HT leads), when the engine is running or being cranked, particularly if components are damp or the insulation is defective. Where an electronic ignition system is used, the secondary (HT) voltage is much higher and could prove fatal.

Remember...

✗ **Don't** start the engine without first ascertaining that the transmission is in neutral.

✗ **Don't** suddenly remove the pressure cap from a hot cooling system - cover it with a cloth and release the pressure gradually first, or you may get scalded by escaping coolant.

✗ **Don't** attempt to drain oil until you are sure it has cooled sufficiently to avoid scalding you.

✗ **Don't** grasp any part of the engine or exhaust system without first ascertaining that it is cool enough not to burn you.

✗ **Don't** allow brake fluid or antifreeze to contact the machine's paintwork or plastic components.

✗ **Don't** siphon toxic liquids such as fuel, hydraulic fluid or antifreeze by mouth, or allow them to remain on your skin.

✗ **Don't** inhale dust - it may be injurious to health (see Asbestos heading).

✗ **Don't** allow any spilled oil or grease to remain on the floor - wipe it up right away, before someone slips on it.

✗ **Don't** use ill-fitting spanners or other tools which may slip and cause injury.

✗ **Don't** lift a heavy component which may be beyond your capability - get assistance.

✗ **Don't** rush to finish a job or take unverified short cuts.

✗ **Don't** allow children or animals in or around an unattended vehicle.

✗ **Don't** inflate a tyre above the recommended pressure. Apart from overstressing the carcass, in extreme cases the tyre may blow off forcibly.

✔ **Do** ensure that the machine is supported securely at all times. This is especially important when the machine is blocked up to aid wheel or fork removal.

✔ **Do** take care when attempting to loosen a stubborn nut or bolt. It is generally better to pull on a spanner, rather than push, so that if you slip, you fall away from the machine rather than onto it.

✔ **Do** wear eye protection when using power tools such as drill, sander, bench grinder etc.

✔ **Do** use a barrier cream on your hands prior to undertaking dirty jobs - it will protect your skin from infection as well as making the dirt easier to remove afterwards; but make sure your hands aren't left slippery. Note that long-term contact with used engine oil can be a health hazard.

✔ **Do** keep loose clothing (cuffs, ties etc. and long hair) well out of the way of moving mechanical parts.

✔ **Do** remove rings, wristwatch etc., before working on the vehicle - especially the electrical system.

✔ **Do** keep your work area tidy - it is only too easy to fall over articles left lying around.

✔ **Do** exercise caution when compressing springs for removal or installation. Ensure that the tension is applied and released in a controlled manner, using suitable tools which preclude the possibility of the spring escaping violently.

✔ **Do** ensure that any lifting tackle used has a safe working load rating adequate for the job.

✔ **Do** get someone to check periodically that all is well, when working alone on the vehicle.

✔ **Do** carry out work in a logical sequence and check that everything is correctly assembled and tightened afterwards.

✔ **Do** remember that your vehicle's safety affects that of yourself and others. If in doubt on any point, get professional advice.

● If in spite of following these precautions, you are unfortunate enough to injure yourself, seek medical attention as soon as possible.

Note: *The Pre-ride checks outlined in your rider's manual covers those items which should be inspected before each journey. These checks should be made with the ignition off.*

Engine oil level

Before you start:

✔ The oil level is viewed through the window in the left-hand side of the engine. Wipe the window clean to make the check easier.

✔ Note that the oil level varies with engine temperature – BMW stress that an accurate reading will only be obtained after the motorcycle has been ridden to allow it to reach normal operating temperature.

✔ If, when the engine is cold, the level is low, topping-up will almost certainly be required – follow the details below.

Caution: Do not run the engine in an enclosed space such as a garage or workshop.

✔ Once the engine has reached normal operating temperature, turn it OFF and support the motorcycle upright on level ground. Allow it to stand for at least five minutes to allow the oil level to stabilise.

The correct oil

● Always top up with a good quality oil of the specified type and viscosity and do not overfill the engine. **Note:** *BMW advise that to ensure the smooth running-in of a new engine, synthetic oil is not used until at least 6000 miles (10,000 km) has been covered.*

● To fill the engine from the bottom to the top of the oil level window requires 0.5 litre of oil.

Oil type	API grade SF or higher
Oil viscosity	20W/50, or see accompanying chart and select the best grade to suit prevailing temperatures

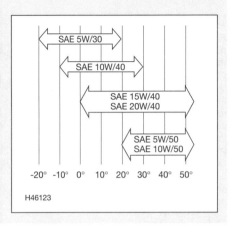

Bike care:

● If you have to add oil frequently, you should check whether there are any oil leaks. Note that oil on the underside of the engine/gearbox joint is a sign that either the engine crankshaft seal or gearbox input shaft seal has failed. If there is no sign of oil leakage from the joints and gaskets the engine could be burning oil (see *Fault Finding*).

● Never run the engine with the oil level below the bottom of the window, and do not fill it above the top of the window.

● Note that on models equipped with an oil level sensor, this doesn't obviate the need to check the oil level via the inspection window.

1 Check the oil level through the inspection window in the left-hand side of the engine. If necessary, wipe the window so that it is clean. With the motorcycle upright, the oil level should lie between the top and bottom of the window.

2 If the level is below the bottom of the window, use the special tool to remove the filler cap from the left-hand valve cover.

3 Top the engine up with the recommended type and grade of oil (see accompanying viscosity chart). The level should be just below the top of the window. Take care not to over-fill the engine.

4 On completion, fit the filler cap, making sure it is secure. If there are any signs of oil leakage from around the cap, renew the sealing O-ring.

Brake fluid levels

Before you start:

✔ When checking the front brake fluid level, position the handlebars so that the top of the master cylinder is as level as possible.

✔ When checking the rear brake fluid level level on ST models, the level can be seen via the cut-out in the body panel. If topping up is required, the body panel must be removed – see Chapter 6. On RT and R models, remove the seat to view the fluid level.

✔ Make sure you have the correct brake fluid, DOT 4 is recommended. Wrap a rag around the reservoir being worked on to ensure that any spillage does not come into contact with painted surfaces.

Bike care:

● On machines not fitted with ABS, the fluid level in the front and rear brake master cylinder reservoirs will drop slightly as the brake pads wear down. If either reservoir requires repeated topping-up this is an indication of a fluid leak somewhere in the system, which should be investigated immediately.

● On ABS equipped machines, the fluid level in the front and rear brake master cylinder reservoirs should not drop below the MAX line. Any drop in the fluid level is an indication of a fault in the system – have the system checked by a BMW dealer immediately.

● Check for signs of fluid leakage from the hydraulic hoses and components – if found, rectify immediately.

● Check the operation of both brakes before taking the machine on the road. If there is evidence of air in the system (spongy feel to lever or pedal), the system must be bled. On machines fitted with ABS, this procedure must be undertaken by a BMW dealer. On machines not fitted with ABS, follow the procedure as described in Chapter 5.

● BMW specify that the pads should be inspected for wear at every second or third fuel tank refill. This amounts to a visual check of the amount of pad material remaining.

 Warning: Brake hydraulic fluid can harm your eyes and damage painted surfaces, so use extreme caution when handling and pouring it and cover surrounding surfaces with rag. Do not use fluid that has been standing open for some time, as it absorbs moisture from the air which can cause a dangerous loss of braking effectiveness.

Front brake fluid level

1 The fluid level is visible through the reservoir body – it must be above the MIN level line.

2 To top up, press the locking tabs in and unscrew the cap.

3 Remove the diaphragm plate and diaphragm.

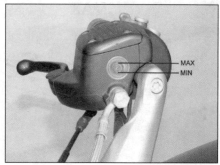

4 On R1200 RT models, the fluid level is visible through the sightglass in the reservoir – it should be midway up the sightglass

5 To top-up, undo the four cover screws and lift off the cover and the diaphragm.

6 Top up with new, clean DOT 4 brake fluid to the MAX level line. Do not overfill and take care to avoid spills (see **Warning** above).

7 Ensure that the diaphragm is correctly seated. If fitted, install the diaphragm plate. Tighten the cap or cover securely.

Rear brake fluid level

1 The fluid level is visible through the reservoir body – on machines not fitted with ABS, it must be between the MIN and MAX level lines. Do not allow it to drop below the MIN line. On ABS equipped machines, the fluid must be level with the MAX level line.

2 To top up, support the reservoir and unscrew the cap, then lift out the diaphragm.

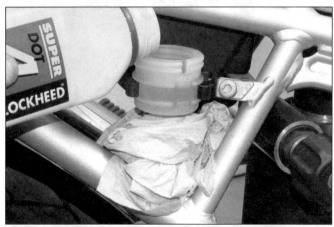

3 Top up with new, clean DOT 4 hydraulic fluid to the MAX level line. Do not overfill and take care to avoid spills (see **Warning** on page 0•12).

4 Ensure that the diaphragm is correctly seated. Install the cap and tighten it securely. Ensure the reservoir is securely clipped into its holder. If applicable, install the body panel (see Chapter 6).

Suspension, steering and drive checks

Suspension and Steering:

● Check that the front and rear suspension operates smoothly without binding.
● Check that the suspension is adjusted as required (where applicable) – see Chapter 4 for details.
● Check that the steering moves smoothly from lock-to-lock.

Gearbox and final drive:

● Check for signs of oil leakage around the gearbox and final drive housings. If there are any signs of leakage from the gearbox, check the oil level (Chapter 1, Section 12). If the final drive housing is leaking, have it checked by a BMW dealer; see Chapter 1, Section 17 for details of oil change and level check.

Clutch fluid level

Before you start:

✔ When checking the fluid level, position the handlebars so that the top of the master cylinder reservoir is as level as possible.

✔ Make sure you have the correct clutch fluid – Vitamol V10, available from BMW dealers. **Do not** use conventional brake and clutch hydraulic fluid. Wrap a rag around the reservoir to ensure that any spillage does not come into contact with painted surfaces.

Bike care:

● If the reservoir requires repeated topping-up this is an indication of a fluid leak somewhere in the system, which should be investigated immediately.

● Check for signs of fluid leakage from the clutch hose and components – if found, rectify immediately.

1 The fluid level is visible through the reservoir body – it must be above the MIN level line.

2 If the level is below the MIN level line, press the locking tabs in and unscrew the cap.

3 Remove the diaphragm plate and diaphragm.

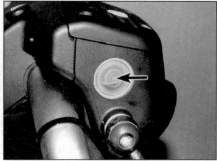

4 On R1200 RT models, the fluid level is visible through the sightglass in the reservoir – it should lie mid-way up the sightglass

5 To top-up, undo the four cover screws and lift off the cover and the diaphragm.

6 Top up with new Vitamol V10 clutch fluid. Do not overfill.

7 Ensure that the diaphragm is correctly seated. If fitted, install the diaphragm plate. Tighten the cap or cover securely.

Tyres

The correct pressures:
● The tyres must be checked when **cold**, not immediately after riding. Note that low tyre pressures may cause the tyre to slip on the rim or come off. High tyre pressures will cause abnormal tread wear and unsafe handling.
● Use an accurate pressure gauge.
● Proper air pressure will increase tyre life and provide maximum stability and ride comfort. Ensure that the pressures are suited to the load the machine is carrying.

Tyre care:
● The need for frequent topping-up indicates an air leak, which should be investigated immediately.
● Check the tyres carefully for cuts, tears, embedded nails or other sharp objects and excessive wear. Operation of the motorcycle with excessively worn tyres is extremely hazardous, as traction and handling are directly affected.
● Check the condition of the tyre valve and ensure the dust cap is in place.
● Pick out any stones or nails which may have become embedded in the tyre tread. If left, they will eventually penetrate through the casing and cause a puncture.
● If tyre damage is apparent, or unexplained loss of pressure is experienced, seek the advice of a tyre fitting specialist without delay.

Tyre tread depth:
● At the time of writing UK law requires that tread depth must be at least 1 mm over 3/4 of the tread breadth all the way around the tyre, with no bald patches. Many riders, however, consider 2 mm tread depth minimum to be a safer limit.
● Many tyres now incorporate wear indicators in the tread. Identify the arrow, triangular pointer or TWI marking on the tyre sidewall to locate the indicator bars and replace the tyre if the tread has worn down level with the bars.

Loading – all models	Front	Rear
Rider only	32 psi (2.2 Bar)	36 psi (2.5 Bar)
With passenger and/or luggage	36 psi (2.5 Bar)	42 psi (2.9 Bar)

1 Check the tyre pressures when the tyres are cold and keep them properly inflated.

2 Measure tread depth at the centre of the tyre using a tread depth gauge.

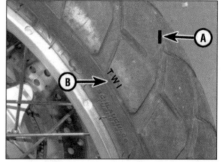

3 Tyre tread wear indicator bar (A) and its location marking (B) – usually either an arrow, a triangle or the letters TWI on the sidewall.

Legal and safety

Lighting and signalling:
● Take a minute to check that the headlight, tail light, brake light, instrument lights and turn signals all work correctly.
● Check that the horn sounds when the switch is operated.
● A working speedometer is a statutory requirement in the UK.

Safety:
● Check that the throttle grip rotates smoothly and snaps shut when released, in all steering positions.
● Check that the engine shuts off when the kill switch is operated.
● Check that the side stand and centre stand return springs hold the stands securely up when retracted.
● Following the procedure in Chapter 1, check the operation of the side stand and starter interlock circuit.

Fuel:
● This may seem obvious, but check that you have enough fuel to complete your journey. Misfiring due to a low fuel level can damage the catalytic converter in the exhaust system.
● If you notice signs of fuel leakage – rectify the cause immediately.
● Ensure you use the correct grade unleaded fuel (see Chapter 3).

Weights and dimensions

R1200GS (2004 to 2007)
Wheelbase . . . . .1519 mm
Overall length . . . . .2210 mm
Overall width. . . . . .915 mm
Overall height . . . . .1380 mm
Seat height . . . . 840 to 860 mm
Weight (with oil and full fuel tank). .256 kg
Maximum payload . . . . .200 kg

R1200GS (2008-on)
Wheelbase . . . . .1519 mm
Overall length . . . . .2210 mm
Overall width. . . . . .930 mm
Overall height . . . . .1450 mm
Seat height . . . . 850 to 870 mm
Weight (with oil and full fuel tank). .229 kg
Maximum payload. . . . . .211 kg

R1200GS Adventure (2006 to 2007)
Wheelbase . . . . .1511 mm
Overall length . . . . .2210 mm
Overall width. . . . . .915 mm
Overall height . . . . .1380 mm
Seat height . . . . 895 to 915 mm
Weight (with oil and full fuel tank). .225 kg
Maximum payload . . . . .179 kg

R1200GS Adventure (2008-on)
Wheelbase . . . . .1511 mm
Overall length . . . . .2240 mm
Overall width. . . . . .950 mm
Overall height . . . . .1525 mm
Seat height . . . . 890 to 910 mm
Weight (with oil and full fuel tank). .259 kg
Maximum payload. . . . . .219 kg

R1200RT
Wheelbase . . . . .1502 mm
Overall length . . . . .2230 mm
Overall width (inc. panniers). . . . . .980 mm
Overall height (screen lowered) .1430 mm
Seat height . . . . 820 to 840 mm
Weight (with oil and full fuel tank). .259 kg
Maximum payload . . . . .236 kg

R1200ST
Wheelbase . . . . .1502 mm
Overall length . . . . .2165 mm
Overall width. . . . . .750 mm
Overall height (screen lowered) .1220 mm
Seat height . . . . 810 to 830 mm
Weight (with oil and full fuel tank). .229 kg
Maximum payload . . . . .231 kg

R1200S
Wheelbase . . . . .1487 mm
Overall length . . . . .2151 mm
Overall width. . . . . .870 mm
Overall height . . . . .1177 mm
Seat height . . . . .830 mm
Weight (with oil and full fuel tank). .213 kg
Maximum payload . . . . .197 kg

R1200R
Wheelbase . . . . .1495 mm
Overall length . . . . .2145 mm
Overall width. . . . . .845 mm
Overall height . . . . .1160 mm
Seat height . . . . 800/770/835 mm
Weight (with oil and full fuel tank). .223 kg
Maximum payload. . . . . .227 kg

Engine

Type	Four-stroke air/oil-cooled horizontal twin
Capacity	1170 cc
Bore and stroke	101 x 73 mm
Compression ratio	
R1200 GS (2004 to 2007)	11.0:1
R1200 RT, ST, R, 2008-on GS	12.0:1
R1200 S	12.5:1
Camshafts	Twin chain-driven camshafts
Valves	4 valves per cylinder
Fuel system	BMS-K electronic engine management
Clutch	Dry, single-plate, hydraulically-operated
Transmission	6-speed constant mesh
Final drive	Shaft

Chassis

Type	Tubular frame, load bearing engine
Rake and trail	
R1200 GS	62.9°, 110 mm
R1200 GS Adventure	63.8°, 97.6 mm
R1200 RT	63.8°, 115.8 mm
R1200 ST	63.0°, 111.6 mm
R1200 S	66.0°, 87 mm
R1200 R	62.9°, 119.1 mm
Front suspension	
Type	BMW Telelever
Travel	
R1200 GS	190 mm
R1200 GS Adventure	210 mm
R1200 RT and R	120 mm
R1200 ST and S	110 mm
Adjustment	Spring preload (see also Chapter 4, Section 10)
Rear suspension	
Type	BMW Paralever
Travel	
R1200 GS	200 mm
R1200 GS Adventure	220 mm
R1200 RT	135 mm
R1200 ST and R	140 mm
R1200 S	120 mm
Adjustment	Spring preload and damping (see also Chapter 4, Section 10)

Tyre sizes	Front	Rear
R1200 GS	110/80 H19 TL	150/70 H17 TL
R1200 RT, ST, S and R	120/70 ZR 17	180/55 ZR 17

Front brake	Twin discs with twin opposed-piston calipers
Rear brake	Single disc with two-piston sliding caliper

Model development

All models covered in this manual are powered by an 1170 cc horizontally opposed, twin-cylinder engine derived from the previous generation R1150 series. Specifications differ according to the state of tune of individual models, however fundamentally, all R1200 engines (known as the K2x series) feature air/oil-cooling, four valves per cylinder and, for the first time on a BMW flat twin, a balancer shaft. The engine drives through a six-speed transmission. Due to the redesign of many components in the engine, frame and suspension, utilisation of the latest manufacturing techniques and adoption of state-of-the-art electronics technology, significant weight-saving has been achieved over the previous 1150 cc model range.

The increased capacity over the earlier 1130 cc engine is achieved by a 2.5 mm increase in piston stroke, although any change to the overall width of the engine is minimised by a compact system of camshafts followers, pushrods and rockers located within the cylinder heads. The camshafts are chain driven off an auxiliary shaft which runs in the crankcase directly below the crankshaft and is itself driven by a chain off the front of the crankshaft. The balancer shaft turns inside the auxiliary shaft and is gear driven off the crankshaft. The shaft has one balance weight at the rear end, below the clutch, and a second weight incorporated in the drive gear at the front.

The cylinder heads, cylinders and crankcase are constructed from aluminium alloy, and the crankcase is divided vertically. The gearbox is a separate unit bolted to the rear of the crankcase. An alternator is mounted externally on the top of the crankcases and is belt driven off the front of the crankshaft.

Engine oil is contained within the crankcase and is pressure-fed for both lubrication and engine cooling by a dual-rotor pump driven by the auxiliary shaft. Oil pressure, oil temperature and, in some cases oil level are monitored by the engine control unit. An oil cooler is mounted at the front of all machines below the headlight unit.

Power from the crankshaft is routed to the transmission input shaft in the gearbox via the clutch. The clutch is operated hydraulically and is of the dry, single-plate type, bolted directly to the rear of the crankshaft.

The transmission is a six-speed, constant-mesh unit, and drive to the rear wheel is by shaft, via a final drive unit.

BMW's own digital engine management system (BMS-K) monitors, controls and co-ordinates both the fuel and ignition system functions. The system is operated by the engine control unit, or ECU. A second unit, the central electronics unit, is responsible for monitoring and control of all other electrical systems such as lighting, switches and accessories. The two units are linked for such functions as starting and engine immobilisation.

The ECU uses engine speed and throttle valve position as the basis for determining optimum engine operation. Additional data, supplied by temperature sensors, oil pressure, gear position and knock sensors, and exhaust gas analysers, when combined with control maps and correction values embedded within the ECU, fine tune injection volume and ignition timing to meet the engine's requirements in any given circumstance. In addition, the engine management system has in-built diagnostic functions which record and store all data should a fault occur.

All models utilise Controlled Area Network (CAN)-bus technology to create an electronic information network between the control units, sensors and power-consuming components. This allows rapid and reliable data transfer around the network. It also allows comprehensive diagnosis of the entire system from one central point.

There is no frame in the traditional sense – the front suspension and its sub-frame, and rear suspension and its sub-frame mount directly to the engine/transmission unit.

Front suspension and steering are managed separately by a modified version of BMW's Telelever system. Telelever uses an arrangement of telescopic fork legs to support the front wheel and provide steering, together with a swingarm and shock absorber to provide suspension control.

At the top of the Telelever system, the fork tubes are held in a yoke, which is mounted to the front sub-frame via the steering head bearing. Midway down the assembly, the fork sliders are linked by a bridge which is attached to the front of the Telelever swingarm via a ball joint. The swingarm pivots around a shaft which passes through the front of the engine crankcases, with the shock absorber located between the swingarm and the front sub-frame.

Rear suspension is provided by a single-sided swingarm and centrally mounted shock absorber. The drive shaft to the rear wheel is housed inside the swingarm. The joint between the swingarm and the final drive unit is pivoted, with a link arm, BMW's Paralever system, controlling movement between the two. The Paralever system, upgraded and strengthened since previous models, counteracts the adverse effect of the shaft drive on suspension movement.

Both front and rear brakes are hydraulically operated disc brakes with optional ABS. The front calipers have two pairs of opposed pistons each and the rear brake has two pistons in a sliding caliper.

R1200 GS (K25)

Launched in January 2004 as the successor to the on/off road R1150 GS. The first model to feature the new R1200 series engine, BMW's own digital engine management system and CAN-bus technology to link on-board control units, sensors and related components. Available with either light alloy cast wheels for road and moderate off-road riding, or wire spoked wheels for high speed, rough terrain use. ABS and the anti-theft warning system were available as options.

A modified model, the K25 11 was introduced for the 2008 model year. It featured a tougher gearbox, derived from the HP2 Sport with revised ratios, new instruments with service indicator, drain plug for the final drive oil, uprated alternator and had an increase of 5 hp in engine power output. Aesthetically the side panels now have stainless steel air deflectors, the upper front mudguard has been redesigned, the front fork tubes, wheel rims and valve covers have a magnesium coated finish, the tail light/brake light is illuminated by LEDs and the wheels are redesigned. An Enduro version of ESA (electronic suspension adjustment) was available as an option.

R1200 GS Adventure (K25 02)

The Adventure was launched in October 2005 for the 2006 model year as the successor to BMW's existing R1150 GS Adventure long distance enduro bike. In fact the use of the R1200 series engine and six-speed gearbox provided the Adventure with more power and tractability yet no gain in weight. Standard equipment included a large capacity (33 litre) fuel tank, larger windshield, adjustable seat height, engine protection bars and extra-wide rider footrests; upgraded front and rear suspension offered longer travel.

A modified model, the K25 12 was introduced for the 2008 model year. Like the standard GS model, it featured a tougher gearbox, derived from the HP2 Sport with revised ratios, new instruments with service indicator, drain plug for the final drive oil, and had an increase of 5 hp in engine power output. Aesthetically there were few changes: the upper front mudguard was been redesigned and the tail light/brake light is now illuminated by LEDs.

R1200 ST (K28)

The ST was launched in January 2005 as the successor to the R1150 RS, the new machine was 17kg lighter than its predecessor, while its engine produced 15 bhp more. The ST gained all the advantages of the R1200 series that originated with the GS, including improved suspension systems, revised handlebar controls and switch units, and a flat screen instrument cluster multi-function display.

The ST was discontinued at the end of 2007.

R1200 RT (K26)

Also launched early in 2005 was the successor to BMW's existing long distance R1150 RT 'Boxer' tourer, the R1200RT. While utilising the new R1200 series engine and transmission, improved front and rear suspension systems and redesigned bodywork with a wider, taller windshield, the overall specification of the tourer remained much the same as its predecessor. Electronic suspension adjustment (ESA), heated seats and cruise control were available as optional extras.

New instruments with a service indicator were fitted for 2008. A special edition model was introduced for 2009 which had tyre pressure control and automatic stability control fitted as standard.

R1200 S (K29)

Available for the 2006 model year, the R1200 S was 16 kg lighter than its predecessor, the R1100 S, and produced 24 bhp more power. A stiffer camshaft design, harder valve springs and reinforced rocker arms increased engine speed to a maximum of 8800 rpm, while variable engine management control permitted the use, when necessary, of 95 octane fuel with a compression ratio of 12.5:1.

The bodywork, rear sub-frame and front fairing bracket were all made from weight-saving materials and the tail light comprised 18 LEDs.

With a view to track use, the ABS fitted to the R1200 S could be deactivated, and Öhlins sports suspension and a wider rear wheel permitting the use of a 190/50 ZR 17 radial sports tyre, could be specified.

New instruments with a service indicator were fitted for 2008 and the R1200 S was discontinued at the end of the year.

R1200R (K27)

A naked style roadster, replacing the R1150R which used the previous generation flat twin engine. It differs from the other models in the range by having new bodywork (without a fairing), new instruments and new lighting.

The R was introduced at the end of 2006, at the time the existing R1200 models changed from servo-assisted brakes to conventional braking and a generation II ABS. Optional equipment was available in the form of ASC (automatic stabilty control), TPC (tyre pressure control) and ESA (electronic suspension adjustment).

Chapter 1
Routine maintenance and Servicing

Contents

Degrees of difficulty

Easy, suitable for novice with little experience	**Fairly easy,** suitable for beginner with some experience	**Fairly difficult,** suitable for competent DIY mechanic	**Difficult,** suitable for experienced DIY mechanic	**Very difficult,** suitable for expert DIY or professional

Servicing specifications

Engine

Spark plugs
  Type . . . . Bosch YR5LDE or NGK DCPR 8 EKC
  Electrode gap
    Standard . . . . 0.7 to 0.9 mm
    Service limit . . . . 1.0 mm
Valve clearances (COLD engine)
  Intake valves . . . . 0.15 mm
  Exhaust valves . . . . 0.30 mm
Rocker arm endplay . . . . 0.05 to 0.4 mm
Engine idle speed
  R1200 R, ST, S, 2004 to 2007 R1200 GS . . . . 1100 to 1200 rpm
  R1200 RT, 2008-on R1200 GS . . . . 1100 to 1300 rpm
Permissible oil consumption . . . . 1.0 litre per 1000 km (600 miles)
Throttle body vacuum differential at idle . . . . 25 mbar (max)

Cycle parts

Throttle cable freeplay
  At handlebar twistgrip . . . . 0.5 mm
  At throttle body. . . . . 0.5 to 1.0 mm
Brake pad minimum friction material thickness . . . . 1.0 mm
Brake disc minimum thickness
  Front . . . . 4.0 mm
  Rear . . . . 4.5 mm

Lubricants and fluids

Engine oil type . . . . API grade SF or higher
Engine oil viscosity. . . . . 20W/50, or see chart in *Pre-ride checks*
Engine oil capacity
  Oil and filter change . . . . 4.0 litres
  Difference between max. and min. levels. . . . . 0.5 litre
Gearbox oil type and viscosity. . . . . API grade GL5 SAE90, or Castrol SAF-XO
Gearbox oil capacity . . . . 0.8 to 0.9 litre
Final drive oil type . . . . Castrol SAF-XO
Final drive oil capacity . . . . 0.22 litre
Brake fluid . . . . DOT 4
Clutch fluid . . . . Vitamol V10
Miscellaneous
  Front wheel bearings . . . . High melting point lithium grease
  Suspension bearings . . . . High melting point lithium grease
  Lever and stand pivot points . . . . Dry film lubricant
  Throttle twistgrip. . . . . Dry film lubricant
  Cables . . . . Aerosol chain lubricant

Torque settings

Centre stand pivot bolts
  R1200 GS . . . . 40 Nm
  R1200 RT and ST . . . . 42 Nm
Cylinder head nuts (see text)
  1st stage setting. . . . . 20 Nm
  2nd stage setting . . . . angle-tighten 90°
  Final setting . . . . angle-tighten 90°
Engine oil drain plug
  Initial setting . . . . 23 Nm
  Final setting . . . . 32 Nm
Engine oil filter . . . . 11 Nm
Engine sump guard
  6 mm bolt . . . . 8 Nm
  19 mm bolt and nuts . . . . 19 Nm
Final drive oil level plug (early models) . . . . 20 Nm
Final drive oil drain plug and oil level plug (later models). . . . . 20 Nm
Front brake caliper mounting bolts . . . . 30 Nm
Fuel tank mounting bolts
  R1200 GS and ST. . . . . 19 Nm
  R1200 S and RT . . . . 16 Nm
  R1200 R . . . . 22 Nm
Gearbox oil filler cap . . . . 30 Nm
Gearbox oil drain plug . . . . 30 Nm
Rear brake caliper mounting bolts. . . . . 24 Nm
Rear wheel mounting bolts. . . . . 60 Nm
Rocker shaft cap bolts. . . . . 18 Nm
Secondary spark plug cover screws . . . . 8 Nm
Spark plugs
  Bosch plugs . . . . 23 Nm
  NGK plugs . . . . 20 Nm
Spoke tension . . . . 4 Nm
Side stand pivot bolt . . . . 56 Nm
Valve cover bolts . . . . 10 Nm
Valve clearance adjuster screw locknuts . . . . 8 Nm

Note: *2008 models onward are fitted with a 'service due' indicator in the instrument display. After the ignition is turned on, the display will momentarily show the mileage or time until the next service. The display can also be configured to display a countdown mileage to the next service. If the service is overdue the word SERVICE will be permanently shown. The service indicator requires resetting by a BMW dealer.*

Pre-ride
☐ Perform the Pre-ride checks listed at the beginning of this manual before carrying out any of the following procedures.

After the initial 600 miles (1000 km)
Note: *This check is usually performed by a BMW dealer after the first 600 miles (1000 km) from new. Thereafter, maintenance is carried out according to the following intervals of the schedule.*

After the initial 6000 miles (10,000 km), and every 12,000 miles (20,000 km) thereafter
☐ Change the engine oil and fit a new filter (Section 1)
☐ Check and adjust the valve clearances (Section 2)
☐ Check the operation of the clutch system (Section 3)
☐ Check the operation of the brake system (Section 4).
☐ Check throttle cable operation and freeplay (Section 5)
☐ Check spoke tension – wire spoked wheels (Section 6)
☐ Check and lubricate the stand pivots (Section 7)
☐ Check the side stand and starter interlock circuit (Section 8)
☐ Check throttle synchronisation (Section 9)
☐ Check battery condition (see Chapter 7)

After the initial 12,000 miles (20,000 km), and every 12,000 miles (20,000 km) thereafter
Carry out all the items listed above under the Initial 6000 miles (10,000 km) check, plus the following:
☐ Fit a new air filter element (Section 10)
☐ Bleed test the ABS (see Note 1)

Every 24,000 miles (40,000 km)
☐ Fit new spark plugs (Section 11).

Every 24,000 miles (40,000 km) or two years
☐ Change the gearbox oil (Section 12)

Every 24,000 miles (40,000 km) or six years
☐ Fit a new alternator drive belt (Section 13)

Every two years
☐ Change the brake fluid – non-ABS equipped machines only (Section 4)

Every four years
☐ Change the brake fluid – ABS equipped machines (see Note 2)

Non-scheduled maintenance
☐ Check the tightness of all nuts and bolts (Section 14)
☐ Check the condition of the wheels, wheel bearings and tyres (Section 15)
☐ Check the front and rear suspension (Section 16)
☐ Change the final drive oil (Section 17). Although a once-only change will be carried out at the 600 mile (1000 km) first service, owners may wish to change the oil again later in the machine's life.

Notes
1 Bleed testing the ABS must be undertaken by a BMW dealer using the BMW diagnostic tester. This ensures that no air is trapped in the system resulting in impaired braking.
2 This procedure must be undertaken by a BMW dealer – it is not possible to change the brake fluid on ABS-equipped machines without the use of a BMW diagnostic tester.

R1200 GS

1 Rear brake fluid reservoir
2 Air filter element
3 Throttle cable adjuster on throttle body
4 Front brake fluid reservoir
5 Throttle cable upper in-line adjuster

6 Fork seals
7 Alternator drive belt cover
8 Valve cover
9 Spark plugs
10 Engine oil drain plug

11 Vacuum take-off point cap
12 Gearbox filler/level plug
13 Gearbox drain plug
19 Final drive oil drain plug (later models)
20 Final drive oil level plug (early models)

R1200 GS

3 Throttle cable adjuster on throttle body
6 Fork seals
8 Valve cover
9 Spark plugs

11 Vacuum take-off point cap
14 Clutch fluid reservoir
15 Engine oil filler cap
16 Battery

17 Engine oil filter
18 Engine oil level window
21 Final drive oil filler plug

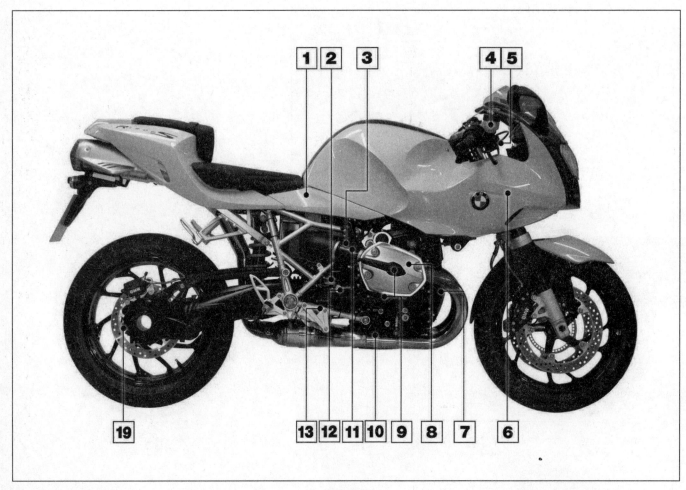

R1200 S

1   Air filter element
2   Rear brake fluid reservoir
3   Throttle cable adjuster on throttle body
4   Front brake fluid reservoir
5   Throttle cable upper in-line adjuster

6   Fork seals
7   Alternator drive belt cover
8   Valve cover
9   Spark plugs
10 Engine oil drain plug

11 Vacuum take-off point cap
12 Gearbox filler/level plug
13 Gearbox drain plug
19 Final drive oil level plug

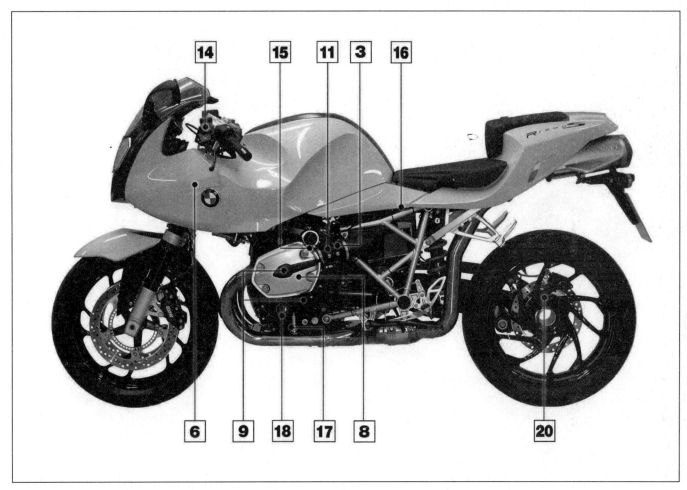

R1200 S

3 Throttle cable adjuster on throttle body
6 Fork seals
8 Valve cover
9 Spark plugs

11 Vacuum take-off point cap
14 Clutch fluid reservoir
15 Engine oil filler cap
16 Battery

17 Engine oil filter
18 Engine oil level window
20 Final drive oil filler plug

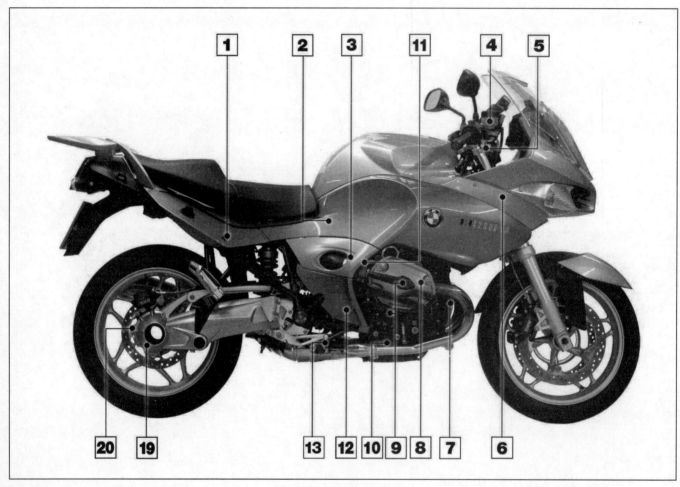

R1200 ST (RT similar)

1 Rear brake fluid reservoir inspection hole (ST only)
2 Air filter element
3 Throttle cable adjuster on throttle body
4 Front brake fluid reservoir
5 Throttle cable upper in-line adjuster

6 Fork seals
7 Alternator drive belt cover
8 Valve cover
9 Spark plugs
10 Engine oil drain plug

11 Vacuum take-off point cap
12 Gearbox filler/level plug
13 Gearbox drain plug
19 Final drive oil drain plug (later models)
20 Final drive oil level plug (early models)

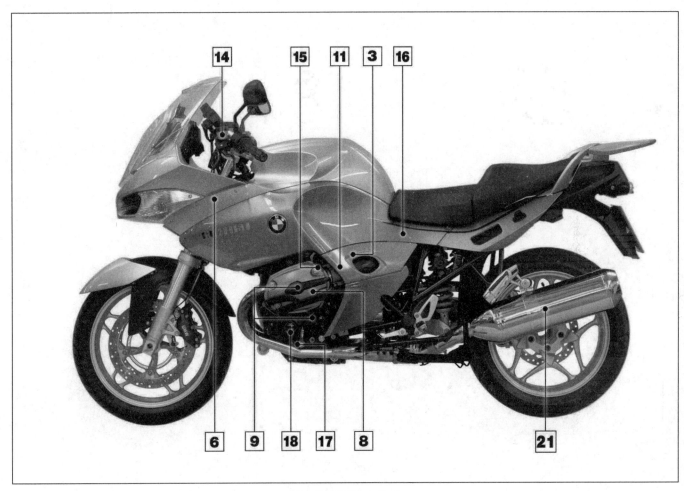

R1200 ST (RT similar)

3   Throttle cable adjuster on throttle body
6   Fork seals
8   Valve cover
9   Spark plugs

11 Vacuum take-off point cap
14 Clutch fluid reservoir
15 Engine oil filler cap
16 Battery

17 Engine oil filter
18 Engine oil level window
21 Final drive oil filler plug

R1200 R

1 Rear brake fluid reservoir
2 Throttle cable adjuster
3 Vacuum take-off point cap
4 Air filter element
5 Front brake fluid reservoir

6 Throttle cable upper in-line adjuster
7 Fork seal
8 Alternator drive belt cover
9 Valve cover
10 Spark plugs

11 Engine oil drain plug
12 Gearbox oil filler/level plug
13 Gearbox oil drain plug
14 Final drive drain plug (later models)
15 Final drive oil level plug (early models)

R1200 R

2 Throttle cable adjuster on throttle body
3 Vacuum take-off point cap
7 Fork seal
9 Valve cover

10 Spark plugs
16 Clutch fluid reservoir
17 Engine oil filler cap
18 Battery

19 Final drive oil filler plug
20 Engine oil filter
21 Engine oil level window

Introduction

1 This Chapter is designed to help the home mechanic maintain his/her motorcycle for safety, economy, long life and peak performance.

2 Deciding where to start or plug into the maintenance schedule depends on several factors. If the warranty period on your motorcycle has just expired, and if it has been maintained according to the warranty standards, you may want to pick up routine maintenance as it coincides with the next mileage or calendar interval. If you have owned the machine for some time but have never performed any maintenance on it, then you may want to start at the nearest interval and include some additional procedures to ensure that nothing important is overlooked.

If you have just had a major engine overhaul, then you may want to start the maintenance routine from the beginning. If you have a used machine and have no knowledge of its history or maintenance record, you may desire to combine all the checks into one large service initially and then settle into the maintenance schedule prescribed.

3 Before beginning any maintenance or repair, the machine should be cleaned thoroughly, especially around the oil filter, spark plugs, valve covers, side panels etc. Cleaning will help ensure that dirt does not contaminate the engine and will allow you to detect wear and damage that could otherwise easily go unnoticed.

4 Certain maintenance information is printed

on labels attached to the motorcycle. If the information on the labels differs from that included here, use the information on the label.

5 Many of the bolts used on R1200 series BMW motorcycles are of the Torx type. Unless you are already equipped with a good range of Torx bits, you are advised to obtain a set. Make sure you get bits that can be used in conjunction with a socket set so that a torque wrench can be applied – a Torx key set will not be adequate on its own, though will be useful in addition to the bits.

⚠️ *Read the Safety first! section of this manual carefully before starting work.*

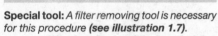

1 Engine oil and filter

Special tool: *A filter removing tool is necessary for this procedure (see illustration 1.7).*

⚠️ *Warning: Be careful when draining the oil, as the exhaust pipes, the engine, and the oil itself can cause severe burns.*

1 Regular oil and filter changes are the single most important maintenance procedure you can perform. The oil not only lubricates the internal parts of the engine, but it also acts as a coolant, a cleaner, a sealant, and a protector. Because of these demands, the oil takes a terrific amount of abuse and should always be changed at the specified interval together with the oil filter.

2 Before changing the oil, warm up the engine so the oil will drain easily. Make sure the bike is on level ground and support it on its centre stand.

3 On R1200 GS models, remove the engine sump guard (see Chapter 6).

4 Position a clean drain tray below the engine. Using the special tool in the bike tool kit, unscrew the oil filler cap on the left-hand valve cover to vent the crankcase and to act as a reminder that there is no oil in the engine (see illustration).

> **HAYNES HINT** *An oil drain tray can be easily made by cutting away the front or back of an old five litre oil container.*

5 Unscrew the oil drain plug from the bottom of the engine and allow the oil to flow into

the drain tray **(see illustrations)**. Discard the sealing washer on the drain plug as a new one should be used.

6 When the oil has completely drained,

1.4 Remove the oil filler cap from the left-hand valve cover

1.5a Unscrew the oil drain plug (arrowed) . . .

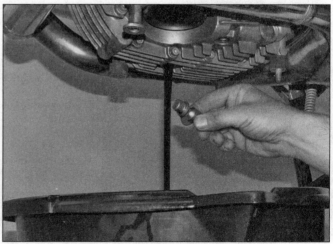

1.5b . . . and allow the oil to drain

1.6a Fit a new sealing washer onto the drain plug . . .

1.6b . . . and tighten the plug to the specified torque setting

install the plug using a new sealing washer and tighten it to the torque setting specified at the beginning of this Chapter, first to the initial setting, then to the final setting **(see illustrations)**. Do not overtighten the plug as the threads in the sump could be damaged.

7 Now place the drain tray below the oil filter. Unscrew the oil filter using an end-cap type oil filter wrench **(see illustration)**. BMW provides

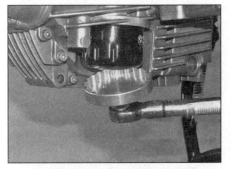

1.7 Use an end-cap type wrench to remove the oil filter

a tool to do this (Part No. 11 4 661). Once the filter has been unscrewed, tip any residual oil into the drain tray.

8 Smear clean engine oil onto the seal of the new filter, then screw the filter onto the engine until it is finger-tight **(see illustrations)**. Now tighten the filter to the specified torque setting using the filter wrench. Take care not to over-tighten the filter as this may damage the seal.

9 Refill the engine to the top of the inspection window using the specified type and amount of oil (see *Pre-ride checks)*. Install the filler cap and tighten it securely.

10 Start the engine and ensure that the oil pressure warning light extinguishes after a few seconds.

11 To ensure an accurate check of the oil level, take the machine for a test ride so that the engine reaches operating temperature, then put it onto the centre stand and allow the oil level to stabilise for five minutes with the engine OFF.

12 Check the level again – it should be just below the top of the window. If necessary,

add more oil to bring it up to the correct level, but take care not to over-fill the engine.

13 Check that there are no oil leaks from around the drain plug and the oil filter.

14 On R1200 GS models, install the engine sump guard.

15 The old oil drained from the engine cannot be re-used and should be disposed of properly. Check with your local refuse disposal company, disposal facility or environmental agency to see whether they will accept the used oil for recycling. Don't pour used oil into drains or onto the ground.

 HAYNES HiNT *Check the old oil carefully – if it is very metallic coloured, then the engine is experiencing wear from running-in (new engine) or from insufficient lubrication. If there are flakes or chips of metal in the oil, then something is drastically wrong internally and the engine will have to be disassembled for inspection and repair.*

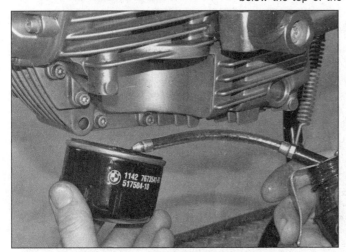

1.8a Lubricate the filter seal with clean engine oil . . .

1.8b . . . then screw the filter on carefully

2.4 Use a spanner to turn the crankshaft pulley nut (arrowed)

2.5 Check for freeplay (arrowed) between the intake and exhaust rocker arms and the valve stems

2 Valve clearances

1 The engine must be cold for this maintenance procedure, so let the machine sit overnight before beginning.

2 Place the motorcycle on its centre stand or on an auxiliary stand. Remove the primary spark plugs (see Section 11).

3 Place a drain tray underneath the side of the engine being worked on to catch any residual oil, then remove the valve covers (see Chapter 2).

4 Work on one side of the engine at a time. To check the valve clearances, the piston must be at top dead centre (TDC) on the compression stroke. To turn the engine to this position, select a high gear and have an assistant turn the rear wheel slowly by hand in the normal direction of rotation. Alternatively, follow the procedure in Section 13 to remove the alternator drive belt cover, then turn the engine with a spanner on the crankshaft pulley nut (see illustration).

Caution: Be sure to turn the engine in its normal direction of rotation only – clockwise.

5 With the piston at TDC on the compression stroke, all the valves will be closed and there should be discernable freeplay in the rocker arms in the form of a clearance between the adjusters and the valve stems (see illustration).

6 Check the clearance on each valve by inserting a feeler gauge of the correct thickness (see Specifications) between the rocker arm adjuster screw and the valve stem – the gauge should be a firm sliding fit (see illustration). Note that the intake valve and exhaust valve clearances are different.

7 If the clearance is incorrect on the valve being checked, loosen the adjuster locknut and turn the adjuster using a suitable Allen key until the correct clearance is obtained. Hold the adjuster in position and tighten the locknut securely (see illustration). Re-check the clearance.

8 When all the valves have been checked on the first cylinder, rotate the engine until the other piston is at TDC on the compression stroke. Check and adjust the valve clearances as described in Steps 6 and 7.

9 After checking the valve clearances, check the rocker arm endplay as follows.

10 Press each rocker arm against the shaft cap and measure the endplay with a feeler gauge, then compare the result with the specification at the beginning of this Chapter (see illustration). If the endplay is outside the specification, loosen the three bolts and the cylinder head nut retaining the cap, then move the cap carefully until the correct clearance is obtained.

11 Tighten the bolts to hold the cap in position, then tighten them to the torque setting specified at the beginning of this Chapter. Tighten the cylinder head nut to the specified torque setting. Check that the endplay is still correct.

12 Check the seals on the valve cover bolts, the inner seal around the spark plug hole and the outer cover seal for damage and deterioration and renew them if necessary (see illustrations).

13 If removed, install the seals ensuring the outer cover seal is fitted the correct way round (see illustration).

14 Lubricate the valve assemblies, rockers and camshafts with clean engine oil, then

2.6 Measure the clearance with a feeler gauge

2.7 Loosen the locknut and turn the adjuster with an Allen key

2.10 Press the rocker arms against the shaft cap (A) and measure the endplay at (B)

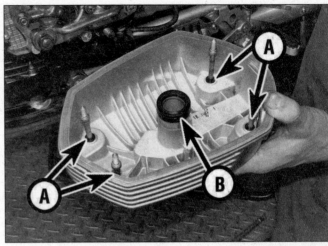

2.12a Check the condition of the seals on the cover bolts (A), the spark plug hole (B) . . .

2.12b . . . and the outer cover seal. Note the seal locating points (arrowed)

2.13 Ensure the outer cover seal is fitted correctly

install the cover and secure it with the bolts. Tighten the bolts evenly in a criss-cross pattern to the specified torque setting.

15 Install the remaining components in the reverse order of removal.

3 Clutch system

1 All models are fitted with an hydraulically operated clutch, for which there is no requirement for adjustment.
2 Check the fluid level in the reservoir (see *Pre-ride checks*).
3 Remove the body panels as applicable (see Chapter 6), and fuel tank (see Chapter 3), then inspect the clutch hose, its connections, the master cylinder on the handlebars and the release cylinder at the rear of the gearbox for signs of fluid leakage, deterioration and wear.
4 If any leaks or damage are found they must be rectified immediately. Refer to Chapter 2 for details of the clutch release mechanism components.

5 Check the operation of the clutch. If there is evidence of air in the system (spongy feel to the lever, difficulty in engaging gear), bleed the system (see Chapter 2). If the lever feels stiff or sticky, check the operation of the master cylinder and the release cylinder (see Chapter 2).
6 The clutch lever has a span adjuster that alters the distance of the lever from the handlebar. On R1200 RT models, each setting

is identified by a number on the adjuster, which must align with the arrowhead on the lever **(see illustration)**. Pull the lever away from the handlebar and turn the adjuster ring until the setting that best suits the rider is obtained. On all other models, the setting is altered by turning the adjuster screw **(see illustration)**. Push the lever forwards, then turn the adjuster clockwise to increase the span and anti-clockwise to decrease it.

3.6a Handlebar lever span adjuster – R1200 RT models

3.6b Handlebar lever span adjuster – R1200 GS shown

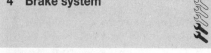

4 Brake system

Brake system check

1 Make sure all brake fasteners are tight.
2 Look for leaks at the hose connections and check for damage to the hoses.
3 Make sure the fluid level in the front and rear brake reservoirs is correct (see *Pre-ride checks*).
4 Check the brake pads and discs for wear (see Steps 10 to 16).
5 If the brake lever or pedal feels spongy, it is likely that there is air in the brake system and it will need bleeding – on machines fitted with ABS, this procedure must be undertaken by a BMW dealer. For machines not fitted with ABS, follow the procedure in Chapter 5.

Front brake lever

6 Check the brake lever for loose fittings, improper or rough action, excessive play, bends, and other damage. Replace any damaged parts with new ones (see Chapter 5).

7 The front brake lever has a span adjuster that alters the distance of the lever from the handlebar. On R1200 RT models, each setting is identified by a number on the adjuster, which must align with the arrowhead on the lever (see illustration 3.6a). Pull the lever away from the handlebar and turn the adjuster ring until the setting that best suits the rider is obtained. On all other models, the setting is altered by turning the adjuster screw (see illustration 3.6b). Push the lever forwards, then turn the adjuster clockwise to increase the span and anti-clockwise to decrease it.

Rear brake pedal

8 Check the brake pedal for loose fittings, improper or rough action, excessive play, bends, and other damage. Replace any damaged parts with new ones. Check the brake pedal stop bolt height, and the clearance between the stop bolt and the tongue of the brake light switch (see Chapter 4, Section 3).

Brake light

9 Make sure the brake light operates when the front brake lever is pulled in and also when

the rear brake pedal is depressed. The brake light switches are not adjustable. If they fail to operate properly, check them (see Chapter 7).

Brake pad wear check

Note: *BMW specify that the pads should be inspected for wear at every second or third fuel tank refill. This amounts to a visual check of the amount of pad material remaining.*

10 Pad wear can be determined without removing them from the caliper. On the front brakes, the friction material has wear indicator grooves (see illustration). If the friction material has worn down to the bottom of the grooves, the pads must be renewed (see Chapter 5). The grooves are visible from the front or rear of the caliper (see illustration), although note that on the R1200 R caliper the pad spring must be removed to view the back edge of the pads (see illustration). On the rear brake, a counter-bored hole in the back of the innermost pad denotes the wear limit (see illustration). If the surface of the brake disc is visible through the hole, the pads must be renewed (see Chapter 5).

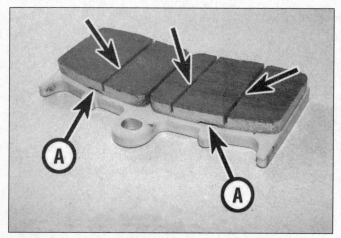

4.10a Front brake pad wear indicator grooves (arrowed). Note also wear indicator cut-outs (A)

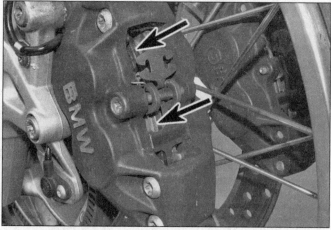

4.10b Grooves can be viewed from the back of the caliper . . .

4.10c . . . but the pad spring must first be detached on the R1200 R caliper; it is retained by two screws (arrowed)

4.10d Wear indicator hole (arrowed) on the innermost pad, rear brake

11 If required, displacing the pads on the front brakes and displacing the caliper on the rear brake will allow closer inspection (see Chapter 5). To measure the amount of friction material remaining, remove the pads from the caliper. If the friction material has worn down to the specified minimum thickness, the pads must be renewed **(see illustration)**. Always renew both pads in the caliper at the same time, and, in the case of the front brake, renew both sets of pads at the same time (see Chapter 5).

12 Inspect the surface of the pads for contamination. If a pad is fouled with oil or grease, or is heavily scored or damaged by dirt and debris, both pads must be renewed as a set. Note that it is not possible to degrease the friction material; if the pads are contaminated in any way, new ones must be fitted. **Note:** *If the pads are contaminated with brake fluid check for leaks at the brake hose banjo union and at the caliper bleed valve. Check for leaks from behind the caliper piston seals (see Step 24).*

13 Check that each pad has the same amount of wear as the other. If uneven wear is noticed, one of the pistons is probably sticking in the caliper, in which case the caliper must be overhauled (see Chapter 5).

14 If the pads are in good condition, clean them carefully using a fine wire brush which is completely free of oil and grease, to remove all traces of road dirt and corrosion. Using a pointed instrument, dig out any embedded particles of foreign matter.

15 Spray the inside of the caliper with a dedicated brake cleaner to remove any dust. Remove any traces of corrosion from the pad pins which might cause sticking of the caliper/pad operation.

16 Follow the procedure in Chapter 5 to install the brake pads.

Brake discs

17 Inspect the front and rear brake discs for wear, damage and distortion. Light scratches are normal after use and won't affect brake operation, but deep grooves and heavy score marks will reduce braking efficiency and accelerate pad wear. If the disc is badly grooved, have it machined by a brake specialist, or fit a new disc (see Chapter 5).

18 Follow the procedure in Chapter 5 to check disc runout

Brake fluid change

19 The brake fluid should be changed at the prescribed service interval. On machines fitted with ABS it is not possible to change the fluid without the use of a BMW diagnostic tester – the procedure must be undertaken by a BMW dealer.

 Warning: Any attempt to drain and refill the ABS in the conventional way will result in air trapped in the system and brake system failure.

20 To change the brake fluid on a machine not fitted with ABS, follow the procedure in Chapter 5.

Brake hoses

21 The flexible hydraulic hoses will deteriorate in time – regular checks should be made for damage and leaks, particularly where the hose joins the banjo union and where it passes through hose guides. Damaged or leaking hoses must be renewed (see Chapter 5).

22 If a brake hose is disconnected, air will enter the brake system and the system will need bleeding – on machines fitted with ABS, this procedure must be undertaken by a BMW dealer. For machines not fitted with ABS, follow the procedure in Chapter 5 to renew a brake hose. Always fit new sealing washers on both sides of a brake hose banjo union.

Brake caliper and master cylinder seals

23 Hydraulic seals will deteriorate over a period of time, particularly if the bike has been in long-term storage, and lose their effectiveness, leading to sticking operation or fluid loss, or allowing the ingress of air and dirt.

24 Remove the brake pads from the caliper (see Chapter 5). Carefully ease up the dust seals around the caliper pistons and check for fluid behind the seals. If brake fluid is leaking from the caliper, the piston seals have failed and the caliper must be overhauled – this procedure must be undertaken by a BMW dealer. **Note:** *This applies to all machines, whether or not they are fitted with ABS.*

25 If brake fluid is leaking from the front or rear master cylinder a new master cylinder must be fitted – seal kits are not available. On machines fitted with ABS, this procedure must be undertaken by a BMW dealer. For machines not fitted with ABS, follow the procedure in Chapter 5 to renew the master cylinder.

5	Throttle cables

Lubrication

Special tool: *A cable lubricating adapter is necessary for this procedure (see illustration 5.3).*

1 Make sure the throttle twistgrip rotates easily from fully closed to fully open with the front wheel turned at various angles. The twistgrip should return automatically from fully open to fully closed when released.

2 If the throttle sticks, this is probably due to a cable fault. Remove the cables (see Chapter 3) and lubricate them as follows.

3 Note which way round the pressure adapter fits onto the inner and outer cables, then slide it over the inner cable **(see illustration)**.

4 Push the outer cable into the recess in the adapter, then tighten the screw so

4.11 If required, measure the thickness of the friction material – note the wear grooves (arrowed)

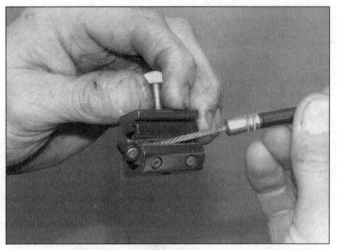

5.3 Fitting the cable lubricating adapter onto the inner throttle cable

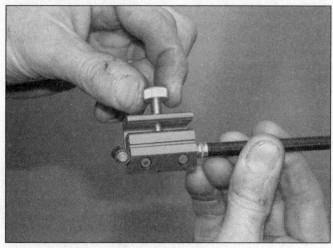
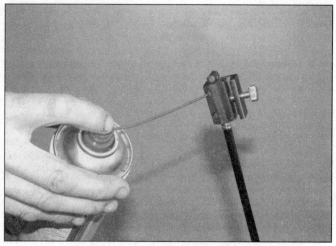

5.4 Ensure that the adapter grips the inner and outer cables firmly

5.5 Connect the can of cable lubricant to the adapter

that the cable is gripped firmly **(see illustration)**. **Note:** *If the screw is not tightened sufficiently, lubricant will leak out of the adapter.*

5 Connect the lubricant can to the adapter and depress the button – lubricant should penetrate between the inner and outer cables along their full length **(see illustration)**. Use an aerosol cable lubricant, such as Silkolene Silkopen.

6 Disconnect the adapter and check that the inner cable slides freely in the outer cable. If not, replace the cable with a new one.

7 With the cables removed, check the operation of the cable splitter (see Chapter 3).

8 Make sure the throttle twistgrip rotates freely on the handlebar – dirt, combined with a lack of lubrication, can cause the action to be stiff. Unscrew the handlebar end-weight and slide the twistgrip off. Clean the bar and inside the twistgrip, then lubricate the components

with dry film lubricant. Install the twistgrip in the reverse order of removal.

9 Install the cables, making sure they are correctly routed (see Chapter 3). If this fails to improve the operation of the throttle, check for a sticking valve in the throttle bodies (see Chapter 3).

⚠ **Warning: Turn the handlebars all the way through their travel with the engine idling. Idle speed should not change. If it does, the cable may be routed incorrectly. Correct this condition before riding the bike.**

Adjustment

10 Check for freeplay in the cable between the twistgrip and the cable splitter, measured in terms of the amount of slack between the outer cable and its seat in the cable adjuster at the twistgrip end. Pull back the boot on the cable before making the check **(see illustration)**. Compare the amount of freeplay

to that listed in this Chapter's Specifications and, if necessary, adjust the cable as follows.

11 Loosen the adjuster lock ring and turn the adjuster in or out as required until the specified amount of freeplay is obtained, then tighten the lock ring. If the adjuster has reached its limit of adjustment, fit a new cable (see Chapter 3). Don't forget to refit the boot afterwards.

12 Pull back the boots on the throttle body ends of the cables and check for freeplay in the cables between the cable splitter and the throttle pulleys, measured in terms of the amount of slack between each outer cable and its seat in the cable adjuster **(see illustration)**. Compare the amount of freeplay to that listed in this Chapter's Specifications and, if necessary, loosen the adjuster locknuts and adjust the cables as described in Step 11. **Note:** *It is essential that freeplay is the same in both cables, otherwise the operation of the throttle valves will not be synchronised (see Section 9).*

5.10 Pull back the boot to measure cable freeplay at upper adjuster (arrowed) . . .

5.12 . . . and at each adjuster (arrowed) on throttle bodies

6 Spokes – wire spoked wheels

Caution: If a machine is ridden off road, BMW recommend that the spoke tension should be checked on a daily basis.
Special tool: *A Torx socket is necessary for this procedure (see illustration 6.3).*

1 Support the machine on its centre stand so that the wheels are free to rotate. Check each spoke for looseness by tapping it gently with a small spanner or screwdriver and listening to the sound **(see illustration)**. The 'tone' of each spoke should sound the same.

2 If a spoke sounds dull or rattles, try to pull it backwards and forwards to confirm that it is loose.

3 A loose spoke can be tightened with the correct size Torx socket and a torque wrench **(see illustration)**. Tighten the spoke carefully to the torque setting specified at the beginning of this Chapter.

4 If several spokes are loose it is likely that the wheel will be out of true – follow the procedure in Chapter 5 to check the radial and axial runout. If necessary, take the wheel to a wheel building expert for correction.

6.1 Check each spoke by tapping with a small screwdriver

5 If a spoke is bent it must be replaced with a new one. First check the wheel runout (see Chapter 5). If the wheel is true, undo the spoke nipple and draw the damaged spoke out from the wheel rim, noting its alignment with adjacent spokes. Insert the new spoke through the rim and screw it into the nipple in the hub, then tighten the spoke to the specified torque setting. If the wheel is out of true, take it to a wheel building expert for correction.

6 If a spoke is damaged, inspect the wheel rim for damage and flat spots also.

7 Stand pivots

1 Since the stands on a motorcycle are exposed to the elements, the pivots should be lubricated periodically to ensure safe and trouble-free operation.

2 In order for the lubricant to be applied where it will do the most good, the component should be disassembled (see Chapter 4). However, if chain or dry film lubricant is being used, it can be applied to the pivot joint gaps and will usually work its way into the areas where friction occurs. If engine oil or light grease is being used, apply it sparingly as it may attract dirt (which could cause the pivots to bind or wear at an accelerated rate).

3 Check the stand springs for damage and distortion **(see illustration)**. The springs must be capable of retracting the stand fully and holding it retracted when the motorcycle is in use. If a spring has sagged or is broken, it must be replaced with a new one (see Chapter 4).

8 Side stand and starter interlock circuit

1 Check the operation of the starter interlock system as follows:

● Make sure the transmission is in neutral, then retract the stand and start the engine. Pull in the clutch lever and select a gear. Extend the side stand – the engine should stop as the side stand is extended.
● Check that when the side stand is down, the engine can only be started if the transmission is in neutral.
● Make sure the engine is in neutral and the side stand is down. Start the engine, pull in the clutch lever and select a gear – the engine should cut out.
● Check that when the side stand is up and the transmission is in gear, the engine can only be started if the clutch lever is pulled in.

2 If the circuit does not operate as described, refer to Chapter 7 and check the operation of the side stand switch, gear position switch and clutch switch, and check the wiring between the switches and the engine control unit (ECU).

9 Throttle synchronisation

⚠️ **Warning: Do not allow exhaust gases to build up in the work area; either perform the check outside or use an exhaust gas extraction system. When carrying out synchronisation, but careful not to allow the engine to overheat.**

1 Throttle synchronisation is simply the process of ensuring the throttle valves pass the same amount of fuel/air mixture to each cylinder. This is done by measuring the vacuum produced in each cylinder. If the valves are out of synchronisation, decreased fuel mileage, increased engine temperature, less than ideal throttle response and higher vibration levels will result.

2 To check throttle synchronisation, you will need a pair of vacuum gauges or calibrated

6.3 Tighten the spokes carefully to the specified torque setting

7.3 Check the condition of the side stand (A) and centre stand (B) springs

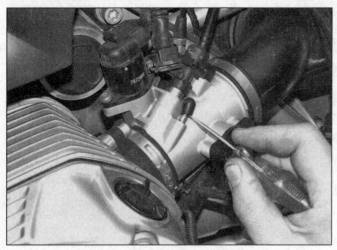

9.7 Remove the caps from both vacuum take-off points

9.8 Note any vacuum difference between the cylinders

tubes to indicate engine vacuum. The equipment used should come complete with the hoses to fit the take-off points. Note: Because of the nature of the synchronisation procedure and the need for special instruments, most owners leave the task to a BMW dealer equipped with the BMW Synchro tester.

3 Before undertaking the procedure, make sure the valve clearances are correct (see Section 2) and that engine compression is within the specified levels (see Chapter 2). Inspect the fixings on the air intake ducts to ensure that they are tightened securely. The engine idle speed should be within the Specification shown at the beginning of this Chapter. Also, turn the handlebars back-and-forth and see if the idle speed changes as this is done. If it does, the throttle cables may not be adjusted or routed correctly, or may be worn out. This is a dangerous condition that can cause loss of control of the bike. Be sure to correct this problem before proceeding (see Section 5).

4 Follow the procedure in Section 5 to ensure that the throttle cables are adjusted correctly.

5 The engine should be at normal operating temperature, which is usually reached after 10 to 15 minutes of stop-and-go riding. Place the

motorcycle on its centre stand, and make sure the transmission is in neutral.

6 On R1200 RT and ST models, remove the fairing side panels and fuel tank side panels (see Chapter 6).

7 Remove the vacuum take-off point blanking cap from each injector throttle body **(see illustration)**. Connect the vacuum gauge hoses, making sure they are a good fit – air leaks will result in false readings.

⚠️ *Warning: Take great care not to burn your hands on the hot engine unit when accessing the gauge take-off points on the intake manifolds.*

8 Start the engine – if using vacuum gauges, set their damping so that needle flutter is just eliminated. Allow the engine to idle and note any vacuum difference between the cylinders **(see illustration)**. Compare the result with the Specification at the beginning of this Chapter. If the differential is greater than the specified figure, refer to Steps 3 and 4 and re-check the engine settings. **Note:** *Do not allow the engine to idle for a prolonged period as over-heating may occur.*

9 Once the vacuum differential is within the specification, start the engine and observe the reading on each vacuum gauge as the throttle twistgrip is slowly opened a small

amount. Both readings should change at the same time as the throttle is opened and remain equal with the twistgrip held steady at approximately 1400 to 1800 rpm. If not, turn the adjuster for the right-hand throttle cable at the throttle valve pulley end until the readings change simultaneously **(see illustration)**. When the correct setting has been achieved, tighten the cable adjuster locknut, taking care not to move the adjuster position whilst this is done.

Caution: Do not adjust the position of the throttle valve stop screws – their positions have been carefully set up and sealed by the manufacturer.

10 Follow the procedure in Section 5 and check the freeplay in the cables between the cable splitter and the pulleys.

11 Remove the vacuum gauges and fit the blanking caps over the take-off points. Ensure that the caps are a tight fit – if not, renew them.

12 On R1200 RT and ST models, install the body panels (see Chapter 6).

13 If acceptable vacuum settings can't be achieved, have the throttle synchronisation checked by a BMW dealer.

10 Air filter

Caution: If the machine is continually ridden in wet or dusty conditions, the filter should be renewed more frequently.

1 Remove the rider's seat (see Chapter 6).

2 The air filter is located in its housing at the rear, right-hand side of the fuel tank. As necessary, according to your machine, remove the right-hand side panel, fairing side panel and tank panel to gain access (see Chapter 6).

3 Release the upper and lower clips securing the air intake duct to the filter housing **(see illustration)**.

9.9 Location of the right-hand throttle cable adjuster (arrowed)

10.3 Pull out the clips (arrowed) securing the air intake duct

10.4 On R1200 S models, undo the screw (arrowed) to release the duct

10.5a Prise the duct off . . .

4 On R1200 S models, undo the screw securing the front of the duct and lift it off **(see illustration)**.
5 On all other models, prise the duct off, noting the location of the peg on the back of the duct **(see illustrations)**.
6 Note the location of the right-hand throttle cable.
7 Prise out the air filter element and discard it **(see illustration)**.
8 Install the new filter, ensuring it is properly seated **(see illustration)**, then install the air intake duct.
9 Ensure that the right-hand throttle cable is not trapped by the underside of the duct.
10 On R1200 S models, secure the duct with the screw.
11 On all other models, press the peg on the back of the duct into the grommet on the frame.

12 Secure the duct to the filter housing with the clips.
13 Install the remaining components in the reverse order of removal.

11 Spark plugs

Special tools: *A spark plug cap/ignition coil extractor and a wire gauge are necessary for this job (see illustrations 11.2a and 11.8).*

Note 1: *The spark plug caps are integral with the ignition coils. To avoid damaging the wiring, always disconnect the wiring connectors before removing the cap/coils. Do not attempt to lever the cap/coils off the primary spark plugs – use the special tool provided. Do not drop the cap/coils.*

10.5b . . . noting the location of the peg (arrowed)

Note 2: *Make sure your spark plug socket is the correct size before attempting to remove the plugs – a suitable one is supplied in the motorcycle's tool kit.*

10.7 Prise out the old air filter element

10.8 Ensure that the new element is fitted all the way into its housing

11.1a Prise off the primary spark plug cover . . .

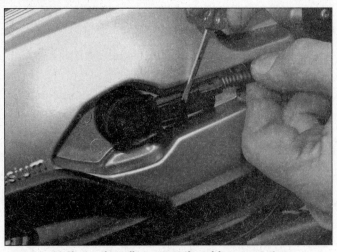

11.1b . . . then disconnect the wiring connector

11.2a Slide the special tool onto the cap/coil . . .

11.2b . . . then pull the cap/coil straight out

1 To remove the primary spark plugs, first prise off the spark plug covers, then carefully release the tab securing the ignition coil wiring connectors and disconnect the connectors **(see illustrations)**.

2 Using the tool provided in the toolkit, pull the cap/coil off the primary spark plug **(see illustrations)**.

3 To remove the secondary spark plugs, first release the tab securing the ignition coil wiring

connectors and disconnect the connectors **(see illustration)**.

4 Undo the screws securing the cap/coil covers and displace the covers and wiring sub looms **(see illustrations)**.

11.3 Disconnect the secondary spark plug wiring connector

11.4a Undo the screws securing the cap/ coil cover (arrowed) . . .

11.4b . . . and displace the cover and wiring

11.5 Pull the cap/coil off the secondary spark plug

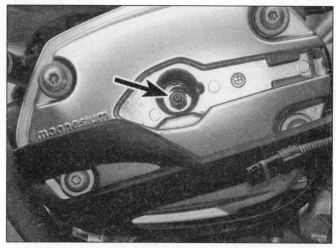

11.6a The primary spark plugs are located in a deep recess (arrowed) . . .

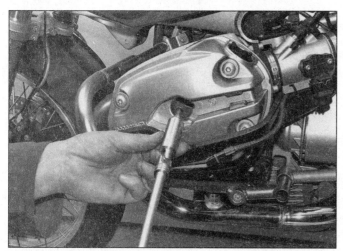

11.6b . . . requiring a long reach socket to remove them

11.6c Access to the secondary spark plugs is easier

5 Pull the cap/coil off the secondary spark plug **(see illustration)**. **Note:** *The secondary spark plug cap/coils are left and right-handed – if necessary, mark them to ensure they are fitted the correct way round.*

6 Using either the plug socket supplied in the bike's toolkit or a 16 mm thin-walled, deep socket type wrench, unscrew the plugs from the cylinder head **(see illustrations)**.

7 Inspect the old spark plugs and compare them with the colour spark plug reading chart at the end of this manual. The condition of the plugs can give an indication of the general condition of the engine. Do not attempt to clean and re-use the old plugs, new ones must be fitted.

8 Before installing the new plugs, make sure they are the correct type and heat range and check the gap between the electrodes – see *Specifications* at the beginning of this Chapter. Measure the gap with a wire gauge **(see illustration)**. New plugs are pre-set to the correct gap – if the plug gap is outside the

specified measurement it is likely the plug has been damaged. Never attempt to bend the plug electrodes, fit another new plug.

9 Make sure the washer is in place before installing each plug.

10 Since the cylinder head is made of aluminium, which is soft and easily damaged, thread the plugs into the heads turning the plug socket by hand. Once the plugs are finger-tight, tighten them to the torque setting specified at the beginning of this Chapter, or, if a torque wrench is not available, according to the manufacturers instructions – do not over-tighten them.

11 Install the spark plug cap/coils, making

> **HAYNES HiNT** *Stripped plug threads in the cylinder head can be repaired with a thread insert – see 'Tools and Workshop Tips' in the Reference section.*

sure they locate correctly onto the plugs. Ensure that the terminals inside the cap/coil wiring connectors are clean, then connect them securely. Install the spark plug covers. Tighten the secondary spark plug cover screws to the specified torque setting.

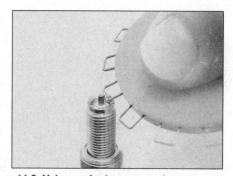

11.8 Using a wire type gauge to measure the spark plug electrode gap

12 Gearbox oil

HAYNES HiNT *An oil drain tray can be easily made by cutting away the front or back of an old oil container – it only needs to hold 1 litre.*

⚠ *Warning: Be careful when draining the oil, as the exhaust pipes, the engine, and the oil itself can cause severe burns.*

1 Before changing the oil, warm up the engine so the oil will drain easily. Make sure the bike is on level ground and support it on its centre stand.

2 The gearbox oil filler and drain plugs are located on the right-hand side of the engine unit **(see illustration)**. As necessary, according to your machine, remove the fairing right-hand side panel to gain access (see Chapter 6).

3 Position a clean drain tray below the gearbox. To avoid the oil running over the hot exhaust system, use a piece of card to channel the oil from the drain plug into the tray.

4 Unscrew the oil filler plug to act as a vent, then unscrew the drain plug and allow the oil to flow into the drain tray **(see illustration)**. Discard the sealing washers on the filler plug and drain plug as a new ones should be used **(see illustration)**. Clean any metal swarf off the drain plug.

5 When the oil has completely drained, fit the drain plug using a new sealing washer and tighten it to the torque setting specified at the beginning of this Chapter. Do not overtighten the plug as the threads in the casing could be damaged.

6 Refill the gearbox to the lower edge of the filler hole using the type and amount of oil specified at the beginning of this Chapter **(see illustration)**.

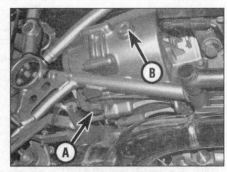

12.2 Location of the gearbox oil drain (A) and filler (B) plugs

7 Install the filler plug, using a new sealing washer, and tighten it to the specified torque setting. Do not over-tighten the plug as the threads in the casing could be damaged **(see illustration)**.

12.4a Draining the gearbox oil – use a piece of card to deflect oil away from the exhaust

12.4b If necessary, cut the old sealing washers off the gearbox plugs

12.6 Refill the gearbox to the lower edge of the filler hole

12.7 Take care not to over-tighten the gearbox plugs

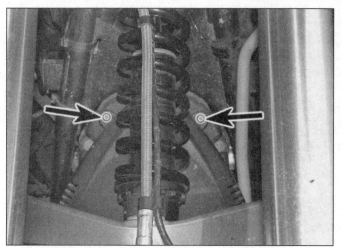

13.3a Undo the two screws at the top (arrowed) . . .

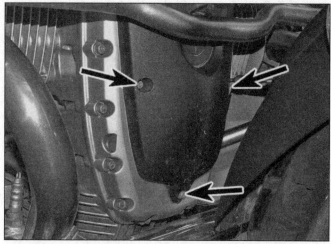

13.3b . . . and the three screws at the bottom (arrowed) . . .

13.3c . . . then lift off the alternator drive belt cover

13.3d Note the location of the brackets for the fairing panels
– R1200 RT

13 Alternator drive belt

Special tool: *A drive belt installation tool is necessary for this job (see illustration 13.8a).*

1 On R1200 RT models, remove the fairing left and right-hand side panels (see Chapter 6). On R1200 R models, remove the oil cooler shroud and unbolt the cooler from the drive belt cover – lean the cooler forwards without straining the oil hoses (see Chapter 2).

2 Where fitted, undo the bolts securing the crash bar and displace the bar to gain clearance for removing the alternator drive belt cover (see Chapter 6).

3 Undo the screws securing the drive belt cover and remove the cover **(see illustrations)**. On R1200 RT models, note the location of the brackets for the fairing panel fixings **(see illustration)**.

4 To remove the drive belt, insert a large screwdriver or tyre lever behind the belt on the left-hand side, just before it engages with the crankshaft pulley, then lever the belt off the edge of the pulley. Turn the pulley clockwise (direction of normal engine rotation) with a spanner on the pulley nut, and carefully guide the belt all the way off with the lever.

5 Alternatively, cut a section out of an old plastic oil bottle, approximately 150 mm x 60 mm. Position the plastic between the pulley and the drive belt, then turn the pulley clockwise and carefully guide the plastic around the pulley underneath the belt **(see illustration)**. When the plastic is trapped around the lower half of the pulley, carefully lever the belt off at its lowest point **(see illustrations)**.

6 Lift the belt off the alternator pulley.

7 To install the new belt you will require BMW service tool Part No. 12 3 591.

8 Position the new belt over the alternator pulley, then fit the service tool over the crankshaft pulley nut and locate the lower end of the belt onto the service tool **(see illustration)**. Turn the crankshaft clockwise and wind the new belt onto the crankshaft pulley until it is fully located over the pulley **(see illustration)**. Remove the service tool when the belt is fully installed, then turn the engine over with a spanner on the pulley nut to settle the belt **(see illustration)**.

Caution: Do not attempt to lever the new belt onto the crankshaft pulley. The belt and/or the surface of the pulley are likely to be damaged resulting in reduced service life of the belt.

9 Install the drive belt cover – take care not to over-tighten the cover screws.

10 Install the remaining components in the reverse order of removal.

13.5a Turn the pulley to trap the plastic (arrowed) underneath the drive belt

13.5b When the plastic is over the lower half of the pulley . . .

13.5c . . . lever the drive belt off carefully

13.8a Locate the new belt over the alternator pulley and the service tool . . .

13.8b . . . then turn the crankshaft to wind the belt onto the crankshaft pulley

13.8c Ensure that the belt is located correctly over both pulleys

14 Nuts and bolts

1 Since vibration of the machine tends to loosen fasteners, all nuts, bolts, screws, etc. should be periodically checked for proper tightness.
2 Pay particular attention to the following:
  Spark plugs
  Engine and gearbox oil filler and drain plugs
  Gearchange lever, front brake lever and rear brake pedal bolts
  Footrest and stand bolts
  Engine mounting bolts
  Shock absorber mounting bolts and Telelever/swingarm pivot bolts
  Handlebar clamp bolts
  Front axle bolt and axle clamp bolts
  Front fork yoke bolts
  Rear wheel bolts
  Brake caliper mounting bolts
  Brake hose banjo bolts and caliper bleed valves
  Brake disc bolts
  Exhaust system bolts/nuts
3 If a torque wrench is available, use it together with the torque specifications at the beginning of this and other Chapters.

15 Wheels and tyres

General
1 Check the valve rubber for signs of damage or deterioration and have it renewed if necessary. Also, make sure the valve stem cap is in place and tight **(see illustration)**.
2 Check that the wheel balance weights are fixed firmly to the wheel rim **(see illustration)**.

If there are signs that a weight has fallen off, have the wheel rebalanced by a motorcycle tyre specialist.
3 Check the wheel runout and front/rear wheel alignment as described in Chapter 5.

Cast wheels
4 Cast wheels are virtually maintenance free, but they should be kept clean and checked periodically for cracks and other damage. Never attempt to repair damaged cast wheels; they must be replaced with new ones.

Wire spoked wheels
5 Follow the procedure in Section 6 to check the spoke tension.
6 Inspect the spokes for damage, breakage or corrosion. A broken or bent spoke must be renewed immediately because the load taken by it will be transferred to adjacent spokes which may in turn fail. Follow the procedure in Chapter 5 to check the radial and axial runout and, if necessary, take the wheel to a wheel building expert for correction.

Front wheel bearings
7 The bearings in the front wheel will wear over a period of time and result in handling problems.
8 Support the motorcycle upright on its centre stand or an auxiliary stand, and take the weight off the front wheel. Check for any play in the bearings by pushing and pulling the wheel against the hub. Also spin the wheel and check that it rotates smoothly.
9 If any play is detected in the hub, or if the wheel does not rotate smoothly (and this is not due to brake drag), remove the wheel and inspect the bearings for wear or damage (see Chapter 5).

Final drive bearings
10 The rear wheel and brake disc are bolted to the final drive unit and pivot on the bearings contained within the drive unit – there are no bearings in the rear wheel. Before checking

for play, first check that the rear wheel bolts are tight – refer to the torque setting in the Specifications section of this Chapter.
11 Support the motorcycle upright on its centre stand or an auxiliary stand, and take the weight off the rear wheel. Grasp the wheel and check for any play between the rear wheel and final drive unit **(see illustration)**. If play is evident the final drive bearings may need attention – have the machine checked a BMW dealer. **Note:** Play felt at the rear wheel may be due to worn pivot bearings between the swingarm and the final drive unit (see Section 16).

16 Suspension

1 The suspension components must be maintained in top operating condition to ensure rider safety. Loose, worn or damaged suspension parts decrease the motorcycle's stability and control and are potentially dangerous.

Front suspension
2 Check that the front suspension operates smoothly and without binding. Note that

15.1 Ensure that the valve cap is tight – front wheel, R1200 S shown

15.2 Balance weights (arrowed) must be firmly attached to the wheel rim – R1200 GS shown

15.11 Checking for play in the final drive bearings

16.3 Displace the dust seals (arrowed) carefully and check for oil leaks

16.5 Inspect the damper rod (arrowed) on the rear shock

due to its unconventional design, the front suspension cannot be checked by pushing and pulling on the handlebars. If problems have been noted whilst riding the bike, the front fork mountings and Telelever pivots should be dismantled and checked thoroughly (see Chapter 4).

3 Inspect the area above the dust seal on the fork tubes for signs of oil leakage, then carefully lever up the dust seal using a flat-bladed screwdriver and inspect the area around the fork seal **(see illustration)**. If leakage is evident, the seals must be renewed (see Chapter 4).

4 Inspect the shock absorber for pitting on the damper rod and fluid leakage. If leakage is found, the shock should be renewed (see Chapter 4). Ensure that the upper and lower mountings are tight.

Rear suspension

5 Remove the bodywork as necessary to access the rear suspension (see Chapter 6). Inspect the shock absorber for pitting on the damper rod and fluid leakage **(see illustration)**. If leakage is found, the shock should be renewed (see Chapter 4). Ensure that the upper and lower mountings are tight.

6 With the aid of an assistant to support the bike, compress the rear suspension several times by pressing down on the passenger grab-rail. It should move up and down freely without binding. If any binding is felt, the worn or faulty component must be identified and replaced. The problem could be due to either the shock absorber or the swingarm components.

7 Grasp the top of the rear wheel and pull it upwards – there should be no discernible freeplay before the shock absorber begins to compress **(see illustration)**. If freeplay is felt, check that the shock absorber mountings are tight, then check for wear in the shock absorber mountings.

8 Support the motorcycle upright on its centre stand or an auxiliary stand, so that the rear wheel is off the ground. Grab the swingarm and rock it from side to side to check for freeplay. If freeplay is detected, this could be due to worn swingarm bearings or loose pivots.

9 First check that the pivots are tightened correctly (see Chapter 4). Then remove the rear wheel (see Chapter 5) and shock absorber (see Chapter 4) to make an accurate assessment of the swingarm components.

10 The swingarm should move smoothly about its pivots, without any binding or rough spots **(see illustration)**. There should be no discernible freeplay felt front-to-back or side-to-side. Next, check for freeplay in the bearings between the swingarm and the final drive unit **(see illustration)**.

11 If bearing damage or freeplay is evident, the swingarm should be removed and the swingarm and final drive unit bearings and pivots inspected (see Chapter 4).

17 Final drive oil change

1 Changing of the final drive oil is necessary after the machine's initial 600 miles of use, after the new components have bedded in. It is performed as part of the initial 600 mile (1000 km) service by a BMW dealer under the terms of the warranty. Successive oil changes should not be necessary unless of course there is evidence of oil leakage from the final drive unit or the unit is overhaul at any time.

2004 to Aug 2007 models

2 The procedure for changing the oil is not straightforward on early machines because no drain plug is provided. Draining of the oil requires disconnection of the Paralever arm

16.7 Checking for play in the shock absorber mountings

16.10a Checking the free movement of the swingarm

16.10b Checking for freeplay in the final drive unit pivot bearings (arrowed)

17.3 Final drive oil level plug (arrowed) is used for oil draining when rotated to 6 o'clock position

17.5a Remove the speed sensor, noting any shims and the O-ring . . .

17.5b . . . and inject the fresh oil into the final drive unit

17.7 Final drive oil drain plug (arrowed)

from the final drive unit so that the unit can be pivoted down at such an angle that the oil level plug is at the lowermost point – the procedure is covered in Chapter 4, Section 12, Steps 1 to 8.

3 Remove the plug and allow the oil to drain – leave it several minuites to drain fully **(see illustration)**. Clean any metal particles off the magnetic tip of the level plug, then refit the plug and tighten it to the specified torque setting.

4 Lubricate the splined end of the bevel gear shaft with molybdenum disulphide grease. Clean the coupling boot and lubricate both its ends with silicone grease, then install it on the drive housing. Referring again to the procedure in Chapter 4, follow Steps 21 to 23 to reconnect the drive housing with the Paralever arm.

5 The oil is injected into the final drive unit housing via the speed sensor hole at the top of the housing. Remove the sensor **(see illustration)**. Use only the specified Castrol

SAF-XO oil in the final drive unit, applying the exact amount specified by injecting it in with a clean syringe – do not use a syringe which has been in contact with any other fluids **(see illustration)**. Note that the oil can be injected through the level plug hole if desired.

6 On completion, refit the speed sensor and all other disturbed components in a reverse of their removal procedure.

Sept 2007-on models

7 Position the machine upright. Make up a cardboard chute which can be used to deflect the final drive oil away from the wheel and tyre and into a container, then remove the drain plug and allow the oil to drain **(see illustration)**. Wait a few minutes for the oil to drain fully, then refit the plug and tigthen it to the specified torque setting.

8 The fresh oil is injected into the final drive unit housing via the filler hole at the top of the housing (see Step 5). Remove the rear wheel for ease of access, then unscrew the plug from

the filler hole **(see illustration)**. Use only the specified Castrol SAF-XO oil in the final drive unit, applying the exact amount specified by injecting it in with a clean syringe – do not use a syringe which has been in contact with any other fluids **(see illustration)**. On completion, refit the filler plug and tighten it to the specified torque setting.

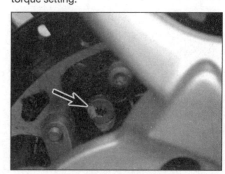

17.8 Oil filler plug (arrowed)

Chapter 2
Engine, clutch and transmission

Contents

Degrees of difficulty

Easy, suitable for novice with little experience	**Fairly easy,** suitable for beginner with some experience	**Fairly difficult,** suitable for competent DIY mechanic	**Difficult,** suitable for experienced DIY mechanic	**Very difficult,** suitable for expert DIY or professional

Specifications

General

Capacity	1170 cc
Bore	101 mm
Stroke	73 mm
Compression ratio	
R1200 GS (2004 to 2007)	11.0 to 1
R1200 RT, ST, R, 2008-on GS	12.0 to 1
R1200 S	12.5 to 1
Valves	4 per cylinder
Cooling system	Air/oil
Clutch	Dry single plate with diaphragm spring

General (continued)

Transmission.	Six-speed constant mesh
Final drive	Shaft

Cylinder compression
Good	above 145 psi (10 Bar)
Normal	125 to 145 psi (8.5 to 10 Bar)
Poor	less than 125 psi (8.5 Bar)
Engine oil pressure (with engine warm)	50 to 87 psi (3.5 to 6.0 Bar)
Cylinder identification.	No. 1 cylinder (left), no. 2 cylinder (right)

Rocker arms

Rocker arm bore diameter	16.016 to 16.034 mm
Rocker shaft diameter	15.973 to 15.984 mm

Arm/shaft clearance
Standard.	0.032 to 0.054 mm
Service limit	0.10 mm
Rocker arm endplay	0.05 to 0.4 mm

Camshafts and followers

Camshafts
Intake valve lift	10.4 mm
Exhaust valve lift.	10.0 mm
Bearing holder diameter	21.02 to 21.04 mm
Camshaft journal diameter	20.97 to 21.00 mm

Journal/holder clearance
Standard.	0.02 to 0.07 mm
Service limit	0.15 mm
Camshaft bearing width	16.0 to 16.05 mm
Cap bearing width	15.92 to 15.95 mm

Camshaft/cap axial play
Standard.	0.08 to 0.13 mm
Service limit	0.25 mm

Followers
Follower diameter.	23.967 to 23.980 mm
Follower bore diameter.	24.000 to 24.021 mm

Follower/bore clearance
Standard.	0.020 to 0.054 mm
Service limit	0.18 mm

Valves and springs

Valve clearances.	see Chapter 1

Intake valves
Head diameter	36.35 mm

Stem diameter
Standard.	4.966 to 4.980 mm
Service limit	4.946 mm

Exhaust valves
Head diameter	31.0 mm

Stem diameter
Standard.	4.956 to 4.970 mm
Service limit	4.936 mm

Spring free length
Standard
R1200 GS, ST, RT and R	48.8 mm
R1200 S	49.2 mm

Service limit
R1200 GS, ST, RT and R	45.2 mm
R1200 S	45.6 mm

Cylinders

Bore diameter	Standard	Service limit
Group A	100.992 to 101.000 mm	101.05 mm
Group B	101.000 to 101.008 mm	101.058 mm
Group A/B.	100.992 to 101.008 mm	101.058 mm

Ovality (out-of-round) service limit
20 mm from top	0.01 mm
100 mm from top	0.015 mm

Piston rings

	Standard	Service limit
Ring installation	'TOP' mark facing up	
Top and second rings		
Ring thickness	1.175 to 1.190 mm	1.10 mm
Ring-to-groove clearance	0.030 to 0.065 mm	0.15 mm
Ring end gap (installed)	0.10 to 0.30 mm	0.80 mm
Oil ring		
Ring thickness	2.475 to 2.490 mm	2.40 mm
Ring-to-groove clearance	0.020 to 0.055 mm	0.15 mm
Ring end gap (installed)	0.30 to 0.60 mm	1.20 mm

Pistons

	Standard	Service limit
Piston diameter – measured 6 mm up from bottom edge at 90° to piston pin axis		
Group A	100.977 to 100.989 mm	100.900 mm
Group B	100.965 to 100.977 mm	100.89 mm
Group A/B	100.973 to 100.981 mm	100.895 mm
Piston-to-bore clearance	0.011 to 0.035 mm	0.12 mm
Piston pin diameter		
Standard	21.995 to 22.000 mm	
Service limit	21.960 mm	
Piston pin bore diameter in piston	22.005 to 22.011 mm	
Piston pin-to-piston clearance service limit	0.06 mm	
Piston weight differential (max)	10 g	

Connecting rods

Small-end internal diameter . . . . 22.015 to 22.025 mm
Small-end to piston pin clearance
  Standard . . . . 0.015 to 0.030 mm
  Service limit . . . . 0.06 mm
Big-end bearing shell identification – colour mark on edge of shells . . . blue or red
Big-end bore diameter without bearing shells . . . . 51.000 to 51.013 mm
Big-end bore diameter with bearing shells
  Stage 0 . . . . 48.016 to 48.050 mm
  Stage 1 (+0.25 mm) . . . . 47.766 to 47.800 mm
Crankpin diameter – paint mark on front crank web
  Stage 0 . . . . no paint mark
  Stage 1 undersize (-0.25 mm) . . . . paint mark
  Stage 0 . . . . 47.975 to 47.991 mm
  Stage 1 (-0.25 mm) . . . . 47.725 to 47.741 mm
Big-end oil clearance
  Standard . . . . 0.025 to 0.075 mm
  Service limit . . . . 0.13 mm
Big-end side clearance
  Standard . . . . 0.130 to 0.312 mm
  Service limit . . . . 0.5 mm
Weight class identification
  2 white dots (class 0) . . . . 559.0 to 564.9 g
  2 blue dots (class 1) . . . . 565.0 to 570.9 g
  3 white dots (class 2) . . . . 571.0 to 576.9 g
  3 yellow dots (class 3) . . . . 577.0 to 582.9 g
  1 blue dot (class 4) . . . . 583.0 to 588.9 g

Oil pump

Engine oil pressure (with engine warm) . . . . 50 to 87 psi (3.5 to 6.0 Bar)
Pressure relief valve opens . . . . 87 psi (6.0 Bar)
Pump housing depth
  Pump 1 (cooling circuit) . . . . 11.020 to 11.050 mm
  Pump 2 (lubricating circuit) . . . . 10.020 to 10.050 mm
Pump rotor thickness
  Pump 1 (cooling circuit) . . . . 10.965 to 10.980 mm
  Pump 2 (lubricating circuit) . . . . 9.965 to 9.980 mm
Clearance (end-float)
  Standard . . . . 0.04 to 0.10 mm
  Service limit . . . . 0.25 mm

Crankshaft and bearings

Crankshaft identification – paint mark on front crank web
   Stage 0 .... no paint mark
   Stage 1 undersize (- 0.25 mm) .... paint mark

Main bearing shell identification – colour mark on edge of shells	Green	Yellow
Stage 0		
Main bearing shell inside diameter	59.964 to 60.003 mm	59.974 to 60.013 mm
Crankshaft journal diameter	59.939 to 59.948 mm	59.949 to 59.958 mm
Stage 1 (re-ground crankshaft)		
Main bearing shell inside diameter	59.714 to 59.753 mm	59.724 to 59.763 mm
Crankshaft journal diameter	59.689 to 59.698 mm	59.699 to 59.708 mm

Main bearing oil clearance (all stages)
   Standard... 0.018 to 0.068 mm
   Service limit .... 0.13 mm
Main bearing bore diameter in crankcase .... 64.960 to 64.979 mm

Guide bearing shell identification – colour mark on edge of shells	Green	Yellow
Stage 0		
Guide bearing shell inside diameter	59.964 to 60.003 mm	59.974 to 60.013 mm
Crankshaft journal diameter	59.939 to 59.948 mm	59.949 to 59.958 mm
Stage 1		
Guide bearing shell inside diameter	59.714 to 59.753 mm	59.724 to 59.763 mm
Crankshaft journal diameter	59.689 to 59.698 mm	59.699 to 59.708 mm

Guide bearing oil clearance (all stages)
   Standard... 0.016 to 0.064 mm
   Service limit .... 0.10 mm
Guide bearing bore diameter in crankcase .... 64.949 to 64.969 mm
Guide bearing width... 24.89 to 24.94 mm
Crankshaft guide bearing journal width .... 25.02 to 25.053 mm
Crankshaft end-float in guide bearing
   Standard... 0.080 to 0.163 mm
   Service limit .... 0.20 mm

Auxiliary shaft

Shaft diameter .... 24.959 to 24.980 mm
Shaft bore diameter (in crankcase)........................... 25.020 to 25.041 mm
Clearance
   Standard... 0.040 to 0.082 mm
   Service limit .... 0.17 mm

Balancer shaft

Shaft diameter
   Front bearing journal .... 16.983 to 16.994 mm
   Rear bearing journal .... 20.991 to 20.000 mm
Bearing bore diameter (in crankcase)
   Front bearing .... 47.0 to 47.016 mm
   Rear bearing... 36.955 to 36.971 mm

Clutch

Friction plate thickness (service limit)........................ 4.4 to 4.6 mm
Clutch fluid .... Vitamol V10

Transmission

Gear ratios (no. of teeth)
  R1200 GS models 2004 to 2007; R1200 R, RT, ST and S models all years
    1st gear.. 2.277 to 1 (41/18T)
    2nd gear... 1.583 to 1 (38/24T)
    3rd gear... 1.259 to 1 (34/27T)
    4th gear... 1.033 to 1 (31/30T)
    5th gear... 0.903 to 1 (28/31T)
    6th gear... 0.805 to 1 (29/36T)
  R1200 GS 2008-on models
    1st gear.. 2.375 to 1 (38/16T)
    2nd gear .... 1.696 to 1 (39/23T)
    3rd gear... 1.296 to 1 (35/27T)
    4th gear... 1.065 to 1 (33/31T)
    5th gear... 0.939 to 1 (31/33T)
    6th gear... 0.848 to 1 (28/33T)

Transmission (continued)

Primary drive ratio
    R1200 GS 2004 to 2007, R1200 R, RT and S all years . . . . 1.824 to 1
    R1200 GS 2008-on. . . . . 1.737 to 1
    R1200 ST . . . . 1.882 to 1
Final drive ratio
    R1200 GS
        2004 to 2007. . . . . 2.82 to 1
        2008-on . . . . 2.91 to 1
    R1200 ST . . . . 2.62 to 1
    R1200 RT
        2005 to 2006. . . . . 2.62 to 1
        2007-on . . . . 2.72 to 1
    R1200 S
        2006 . . . . 2.75 to 1
        2007-on . . . . 2.62 to 1
    R1200R. . . . . 2.75 to 1
Output shaft
    Partial assembled length . . . . 115.55 to 115.6 mm
    Total assembled length. . . . . 182.64 to 182.69 mm
Input shaft
    Pre-damper travel. . . . . 0.4 to 0.6 mm
    Total assembled length. . . . . 163.1 to 163.15 mm

Torque settings

Alternator belt cover screws. . . . . 5 Nm
Alternator belt drive pulley nut
    Initial stage setting . . . . 40 Nm
    Final setting . . . . 140 Nm
Auxiliary shaft bearing cover screws . . . . 8 Nm
Auxiliary shaft drive chain lower sprocket bolts. . . . . 6 Nm
Auxiliary shaft drive chain upper sprocket bolts . . . . 8 Nm
Auxiliary shaft drive chain tensioner bolts . . . . 8 Nm
Balancer shaft gear nut (Oct 2007-on) . . . . 75 Nm
Balancer shaft cover screws . . . . 8 Nm
Balancer shaft front bolt. . . . . 19 Nm
Balancer shaft weight bolt
    Initial setting . . . . 10 Nm
    Final setting . . . . 90°
Camchain guide and tensioner blade pivot bolts. . . . . 18 Nm
Camchain tensioner . . . . 32 Nm
Camshaft bearing cap bolts. . . . . 15 Nm
Camshaft sprocket bolt . . . . 65 Nm
Camshaft sprocket cover bolts . . . . 8 Nm
Clutch cover plate bolts . . . . 12 Nm
Clutch flywheel bolts
    Initial setting . . . . 40 Nm
    Final setting . . . . angle-tighten 40°
Clutch hose banjo bolts . . . . 24 Nm
Clutch release cylinder mounting bolts . . . . 8 Nm
Clutch top cover screws. . . . . 8 Nm
Connecting rod big-end bolts
    1st stage setting. . . . . 5 Nm
    2nd stage setting . . . . 20 Nm
    Final setting
        Models up to Mar 2006 (M10 x 1.25) . . . . 90°
        Models after Mar 2006 (M10 x 1.00). . . . . 105°
Crankcase bolts
    10 mm bolts
        Initial setting . . . . 25 Nm
        Final setting . . . . angle-tighten 90°
    8 mm bolts . . . . 19 Nm
    6 mm bolts . . . . 8 Nm
Crankshaft position sensor screw . . . . 8 Nm
Cylinder 8 mm bolt. . . . . 19 Nm
Cylinder 6 mm screws . . . . 8 Nm
Cylinder head 10 mm bolt . . . . 40 Nm

Torque settings (continued)

Cylinder head 6 mm screws . . . . 9 Nm
Cylinder head nuts
  1st stage setting . . . . 20 Nm
  2nd stage setting . . . . angle-tighten 90°
  Final setting . . . . angle-tighten 90°
Engine mountings
  Front sub-frame
    Front strut-to-engine through-bolt
      R1200 GS, RT, ST and R . . . . 110 Nm
      R1200 S . . . . 130 Nm
    Rear strut to rear frame/engine bolts
      R1200 GS, RT, ST and R . . . . 38 Nm
      R1200 S . . . . 58 Nm
    Telelever pivot bolt – all models
      Initial stage setting . . . . 45 Nm
      Final setting . . . . 73 Nm
  Rear sub-frame
    Top mounting bolt . . . . 38 Nm
    Bottom mounting bolt . . . . 55 Nm
    Rear front strut to rear frame/engine bolts . . . . 38 Nm
    Frame to gearbox . . . . 28 Nm
Gear position sensor bolts . . . . 9 Nm
Gearbox cover bolts . . . . 9 Nm
Gearbox mounting bolts . . . . 19 Nm
Gearchange lever pinch bolt . . . . 8 Nm
Knock sensor bolt . . . . 19 Nm
Oil cooler mounting bolts
  R1200 GS and RT . . . . 8 Nm
  R1200 S and ST . . . . 6 Nm
  R1200 R . . . . 4 Nm
Oil cooler return pipe banjo bolt . . . . 35 Nm
Oil pump mounting bolts
  Initial setting . . . . 4 Nm
  Final setting . . . . angle-tighten 90°
Oil pipe banjo bolt (internal) . . . . 25 Nm
Oil pipe bracket bolts (internal) . . . . 8 Nm
Oil pressure relief valve . . . . 42 Nm
Oil pressure switch . . . . 30 Nm
Oil strainer bolts . . . . 8 Nm
Oil thermostat/cooler feed pipe flange bolts . . . . 8 Nm
Rocker holder bolts . . . . 8 Nm
Rocker shaft cap bolts . . . . 18 Nm
Starter motor mounting bolts . . . . 19 Nm
Timing case cover screws . . . . 8 Nm
Valve cover bolts . . . . 10 Nm

1 General information

The engine unit is an air/oil-cooled, horizontally-opposed twin. There are four valves per cylinder, each operated by a single camshaft via followers, pushrods and rockers. The camshafts are located in the cylinder heads and are chain driven off the auxiliary shaft, which in turn is driven by chain off the crankshaft. The auxiliary shaft runs at half crankshaft speed.

The engine incorporates a balancer shaft.

The separate engine and gearbox cases are constructed from aluminium alloy. The engine and gearbox units are bolted together with a dry, single plate diaphragm clutch located between the two. The engine/gearbox unit supports the front and rear suspension systems – there is no motorcycle frame in the conventional sense.

The crankcase is divided vertically and incorporates a wet sump, pressure-fed lubrication system which utilises a dual-rotor oil pump driven by the auxiliary shaft. An oil filter is externally located on the underside of the crankcase. To assist engine cooling, oil is pumped to a cooler mounted at the front of the machine, underneath the headlight.

Power from the crankshaft is routed to the transmission input shaft in the gearbox via the clutch. The input shaft has a sprung damper. The transmission is a six-speed constant-mesh unit, and drive to the rear wheel is by shaft via a final drive unit.

2 Component access

Operations possible with the engine in the frame

The components and assemblies listed below can be removed without having to remove the front or rear sub-frames and suspension systems.

Oil cooler and hoses
Valve covers
Camchain tensioners
Rocker/camshaft assemblies
Cylinder heads and valves
Cylinders, pistons and piston rings
Connecting rods and bearings

Alternator drive belt and pulleys
Alternator
Balancer shaft gears
Auxiliary shaft sprockets and chain
Oil pump and pressure relief valve
Starter motor
Clutch release cylinder

Operations requiring removal of the front or rear sub frames

It is necessary to remove either the front or rear sub-frames and suspension systems, or both, to gain access to the following components.

Gearbox
Clutch
Auxiliary shaft
Camchains, tensioner blades and guide blades
Crankshaft and bearings
Oil strainer

| 3 | Engine wear assessment | |

 Warning: Be careful when working on the hot engine – the exhaust pipes, the engine and engine components can cause severe burns.

Cylinder compression test

Special tools: *A compression gauge with an appropriate threaded adapter (see illustration 3.6) and spark plug cap/ignition coil extractor are necessary for this procedure.*

1 Among other things, poor starting and engine performance may be caused by leaking valves, a leaking head gasket or worn pistons, rings and/or cylinder walls. A cylinder compression check will help pinpoint these conditions.
2 Before carrying out the test, check that the valve clearances are correct (see Chapter 1).
3 Run the engine until it reaches normal operating temperature, then turn the ignition OFF. Support the machine on its centre stand or on an auxiliary stand.
4 Follow the procedure in Chapter 1, Section 11, and pull the ignition cap/coils off all four spark plugs, then unscrew the primary spark plugs from both cylinder heads.

3.6 Using the cylinder compression gauge and adapter

5 Install the primary spark plugs back into their cap/coils and install two spare spark plugs into the secondary cap/coils. Arrange the plugs so that their metal bodies are earthed against the adjacent cylinder. **Note:** *Do not earth the plugs against the magnesium valve covers which may be damaged by the procedure.*
6 Working on the first cylinder to be tested, thread the adapter into the spark plug hole then install the compression gauge **(see illustration)**.
7 Open the throttle fully and crank the engine over on the starter motor until the gauge reading stabilises – after one or two revolutions the pressure should build up to a maximum figure and then remain stable. Make a note of the pressure reading and then repeat the procedure on the other cylinder. Turn the ignition OFF when the test has been completed.
8 Compare the results with the specifications at the beginning of this Chapter. If they are both within the specified range (normal to good) and relatively equal, the engine is in good condition. If there is a marked difference between the readings, or if the readings are lower than specified, inspection of one or both engine top-ends is required (see Sections 12 to 14).
9 Follow the procedure in Chapter 1, Section 11, and install the spark plugs and cap/coils. **Note:** *High compression pressure indicates excessive carbon build-up in the combustion chamber and on the top of the piston. If this is the case, remove the cylinder heads and clean the carbon deposits off. Note that excessive carbon build-up is less likely with the use of modern fuels.*

Engine oil pressure check

Special tools: *An oil pressure gauge with an appropriate threaded adapter is necessary for this procedure.*
Note: *Even if the engine appears to be in good condition and the oil pressure warning light is not coming on, an oil pressure check can provide useful information about the internal condition of the engine.*

10 The oil pressure warning light should come on together with a red general warning light when the ignition (main) switch is first turned ON – this is part of the electronic 'self-checking' system and serves as a check that the warning indicators are working. If the oil pressure light comes on whilst the engine is running, low oil pressure is indicated – stop the engine immediately and carry out an oil level check (see *Pre-ride checks*).
11 If the oil level is correct, test the oil pressure switch (see Chapter 7). If the switch is good, carry out an oil pressure check.
12 To check the oil pressure, a suitable gauge and adapter piece (which screws into the crankcase) will be needed – see the example shown in Section 3 of *Reference* at the end of this manual.
13 Run the engine until it reaches normal

operating temperature then turn the ignition OFF. Support the bike upright on its centre stand or on an auxiliary stand.
14 Unscrew the oil pressure switch (see Chapter 7) then quickly screw the adapter into the crankcase threads. Connect the pressure gauge to the adapter.
15 Start the engine and increase the engine speed whilst watching the gauge reading. Make a note of the pressure reading, then stop the engine, unscrew the gauge and adapter from the crankcase and install the oil pressure switch.
16 The oil pressure should be similar to that given in the *Specifications* at the beginning of this Chapter. If the pressure is significantly lower than that specified, either the pressure relief valve is stuck open, the oil strainer or filter is blocked, the oil pump is worn or there is other engine wear or damage.
17 Begin diagnosis by checking the pressure relief valve (see Section 22) and fitting a new oil filter (see Chapter 1). Next inspect the oil pump (see Section 22) and finally the strainer – this last procedure requires engine removal and crankcase separation (see Section 25). If everything is in good condition, it is likely that the crankshaft bearing oil clearances are excessive and the engine needs to be overhauled.
18 If the pressure is too high, either an oil passage is clogged, the relief valve is stuck closed or the wrong grade of oil is being used.

| 4 | Engine removal and installation | |

Note 1: *The engine is not removed from the bike, rather the rest of the bike is removed from around the engine. For ease of operation, the rear suspension and its sub-frame are removed first, followed by the front suspension and its sub-frame. If required, only one of the sub-frames can be removed independently of the other to gain access to a specific area of the engine/gearbox unit.*
Note 2: *On machines fitted with ABS, the modulator must be disconnected from the front and rear brake systems before it is removed from its location on top of the engine unit – on reassembly, once the brake pipes have been reconnected, the system must be topped-up and bled by a BMW dealer using the BMW diagnostic tester. This ensures that no air is trapped in the system resulting in impaired braking.*
Note 3: *The machines covered in this manual were available from new fitted with a range of optional electrical extras. A list of model specific extras can be found at the end of Chapter 7. When working on your machine, take care to ensure that all relevant electrical components are disconnected on disassembly and subsequently reconnected during the rebuild. Always take the precaution*

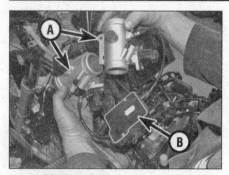

4.12 Remove the throttle bodies (A) and cable splitter (B) as an assembly

4.13a Undo the screw (arrowed) . . .

4.13b . . . then manoeuvre the starter motor cover out

of disconnecting the battery negative (-ve) terminal before disconnecting an electrical wiring connector.

Removal

1 Support the bike upright on its centre stand or on an auxiliary stand. Prior to removing the swingarm (R1200 S models) and rear sub-frame (all other models), the engine will have to be supported underneath the crankcase and provision will have to be made to secure the engine unit to prevent it toppling over. This was achieved on the machine photographed by securing the cylinders to both sides of the motorcycle ramp with tie-down straps **(see illustration 4.26)**.

2 Remove the seat, the frame side panels and the fairing side panels, as required according to your model, to gain access to the engine and related components (see Chapter 6).

3 Remove the fuel tank panels (see Chapter 6).

4 Remove the battery (see Chapter 7).

5 If the engine is dirty, particularly around its mountings, wash it thoroughly before starting any major dismantling work. This will make work much easier and rule out the possibility of dirt falling into some vital component.

6 Drain the engine oil and remove the oil filter (see Chapter 1). If work is being carried out on the gearbox, drain the gearbox oil (see Chapter 1).

7 Remove the air intake duct (see Chapter 1, Section 10).

8 Remove the fuel tank (see Chapter 3).

9 Follow the procedure in Chapter 1, Section 11, and remove the primary and secondary spark plug caps/coils.

10 Remove the exhaust system (see Chapter 3).

11 Where fitted, remove the crash bars (see Chapter 6).

12 Follow the procedure in Chapter 3 and disconnect the throttle cable from the handlebar twistgrip. Feed the cable back to the cable splitter and unclip the splitter from the front of the air filter housing. Follow the procedure in Chapter 3 and remove both throttle bodies from the intake manifolds, then lift the throttle bodies, splitter and cables off as an assembly **(see illustration)** – there is no need to disconnect the throttle cables from the injector pulleys.

13 Where fitted, undo the screw securing the starter motor cover and lift the cover off, noting how it fits **(see illustrations)**.

14 Check for the mark on the gearchange shaft that aligns with the slot in the lever **(see illustration)**. If the mark isn't visible, make your own with a sharp punch, then remove the pinch bolt and pull the lever off the shaft.

15 Note the location of the cable ties securing the clutch hose to the frame, then cut the ties **(see illustration)**. Undo the bolts securing the clutch release cylinder to the back of the gearbox and position the cylinder clear of the rear sub-frame **(see illustrations)**.

16 Remove the rear wheel (see Chapter 5). At this point, on R1200S models, it will be necessary to place a support underneath the crankcase and secure the engine unit to prevent it toppling over.

17 On machines fitted with ABS, lift out the document tray, where fitted **(see**

4.13c Note the peg (arrowed) on the cover that locates in a hole in the engine casing

4.14 Punch mark on shaft (arrowed) should align with slot in lever

4.15a Release the clutch hose from the frame

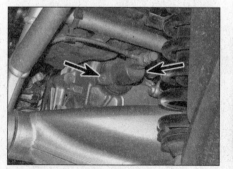

4.15b Undo the bolts (arrowed) . . .

4.15c . . . and displace the clutch release cylinder

4.17a Lift out the document tray

4.17b Undo the screws (arrowed) . . .

4.17c . . . and lift off the brake hose guide

4.17d Disconnect the rear wheel ABS sensor wiring connector

4.18a Displace the rear brake caliper . . .

4.18b . . . and secure it to the rear sub-frame

illustration). Undo the screws securing the rear brake hose guide and lift the guide off the Paralever arm (see illustrations). Trace the wiring from the rear wheel ABS sensor to the wiring connector and disconnect it (see illustration). Note the location of the cable ties securing the wiring to the frame, then cut the ties and secure the wiring next to the final drive unit, well clear of the rear sub-frame.

18 Displace the rear brake caliper (see Chapter 5), then secure the caliper to the rear sub-frame (see illustrations). Note that it is not necessary to disconnect the brake hose from the caliper.

19 Follow the procedure in Chapter 4 and remove the rear shock absorber and swingarm/final drive unit assembly (see illustrations).
20 Remove the rear light unit (see Chapter 7). Displace any electrical units (such as the starter relay and the diagnostic tester connector) located on the rear sub-frame (see illustration). Note the location of the cable ties securing the wiring to the frame, then cut the ties and secure the wiring well clear of the rear sub-frame.
21 Disconnect the rear brake light switch and side stand switch wiring connectors (see

4.19a Remove the rear shock absorber . . .

4.19b . . . and swingarm/final drive unit assembly

4.20 Displace any electrical units from the rear sub-frame

4.21a Disconnect the rear brake light switch . . .

4.21b . . . and side stand switch wiring connectors

4.21c Undo the screws (arrowed) to release the trunking from the frame

4.22a Release the clip . . .

4.22b . . . and pull the hose off the air filter housing

illustrations). Note the location of the cable ties securing the wiring loom to the frame, then cut the ties. Where fitted, undo the screws securing the wiring loom trunking to the frame and ensure the trunking is free (see illustration).

22 Release the clip securing the engine breather hose to the air filter housing and pull the hose off (see illustrations).

23 On machines fitted with ABS, trace the rear brake pipes from the rear brake hose-to-pipe union on the rear sub-frame, and from the rear master cylinder, to the ABS modulator and disconnect them (see Note 2 at the beginning of this Section). Wrap a clean rag around the modulator to catch any spilled hydraulic fluid. On some machines, the pipes are secured by spring clips, on others they are secured by union nuts (see illustrations). Use one of the modulator bleed valve caps to cover the open end of the pipe from the master cylinder. Cover the unions to prevent dirt entering the modulator. Disconnect the rear brake hose-to-pipe union, being prepared to catch any residual fluid in the brake pipe, and lift the pipe off (see illustrations).

24 Check that all the wiring is free from the rear sub-frame. Note that some of the wiring is secured by push-in clips – use pliers to compress the ends of the clips together to release them (see illustration). If any optional electrical extras are fitted to the rear sub-frame, ensure the wiring has been

4.23a Pull out the spring clip . . .

4.23b . . . and disconnect the brake pipes

4.23c Disconnect the brake hose-to-pipe union . . .

4.23d . . . and lift the pipe off

4.24 Ensure that all the wiring clips are free from the rear sub-frame

4.25 Disconnect the intake air temperature sensor

4.26 Ensure that the engine/front suspension assembly is securely supported

disconnected (see **Note 3** at the beginning of this Section).

25 Disconnect the intake air temperature sensor **(see illustration)**.

26 If not already done, place a support underneath the crankcase and secure the engine unit to prevent it toppling over **(see illustration)**.

27 Undo the bolt securing the rear sub-frame to the rear of the gearbox **(see illustration)**.

28 Loosen the bolts on both sides securing the upper and lower struts of the rear sub-frame to the engine unit – note that the bolts through the brackets on the upper struts also secure the rear front struts **(see illustrations)**.

29 Have an assistant support the rear sub-frame, then withdraw the bolts, noting the location of any washers **(see illustration)**. Note that the brackets on the rear sub-frame fit outside the front struts **(see illustration)**.

30 Ease the rear sub-frame away carefully from the engine unit, ensuring the wiring is free of the frame members. Unclip the fuel pressure regulator from the front of the air filter housing **(see illustration)**.

31 Lift the rear sub-frame off **(see illustration)**. Support the sub-frame in an upright position to avoid brake fluid leaking from the fluid reservoir.

4.27 Undo the bolt (arrowed) on the rear of the gearbox

4.28a Loosen the bolts (arrowed) securing the upper . . .

4.28b . . . and lower ends of the rear sub-frame

4.29a Note the location of any washers on the bolts

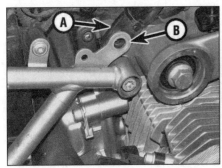

4.29b Note how the front struts (A) fit inside the rear sub-frame struts (B)

4.30 Displace the fuel pressure regulator (arrowed)

4.31 Lift off the rear sub-frame

4.32a Undo the terminal nut (arrowed) and disconnect the battery lead

4.32b Disconnect the wiring connector . . .

4.32c . . . and remove the solenoid cover

4.32d Undo the bolts (arrowed) . . .

4.32e . . . and lift off the starter motor. Note the location of the clutch ring gear (arrowed)

32 Undo the terminal nut and disconnect the battery lead from the starter solenoid, then disconnect the wiring connector and lift off the solenoid cover (**see illustrations**). If required, undo the bolts securing the starter motor and lift it off, noting how the starter gear engages with the clutch ring gear (**see illustrations**). Note that if the gearbox is going to be removed (see Step 34), the starter motor must be removed.

33 Disconnect the gear position sensor wiring connector (**see illustration**).

34 At this point, if required, the gearbox can be separated from the engine, either to gain access to the clutch or to reduce the overall weight of the engine unit if it is to be lifted onto the workbench. If the gearbox is not going to be removed, proceed to Step 39.

35 To remove the gearbox, first withdraw the clutch pushrod from the centre of the transmission input shaft, noting which way round it fits (**see illustration**). Note the location of the seal on the pushrod.

36 Undo the bolts securing the clutch top cover and lift the cover off (**see illustrations**). On machines fitted with ABS, temporarily install the two upper bolts to support the ABS modulator (**see illustration**).

37 Undo the bolts securing the gearbox to the engine crankcases, noting where they fit –

4.33 Disconnect the gear position sensor wiring connector

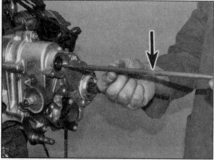

4.35 Withdraw the clutch pushrod – note the location of the seal (arrowed)

4.36a Undo the bolts (arrowed) . . .

4.36b . . . and lift the clutch top cover off

4.36c The two upper bolts (arrowed) support the ABS modulator, where fitted

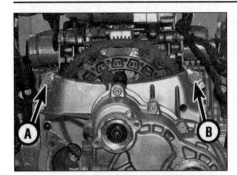

4.37a Undo the two upper bolts (A) and (B) . . .

4.37b . . . and lower bolt (C) securing the gearbox

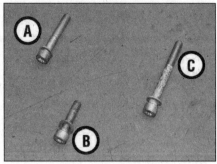

4.37c Note the different lengths of the bolts

the bolts are different lengths **(see illustrations)**.
38 Draw the gearbox off the back of the engine – this procedure is best performed with the aid of an assistant to support the gearbox and ensure it is drawn back level with the engine to avoid damaging the transmission input shaft which locates inside the centre of the clutch **(see illustrations)**. On the machine photographed, corrosion on the two crankcase-to-gearbox case locating dowels made separation difficult. If the gearbox is stuck, tap around the joint face with a soft-faced mallet and drive a wood wedge behind the prise point on the lower edge of the gearbox case – don't exert too much pressure with the wedge or the case may be damaged **(see illustrations)**. Apply heat in the area of the dowels and, once the gearbox starts to come free, soak the

dowels with penetrating fluid **(see illustration)**.
39 Disconnect the wiring connectors for the left and right-hand knock sensors and temperature sensors, noting that on models from Aug 2006

4.38a Draw the gearbox off, keeping it level . . .

there is only a temperature sensor on the left cylinder head **(see illustration)**.
40 Undo the screws securing the earth wires to both cylinder heads **(see illustration)**.

4.38b . . . to avoid damaging the transmission input shaft (arrowed)

4.38c If the gearbox is stuck, tap around the joint face . . .

4.38d . . . and use a wood wedge (arrowed) as described

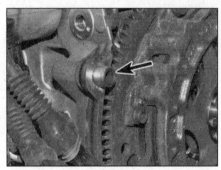

4.38e Location of the dowel in the engine casing . . .

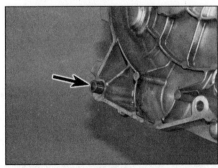

4.38f . . . and the dowel in the gearbox casing

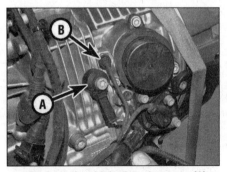

4.39 Location of the knock sensor (A) and temperature sensor (B) – right-hand cylinder shown

4.40 Location of the earth wire terminal screw – left-hand cylinder shown

4.41 Location of the camshaft position sensor

4.42 Location of the oil pressure switch wiring connector

4.43a Trace the wiring from the crankshaft position sensor (arrowed) . . .

4.43b . . . and disconnect it at the connector (arrowed)

4.44 Location of the oil temperature sensor wiring connector

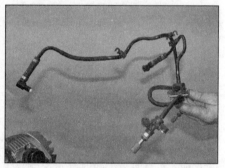

4.45 Remove the fuel pressure regulator assembly

41 Disconnect the wiring connector for the camshaft position sensor on the right-hand cylinder head (see illustration).
42 Disconnect the wiring connector for the oil pressure switch on the left-hand side of the crankcase (see illustration). Where fitted, disconnect the wiring connector for the oil level warning sensor on the right-hand side of the crankcase.
43 Trace the wiring from the crankshaft position sensor on the top of the timing cover and disconnect it at the connector (see illustrations).
44 Disconnect the wiring connector for the oil temperature sensor (see illustration).
45 Lift off the fuel pressure regulator and fuel hose assembly, noting how it fits (see illustration).
46 On machines fitted with ABS, disconnect the front and rear wheel sensor wiring

connectors from the control unit/modulator (see illustration). Release the catch and disconnect the multi-pin wiring connector from the modulator (see illustrations). If required, ease the modulator breather hoses

off their unions and remove the breather assembly (see illustration). Undo the bolt securing the front brake pipes to the front sub-frame (see illustration). Follow the procedure in Step 23 and disconnect the front brake

4.46a Disconnect the ABS wheel sensor connectors (arrowed)

4.46b Release the catch . . .

4.46c . . . and disconnect the multi-pin wiring connector

4.46d Remove the modulator breather assembly carefully

4.46e Separate the brake pipes from the front sub-frame

4.46f Cover the ends of the brake pipes with bleed valve caps

4.46g Undo the bolt (arrowed) securing the front of the modulator . . .

4.46h . . . and lift the ABS modulator off

4.47 Location of the earth wire terminal (arrowed)

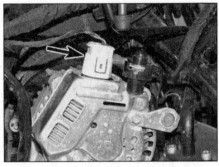

4.48a Disconnect the wiring connector (arrowed) . . .

4.48b . . . and the lead from the alternator terminal (arrowed)

pipes from the modulator, then use two of the bleed valve caps to cover the open ends of the brake pipes (see illustration). Cover the unions to prevent dirt entering the modulator. Undo the two bolts securing the rear of the modulator (see illustration 4.36c). Undo the bolt securing the front of the modulator and lift the modulator off (see illustrations).

47 Undo the screw securing the earth wire to the top of the crankcase (see illustration).

48 Disconnect the wiring connector from the alternator, then remove the cover and undo the terminal nut to disconnect the lead from the alternator (see illustrations).

49 Undo the screw securing the right-hand oil pipe to the fairing bracket (see Section 6). Undo the bolts securing the oil pipe to the crankcase, then lift the pipe and displace it, noting the location of the baffle on top of the

oil thermostat (see illustration). If required, remove the baffle for safekeeping.

50 Undo the banjo bolt securing the left-hand oil pipe to the crankcase and disconnect the pipe, noting the sealing washers on both sides of the banjo union (see Section 6).

51 Check that all the wiring, pipes and hoses are free from the engine unit, and that the engine unit is secure. When the Telelever pivot shaft and engine mounting through-bolt are removed, the front sub-frame and suspension assembly will be unsupported and must be lifted away immediately – ensure all wiring, pipes and hoses on the sub-frame assembly are clear of the engine unit.

52 Prise off the covers on both ends of the Telelever pivot shaft, then counter-hold the head of the pivot shaft and undo the bolt on the right-hand side (see illustrations).

Position small blocks of wood underneath both sides of the Telelever arm to support it as the pivot shaft is withdrawn, then pull out the shaft (see illustration). The wood blocks

4.49 Note the location of the baffle (arrowed) above the oil thermostat

4.52a Counter-hold the pivot shaft (arrowed) . . .

4.52b . . . and undo the bolt (arrowed) on the right-hand side

4.52c Withdraw the Telelever pivot shaft

4.52d Support the Telelever arm to maintain access to the engine mounting bolt (arrowed)

4.53a Undo the nut on the through bolt . . .

4.53b . . . then withdraw the through bolt . . .

will prevent the Telelever arm dropping down over the engine mounting through-bolt **(see illustration)**.

53 Undo the nut on the left-hand end of the engine mounting through-bolt **(see illustration)**. Have an assistant support the front sub-frame and suspension assembly and withdraw the through-bolt, then lift the rear ends of the Telelever arm to prevent them dropping onto the cylinders and manoeuvre the sub-frame and suspension assembly off **(see illustration)**. Support the sub-frame and suspension assembly in an upright position to avoid fluid leaking from the reservoirs.

54 Wrap clean rag around the ends of the left and right-hand oil pipes to prevent spillage of any residual oil from the oil cooler.

 Warning: The engine is very heavy. It is strongly recommended that you have at least one assistant to help lift the engine if it is being moved. Personal injury or damage could occur if the engine falls or is dropped.

Installation

55 Installation is the reverse of removal, noting the following:
● Tighten all bolts to the torque settings specified at the beginning of this Chapter.
● Ensure the engine unit is supported at the right height for the installation of the front and rear sub-frame assemblies, and is held securely.
● If the alternator has been removed, install it before fitting the front sub-frame and suspension assembly (see Chapter 7).

4.53c . . . and lift the front sub-frame/ suspension assembly off

● When installing the front sub-frame and suspension assembly, ensure the left-hand oil pipe is located inside the Telelever arm.
● Install the Telelever pivot shaft first, then the engine mounting though-bolt. Tighten the pivot shaft bolt and through-bolt nut finger-tight initially. Only tighten them to the specified torque settings when all the wiring, pipes and hoses have been correctly routed and secured. Don't forget that the bolts for the rear front struts also secure the brackets on the upper struts of the rear sub-frame.
● Fit a new O-ring onto the right-hand oil pipe and don't forget to install the baffle on top of the oil thermostat before installing the pipe (see Section 6).
● Fit new sealing washers to both sides of the left-hand oil pipe banjo union (see Section 6).
● On machines fitted with ABS, reconnect all the wiring and oil pipes before installing the ABS control unit/modulator. The brake pipes should be connected temporarily onto the modulator, but note that before the machine is ridden it is essential that the brake system is topped-up and bled by a BMW dealer using a BMW diagnostic tester.
● If the gearbox has been removed, smear the crankcase-to-gearbox case dowels and the splines on the transmission input shaft with clutch assembly grease (BMW specify Optimoly MP 3) before installing the gearbox. Ensure the gearbox mounting bolts are positioned in their correct locations – their lengths differ.
● If the starter motor has been removed, install it before fitting the rear sub-frame (see Step 32).
● Position the fuel pressure regulator and fuel hose assembly before installing the rear sub-frame.
● Ensure no wiring becomes trapped between the engine unit and the rear sub-frame when the sub-frame is installed. Note that the brackets on the upper struts fit outside the front struts (see Step 29). Only tighten the mounting bolts to the specified torque settings when all the wiring and hoses have been correctly routed and secured.
● Don't forget to install the clutch pushrod before installing the clutch release cylinder to the back of the gearbox

● Follow the procedure in Chapter 4 to install the rear shock absorber and swingarm/ final drive unit assembly.
● Follow the procedure in Chapter 5 to install the rear brake caliper and rear wheel.
● Follow the procedure in Chapter 3 to install the throttle bodies and throttle cables.
● Refill the engine and gearbox with the correct amount of oil (see Chapter 1).
● Check the operation of all electrical systems before taking the bike on the road.
● On machines not fitted with ABS, check the operation of the brakes before taking the bike on the road. On ABS-equipped models, have the braking system bled and its operation restored by a BMW dealer **before** the machine is ridden.

5 Engine overhaul – general information

Disassembly

1 Before disassembling the engine, the external surfaces of the unit should be thoroughly cleaned and degreased. This will prevent contamination of the engine internals, and will also make working a lot easier and cleaner. A high flash-point solvent, such as paraffin (kerosene) can be used, or better still, a proprietary engine degreaser such as Gunk. Use old paintbrushes and toothbrushes to work the solvent into the various recesses of the engine casings. Take care to exclude solvent or water from the electrical components and from the intake and exhaust ports.

 Warning: The use of petrol (gasoline) as a cleaning agent should be avoided because of the risk of fire.

2 When the engine is clean and dry, clear a suitable clear area for working – a workbench is desirable for all operations once a component has been removed from the machine. Gather a selection of small containers and plastic bags so that parts can be grouped together in an easily identifiable manner. Some paper and a pen should be on hand so that notes can be

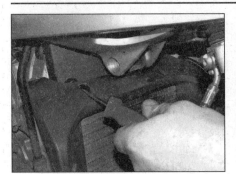

6.1a Oil cooler shroud is retained by screws at top . . .

6.1b . . . and tabs at the bottom on R1200 R

6.3 Release the oil hose clips

made and labels attached where necessary. A supply of clean rag is also required. If the engine has been removed from the bike (see Section 4), have an assistant help you lift it onto the workbench.

3 Before commencing work, read through the appropriate section so that some idea of the necessary procedure can be gained. When removing components it should be noted that great force is seldom required, unless specified. In many cases, a component's reluctance to be removed is indicative of an incorrect approach or removal method – if in any doubt, re-check with the text.

4 When disassembling the engine, keep 'mated' parts together (e.g. valve and camshaft assemblies, cylinders, pistons and connecting rods, that have been in contact with each other during engine operation). These 'mated' parts must be reused or renewed as assemblies.

5 A complete engine stripdown should be done in the following general order with reference to the appropriate Sections.

> Remove the starter motor (if not done when removing the engine)
> Remove the gearbox (if not done when removing the engine)
> Remove the alternator (see Chapter 7)
> Remove the valve covers
> Remove the camchain tensioners
> Remove the rocker/camshaft assemblies
> Remove the cylinder heads
> Remove the cylinders
> Remove the pistons
> Remove the balancer gears and balancer shaft

> Remove the auxiliary shaft drive chain, tensioner and sprockets
> Remove the oil pump
> Separate the crankcase halves
> Remove the crankshaft and connecting rods
> Remove the auxiliary shaft, camchains and tensioner blades

6 Access to the clutch, selector drum/forks and gearshafts can be gained after removing the gearbox.

Reassembly

7 Reassembly is accomplished by reversing the general disassembly sequence.

6 Oil cooler and hoses

Special tool: *A pair of hose clip pliers is necessary for this procedure (see illustration 6.7).*

Oil cooler

Note: *If the engine has been running, allow it to cool before commencing work. If the machine is left to stand, oil will drain down from the cooler into the crankcase, reducing the amount of residual oil in the cooler.*

1 The oil cooler is located at the front of the machine behind the fairing centre panel. Remove the fairing panels as required according to your model to gain access to the oil cooler (see Chapter 6). On R1200 R models, remove the plastic shroud from the

oil cooler – it is retained by two screws on the top edge and two grommets which locate over lugs on the oil cooler at the bottom edge **(see illustrations)**.

2 If required, drain the engine oil (see Chapter 1). Alternatively, have a suitable container ready to catch any residual oil from the cooler when the feed and return hoses are disconnected.

> ⚠ **Warning: Be careful when disconnecting the oil hoses – hot oil can cause severe burns.**

3 Release the clips securing the oil hoses to the unions on the back of the cooler **(see illustration)**. Pull the hoses off carefully, being prepared to catch any residual oil. Secure the hoses in an upright position to avoid leakage and cover the open ends to prevent dirt getting in.

4 On R1200 RT, ST, GS and S models, loosen the left and right-hand bolts securing the cooler to the fairing bracket, then support the cooler and withdraw the bolts **(see illustrations)**. On R1200 R models, remove the two bolts securing the cooler to the timing cover and disengage its top mounting from the lug on the cover **(see illustration)**.

5 Check the oil cooler for signs of damage and clear any dirt or debris that might obstruct air flow using water or low pressure compressed air directed through the fins from the back. If the fins are bent or distorted, straighten them carefully with a screwdriver. Bent or damaged fins will restrict the air flow and impair the efficiency of the cooler causing the engine to overheat. If there is substantial damage to the oil cooler's surface area, renew it.

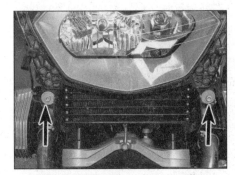

6.4a Undo the oil cooler mounting bolts . . .

6.4b . . . noting the location of the washers

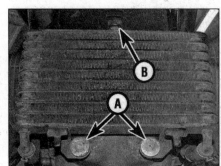

6.4c Oil cooler bolts (A) and tab (B) – R1200 R

6.7 Using special pliers to secure the oil cooler hose clips

6.10a Location of the left-hand oil pipe banjo union

6.10b Location of the right-hand oil hose union on top of the crankcase

6.11 Fit new sealing washers on both sides of the oil pipe banjo union

6.12a Location of the left-hand oil pipe mounting screw on the fairing bracket

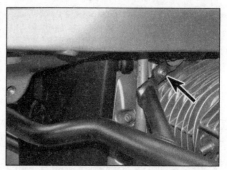

6.12b Location of the oil pipe mounting screw in front of the left-hand cylinder

6 Check the oil cooler mounting bushes, and renew them if necessary.

7 Installation is the reverse of removal. Tighten the cooler mounting bolts to the torque setting specified at the beginning of this Chapter. Secure the hoses with new clips and tighten the clips with the correct type of pliers to avoid damaging them **(see illustration)**.

8 Check the engine oil level and top-up or refill the engine as necessary (see *Pre-ride checks* and Chapter 1)

Oil hoses

9 Remove the fairing side panels according to your model (see Chapter 6), then follow the procedure in Chapter 3 and remove the fuel tank.

10 Examine the oil hoses and pipes for damage and signs of deterioration, and check the unions on the crankcase for signs of leakage **(see illustrations)**.

11 If the left-hand (return) pipe union is leaking, undo the banjo bolt, being prepared to catch any residual oil (see *Note* at the beginning of this Section) and remove the sealing washers. Ensure the sealing surfaces of the crankcase, the banjo union and the banjo bolt are clean and smooth. Fit new sealing washers to both sides of the union, then install the bolt and tighten it to the torque setting specified at the beginning of this Chapter **(see illustration)**.

12 To remove the pipe from the machine, first free the upper end from the oil cooler (see above) and the lower end from the crankcase. Undo the mounting screw on the left-hand side of the fairing bracket **(see illustration)**. Undo the mounting screw in front of the left-hand cylinder – on machines fitted with a crash bar, this screw also supports the crash bar **(see illustration)**. Manoeuvre the pipe off. Installation is the reverse of removal. Check

the engine oil level and top-up as necessary (see *Pre-ride checks*).

13 If the right-hand (feed) pipe union is leaking, first undo the mounting screw securing the pipe to the fairing bracket **(see illustration)**. Undo the flange bolts securing the pipe to the top of the crankcase **(see illustration 6.10b)**. Lift the pipe out of its socket, being prepared to catch any residual oil (see *Note* at the beginning of this Section) then ease off the O-ring from the end of the pipe **(see illustration)**. Take care not to displace the baffle on top of the oil thermostat. Ensure the mating surfaces of the crankcase and the pipe flange are clean and smooth. Fit a new O-ring onto the pipe and lubricate it with a smear of clean engine oil, then press the pipe into its socket and tighten the flange bolts to the torque setting specified at the beginning of this Chapter.

14 To remove the pipe from the machine, free the upper end from the oil cooler (see above) and the lower end from the top of the crankcase, then manoeuvre it free, noting the routing around the front sub-frame and suspension. Installation is the reverse of removal. Check the engine oil level and top-up as necessary (see *Pre-ride checks*).

7 Valve covers

Removal

1 Support the bike upright on its centre stand or on an auxiliary stand. Working on one side

6.13a Location of the right-hand oil pipe mounting screw on the fairing bracket

6.13b Note the location of the O-ring on the end of the oil feed pipe

7.2a Cylinder head protector is secured by one screw at the front . . .

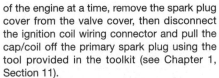

7.2b . . . and two screws (arrowed) at the back

7.5 . . . and pull the cover off

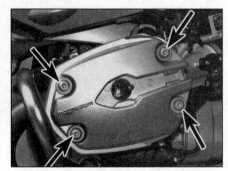

7.4 Undo the valve cover bolts (arrowed) . . .

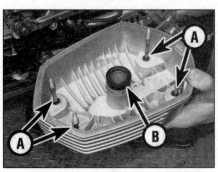

7.7 Location of the bolt sealing grommets (A). Note the inner cover seal (B)

of the engine at a time, remove the spark plug cover from the valve cover, then disconnect the ignition coil wiring connector and pull the cap/coil off the primary spark plug using the tool provided in the toolkit (see Chapter 1, Section 11).

2 Where fitted, undo the screws securing the cylinder head protector and lift it off **(see illustrations)**.

3 Position a drain tray below the valve cover to catch any residual oil when the cover is removed.

4 Undo the valve cover bolts – the bolts are retained in the cover by sealing grommets, so do not attempt to pull them all the way out **(see illustration)**.

5 Pull the cover off the cylinder head **(see illustration)**. If it is stuck, tap it gently around the sides with a soft-faced mallet or block of wood to dislodge it – do not try to lever it off and risk damaging the sealing surface.

6 Note the location of the inner and outer cover seals and remove them if they are loose.

7 Check the condition of the cover bolt sealing grommets **(see illustration)**. If they are in good condition, leave them in place. If they are damaged or deteriorated, or if there are signs of oil leakage, prise them out of the cover from the outside, then pull out the bolts

and washers, noting which way round the washers fit.

8 With the washers in place on the bolts, lubricate the new grommets with clean engine oil and ease them onto the bolts, then ease the bolt assemblies into the cover.

9 The inner and outer cover seals are reusable; however, if they are damaged or deteriorated, or if there are signs of oil leakage, renew them.

Installation

10 Clean the sealing surfaces of the cylinder head and the valve cover with suitable solvent.

Note that the left-hand cover incorporates the oil filler cap.

11 Fit the outer cover seal onto the cylinder head, making sure the half-circles locate around the castings in the head **(see illustration)**. Fit the inner seal onto the spark plug location **(see illustration 7.7)**.

12 Position the cover on the cylinder head, making sure the seals stay in place, then tighten the bolts finger-tight **(see illustration)**.

13 Once the cover is correctly seated on the seals, tighten the bolts to the torque setting specified at the beginning of this Chapter.

14 Check the engine oil level and top-up as necessary (see *Pre-ride checks*).

7.11 Note how the locating points on the seal (arrowed) fit against the castings

7.12 Tighten the bolts carefully to ensure the cover seals are correctly seated

8.1a Location of the right-hand cam chain tensioner

8.1b Location of the left-hand cam chain tensioner

8.4 Removing the right-hand cam chain tensioner

8.5 Removing the left-hand cam chain tensioner

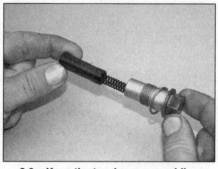

8.6a Keep the tensioner assemblies separate – the plungers differ

8.6b One-piece plunger assembly – left-hand side

8 Camchain tensioners

Note: *The camchain tensioners can be removed with the engine in the frame, although access to the left-hand cylinder's tensioner is extremely limited. To access the tensioner blades and guide blades the engine must be removed and the crankcases split.*

Removal

1 The right-hand chain tensioner is located on the underside of the cylinder, the left-hand tensioner is located on the top of the cylinder immediately below the Telelever pivot point **(see illustrations)**.
2 Support the bike upright on its centre stand or on an auxiliary stand.
3 On R1200 RT and ST models, remove the fairing side panels as appropriate; on R1200 GS models, remove the left-hand frame side panel (see Chapter 6).
4 If the right-hand tensioner is being removed, either drain the engine oil (see Chapter 1) or position a drain tray below the engine to catch any residual oil when the tensioner is withdrawn from the cylinder. Unscrew the tensioner and pull it out – discard the sealing washer as a new one must be used **(see illustration)**.
5 If the left-hand tensioner is being removed, first displace the left-hand throttle body (see Chapter 3). Unscrew the tensioner and pull it out – discard the sealing washer as a new one

must be used **(see illustration)**. **Note:** *If the engine has not been removed from the frame, BMW recommends that the left-hand camshaft sprocket is removed to allow more space to manoeuvre the tensioner out (see Section 10).*
6 Mark the tensioners so that they can be installed in their original locations. Don't mix up the plungers for the right and left-hand tensioners as they are different **(see illustration)**. On some machines, a one-piece plunger assembly is fitted in the left-hand side **(see illustration)**.

Inspection

7 Examine the tensioner components for signs of wear, scoring or damage.
8 Check that the plunger moves freely in and out of the tensioner body, and that the spring tension is good.
9 If the any of the tensioner components are

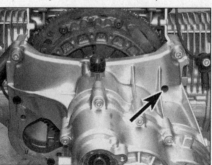

9.1 Location (arrowed) for the TDC locating pin

worn or damaged, they must be replaced with new ones.

Installation

10 Fit a new sealing washer on the tensioner, then install the tensioner into the cylinder. Tighten the tensioner to the torque setting specified at the beginning of this Chapter.
11 Check the engine oil level and top-up or refill the engine as necessary (see Chapter 1 and *Pre-ride checks*)
12 Install the remaining components in the reverse order of removal.

9 Rocker arms and shafts

Caution: The engine must be completely cool before beginning this procedure or the cylinder head(s) may become warped.
Note: *The rocker arms and shafts can be removed with the engine in the frame. If the engine has been removed, ignore the steps which do not apply.*
Special tool: *A top dead centre (TDC) locating pin is required for this procedure (see* ***Tool Tip****). A degree disc is required for angle-tightening the cylinder head nuts.*

Removal

1 During this procedure the engine should be locked in the TDC position by inserting a locating pin through the hole in the right-hand side of the gearbox case **(see illustration)**. Remove the

9.5 Check for freeplay (arrowed) between the intake and exhaust rocker arms and the valve stems

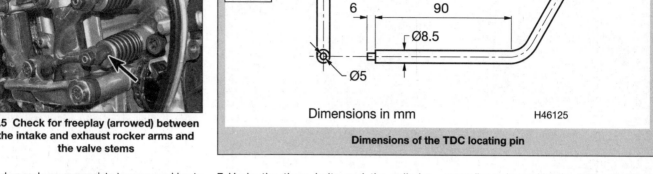

Dimensions in mm   H46125

Dimensions of the TDC locating pin

body panels as appropriate to your machine to access the hole (see Chapter 6).

2 Remove the valve cover from the side of the engine being worked on (see Section 7).

3 Remove both primary spark plugs (see Chapter 1, Section 11).

4 Before removing the rocker arms and shafts, the piston on the side of the engine being worked on must be at top dead centre (TDC) on the compression stroke. To turn the engine to this position, select a high gear and have an assistant turn the rear wheel slowly by hand in the normal direction of rotation. Alternatively, follow the procedure in Chapter 1, Section 13 to remove the alternator drive belt cover, then turn the engine with a spanner on the crankshaft pulley nut.

Caution: Be sure to turn the engine in its normal direction of rotation only – i.e. clockwise.

5 With the piston at TDC on the compression stroke, all the valves will be closed and there should be discernable freeplay in the rocker arms in the form of a clearance between the adjusters and the valve stems **(see illustration)**.

6 Insert the TDC locating pin into the hole in the right-hand side of the gearbox case **(see illustration 9.1)**. The pin should pass through the clutch assembly and locate in a 5 mm diameter hole in the crankcase. BMW provide a service tool for this purpose (Part No. 11 2 650). Alternatively, a similar tool can be made (see *Tool Tip*).

7 Undo the three bolts and the cylinder head nut which secure the rocker shaft cap and remove the cap **(see illustrations)**. Also remove the lower rear cylinder head nut to provide clearance for the intake rocker shaft to be withdrawn from the holder. Note the washers on the studs.

8 Working on one shaft at a time, undo the bolt retaining the end of the shaft in the holder, then hold the rocker arm and remove the bolt, noting the location of the contact plate **(see illustration)**.

9 Withdraw the rocker shaft from the holder together with the rocker arm – note the location of the pushrod in the follower and lift it out **(see illustration)**. Note the cut-out in the end of the shaft for the retaining bolt.

10 Mark each rocker shaft, arm and pushrod

according to its position (i.e. left or right-hand cylinder, intake or exhaust valve), and keep matched assemblies together. **Note:** *If you wish to remove the rocker arms and shafts from both sides of the engine before further work, it is essential to keep a note of which piston is at TDC on the compression stroke (i.e. all valves closed). Damage is likely to occur if the rocker arms and shafts are installed on a cylinder where the camshaft is in the valves open position.*

Inspection

11 Inspect the rocker arm contact points for wear, pitting, spalling, score marks and cracks **(see illustration)**. Check that the articulated tips of the adjusting screws are free to move, but not loose. If any components are worn or damaged, they must be renewed.

9.7a Undo the bolts (A) and the nut (B) . . .

9.7b . . . and lift off the rocker shaft cap

9.8 Rocker shafts are retained by bolts (arrowed)

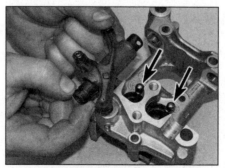

9.9 Remove the shaft and rocker arm. Note the location of the pushrods (arrowed)

9.11 Inspect the contact points (arrowed) for wear

9.12a Inspect the rocker shafts for wear and damage

9.12b Measuring the rocker shafts with a micrometer

9.16 Install the pushrods

12 Inspect the surface of the rocker shafts for pitting and score marks **(see illustration)**. Measure the diameter of the shafts in the area of contact with the rocker arms and compare the result with the specifications at the beginning of this Chapter **(see illustration)**. Also measure the internal diameter of the rocker arms. Subtract the shaft diameter from the internal bore diameter to obtain the clearance and compare the result with the specifications. If the clearance is beyond the service limit, use the specifications to determine whether it is the shaft or the bore that is worn, and replace either or both as required.

13 Check the pushrods for any signs of damage or wear, particularly on their ends.

14 If available, blow through any oil passages with compressed air.

Installation

15 Make sure that the piston on the side of the engine being worked on is at TDC on the compression stroke.

16 Place the pushrods into the followers, making sure they are returned to their original locations **(see illustration)**. A dab of grease will hold the pushrods in the followers while the rocker shafts are installed.

17 Lubricate the rocker shafts with clean engine oil and assemble the rocker arms on the shafts. Install the shaft assemblies into the holder so that the cut-outs in the shafts align with the retaining bolt holes and the

pushrods locate in the rocker arms **(see illustration 9.9)**.

18 Install the retaining bolts – don't forget to install the contact plate with the bolts **(see illustration)**. Tighten the bolts to the torque setting specified at the beginning of this Chapter.

19 Install the rocker shaft cap, making sure it is the correct way round, then install the three bolts **(see illustration)**. Follow the procedure in Chapter 1, Section 2 and check the rocker arm endplay, then tighten the cap bolts to the specified torque setting.

20 Lubricate the cylinder head nuts with clean engine oil, then install them with their washers, with the collared end of the nuts facing the cylinder head **(see illustration)**. Tighten the nuts evenly, a little at a time, to the initial torque setting specified at the beginning of this Chapter. Next, using a degree disc (see *Tools and Workshop Tips*) , angle tighten each nut in the same sequence to the second, and then the final stage settings.

21 Withdraw the TDC locating pin and rotate the crankshaft to check that the rocker arms move freely on the shafts, then check the valve clearances (see Chapter 1).

22 As required, carry-out the procedure on the other side of the engine.

23 Install the valve cover(s) (see Section 7).

24 Check the engine oil level and top-up if necessary (see *Pre-ride checks*).

25 Install the remaining components in the reverse order of removal.

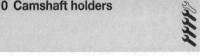

10 Camshaft holders

Caution: The engine must be completely cool before beginning this procedure or the cylinder head(s) may become warped.

Note: *The camshaft holders can be removed with the engine in the frame. If the engine has been removed, ignore the steps which do not apply.*

Special tools: *A top dead centre (TDC) locating pin is required for this procedure (see* **Tool Tip,** *Section 9). A degree disc is required for angle-tightening the cylinder head nuts.*

Removal

1 During this procedure the engine should be locked in the TDC position by inserting a locating pin through the hole in the right-hand side of the gearbox case **(see illustration 9.1)**. Remove the body panels as appropriate to your machine to access the hole (see Chapter 6).

2 Remove the valve cover from the side of the engine being worked on (see Section 7).

3 Remove both primary spark plugs (see Chapter 1, Section 11).

4 Before removing the camshaft holder, the piston on the side of the engine being worked on must be at top dead centre (TDC) on the compression stroke. To turn the engine to this position, select a high gear and have an assistant turn the rear wheel slowly by hand in

9.18 Contact plate is retained by rocker shaft retaining bolts

9.19 Secure the rocker shaft cap with the three bolts

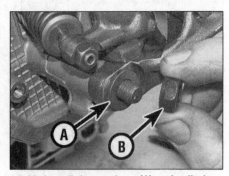

9.20 Install the washers (A) and cylinder head nuts (B) as described

10.8 Pull the breather hose off the air filter housing

10.9 Remove the camshaft sprocket cover, noting the O-ring (arrowed)

10.10 Undo the bolt and remove the breather rotor

the normal direction of rotation. Alternatively, follow the procedure in Chapter 1, Section 13 to remove the alternator drive belt cover, then turn the engine with a spanner on the crankshaft pulley nut.

Caution: Be sure to turn the engine in its normal direction of rotation only – i.e. clockwise.

5 With the piston at TDC on the compression stroke, all the valves will be closed and there should be discernable freeplay in the rocker arms in the form of a clearance between the adjusters and the valve stems **(see illustration 9.5)**.

6 Insert the TDC locating pin into the hole in the right-hand side of the gearbox case **(see illustration 9.1)**. The pin should pass through the clutch assembly and locate in a 5 mm diameter hole in the crankcase. BMW provide a service tool for this purpose (Part No. 11 2 650). Alternatively, a similar tool can be made (see *Tool Tip* in Section 9).

Left-hand camshaft holder

7 Displace the left-hand throttle body (see Chapter 3).

8 Release the clips securing the engine breather hose to the air filter housing and pull the hose off **(see illustration)**.

9 Undo the bolts securing the camshaft sprocket cover and remove the cover, noting the location of the cover O-ring **(see illustration)**.

10 Undo the camshaft sprocket bolt and

remove the breather rotor **(see illustration)**. Note the tab on the inner face of the rotor that locates in one of the holes in the sprocket.

11 At TDC on the compression stroke, an arrow on the sprocket should be in alignment with a static mark on the holder and the locating lug in the centre of the sprocket should be facing up. If no marks are visible, make your own with a dab of paint to aid reassembly.

12 Thread a cable tie through one of the holes in the sprocket and over the camchain, and lock the sprocket and chain together, then ease the sprocket off the end of the camshaft, noting how the locating lug on the sprocket locates in the cut-out on the camshaft.

13 Follow the procedure in Section 8 and remove the camchain tensioner.

14 Thread a rubber band around the rocker arms to hold them in tension against the pushrods – this will prevent the pushrods falling out when the camshaft holder is removed **(see illustration 10.16)**. Remove the bolts securing the camshaft holder to the cylinder head, noting the location of the contact plate **(see illustrations)**.

15 Undo the cylinder head nuts evenly and in a criss-cross pattern **(see illustration)**. Remove the washers from the studs.

16 Lift off the camshaft holder, noting how it fits **(see illustration)**.

17 If required, remove the rocker arms and shafts and the camshafts from the holder (see Sections 9 and 11).

Right-hand camshaft holder

18 Follow the procedure in Steps 4 and 5 to position the right-hand piston at TDC on the compression stroke.

Note: *If the left-hand camshaft holder has already been removed, take extreme care when turning the engine to the TDC position, compression stroke, for the right-hand piston. Temporarily release the left-hand camshaft sprocket from the chain and hold the chain in tension against the auxiliary shaft to prevent it slipping off the sprocket on the shaft, then turn the engine 360°. Don't forget to withdraw the TDC locating pin.*

19 Insert the TDC locating pin into the hole in the right-hand side of the gearbox case (see Step 6). If the left-hand camshaft holder has

10.14a Undo the camshaft holder bolts (arrowed) . . .

10.14b . . . noting the location of the contact plate

10.15 Undo the cylinder head nuts evenly

10.16 Lift off the camshaft holder. Note the rubber band (arrowed)

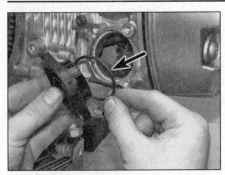

10.20 Remove the camshaft sprocket cover, noting the O-ring (arrowed)

10.21a Camshaft sprocket bolt (A) secures trigger (B) for camshaft position sensor

10.21b Tab (arrowed) locates in small hole in camshaft sprocket

already been removed, lock the sprocket and chain together as before (see Step 12).

20 Disconnect the wiring connector for the camshaft position sensor, then undo the bolts securing the camshaft sprocket cover and remove the cover, noting the location of the cover O-ring **(see illustration)**.

21 Undo the camshaft sprocket bolt and remove the trigger for the camshaft position sensor **(see illustration)**. Note the tab on the back of the trigger that locates in the small hole in the sprocket **(see illustration)**.

22 At TDC on the compression stroke, an arrow on the sprocket should be in alignment with a static mark on the holder and the locating lug in the centre of the sprocket should be facing down **(see illustration)**. If no marks are visible, make your own with a dab of paint to aid reassembly.

23 Thread a cable tie through one of the holes in the sprocket and over the camchain, and lock the sprocket and chain together, then ease the sprocket off the end of the camshaft **(see illustration)**. Note how the locating lug on the sprocket locates in the cut-out on the camshaft.

24 Follow the procedure in Section 8 and remove the camchain tensioner.

25 Follow the procedure in Steps 14 to 16 to remove the camshaft holder.

26 If required, remove the rocker arms and shafts and the camshafts from the holder (see Sections 9 and 11). If both camshaft holders have been removed, work on them separately to avoid getting parts mixed up.

Note: *If further engine disassembly is to be undertaken, requiring the removal of the TDC*

locating pin, it will be necessary to remove the timing cover and retime the engine with reference to the timing marks on the crankshaft and balancer shaft gears (see Section 20).

Installation

27 Make sure that the cylinder being worked on is at TDC on the compression stroke. If both cylinders are being worked on, start with the right-hand cylinder. Ensure that the TDC locating pin is in position.

28 If removed, install the camshafts (see Section 11) and the rocker arms and shafts (see Section 9).

29 Thread a rubber band around the rocker arms to hold them in tension against the pushrods – this will prevent the pushrods falling out when the camshaft holder is installed **(see illustration 10.16)**.

30 Ensure that the camshaft is in the valves closed position, then install the camshaft holder onto the cylinder head **(see illustration)**.

31 Lubricate the cylinder head nuts with clean engine oil, then install them with their washers, with the collared end of the nuts facing the cylinder head **(see illustration 9.20)**. Tighten the nuts finger-tight.

32 Install the camshaft holder bolts finger-tight – don't forget to install the contact plate **(see illustrations 10.14a and b)**.

33 Tighten the cylinder head nuts evenly, a little at a time and in a criss-cross sequence, to the initial torque setting specified at the beginning of this Chapter **(see illustration 10.15)**. Next, using a degree disc (see *Tools and Workshop Tips*) ,

angle-tighten each nut in the same sequence to the second, and then to the final stage settings.

34 Tighten the camshaft holder bolts to the specified torque setting.

35 Follow the procedure in Section 8 and install the camchain tensioner. **Note:** *The camchain tensioners must be installed before the camshaft sprocket bolts are tightened, otherwise the camchain my jump over the sprocket teeth.*

36 When working on the right-hand camshaft holder, check that the locating lug in the centre of the camshaft sprocket is facing down and aligns with the corresponding cut-out on the camshaft. Ease the sprocket onto the camshaft and ensure that the arrow on the sprocket aligns with a static mark on the holder, or that any previously made match marks align **(see illustration 10.22)**. Install the camshaft position sensor trigger, locating the tab on the back of the trigger in the small hole in the sprocket, then install the camshaft sprocket bolt and tighten it to the specified torque setting **(see illustration 10.21b)**. Cut the cable tie locking the sprocket and chain together.

37 When working on the left-hand camshaft holder, check that the locating lug in the centre of the camshaft sprocket is facing up and aligns with the corresponding cut-out on the camshaft. If both cylinders are being worked on, and the right-hand camshaft sprocket has been installed, it will be necessary to turn the engine to the TDC position, compression stroke, for the left-hand piston. Cut the cable tie locking the sprocket and chain together and hold the chain in tension against the auxiliary shaft to prevent it slipping off the sprocket

10.22 Arrow (A) aligns with static mark (B). Locating lug (C) points down

10.23 Ease the sprocket off the end of the camshaft

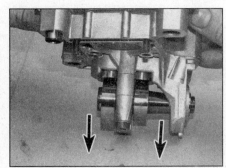

10.30 When both lobes are pointing down, camshaft is in the valves closed position

on the shaft, then turn the engine 360°. Don't forget to withdraw the TDC locating pin, and install it again when the piston is in the correct position. Ease the sprocket onto the camshaft and ensure that the arrow on the sprocket aligns with a static mark on the holder, or that any previously made match marks align. If not already done, cut the cable tie locking the sprocket and chain together. Install the breather rotor, locating the tab on the inner face of the rotor in one of the holes in the sprocket, then install the camshaft sprocket bolt and tighten it to the specified torque setting.

38 Rotate the crankshaft and check that the valve timing for both cylinders is correct (see Step 5).

39 Check the valve clearances and adjust if necessary (see Chapter 1).

40 Install the camshaft sprocket cover(s) using a new O-ring if necessary, and tighten the bolts to the specified torque setting **(see illustrations 10.9 and 10.20).**

41 Install the engine breather hose and/or connect the camshaft position sensor wiring connector, as applicable.

42 Install the remaining components in the reverse order of removal.

43 Check the engine oil level and top-up if necessary (see *Pre-ride checks*).

11 Camshafts and followers

Note: *The camshafts can be removed with the engine in the frame. If the engine has been removed, ignore the steps which do not apply.*
Special tools: *See Section 10*

Removal

1 Remove the camshaft holder (see Section 10).

2 Mark the pushrods according to their position and lift them out (see Section 9).

3 Unscrew the bolts securing the camshaft bearing cap and remove the cap **(see illustrations).**

4 Withdraw the camshaft and the bearing base from the holder **(see illustration).**

5 Mark the followers according to their position and lift them out **(see illustration).**

6 If both camshaft holders have been removed, work on them separately to avoid getting parts mixed up.

Inspection

7 Inspect the bearing surfaces of the holder and the camshaft bearing cap and base, and the corresponding journals on the camshaft **(see illustration).** Look for score marks, deep scratches and evidence of spalling.

8 Check the camshaft lobes for heat discoloration (blue appearance), score marks, chipped areas, flat spots and spalling **(see illustration).** If any components appear worn or damaged they must be renewed.

9 Clean the mating surfaces of the camshaft bearing base and bearing cap and assemble them on the holder, ensuring the alignment marks match. Tighten the cap bolts to the torque setting specified at the beginning of this Chapter. Use a telescoping gauge and micrometer to measure the internal diameter of the bearing holder **(see illustration).** Compare the result with the specifications at the beginning of this Chapter.

10 Use a micrometer to measure the camshaft journal diameter – take several measurements to ensure the journal has not worn unevenly **(see illustration).** Compare the result with the specifications at the beginning of this Chapter.

11.3a Undo the bolts . . .

11.3b . . . and lift off the bearing cap

11.4 Remove the bearing base with the camshaft

11.5 Lift the followers out of the camshaft holder

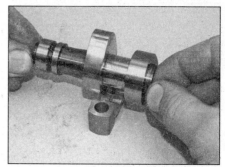

11.7 Inspect the bearing surfaces for wear and damage

11.8 Inspect the cam lobes for wear and damage

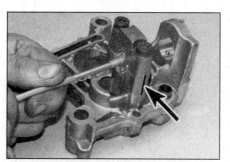

11.9 Measuring the internal diameter of the bearing holder. Note the alignment marks (arrowed)

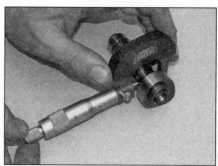

11.10 Measuring the diameter of the camshaft journal

11.12a Subtract the cam follower diameter . . .

11.12b . . . from the follower bore diameter to calculate the clearance

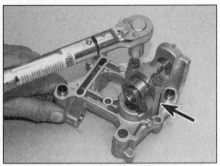

11.17 Ensure that the marks (arrowed) are aligned, then tighten the cap bolts

11 Subtract the camshaft journal diameter from the bearing holder diameter to determine the journal/holder oil clearance. If the clearance is greater than the specified service limit, use the measurements to determine which components are worn and renew them accordingly.

12 Inspect the outer surfaces of the cam followers for evidence of scoring and other damage. If the surface of a follower is in poor condition, it is probable that the bore in which it runs is also damaged. Measure the external diameter of each follower and the internal diameter of the corresponding bore and compare the results with the specifications at the beginning of this Chapter **(see illustrations)**.

13 Calculate the follower/bore clearance by subtracting the follower diameter from the bore diameter and compare the result with the specifications at the beginning of this Chapter. If the clearance is greater than the specified service limit, use the measurements to determine which components are worn and renew them accordingly

14 If available, blow through any oil passages with compressed air.

15 Except in cases of oil starvation, the camchains and sprockets wear very little. Check the sprockets for wear on the sides and tips of the teeth and for signs of damage. If a sprocket needs renewing, then a new chain must also be fitted, and it is very likely the sprocket on the auxiliary shaft will be worn also. Refer to Section 28 for details of chain and auxiliary shaft renewal.

Installation

16 Install the followers into the holder, making sure each is returned to its original location **(see illustration 11.5)**.

17 Lubricate the camshaft journals with clean engine oil and fit the camshaft into the bearing base, then install the camshaft and base onto the holder **(see illustration 11.4)**. Fit the bearing cap and check that the alignment marks on the holder, bearing base and cap all match. Tighten the cap bolts to the torque setting specified at the beginning of this Chapter **(see illustration)**.

18 Install the camshaft holder (see Section 10).

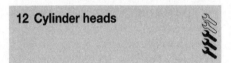

12 Cylinder heads

Caution: The engine must be completely cool before beginning this procedure or the cylinder head(s) may become warped.

Note: *The cylinder heads can be removed with the engine in the frame. If the engine has been removed, ignore the steps which do not apply.*

Special tools: *A top dead centre (TDC) locating pin is required for this procedure (see Tool Tip, Section 9). A degree disc is required for angle-tightening the cylinder head nuts.*

Removal

1 During this procedure the engine should be locked in the TDC position by inserting a locating pin through the hole in the right-hand side of the gearbox case **(see illustration 9.1)**. Remove the body panels as appropriate to your machine to access the hole (see Chapter 6).

2 Disconnect the battery negative (-ve) terminal (see Chapter 7).

3 Remove the exhaust system (see Chapter 3).

4 Remove the primary and secondary spark plugs (see Chapter 1, Section 11).

5 Displace the throttle bodies (see Chapter 3).

6 Trace the wiring from the cylinder head temperature sensors (sensor on left head only after Aug 2006) and disconnect it at the connectors – free the wiring from any clips or ties **(see illustration)**.

7 Undo the screws securing the earth wires to both cylinder heads **(see illustration 12.6)**.

8 Remove the valve covers (see Section 7).

9 Before removing the cylinder heads, the piston on the side of the engine being worked on must be at top dead centre (TDC) on the compression stroke. To turn the engine to this position, select a high gear and have an assistant turn the rear wheel slowly by hand in the normal direction of rotation. Alternatively, follow the procedure in Chapter 1, Section 13 to remove the alternator drive belt cover, then turn the engine with a spanner on the crankshaft pulley nut.

Caution: Be sure to turn the engine in its normal direction of rotation only – i.e. clockwise.

10 With the piston at TDC on the compression stroke, all the valves will be closed and there should be discernable freeplay in the rocker arms in the form of a clearance between the adjusters and the valve stems **(see illustration 9.5)**.

11 Insert the TDC locating pin into the hole in the right-hand side of the gearbox case **(see illustration 9.1)**. The pin should pass through the clutch assembly and locate in a 5 mm diameter hole in the crankcase. BMW provide a service tool for this purpose (Part No. 11 2 650). Alternatively, a similar tool can be made (see *Tool Tip* in Section 9).

12 Working on one side of the engine at a time, follow the procedure in Section 10 to remove the camshaft sprocket, ensuring the sprocket and chain are locked together with a cable tie as described. Next, follow the procedure in Section 8 and remove the camchain tensioner.

13 Stuff clean rag into the camchain tunnel to prevent anything falling inside, then undo the three 6 mm screws securing the cylinder head to the cylinder and remove the screws and washers **(see illustration)**.

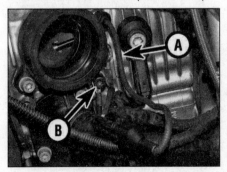

12.6 Temperature sensor wiring (A), earth wire terminal (B)

12.13 Undo the 6 mm screws (arrowed)

12.14 Undo the 10 mm bolt (arrowed)

12.15a Undo the cylinder head nuts . . .

12.15b . . . and remove the washers

14 Undo the 10 mm bolt securing the cylinder head to the cylinder and remove the bolt and washer **(see illustration)**.

15 Undo the cylinder head nuts evenly and in a criss-cross pattern **(see illustration)**. Remove the washers from the studs **(see illustration)**.

16 Pull the cylinder head up off the studs **(see illustration)**. If it is stuck, tap around the joint face between the head and the cylinder with a soft-faced mallet to free it. Do not attempt to free the head by levering with a screwdriver between the head and cylinder – you'll damage the sealing surfaces. Remove the cylinder head gasket.

17 Ensure that the dowels are a tight fit in the top of the cylinder and check that the four studs are tight **(see illustration)**.

18 Check the old cylinder head gasket and the sealing surfaces on the cylinder head and cylinder for signs of leakage, which could indicate a warped head. Discard the gasket once it has been inspected as a new one must be used.

19 Clean any traces of old gasket material from the cylinder head and cylinder. If a scraper is used, take care not to scratch or gouge the soft aluminium. Be careful not to let any of the gasket material fall into the crankcase or the oil passages.

Installation

20 Make sure that the cylinder being worked on is at TDC on the compression stroke. Work on one side of the engine at a time.

21 If removed, install the two dowels into the top of the cylinder.

22 Fit the new head gasket in place on the cylinder, making sure all the holes are correctly aligned **(see illustration)**. Never re-use the old gasket.

23 Ensure that the camshaft is in the valves closed position.

24 Carefully fit the cylinder head over the studs and onto the cylinder, feeding the camchain and sprocket up through the tunnel.

25 Lubricate the cylinder head nuts with clean engine oil, then install them with their washers, with the collared end of the nuts facing the cylinder head **(see illustration 9.20)**. Tighten the nuts finger-tight.

26 Stuff clean rag into the camchain tunnel to prevent anything falling inside, then install the 10 mm bolt and the three 6 mm screws and tighten them all finger-tight **(see illustrations 12.14 and 13)**.

27 Tighten the cylinder head nuts evenly, a little at a time and in a criss-cross sequence, to the initial torque setting specified at the beginning of this Chapter **(see illustration 10.15)**. Next, using a degree disc (see *Tools and Workshop Tips*) , angle-tighten each nut in the same sequence to the second, and then to the final stage settings.

28 Tighten the 10 mm bolt to the specified torque setting, then tighten the three 6 mm screws to the specified torque setting. Remove the rag from the camchain tunnel.

29 Follow the procedure in Section 8 and

install the camchain tensioner, then follow the procedure in Section 10 to install the camshaft sprocket.

30 Install the remaining components in the reverse order of removal, noting the following:
● Check the valve clearances and adjust if necessary (see Chapter 1).
● Check the engine oil level and top-up if necessary (see Pre-ride checks).

13 Valve/valve seat/valve guide servicing

1 Because of the complex nature of this job and the special tools and equipment required, most owners leave servicing of the valves, valve seats and valve guides to a professional. However, you can make an initial assessment of whether the valves are seating, and therefore sealing, correctly by pouring a small amount of solvent into each of the valve ports. If the solvent leaks past any valve into the combustion chamber the valve is not seating and sealing correctly.

2 Once the camshaft holder has been removed, you can remove the valves from the cylinder head, clean the components, check them for wear to assess the extent of the work needed and, unless a valve service is required, grind in the valves (see Section 14). The head can then be reassembled.

3 The dealer service department will remove the valves and springs, renew the valves and guides, recut or renew the valve seats, check

12.16 Pull the cylinder head off

12.17 Location of the cylinder head dowels (arrowed)

12.22 Install the new head gasket carefully

14.4a Make sure the compressor is located squarely onto the valve assembly

14.4b Remove the collets once they are free

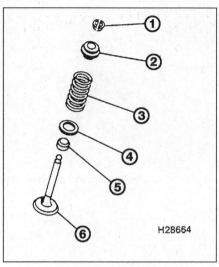

H28664

14.5 Valve assembly

1 Collets
2 Spring retainer
3 Valve spring
4 Spring seat
5 Valve stem seal
6 Valve

and renew the valve springs, spring retainers and collets (as necessary), replace the valve seals with new ones and reassemble the valve components.

4 After the valve service has been performed, the head will be in like-new condition. When the head is returned, be sure to clean it again very thoroughly before installation on the engine, to remove any metal particles or abrasive grit that may still be present from the valve service operations. Use compressed air, if available, to blow out all the holes and passages.

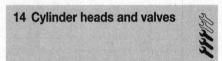

14 Cylinder heads and valves

Special tool: *A valve spring compressor suitable for motorcycle work is absolutely necessary for this procedure.*

1 As mentioned in the previous Section, valve overhaul should be left to a BMW dealer or engine specialist. However, disassembly, cleaning and inspection of the valves and related components can be done by the home mechanic if the necessary tools are available. This way no expense is incurred if the inspection reveals that overhaul is not required at this time.

Disassembly

2 Before proceeding, arrange to label and store the valves along with their related components in such a way that they can be returned to their original locations without

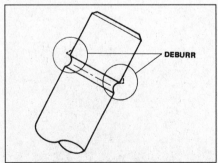

14.6 If necessary, deburr the valve stem above the collet groove

getting mixed up. A good way to do this is to obtain a container which is divided into eight compartments, and to label each compartment with the identity of the valve which will be stored in it (i.e. left or right-hand cylinder, intake top or bottom and exhaust top or bottom valve). Alternatively, labelled plastic bags will do just as well.

3 If not already done, clean any traces of old gasket material from the cylinder head. If a scraper is used, take care not to scratch or gouge the soft aluminium.

 Refer to Tools and Workshop Tips for details of gasket removal methods.

4 Using a suitable valve spring compressor, compress the spring on the first valve, making sure the tool is correctly located onto each end of the valve assembly **(see illustration)**. Do not compress the spring any more than is absolutely necessary, then remove the collets, using either needle-nose pliers, tweezers, a magnet, or a screwdriver with a dab of grease on it **(see illustration)**.

5 Carefully release the valve spring compressor and remove the spring retainer, noting which way up it fits, the spring, and the spring seat, noting which way up it fits **(see illustration)**.

6 Push the valve down into the head and withdraw it from the underside. If the valve binds in the guide (won't pull through), push it back into the head and deburr the area

14.8 Pull off the old valve stem seals

above the collet groove with a very fine file or whetstone **(see illustration)**.

7 Repeat the procedure for the remaining valves. Remember to keep the components for each valve assembly together and in order so they can be reinstalled in the same location **(see illustration 14.5)**. Repeat the procedure for the other valves.

8 Once the valves have been removed and labelled, pull the valve stem seals off the top of the valve guides using either a special removing tool or pliers **(see illustration)**. Discard the old seals as new ones must be fitted.

9 Carefully scrape all carbon deposits out of the combustion chamber area. A hand held wire brush or a piece of fine emery cloth can be used once the majority of deposits have been scraped away. Do not use a wire brush mounted in a drill motor as the head material is soft and may be eroded away. Next, wash the cylinder head with solvent and dry it thoroughly. Compressed air will speed the drying process and ensure that all holes, recessed areas and oil passages are clean.

10 Scrape off any deposits that may have formed on the valves, then use a motorized wire brush to remove deposits from the valve heads and stems. Make sure the valves do not get mixed up.

11 Clean the valve springs, collets, retainers and spring seats with solvent and dry them thoroughly. Clean the parts from one valve at a time so as not to mix them up.

Inspection

12 Inspect the head very carefully for cracks and other damage. If cracks are found, a new head will be required.

13 Examine the valve seats in the combustion chamber. If they are pitted, cracked or burned,

14.13 Inspect the valve seat (arrowed) for wear and pitting

14.14a Inspect the valve face – it should be the same width all the way around

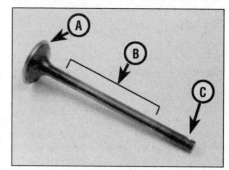

14.14b Valve face (A), stem (B) and collet groove (C)

the head will require work beyond the scope of the home mechanic. Check that the width of the valve seat-to-valve contact area is the same around the entire circumference of the seat **(see illustration)**. If the width varies, valve overhaul is required (see Section 13).

14 Carefully inspect each valve face for cracks, pits and burned spots, and check the valve stem and the collet groove area for scoring and cracks **(see illustrations)**. Rotate the valve and check for any obvious indication that it is bent. Check the end of the stem for pitting and excessive wear. Any of the above conditions indicates the need for new valves.

15 Measure each valve stem diameter and valve head diameter and compare the results with the specifications at the beginning of this Chapter **(see illustrations)**. If any valve heads are under-size, or the stems are worn below the service limit, a new valve will have to be fitted. **Note:** Carbon build-up inside the lower ends of the exhaust valve guides indicates worn valve stems and/or valve guides. Have the head inspected by a BMW dealer.

16 Check the end of each valve spring for wear and pitting. Measure the spring free length and compare it to that listed in the specifications **(see illustration)**. If any spring is shorter than specified it has sagged and must be replaced – always renew the valve springs as a set.

17 Check the spring retainers and collets for obvious wear and cracks. Any questionable

14.15a Measuring the valve stem diameter

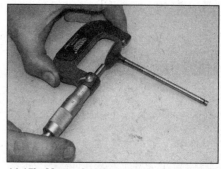

14.15b Measuring the valve head diameter

parts should not be reused, as extensive damage will occur in the event of failure during engine operation.

18 If the inspection indicates that no overhaul work is required, the valve components can be reinstalled in the head.

Reassembly

19 Unless a valve service has been performed, before installing the valves in the head they should be ground in (lapped) to ensure a positive seal between the valves and seats. This procedure requires coarse and fine valve grinding compound and a valve grinding tool. If a grinding tool is not available, a piece of rubber or plastic hose can be slipped over the valve stem (after the valve has been installed in the guide) and used to turn the valve.

20 Apply a small amount of coarse grinding compound to the valve face, then oil the valve stem and insert it into the guide **(see illustration)**. **Note:** Make sure each valve is installed in its correct guide and be careful not to get any grinding compound on the valve stem.

21 Attach the grinding tool (or hose) to the valve and rotate the tool between the palms of your hands. Use a back-and-forth motion (as though rubbing your hands together) rather than a circular motion (i.e. so that the valve rotates alternately clockwise and anti-clockwise rather than in one direction only) **(see illustration)**. Lift the valve off the seat and turn it at regular intervals to distribute the grinding compound properly. Continue the grinding procedure until the valve face and seat contact area is of uniform width and

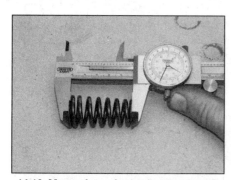

14.16 Measuring valve spring free length

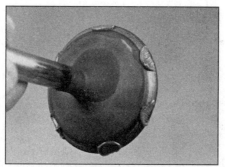

14.20 Apply grinding compound sparingly to the valve face only

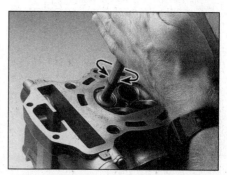

14.21a Rotate the valve grinding tool back and forth between the palms of your hands

14.21b Valve face . . .

14.21c . . . and valve seat should be of uniform width

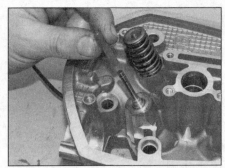

14.24a Slide a plastic sleeve over the valve stem . . .

unbroken around the entire circumference of the valve face and seat **(see illustrations)**.

22 Carefully remove the valve from the guide and wipe off all traces of grinding compound. Use solvent to clean the valve and wipe the seat area thoroughly with a solvent soaked cloth.

23 Repeat the procedure with fine valve grinding compound, then repeat the entire procedure for the remaining valves.

24 Working on each valve in turn, lubricate the stem with clean engine oil and install the valve into its guide. Slide a suitable plastic sleeve over the upper end of the valve stem, then slide the valve stem new seal down over the sleeve **(see illustrations)**. The purpose of the plastic sleeve is to prevent the edges of

the collet groove damaging the inside of the stem seal – electrical heat shrink sleeving is ideal. If a suitable sleeve is not available, take great care when installing the seal.

25 If used, remove the sleeve, then press the seal over the end of the valve guide with an appropriate size deep socket until it is felt to clip into place **(see illustrations)**. Don't twist or cock the seal, or it will not seal properly against the valve stem. Also, don't remove it again or it will be damaged.

26 Install the spring seat with its shouldered side facing up, then install the spring with the coloured end facing down (the springs photographed were marked with green paint on their lower ends) **(see illustrations)**.

27 Install the spring retainer, with its

shouldered side facing down so that it fits into the top of the spring **(see illustration)**.

28 Apply a small amount of grease to the collets to hold them in place during installation, then compress the spring with the valve spring compressor and install the collets **(see illustration 14.4b)**. Do not compress the spring any more than is absolutely necessary to slip the collets into position. Make certain that the collets are securely located in the collet groove, then release the spring compressor.

29 Repeat the procedure for the remaining valves.

30 Support the cylinder head on blocks so the valves can't contact the workbench top, then gently tap each of the valve stems

14.24b . . . then slide the stem seal on

14.25a Remove the plastic sleeve . . .

14.25b . . . and press the seal into place

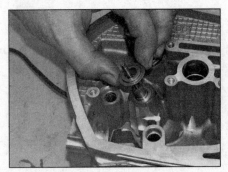

14.26a Install the spring seat . . .

14.26b . . . and the spring, painted end down

14.27 Install the retainer, shouldered side down

14.30 Tap the end of the valve stem to seat the collets

15.2a Undo the mounting bolt (arrowed) . . .

15.2b . . . and remove the knock sensor

to seat the collets in their grooves (see illustration).

 HAYNES HINT *Check for proper sealing of the valves by pouring a small amount of solvent into each of the valve ports. If the solvent leaks past any valve into the combustion chamber the valve grinding operation on that valve should be repeated.*

15 Cylinders

Note: *The cylinders can be removed with the engine in the frame.*

Removal

1 Remove the cylinder heads (see Section 12). Ensure that the TDC locating pin is left in place.

2 Working on one side of the engine at a time, disconnect the wiring connector for the knock sensor. If required, undo the mounting bolt and lift the sensor off (see illustrations).

3 Unscrew the camchain guide blade pivot bolt and remove it with its sealing washer (see illustration).

4 To prevent the camchain slipping into the crankcase, wrap an elastic band around the chain and guide blade (see illustration).

5 Stuff clean rag into the camchain tunnel to prevent anything falling inside, then undo the three 6 mm screws and single 8 mm bolt securing the cylinder to the crankcase and remove the screws, bolt and washers (see illustration).

6 Draw the cylinder off the studs, supporting the piston as you do to prevent the connecting rod hitting the crankcase (see illustrations). The sealant used between the cylinder and the crankcase can form a strong bond - if the cylinder is stuck, tap around the joint with a soft-faced mallet to free it from the crankcase. Do not attempt to free the cylinder by levering with a screwdriver between the cylinder and the crankcase – you'll damage the sealing surfaces. Once the cylinder has been removed, stuff clean rag around the connecting rod to protect it and to prevent anything falling into the crankcase.

7 Remove the two oil passage O-rings from the crankcase and discard them as new ones must be used (see illustration). Remove the two dowels from the crankcase if they are loose.

8 Clean all traces of sealant from the cylinder

15.3 Remove the cam chain guide blade pivot bolt and sealing washer

15.4 Secure the chain to the guide blade with an elastic band

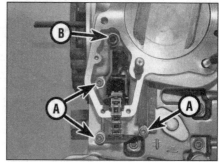

15.5 Undo the 6 mm screws (A) and 8 mm bolt (B)

15.6a Draw the cylinder off . . .

15.6b . . . supporting the piston to prevent the rod striking the crankcase

15.7 Remove the O-rings (arrowed)

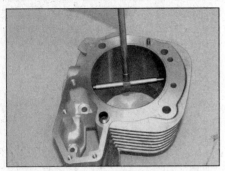

15.12a Measuring the cylinder bore with a telescoping gauge

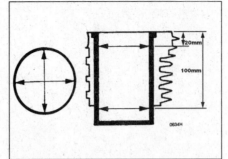

15.12b Take measurements in the directions shown

15.22 Feed the piston rings into the bottom of the cylinder bore (arrowed)

and crankcase mating surfaces. If a scraper is used, take care not to scratch or gouge the soft aluminium. Be careful not to let any of the old sealant fall into the crankcase or the oil passages.

Inspection

9 The cylinder bores have a wear resistant coating which should last the life of the engine unless damage, caused by a broken piston ring or seizure, has occurred.

10 Working on one cylinder at a time, inspect the cylinder walls carefully for scratches and score marks. If damage is noted, yet the bore diameter is still within the service limit, seek the advice of a BMW dealer or engine specialist as to the suitability of the cylinder for continued use. The cylinders cannot be rebored.

11 Cylinders and pistons, as fitted at the BMW factory, are designated as either tolerance Group A or Group B. Replacement components (available from the BMW dealer) are designated as tolerance Group A/B. The group letter is stamped into the top of the cylinder, just outside the machined cylinder-to-cylinder head sealing surface **(see illustration 17.3)**.

12 Using telescoping gauges and a micrometer (see *Tools and Workshop Tips* in the Reference section), check the dimensions of each cylinder to assess the amount of wear and ovality **(see illustration)**. Take measurements 20 mm and 100 mm from the top of the bore, both parallel with the piston pin and at 90° to it, taking a total of four measurements **(see illustration)**.

13 Compare the results with the specifications at the beginning of this Chapter, then calculate any difference between the measurements to determine ovality in the bore.

14 If the cylinder is worn beyond the service limit, or bore ovality exceeds the service limits, the cylinder must be renewed. Make sure you supply the dealer with the tolerance group letter when purchasing new parts. **Note:** *Cylinders and pistons must be fitted as paired sets, so a new piston will also be required (see Section 16).*

Installation

Note: *The following procedure assumes that the pistons are on the connecting rods. If the pistons have been removed, follow the installation procedure in Section 16, Steps 16 to 31.*

15 Ensure that the TDC locating pin is in place.

16 Working on one side of the engine at a time, check that the sealing surfaces of the cylinder and crankcase are clean and free from oil and old sealant. Check the four cylinder studs are tight.

17 If removed, install the two dowels in the crankcase, then fit new O-rings on the dowels **(see illustration 15.7)**.

18 Ensure that the piston ring end gaps are correctly staggered (see Section 17).

19 Apply an even bead of suitable sealant to the sealing surface of the cylinder **(see illustration 16.27)**.

Caution: Do not apply an excessive amount of sealant as it will ooze out and may obstruct oil passages.

20 Lubricate the cylinder bore and piston with clean engine oil. Install the cylinder over the studs until the piston crown fits into the bore **(see illustration 15.6a)**. Make sure the camchain is positioned so that it enters the tunnel without causing an obstruction.

21 Remove the rag from around the connecting rod.

22 Gently push on the cylinder, making sure the piston enters the bore squarely and does not get cocked sideways. Carefully compress and feed each ring into the bore in turn as the cylinder is installed **(see illustration)**.

23 When the piston is fully installed in the bore, ensure that the camchain is aligned with the tunnel and press the cylinder down onto the crankcase **(see illustrations)**.

24 Stuff clean rag into the camchain tunnel to prevent anything falling inside, then take the elastic band off the chain and guide blade.

25 Install the single 8 mm bolt and washer, three 6 mm screws and washers, and tighten them to the torque setting specified at the beginning of this Chapter **(see illustration 15.5)**.

26 Remove the rag from the camchain tunnel. Install the camchain guide blade pivot bolt using a new sealing washer and tighten it to the specified torque setting **(see illustration 15.3)**.

27 If removed, install the knock sensor and tighten the bolt to the specified torque setting – note that the correct torque for the sensor bolt is critical, otherwise the sensor will not function correctly. Connect the sensor wiring connector.

28 Install the cylinder head (see Section 12).

16 Pistons

Note: *The pistons can be removed with the engine in the frame.*

Special tool: *A piston ring clamp is desirable for this procedure.*

Removal

1 Remove the cylinder (see Section 15). Once the cylinder has been removed, don't forget to stuff clean rag around the connecting rod to protect it and to prevent anything falling into the crankcase.

15.23a Ensure that the camchain (arrowed) is aligned with the tunnel . . .

15.23b . . . then press the cylinder onto the crankcase

16.2 Mark the piston with its identity (arrowed) for future reference

16.3a Remove the circlips . . .

16.3b . . . and draw the piston pin out

2 The left and right-hand pistons are different. Identification marks (weight class, tolerance group, left or right-hand fitment and direction of installation arrow) are printed on the top of new pistons, but these marks will not be visible once the engine has been run. Before removing a piston, use a marker pen to write the cylinder identity (i.e. left or right-hand cylinder) on the piston crown or on the side of the skirt **(see illustration)**. Note that the valve cut-out in the piston crown is larger for the intake valves – this cut-out faces the rear of the engine. **Note:** *Pistons and cylinders are supplied as paired sets – check for the tolerance group letter on the top of the cylinder (see Section 15, Step 11).*

3 Carefully remove the circlip from both ends of the piston pin using external circlip pliers **(see illustration)**. Discard the circlips as new ones must be used. Push the piston pin out to free the piston from the connecting rod **(see illustration)**. Once the piston has been removed, fit the pin back into the piston to ensure it can be installed the right way round on reassembly.

 If a piston pin is a tight fit in the piston bosses, heat the piston with a hot air gun to release the pin. Support the piston (wrap rag around the piston to avoid burning your hands) and press the pin out with a suitable length of rod. Never drive a piston pin out with a hammer and drift.

Inspection

4 If both pistons have been removed, work on them separately to avoid getting parts mixed up.
5 Before the inspection process can be carried out, remove the piston rings and clean the piston.
6 Using your thumbs or a thin blade, carefully remove the rings from the piston **(see illustrations)**. Do not nick or gouge the piston in the process. Note which way up each ring fits and in which groove as they must be installed in their original positions if being re-used. The upper surface of each ring is marked 'TOP'. Note that the oil control ring

(lowest on the piston) has an expander fitted behind it **(see illustration 17.5)**.
7 Scrape all traces of carbon from the piston crown. A hand-held wire brush or a piece of fine emery cloth can be used once most of the deposits have been scraped away. Do not, under any circumstances, use a wire brush mounted in a drill motor to remove deposits from the piston – the piston material is soft and will be eroded away by the wire brush.
8 Use a piston ring groove cleaning tool to remove any carbon deposits from the ring grooves. If a tool is not available, a piece broken off an old ring will do the job. Be very careful to remove only the carbon deposits. Do not remove any metal and do not nick or gouge the sides of the ring grooves.
9 Once the deposits have been removed, wash the piston with solvent and dry it thoroughly. Make sure the oil return holes

in the back of the oil ring groove are clear. If the identification mark made on removal is cleaned off, be sure to re-mark the piston with the correct identity **(see illustration)**.
10 Inspect the piston for cracks and damage around the skirt, at the pin bosses and at the ring lands **(see illustration)**. Normal wear appears as light, vertical marks on the thrust surfaces of the skirt and slight looseness of the top ring in its groove. If the skirt is scored or scuffed, the piston and cylinder are probably worn beyond the service limit. Alternatively, the engine may have been suffering from overheating caused by lack of lubrication or abnormal combustion. Check the operation of the oil pump (see Section 22) and, if necessary, have the engine management system checked by a BMW dealer.
11 A hole in the top of the piston (only likely in extreme circumstances) or burned areas

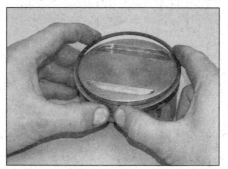

16.6a Remove the rings carefully, using your thumbs . . .

16.6b . . . or a thin blade – a feeler gauge is ideal

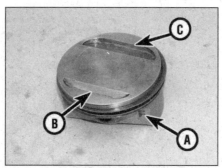

16.9 Cylinder identity (A). Note the smaller exhaust valve cut-out (B) and larger intake valve cut-out (C)

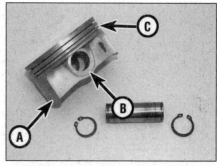

16.10 Inspect the piston skirt (A), pin boss (B) and ring lands (C)

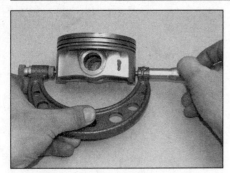

16.12 Measuring piston diameter

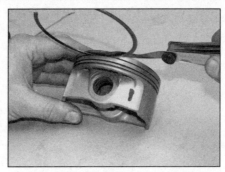

16.13 Measuring piston ring-to-groove clearance

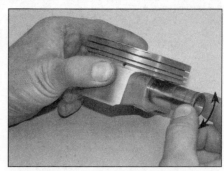

16.14a Try to rock the piston pin back and forth. If it's loose, renew the piston and pin

around the edge of the piston crown, indicate that pre-ignition or knocking under load have occurred. The knock sensors fitted to the cylinders should ensure correct ignition under all circumstances, but if a sensor fails, or if it is fitted incorrectly, the engine management system will not be able to set the correct ignition timing. If you find evidence of any problems, the causes must be corrected or the damage will occur again.

12 Calculate the piston-to-bore clearance by measuring the cylinder bore (see Section 15) and the piston diameter. Make sure the piston is matched to its correct cylinder. Measure the piston 6 mm up from the bottom of the skirt and at 90° to the piston pin axis **(see illustration)**. Subtract the piston diameter from the bore diameter to obtain the clearance and compare the result with the service limit specified at the beginning of this Chapter. If it is greater than specified, a new piston and cylinder will have to be fitted (see Step 15).

13 Measure the piston ring-to-groove clearance by laying each piston ring in its groove and slipping a feeler gauge in beside it **(see illustration)**. Make sure you have the correct ring for the groove. Check the clearance at three or four locations around the groove. If the clearance is greater than specified, measure the thickness of the ring and compare the result with the specifications. If the ring is worn, and fitting a new ring will restore the clearance to within the service limit, fit a new set of rings. **Note:** *Piston ring-to-groove clearance must be within the*

service limit for all rings, otherwise the piston is unserviceable and must be renewed (see Step 15).

14 Apply clean engine oil to the piston pin, insert it part way into the piston and check for any freeplay between the two **(see illustration)**. Measure the pin external diameter and the pin bore in the piston **(see illustration)**. Subtract the pin diameter from the bore diameter to obtain the clearance. If it is greater than the specified figure, check whether it is the piston or pin that is worn beyond its service limit and renew them as required. Repeat the checks between the pin and the connecting rod small end (see Section 18).

15 Pistons and cylinders must be fitted as paired sets, so if a new piston is required, a new cylinder will be required also. The tolerance group letter for piston and cylinder sets is stamped on the top of the cylinder (see Section 15, Step 11). Also, when purchasing new parts, it is essential to determine the piston's weight category – left and right-hand pistons must be within 10 grams of each other to ensure smooth running of the engine. The weight category is printed on the top of a new piston, but this mark will not be visible once the engine has been run. If only one new piston is required, supply the BMW dealer with the old piston, complete with piston pin and piston rings, from the other side of the engine so that a match can be made. **Note:** *All piston weights are inclusive of the piston pin and piston rings.*

Installation

16 Ensure that the TDC locating pin is in place. Work on one side of the engine at a time.

17 Install the piston rings and ensure that the ring end gaps are correctly staggered (see Section 17).

18 If a piston ring clamp is being used, proceed as follows, otherwise go to Step 22. Lubricate the piston, rings and the inside of the clamp with clean engine oil. Install the clamp over the rings and tighten it enough to compress the rings into their grooves, but not so tight that it locks onto the piston – as the piston is pressed into the cylinder bore, the clamp must be able to slide off. Once the clamp is in place, don't rotate it as the position of the ring end gaps will alter.

19 Lubricate the appropriate cylinder bore with clean engine oil, then install the lower end of the piston into the top of the bore **(see illustration)** – if both pistons have been removed, check the identification marks (see Step 2). Also ensure that the piston is installed the right way round with the larger valve cut-outs facing the rear of the cylinder – again, don't rotate the piston once it had been pressed all the way into the cylinder as the position of the ring end gaps will alter.

20 Press down on the top of the piston and slowly ease it into the bore **(see illustration)**. If the rings snag on the top lip of the bore, tighten the clamp slightly to compress the rings further into their grooves.

16.14b Measuring the piston pin external diameter

16.19 Install the lower end of the piston into the top of the cylinder bore

16.20 Ease the piston into the bore

16.21a Once the piston is safely installed ...

16.21b ... push it down until the pin bore (arrowed) is just visible

16.25a Compress the rings carefully ...

Caution: Do not force the piston down – this will only result in broken rings.

21 Only lift the ring clamp off once the piston is safely inside the cylinder, then carefully push the piston down until the piston pin bore is visible below the lower edge of the bore **(see illustrations)**. Don't push the piston too far, otherwise the oil control ring will come out of its groove. Now go to Step 27.

22 To install the piston without a ring clamp, stand the cylinder upside down on the work surface and lubricate the bore with clean engine oil.

23 Lubricate the piston and rings with clean engine oil – if both pistons have been removed, check the identification marks (see Step 2).

24 Position the top of the piston on the lower edge of the cylinder bore. Ensure that the piston is positioned the right way round with the larger valve cut-outs facing the rear of the cylinder – don't rotate the piston once it had been pressed into the cylinder as the position of the ring end gaps will alter.

25 Carefully compress and feed each ring into the bore in turn as the piston is pressed down – use your finger-tips and a small screwdriver to do this **(see illustration)**. Don't press the piston down too hard as this will only cause the rings to snag and take care not

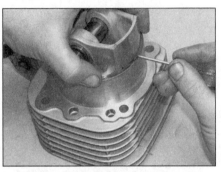

16.25b ... feeding each one into the cylinder bore in turn

to score the surface of the piston skirt with the screwdriver **(see illustration)**.

26 Press the piston down far enough to ensure the oil control ring is safely inside the bore, but leave clearance for the piston pin to be installed **(see illustration)**.

27 Apply an even bead of suitable sealant to the sealing surface of the cylinder **(see illustration)**. Fit new O-rings to the crankcase dowels **(see illustration 15.7)**.

Caution: Do not apply an excessive amount of sealant as it will ooze out and may obstruct oil passages.

28 Install the cylinder over the studs and slide

16.26 Leave clearance for installation of the piston pin

it towards the crankcase **(see illustration)**. Check that the piston is positioned the correct way round, with the larger valve cut-outs facing the rear of the engine.

29 Make sure the camchain is positioned so that it enters the tunnel without causing an obstruction and guide the connecting rod small-end into the piston – it may be necessary to adjust the position of the piston slightly so that the piston pin bore aligns with the small-end, but take care not to pull the piston out from the cylinder.

30 Lubricate the piston pin with clean engine oil and press it into position, then secure

16.27 Apply sealant to the cylinder sealing surface

16.28 Install the cylinder over the studs

16.30a Align the piston and connecting rod, then press the piston pin through the rod . . .

16.30b . . . to secure the piston to the rod . . .

16.30c . . . then install the circlips

the pin with a new circlip at both ends **(see illustrations)**.

31 Remove the rag from around the connecting rod and press the cylinder down onto the crankcase.

32 Follow the procedure in Section 15, Steps 24 to 28, to complete the installation of the cylinder and cylinder head.

17 Piston rings

1 It is good practice to replace the piston rings when an engine is being overhauled. Before installing the new piston rings, the ring end gaps must be checked with the rings installed in the cylinder.

2 Lay out the pistons and the new ring sets so the rings will be matched with the same piston and cylinder during the end gap measurement procedure and engine assembly. The upper surface of each ring is marked 'TOP' **(see illustration)**. Note that the oil control ring (lowest on the piston) has an expander fitted behind it **(see illustration 17.5)**.

3 To measure the installed ring end gap, insert each ring into the top of the cylinder and square it up with the cylinder walls by pushing it in with the top of the piston. The ring should be about 20 mm below the top edge of the cylinder. To measure the end gap, slip a feeler gauge between the ends of the ring and compare the measurement to the specifications at the beginning of the Chapter **(see illustration)**. Note that the end gaps for the top and second ring are different from the oil control ring.

4 If the gap is larger or smaller than specified, double check to make sure that you have the correct rings before proceeding. Excess end gap is not critical unless it exceeds the service limit. Also, check to ensure that the cylinder bore is not worn beyond the service limit (see Section 15). Remember to keep the rings, pistons and cylinders matched up.

5 The oil control ring (lowest on the piston) is installed first. It is composed of two separate components – the expander and the ring. Pull the ends of the expander apart enough to fit it over the top of the piston and slip it into its groove, then press the ends back together **(see illustration)**. Ensure that the straight wire is not pulled out of either end of the coiled wire. Now install the oil control ring over the expander. Make sure that the 'TOP' mark is facing up and that the end gap in the ring is on the opposite side of the piston to the end gap in the expander. Do not expand the ring any more than is necessary to slide it into place. To avoid breaking the ring, slide a thin blade around the piston while easing the ring on **(see illustration 16.6b)**.

6 After the oil ring components have been installed, check that the ring can be turned smoothly in the ring groove.

7 Install the second ring next. Make sure that the 'TOP' mark is facing up. Fit the ring into the middle groove in the piston and use a thin blade, as with the oil ring, to ease the ring on without breaking it.

8 Finally, install the top ring in the same manner into the top groove in the piston.

9 Once the rings are correctly installed, check they move freely without snagging **(see illustration)**.

10 Before fitting the piston into the cylinder, stagger the ring end gaps 120° apart. Viewed as fitted onto the connecting rod, the oil control ring end gap should be facing up, the second ring gap facing forward and down, and the top ring gap facing back and down.

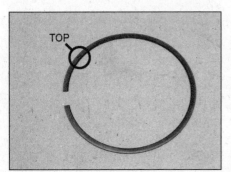

17.2 Upper surface of each piston ring is marked TOP

17.3 Measuring piston ring end gap with a feeler gauge. Note the cylinder tolerance group letter (arrowed)

17.5 Installing the oil control ring expander

17.9 Ensure that the rings move freely in their grooves

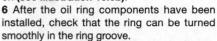

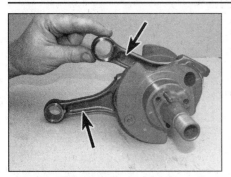

18.10a Mark the cylinder identity on the connecting rods . . .

18.10b . . . and on the big-end caps

18.11a Undo the big-end bolts . . .

18 Connecting rods

Note 1: *The connecting rods can be removed with the engine in the frame, gaining access to the big-end bolts for each rod via the cylinder aperture in the crankcase on the opposite side of the engine. However, accurate assessment of wear to the crankshaft crankpins requires the engine removed from the frame and the crankcase halves separated to gain access to the crankshaft.*

Note 2: *The big-end bolts are of the stretch type – new bolts must be fitted when the engine is fully reassembled. Note that the bolt thread pitch changed from 1.25 to 1.00 mm in Mar 2006. It is important to identify the type fitted if working on a machine built around this period because this information is necessary when tightening through the correct torque angle (see Torque settings at the beginning of this Chapter). Thread pitch can be measured with a gauge (see Tools and Workshop Tips in the Reference section).*

Special tool: *A degree disc is required for angle-tightening the connecting rod big-end bolts.*

Removal – with engine in the frame

1 Remove the pistons (see Section 16). If necessary, remove the TDC locating pin and position the crankshaft to provide the best access to the big-end bolts on the connecting rod being removed. Note the amount of

crankshaft movement so that the pin can be refitted afterwards, otherwise it will be necessary to remove the timing cover and retime the engine with reference to the timing marks on the crankshaft and balancer shaft gears (see Section 20).

2 Before removing the rod from the crankshaft, push it to one side on the crankpin and measure the side clearance between the big-end and the crankshaft with a feeler gauge. If the clearance is greater than the service limit listed in the *Specifications* at the beginning of this Chapter, the rod must be renewed.

3 Using paint or a marker pen, mark the cylinder identity (L or R) on the connecting rod and cap **(see illustration 18.10a and b)**. Use the marks to indicate which way round the rod is fitted.

4 Undo the big-end bolts and separate the cap and its bearing shell from the crankpin **(see illustrations 18.11a and b)**.

Caution: Ensure the bearing shells do not fall out of either the cap or the rod and into the crankcase.

5 Withdraw the connecting rod and its bearing shell from the other side of the engine. Keep the rod, cap and the bearing shells together to ensure correct installation.

6 If required, follow the same procedure to remove the other connecting rod from the crankshaft.

Removal – engine out of the frame

7 Separate the crankcase halves (see Section 25).

8 Lift out the crankshaft assembly, taking care not to dislodge the crankshaft main and guide bearing shells (see Section 27).

9 Before removing the rods from the crankshaft, measure the big-end side clearance. Working on one rod at a time, push it to one side on the crankpin and measure the clearance between the big-end and the crankshaft with a feeler gauge. If the clearance is greater than the service limit listed in the *Specifications* at the beginning of this Chapter, the rod must be renewed.

10 Using paint or a marker pen, mark the cylinder identity (L or R) on the connecting rod and cap. Use the marks to indicate which way round the rod is fitted **(see illustrations)**.

11 Undo the big-end bolts and separate the rod and cap from the crankpin **(see illustrations)**. Keep the rod, cap and the bearing shells together to ensure correct installation **(see illustration)**.

12 Follow the same procedure to remove the other connecting rod from the crankshaft.

Inspection

13 The connecting rods are fitted as paired sets dependant upon their weight. Weight class identification is represented by coloured dots (white, blue or yellow) painted on the sides of the rods (see *Specifications* at the beginning of this Chapter for details) **(see illustration)**.

14 The joint between the connecting rod and the cap is a fractured joint that can only be

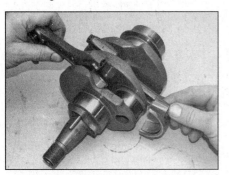

18.11b . . . and separate the rod and cap

18.11c Note the location of the bearing shells

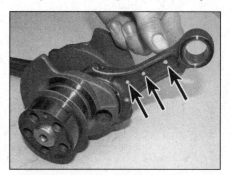

18.13 Dots (arrowed) indicate the weight class of the rod

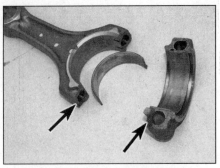

18.14 Note the uneven surface of the fractured joint (arrowed)

18.16a Measuring the piston pin external diameter . . .

18.16b . . . and the small-end bore diameter

assembled one way round **(see illustration)**. Take care not to damage the joint surfaces – if the surfaces are not a perfect match, the two halves of the big-end will not come-together properly and a new connecting rod will have to be fitted.

15 Check the connecting rods for cracks and other obvious damage.

16 To check the rod small-end, lubricate the appropriate piston pin with clean engine oil, then insert it in the rod and check for any freeplay between the two. Measure the pin external diameter and the small-end bore diameter **(see illustrations)**. Subtract the pin diameter from the bore diameter to obtain the clearance. If it is greater than the specified figure, check whether it is the pin or the small-end that is worn beyond its service limit and renew the pin or the rod as required. Repeat the check with the other connecting rod. **Note:** *If a new connecting rod is fitted, it must be of the same weight class as the other rod in the engine (see Step 13).*

17 Examine the big-end bearing shells **(see illustration)**. If there are any signs of wear on the bearing surfaces they should be renewed – always renew the shells in both big-ends as a set. The shells are colour-coded red or blue according to their original tolerance fit – the colour mark is on the edge of the shell. Always fit new shells of the same colour code.

18 Refer to the general information in Section 26. If the bearing shells are scored,

badly scuffed or appear to have seized, check the corresponding crankpin. Damage to the surface of the crankpin on a standard crankshaft can be corrected by re-grinding and fitting oversize (+0.25 mm) bearing shells. If the crankshaft has already been reground, indicated by paint marks on the front crankshaft web, a new crankshaft will have to be fitted. If there is any doubt about the condition of the crankshaft, have it checked by a BMW dealer.

19 To check the rod big-end, first remove the bearing shells by easing them out to one side with your fingers, noting how they fit **(see illustration)**. Assemble the cap on the rod, ensuring that the two halves of the fractured joint are a perfect fit, then install the bolts and tighten them to the second stage setting (see *Specifications* at the beginning of this Chapter). Use the old bolts for the purpose of the check. Measure the diameter of the big-end bore with a telescoping gauge and micrometer and compare the result with the specification at the beginning of this Chapter **(see illustration)**. If it is greater than the specified figure, renew the connecting rod (see **Note**, Step 16).

20 If you are in doubt about their straightness, have the rods checked for twist and bending by a BMW dealer. Note that the sintered-metal type connecting rods used in this engine cannot be straightened due to risk of fracture.

Oil clearance check

Note: *This procedure can only be undertaken with any degree of accuracy once the crankshaft has been removed from the engine (see Section 27).*

21 Whether new bearing shells are being fitted or the original ones are being re-used, the connecting rod big-end bearing oil clearance should be checked prior to reassembly. Bearing oil clearance can be measured either by using a micrometer and telescoping gauge, or with a product called Plastigauge.

22 To measure the oil clearance using Plastigauge, first clean the backs of the bearing shells, the shell locations in both the connecting rod and cap, and the corresponding crankshaft crankpin with a suitable solvent. Work on one connecting rod at a time to avoid getting parts mixed up.

23 Press the shells into their locations, ensuring that the tab on each shell engages in the notch in the connecting rod or cap **(see illustration 18.19a)**. Make sure the shells are fitted in their correct locations and take care not to touch any shell's bearing surface with your fingers.

24 Support the crankshaft on the work bench so that it cannot move during the check procedure – it is essential that the crankshaft and the connecting rod remain in the same position throughout.

25 Cut an appropriate size length of Plastigauge (it should be slightly shorter than

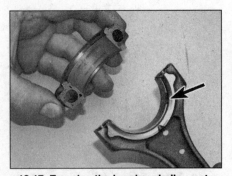

18.17 Examine the bearing shells – note the location of the colour mark (arrowed)

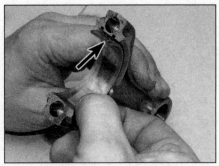

18.19a Ease the shells out carefully – note the locating tab (arrowed)

18.19b Measuring the big-end bore diameter

18.25 Lay a strip of Plastigauge on the crankpin

18.27 Tighten the big-end bolts using a degree disc

18.29 Measuring the crushed Plastigauge using the printed scale

the width of the crankpin) and place it on the crankpin **(see illustration)**. Do not place the Plastigauge over any oil holes.

26 Lubricate the big-end bolts with clean engine oil – use the old bolts for the purpose of the check.

27 Install the connecting rod and cap on the crankpin, ensuring they are the right way round (see Step 10). Ensure that the two halves of the fractured joint are a perfect fit, then install the bolts and tighten them finger-tight. Ensure that the crankshaft is held securely and tighten the bolts evenly to the second stage setting (see *Specifications* at the beginning of this Chapter), then use a degree disc (see *Tools and Workshop Tips)* to tighten them to the final setting in one continuous movement **(see illustration)**.

28 Unscrew the bolts and remove the connecting rod and cap from the crankpin, being careful not to disturb the Plastigauge.

29 Compare the width of the crushed Plastigauge on the crankpin to the scale printed on the Plastigauge envelope to obtain the bearing oil clearance **(see illustration)**. Compare the result with the specifications at the beginning of the Chapter.

30 If the original bearing shells have been used for the check and the clearance is within the service limit, they can be reused. If the clearance is beyond the service limit, but the crankpin journal is good (see Step 32) , fit new bearing shells and check the oil clearance once again. **Note:** *Always renew the bearing shells in both connecting rods at the same time.*

31 Carefully clean away all traces of the Plastigauge material from the crankpin and bearing shells using a fingernail or other object which will not score the bearing surfaces.

32 To measure the oil clearance using a micrometer and telescoping gauge, first measure the diameter of the crankpin in two different planes with the micrometer and note the results **(see illustration)**. Wear on the crankpin can be determined by comparing the results with the specifications at the beginning of this Chapter. Note that a re-ground (Stage 1) crankshaft is identified by paint marks on the front crankshaft web.

33 Next, working on the corresponding

connecting rod, clean the backs of the bearing shells and the shell locations in both the rod and cap with a suitable solvent. Press the shells into their locations, ensuring that the tab on each shell engages the notch in the connecting rod or cap **(see illustration 18.19a)**. Make sure the shells are fitted in the correct locations and take care not to touch the bearing surfaces with your fingers.

34 Assemble the cap on the rod, ensuring that the two halves of the fractured joint are a perfect fit, then install the bolts and tighten them to the second stage setting (see *Specifications* at the beginning of this Chapter). Use the old bolts for the purpose of the check. Measure the diameter of the big-end bore with bearing shells with a telescoping gauge and micrometer and note the result **(see illustration 18.19b)**. With reference to Step 32, note that a re-ground crankshaft will be fitted with appropriately sized Stage 1 shells.

35 Subtract the crankpin diameter from the bore diameter to obtain the clearance and compare the result with the specifications at the beginning of this Chapter.

36 If the original bearing shells have been used for the check and the clearance is within the service limit, they can be reused. If the clearance is beyond the service limit, but the crankpin journal is good (see Step 32) , fit new bearing shells and check the oil clearance once again. **Note:** *Always renew the bearing shells in both connecting rods at the same time.*

Installation

37 Working on one connecting rod at a time, press the bearing shells into their locations (see Step 23). Lubricate the shells and the crankpin with clean engine oil **(see illustration)**.

38 Lubricate a set of new big-end bolts with clean engine oil.

39 Install the connecting rod and cap on the crankpin, ensuring that they are the right way round (see Step 10). Ensure that the two halves of the fractured joint are a perfect fit, then install the new bolts and tighten them finger-tight.

40 Tighten the bolts evenly to the second stage setting (see *Specifications* at the beginning of this Chapter), then use a degree disc (see *Tools and Workshop Tips* in the *Reference* section) to tighten them to the final setting in one continuous movement **(see illustration 18.27)**.

41 Check that the connecting rod is free to rotate smoothly and freely on the crankpin. If the rod feels tight, tap on the bottom of the cap with a soft-faced mallet to free it. If there are still signs of roughness or tightness, detach the rod and recheck the assembly. **Note:** *New big-end bolts must be used each time they are disturbed.*

42 Install the other rod in the same way. Ensure that all components have been returned to their original locations using the marks made on disassembly.

43 As appropriate, follow the procedure in Section 16 and install the pistons, or Section 27 and install the crankshaft assembly in the crankcase.

18.32 Measuring the diameter of the crankpin

18.37 Lubricate the shells generously with clean engine oil

19.4 Remove the alternator drive belt top cover

19.5 Undo the screw and remove the crankshaft position sensor

19.8 Remove the alternator drive pulley

19 Alternator drive and engine timing cover

Note: *The alternator drive components and the engine timing cover can be removed with the engine in the frame.*

Special tools: *A top dead centre (TDC) locating pin is required for this procedure (see* **Tool Tip***, Section 9). On models up to Sept 2007, a two-legged puller is required to remove the timing cover and seal installation guides are required to fit the crankshaft oil seal (see* **Tool Tip***, Step 21).*

Removal – 2004 to Sept 2007 models

1 During this procedure the engine should be locked in the TDC position by inserting a locating pin through the hole in the right-hand side of the gearbox case **(see illustration 9.1)**. Remove the body panels as appropriate to your machine to access the hole (see Chapter 6).

2 Drain the engine oil (see Chapter 1, Section 1).

3 Remove the alternator drive belt (see Chapter 1, Section 13).

4 Undo the screws securing the alternator drive belt top cover and remove the cover **(see illustration)**.

5 Undo the screw securing the crankshaft position sensor and pull the sensor out of its location in the top of the timing cover, noting the location of the sealing O-ring **(see illustration)**.

6 Remove both primary spark plugs (see Chapter 1, Section 11).

19.9a Undo the screws (arrowed) . . .

19.9b . . . and lift off the cover and O-ring (arrowed)

7 Turn the engine with a spanner on the crankshaft pulley nut until both pistons are at TDC. Insert the TDC locating pin into the hole in the right-hand side of the gearbox case. The pin should pass through the clutch assembly and locate in a 5 mm diameter hole in the crankcase.

8 Undo the nut securing the alternator belt drive pulley, remove the nut and washer, then lift off the pulley, noting which way round its fits **(see illustration)**.

9 Undo the screws securing the balancer shaft cover, then lift off the cover and the cover O-ring **(see illustrations)**.

10 Undo the balancer shaft front bolt and remove the bolt and washer **(see illustration)**.

Note: *Take care not to press the balancer shaft into the engine in case the lip on the oil seal on the rear end of the shaft is damaged.*

11 Undo the screws securing the timing cover to the crankcase **(see illustration)**.

12 Position a suitable spacer over the centre of the balancer shaft drive gear, inside the inner race of the bearing in the timing cover, then assemble a two-legged puller as shown **(see illustration)**. Take care to ensure that the spacer rests on the rim of the drive gear and not on the end of the balancer shaft which is in the centre of the drive gear.

13 Ease the timing cover off carefully. The sealant used between the cover and the crankcase can form a strong bond – if the cover is stuck, tap around the joint with a soft-faced mallet to free it from the crankcase. Do not attempt to free the cover by levering

19.10 Remove the balancer shaft bolt and washer

19.11 Timing cover screws (arrowed)

19.12 Set-up for drawing the timing cover off

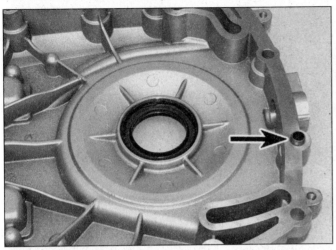

19.14a Note the location of the dowel (arrowed) in the cover . . .

19.14b . . . and the dowel (arrowed) in the crankcase

19.16 Bearing is retained by a circlip (arrowed)

19.17 Driving out the old crankshaft oil seal

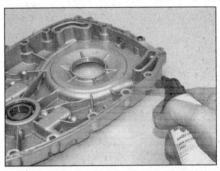

19.19 Apply an even bead of sealant to the cover

with a screwdriver between the cover and the crankcase – you'll damage the sealing surfaces.

14 Note the location of the dowels in either the cover or the crankcase and remove them if they are loose **(see illustrations)**.

15 Clean all traces of sealant from the cover and crankcase mating surfaces. If a scraper is used, take care not to scratch or gouge the soft aluminium. Be careful not to let any of the old sealant fall into the crankcase.

16 Check the condition of the bearing in the cover (see *Tools and Workshop Tips* in the *Reference* section). To renew the bearing, first remove the retaining circlip **(see illustration)**. Heat the cover around the bearing housing

with a hot air gun, then press the bearing out with a bearing driver or suitably sized socket. Note which way round the bearing is fitted. Ensure the cover is still hot, then install the new bearing in the reverse order of removal and secure it with a new circlip.

17 Drive out the old crankshaft seal, noting which way round it fits **(see illustration)**.

Installation – 2004 to Sept 2007 models

18 If removed, fit the dowels into the crankcase or cover (see Step 14).

19 Apply an even bead of suitable sealant to the sealing surface of the cover **(see illustration)**.

20 Install the cover, then install the cover screws and tighten them to the torque setting specified at the beginning of this Chapter **(see illustration 19.11)**.

21 Care must be taken to avoid damaging the inner lip of the new crankshaft seal when it is installed – a suitable seal guide and sleeve must be used (see *Tool Tip overleaf*). BMW provide a set of tools for this purpose. Slip the seal, inner side first, over the shaped end of the guide (BMW Part No. 11 5 713) **(see illustration)**. Install the guide on the end of the crankshaft and press the seal into position with the sleeve (BMW Part No. 11 5 711) **(see illustration)**. Withdraw the guide, then screw

19.21a Slip the seal over the end of the guide . . .

19.21b . . . then install the guide on the crankshaft and press the seal onto the crankshaft with the sleeve

19.21c Withdraw the guide . . .

19.21d ...and press the seal into the cover

19.21e The installed seal should look like this

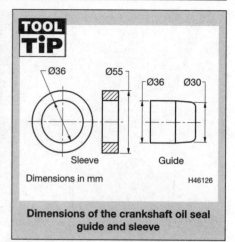

Dimensions in mm   H46126

Dimensions of the crankshaft oil seal guide and sleeve

on the threaded sleeve (BMW Part No. 11 5 712) to press the seal into the cover **(see illustrations)**. The outer face of the installed seal should be level with the edge of the seal housing **(see illustration)**.

22 Install the alternator belt drive pulley, writing facing out, then install the washer and nut **(see illustration)**. Ensure that the TDC locating pin is securely in place and tighten the pulley nut to the first stage torque setting, then tighten the nut to the final torque setting specified at the beginning of this Chapter.

23 Install the washer on the balancer shaft front bolt and install the bolt, then tighten the bolt to the specified torque **(see illustration 19.10)**.

24 Install a new O-ring and the balancer shaft cover, then tighten the cover screws to the specified torque **(see illustration)**.

25 Install a new O-ring on the crankshaft position sensor and install the sensor **(see illustration)**. Tighten the sensor screw to the specified torque.

26 Install the alternator drive belt top cover and tighten the screws to the specified torque **(see illustration 19.4)**.

27 Follow the procedure in Chapter 1, Section 13, and install the alternator drive belt.

28 Refill the engine with oil (see Chapter 1).

29 Install the remaining components in the reverse order of removal.

Removal – Oct 2007-on models

30 Follow Steps 1 to 4 at the beginning of this Section.

31 Remove both primary spark plugs (see Chapter 1, Section 11).

32 Turn the engine with a spanner on the crankshaft pulley nut until both pistons are at TDC. Insert the TDC locating pin into the hole in the right-hand side of the gearbox case. The pin should pass through the clutch assembly and locate in a 5 mm diameter hole in the crankcase.

33 Undo the nut securing the alternator belt drive pulley, remove the nut and washer, then lift off the pulley, noting which way round its fits **(see illustrations 19.8)**.

34 Undo the screws securing the timing cover to the crankcase **(see illustration 19.11)**.

35 Ease the timing cover away slightly so that access can be gained to the crankshaft position sensor. The sealant used between the cover and the crankcase can form a strong bond – if the cover is stuck, tap around the joint with a soft-faced mallet to free it from the crankcase. Do not attempt to free the cover by levering with a screwdriver between the cover and the crankcase – you'll damage the sealing surfaces. Undo the screw securing the crankshaft position sensor and pull the sensor out of its location in the top of the timing cover, noting the location of the sealing O-ring **(see illustration 19.5)**. Now remove the timing cover fully.

36 Note the location of the dowels in either the cover or the crankcase and remove them if they are loose **(see illustrations 19.14a and b)**.

37 Clean all traces of sealant from the cover and crankcase mating surfaces. If a scraper

is used, take care not to scratch or gouge the soft aluminium. Be careful not to let any of the old sealant fall into the crankcase.

38 Drive out the old crankshaft seal, noting which way round it fits **(see illustration 19.17)**.

Installation – Oct 2007-on models

39 If removed, fit the dowels into the crankcase or cover.

40 Apply an even bead of suitable sealant to the sealing surface of the cover **(see illustration 19.19)**. Install the cover, then install the cover screws and tighten them to the torque setting specified at the beginning of this Chapter **(see illustration 19.11)**.

41 Care must be taken to avoid damaging the inner lip of the new crankshaft seal when it is installed – a suitable seal guide and sleeve must be used (see **Tool Tip**). BMW provide a set of tools for this purpose. Slip the seal, inner side first, over the shaped end of the guide (BMW Part No. 11 5 713) **(see illustration 19.21a)**. Install the guide on the end of the crankshaft and press the seal into position with the sleeve (BMW Part No. 11 5 711) **(see illustration 19.21b)**. Withdraw the guide, then screw on the threaded sleeve (BMW Part No. 11 5 712) to press the seal into the cover **(see illustrations 19.21c and d)**. The outer face of the installed seal should be level with the edge of the seal housing **(see illustration 19.21e)**.

19.22 Install the pulley washer and nut

19.24 Fit a new O-ring inside the balancer shaft cover

19.25 Fit a new O-ring on the crankshaft position sensor

20.2a Location of the marks on the crankshaft gear (A) and the balancer shaft gear (B)

20.2b Check that the circlip (arrowed) is secure

42 Install the alternator belt drive pulley, writing facing out, then install the washer and nut **(see illustration 19.22)**. Ensure that the TDC locating pin is securely in place and tighten the pulley nut to the first stage torque setting, then tighten the nut to the final torque setting specified at the beginning of this Chapter.

43 Install a new O-ring on the crankshaft position sensor and install the sensor **(see illustration 19.25)**. Tighten the sensor screw to the specified torque.

44 Install the alternator drive belt top cover and tighten the screws to the specified torque **(see illustration 19.4)**.

45 Follow the procedure in Chapter 1, Section 13, and install the alternator drive belt.

46 Refill the engine with oil (see Chapter 1).

47 Install the remaining components in the reverse order of removal.

20 Balancer shaft gears and balancer shaft

Note: *The balancer shaft gears can be removed with the engine in the frame. To remove the balancer shaft, shaft bearing and oil seal, first remove the gearbox (see Section 4).*

Special tools: *A two-legged puller is required to remove the crankshaft gear on all models. On 2004 to Sept 2007 models, a knife-edged bearing puller is required to remove the balancer shaft bearing. On models from Oct 2007, a centre bolt puller is required to remove the balancer shaft gear.*

Balancer shaft gears

Removal

1 Remove the alternator drive and engine timing cover (see Section 19).

2 Note the position of the register marks on the balancer shaft gear and the crankshaft gear **(see illustration)**. On 2004 to Sept 2007 models, draw the balancer shaft gear off, noting that it is a two-piece, spring loaded assembly; when the teeth of the two halves

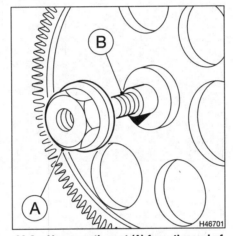

20.2c Unscrew the nut (A) from the end of the balancer shaft (B) . . .

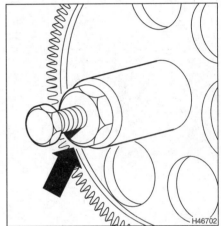

20.2d . . . then use a puller (arrowed) to draw the balancer gear off the shaft

are aligned they are under spring tension which eliminates any back-lash between the balancer shaft gear and the crankshaft gear when they are in mesh. Check that the circlip on the back of the balancer shaft gear is secure **(see illustration)**. If the spring between the two gears has lost its tension, a new balancer shaft gear assembly must be fitted. On models from Oct 2007, the gear is retained by a nut. Unscrew the nut and use a centre bolt puller on the shaft threads (BMW

No. 11 2 742) to draw the gear off the shaft **(see illustrations)**. On all models, note the location of the key on the balancer shaft.

3 Temporarily screw the alternator belt drive pulley nut onto the end of the crankshaft to protect the threads, position a suitable block of soft metal (see photo) over the nut and assemble a two-legged puller as shown **(see illustration)**. Pull the crankshaft gear off the taper on the shaft, noting the position of the locating pin **(see illustration)**.

20.3a Set-up for drawing the crankshaft gear off

20.3b Note the position of the locating pin (arrowed)

20.4 Clean the components with a suitable solvent

20.6 Install the crankshaft gear, pulley, washer and nut

20.7a Tighten the nut to the specified torque to seat the crankshaft gear . . .

20.7b . . . then remove the nut, washer and pulley

Installation

4 Ensure the taper on the crankshaft and the inside of the crankshaft gear are clean and free from oil **(see illustration)**.

5 Ensure the crankshaft is in the TDC position – the locating pin for the crankshaft gear should be facing up.

6 Install the crankshaft gear onto the shaft, then temporarily install the alternator belt drive pulley, washer and nut **(see illustration)**.

7 Ensure that the TDC locating pin is securely in place and tighten the pulley nut to the first stage torque setting, then tighten the nut to the final torque setting specified at the beginning of this Chapter **(see illustration)**. With the gear pressed firmly onto the crankshaft taper, undo the nut and remove the washer and pulley **(see illustration)**.

8 The register mark on the crankshaft gear should be facing down. Position the balancer shaft gear with its register mark facing up and

rotate the balancer shaft so that the key on the shaft aligns with the slot in the centre of the gear **(see illustration)**. Align the teeth of the balancer shaft gear and press it into position on the shaft. With the gear installed, check the alignment of the register marks **(see illustration 20.2a)**.

9 Install the engine timing cover and alternator drive (see Section 19).

Balancer shaft, oil seal and bearing – 2004 to Sept 2007 models

10 Remove the gearbox (see Section 4).

11 Follow the procedure in Steps 1 and 2 and remove the balancer shaft gear.

12 Draw the balancer shaft out carefully to avoid damaging the shaft seal **(see illustration)**.

13 To renew the seal or to gain access to the balancer shaft bearing, first remove the clutch (see Section 23).

14 Note the location of the old seal in its housing, then lever out the old seal taking care not to damage the housing **(see illustration)**. Discard the old seal as a new one must be fitted.

20.8 Key on the balancer shaft (A) must align with the slot (B) in the gear

20.12 Avoid damaging the seal (arrowed) when withdrawing the balancer shaft

20.14 Note the location of the old seal

20.15 Bearing is retained by a circlip (arrowed)

20.17a Ensure the new bearing is the right way round . . .

20.17b . . . and drive it all the way in

20.17c With the circlip groove (arrowed) visible . . .

20.17d . . . secure the bearing with the circlip

15 Inspect the balancer shaft bearing (see *Tools and Workshop Tips* in the *Reference* section). To remove the bearing, first remove the retaining circlip **(see illustration)**.
16 Heat the bearing housing with a hot air gun, then draw the bearing out with a knife-edged bearing puller and slide-hammer attachment (see *Tools and Workshop Tips* in the *Reference* section). Note which way round the bearing is fitted.
17 Install the new bearing in its housing and drive it all the way in with a bearing driver or suitably sized socket **(see illustrations)**. With the bearing fully installed, the circlip groove should

be visible all the way round **(see illustration)** Secure the bearing with a new circlip.
18 Install the new seal and press it into its housing until the outer edge of the seal is level with the outer face of the housing **(see illustrations)**.
19 Install the clutch (see Section 23).
20 Install the balancer shaft carefully to avoid damaging the shaft seal.
21 To install the balancer shaft gear before installing the gearbox, have an assistant support the rear end of the shaft while the gear is pressed into place to avoid damaging the inner lip of the seal **(see illustration)**.

20.18a Install the new seal . . .

20.18b . . . and press it in using a suitable driver

20.21 Avoid damaging the inner lip of the seal (arrowed)

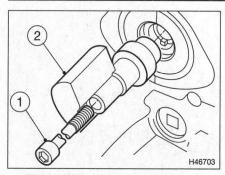

20.24a With the balancer gear held, unscrew the balancer weight screw (1) and remove the weight (2) from the end of the shaft – shown with clutch removed

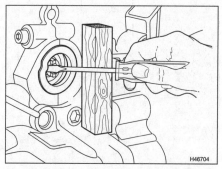

20.24b Prise out the balancer shaft oil seal from the rear of the engine. Note the use of the wood block to protect the engine casting

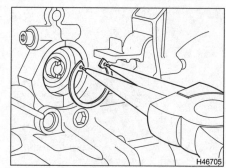

20.26a Remove the circlip from the rear of the engine . . .

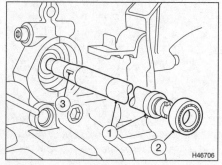

20.26b . . . then push the balancer shaft (1) and bearing (2) out. Woodruff key (3) must remain in shaft slot

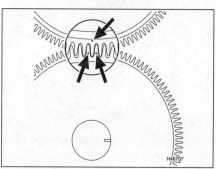

20.28 Align the scribed lines on the balancer shaft gear teeth each side of the punch marked tooth on the crankshaft gear

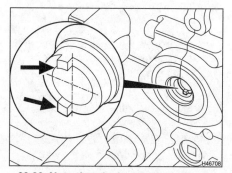

20.30 Note that the lugs in the balancer shaft end are off-set

Balancer shaft, oil seal and bearing – Oct 2007-on models

22 Remove the gearbox (see Section 4).
23 Remove the alternator drive and engine timing cover (see Section 19).
24 Hold the balancer shaft gear with a suitable tool inserted through the gear holes (or use the BMW tool No. 12 4 600) and unscrew the balancer weight screw from the rear of the engine. Lift off the balancer weight **(see illustration)**. The shaft oil seal can be prised out of the crankcase using a flat-bladed screwdriver; use a piece of wood between the screwdriver and crankcase so that the casing is not damaged **(see illustration)**.
25 Hold the balancer shaft gear again and unscrew its retaining nut **(see illustration 20.2c)**. Use a centre bolt puller on the shaft threads (BMW No. 11 2 742) to draw the gear off the shaft. Note the location of the key on the balancer shaft **(see illustration 20.2d)**.
26 Working from the rear of the crankcase, remove the bearing retaining circlip **(see illustration)**. Withdraw the balancer shaft complete with the bearing, pushing it out from the front **(see illustration)**. Make sure the Woodruff key is fully seated in the shaft to allow it to pass through the auxiliary shaft bore. Note that the bearing must be renewed.
27 Slide the balancer shaft into the crankcase from the rear. Drive the new bearing into the casing until it is seated over the end of the balancer shaft. Note that BMW have an installing

tool (No. 11 5 742 and driver 11 5 741) for driving the bearing into place. Install the circlip, ensuring it locates in its groove in the casing.
28 Install the balancer shaft gear over the front end of the balancer shaft so that its marks align with those of the crankshaft gear **(see illustration)**. The gear must locate over the Woodruff key. Hold the gear via its holes (or using BMW tool No. 11 4 600) and tighten the balancer shaft gear nut to the specified torque setting (see Specifications).
29 Fit a new oil seal to the rear of the casing, noting that a guide (BMW tool No. 11 5 742) must be used to ensure it locates over the end of the balancer shaft without damaging the seal lips – don't use any lubricant on the seal. Use a driver (No. 11 5 741) to tap the seal in until it is seated.

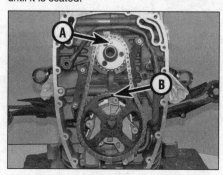

21.2 Locating pin (A) and notch (B) should be facing up

30 Lightly lubricate the balancer weight friction face with engine oil and install it on the shaft end noting that the locating lugs on the shaft are off-set **(see illustration)**. Install the balancer shaft screw, hold the balancer shaft gear as described in Step 24 and tighten the gear to the specified torque, then though a quarter turn (90°).
31 Install the engine timing cover and alternator drive (see Section 19).

21 Auxiliary shaft drive chain, tensioner and sprockets

Note 1: *The auxiliary shaft drive chain, tensioner and sprockets can be removed with the engine in the frame.*
Note 2: *New bolts must be used to secure the auxiliary shaft sprocket on installation.*
Special tool: *A degree disc is required for angle-tightening the oil pump mounting bolts.*

Removal

1 Remove the balancer shaft gears (see Section 20).
2 Ensure that the crankshaft is in the TDC compression position for the right-hand cylinder. To confirm this position, the locating pin for the crankshaft sprocket should be facing up, and the notch on the auxiliary shaft sprocket should also be facing up **(see illustration)**.
3 Undo the internal oil pipe banjo bolt and

21.3a Remove the banjo bolt and washers

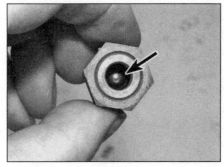

21.3b Note the location of the ball valve (arrowed)

21.3c Undo the bracket bolts (arrowed) . . .

remove the bolt and sealing washers **(see illustration)**. Discard the washers as new ones must be used. Note the location of the ball valve inside the banjo bolt and ensure that it is free to move **(see illustration)**. Undo the oil pipe bracket bolts, then ease the lower end of the pipe out from the side of the oil pump and remove it **(see illustrations)**.

4 Undo the bolts securing the chain tensioner to the crankcase, then hold the tensioner piston in position and lift the tensioner off **(see illustrations)**. Note how the lip on the inner (straight) edge of the top of the piston locates behind the edge of the tensioner blade **(see illustration)**. Note the location of the gasket on the back of the tensioner and discard it as a new one must be fitted.

5 Remove the E-clips and washers securing the chain tensioner blade and the guide blade

21.3d . . . then ease the end of the pipe (arrowed) out of the oil pump . . .

(see illustrations). Note which way round the blades are fitted, then slide them off their lugs **(see illustration)**.

21.3e . . . and lift the pipe off

6 Undo the bolts securing the auxiliary shaft sprocket to the shaft, then undo the bolts securing the crankshaft sprocket **(see**

21.4a Undo the bolts (arrowed) . . .

21.4b . . . then lift the tensioner off

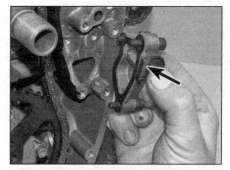

21.4c Note how the lip (arrowed) locates behind the tensioner blade

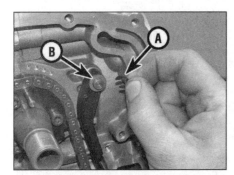

21.5a Remove the E-clip (A) and washer (B) securing the tensioner blade washer . . .

21.5b . . . and the guide blade (arrowed)

21.5c Note which way round the blades are fitted

21.6a Undo the bolts securing the auxiliary shaft sprocket . . .

21.6b . . . and the bolts securing the crankshaft sprocket

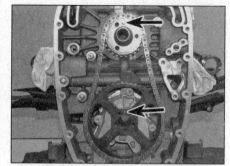

21.6c Note the alignment of the pins (arrowed)

21.6d Lift the sprockets and chain off as an assembly

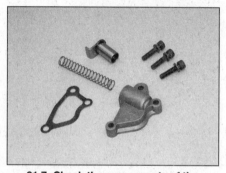

21.7 Check the components of the tensioner for wear

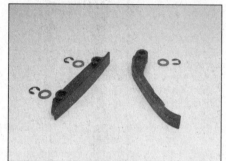

21.8 Check the blades for wear and damage

illustrations). Note that the locating pin for the auxiliary shaft sprocket is facing up in alignment with the pin on the crankshaft, then lift the sprockets and chain off as an assembly (see illustrations).

Inspection

7 Check that the tensioner piston is not scored and that it moves freely in its bore, and that the spring has not sagged (see illustration).
8 Check the tensioner blade and the guide blade for wear or damage and renew them if necessary (see illustration).
9 Check the sprockets for worn or damaged teeth and renew the sprockets and chain as a set.

Installation

10 Ensure that the crankshaft is in the TDC compression position for the right-hand cylinder. To confirm this position, the locating pins for the crankshaft sprocket and the auxiliary shaft sprocket should be facing up. Ensure that the TDC locating pin is securely in place.
11 Install the two sprockets in the chain so that the holes for the locating pins are in alignment, then install the sprockets onto the shafts and tighten the bolts finger-tight (see illustrations 21.6c, b and a). Note that new bolts must be used to secure the auxiliary shaft. Tighten the bolts to the torque settings specified at the beginning of this Chapter.
12 Check that the locating pins and the notch in the auxiliary shaft sprocket are all in alignment and facing up.
13 Install the chain tensioner blade and guide blade on their lugs, then fit the washers

and secure them with new E-clips (see illustrations 21.5c, a and b). Check that the tensioner blade pivots freely on its lug.
14 Fit the spring and piston into the tensioner, then install the tensioner with a new gasket, making sure the lip on the piston locates behind the edge of the tensioner blade (see illustration 21.4b). Tighten the tensioner mounting bolts to the specified torque setting.
15 Lubricate the lower end of the internal oil pipe with clean engine oil, then carefully ease it into the socket in the side of the oil pump so as not to displace the sealing O-ring (see Section 22, Step 9). Align the banjo union with the oilway in the crankcase, install the banjo bolt using new sealing washers on both sides of the union, then tighten the bolt finger-tight (see illustration 21.3a).
16 Install the oil pipe bracket bolts, then tighten the banjo bolt and the bracket bolts to the specified torque settings.

17 Install the balancer shaft gears (see Section 20).

22 Oil pump, pressure relief valve and thermostat

Note 1: *The oil pump can be removed with the engine in the frame.*
Note 2: *New mounting bolts must be used when the oil pump is reassembled.*

Oil pump
Removal

1 Remove the auxiliary shaft drive chain, tensioner and the lower sprocket (see Section 21).
2 Undo the bolts securing the oil pump, noting which length fits where, then lift off the pump cover (see illustrations).

22.2a Location of 40 mm oil pump bolts (arrowed)

22.2b Location of 45 mm oil pump bolts (arrowed)

22.2c Lift off the cover . . .

22.3 Note the register marks (A) and the key (B)

22.4a Draw the inner . . .

22.4b . . . and outer cooling oil rotors off

22.5a Remove the oil pump housing . . .

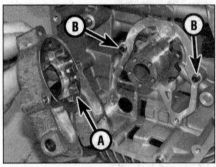

22.5b . . . noting the location of the outer lubricating oil rotor (A) and the dowels (B)

3 Note the register marks on the outside face of the cooling oil rotors, and the key that locates the inner rotor on the auxiliary shaft **(see illustration)**.

4 Draw the inner and outer cooling oil rotors off **(see illustrations)**.

5 Lift off the oil pump housing **(see illustrations)**. Note the location of the outer lubricating oil rotor which may remain inside the housing – note the register mark on the outside face of the rotor **(see illustration)**. **Note:** *Take care not to mix-up the outer cooling oil and lubricating oil rotors.*

6 The inner lubricating oil rotor is an integral part of the auxiliary shaft **(see illustration)**. Note the location of the dowels in the crankcase.

7 Note the location of the Woodruff key and remove it if it is loose **(see illustration 22.6)**.

Inspection

8 Clean all the components in a suitable solvent.

9 Carefully ease out the internal oil pipe O-ring from the socket in the side of the oil pump housing, noting how it fits **(see illustration)**. Discard the O-ring as a new one must be fitted.

10 Inspect the pump cover, housing and rotors for scoring and wear. If any damage or wear is evident, renew the components as required.

11 Measure the depth of the pump cover (cooling circuit) and housing (lubricating circuit) and the thickness of the corresponding rotors with a Vernier gauge. Calculate the difference to determine the amount of clearance (end-float) between the rotors and the housing and compare the results to

the specifications at the beginning of this Chapter. If the clearance is greater than specified, use your measurements to determine whether the rotors or the housing, or both, are worn, and renew the components as required. **Note:** *If a Vernier gauge is not available, install the rotors and lay a straight-edge across the joint surface of the pump. Measure the gap between the rotors and the straight-edge with a feeler gauge to assess the end-float.*

12 If the inner lubricating oil rotor is worn or damaged, refer to Section 28 to access the auxiliary shaft.

Installation

13 During installation, ensure that the pump rotors are generously lubricated with clean engine oil. The register marks on the pump

22.5c Note the register mark (arrowed) on the outer lubricating oil rotor

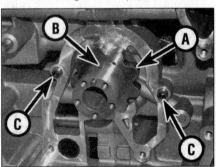

22.6 Inner rotor (A) is integral with the shaft. Note the Woodruff key (B) and the dowels (C)

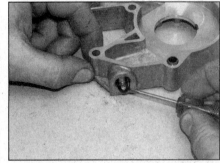

22.9 Ease the O-ring out carefully

22.14 Ensure that the O-ring is correctly installed

22.21 Location of the oil pressure relief valve (arrowed)

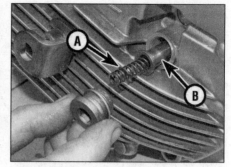

22.22 Remove the cap and withdraw the spring (A) and relief valve (B)

rotors must face forward, i.e. towards the front of the machine

14 Lubricate a new O-ring with clean engine oil and fit it into the groove in the socket in the side of the pump housing **(see illustration)**.

15 If removed, fit the Woodruff key into its slot in the auxiliary shaft **(see illustration 22.6)**.

16 Install the outer lubricating oil rotor into the housing, then fit the housing over the end of the auxiliary shaft and onto the crankcase dowels **(see illustration 22.5b)**.

17 Install the outer cooling oil rotor, then align the slot in the inner rotor with the key on the auxiliary shaft and install the inner rotor **(see illustrations 22.4b and a)**. Check that the lobes on the inner and outer rotors are correctly aligned **(see illustration 22.3)**.

18 Install the pump cover, making sure it fits over the dowels in the housing **(see illustration 22.2c)**.

19 Install the new oil pump mounting bolts – ensure the bolts are fitted in their correct positions **(see illustration 22.2a and b)**. Tighten the bolts to the initial torque setting specified at the beginning of this Chapter. Next, using a degree disc (see *Tools and Workshop Tips*) , angle-tighten each bolt in a criss-cross sequence to the final stage torque setting.

20 Install the auxiliary shaft drive chain, tensioner and the lower sprocket (see Section 21).

Oil pressure relief valve

21 The pressure relief valve cap is located on the right-hand side of the crankcase **(see**

illustration). If the engine oil has not been drained, position a drain tray below the engine to catch any residual oil when the valve is removed.

22 Unscrew the cap and sealing washer, then withdraw the spring and relief valve **(see illustration)**.

23 Wash the components in a suitable solvent and examine them for signs of wear, scoring or damage **(see illustration)**.

24 No specifications are available for checking the valve. If the any of the valve components are worn or damaged, or if an oil pressure test (see Section 3) suggests the valve is not operating correctly, fit a new valve assembly.

25 Installation is the reverse of removal. Fit a new sealing washer to the cap and tighten it to the torque setting specified at the beginning of this Chapter.

26 Check the engine oil level and top-up as necessary (see *Pre-ride checks*)

Oil thermostat

27 The oil thermostat is located in the top of the crankcase on the right-hand side, below the flange for the oil cooler feed pipe (see Section 6).

28 To gain access to the thermostat, follow the procedure in Section 6 and displace the feed pipe, noting the O-ring on the end of the pipe.

29 Lift out the baffle, then withdraw the thermostat and spring **(see illustrations)**.

30 No specifications are available for checking the thermostat. If the engine oil

is not circulating through the oil cooler, resulting in high oil temperatures, oil thinning and a possible loss in oil pressure, fit a new thermostat assembly. **Note:** *Check that the oil cooler itself is not damaged or blocked internally.*

31 Installation is the reverse of removal. Follow the procedure in Section 6 to install the oil cooler feed pipe.

23 Clutch

Note 1: *To gain access to the clutch, it is first necessary to remove the rear shock absorber and swingarm/final drive unit assembly (see Chapter 4), the rear sub-frame and the gearbox (see Section 4).*
Note 2: *New bolts must be used to secure the flywheel and clutch cover plate on installation.*
Special tools: *A top dead centre (TDC) locating pin is required for this procedure (see Tool Tip, Section 9). A clutch centering tool is required for this procedure (see Tool Tip on page 2•51). A degree disc is required for angle-tightening the flywheel mounting bolts. Seal installation guides are required to fit the crankshaft oil seal (see Steps 15 and 16).*

Removal

1 Remove both primary spark plugs (see Chapter 1, Section 11).

2 Remove the alternator drive belt cover (see Chapter 1, Section 13).

22.23 Examine the pressure relief valve components for wear

22.29a Lift out the baffle . . .

22.29b . . . then withdraw the thermostat and spring

23.4 Loosen the bolts (arrowed) in a criss-cross sequence

23.5 Lift off the clutch assembly

3 Turn the engine with a spanner on the crankshaft pulley nut until both pistons are at TDC. Insert the TDC locating pin into the hole in the clutch assembly and locate it in the hole in the crankcase.

4 Undo the cover plate bolts evenly and a little at a time in a criss-cross sequence until spring pressure has been released **(see illustration)**. Remove the bolts and discard them as new ones must be used.

5 Lift off the clutch assembly **(see illustration)**.

6 The cover plate, friction plate and pressure plate will come away together, joined by the locating pins between the cover and pressure plate **(see illustration)**. Carefully lever the cover and pressure plates apart, noting which way round they fit. Lift off the friction plate **(see illustration)**.

7 If required, undo the bolts securing the flywheel to the end of the crankshaft, noting the location of the reinforcing disc **(see illustration)**. Remove the flywheel, noting how the peg on the back of the flywheel locates

in the hole in the end of the crankshaft **(see illustration)**. Discard the bolts as new ones must be used.

Inspection

8 After an extended period of service the friction plate will wear resulting in clutch slip. Measure the thickness of the plate in several places and compare the result with the specification at the beginning of this Chapter **(see illustration)**. If the plate has worn down to the service limit it must be renewed. If the plate smells burnt, is contaminated with oil or grease or is glazed, it must be replaced with a new one. **Note:** *If there is oil contamination on the clutch plate or in the clutch housing, check the crankshaft rear oil seal (see Steps 14 to 16) and the gearbox front oil seal (see Section 30) for leakage.*

9 Check the friction plate splines and the corresponding splines on the gearbox input shaft for signs of wear and damage. Fit the friction plate on the input shaft splines and check that it is able to move freely on the splines, but without undue freeplay – note that wear between the two components may result in a rattle when the machine is in neutral.

10 Check the surface of the pressure plate and the cover plate for distortion using a

23.6a Locating pins (arrowed) hold clutch assembly together

23.6b Lift off the friction plate

23.7a Reinforcing disc (arrowed) is secured by flywheel bolts

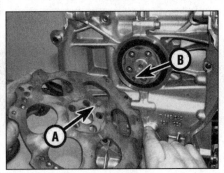

23.7b Note how peg (A) locates on hole (B)

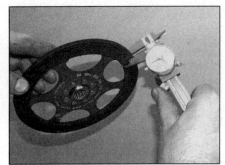

23.8 Measuring the thickness of the clutch friction plate

23.10a Check the surface of the pressure plate (arrowed) . . .

23.10b . . . and the cover plate (arrowed) for wear and damage

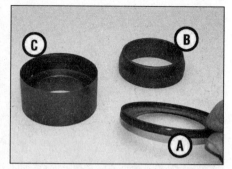

23.15a Crankshaft oil seal (A), seal guide (B) and sleeve (C)

23.15b Position the seal on the guide . . .

23.15c . . . then position the guide on the sleeve

23.15d Slide the seal onto the sleeve . . .

23.15e . . . then remove the guide

straight-edge (see illustrations). If the surface of either plate is distorted, badly scored or blued through overheating, renew the pressure plate, cover plate and friction plate as a set. Inspect the teeth of the starter motor ring gear for wear and damage. The gear is an integral part of the pressure plate assembly – renew the pressure plate if necessary.

11 If the clutch has been slipping and the friction plate thickness is satisfactory, it is likely the diaphragm spring in the pressure plate has lost its tension. Renew the pressure plate.

12 Slide the seal off the clutch pushrod (see illustration 4.35). Check that the pushrod is straight by rolling it on a flat surface such as a piece of glass, or setting it up in V-blocks and measuring runout with a dial gauge. If the pushrod is bent, it must be renewed.

13 Check around the clutch housing for signs of any oil leakage from either the crankcase or the gearbox. If the gearbox front oil seal on the transmission input shaft has failed, follow the procedure in Section 30 to renew it. If the crankshaft rear oil seal has failed, renew it as follows.

14 Using a 3 mm drill bit, drill two holes on opposite sides of the seal. Take care to only drill through the outer surface of the seal. Next, thread two self-tapping screws part-way into the holes. Position a piece of thick card over the outer surface of the seal housing to protect it, then carefully lever out the seal using a pair of curved, thin-nosed pliers. Work evenly on both sides of the seal (see illustration 30.17).

15 Take care to avoid damaging the inner lip of the new crankshaft oil seal when it is installed – a suitable seal guide and sleeve must be used. BMW provide a set of tools for this purpose (see illustration). Slip the seal over the end of the guide (BMW Part No. 11 5 702), position the guide on the sleeve (BMW Part No. 11 5 703), then slide the seal onto the sleeve and remove the guide (see illustrations).

16 Locate the sleeve over the end of the crankshaft and press the seal into position with a suitable driver (BMW Part No. 11 5 704 and Part No. 11 5 701) (see illustrations). When

23.16a Locate the sleeve over the end of the crankshaft . . .

23.16b . . . then use the driver . . .

23.16c . . . to install the seal

23.16d Remove the sleeve. Note the alignment of the outer edge of the seal (arrowed)

23.18 Lightly oil the new flywheel bolts before installation

23.19 Lock the flywheel with the TDC locating pin

23.20 Tighten the bolts to the final setting with a degree disc

23.22a Align the clutch assembly with the flywheel . . .

23.22b . . . and install the new cover plate bolts

installed, the outer edge of the seal should be level with the outer face of the housing. Withdraw the sleeve **(see illustration)**.

Installation

17 Make sure all the components are clean and dry.

18 Align the peg on the back of the flywheel with the hole in the end of the crankshaft and install the flywheel **(see illustration 23.7b)**. Lightly oil the threads and the underside of the heads of the new flywheel bolts, then fit the reinforcing disc and install the bolts finger-tight **(see illustration)**.

19 Align the cut-out on the edge of the flywheel with the hole in the crankcase for the TDC locating pin and install the pin **(see illustration)**.

20 Tighten the bolts evenly and in a criss-cross pattern to the initial torque setting specified at the beginning of this Chapter, then use a degree disc (see *Tools and Workshop Tips* in the *Reference* section) to tighten them to the final setting in one continuous movement **(see illustration)**. Remove the TDC locating pin.

21 Position the friction plate on the pressure plate, then align the locating pins on the cover plate with the holes in the pressure plate and press the cover plate into position **(see illustrations 23.6b and a)**.

22 Align the clutch assembly with the flywheel and install the new cover plate bolts finger-tight **(see illustrations)**.

23 Before the cover plate bolts are tightened, the clutch friction plate, pressure plate and crankshaft centres must be aligned. BMW provide a service tool for this purpose (Part No. 21 2 673). Alternatively, a similar tool can be made (see *Tool Tip*). Insert the aligning tool into the centre of the clutch, ensuring it goes all the way in – if necessary, slacken

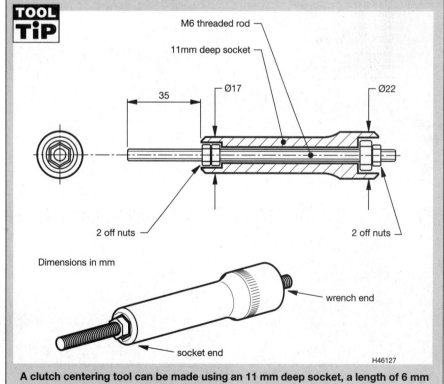

TOOL TiP

M6 threaded rod
11mm deep socket
35
Ø17
Ø22
2 off nuts
2 off nuts
Dimensions in mm
wrench end
socket end
H46127

A clutch centering tool can be made using an 11 mm deep socket, a length of 6 mm diameter threaded rod and a handful of nuts.

23.23 Using the home-made clutch centering tool

23.24 Tighten the cover plate bolts in a criss-cross sequence

the cover plate bolts to aid installation **(see illustration)**.

24 Install the TDC locating pin, then tighten the cover plate bolts evenly and a little at a time in a criss-cross sequence to the specified torque setting **(see illustration)**.

25 Install the remaining components in the reverse order of removal.

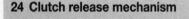

24 Clutch release mechanism

1 All the models covered in this manual are fitted with an hydraulic clutch. The clutch system comprises the master cylinder on the handlebars, the hose and the release cylinder at the rear of the gearbox. The system requires

no maintenance other than inspection at the specified service interval (see Chapter 1) and pre-ride checks of the hydraulic fluid level (see *Pre-ride checks*).

2 If there is evidence of air in the system (spongy feel to the lever, difficulty in engaging gear), bleed the system (see Steps 28 to 38).

3 If clutch fluid is leaking from any part of the system, first check that the hose banjo union bolts are tight. If necessary, renew the sealing washers on both sides of the banjo unions. If either the master cylinder or the release cylinder is leaking, a new component will have to be installed – no rebuild kits are available for the cylinders.

4 If the clutch handlebar lever feels stiff, check the lever and the lever bracket for damage.

5 Turn the lever span adjuster to its lowest setting (see Chapter 1). On R1200 ST and S models, undo the lever pivot bolt locknut

on the underside of the lever, then withdraw the pivot bolt and lift the lever off **(see illustration)**. Note that on R1200 GS models, it is first necessary to remove the hand protector (see Chapter 6) and the upper half of the lever mounting bracket to access the pivot bolt **(see illustration)**. On R1200 RT models, first remove the lower cover from the handlebar assembly, then undo the lever pivot bolt and lift the lever off **(see illustrations)**.

6 Clean the contact surfaces of the lever, bracket and pivot bolt. If they are in good condition, lubricate the components with dry film lubricant prior to assembly.

7 If, after cleaning and lubricating the lever, the clutch action is still stiff, the master cylinder will have to be removed from the machine and checked.

Master cylinder

Removal

8 Before starting, make sure you have some new Vitamol V10 clutch fluid, some clean rags and a suitable container for the old clutch fluid.

9 Refer to the procedure in Chapter 7 and displace the clutch switch from the underside of the master cylinder.

10 On R1200 RT models, undo the screws securing the switch unit to the back of the master cylinder and displace the unit (see Chapter 7).

11 On R1200 GS models, remove the hand protector (see Chapter 6). On R1200 GS and ST models, remove the left-hand rear view mirror (see Chapter 6).

12 Undo the clutch hose banjo bolt and separate the hose from the master cylinder, noting its alignment **(see illustration)**. Be prepared to catch any residual fluid in the union. Discard the sealing washers as new ones must be used. Wrap a clean plastic bag over the end of the hose to prevent dirt entering the system and secure the hose in an upright position to minimise fluid loss.

Caution: Do not operate the clutch lever while the hose is disconnected.

13 Support the master cylinder, then undo the handlebar clamp screws and remove the

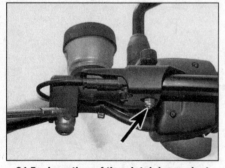

24.5a Location of the clutch lever pivot bolt locknut (arrowed)

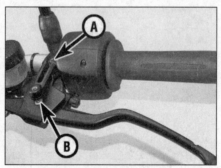

24.5b Remove the bracket (A) to access the pivot bolt (B) – R1200 GS

24.5c On R1200 RT models, undo the screw . . .

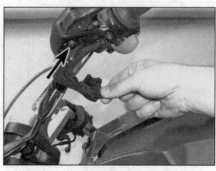

24.5d . . . remove the lower cover to access the pivot bolt (arrowed)

24.12 Undo the clutch hose banjo bolt (arrowed)

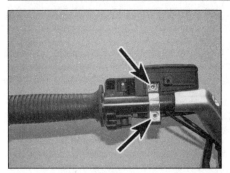

24.13 Handlebar clamp screws – R1200 RT shown

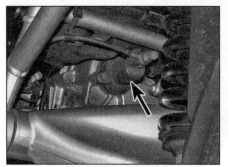

24.19 Location of the clutch release cylinder (arrowed)

24.23 Cut the ties securing the clutch hose . . .

clamp **(see illustration)**. Note the alignment of the master cylinder with the handlebar, then lift the master cylinder off.

14 On R1200 RT models, undo the screws securing the reservoir cover and lift off the cover and diaphragm (see *Pre-ride checks*).

15 On all other models, press the locking tabs in and unscrew the cap, then remove the diaphragm plate and diaphragm (see *Pre-ride checks*).

16 Empty the clutch fluid into a suitable container.

17 To check the action of the master cylinder piston, temporarily install the reservoir cover or cap. Wrap some clean rag over the open end of the master cylinder hose union and operate the lever. If the lever sticks, or the action is stiff, there is a fault with the master cylinder piston. No rebuild kit is available for the master cylinder – if it is not working correctly, a new one will have to be fitted. If the lever moves smoothly, it is likely that the release cylinder is faulty (see below).

Caution: Do not, under any circumstances, use a petroleum-based solvent to clean the master cylinder.

Installation

18 Installation is the reverse of removal, noting the following:
● Align the master cylinder as noted on removal and tighten the handlebar clamp screws securely.
● Align the clutch hose with the master cylinder and fit new sealing washers on each side of the banjo union.

● Tighten the banjo bolt to the torque setting specified at the beginning of this Chapter.
● Fill the fluid reservoir with new Vitamol V10 clutch fluid (see Pre-ride checks). Bleed the air from the system (see Steps 28 to 38).
● Check the operation of the clutch before riding the motorcycle.

Release cylinder

19 The release cylinder is located at the back of the gearbox **(see illustration)**.

20 If the clutch action is stiff, and the master cylinder is good, it is likely that the release cylinder is faulty. No rebuild kit is available for the release cylinder – if it is not working correctly, a new one will have to be fitted.

Removal

21 Before starting, make sure you have some new Vitamol V10 clutch fluid, some clean rags and a suitable container for the old clutch fluid.

22 Remove the body panels as applicable to gain access to the release cylinder and to the clutch hose where it is secured to the rear sub-frame (see Chapter 6).

23 Release the ties securing the clutch hose to the rear sub-frame **(see illustration)**.

24 Slacken the clutch hose banjo bolt, then tighten it lightly as an aid to removal. Undo the release cylinder mounting bolts and lift the cylinder off **(see illustration)**.

25 Undo the clutch hose banjo bolt and separate the hose from the master cylinder, noting its alignment. Be prepared to catch any

residual fluid in the union. Discard the sealing washers as new ones must be used. Wrap a clean plastic bag over the end of the hose to prevent dirt entering the system and secure the hose in an upright position to minimise fluid loss.

Caution: Do not operate the clutch lever while the hose is disconnected.

26 Check that the clutch push rod is free to move inside the transmission input shaft – if necessary, remove the rear shock absorber (see Chapter 4), then withdraw the pushrod and check that it is clean and free from corrosion **(see illustration)**. Note the location of the seal on the pushrod and renew it if necessary. Lubricate the pushrod with a smear of clutch assembly grease (BMW recommend Optimoly MP 3) before installation.

Installation

27 Installation is the reverse of removal, noting the following:
● Align the release cylinder with the clutch pushrod and tighten the mounting bolts to the torque setting specified at the beginning of this Chapter.
● Align the clutch hose with the release cylinder and fit new sealing washers on each side of the banjo union.
● Tighten the banjo bolt to the specified torque setting.
● Secure the clutch hose to the sub-frame as noted on removal.
● Top-up the fluid reservoir with new Vitamol V10 clutch fluid (see Pre-ride checks). Bleed the air from the system (see Steps 28 to 38).
● Check the operation of the clutch before riding the motorcycle.

Bleeding the clutch release mechanism

Note: *You will need an assistant to help carry out this procedure.*

28 Bleeding the clutch is simply the process of removing air from the master cylinder, hose and the release cylinder. Bleeding is necessary whenever a hydraulic connection is loosened, or when a component or hose is renewed. Leaks in the system may also allow air to enter, but leaking clutch fluid will reveal their presence and warn you of the need for repair.

29 To bleed the clutch, you will need some

24.24 . . . then undo the mounting bolts and lift the release cylinder off

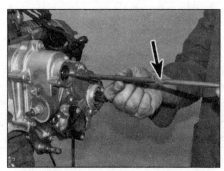

24.26 Withdraw the clutch pushrod. Note the location of the seal (arrowed)

new Vitamol clutch fluid, a length of clear vinyl or plastic tubing, a small container partially filled with clean clutch fluid, some rags and a spanner to fit the release cylinder bleed valve.

30 On R1200 RT models, undo the screws securing the reservoir cover and lift off the cover and diaphragm (see *Pre-ride checks*).

31 On all other models, press the locking tabs in and unscrew the cap, then remove the diaphragm plate and diaphragm (see *Pre-ride checks*).

32 Slowly pump the clutch lever a few times until no air bubbles can be seen floating up from the holes in the bottom of the reservoir. Doing this bleeds the air from the master cylinder end of the hose. Make sure there is plenty of fluid in the reservoir – do not allow the level to drop below the MIN level during the bleeding process. Loosely refit the cover.

33 If using a ring spanner, fit it over the bleed valve now. Attach one end of the clear tubing to the bleed valve and submerge the other end in the clutch fluid in the container.

34 Carefully pump the clutch lever three or four times, then hold it in while opening the bleed valve. When the valve is opened, clutch fluid will flow into the clear tubing and the lever will move toward the handlebar.

35 Retighten the bleed valve, then release the clutch lever gradually. Repeat the process until no air bubbles are visible in the fluid leaving the valve.

36 On completion, disconnect the hose from the bleed valve and ensure that the valve is tightened securely. Wipe up any spilled brake fluid.

37 Check the fluid level in the reservoir (see *Pre-ride checks*), then install the reservoir cover or cap.

38 Check the operation of the clutch before riding the motorcycle.

---

25 Crankcase

Note: *To separate the crankcase halves, the engine must be removed from the frame (see Section 4).*

Special tools: *A degree disc is required for angle-tightening the 10 mm crankcase bolts. Seal installation guides are required to fit the crankshaft oil seal (see Section 23).*

Separation

1 To access the crankshaft and its bearings, the auxiliary shaft, camchains, tensioner and guide blades, and the oil strainers, the crankcase must be split into two parts.

2 Before the crankcase halves can be separated, the following components must be removed:

● Gearbox (if not done when removing the engine – see Section 4)
● Alternator (see Chapter 7)
● Cylinder heads (see Section 12)
● Cylinders (see Section 15)
● Pistons (see Section 16)
● Balancer shaft gears and balancer shaft (see Section 20)
● Auxiliary shaft drive chain, tensioner and sprockets (see Section 21)
● Oil pump (see Section 22)
● Clutch and flywheel (see Section 23)

3 If not already done, wrap clean rag around the connecting rods to prevent them striking the crankcase.

4 Unscrew the cylinder/cylinder head studs from both sides of the crankcase. To do this, lock two nuts together on the threaded end of each stud, then unscrew the stud using a

spanner on the lower nut **(see illustration)**. Mark each stud with its location as an aid for installation.

5 Before separating the crankcase halves, measure the amount of crankshaft end-float using a dial gauge (see *Tools and Workshop Tips* in the *Reference* section). Press the crankshaft into the crankcase, then mount the dial gauge with its pointer sitting against the front end of the crankshaft. Zero the gauge, then pull the crankshaft out of the casing and record the end-float. Compare the result to the specifications at the beginning of this Chapter. If the end-float exceeds the service limit, measure the width of the crankshaft guide bearing journal and the width of the guide bearing, then compare the results with the specifications at the beginning of this Chapter to determine which component has worn (see Section 27).

> **HAYNES HINT** *Make a cardboard template for both sides of the crankcase and punch a hole for each bolt location.* **As each bolt is removed, store it in its relative position in the template. This will ensure all bolts are installed correctly on reassembly – this is important, as many bolts differ slightly in length.**

6 Lay the engine onto its left-hand side, making sure it is properly supported using blocks of wood. Unscrew the two 6 mm bolts followed by the four 8 mm bolts, then the two 10 mm bolts **(see illustrations)**. Unscrew the bolts evenly, a little at a time, until they are loose, then remove them and their washers and store them on the cardboard crankcase template for the right-hand side. Note that the 8 mm x 60 mm bolt is fitted with a sealing washer – a new sealing washer must be used on reassembly.

7 Turn the engine over so that it rests on its right-hand side, making sure it is properly supported using blocks of wood.

8 Unscrew the fifteen 6 mm bolts followed by the single 8 mm bolt, then the two 10 mm

---

> **HAYNES HINT** *If it's not possible to produce the correct feel to the lever the clutch fluid may be aerated. Let the fluid in the system stabilise for a few hours and then repeat the procedure. Also check to make sure that there are no 'high-spots' in the hose in which an air bubble can become trapped – moving the hose around will normally dislodge any trapped air. A vacuum type brake bleeder may also prove useful for bleeding the clutch if problems are experienced with the above method – see Chapter 5, Section 10 for details.*

25.4 Use locked nuts (arrowed) to unscrew the cylinder studs from both sides of the crankcase

25.6a Location of the crankcase 6 mm bolts (arrowed) – right-hand side

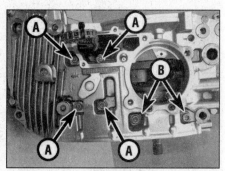

25.6b Location of the crankcase 8 mm (A) and 10 mm (B) bolts – right-hand side

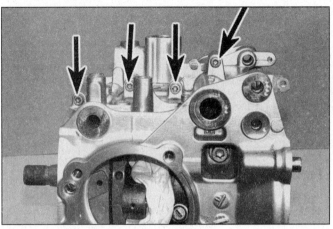

25.8a Location of the crankcase upper 6 mm bolts (arrowed) – left-hand side

25.8b Location of the crankcase centre rear 6 mm bolts (arrowed) – left-hand side

bolts **(see illustrations)**. Unscrew the bolts evenly, a little at a time, until they are loose, then remove them and their washers store them on the cardboard crankcase template for the left-hand side. Note that the 8 mm bolt is fitted with a sealing washer – a new sealing washer must be used on reassembly.

9 Carefully lift the left-hand crankcase half off the right-hand half **(see illustration)**. If the halves do not separate easily, first make sure all the bolts have been removed. The sealant used between the crankcase halves can form a strong bond – if the two halves are stuck, tap around the joint with a soft-faced mallet to

free them. Do not attempt to lever the cases apart with a screwdriver – you'll damage the sealing surfaces.

10 Note the location of the crankshaft main bearing and guide bearing shells in the left-hand crankcase half and take care not to dislodge them **(see illustration)**.

25.8c Location of the crankcase lower 6 mm bolts (arrowed) – left-hand side

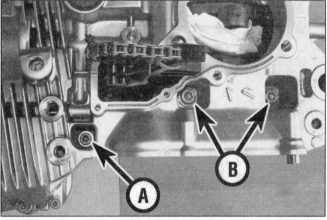

25.8d Location of the crankcase 8 mm (A) and 10 mm (B) bolts – left-hand side

25.9 Lift the left-hand crankcase half off the right-hand half

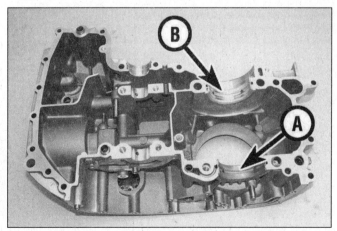

25.10 Location of the crankshaft main bearing (A) and guide bearing (B) shells

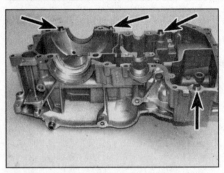

25.12 Location of the dowels (arrowed) in the left-hand crankcase half

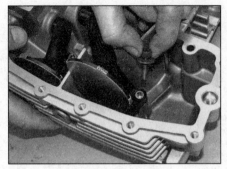

25.14a Undo the bolts . . .

25.14b . . . and ease out the oil strainers

11 Note the location of the balancer shaft oil seal, bearing and bearing retaining circlip and remove them from the crankcase. All three components can be installed after the crankcases have been reassembled – discard the old oil seal as a new one must be fitted (see Section 20).

12 Note the location of the four dowels in the left-hand crankcase half and remove them if they are loose **(see illustration)**.

Inspection

13 Before the crankcase halves can be inspected, the following components must be removed:

● Crankshaft and crankshaft bearings (see Section 27)
● Auxiliary shaft and camchains, camchain tensioner blades and guide blades (see Section 28)
● Oil pressure relief valve and oil thermostat (see Section 22)
● Oil temperature sensor (see Chapter 3)
● Oil pressure switch and oil level warning sender (see Chapter 7)

14 Undo the bolts securing the oil strainers and ease the strainers out from their sockets **(see illustrations)**. The larger strainer is for the lubricating oil and the smaller strainer is for the cooling oil. Carefully ease out the O-rings from the grooves in the sockets, taking care not to damage the soft aluminium – discard the O-rings as new ones must be used **(see illustration)**.

15 Ease the crankcase vent valve out, noting which way round it is fitted **(see illustration)**.

16 Clean the crankcases thoroughly with

suitable solvent and dry them with compressed air. Blow out all oil passages with compressed air.

17 Remove all traces of old sealant from the mating surfaces. If a scraper must be used, be very careful not to nick or gouge the soft aluminium or oil leaks will result.

18 Check the cases for any damage. Small cracks or holes in aluminium castings can be repaired with an epoxy resin adhesive as a temporary measure or a more secure repair can be made with one of the low temperature home welding kits, such as Lumiweld. Argon-arc welding is another solution, but only a specialist in this process is in a position to advise on the economy or practical aspect of such a repair. If any damage is found that can't be repaired, renew the crankcase halves as a set.

19 Damaged threads can be economically reclaimed by using a diamond section wire insert. These are easily fitted after drilling and re-tapping the affected thread.

20 Sheared studs or screws can usually be removed with stud extractors – if you are in any doubt, consult a BMW dealer or a specialist motorcycle engineer.

HAYNES HiNT *Refer to Tools and Workshop Tip in the Reference sections for details of installing a thread insert and using stud extractors.*

Reassembly

21 Clean the threads of all the crankcase bolts.

22 Check the crankcase vent valve for

particles of trapped dirt. If necessary, wash the valve with suitable solvent and dry it with compressed air. Do not attempt to scrape dirt off the surface of the valve reeds – they are fragile and easily damaged. The reeds should lay flat against the body of the valve – hold the valve up to the light to check. If the reeds have been sprained, fit a new valve, otherwise oil mist from the lower crankcase will be forced into the top of the engine and cause a smoky exhaust. Ensure that the screws securing the reed stopper plates are secure, then install the vent valve in the right-hand crankcase.

23 Lubricate the new oil strainer O-rings with clean engine oil and install them in the grooves in the strainer sockets **(see illustration 25.14c)**. Note that the lower O-ring is smaller than the upper O-ring.

24 Ensure that the oil strainers are thoroughly clean. Do not attempt to prise the gauze filters off the strainers – they must remain a tight fit. If necessary, wash the strainers with suitable solvent and dry them with compressed air. Install the strainers carefully, taking care not to displace the O-rings, then install the bolts and washers and tighten them to the torque setting specified at the beginning of this Chapter **(see illustration)**.

25 Install the oil temperature sensor (see Chapter 3). Install the oil pressure switch and oil level warning sender (see Chapter 7).

26 Install the oil pressure relief valve and oil thermostat (see Section 22).

27 Make sure that the auxiliary shaft and camchains, camchain tensioner blades and right-hand guide blade (see Section 28)

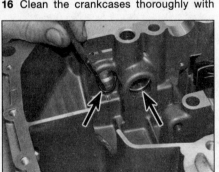

25.14c Remove the O-rings carefully (arrowed)

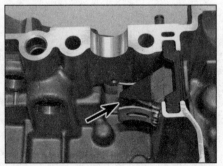

25.15 Location of the crankcase vent valve (arrowed)

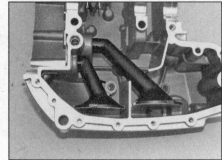

25.24 Arrangement of the oil strainers

25.29a Apply an even bead of sealant to the right-hand crankcase half

25.29b Apply sealant to the end of the camchain guide blade pivot pin (arrowed)

26 Crankshaft bearings and connecting big-end rod bearings – general information

1 Even though the crankshaft and connecting rod bearings are generally replaced with new ones during the engine overhaul, the old bearings should be retained for close examination as they may reveal valuable information about the condition of the engine.
2 Bearing failure occurs mainly because of lack of lubrication, the presence of dirt or other foreign particles, overloading the engine and/or corrosion. Regardless of the cause of bearing failure, it must be corrected before the engine is reassembled to prevent it from happening again.
3 When examining the bearings, match them with their corresponding journal on the crankshaft to help identify the cause of any problem. Note that the bearing shells are pressed into their locations in the crankcase halves and connecting rods and caps, and should only be disturbed when required for examination. It is essential to keep the bearing shells in the right order – lay them on a clean sheet of card and mark the locations on the card.
4 Dirt and other foreign particles get into the engine in a variety of ways. They may be left in the engine during assembly or they may pass through filters or breathers, then get into the oil and from there into the bearings. Metal chips from machining operations and normal engine wear are often present. Abrasives are sometimes left in engine components after reconditioning operations, especially when parts are not thoroughly cleaned using the proper cleaning methods. Whatever the source, foreign objects often end up imbedded in the soft bearing material and are easily recognised. Large particles will not imbed in the bearing and will score or gouge the bearing and journal. The best prevention for this type of bearing failure is to clean all parts thoroughly and keep everything spotlessly clean during engine reassembly. Regular oil and filter changes are also essential.
5 Lack of lubrication or lubrication breakdown has a number of interrelated causes. Excessive heat (which thins the oil), overloading (which squeezes the oil from the bearing face) and oil leakage or throw off (from excessive bearing clearances, worn oil pump or high engine speeds) all contribute to a breakdown of the protective lubricating film. Blocked oil passages will starve a bearing of lubrication and destroy it. When lack of lubrication is the cause of bearing failure, the bearing material is wiped or extruded from the steel backing of the bearing. Temperatures may increase to the point where the steel backing and the journal turn blue from overheating.

 HAYNES HiNT *Refer to Tools and Workshop Tips in the Reference section for bearing fault finding.*

and the crankshaft and crankshaft bearings (see Section 27) are correctly positioned in the right-hand crankcase half. Ensure the crankcase half is properly supported using blocks of wood. Generously lubricate all the components with clean engine oil, then use a rag soaked in high flash-point solvent to wipe over the mating surfaces of both crankcase halves to remove all traces of oil.
28 Make sure the left-hand guide blade (see Section 28) and the crankshaft bearings are correctly positioned in the left-hand crankcase half (see Section 27). If removed, install the four locating dowels in the left-hand crankcase half **(see illustration 25.12)**.
29 Apply a thin, even bead of suitable sealant to the mating surface of the right-hand crankcase half **(see illustration)**. Apply sealant to the rear end of the right-hand camchain guide blade pivot pin to prevent oil leaking into the clutch housing **(see illustration)**.
Caution: Don't apply an excessive amount of sealant as it will ooze out when the case halves are assembled and may obstruct oil passages. Do not apply the sealant on or too close to any of the bearing shells or surfaces.
30 Carefully lower the left-hand crankcase half down onto the right-hand half – it is worthwhile having an assistant to support the connecting rod and the camchain assembly as the left-hand crankcase half as it is fitted. Ensure the crankshaft bearings remain in position in the left-hand crankcase half and make sure the dowels all locate correctly **(see illustration 25.9)**. Check that the crankcase halves are correctly seated all the way round.
Caution: The crankcase halves should fit together without being forced. If they're not correctly seated, separate them and investigate the problem. DO NOT attempt to pull them together by tightening the crankcase bolts.
31 Install the two 10 mm bolts and their washers, followed by the single 8 mm bolt with a new sealing washer, then the fifteen 6 mm bolts and their washers **(see illustrations 25.8d, 8c, 8b and 8a)**. Secure all the bolts finger-tight.
32 Tighten the 10 mm bolts to the initial torque setting specified at the beginning of this Chapter, then use a degree disc (see

Tools and Workshop Tips in the *Reference* section) to tighten them to the final setting in one continuous movement.
33 Tighten the 8 mm bolt to the specified torque setting, then tighten the 6 mm bolts evenly and a little at a time in a criss-cross sequence to the specified torque setting.
34 Turn the engine over so that it rests on its left-hand side, making sure it is properly supported using blocks of wood.
35 Install the two 10 mm bolts and their washers, followed by the four 8 mm bolts and their washers, then the two 6 mm bolts and their washers **(see illustrations 25.6b and 6a)**. Don't forget to fit a new sealing washer on the 8 mm x 60 mm bolt.
36 Tighten the 10 mm bolts to the initial torque setting specified at the beginning of this Chapter, then use a degree disc (see *Tools and Workshop Tips* in the *Reference* section) to tighten them to the final setting in one continuous movement.
37 Tighten the 8 mm bolts evenly and a little at a time in a criss-cross sequence to the specified torque setting, then tighten the 6 mm bolts to the specified torque setting.
38 With all crankcase fasteners tightened, check that the crankshaft and auxiliary shaft are free to rotate. Support the connecting rods to prevent them striking the crankcase and take care not to dislodge the camchains from the auxiliary shaft. If there are any signs of undue stiffness or rough spots, or of any other problem, the fault must be rectified before proceeding further.
39 Follow the procedure in Section 23, Steps 15 and 16, and install a new crankshaft oil seal.
40 Follow the procedure in Section 20, Steps 17 and 18, and install the balancer shaft bearing, circlip and new balancer shaft oil seal.
41 Install the cylinder/cylinder head studs using the two nuts locked together to screw them into the crankcases. Ensure the studs are tight, then unlock the nuts without disturbing the studs, and screw the nuts off.
42 Install the remaining components in the reverse order of removal, noting that the auxiliary shaft drive chain and sprockets should be left off until after the cylinder heads and camshafts are installed to enable the timing to be set up correctly.

6 Riding habits can have a definite effect on bearing life. Full throttle, low speed operation, or labouring the engine, puts very high loads on bearings, which tend to squeeze out the oil film. These loads cause the bearings to flex, which produces fine cracks in the bearing face (fatigue failure). Eventually the bearing material will loosen in pieces and tear away from the steel backing. Short trip riding leads to corrosion of bearings, as insufficient engine heat is produced to drive off the condensed water and corrosive gases produced. These products collect in the engine oil, forming acid and sludge. As the oil is carried to the engine bearings, the acid attacks and corrodes the bearing material.

7 Incorrect bearing installation during engine assembly will lead to bearing failure as well. Tight fitting bearings which leave insufficient bearing oil clearances result in oil starvation. Dirt or foreign particles trapped behind a bearing shell result in high spots on the bearing which lead to failure.

8 To avoid bearing problems, clean all parts thoroughly before reassembly, double check all bearing clearance measurements and lubricate the new bearings with clean engine oil during installation.

27 Crankshaft main and guide bearings

Note: *To remove the crankshaft the engine must be removed from the frame (see Section 4).*

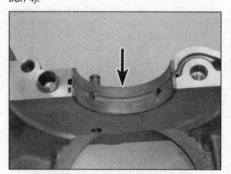

27.5a Examine the crankshaft main bearing shells (arrowed) . . .

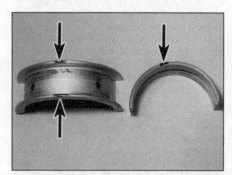

27.5c Location of the colour coding on the bearing shells (arrowed)

27.2a Location of the crankshaft main bearing (arrowed) . . .

Special tools: *Several special tools are required for this procedure – see Sections 23 and 25.*

Removal

1 Follow the procedure in Section 25 and separate the crankcase halves.
2 Lift the crankshaft assembly out of the right-hand crankcase half, taking care not to dislodge the crankshaft main and guide bearing shells **(see illustrations)**. Note the location of the oil seal on the rear of the crankshaft and discard it as a new one must be fitted after the crankcases have been reassembled.
3 Remove the auxiliary shaft and camchains, camchain tensioner blades and guide blades (see Section 28).
4 Follow the procedure in Section 18 and remove the connecting rods from the crankshaft.

27.5b . . . and the guide bearing shells (arrowed)

27.7a Remove the main bearing shells by pushing the centres to one side

27.2b . . . and guide bearing (arrowed) shells

Inspection

5 Examine the crankshaft bearing shells in both halves of the crankcase **(see illustrations)**. If there are any signs of wear on the bearing surfaces they should be renewed – always renew the main bearing and guide bearing shells as a set. The shells are colour-coded green or yellow according to their original tolerance fit – the colour mark is on the edge of the shell **(see illustration)**. Always fit new shells of the same colour code.
6 Refer to the general information in Section 26. If the bearing shells are scored, badly scuffed or appear to have seized, check the corresponding crankshaft journal. Damage to the surface of the journal on a standard crankshaft can be corrected by re-grinding and fitting oversize (+0.25 mm) bearing shells. If the crankshaft has already been reground, indicated by paint marks on the front crankshaft web, a new crankshaft will have to be fitted. If there is any doubt about the condition of the crankshaft, have it checked by a BMW dealer.
7 Remove the main bearing shells from each crankcase half by pushing their centres to the side, then lifting them out **(see illustration)**. Remove the guide bearing shells by pressing down on one end of the shell so that it slips round in the housing **(see illustration)**. If there are no obvious signs of damage, keep the shells in order so that they can be returned to their original locations for accurate oil clearance measurement prior to reassembly.
8 Clean the crankshaft with suitable solvent and blow dry it with compressed air – also

27.7b Remove the guide bearing shells by rotating them in the housing

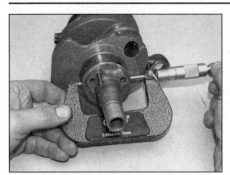

27.10a Measuring the diameter of the crankshaft main bearing journal

27.10b Measuring the diameter of the crankshaft guide bearing journal

blow through the oil passages to ensure they are clear.

Oil clearance check

9 Whether new bearing shells are being fitted or the original ones are being re-used, the crankshaft bearing oil clearance should be checked before the engine is reassembled. Bearing oil clearance can be measured by using a micrometer and telescoping gauge.

10 First measure the diameter of both crankshaft journals in two different planes with the micrometer and note the results **(see illustrations)**. Wear on the journals can be determined by comparing the results with the specifications at the beginning of this Chapter. **Note:** *A re-ground (Stage 1) crankshaft is identified by paint marks on the front crankshaft web.*

11 Next, clean the backs of the bearing shells and the bearing housings in both crankcase halves with a suitable solvent. Press the shells into their locations, ensuring that the tab on each shell engages in the notch in the crankcase **(see illustration)**. Make sure the shells are fitted in their correct locations and take care not to touch any shell's bearing surface with your fingers.

12 Carefully lower the left-hand crankcase half down onto the right-hand half. Ensure the crankshaft bearings remain in position in the

left-hand half and make sure the crankcase dowels all locate correctly. Check that the crankcase halves are correctly seated all the way round.

13 Ensure that the threads of all the crankcase bolts are clean, then follow the procedure in Section 25, Steps 31 to 37, to tighten the crankcase bolts. Note that for the purpose of this check it is not necessary to fit new sealing washers to the 8 mm bolts.

14 Measure the inside diameter of the crankshaft bearing shells with a telescoping gauge and micrometer and note the results **(see illustration)**. With reference to Step 10, note that a re-ground crankshaft will be fitted with appropriately sized Stage 1 main and guide bearing shells.

15 Subtract each crankshaft journal diameter from the appropriate bearing shells inside diameter to obtain the oil clearances and compare the results with the service limits specified at the beginning of this Chapter.

16 If the original bearing shells have been used for the check and the clearances are within the service limit, they can be reused. If the clearances are beyond the service limit, but the crankpin journals are good (see Step 10) , fit new bearing shells and check the oil clearances once again. Always renew the main bearing and guide bearing shells as a set. The shells are colour-coded green or

yellow according to their original tolerance fit – the colour mark is on the edge of the shell **(see illustration 27.5c)**. Always fit new shells of the same colour code.

End-float check

17 To check the crankshaft end-float in the guide bearing, measure the crankshaft guide bearing journal width, then measure the overall width of both guide bearing shells – unless they have worn unevenly, both shells should be the same overall width.

18 To calculate the end-float, subtract the shell width from the journal width, then compare the result with the specifications at the beginning of this Chapter.

19 If the end-float is greater than the service limit, compare your measurements with the specifications to determine which component is worn and renew it as necessary.

Installation

20 Ensure the backs of the bearing shells and the bearing housings in both crankcase halves are clean. If new shells are being fitted, ensure that all traces of the protective grease are cleaned off using suitable solvent.

21 Press the shells into their locations, ensuring that the tab on each shell engages in the notch in the crankcase **(see illustration 27.11)**. Make sure the shells are fitted in their correct locations and take care not to touch any shell's bearing surface with your fingers.

22 Follow the procedure in Section 18 and install the connecting rods onto the crankshaft.

23 Install the auxiliary shaft and camchains, camchain tensioner blades and guide blades (see Section 28).

24 Lubricate the crankshaft bearings with clean engine oil, then install the crankshaft assembly **(see illustrations 27.2a and 2b)**. **Note:** *The rear crankshaft oil seal is fitted after the crankcase halves have been reassembled (see Section 23).*

25 Reassemble the crankcase halves (see Section 25).

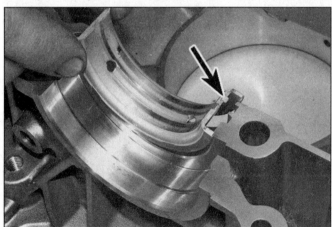

27.11 Make sure the tab (arrowed) engages with the notch in the case

27.14 Measuring the inside diameter of the crankshaft bearing shells

28.3a Undo the pivot bolt (arrowed) . . .

28.3b . . . and lift out the right-hand camchain tensioner blade

28.4a Support the left-hand camchain . . .

28 Auxiliary shaft, camchains and tensioner/guide blades

Note: *To remove the auxiliary shaft and associated components the engine must be removed from the frame.*

Removal

1 Follow the procedure in Section 25 and separate the crankcase halves.
2 Follow the procedure in Section 27 and lift the crankshaft assembly out of the right-hand crankcase half.
3 Working on the right-hand crankcase half, undo the pivot bolt securing the right-hand camchain tensioner blade and withdraw the blade from the crankcase half **(see illustrations)**.

4 Support the left-hand camchain and camshaft sprocket (the camshaft sprockets should still be secured to the camchains with cable ties – see Section 10) and lift the auxiliary shaft, together with the right-hand camchain and camshaft sprocket, out **(see illustrations)**.
5 Lift the left-hand tensioner blade/right-hand guide blade assembly out **(see illustration)**.
6 Working on the left-hand crankcase half, remove the E-clip securing the left-hand guide blade to the pivot pin, then remove the washer and withdraw the guide blade from the crankcase half **(see illustrations)**.
7 Mark or label all the components to avoid mixing them up.

Inspection

8 Except in cases of oil starvation, the camchains wear very little. If the chains have

stretched, indicated by play between the links, they must be renewed **(see illustration)**. If the chains have worn, it is likely that the auxiliary shaft sprockets and camshaft sprockets are worn also. **Note:** *If new camshaft sprockets are fitted, or the sprockets are separated from the camchains, note which way round the sprockets are fitted in relation to the auxiliary shaft. It is essential that any reference marks, timing marks and the locations for the breather rotor and camshaft position sensor trigger are in the right position on reassembly.*
9 Check the auxiliary shaft sprockets for wear and other damage and renew the shaft if necessary **(see illustration)**. Note that if a new shaft is installed, new camchains and camshaft sprockets should also be installed.
10 Inspect the bearing surfaces of the auxiliary shaft and the corresponding surfaces

28.4b . . . and lift out the auxiliary shaft and right-hand camchain

28.5 Lift out the blade assembly

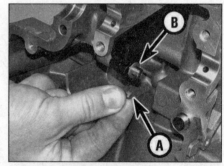

28.6a Remove the E-clip (A) and washer (B) . . .

28.6b . . . and lift out the left-hand guide blade

28.8 Check the camchains for stretch

28.9 Inspect the sprockets on the auxiliary shaft (A). Note the oil pump rotor (B)

28.10 Auxiliary shaft bearing surfaces in the left-hand crankcase half (arrowed)

28.11a Inspect the surfaces of the tensioner and guide blades for wear

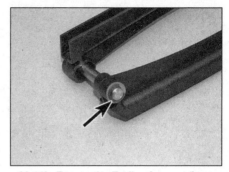

28.11b Ensure the E-clips (arrowed) are secure

in the crankcase halves **(see illustration)**. If there is any wear, scoring or other damage, renew the components as necessary.

11 Check the tensioner and guide blades and their pivots for signs of wear and damage and renew them if necessary **(see illustration)**. Ensure that the retaining E-clips are secure and renew them if necessary **(see illustration)**. If an E-clip is removed, fit a new one on installation.

Installation

12 Install the left-hand guide blade in the left-hand crankcase half, making sure it is the right way up, and secure it with the washer and new E-clip **(see illustrations 28.6b and a)**.

13 Ensure the right-hand crankcase half is properly supported using blocks of wood. Apply a smear of suitable sealant to the outside edge of the pivot pin location, then install the left-hand tensioner blade/right-hand guide blade assembly **(see illustration)**. Make sure the assembly is fitted the right way round **(see illustration 28.5)**.

14 Ensure the camshaft sprockets are correctly installed and secured to the camchains (see **Note**, Step 8). Apply clean engine oil to the auxiliary shaft bearing surfaces in the crankcase **(see illustration)**. Slip the camchains around their sprockets on the auxiliary shaft, making sure the chains are properly engaged with the sprocket teeth, then install the auxiliary shaft in the right-hand

crankcase half **(see illustration 28.4b and a)**.

15 Install the right-hand tensioner blade, ensuring it is located over the sides of the camchain, and secure it with the pivot bolt **(see illustration)**. Tighten the pivot bolt to the torque setting specified at the beginning of this Chapter.

16 Follow the procedure in Section 27 and install the crankshaft assembly in the right-hand crankcase half.

17 Reassemble the crankcase halves (see Section 25).

29 Gearbox removal and installation

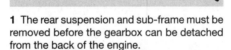

1 The rear suspension and sub-frame must be removed before the gearbox can be detached from the back of the engine.

2 Note that on machines fitted with ABS, the rear brake system must be disconnected from the control unit/modulator in order to remove the sub-frame. On reassembly, once the brake pipe has been reconnected, the system must be topped-up and bled by a BMW dealer using a BMW diagnostic tester - this is essential to restore brake operation.

3 To remove the gearbox, follow the procedure in Section 4, Steps 1 to 38. **Note:** *If work is being carried out on the gearbox, drain its oil prior to removal (see Chapter 1).*

4 Installation is the reverse of removal (see Section 4, Step 55).

30 Gearbox oil seals

Special tools: *BMW seal installation tools are referred to in Steps 6, 7, 13 and 18. These are not essential – alternative methods are described.*

1 The gearbox oil seals should be renewed whenever there are signs of oil leakage, or when the gearbox housing or transmission shafts have been removed.

2 Great care should be taken when installing new seals, especially over splined shafts which can damage the inner lip of the seal. BMW provide a number of guides, sleeves and drivers for this purpose.

Transmission input shaft seals

Rear seal

3 To access the rear oil seal, first remove the rear wheel (see Chapter 5) and the rear shock absorber (see Chapter 4). Follow the procedure in Section 24 to displace the clutch release cylinder – note that it is not necessary to disconnect the clutch hose from the cylinder. Withdraw the clutch pushrod from the input shaft.

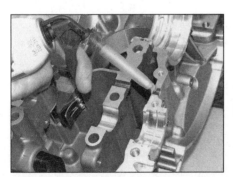

28.13 Apply a smear of sealant to the pivot pin location in the right-hand crankcase half

28.14 Lubricate the auxiliary shaft bearing surfaces

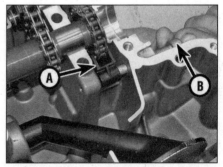

28.15 Secure the right-hand tensioner blade (A) with the pivot bolt (B)

30.4 Location of the input shaft rear oil seal (arrowed)

30.5 Removing the oil seal as described

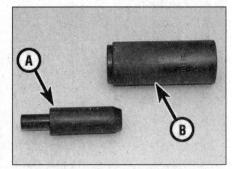

30.6 BMW installation guide (A) and sleeve (B) – input shaft rear oil seal

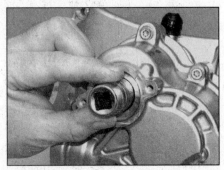

30.8 Installing the seal with a suitably sized socket

30.11 Measuring the installed depth of the input shaft front oil seal

30.12a Drill a small hole in one side of the old seal . . .

4 Note the location of the oil seal on the end of the transmission shaft (see illustration).
5 To avoid damaging the seal housing or the surface of the shaft, use a 3 mm drill bit to drill a hole on one side of the seal. Take care to only drill through the outer surface of the seal. Thread a self-tapping screw part-way into the hole and position a piece of thick card over the outer surface of the seal housing to protect it, then carefully lever out the seal using a pair of curved, thin-nosed pliers (see illustration).
6 If available, use the BMW tools to install the new seal (see illustration). Lubricate the inner lip of the seal with a smear of clean gearbox oil, then slip the seal over the end of the guide

(Part No. 23 4 722) and install the smaller diameter end of the guide into the end of the input shaft.
7 Position the sleeve (Part No. 23 4 723) over the end of the guide, and press the seal into position with the sleeve.
8 Alternatively, press the seal into position carefully with a suitably sized socket that locates on the outer edge of the seal only (see illustration).
9 When installed, the outer edge of the seal should be level with the inner face of the housing and the end of the shaft should protrude through the centre of the seal (see illustration 30.4).

Front seal

10 To access the front oil seal, the gearbox must be removed (see Section 29).
11 If the BMW installation tools are not available, measure the installed depth of the old seal before it is removed (see illustration).
12 Follow the procedure in Step 5 to remove the old seal (see illustrations).
13 If available, use the BMW tools to install the new seal (see illustration). Lubricate the inner lip of the seal with a smear of clean gearbox oil, then slip the seal over the end of the guide (Part No. 23 4 712). Locate the guide over the end of the shaft, then position

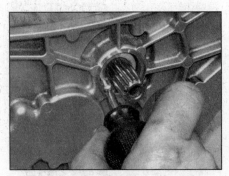

30.12b . . . then thread a self-tapping screw into the seal . . .

30.12c . . . and pull the seal out with thin-nosed pliers

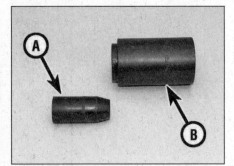

30.13a BMW installation guide (A) and driver (B) – input shaft front oil seal

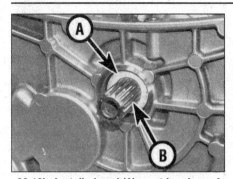

30.13b Installed seal (A) must be clear of the splines (B) on the input shaft

30.14a Cover the shaft splines with tape to protect the oil seal . . .

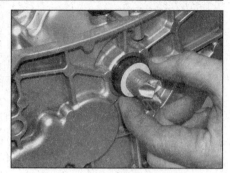

30.14b . . . then install the seal . . .

the driver (Part No. 23 4 711) over the end of the guide, and press the seal into position with the driver. The end of the driver is shaped to ensure that the seal is pressed fully home inside its housing, clear of the splines on the shaft (see illustration).

14 Alternatively, wrap self-adhesive tape around the splines of the shaft to protect the inner lip of the seal, then install the seal on the shaft and press it into position carefully with a suitably sized driver that locates on the outer edge of the seal only (see illustrations). Check that the seal has been installed evenly and to the depth measured before the old seal was removed, then remove the self-adhesive tape.

Transmission output shaft seal

15 To access the output shaft oil seal, first remove the rear shock absorber and swingarm/final drive unit assembly (see Chapter 4).

16 Note the location of the seal in its housing and on the output shaft (see illustration).

17 Follow the procedure in Step 5 to remove the old seal, this time drilling two holes on opposite sides of the old seal to ensure the seal is levered out evenly (see illustration).

18 If available, use the BMW tools to install

30.14c . . . and press it into place with a suitably sized driver

the new seal (see illustration). Lubricate the inner lip of the seal with a smear of clean gearbox oil, then slip the seal over the end of the guide (Part No. 23 4 732). Locate the guide over the end of the shaft, then position the driver (Part No. 23 4 731) over the end of the guide, and press the seal into position with the driver. The end of the driver is shaped to ensure that the seal is pressed fully home inside its housing, clear of the splines on the shaft (see illustration 30.16).

30.16 Location of the output shaft rear oil seal (arrowed)

19 Alternatively, wrap self-adhesive tape around the shaft to protect the inner lip of the seal, then install the seal on the shaft and press it into position carefully with a suitably sized driver that locates on the outer edge of the seal only.

20 When installed, the outer edge of the seal should be level with the inner face of the housing and the inner lip should be clear of the splines on the shaft. Remove the self-adhesive tape.

30.17 Levering out the old output shaft oil seal

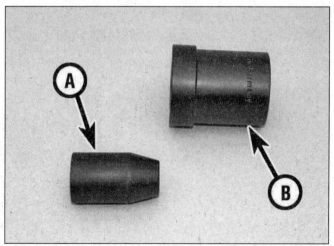

30.18 BMW installation guide (A) and driver (B) – output shaft oil seal

31.1a Undo the sensor mounting bolts (arrowed)

31.1b Location of the sensor O-ring (arrowed)

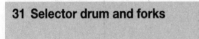

31 Selector drum and forks

Note: *To remove the selector drum and forks the gearbox must first be removed (see Section 29).*

Special tools: *A stand is required to support the gearbox during this procedure (see Tool Tip). A knife-edged bearing puller is required to remove the selector drum bearings.*

Removal

1 Ensure that the transmission is in neutral

– the input and output shafts should rotate independently from each other. If not, temporarily install the gearchange lever and select neutral. To avoid damage, undo the bolts securing the gear position sensor and lift the sensor off, noting the location of the sensor O-ring **(see illustrations)**. If there is evidence of oil leakage, the oil seal in the gearbox end cover must be renewed (see Step 19).

2 Undo the bolts securing the gearbox end cover to the gearbox housing, then remove the bolts together with the exhaust system bracket **(see illustration)**.

3 Support the gearbox on its rear end,

making sure it is secure. A suitable stand can be made from two lengths of wood secured to a baseboard (see *Tool Tip*).

4 Using a hot air gun, heat the gearbox housing around the locations for the internal bearings to release the bearings from the housing, then tap around the joint between the housing and the end cover with a soft-faced mallet to separate them **(see illustration)**. The sealant used between the casings can form a strong bond, but do not attempt to lever them apart with a screwdriver – you'll damage the sealing surfaces. If the housing won't lift off, it isn't hot enough – BMW suggest a separation temperature between 50°C to 80°C.

> ⚠ **Warning: Be careful when separating the gearbox casings – when heated, the housing could cause severe burns.**

5 Lift off the gearbox housing – the gearbox internal components will remain in the end cover **(see illustration)**. Note the location of the two dowels in the end cover and remove them if they are loose **(see illustration)**.

6 Before removing the selector forks, mark each one according to its location and which way up it fits as an aid to installation **(see illustration)**. Note how the guide pins on the forks locate in the grooves in the selector drum.

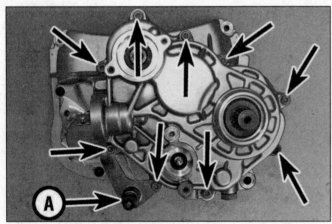

31.2 Location of the gearbox end cover bolts and exhaust bracket (A)

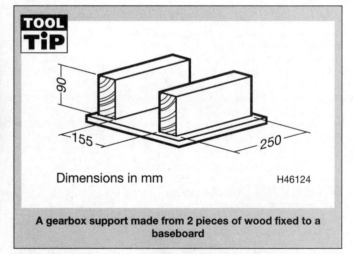

TOOL TiP

Dimensions in mm   H46124

A gearbox support made from 2 pieces of wood fixed to a baseboard

31.4 Heat the gearbox housing to release the internal bearings

31.5a Lift off the gearbox housing

31.5b Note the location of the dowels (arrowed)

31.6 Gear selector forks – 1st/5th gear (A), 2nd/3rd gear (B), 4th/6th gear (C). Selector drum (D)

31.7 Lift out the selector fork shaft

7 Lift out the fork shaft supporting the upper 1st/5th and lower 2nd/3rd gear selector forks **(see illustration)**.

8 Note how the 1st/5th gear selector fork locates in its shift sleeve on the transmission output shaft and lift the selector fork off **(see illustration)**. Slide the fork back onto its shaft the right way round.

9 Note the location of the plain and wave washers between the 4th/6th gear selector fork and the selector arm **(see illustration)**. Carefully lift out the fork shaft and remove the washers **(see illustration)**. Slide the washers onto the fork shaft for safekeeping.

10 Disengage the guide pin on the 4th/6th gear selector fork from the selector drum, then withdraw the fork from the shift sleeve on the transmission intermediate shaft **(see illustrations)**. Slide the fork back onto its shaft the right way round.

11 Note the location of the selector arm – the centralising spring locates on the pivot pin for the stopper arm and the selector arm pawls engage with the pins on the lower end of the selector drum **(see illustration)**. Lift the selector arm out **(see illustration)**.

12 Manoeuvre the 2nd/3rd gear selector fork to disengage the guide pin from the selector drum, then ease the stopper arm away from

31.8 Pull the selector fork out of the shift sleeve (arrowed)

31.9a Note the location of the washers (arrowed) . . .

31.9b . . . then lift the fork shaft and remove the washers

31.10a Disengage the guide pin (arrowed) from the selector drum

31.10b Withdraw the fork from the shift sleeve on the intermediate shaft (arrowed)

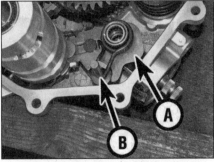

31.11a Selector arm (A), pivot pin for stopper arm (B)

31.11b Lift out the selector arm

31.12a Disengage the guide pin (arrowed) from the selector drum . . .

31.12b . . . then ease the stopper arm (arrowed) away from the gearchange cam . . .

31.12c . . . and lift the selector drum out

the gearchange cam on the lower end of the selector drum and lift the selector drum out **(see illustrations)**. Note the location of the shim on the lower end of the selector drum shaft **(see illustration)**.

13 To remove the 2nd/3rd gear selector fork, the transmission shafts must be removed from the gearbox end cover (see Section 33). Note which way round the selector fork is fitted, then withdraw it from the shift sleeve on the transmission output shaft **(see illustration 33.4a)**. Slide the fork back onto its shaft the right way round.

Inspection

14 Inspect the selector forks for any signs of wear or damage, especially around the fork ends where they engage with the grooves in the shift sleeves **(see illustration)**. Check that each fork fits correctly in its groove. Check closely to see if the forks are bent. If the

forks are in any way damaged they must be renewed.

15 Check that the forks fit correctly on their shafts. They should move freely with a light fit but no appreciable freeplay. Replace the forks and/or shaft if excessive wear is noted. Check that the fork shaft holes in the casing and end cover are not worn or damaged.

16 Check that the selector fork shafts are straight by rolling them along a flat surface. A bent shaft will cause difficulty in selecting gears and make the gearchange action heavy, and should be replaced with a new one.

17 Inspect the grooves in the selector drum and guide pins on the selector forks for signs of wear or damage **(see illustration)**. Any components with wear or damage should be renewed.

18 Check that the bearing in the end of the selector drum rotates freely. To renew the bearing, heat the end of the drum with

a hot air gun and pull the bearing out with a knife-edged bearing puller (see *Tools and Workshop Tips* in the *Reference* section). Note which way round the bearing is fitted. Drive the new bearing in with a bearing driver or suitably sized socket. Take great care not to damage the components on the lower end of the selector drum shaft when renewing the bearing.

19 Check that the selector drum bearing in the gearbox end cover rotates freely, and check the oil seal in the outside of the cover for signs of leakage **(see illustrations)**. To renew the seal, lever it out carefully with a flat-bladed screwdriver, taking care not to damage the surface of the housing. Press the new seal in with a suitably sized socket. To renew the bearing, heat the housing with a hot air gun and pull the bearing out with a knife-edged bearing puller. Note which way round the bearing is fitted. Drive the new bearing in with a bearing driver or suitably sized socket.

Installation

20 Ensure that the gearbox end cover is securely supported (see Step 3).

21 If the 2nd/3rd gear selector fork has been removed, install it in its shift sleeve on the transmission output shaft, making sure it is the right way round, then install the shafts into the gearbox end cover (see Section 33).

22 Secure the shim on the lower end of the selector drum shaft with a dab of grease, then install the selector drum in the gearbox end cover. Locate the guide pin on the 2nd/3rd gear selector fork in the lower groove in the

31.12d Note the shim (arrowed) on the selector drum shaft

31.14 Inspect the selector forks for wear

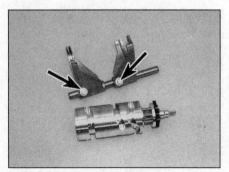

31.17 Inspect the guide pins (arrowed) and the grooves in the drum

31.19a Location of the selector drum bearing (arrowed)

31.19b Location of the selector drum shaft seal (arrowed)

31.22 Roller (arrowed) should engage in the neutral detent

31.31 Apply an even bead of sealant to the end cover mating surface

selector drum (see illustration 31.12a). Ensure that the stopper arm roller is located in the neutral detent on the gearchange cam (see illustration).

23 Install the selector arm, centralising spring uppermost (see Step 11).

24 Install the 4th/6th gear selector fork in the shift sleeve on the transmission intermediate shaft, then locate the guide pin in the middle groove on the selector drum (see illustrations 31.10b and a). Slide the fork shaft through the selector fork, the plain and wave washers, the selector arm and into its location in the gearbox end cover (see illustration 31.9b). Ensure shaft is pressed fully into place.

25 Install the 1st/5th gear selector fork in its shift sleeve on the transmission output shaft, then locate the guide pin in the upper groove in the selector drum (see illustration 31.8). Slide the fork shaft through the upper and lower selector forks and into its location in the gearbox end cover (see illustration 31.7). Ensure the shaft is pressed fully into place.

26 Check that each selector fork is correctly installed (see illustration 31.6).

27 Remove all traces of old sealant from the mating surfaces of the gearbox housing and end cover. If a scraper must be used, be very careful not to nick or gouge the soft aluminium or oil leaks will result. Take care not to let any old sealant fall into the end cover.

28 If removed, fit the dowels into the end cover (see illustration 31.5b).

29 Clean the threads of all the cover bolts.

30 Generously lubricate all the components

with clean gearbox oil (see Chapter 1), then use a rag soaked in high flash-point solvent to wipe over the mating surfaces of the casings to remove all traces of oil.

31 Apply a thin, even bead of suitable sealant to the mating surface of the end cover (see illustration).

Caution: Don't apply an excessive amount of sealant as it will ooze out when the gearbox housing and end cover are assembled.

32 Carefully lower the housing over the transmission components – align the input shaft with the bearing in the housing and align the mating surfaces of the housing and end cover (see illustration 31.5a). Using a hot air gun, heat the gearbox housing around the locations for the internal bearings, then tap the housing down onto the end cover with a soft-faced mallet. If the housing won't drop into place, either the shafts are not properly aligned with their locations in the housing, or the housing isn't hot enough – BMW suggest an assembly temperature between 50°C to 80°C. Check that the gearbox casings are correctly seated all the way round.

Caution: The gearbox casings should fit together without being forced. If they're not correctly seated, separate them and investigate the problem. DO NOT attempt to pull them together by tightening the cover bolts.

33 Carefully turn the gearbox over, then install the cover bolts and the exhaust system bracket (see illustration 31.2). Tighten the bolts in a criss-cross sequence to the torque

setting specified at the beginning of this Chapter.

34 Temporarily install the gearchange lever and check that all the gears can be selected and that the transmission shafts rotate smoothly in every gear.

35 Fit a new O-ring to the gear position sensor and lubricate it with a smear of clean gearbox oil, then press the sensor into position and secure it with the bolts (see illustrations 31.1b and 1a). Tighten the bolts to the specified torque setting.

36 Before installing the gearbox, renew the transmission input and output shaft oil seals (see Section 30).

32 Gearchange mechanism

Note: To remove the gearchange mechanism the gearbox must first be removed (see Section 29).

Special tools: A stand is required to support the gearbox during this procedure (see Tool Tip on page 2•64). A knife-edged bearing puller is required to remove the inner gearchange shaft bearing.

Removal

1 Follow the procedure in Section 31 to remove the selector drum and forks.

2 Note the location of the return spring on the stopper arm and how the spring holds the stopper arm roller against the selector drum cam (see illustration 31.22). Pull out the stopper arm pivot pin and remove the stopper arm and return spring.

3 If the gearchange shaft oil seal is leaking, or to inspect the shaft bearings, first remove the old seal as follows. Using a 3 mm drill bit, drill a hole on one side of the seal (see illustration). Take care to only drill through the outer surface of the seal. Next, thread a self-tapping screw part-way into the hole. Position a small piece of wood over the outer edge of the seal housing to protect it, then carefully lever out the seal using a pair of curved, thin-nosed pliers (see illustrations).

4 The gearchange shaft and caged ball bearing are retained by a circlip – remove

32.3a Drill a small hole in one side of the old seal ...

32.3b ... then thread in a self-tapping screw ...

32.3c ... and pull the old seal out

32.4a Remove the circlip . . .

32.4b . . . and draw out the gearchange shaft assembly

32.4c Note the location of the needle roller bearing (arrowed)

the circlip and draw the shaft assembly out **(see illustrations)**. The inner end of the shaft is supported by a needle roller bearing **(see illustration)**.

Inspection

5 Inspect the pawls on the selector arm and the pins on the selector drum **(see illustration)**. Note the location of the small spring on the pawl mechanism – the mechanism should move smoothly, but not be loose **(see illustration)**. Ensure that the centralising spring is a tight fit on the selector arm.
6 Inspect the stopper arm return spring, the stopper arm and the roller and the corresponding lobes on the gearchange cam **(see illustration)**.

7 If any of the components are found to be worn or damaged, or the springs fatigued, they must be renewed.
8 Inspect the gearchange shaft for damage to the splines and renew the shaft if necessary **(see illustration)**. Check the peg on the shaft and the corresponding fork on the selector arm for wear. Check the condition of the shaft bearings. The caged ball bearing is secured on the shaft by a circlip – if required, remove the circlip and press the shaft out. Only remove the shaft needle roller bearing if it is going to be renewed – draw the old bearing out with a knife-edged bearing puller and press the new bearing in carefully with a suitably sized socket.

Installation

9 If removed, secure the caged ball bearing

on the gearchange shaft with the circlip, then install the shaft assembly and secure it with the circlip **(see illustrations 32.4b and a)**. Ensure both circlips are correctly fitted in their grooves – it is good practice to renew the circlips, especially if they are corroded or fatigued. Fit a new gearchange shaft oil seal, ensuring it is the right way round **(see illustration)**. Press the seal in with a suitably sized socket that bears on the outer edge of the seal only **(see illustration)**.
10 Install the return spring and stopper arm on the lower end of the pivot pin. Ensure that the stopper arm is located onto the shoulder on the pivot pin. Install the assembly in the gearbox making sure that the pivot pin is pressed all the way in to its location, and position the ends of the spring so that the stopper arm roller is held under tension

32.5a Inspect the pawls (A) and the pins (B)

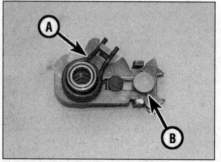

32.5b Inspect the pawl mechanism – note the centralising spring (A) and pawl spring (B)

32.6 Inspect the stopper arm return spring (A), roller (B) and gearchange cam lobes (C)

32.8 Inspect the gearchange shaft splines (arrowed)

32.9a Ensure the gearchange shaft oil seal is fitted the correct way round

32.9b Note the alignment of the seal with the casing

33.2 Note the location of the three transmission shafts

against the selector drum cam **(see illustration 31.22)**.

11 Follow the procedure in Section 31 to install the selector drum and forks.

33 Transmission shafts

Note 1: *To remove the transmission shafts the gearbox must first be removed (see Section 29).*
Note 2: *The assembled length of the transmission shafts is critical to ensure that they fit inside the gearbox casings. If the shafts are disassembled for inspection, or any components are renewed, be sure to check the assembled length before installation.*
Special tools: *A bearing puller with both long and short-reach arms is required for this procedure.*

33.3 Lift the transmission shafts out as an assembly

Removal

1 Follow the procedure in Section 31 to remove the selector drum and forks.
2 Note the relative positions of the three transmission shafts and how they fit together **(see illustration)**.
3 Using a hot air gun, heat the gearbox end cover around the locations for the internal bearings to release the bearings from the cover, then lift the transmission shafts out as an assembly **(see illustration)**. Don't try to pull the shafts out individually, if the assembly won't lift out, the cover isn't hot enough – BMW suggest a separation temperature between 90°C to 100°C.

⚠️ *Warning: Be careful when removing the transmission shafts – when heated, the end cover could cause severe burns.*

4 Lay the transmission shafts on a clean work

surface. Note which way round the 2nd/3rd gear selector fork is fitted, then withdraw it from the shift sleeve on the transmission output shaft **(see illustration)**. Slide the fork back onto its shaft the right way round (see Section 31). Keep the shafts in their correct order **(see illustration)**.
5 If necessary, the input shaft and output shaft can be disassembled and inspected for wear or damage. The intermediate shaft cannot be disassembled other than to renew the bearings.
6 Always disassemble the transmission shafts separately to avoid mixing up the components.

> **HAYNES HINT** *When disassembling the transmission shafts, place the parts on a long rod or thread a wire through them to keep them in order and facing the proper direction.*

Input shaft

Disassembly

7 Using a bearing puller, pull the rear bearing off the shaft, noting which way round it is fitted **(see illustration)**.
8 Slide off the shim and splined collar **(see illustrations)**.
9 Assemble a puller on the shaft as shown **(see illustration)**. Protect the splined end of the shaft with a piece of soft metal (brass is ideal) and position the lower jaws of the puller

33.4a Remove the 2nd/3rd gear selector fork

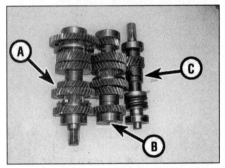

33.4b Keep the output (A), intermediate (B) and input shaft (C) in their correct order

33.7 Set-up for pulling the rear bearing off the input shaft

33.8a Slide off the shim . . .

33.8b . . . and the splined collar

33.9a Set-up for compressing the input shaft damper spring – note the piece of brass (arrowed)

33.9b Location of the collets (arrowed) inside the spring retainer

33.10 Remove the collets carefully

33.11a Slide off the spring retainer . . .

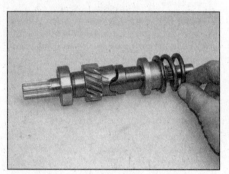

33.11b . . . and the damper spring

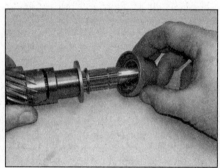

33.12a Slide off the sleeve . . .

each side of the collets inside the spring retainer **(see illustration)**.

10 Compress the damper spring with the puller and remove the collets with a magnet or small screwdriver **(see illustration)**.

11 Release the spring tension and remove the spring retainer and spring **(see illustrations)**.

12 Slide off the sleeve, noting the location of the wave washer **(see illustrations)**.

13 Slide off the splined damper adjusting washer **(see illustration)**.

14 Remove the circlip, then slide off the stop washer **(see illustrations)**. Discard the circlip as a new one must be fitted.

15 Slide off the drive cam and the driven gear **(see illustrations)**.

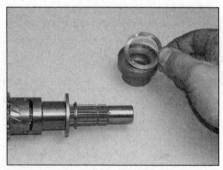

33.12b . . . noting the location of the wave washer

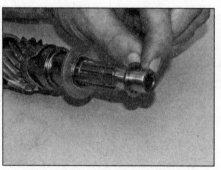

33.13 Slide off the splined damper adjusting washer

33.14a Remove the circlip . . .

33.14b . . . then slide off the stop washer

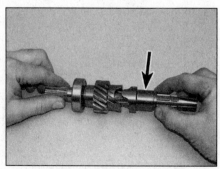

33.15a Slide off the drive cam (arrowed) . . .

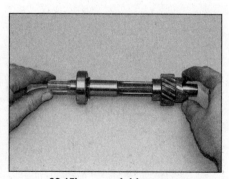

33.15b . . . and driven gear

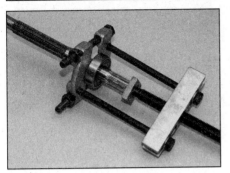

33.17 Set-up for pulling the front bearing off the input shaft

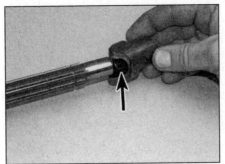

33.18a Inspect the splines on the shaft and inside the drive cam (arrowed)

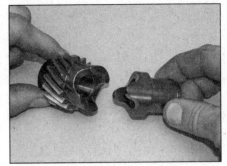

33.18b Inspect the cam faces and gear teeth for wear and damage

Inspection

16 Wash all of the components in suitable solvent and dry them thoroughly.

17 Check the input shaft bearings for wear or damage (see *Tools and Workshop Tips* in the *Reference* section), replacing them with new ones if necessary. If required remove the front bearing using a puller, noting which way round it is fitted **(see illustration)**.

18 Inspect the shaft splines and the corresponding splines inside the drive cam for signs of wear or damage **(see illustration)**. Inspect the faces of the drive cam and driven gear for wear, and inspect the gear teeth for chipping, pitting and wear **(see illustration)**. If any components are worn or damaged, renew them. Note that the drive cam and driven gear should be renewed as a set. If the driven gear teeth are worn or damaged, check the teeth on the corresponding gear on the intermediate shaft.

19 Inspect the collets and the collet groove in the shaft for wear. If the inner edges of the collets are rounded, renew them.

20 No specifications are available for the damper spring – if required, compare the length of the spring with a new item and fit a new spring if the old one has sagged.

Reassembly

21 If removed, install the front bearing with a driver that locates on the inner race of the bearing only, and drive the bearing all the way on **(see illustration)**.

22 Lubricate the shaft lightly with clean

gearbox oil. Slide on the driven gear and drive cam, then slide on the stop washer and secure it with a new circlip **(see illustrations 33.15b, 15a and 14b)**. Ensure that the circlip is secure in its groove and align the ends of the circlip as shown **(see illustration)**.

23 Slide on the splined damper adjusting washer **(see illustration 33.13)**. Slide on the sleeve without the wave washer **(see illustration)**. Push the sleeve against the damper adjusting washer and measure the distance between the front bearing stop and the front end of the driven gear (pre-damper travel) with a feeler gauge **(see illustration)**. Compare the result with the specification at the beginning of this Chapter – if the travel is too great fit a thinner adjusting washer to correct it, if the travel is too small fit a thicker adjusting washer. Four thicknesses of

adjusting washer are available, from 1.5 to 2.1 mm thickness – see a BMW dealer for details.

24 When the pre-damper travel is correct, install the wave washer in the sleeve, then slide on the sleeve, damper spring and spring retainer **(see illustrations 33.12b, 12a, 11b and 11a)**.

25 Assemble the puller as used on disassembly, then compress the damper spring and slip the collets into place **(see illustration 33.10)**. Make sure the collets are securely located in the collet groove and release the spring tension.

26 Slide on the splined collar and the shim **(see illustrations 33.8b and 8a)**.

27 Press on the rear bearing with a driver that locates on the inner race of the bearing only, and drive the bearing all the way on **(see illustration)**.

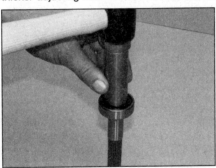

33.21 Install the front bearing with a suitable driver

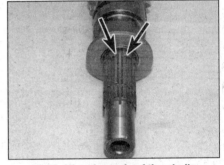

33.22 Align the ends of the circlip (arrowed) with the raised splines on the shaft

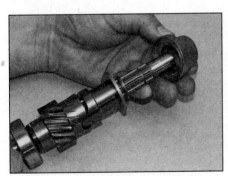

33.23a Slide on the sleeve without the wave washer

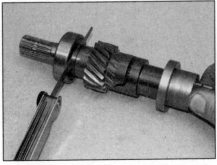

33.23b Measuring the predamper travel with a feeler gauge

33.27 Install the rear bearing with a suitable driver

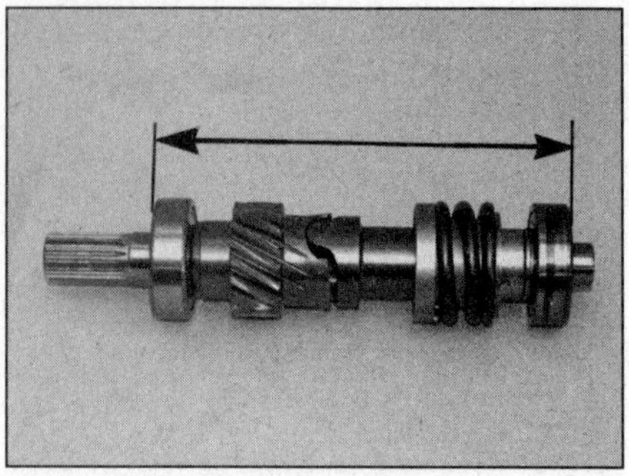

33.28 Assembled input shaft – measure the assembled length between the points shown

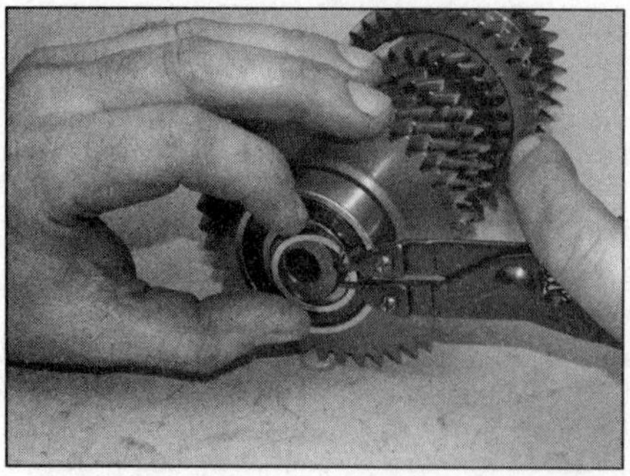

33.33 Remove the circlip from the front end of the output shaft

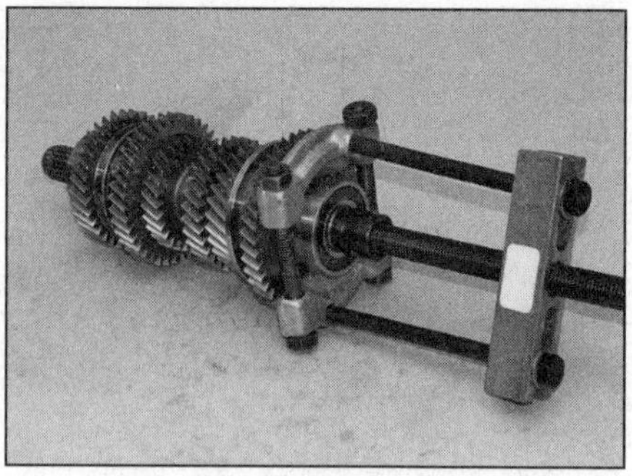

33.34a Set-up for pulling the front bearing off the output shaft

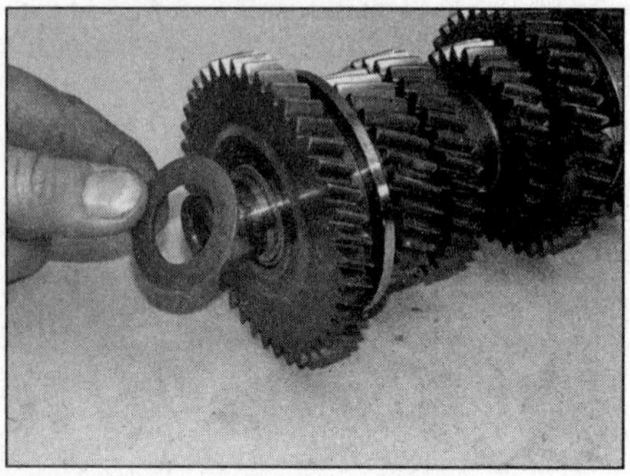

33.34b Remove the shim . . .

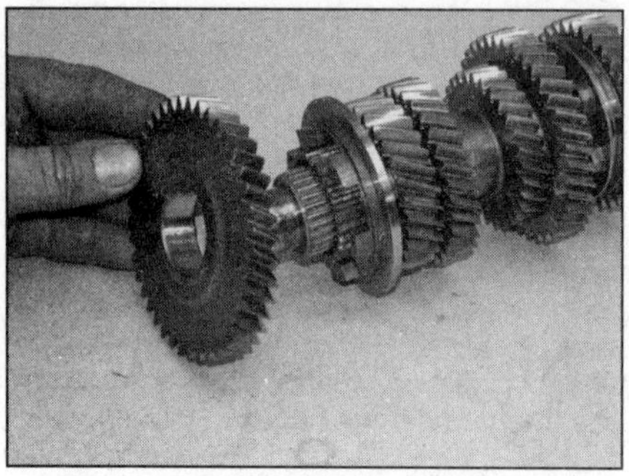

33.34c . . . and the 1st gear pinion

28 The assembled input shaft should look like this **(see illustration)**. Measure the assembled length of the input shaft and compare the result with the specification at the beginning of this Chapter. If the length is too great, pull off the rear bearing and fit a thinner shim to correct it. There are 17 thicknesses of shim available, from 3.0 to 3.4 mm thickness – see a BMW dealer for details.

Intermediate shaft

29 The intermediate shaft cannot be disassembled and, with the exception of the bearings, no replacement parts are available. If any of the shaft gears, or the 4th/6th gear selector fork shift sleeve, is damaged or worn, the complete intermediate shaft must be renewed.

30 Check the bearings for wear or damage and renew them if necessary (see *Tools and Workshop Tips* in the *Reference* section). Both bearings are a press fit on the shaft – note which way round they are fitted, then remove them using a puller **(see illustration 33.7)**.

31 A shim is fitted behind the front bearing – note the combined width of the old bearing and the shim, and ensure the combined width of the new bearing and shim is the same. If the width is too great, fit a thinner shim to correct it. There are 29 thicknesses of shim available, from 1.5 to 2.3 mm thickness – see a BMW dealer for details.

32 Drive the new bearings into place using a suitable socket or bearing driver.

Output shaft

Disassembly

33 Remove the circlip from the front end of the shaft **(see illustration)**. Discard the circlip as a new one must be fitted.

34 Using a bearing puller, pull the front bearing off the shaft, noting which way round it is fitted **(see illustration)**. If a knife-edged puller is not available, position the puller behind the 1st gear pinion to displace the bearing. Remove the shim, noting which way round it is fitted, and the 1st gear pinion **(see illustrations)**.

35 Slide off the green needle bearing and the 1st/5th gear shift sleeve, noting which way round it is fitted **(see illustrations)**.

36 Position the puller behind the 5th gear pinion to displace the bush, then slide off the bush and the splined sleeve, noting which way round the sleeve is fitted **(see illustrations)**.

37 Slide off the 5th gear pinion, noting which

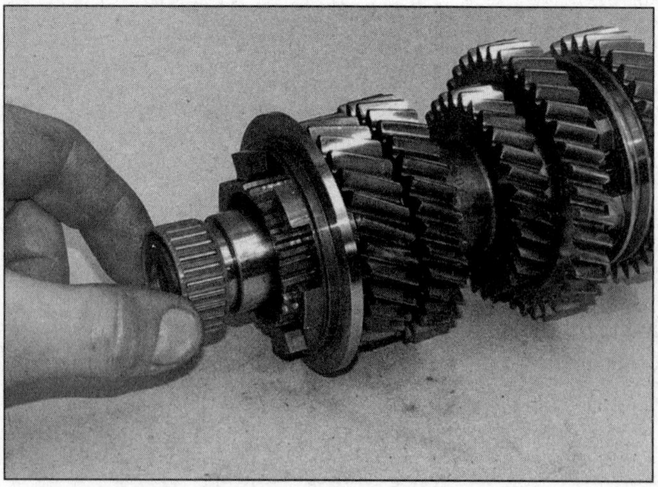

33.35a Slide off the green needle bearing . . .

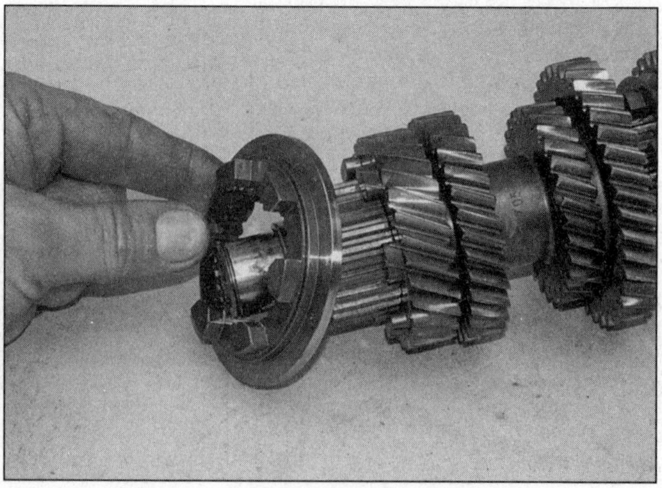

33.35b . . . and the 1st/5th gear shift sleeve

33.36a Position the puller behind the 5th gear pinion (A) – note the piece of brass (B)

33.36b Slide off the bush . . .

way round it fits, and the black needle bearing – note that the black needle bearing has a split race to facilitate removal **(see illustrations)**.

38 The 4th gear pinion is an integral part of the transmission shaft **(see illustration)**.

39 Remove the circlip from the rear end of the shaft **(see illustration)**. Discard the circlip as a new one must be fitted.

40 Using a bearing puller, pull the rear bearing off the shaft, noting which way round it is fitted **(see illustration)**. If a knife-edged puller is not available, position the puller behind the 3rd gear pinion to displace the bearing. Remove the shim and the 3rd gear pinion **(see illustrations)**.

33.36c . . . and the splined sleeve

33.37a Slide off the 5th gear pinion

33.37b Note the split (arrowed) in the race of the black needle bearing

33.38 Location of the 4th gear pinion (arrowed)

33.39 Remove the circlip from the rear end of the output shaft

33.40a Set-up for pulling the rear bearing off the output shaft

33.40b Remove the shim . . .

33.40c . . . and the 3rd gear pinion

33.41a Slide off the green needle bearing . . .

33.41b . . . and the 2nd/3rd gear shift sleeve

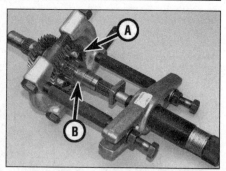

33.42a Position the puller behind the 2nd gear pinion (A) to displace the bush (B)

33.42b Slide off the bush . . .

33.42c . . . and the splined sleeve

33.43a Slide off the 2nd gear pinion . . .

41 Slide off the green needle bearing and the 2nd/3rd gear shift sleeve, noting which way round it is fitted **(see illustrations)**.
42 Position the puller behind the 2nd gear pinion to displace the bush, then slide off the bush and the splined sleeve **(see illustrations)**.
43 Slide off the 2nd gear pinion, noting which way round it fits, and the green needle bearing **(see illustrations)**.
44 The 6th gear pinion is an integral part of the transmission shaft **(see illustration)**.

Inspection

45 Wash all of the components in clean solvent and dry them thoroughly.
46 Check the gear teeth for cracking,

chipping, pitting and other signs of wear or damage. Any gear pinion that is damaged must be renewed – don't forget to check for wear on the corresponding intermediate shaft gears.
47 Inspect the dogs and the dog holes in the gears and the shift sleeves for cracks, chips and excessive wear, especially in the form of rounded edges. Make sure mating gears engage properly. Check for signs of wear on the selector fork grooves.
48 The shaft is unlikely to sustain damage unless the engine has seized, placing an unusually high loading on the transmission, or the machine has covered a very high mileage. Check the surface of the shaft, especially where a pinion turns on it, and renew the shaft if it is worn, scored or pitted. Similarly,

check the pinion bushes and the needle roller bearings for damage.
49 Check the output shaft caged ball bearings for wear or damage (see *Tools and Workshop Tips* in the *Reference* section), replacing them with new ones if necessary.

Reassembly

50 During reassembly, lubricate the components lightly with clean gearbox oil.
51 Slide the black needle bearing onto the front end of the shaft, then slide the 5th gear pinion onto the bearing with its dogs facing away from the fixed 4th gear pinion **(see illustrations 33.37b and a)**.
52 Slide on the splined sleeve with the recessed end facing out, then slide on the bush **(see illustration)**. Using a suitably sized

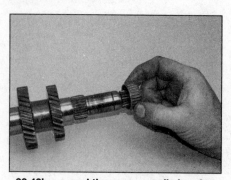

33.43b . . . and the green needle bearing

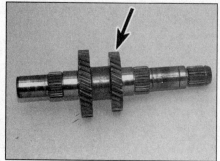

33.44 Location of the 6th gear pinion (arrowed)

33.52a Location of the splined sleeve (A) and bush (B)

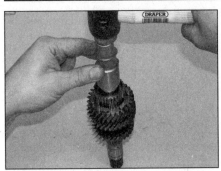

33.52b Drive the bush all the way on

33.54 Dog holes (arrowed) on 1st gear pinion

33.55a Fit the shim with the tapered face (arrowed) facing out . . .

33.55b . . . then press on the bearing

33.56 Partially assembled output shaft – measure the partially assembled length between the points shown

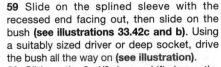

33.58 Dog holes (arrowed) on 2nd gear pinion

driver or deep socket, drive the bush all the way on **(see illustration)**.

53 Slide on the 1st/5th gear shift sleeve and the green needle bearing **(see illustrations 33.35b and a)**.

54 Slide on the 1st gear pinion with its dog holes facing the dogs on the shift sleeve **(see illustration)**.

55 Install the shim with its tapered face facing out **(see illustration)**. Press the front bearing onto the end of the shaft with a driver that locates on the inner race of the bearing only **(see illustration)**.

56 The partially assembled output shaft should look like this **(see illustration)**. Measure the partial assembled length of the output shaft and compare the result with the specification at the beginning of this Chapter.

If the length is too great, pull off the front bearing and fit a thinner shim to correct it. There are 29 thicknesses of shim available, from 1.8 to 2.5 mm thickness – see a BMW dealer for details.

57 When the partial assembled length is correct and the bearing is fully installed, measure the width of the circlip groove on the end of the shaft with a feeler gauge and fit the appropriate sized new circlip **(see illustration 33.33)**. Three thicknesses of circlip are available, from 1.1 to 1.3 mm in thickness – see a BMW dealer for details.

58 Slide the green needle bearing onto the rear end of the shaft **(see illustration 33.43b)**. Slide the 2nd gear pinion onto the bearing with its dog holes facing away from the fixed 6th gear pinion **(see illustration)**.

59 Slide on the splined sleeve with the recessed end facing out, then slide on the bush **(see illustrations 33.42c and b)**. Using a suitably sized driver or deep socket, drive the bush all the way on **(see illustration)**.

60 Slide on the 2nd/3rd gear shift sleeve, the green needle bearing and the 3rd gear pinion **(see illustrations 33.41b, 41a and 40c)**.

61 Install the shim with its tapered face facing out **(see illustration)**. Press the rear bearing onto the end of the shaft.

62 The assembled output shaft should look like this **(see illustration)**. Measure the total assembled length of the output shaft and compare the result with the specification at the beginning of this Chapter. If the length is too great, pull off the rear bearing and fit a thinner shim to correct it. There are 29 thicknesses of

33.59 Drive the bush all the way on

33.61 Fit the shim with the tapered face (arrowed) facing out

33.62 Assembled output shaft – measure the assembled length between the points shown

33.63 Measuring the width of the circlip groove

shim available, from 1.8 to 2.5 mm thickness – see a BMW dealer for details.

63 When the total assembled length is correct and the bearing is fully installed, measure the width of the circlip groove on the end of the shaft with a feeler gauge and fit the appropriate sized new circlip **(see illustration)**. Three thicknesses of circlip are available, from 1.1 to 1.3 mm in thickness – see a BMW dealer for details.

Installation

64 Installation is the reverse of removal, noting the following:
● Ensure that the gearbox end cover is supported securely.
● Lay the assembled shafts in the correct order **(see illustration 33.4b)**.
● Don't forget to install the 2nd/3rd gear selector fork in its shift sleeve on the transmission output shaft **(see illustration 33.4a)**.

● Heat the gearbox end cover around the locations for the shaft bearings – BMW suggest an installation temperature between 90°C to 100°C.
● Install the transmission shafts as an assembly.
● Check that the relative positions of the three transmission shafts is as noted on removal **(see illustration 33.2)**.
● Generously lubricate all the components with clean gearbox oil (see Chapter 1).
● Install the selector drum and forks (see Section 31).
● Don't forget to renew the transmission input and output shaft oil seals (see Section 30).

34 Running-in procedure

1 Make sure the engine and gearbox oil levels are correct (see *Pre-ride checks* and Chapter 1).
2 Check that the kill switch is in the RUN position and the gearbox is in neutral, then turn the ignition switch ON
3 Start the engine and allow it to run until it reaches operating temperature.

 Warning: If the oil pressure indicator light doesn't go off, or it comes on while the engine is running, stop the engine immediately.

4 If a lubrication failure is suspected, stop the engine immediately and try to find the cause. If an engine is run without the oil circulating,

even for a short period of time, severe damage will occur.
5 Check carefully for oil leaks and make sure the transmission and controls, especially the brakes, function properly before road testing the machine.
6 On machines fitted with ABS, if any part of the brake system has been disconnected, the system must be topped-up and bled by a BMW dealer using a BMW diagnostic tester – this is essential to restore brake operation.
7 Treat the machine gently for the first few miles to make sure oil has circulated throughout the engine and any new parts installed have started to seat.
8 Extra care is necessary if new pistons, rings or bearing shells have been fitted. If this is the case, the bike will have to be run in as when new. This means greater use of the transmission and a restraining hand on the throttle until at least 600 miles (1000 km) have been covered.
9 Upon completion of the road test, and after the engine has cooled down completely, recheck the valve clearances (see Chapter 1) and check the engine and gearbox oil levels (see *Pre-ride checks* and Chapter 1).
10 BMW advise that the engine should not exceed 4000 rpm during the running-in period. There's no point in keeping to any set speed limit – the main idea is to keep from labouring the engine and to gradually increase performance, varying the throttle position, up to the 600 mile (1000 km) mark. Experience is the best guide, since it's easy to tell when an engine is running freely.

Chapter 3
Engine management systems

Contents

Degrees of difficulty

Easy, suitable for novice with little experience	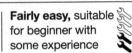	Fairly easy, suitable for beginner with some experience		Fairly difficult, suitable for competent DIY mechanic		Difficult, suitable for experienced DIY mechanic		Very difficult, suitable for expert DIY or professional	

Specifications

Fuel

Grade
R1200 GS	Unleaded, minimum 95 RON (Research Octane Number)
R1200 RT, ST, S and R	Unleaded, minimum 98 RON (Research Octane Number)

Tank capacity
R1200 GS	20 litres
R1200 GS Adventure	33 litres
R1200 RT	27 litres
R1200 ST	21 litres
R1200 S	17 litres
R1200 R	18 litres

Quantity remaining when level warning light comes on
R1200 R	3 litres
All other models	4 litres

Throttle bodies

Internal diameter
R1200 S	45 mm
All other models	42 mm
Idle speed	see Chapter 1

General information

Spark plugs and gaps	See Chapter 1

Ignition HT coils

Primary winding resistance	0.87 ohms
Secondary winding resistance	6 K-ohms

Torque settings

Exhaust system
  Silencer rear mounting bolt
    R1200 S . . . . 12 Nm
    All other models . . . . 19 Nm
  Silencer clamp bolt. . . . . 55 Nm
  Downpipe assembly clamp bolts . . . . 8 Nm
  Downpipe manifold nuts. . . . . 21 Nm
  Oxygen sensors . . . . 45 Nm
Fuel tank bolt
  R1200 GS and ST . . . . 19 Nm
  R1200 S and RT . . . . 16 Nm
  R1200 R . . . . 22 Nm
Fuel pump retaining ring. . . . . 35 Nm
Fuel injector mounting screws . . . . 5 Nm
Intake manifold bolts . . . . 8 Nm
Sensors
  Camshaft position sensor screw . . . . 8 Nm
  Crankshaft position sensor screw . . . . 8 Nm
  Cylinder head temperature sensor . . . . 10 Nm
  Gear position sensor . . . . 9 Nm
  Knock sensor bolt. . . . . 19 Nm
  Engine oil temperature sensor . . . . 30 Nm
  Engine oil level sensor . . . . 9 Nm

1 General information and precautions

General information

All models covered in this manual are fitted with BMW's own digital engine management system (BMS-K) which monitors, controls and co-ordinates both the fuel and ignition system functions.

The system is operated by the engine control unit, or ECU. A second unit, the central electronics unit, is responsible for monitoring and control of all other electrical systems such as lighting, switches and accessories. The two units are linked for such functions as starting and engine immobilisation.

The ECU uses engine speed and throttle valve position as the basis for determining optimum engine operation. Additional data, supplied by temperature sensors, oil pressure, gear position and knock sensors, and exhaust gas analysers, when combined with control maps and correction values embedded within the ECU, fine tune injection volume and ignition timing to meet the engine's requirements in any given circumstance.

The engine management system has in-built diagnostic functions which record and store all data should a fault occur. If this happens, the engine warning light in the instrument cluster illuminates and, unless the fault is serious, the engine runs in emergency 'limp home' mode. Otherwise, the engine will stop. BMW advise that in 'limp home' mode, full engine power may not be available and the machine should be ridden with this in mind. Have the machine checked by a BMW dealer – recorded faults can then be analysed using the BMW diagnostic tester and remedial action taken.

Because of their nature, individual system components cannot be repaired. Once the faulty component has been isolated, the only cure is to replace the part with a new one. Keep in mind that most electrical parts, once purchased, cannot be returned. To avoid unnecessary expense, make very sure the faulty component has been positively identified before buying a new part.

Fuel system

The fuel system consists of the fuel tank, fuel pump and filter, fuel hoses and pressure regulator, throttle bodies, fuel injectors and throttle control cables, and the air intake system.

The fuel pump is housed inside the tank. The fuel filter is integral with the pump on all models except the R1200 ST and R which have an external filter. The low fuel warning circuit is operated by a level sensor inside the tank.

There is an injector for each cylinder, housed in the throttle body. Cold starting, warm-up and engine idle speed are controlled by the ECU acting on information sent by the engine and intake air temperature sensors – there is no manual method (i.e. a choke) for assisting cold starting.

Information on fuel level is provided by a level sensor in the tank which is linked to a low fuel level warning light in the instrument cluster. The tripmeter will calculate the range available on the remaining fuel and present this information on the multi-function panel in the instrument cluster.

The exhaust system is a two-into-one design, incorporating a catalytic converter and oxygen sensors.

 Warning: Petrol (gasoline) is extremely flammable, so take extra precautions when you work on any part of the fuel system. Don't smoke or allow open flames or bare light bulbs near the work area, and don't work in a garage where a natural gas-type appliance is present. If you spill any fuel on your skin, rinse it off immediately with soap and water. When you perform any kind of work on the fuel system, wear safety glasses and have a fire extinguisher suitable for a class B type fire (flammable liquids) on hand.

Ignition system

The ignition system, due to its lack of mechanical parts, is totally maintenance free.

On all models, the HT coil for each spark plug (there are two per cylinder) is incorporated in the spark plug cap. The system incorporates ignition advance controlled by the ECU, which reacts to the information sent to it from the various sensors to provide the sparks at the optimum time – during low speed engine operation, the primary and secondary plugs fire independently of each other to ensure maximum fuel burn efficiency.

Knock sensors located on both cylinders allow the ECU to adjust ignition timing to protect the engine from detonation due to high operating temperatures or poor quality fuel.

The system incorporates a safety interlock circuit which prevents the engine from being started with the side stand down unless the gearbox is in neutral. The interlock circuit will also cut the ignition if the side stand is put down whilst the engine is running and in gear, or if a gear is selected whilst the engine is running and the side stand is down.

 Warning: The very high output of the engine management system means that it can be very dangerous or even fatal to touch live components or terminals of any part of the system while in operation. Take care not to touch any part of the system when the engine is running, or even with it stopped and the ignition ON. Before working on an electrical component, make sure that the ignition switch is OFF, then disconnect the

2.3a Disconnect the fuel return hose

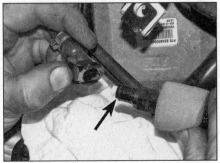

2.3b Note the O-ring (arrowed) on the hose union

2.4a Note the routing of the breather and drain hoses . . .

2.4b . . . and release them from the clips (arrowed)

battery negative lead (-ve) and insulate it away from the battery terminal.

Precautions

Always perform fuel-related procedures in a well-ventilated area to prevent a build-up of fumes.

Never work in a building containing a gas appliance with a pilot light, or any other form of naked flame. Ensure that there are no naked light bulbs or any sources of flame or sparks nearby.

Do not smoke (or allow anyone else to smoke) while in the vicinity of petrol (gasoline) or of components containing it. Remember the possible presence of vapour from these sources and move well clear before smoking.

Check all electrical equipment belonging to the house, garage or workshop where work is being undertaken (see the Safety first! section of this manual). Remember that certain electrical appliances such as drills, cutters etc. create sparks in the normal course of operation and must not be used near petrol (gasoline) or any component containing it. Again, remember the possible presence of fumes before using electrical equipment.

Always mop up any spilt fuel and safely dispose of the rag used.

Any stored fuel that is drained off during servicing work must be kept in sealed containers that are suitable for holding petrol (gasoline), and clearly marked as such; the containers themselves should be kept in a safe place. Note that this last point applies equally to the fuel tank if it is removed from the machine; also remember to keep its filler cap closed at all times.

Read the Safety first! section of this manual carefully before starting work.

Owners of machines used in the US, particularly California, should note that their machines must comply at all times with Federal or State legislation governing the permissible levels of noise and of pollutants such as unburnt hydrocarbons, carbon monoxide etc. that can be emitted by those machines. All vehicles offered for sale must comply with legislation in force at the date of manufacture and must not subsequently be altered in any way which will affect their emission of noise or of pollutants.

In practice, this means that adjustments may not be made to any part of the fuel, ignition or exhaust systems by anyone who is not authorised or mechanically qualified to do so, or who does not have the tools, equipment and data necessary to properly carry out the task. Also if any part of these systems is to be replaced it must be replaced with only genuine BMW components or by components which are approved under the relevant legislation. The machine must never be used with any part of these systems removed, modified or damaged.

2 Fuel tank

⚠ *Warning: Refer to the precautions given in Section 1 before starting work.*

R1200 GS

1 Remove the seats (see Chapter 6).

2 Remove the frame side panels and the fairing side panels, then remove the fuel tank side panels (see Chapter 6).

3 Release the clip securing the union on the fuel return hose on the right-hand side and disconnect the hose, being prepared to catch any residual fuel **(see illustration)**. Note the location of the O-ring on the union **(see illustration)**.

4 Feed the fuel tank breather and drain hoses up from the guide behind the engine unit on the left-hand side and release them from the clips on the right-hand side **(see illustrations)**. Note the routing of the hoses.

5 Lift off the fuel pump cover **(see illustration)**. Release the tabs securing the wiring connectors for the fuel pump and fuel level sensor and disconnect the connectors **(see illustrations)**.

6 Release the clip securing the fuel delivery hose union and disconnect the hose from the

2.5a Lift off the fuel pump cover . . .

2.5b . . . then release the tabs . . .

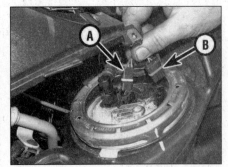

2.5c . . . and disconnect the fuel pump (A) and fuel level sender (B) wiring connectors

2.6 Disconnect the fuel delivery hose

2.7 Remove the fuel filler cap assembly

2.8a Note the right-hand fairing side panel bracket (arrowed)

2.8b Location of the left-hand fairing side panel bracket (arrowed)

2.9 Draw the tank back and lift it off

2.10a Check the condition of the fuel tank mounting bushes (arrowed)

tank **(see illustration)**. Note the location of the O-ring on the union.

7 On GS Adventure models, undo the screws securing the tank centre panel from the surrounding bodywork; if required, undo the screws securing the fuel filler cap assembly **(see illustration)**, remove the assembly and lift off the tank centre panel (see Chapter 6). Temporarily install the fuel filler cap. Remove the air intake duct (see Chapter 1, Section 10).

8 Note the location of the fairing side panel bracket on the right-hand side, then undo the bolts securing the left and right-hand sides of the fuel tank, noting the location of the washers **(see illustration)**. The fairing side panel bracket on the left-hand side is a press fit in the fuel tank mounting hole **(see illustration)**.

9 Make sure the fuel filler cap is secure, then draw the tank back off the front mounting bushes and lift it off **(see illustration)**.

10 Installation is the reverse of removal, noting the following:
● Check the condition of the front mounting bushes and renew them if they are damaged or deteriorated **(see illustration)**.
● Ensure that the left-hand fairing side panel bracket is in place **(see illustration)**.
● Ensure that the fuel delivery and return hoses are correctly routed – renew the union O-rings if they are flattened or cracked.
● Ensure that the fuel hose unions are firmly clipped together.
● Ensure that the breather and drain hoses are clipped in position and not trapped underneath the tank **(see illustration)**.
● Check the hose unions for leaks before installing the bodywork.
● Align the right-hand fairing side panel bracket with the panel.

● Tighten the mounting bolts to the torque setting specified at the beginning of this Chapter.

R1200 RT

11 Remove the seats (see Chapter 6).
12 Remove the front fairing side panels and the main fairing side panels (see Chapter 6).
13 Remove the tank centre panel (see Chapter 6). Remove the air intake duct (see Chapter 1, Section 10).
14 Disconnect the breather hose from the front of the fuel tank.
15 Release the clip securing the fuel delivery hose union and disconnect the hose from the tank **(see illustration)**. Note the location of the O-ring on the union.
16 Release the clip securing the union on the fuel return hose and disconnect the hose,

2.10b Note how the fairing bracket locates in the fuel tank mounting (arrowed)

2.10c Ensure that the hoses (arrowed) are not trapped underneath the fuel tank

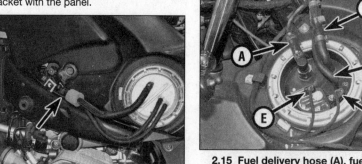

2.15 Fuel delivery hose (A), fuel return hose (B), fuel tank drain hose (C), fuel level sensor connector (D) and fuel pump connector (E) – R1200 RT

2.19 Location of left-hand fuel tank mounting bolt (arrowed)

2.21 Location of right-hand fuel tank mounting bush (arrowed)

2.27 Disconnect the fuel delivery hose (arrowed) from the tank – R1200 ST

being prepared to catch any residual fuel **(see illustration 2.15)**. Note the location of the O-ring on the union.

17 Disconnect the drain hose **(see illustration 2.15)**.

18 Release the tabs securing the wiring connectors for the fuel level sensor and the fuel pump and disconnect the connectors **(see illustration 2.15)**. Undo the screws securing the wiring guides to the fuel tank.

19 Undo the bolts securing the left and right-hand sides of the fuel tank, noting the location of the washers **(see illustration)**.

20 Make sure the fuel filler cap is secure and check that the wiring and hoses are clear of the tank.

21 Draw the tank back off the front mounting bushes and lift it off **(see illustration)**.

22 Installation is the reverse of removal, noting the points in Step 10, where applicable.

R1200 ST

23 Remove the seats (see Chapter 6).

24 Remove the fairing side panels (see Chapter 6).

25 Remove the fairing trim panels (see Chapter 6).

26 Disconnect the breather hose from the front of the fuel tank.

27 Release the clip securing the fuel delivery hose union and disconnect the hose from the tank **(see illustration)**. Note the location of the O-ring on the union.

28 Release the clip securing the union on

the fuel return hose and disconnect the hose, being prepared to catch any residual fuel **(see illustration)**. Note the location of the O-ring on the union.

29 Disconnect the drain hose.

30 Release the tabs securing the wiring connectors for the fuel level sensor and the fuel pump and disconnect the connectors **(see illustration 2.28)**.

31 Undo the bolts securing the left and right-hand sides of the fuel tank, noting the location of the washers and rubber bushes **(see illustration)**.

32 Make sure the fuel filler cap is secure and check that the wiring and hoses are clear of the tank.

33 Draw the tank back off the front mounting bushes and lift it off.

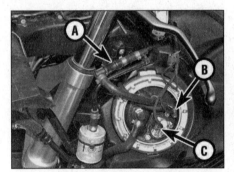

2.28 Fuel return hose (A), fuel level sensor connector (B) and fuel pump connector (C)

34 Installation is the reverse of removal, noting the points in Step 10, where applicable.

R1200 S

35 Remove the rider's seat (see Chapter 6).

36 Remove the tank/fairing side panels (see Chapter 6).

37 Remove the air intake duct (see Chapter 1, Section 10).

38 Undo the screws securing the fuel filler cap assembly and remove the assembly **(see illustrations)**. Lift off the tank centre panel (see Chapter 6).

39 Disconnect the breather hose and the drain hose from the fuel filler neck **(see illustration)**.

40 Release the clip securing the fuel delivery hose union and disconnect the hose from the

2.31 Location of right-hand fuel tank mounting bolt (arrowed)

2.38a Undo the screws (arrowed) . . .

2.38b . . . and remove the fuel filler cap

2.39 Disconnect the hoses from the fuel filler neck

2.40 Release the clip (arrowed) securing the fuel delivery hose union

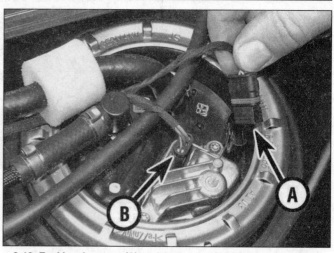

2.42 Fuel level sensor (A) and fuel pump (B) wiring connectors

tank **(see illustration)**. Note the location of the O-ring on the union.

41 Release the clip securing the union on the fuel return hose and disconnect the hose, being prepared to catch any residual fuel. Note the location of the O-ring on the union.

42 Release the tabs securing the wiring connectors for the fuel level sensor and the fuel pump and disconnect the connectors **(see illustration)**.

43 Undo the bolts securing the left and right-hand sides of the fuel tank, noting the

location of the washers and spacers **(see illustrations)**.

44 Make sure the fuel filler cap is secure, then draw the tank back off the front mounting bushes and lift it off **(see illustration)**.

45 Installation is the reverse of removal, noting the points in Step 10, where applicable.

R1200 R

46 Remove the seat and the sidepanels from each side (see Chapter 6).

47 Free the fuel pump wiring connector from its clip on the left side of the frame and disconnect it **(see illustration)**.

48 Remove the black plastic trim panel from the front of the tank. It is retained to the tank by two screws on each side **(see illustration)**. Note that the throttle cable must be freed from its grommet in the trim panel.

49 Disconnect the breather hose and the drain hose from the unions on the right inner side of the tank – they are a push fit **(see illustration)**. Label the hoses to ensure you refit them to the correct union.

50 Remove the bolt and washer from the left side of the tank, then lift the tank at the rear sufficiently to gain access to the fuel lines (see

2.43a Location of right-hand fuel tank mounting bolt (arrowed)

2.43b Note the washer and spacer on each bolt

2.44 Location of front fuel tank mounting bush (arrowed)

2.47 Separate the fuel pump wiring connector

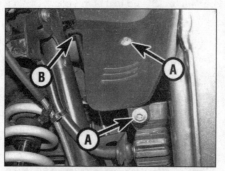

2.48 Trim is retained by two screws (A) on each side. Throttle cable (B) locates in trim panel slot

2.49 Disconnect breather and drain hoses at this point

2.50 Fuel tank mounting bolt

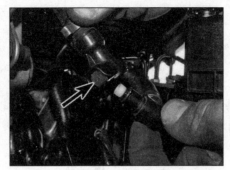
2.51 Press in the fuel line coupling clip (arrowed) to release it

2.52 Ensure tank locates over mounting rubbers at the front

illustration). It's handy to have an assistant hold the tank at this stage, especially if it's quite full.

51 Release the two quick-release couplings by pressing in their clips and disconnect the fuel lines (see illustration). There should only be slight fuel spillage, but have some rag on hand to mop it up. Now ease the tank rearwards off its front mounting bushes and lift it off.

52 Installation is the reverse of removal, noting the following points:
- Check the condition of the front mounting rubbers and renew them if they are damaged or deteriorated (see illustration).
- Ensure that the fuel delivery and return hoses are correctly routed – renew the union O-rings if they are flattened or cracked.
- Ensure that the fuel couplings are firmly clipped together.
- Ensure that the breather and drain hoses are clipped in position and not trapped underneath the tank.
- Check the hose unions for leaks before installing the bodywork.

Fuel tank cleaning and repair - all models

53 All repairs to the fuel tank should be carried out by a professional who has experience in this critical and potentially dangerous work. Even after cleaning and flushing of the fuel system, explosive fumes can remain and ignite during repair of the tank. If sending the tank for repair, first remove the fuel pump and filter assembly from inside the tank.

54 If the fuel tank is removed from the bike, it should not be placed in an area where sparks or open flames could ignite the fumes coming out of the tank. Be especially careful inside garages where a natural gas-type appliance is located, because the pilot light could cause an explosion.

3 Evaporative emission control system – US models

1 When the engine is stopped, fuel vapour from the tank vents into a cylindrical charcoal filter, rather than venting directly into the atmosphere as on other market models. A regeneration valve, operated by the ECU, directs fuel vapours stored in the canister back into the fuel system when the engine is running. Apart from periodic checks of the hoses, the system is essentially maintenance-free.

R1200GS

2 The regeneration valve is located under the fuel tank on the left-hand side of the air filter housing – remove the fuel tank as described in the previous section for access. The charcoal filter is mounted to the rear sub-frame on the left-hand side and is easily assessable.

R1200RT and ST

3 The regeneration valve and charcoal filter are located at the front of the machine on the right-hand side. On RT models, remove the fairing upper right-hand side panel for access. On ST models, remove the cockpit trim panel and the fairing side panel on that side for full access.

R1200S

4 The regeneration valve is mounted on the front sub-frame, beneath the fairing/fuel tank right-hand side panel (see Chapter 6, Section 5 for removal details). The charcoal filter is at the front of the machine, between the fork legs.

R1200R

5 The regeneration valve is mouned on the left-hand side of the front sub-frame. The charcoal filter is at the front of the machine, between the fork legs.

4 Fuel filter and pump

⚠ **Warning: Refer to the precautions given in Section 1 before starting work.**

Note: *Cleaning the fuel filter is not a service item. However, if fuel delivery problems are suspected, the filter should be inspected. A clogged in-line filter on R1200 ST and R models will result in a loss of fuel pressure.*

1 The fuel pump is located inside the fuel tank on the left-hand side. The pump incorporates the fuel level sensor (see Chapter 7) and the fuel filter. On R1200 ST and R models, an additional external in-line filter is fitted.

2 On R1200 GS models, a balance pump is located in the right-hand side of the tank. The balance pump transfers fuel from the right to the left-hand side of the tank. No filter is fitted to the balance pump.

3 Before attempting to unscrew the pump from the tank, any fuel should be emptied from the tank using a commercially available pump.

Fuel filter

4 Refer to Section 2 and remove the body panels applicable to your machine to access the pump.

RS1200 ST and R

5 The external in-line filter is a sealed unit. If it is clogged, fit a new one.

6 Note the direction of fuel flow arrow on the filter body, then cut the cable tie(s) securing the filter (see illustrations). Release the clips securing the hoses to the filter and detach the

4.6a Direction of fuel flow is marked (arrowed) on the filter body – ST

4.6b Fuel filter location on R1200 R

4.10a Fuel pump is retained by large diameter ring (arrowed)

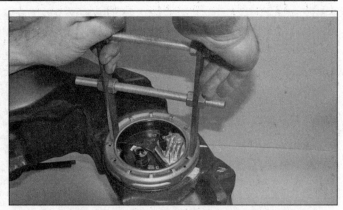

4.10b Set-up for unscrewing the retaining ring

4.11 Withdraw the pump assembly from the tank

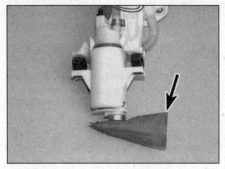

4.12 Location of the fuel filter (arrowed)

4.15 Inspect the seal for damage

hoses from the filter unions, being prepared to catch any residual fuel.

7 Inspect the hoses for deterioration or damage and renew them if necessary. If the hose clips are corroded or deformed, fit new clips.

8 Make sure that the clips are on the hoses, then push the hoses all the way onto the filter unions – make sure that the direction of fuel flow arrow is pointing away from the tank. Secure the hoses with the clips.

All other models

9 Make sure the ignition is switched OFF. To access the filter, first disconnect the fuel hose unions and wiring connectors for the fuel level sender and the fuel pump (see Section 2). Where fitted, disconnect the breather/drain hose from the back of the pump.

10 Unscrew the pump retaining ring **(see illustration)**. BMW provide a special tool to do this (Part No. 16 1 021). Alternatively, use the set-up shown, taking care not to damage the tabs on the ring **(see illustration)**.

11 Lift off the ring, then withdraw the pump assembly from the tank, noting which way round it is fitted **(see illustration)**. Take care not to damage the arm of the fuel level sensor float.

12 The filter is located on the lower end of the pump assembly – if required, twist the filter neck to remove it **(see illustration)**.

13 Allow the filter element to dry, they use a soft brush to remove any dirt or sediment. If

the filter is heavily soiled, clean accumulated dirt out of the tank.

14 Inspect the filter element for splits and holes – if any damage is found, fit a new filter.

15 Installation is the reverse of removal, noting the following:
● Check the sealing ring for splits and deterioration and renew it if necessary **(see illustration)**.
● Ensure the pump assembly is installed the right way round.
● If a suitable tool is available, tighten the retaining ring to the torque setting specified at the beginning of this Chapter.
● Connect the wiring connectors and hoses as noted on removal.
● Part-fill the tank with fuel, then check that there are no leaks from the pump seal and hose union seals before installing the bodywork.

Fuel pump

16 Pump efficiency will be severely restricted if the filter is blocked. If the filter is good, test the pump as follows.

17 If not already done, follow the procedure in Steps 10 and 11 to remove the pump from the fuel tank. On R1200 R models, prior to unscrewing the pump retaining ring disconnect the wiring plugs for the fuel level sensor and the fuel pump, then disconnect the fuel hoses from the pump base **(see illustration)**.

18 Using a fully charged 12 volt battery and two insulated jumper wires, connect the positive (+ve)

terminal of the battery to the pump's positive terminal, and the negative (-ve) terminal of the battery to the pump's negative terminal. The pump should operate. If not, replace it with a new one.

19 Ensure that the terminals in the pump wiring connector are clean, then connect the connector and turn the ignition ON. The pump should operate. If not, inspect the wiring and terminals for physical damage or loose or corroded connections. Turn the ignition OFF when the test is complete.

20 If the pump operates but is thought to be delivering an insufficient amount of fuel, check that the fuel tank breather hose is not obstructed, pinched or trapped.

21 If all appears to be good, have the fuel pump's output pressure, and the operation

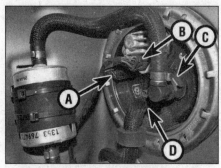

4.17 Level sensor wiring (A), pump wiring (B), delivery hose (C) and return hose (D) – R1200 R

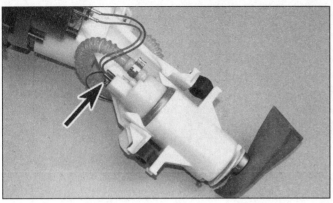

4.22 Fuel pump wiring connector (arrowed)

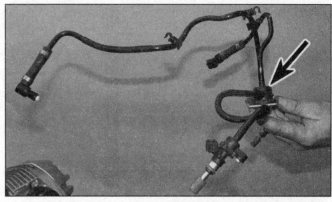

5.1 Fuel hose and pressure regulator (arrowed) assembly

of the fuel pressure regulator (see Section 5), checked by a BMW dealer.

22 To renew the pump, first disconnect the wiring connector **(see illustration)**.

23 The pump is secured to the assembly by three rubber bushes - prise the bushes off their lugs and ease the pump off the bottom of the assembly.

24 Installation is the reverse of removal, noting the following:

● Check the condition of the rubber bushes and renew them if necessary.

● Ensure that the terminals in the wiring connector are good.

5 Fuel hoses and pressure regulator

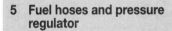

⚠️ **Warning: Refer to the precautions given in Section 1 before starting work.**

1 The fuel hoses, between the tank unions and the fuel injectors, are part of a one-piece distribution assembly that incorporates the fuel pressure regulator **(see illustration)**.

2 The quick-release unions on the delivery and return hoses are secured to the main assembly by clips and short sections of flexible hose. Whenever the quick-release unions are disconnected, check the condition of the flexible hose and renew the hose and hose clips if there are signs of deterioration, cracking or fuel leakage.

3 The pressure regulator monitors fuel supply from the pump to the injectors and maintains delivery at a constant pressure. At high engine speeds, the regulator opens to allow the injectors to draw more fuel from the system; at low engine speeds, the regulator closes and diverts excess fuel back into the tank via the return hose. This prevents any risk of the pump overloading.

4 BMW provide no test data or procedure for checking the regulator. If a known good regulator is available, substitute that for the suspect one and see if the fault is cured.

5 To remove the fuel distribution assembly, first remove the fuel tank (see Section 2).

6 Release the clips securing the fuel hoses to

5.6 Clip (arrowed) secures fuel hose to the injector

the fuel injectors **(see illustration)**.

7 Unclip the assembly from the front of the air filter housing **(see illustration)**. On machines fitted with ABS, unclip the fuel hoses from the brake hoses.

8 Carefully ease the assembly off the bike, noting the routing of the fuel hoses.

9 The pressure regulator is secured in its holder by a large U-clip – withdraw the clip and pull the regulator off, noting the location of the sealing O-ring. Discard the O-ring as a new one must be used.

10 Installation is the reverse of removal, noting the following:

● Install a new O-ring on the pressure regulator.

● Check that there are no leaks from the pressure regulator and hose union seals before installing the bodywork.

6.3a Air ducts are secured by two clamps (arrowed)

5.7 Release the pressure regulator (arrowed) from its clip

6 Throttle bodies

⚠️ **Warning: Refer to the precautions given in Section 1 before starting work.**

Removal

1 Remove the frame side panels and the fairing side panels to gain access to the throttle bodies (see Chapter 6).

2 Make sure the ignition is switched OFF.

3 Release the clamps securing the air ducts to the air filter housing and the throttle bodies **(see illustration)**. If available, use special hose clamp pliers to release the clamps without damaging them **(see illustration)**. Pull

6.3b Using hose clamp pliers to release the clamps

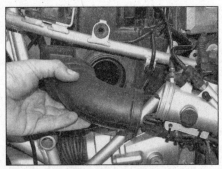

6.3c Note how the air ducts fit . . .

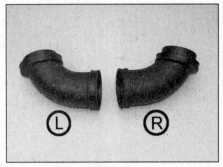

6.3d . . . and if necessary mark them to aid reassembly

6.4 Release the fuel injector wiring connector

the air ducts off carefully, noting which way round they fit – the ducts should be marked L (left) and R (right), if not mark them to aid reassembly **(see illustrations)**.

4 Working on one throttle body at a time, release the clip securing the fuel injector wiring connector and disconnect the connector **(see illustration)**.

5 Release the clip securing the idle speed actuator connector and disconnect the connector **(see illustration)**.
6 Undo the screw securing the fuel injector, then carefully withdraw the injector from the throttle body **(see illustrations)**. Note the location of the O-ring on the injector – a new O-ring must be fitted on reassembly. Cover the end of the injector to prevent it getting damaged **(see illustration)**.
7 Cut the cable ties securing the wiring to the underside of the throttle body **(see illustration)**.
8 On the left-hand throttle body, note the location of the security tab on the throttle position sensor wiring connector **(see illustration)**. Prise out the tab, then release the clip securing the connector and disconnect it **(see illustrations)**.

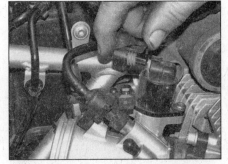

6.5 Disconnect the idle speed actuator

6.6a Undo the screw (arrowed) . . .

6.6b . . . and withdraw the injector

6.6c Note the O-ring. Cover the end of the injector to avoid damage

6.7 Wiring is secured by cable ties (arrowed)

6.8a Location of the security tab (arrowed)

6.8b Prise out the tab . . .

6.8c . . . and disconnect the connector

6.9a Release the clamp . . .

6.9b . . . and ease the throttle body off

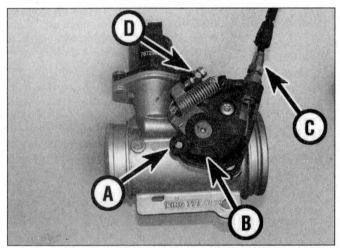

6.11 Disconnect the inner cable end (A) from the cam (B). Note the cable adjuster (C) and cam stop screw (D)

6.13 Intake manifolds are secured by three bolts (arrowed)

9 Release the clamp securing the throttle body to the intake manifold and ease the throttle body off (see illustrations). Stuff clean rag into the intake manifold to prevent anything falling inside.

10 If required, the left and right-hand throttle bodies and the cable splitter can be displaced or removed as an assembly (see Section 8).

11 Displace the cover from the throttle valve actuating mechanism (see illustration). Rotate the throttle cam to the fully open position and detach the end of the inner cable from the cam, then unclip the cable adjuster from the mechanism backplate. Do not disturb the setting of the throttle cam stop screw.

12 If required, undo the screws securing the idle speed actuator and remove the actuator. Caution: Do not remove the throttle position sensor from the left-hand throttle body as its position is pre-set. If it is disturbed, its position will have to be reset by a BMW dealer using the BMW diagnostic tester.

Inspection

13 Inspect the throttle bodies and air ducts

for cracks or any other damage which may result in air leakage and renew any components as necessary. The joints between the intake manifolds and the cylinder heads are sealed with O-rings. If the manifolds are removed, fit new O-rings on installation and tighten the manifold bolts to the torque setting specified at the beginning of this Chapter (see illustration).

14 Check that the throttle butterfly moves smoothly and freely in the body, and make sure that the inside of the body is completely clean.

15 Check that the throttle actuating cam moves smoothly and freely, taking into account spring pressure. Clean any dirt from around the cam.

16 Check the condition of the clamps for the air ducts and the throttle bodies – if the clamps were damaged during removal, renew them.

Installation

17 Installation is the reverse of removal, noting the following:

● Install the throttle cable on the actuating cam and secure the actuating mechanism cover before installing the throttle body.

● Fit the throttle body clamp loosely over the intake manifold, then align the tab on the throttle body with the notch in the manifold and press the throttle body all the way in (see illustration).

● Secure the throttle body clamps with the

6.17a Tab (arrowed) must align with notch in the manifold

6.17b Make sure the clamps are tightened securely

6.17c Fit new O-rings on the injectors

correct clamp pliers to avoid damage (see illustration).
● Check the operation of the throttle cables and adjust them if necessary (see Chapter 1).
● Install new O-rings on the injectors (see illustration).
● Tighten the injector screws to the torque setting specified at the beginning of this Chapter.
● Check the throttle synchronisation and adjust as necessary (see Chapter 1).

7 Fuel injectors

> ⚠ Warning: Refer to the precautions given in Section 1 before starting work.

Removal

1 Remove the frame side panels and the fairing side panels to gain access to the throttle bodies (see Chapter 6).
2 Make sure the ignition is switched OFF.
3 Release the clip securing the fuel injector wiring connector and disconnect the connector (see illustration).
4 Undo the screw securing the fuel injector,

then carefully withdraw the injector from the throttle body (see illustrations 6.6a and b).
5 Release the clip securing the fuel hose connector and disconnect the injector from the connector, being prepared to catch any residual fuel (see illustration).
6 Note the location of the two O-rings on the injector body, then carefully ease them off – new O-rings must be fitted on reassembly (see illustrations).
7 Modern fuels contain detergents which should keep the injectors clean and free of gum or varnish. If either injector is suspected of being blocked, flush it through with injector cleaner.

7.3 Disconnect the fuel injector wiring connector

Installation

8 Installation is the reverse of removal, noting the following:
● Install new O-rings on the injectors.
● Tighten the injector screws to the torque setting specified at the beginning of this Chapter.
● Ensure that the fuel hose connections are secure.
● Check the fuel hose unions for leaks before installing the bodywork.

8 Throttle cables

1 Three separate cables are fitted – the cable from the throttle twistgrip goes into a splitter located on the front of the air filter housing, then two cables go from the splitter to the throttle bodies, one on either side. All three cables are available individually.

Removal

2 The throttle cables, splitter and throttle bodies must be removed as an assembly. Individual cables can then be removed for inspection, lubrication and renewal.
3 Remove the fuel tank (see Section 2).
4 Displace the throttle bodies (see Section 6).

7.5 Disconnect the fuel hose connector

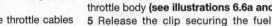

7.6a Note the location of the O-rings (arrowed) . . .

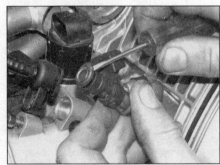

7.6b . . . ease them off carefully

8.5a Release the clip securing the throttle cable splitter

8.5b Secure the throttle bodies and splitter to avoid damage

8.6 Throttle cable adjuster lock ring (arrowed)

8.7 Screw (arrowed) secures lower half of twistgrip housing – R1200 RT models

8.8a Remove the top half of the twistgrip housing

8.8b Cable elbow is secured by lock ring (arrowed)

5 Release the clip securing the cable splitter to the air filter housing and displace the splitter (see illustration). Temporarily secure the throttle bodies and the splitter on the machine (see illustration).
6 Loosen the lock ring on the adjuster at the twistgrip end of the cable and turn the adjuster all the way in to create slack in the cable (see illustration).
7 On R1200 RT models, undo the screw securing the lower half of the twistgrip housing and lift the lower half off (see illustration). Disconnect the inner cable end from the throttle pulley, then remove the cable guide and pull the cable out of the housing.
8 On all other models, undo the screw

securing the top half of the twistgrip housing and lift the top half off (see illustration). Disconnect the inner cable end from the throttle pulley. Undo the lock ring securing the cable elbow in the lower half of the housing (see illustration). Draw the cable out of the housing.
9 Feed the cable back to the splitter, noting its routing (see illustration). Release the cable from any clips or ties.
10 Remove the cables, splitter and throttle bodies from the machine and lay them on a clean surface (see illustration). Carefully unclip the cover on the splitter and note the location of the three cables on the splitter pulley (see illustration).

8.9 Note any guides (arrowed) that secure the cable

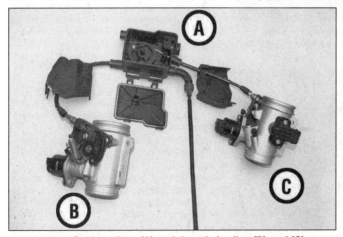

8.10a Cable splitter (A) and throttle bodies (B) and (C)

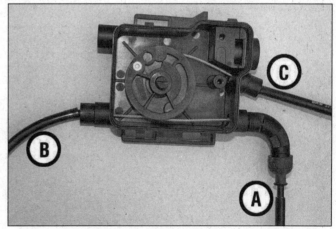

8.10b Main cable to twistgrip (A), cable to right-hand throttle body (B), cable to left-hand throttle body (C)

9.1 Loosen the silencer clamp bolt (arrowed)

9.2a Silencer to rear sub-frame bolt (arrowed)

9.2b Location of silencer clamp bolt (A) and support bolt (B) – R1200 RT

11 Detach the inner cable ends from the splitter pulley and withdraw the cables from the splitter housing. If necessary, mark the cables to ensure they are installed in their original positions.

12 Detach the end of each inner cable from the throttle body cams, then unclip the cable adjusters from the mechanism backplates **(see illustration 6.11)**.

Installation

13 Installation is the reverse of removal, noting the following:

● Install the cable onto the throttle bodies first.
● Install all three cables onto the splitter pulley. Adjust the cables between the splitter and the throttle bodies, then check the operation of the splitter.

● Follow the procedure in Section 6 to install the throttle bodies.
● Ensure that the cable to the handlebar twistgrip is correctly routed and secured with any clips or ties.
● On R1200 RT models, don't forget to install the cable guide in the twistgrip housing.
● On R1200 GS, ST, R and S models, tighten the lock ring securing the cable elbow securely.
● Check the throttle synchronisation and adjust as necessary (see Chapter 1).
● Adjust the throttle cables (see Chapter 1).

⚠ *Warning: Turn the handlebars all the way through their travel with the engine idling. Idle speed should not change. If it does, the cable may be routed incorrectly. Correct this condition before riding the bike.*

9 Exhaust system

⚠ *Warning: If the engine has been running the exhaust system will be very hot. Allow the system to cool before carrying out any work.*

Silencer

R1200 GS, RT, ST and R

1 Loosen the bolt on the clamp securing the silencer to the downpipe assembly **(see illustration)**.

2 Undo the bolt securing the silencer to the rear sub-frame, then support the silencer and withdraw the bolt **(see illustrations)**. Note the location of the washer, spacer and rubber bush on the bolt.

3 Draw the silencer off **(see illustration)**.

4 Installation is the reverse of removal, noting the following:

● Tighten the bolts to the torque settings specified at the beginning of this Chapter.
● Ensure that the rubber bush is in good condition and renew it if necessary.
● On R1200 RT models, check the gap between the silencer and the rear tyre. BMW specify a minimum of 15 mm. If necessary, loosen the silencer mounting clamp bolts and adjust the position of the clamp to achieve the correct gap.

R1200 S

5 Ensure the machine is securely supported in an upright position.

6 Remove the seat cowling (see Chapter 6).

7 Disconnect the wiring connector for the rear turn signals/number plate light assembly **(see illustration)**.

8 Disconnect the springs securing the silencer front pipe to the downpipe assembly **(see illustration)**.

9 Undo the two bolts securing the silencer to the rear sub-frame, then support the silencer and withdraw the bolts **(see illustration)**.

10 Draw the silencer off. If required, undo the screws securing the number plate bracket and turn signals assembly and remove the assembly (see Chapter 7).

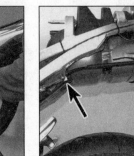

9.3 Draw the silencer off

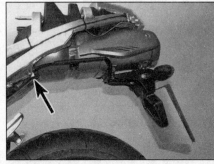

9.7 Wiring connector (arrowed) for the rear turn signals/number plate light assembly

9.8 Disconnect the springs (arrowed) on both sides of the downpipe

9.9 Silencer is secured by bolts (arrowed) underneath the passenger's seat

9.14 Disconnect the oxygen sensor wiring connectors

9.15a Undo the nuts (arrowed) . . .

9.15b . . . and draw the collar off the studs

11 Installation is the reverse of removal, noting the following:
● Fit the silencer front pipe onto the exhaust downpipe and install the two under-seat mounting bolts before fitting the springs.
● Tighten the bolts to the torque setting specified at the beginning of this Chapter.
● Ensure that the connector for the rear turn signals/number plate light assembly is secure.

Downpipe assembly

Removal

12 On R1200 RT models, to avoid damage, remove the fairing side panels (see Chapter 6).
13 On all models, remove the silencer (see above).
14 Disconnect the wiring connectors for the left and right-hand oxygen sensors **(see illustration)**.
15 Undo the nuts securing the downpipes to the cylinder heads, then draw the collars off the studs **(see illustrations)**.
16 Carefully manoeuvre the rear support bracket off the mounting on the back of the gearbox, then lower the assembly off the bike **(see illustrations)**.
17 Remove the old gaskets from the exhaust ports and discard them as new ones must be fitted. Clean any corrosion off the cylinder head studs with a wire brush.
18 If required, unscrew the oxygen sensors from the exhaust pipes (see Section 10).

Installation

19 Check that the rear support bracket is clamped securely in position. Check the condition of the bush in the bracket and renew

it if it is deformed or deteriorated – the bracket should be a firm push fit onto its mounting.
20 If removed, ensure the threads of the oxygen sensors are clean and lubricate them with a smear of high temperature assembly grease. If a suitable tool is available, tighten the oxygen sensors to the torque setting specified at the beginning of this Chapter.
21 Fit a new gasket into each exhaust port **(see illustration)**. Apply a smear of grease to the gaskets to keep them in place whilst fitting the downpipe if necessary. Lubricate the cylinder head studs with a smear of copper-based grease.
22 Manoeuvre the assembly into position – locate the rear support bracket on its mounting, then align the front of the downpipes with the exhaust ports and slide the collars onto the studs.
23 Install the nuts on the cylinder head studs and tighten them to the torque setting specified at the beginning of this Chapter.
24 Ensure that the wiring connectors for the left and right-hand oxygen sensors are secure **(see illustration)**.
25 Install the silencer.
26 Run the engine and check that there are no air leaks from the joints.
27 Install any body panels as required according to model (see Chapter 6).

---

10 Catalytic converter and oxygen sensors

 Warning: If the engine has been running the exhaust system will be very hot. Allow the system to cool before carrying out any work.

Catalytic converter

1 All models have a three-way catalytic converter located in the rear end of the exhaust downpipe assembly. The purpose of the catalytic converter is to minimise the amount of pollutants which escape into the atmosphere. Hot exhaust gasses pass through the flow channels in the converter which are coated with a precious metal catalyst. The catalyst reduces nitrous oxides into nitrogen and oxygen, and oxidises unburned harmful hydrocarbons and carbon monoxide into water and carbon

9.16a Manoeuvre the rear support bracket off the mounting (arrowed) . . .

9.16b . . . and lower the assembly off the bike

9.21 Fit new gaskets into the exhaust ports (arrowed)

9.24 Ensure the oxygen sensor wiring connectors are secure

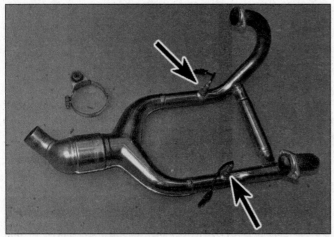

10.4 Location of the oxygen sensors (arrowed)

10.10 Lubricate the sensor threads with high temperature assembly grease before installation

dioxide. The efficiency of the catalyst is reduced if the flow channels become clogged or if the precious metal coating becomes covered with carbon, lead or oil.

2 The catalytic converter is simple in operation and requires no maintenance, although the following precautions should be noted.

● Always use unleaded fuel – the use of leaded fuel will destroy the converter.
● Do not use any fuel or oil additives.
● Keep the fuel and ignition systems in good order.
● Handle the downpipe assembly with care when it is off the machine - the catalyst is fragile.

Oxygen sensors

3 The oxygen sensors measure exhaust gas oxygen content and relay this information to the ECU. The ECU compares exhaust gas oxygen content with the oxygen content in the ambient air and, depending on whether the engine is running rich or lean, adjusts the fuel/air mixture accordingly.

4 The sensors are threaded into the left- and right-hand exhaust downpipes **(see illustration)**.

5 To remove the sensor, first disconnect the wiring connector **(see illustration 9.14)**.

6 Unscrew the sensor carefully to avoid damage to its tip. If the sensor threads are corroded, soak them with penetrating oil before proceeding.

7 Deposits on the sensor tip are an indication of poor engine running – light rust coloured deposits indicate lead contamination through the use of the wrong fuel, black or dark brown deposits are a sign that oil is getting into the combustion chamber through worn valve stem seals or piston rings.

8 A contaminated sensor will send an inaccurate signal to the ECU, which should, in turn, illuminate the engine warning light in the instrument cluster. Do not attempt to clean the sensor – if it is contaminated, a new one will have to be fitted.

9 No data is available for checking the oxygen

sensors individually – have the overall engine efficiency checked by a BMW dealer using the diagnostic tester.

10 Before installing the oxygen sensor, clean the threads and lubricate them with a smear of high temperature assembly grease **(see illustration)**. If a suitable tool is available, tighten the sensor to the torque setting specified at the beginning of this Chapter.

11 Ensure that the terminals in the wiring connector are clean and make sure that the connection is secure.

11 Ignition system checks

⚠️ *Warning: Refer to the Warning given in Section 1 before starting work.*

1 As no means of adjustment is available, any failure of the system can be traced to failure of a system component or a simple wiring fault. Of the two possibilities, the latter is by far the most likely. In the event of failure, check the system in a logical fashion, as described below. **Note:** *Before making any tests, check that the battery is in good condition and fully charged.*

2 Ignition faults can be divided into two categories, namely those where the ignition system has failed completely, and those which are due to a partial failure. The likely faults are listed below, starting with the most probable source of failure. Work through the list systematically, referring to the subsequent sections for full details of the necessary checks and tests, where information is available.

● Loose, corroded or damaged wiring connections, broken or shorted wiring between any of the component parts of the ignition system (see Chapter 7).
● Faulty spark plug, dirty, worn or corroded plug electrodes, or incorrect gap between electrodes (see Chapter 1).
● Faulty ignition HT cap/coil (see Section 12).

● Faulty ignition (main) switch or engine kill switch (see Chapter 7).
● Faulty clutch switch, gear position switch or sidestand switch (see Chapter 7).
● Faulty crankshaft position sensor or camshaft position sensor.
● Faulty engine control unit (ECU).

3 If the above checks don't reveal the cause of the problem, have the ignition system tested by a BMW dealer equipped with the diagnostic tester. The diagnostic tester permits full testing of the ignition system components and reads the ECU fault code memory.

12 Ignition HT cap/coils

⚠️ *Warning: Refer to the Warning given in Section 1 before starting work.*

1 Working on one cap/coil at a time, follow the procedure in Chapter 1, Section 11, disconnect the wiring connector and pull the cap/coil off the spark plug.

2 Ensure that the terminals inside the wiring connector are clean, then reconnect the wiring connector **(see illustration)**. Connect the cap/coil to a new spark plug of the correct type and lay the plug on the engine with the

12.2 Check the terminals inside the cap/coil wiring connectors

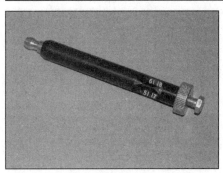

12.4 A commercially available spark gap test tool

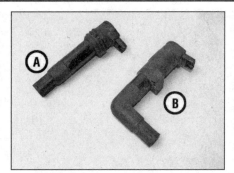

12.6 Check the primary (A) and secondary (B) coils for damage

13.5 Location of the BMW diagnostic tool plug (arrowed) – R1200 RT shown

threads contacting the engine. If necessary, hold the plug in position with an insulated tool. Do not hold the plug against the magnesium valve cover as this could be damaged.

⚠️ *Warning: Do not remove any of the spark plugs from the engine to perform this check – atomised fuel being pumped out of the open spark plug hole could ignite, causing severe injury!*

3 Check that the kill switch is in the RUN position and the transmission is in neutral, then turn the ignition switch ON and turn the engine over on the starter motor. If the system is in good condition a regular, fat blue spark should be evident at the plug electrodes. If the spark appears thin or yellowish, or is non-existent, further investigation is necessary. Turn the ignition OFF. Repeat the check for the other cap/coils.

4 The ignition system must be able to produce a spark which is capable of jumping a particular size gap. BMW provide no specification, but a healthy system should produce a spark capable of jumping at least 6 mm. A commercially available ignition spark gap tester tool will be required for this check (see illustration).

5 Connect the cap/coil to the protruding electrode on the test tool, and connect the tool to a good earth (ground) on the engine. Check that the kill switch is in the RUN position, turn the ignition switch ON and turn the engine over on the starter motor. If the system is in good condition a regular, fat blue spark should be seen to jump across the gap on the tool. Repeat the test for the other cap/coils. If the test results are good the entire ignition system can be considered good. If the spark appears thin or yellowish, or is non-existent, further investigation is necessary.

6 In order to determine conclusively that an ignition HT coil is defective, it should be tested by a BMW dealer equipped with the diagnostic tester. However, the cap/coil can be checked visually for damage, and the primary and secondary resistances can be measured with a multimeter (see illustration). If the cap/coil is undamaged, and if the resistance readings are within the specification, it is probably capable of proper operation.

7 To check the cap/coil primary resistance, set the multimeter to the ohms x 1 scale and connect its probes across the two primary wire terminals on the coil, marked 1 and 3. Compare

the result with the specification at the beginning of this Chapter. **Note:** *The terminal numbers are very small and are located inside the connector socket on the cap/coil - you made need to view them with a flash-light.*

8 To check the cap/coil secondary resistance, set the meter to the K-ohms scale. Connect the positive (+) meter probe to the spark plug terminal inside the cap/coil and the negative (-) meter probe to the No. 2 wire terminal on the coil. Compare the result with the specification at the beginning of this Chapter.

9 If either of the results are not as specified, the cap/coil is probably faulty and should be renewed.

10 Follow the procedure in Chapter 1, Section 11, to install the ignition HT cap/coil.

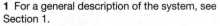

13 Engine management system and ECU – fault finding

1 For a general description of the system, see Section 1.

Diagnostic tester and fault identification

2 To diagnose the exact cause of a failure in the system, the BMW diagnostic tester, specifically designed for this system, is essential. Hence if a problem occurs, the motorcycle should be taken to a BMW dealer.

3 The engine management system has in-built diagnostic functions which record and store all data should a fault occur. Recorded faults can then be checked using BMW's diagnostic tester, which analyses the data and identifies the exact fault.

4 Should a fault occur, the engine warning light in the instrument cluster illuminates. If this happens, the management system switches itself into 'limp home' mode, so that in theory you should not be left stranded. Depending on the problem, it is possible that you will notice no difference in the running of the motorcycle. However, BMW advise that in 'limp home' mode, full engine power may not be available and the machine should be ridden with this in mind.

5 In order to diagnose the problem and to turn the warning light off, the diagnostic tester is essential. Take your machine to a BMW dealer and have them check the system. For

information, the diagnostic tool plugs into the main wiring harness at a connection point under the rider's seat on RT, ST and R models (see illustration), underneath the seat cowling on GS models (see illustration 16.10b in Chapter 5) and at the rear of the fuel tank on S models (see illustration 5.10 in Chapter 6).

6 It is possible to perform certain tests and checks to identify a particular fault, but the difficulty is knowing in which part of the system the fault has occurred, and therefore where to start checking. Further details on the location and function of the individual sensors are given in the following Sections.

Fault tracing

7 If a fault is indicated, first check the wiring and connectors to and from the ECU and the various sensors and all their related components. It may be that a connector is dirty or corroded or has come loose – a dirty or corroded terminal or connector will affect the resistance in that circuit, which will distort the information transmitted to the ECU, and therefore affect its control of the system. To deter corrosion, spray the wiring loom connector pins lightly with electrical contact cleaner.

8 A wire could be pinched and is shorting out – a continuity test of all wires from connector to connector will locate this. Albeit a fiddly and laborious task, the only way to determine any wiring faults is to systematically work through the wiring diagrams at the end of Chapter 7 and test each individual wire and connector for continuity – all wires are colour-coded. The wiring diagrams show the terminal number for each wire on the ECU – match these to the terminals on the ECU connector when making the tests (see illustration 14.6b). Refer also to Section 29 of Chapter 7.

14 ECU removal and installation

⚠️ *Warning: Refer to the Warning given in Section 1 before starting work.*

Removal

1 Disconnect the battery negative (-ve) lead (see Chapter 7).

14.3a Release the catch . . .

14.3b . . . and disconnect the connector

14.4 Remove the central electronics unit

14.5a Release the clips . . .

R1200 GS, ST, RT and R

2 Remove the fuel tank (see Section 2). The ECU and the central electronics unit are mounted on the frame behind the steering head.

3 Release the catch(es) securing the multi-pin wiring connector(s) for the central electronics unit and disconnect the connector(s) **(see illustrations)**.

4 Release the clips securing the central electronics unit in its holder and lift the unit off **(see illustration)**.

5 Unclip the holder and fold it forwards to access the ECU **(see illustrations)**.

6 Release the catches securing the two multi-pin wiring connectors to the ECU and disconnect the connectors, then lift the ECU off **(see illustrations)**.

R1200 S

12 Remove the left-hand tank/fairing side panel (see Chapter 6). The ECU and the central electronics unit are located in a holder on the left-hand side of the fuel tank **(see illustration)**.

13 Ease the top edge of the central electronics unit out of the holder, then release the catch securing the multi-pin wiring connector for

14.5b . . . and fold the holder forwards

14.6a Release the catches . . .

14.6b . . . and disconnect both wiring connectors from the ECU

14.12 Location of the central electronics unit (A) and ECU (B) – R1200 S

14.13a Ease the unit out of the holder . . .

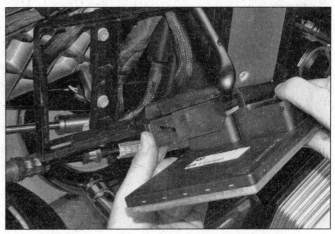

14.13b . . . and disconnect the wiring connector

the unit and disconnect the connector **(see illustrations)**.

14 Release the clips securing the ECU in the holder and ease it out **(see illustrations)**.

15 Release the catches securing the two multi-pin wiring connectors for the ECU and

disconnect the connectors, then lift the ECU off **(see illustrations)**.

Installation

16 Installation is the reverse of removal, noting the following:

● Ensure that the terminals in the multi-pin connectors are clean and undamaged.
● Spray the connector pins lightly with electrical contact cleaner.
● Ensure the connectors are locked in position with the catches.

14.14a Release the clips . . .

14.14b . . . and ease the ECU out of its holder

14.15a Release the wiring connector catches . . .

14.15b . . . and disconnect both wiring connectors from the ECU

15.3 Location of the crankshaft position sensor (arrowed)

15.6a Undo the screw and remove the sensor . . .

15.6b . . . noting the location of the O-ring

15 Sensors

Warning: Refer to the Warning given in Section 1 before starting work.
Caution Before disconnecting the wiring connector from any sensor, make sure the ignition is switched OFF, then disconnect the battery (see Chapter 7).

1 No data is available for testing the sensors which supply data to the ECU. If a sensor is faulty, the engine warning light in the instrument cluster will illuminate. The machine must then be taken to a BMW dealer who will be able to

15.10 Location of the camshaft position sensor (arrowed)

identify the faulty component using the BMW diagnostic tester. Once the faulty component had been renewed, the fault code can be erased from the engine management system.

Crankshaft position sensor

Function

2 The sensor reads the position of the crankshaft and how fast it is turning; this information is used by the ECU to determine which cylinder is on its ignition stroke and when it should fire. The ECU combines engine speed with information from other sensors to determine fuelling and ignition requirements.

Removal and installation

3 The crankshaft position sensor is located on the front top edge of the timing cover, just below the alternator pulley **(see illustration)**. Follow the procedure in Chapter 1, Section 13, to remove the alternator drive belt cover.
4 Remove the fuel tank (see Section 2).
5 Trace the wiring from the sensor and disconnect it at the connector. Free the wiring from any ties.
6 Undo the screw securing the sensor and pull it out **(see illustration)**. Note the location of the O-ring and discard it as a new one must be fitted **(see illustration)**.
7 The sensor is triggered by the teeth on the crankshaft gear inside the engine timing cover. To inspect the gear teeth, follow the procedure in Chapter 2, Section 19, and remove the cover.

8 Installation is the reverse of removal, noting the following:
● Fit a new O-ring to the sensor and lubricate it with a smear of clean engine oil.
● Tighten the sensor screw to the torque setting specified at the beginning of this Chapter.
● Ensure the terminals in the wiring connector are clean.
● Ensure the wiring is securely connected and renew any cable ties.

Camshaft position sensor

Function

9 The sensor reads the position of the camshaft and how fast it is turning. This information is used by the ECU to determine which cylinder is on its ignition stroke and when it should fire.

Removal and installation

10 The camshaft position sensor is located on the right-hand cylinder's camshaft sprocket cover **(see illustration)**. Remove the body panels as appropriate to your machine to access the sensor (see Chapter 6).
11 Free the wiring from the ties on the underside of the throttle body, then disconnect the sensor wiring connector
12 Undo the screw securing the sensor and pull it out **(see illustration)**. Note the location of the O-ring and discard it as a new one must be fitted **(see illustration)**.

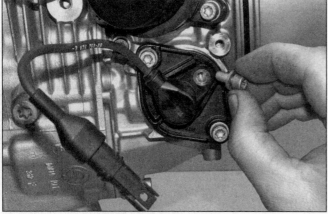

15.12a Undo the screw . . .

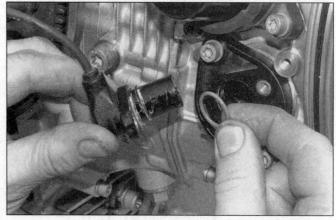

15.12b . . . and pull the sensor out. Note the location of the O-ring

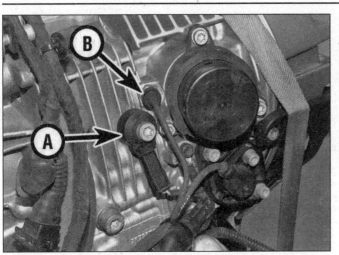

15.16 Location of the knock sensor (A) and cylinder head temperature sensor (B)

15.20 Location of the intake air temperature sensor (arrowed)

13 The sensor is activated by a trigger retained by the camshaft sprocket bolt. To inspect the trigger, follow the procedure in Chapter 2, Section 10. Note that the position of the trigger is determined by a tab which locates in a small hole in the camshaft sprocket.

14 Installation is the reverse of removal, noting the points in Step 8.

Knock sensors

Function

15 The sensors detect the precise frequency vibrations caused by detonation or 'pinking' inside the combustion chambers. When detonation occurs, a signal is sent to the ECU

15.21 Disconnect the wiring connector

which then retards the ignition timing to avoid engine damage through mechanical stress or over-heating.

Removal and installation

16 The knock sensors are located on the left and right-hand cylinders, inboard of the throttle bodies **(see illustration)**. Remove the throttle bodies to access the sensors (see Section 6).

17 Follow the procedure in Chapter 2, Section 15 to remove the sensors.

18 Installation is the reverse of removal, noting the relevant points in Step 8. Note that the correct torque for the sensor bolt is critical, otherwise the sensor will not function correctly.

Intake air temperature sensor

Function

19 The sensor reads the temperature of the air in the airbox. As changes in temperature affect air density, the ECU uses the information to determine fuelling requirements.

Removal and installation

20 The intake air temperature sensor is located in the left-hand side of the airbox at the front **(see illustration)**. Remove the body panels as appropriate to your machine to access the sensor (see Chapter 6).

21 Release the clip securing the sensor wiring connector and disconnect the connector **(see illustration)**.

22 Release the clip securing the sensor in the airbox, then draw the sensor out, noting the location of the O-ring **(see illustrations)**.

23 Check the condition of the sensor O-ring and renew it if it is deformed or deteriorated.

24 Installation is the reverse of removal, noting the relevant points in Step 8.

Engine oil temperature sensor

Function

25 The sensor reads the temperature of the oil in the cooling circuit and the ECU uses the information to determine fuelling and ignition requirements, particularly for hot and cold starting.

Removal and installation

Note: *If the engine has been running, allow it to cool before commencing work. If the machine is left to stand, oil will drain down from the cooler into the crankcase, reducing the amount of residual oil in the cooler.*

26 The engine oil temperature sensor is located on the top of the engine on the right-hand side **(see illustration)**. Remove the fuel tank to access the sensor (see Section 2).

15.22a Release the clip . . .

15.22b . . . and pull the sensor out. Note the O-ring (arrowed)

15.26 Location of the oil temperature sensor (arrowed)

27 Release the clip securing the sensor wiring connector and disconnect the connector.

28 Unscrew the sensor and lift it out, being prepared to catch any residual oil (see *Note* above). Note the location of the sealing washer and discard it as a new one must be fitted **(see illustration)**.

29 Installation is the reverse of removal, noting the relevant points in Step 8. Don't forget to fit a new sealing washer and tighten the sensor to the torque setting specified at the beginning of this Chapter.

Oxygen sensors

30 The oxygen sensors measure exhaust gas oxygen content and the ECU uses the information to determine fuelling requirements.

31 Refer to the procedure in Section 10 to remove and install the oxygen sensors.

Cylinder head temperature sensors

Function

32 A temperature sensor is fitted to each cylinder head on models up to Aug 2006; later models just have a sensor in the left cylinder head. The sensor(s) read the temperature of the cylinder head and the ECU uses this information to determine fuelling and ignition requirements.

Removal and installation

33 The cylinder head temperature sensor(s) is located inboard of the throttle body **(see illustration 15.16)**. Remove the throttle body to access the sensor (see Section 6).

34 Free the sensor wiring from the tie, then release the clip securing the sensor wiring connector and disconnect the connector **(see illustration)**.

35 Unscrew the sensor and lift it out.

36 Installation is the reverse of removal, noting the relevant points in Step 8.

Engine oil pressure switch

37 While the engine is running under normal circumstances, the switch is held in the OFF position by oil pressure in the lubricating circuit. If the pressure drops, the switch illuminates the oil pressure warning light in the

15.28 Unscrew the temperature sensor. Note the sealing washer (arrowed)

instrument cluster. If this happens, the engine should be stopped immediately and the cause of the loss of pressure investigated.

38 Refer to the procedure in Chapter 7 for testing, removal and installation of the oil pressure switch.

Throttle position sensor

Function

39 The sensor monitors the position of the butterfly valve in the left-hand throttle body and the ECU uses the information to determine fuelling and ignition requirements.

Removal and installation

Note: *The sensor should not be removed unless it is known to be faulty. When a new sensor is installed its position must be reset using the BMW diagnostic tester.*

40 The throttle position sensor is located on the side of the left-hand throttle body **(see**

15.40 Location of the throttle position sensor (arrowed)

15.34 Release the clip to disconnect the wiring connector

illustration). Disconnect the sensor wiring connector (see Section 6, Step 8), then undo the screws securing the sensor and lift it off. Note how the valve spindle locates inside the sensor.

Gear position sensor

41 The sensor monitors the position of the selector drum in the gearbox and the ECU uses the information, combined with engine speed, to determine fuelling and ignition requirements.

Removal and installation

42 To gain access to the gear position sensor, follow the procedure in Section 9 and remove the exhaust silencer and downpipe assembly.

43 Disconnect the sensor wiring connector **(see illustration)**.

44 Refer to the procedure in Chapter 2, Section 31, for removal and installation of the sensor.

15.43 Disconnect the gear position sensor wiring connector

Chapter 4
Frame, suspension and final drive

Contents

Degrees of difficulty

Easy, suitable for novice with little experience	**Fairly easy,** suitable for beginner with some experience	**Fairly difficult,** suitable for competent DIY mechanic	**Difficult,** suitable for experienced DIY mechanic	**Very difficult,** suitable for expert DIY or professional

Specifications

Front suspension

Type	BMW Telelever
Fork oil type	BMW telescopic fork oil (10W)
Fork oil capacity	
R1200 GS, Adventure and R1200 ST	0.65 litre
R1200 RT	0.62 litre
R1200S	0.6 litre
R1200 R	0.46 litre
Fork tube runout limit	0.1 mm

Rear suspension

Type	BMW Paralever

Brake pedal

Stop bolt height	
R1200 GS	10.5 to 11.5 mm
R1200 RT	17.0 to 18.0 mm
R1200 ST	15.2 to 16.2 mm
R1200 R	15.7 to 16.2 mm
Stop bolt clearance	2.0 to 3.0 mm
Brake pedal to stop bolt clearance	
R1200 S	2.0 to 3.0 mm
R1200 R	2.5 to 3.0 mm

Torque settings

Brake and clutch lever pivot bolt	
R1200 RT 2005 to 2006	11 Nm
R1200 GS, ST and S 2004 to 2006	6 Nm
R1200 RT and ST 2007-on, all R	8 Nm
R1200 GS 2007-on	9 Nm
Brake pedal pivot bolt	
R1200 GS, ST and R	21 Nm
R1200 RT	38 Nm
R1200 S	19 Nm
Centre stand pivot bolts	
R1200 GS	40 Nm
R1200 RT and ST	42 Nm
Sidestand pivot bolt	42 Nm
Footrest mounting bracket bolts	19 Nm

Torque settings (continued)

Handlebar mountings

R1200 GS and Adventure – 2004 to 2007 models

Handlebar clamp bolts (front first)	28 Nm
Handlebar end-weights	21 Nm

R1200 GS and Adventure – 2008-on

Handlebar clamp bolts (front bolts, tighten first)	36 Nm
Handlebar clamp bolts (rear bolts)	16 Nm
Handlebar end-weights	21 Nm

R1200 RT

Handlebar mounting bolts (front first)	19 Nm
Handlebar end-weights	19 Nm

R1200 ST

Handlebar clamp bolts	19 Nm
Handlebar end-weights	21 Nm

R1200 S

Handlebar clamp bolts (inner first)	10 Nm
Handlebar end-weights	19 Nm

R1200 R

Handlebar clamp bolts	24 Nm
Handlebar end-weight bolts	19 Nm

Final drive unit pivot bolt	100 Nm

Front suspension

Top yoke (steering head) bearing nut – R1200 GS, RT and R	130 Nm
Top yoke clamp bolts – R1200 ST and S	21 Nm
Top yoke (steering head) ball joint – R1200 ST and S	230 Nm
Top yoke (steering head) ball joint nut – R1200 ST and S	130 Nm
Fork tube top stud nut – R1200 GS, RT and R	40 Nm
Fork air bleed screw	3 Nm
Fork bridge clamp bolts – R1200 GS, ST and S	25 Nm
Fork bridge-to-slider bolts – RT and R	25 Nm
Fork bridge ball joint nut	130 Nm
Fork bridge ball joint	230 Nm

Front shock absorber – R1200 RT

Upper mounting nut	34 Nm
Lower mounting bolt	40 Nm

Front shock absorber – R1200 R, S, ST and GS

Upper and lower mounting bolts	34 Nm

Telelever pivot shaft bolt

Initial setting	45 Nm
Final setting	73 Nm
Steering damper-to-fork bridge nut – R1200 S and R	19 Nm
Steering damper-to-Telelever bolt – R1200 S and R	19 Nm

Rear suspension

Paralever mounting bolts

Front	42 Nm
Rear	43 Nm

Rear shock absorber

Upper mounting bolt nut	50 Nm

Lower mounting bolt

Initial setting	20 Nm
Final setting	58 Nm
Swingarm left-hand bearing pin	7 Nm
Swingarm left-hand bearing pin locknut	145 Nm
Swingarm right-hand bearing pin screws	9 Nm

1 General information

There is no frame in the traditional sense – the front suspension and sub-frame and rear suspension and sub-frame mount directly to the engine/transmission unit.

Front suspension and steering are managed separately by BMW's Telelever system. Telelever uses an arrangement of telescopic fork legs to support the front wheel and provide steering, together with a swingarm and shock absorber to provide suspension control – unlike conventional front forks, the Telelever forks contain neither damping mechanism nor springs, only oil to lubricate the friction surfaces.

At the top of the Telelever system, the fork tubes are held in a yoke, which is mounted to the front sub-frame via the steering head bearing. Midway down the assembly, the fork sliders are linked by a bridge which is attached to the front of the Telelever swingarm via a ball joint. The swingarm pivots around a shaft which passes through the front of the engine crankcases, with the shock absorber located between the swingarm and the front sub-frame.

Rear suspension is provided by a single-sided swingarm and centrally mounted shock absorber. The drive shaft to the rear wheel is housed inside the swingarm. The joint between the swingarm and the final drive unit is pivoted, with a link arm, BMW's Paralever

3.1 Remove the E-clip from the pivot pin (arrowed) – R1200 GS rider's footrest

3.2 Remove the E-clip from the pivot pin (arrowed) – R1200 GS passenger's footrest

3.3 Footrest bracket mounting bolts (arrowed) – R1200 RT right-hand side shown

system, controlling movement between the two. The Paralever system counteracts the adverse effect of the shaft drive on suspension movement.

The rear shock absorber is located between the swingarm and the rear sub-frame.

2 Front and rear sub-frames

1 The front sub-frame supports the steering and suspension, the fuel tank and a number of electrical components, including the engine control unit and the central electronics unit. The sub-frame bolts directly to the engine's crankcase.

2 The rear sub-frame supports the swingarm and provides the top mounting for the rear shock absorber. The sub-frame also supports the seat, rear mudguard, air filter housing, battery and electrical components. The sub-frame bolts directly to the engine's crankcase.

3 The sub-frames should not require attention unless accident damage has occurred. In most cases, renewal is the only satisfactory remedy for such damage. A few frame specialists have the jigs and other equipment necessary for straightening the sub-frame assemblies to the required standard of accuracy, but even then there is no simple way of assessing to what extent the frame components may have been over-stressed.

4 Remember that misalignment of the front and rear suspension/sub-frame assemblies will cause handling problems. If misalignment is suspected, first check the wheel alignment (see Chapter 5).

5 To check the sub-frame assemblies it will be necessary to remove the body panels (see Chapter 6) and fuel tank (see Chapter 3).

6 Loose bolts can cause ovaling or fracturing of the sub-frame mountings. On a high mileage bike, the sub-frame assemblies should be examined closely for signs of cracking or splitting at the welded joints. Minor damage can often be repaired by welding, depending on the extent and nature of the damage, but this is a task for an expert. Always remove the battery, engine control unit, central electronics

unit and instrument cluster before using electric welding equipment.

7 Follow the relevant Steps in Chapter 2, Section 4, to remove the front and rear sub-frames. Note that the wiring loom remains connected to the front sub-frame when it is removed.

3 Footrests, brake pedal and gearchange lever

Footrests

R1200 GS and Adventure

1 To remove the rider's footrests, first remove the E-clip from the bottom of the footrest pivot pin, then withdraw the pivot pin and remove the return spring and the footrest **(see illustration)**. Note how the spring ends locate in the footrest and on the mounting bracket.

2 To remove the passenger's footrests, first remove the E-clip from the bottom of the footrest pivot pin, then withdraw the pivot pin and remove the footrest **(see illustration)**.

R1200 RT

3 The rider's and passenger's footrests are located on mounting brackets. To remove the left-hand bracket, first undo the screws securing the fairing side panel to the top edge of the bracket, then undo the bracket mounting bolts and lift the bracket off **(see illustration)**. Follow the procedure in Steps

1 and 2 to remove the footrests from the bracket.

4 The right-hand bracket also supports the rear brake pedal and master cylinder. Before removing the bracket, release the clip securing the pedal to the master cylinder pushrod and separate the pushrod from the brake pedal (see below), then undo the two bolts securing the master cylinder to the rear of the bracket and displace the master cylinder. Trace the wiring from the rear brake light switch on the back of the panel to the wiring connector and disconnect it. Release the wiring from any ties. Undo the bracket mounting bolts and remove the bracket, footrests and rear brake pedal as an assembly.

R1200 ST and R

5 The rider's footrests are located on mounting brackets. To remove the left-hand bracket, undo the bracket mounting bolts and lift the bracket off **(see illustration)**. Follow the procedure in Step 1 to remove the footrest from the bracket.

6 The right-hand bracket also supports the rear brake pedal and master cylinder – follow the procedure in Step 1 to remove the footrest only **(see illustration)**. Alternatively, follow the procedure in Chapter 5 and displace the master cylinder. Undo the bracket mounting bolts, then undo the screw securing the rear brake light switch to the back of the panel. Remove the bracket, footrest and rear brake pedal as an assembly.

7 The passenger's footrests are located on mounting brackets. Undo the bracket mounting bolts and lift the bracket off **(see**

3.5 Footrest bracket mounting bolts (arrowed) – R1200 ST left-hand side

3.6 Remove the E-clip from the pivot pin (arrowed) – R1200 ST rider's footrest

3.7a Passenger's footrest bracket mounting bolts (arrowed) – R1200 ST left-hand side

3.7b Remove the E-clip from the pivot pin (arrowed) – R1200 ST passenger's footrest

3.8a Disconnect the rod from the gearchange lever (arrowed)

illustration). To remove the footrest from the bracket, remove the E-clip from the bottom of the footrest pivot pin, then withdraw the pivot pin and remove the footrest **(see illustration)**.

R1200 S

8 The rider's footrests are located on mounting brackets. To remove the left-hand bracket, first disconnect the gearchange rod from the upper end of the gearchange lever **(see illustration)**. Undo the nut on the upper mounting bolt and withdraw the bolt, then undo the lower mounting bolt and lift the bracket and lever assembly off **(see illustration)**. Follow the procedure in Step 1 to remove the footrest from the bracket.

9 To remove the right-hand bracket, undo the mounting bolts and lift the bracket off. Follow the procedure in Step 1 to remove the footrest from the bracket.

10 To remove the passenger's footrests, first remove the E-clip from the bottom of the footrest pivot pin, then withdraw the pivot pin and remove the footrest.

Installation

11 If they are worn, the footrest rubbers can be drawn off the footrest or released by undoing the screws on the bottom (according to model) and replaced with new ones.

12 Installation is the reverse of removal. Always use new E-clips to secure the pivot pins.

Brake pedal

R1200 GS and Adventure

13 Note the location of the clip securing the brake master cylinder pushrod clevis pin, then ease the clip off the pushrod and withdraw the

pin **(see illustrations)**. Separate the pushrod from the brake pedal **(see illustration)**.

14 Note how the ends of the pedal return spring locate on the bracket and the underside of the pedal **(see illustrations)**. Undo the pivot bolt and lift the pedal and spring off.

R1200 RT

15 Separate the pushrod from the brake pedal (see Steps 13 and 14).

16 Undo the nut on the pedal pivot bolt and remove the washer and return spring – note how the spring locates against the lugs on the back of the mounting bracket. Support the pedal and withdraw the bolt, then lift the pedal off.

R1200 ST and R

17 Separate the pushrod from the brake pedal (see Steps 13 and 14).

18 Note how the ends of the pedal return spring locate on the bracket and the underside

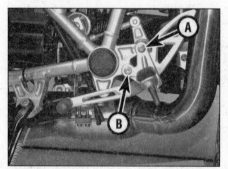

3.8b Footrest bracket upper mounting bolt (A) and lower mounting bolt (B) – R1200 S

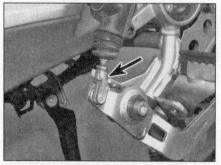

3.13a Release the clip (arrowed) . . .

3.13b . . . and pull out the clevis pin . . .

3.13c . . . then remove the pushrod

3.14a One end of the spring (arrowed) locates on the bracket . . .

3.14b . . . the other end (arrowed) locates underneath the pedal

3.18 Note the location of the pedal return spring (arrowed) – R1200 ST

3.20 Note the location of the pedal return spring (arrowed) – R1200 S

3.22a Location of the brake pedal stop – R1200 GS

of the pedal **(see illustration)**. Undo the pivot bolt and lift the pedal and spring off.

R1200 S

19 Separate the pushrod from the brake pedal (see Steps 13 and 14).
20 Note the location of the pedal return spring **(see illustration)**. Undo the nut on the pedal pivot bolt and remove the washer, then withdraw the bolt and lift the pedal and spring off.

Installation

21 Installation is the reverse of removal, noting the following:
● Lubricate the pedal pivot with a smear of grease.
● Make sure the spring ends are correctly positioned.
● Tighten the pivot bolt to the torque setting specified at the beginning of this Chapter.
● Renew the clevis pin and clip assembly if the clip is sprained or corroded.

Adjusting the brake pedal stop

22 Measure the distance between the top edge of the brake pedal and the top of the stop bolt to check that the stop bolt is set at the correct height **(see illustrations)**. If the bolt height is outside the specification shown at the beginning of this Chapter, loosen the lock nut and adjust the stop bolt, then tighten the lock nut. Note that no stop bolt is fitted to R1200 S models.
23 Using a feeler gauge, measure the clearance between the tongue of the brake light switch and the pedal stop on the bracket. Compare the result with the specification. If the clearance is outside the specification, loosen the lock nut on the master cylinder pushrod and turn the pushrod in or out until the gap is correct. Tighten the lock nut.

Gearchange lever

R1200 S

24 Remove the rider's left-hand footrest bracket (see Step 8). Remove the circlip securing the lever and remove the lever. Lubricate the lever pivot with a smear of grease and secure the lever with a new circlip on reassembly.
25 To remove the gearchange linkage, check for the mark on the gearchange shaft that aligns with the slot in the lever **(see illustration**

3.25a). If the mark isn't visible, make your own with a sharp punch, then remove the pinch bolt and pull the lever off the shaft.

All other models

26 Check for the mark on the gearchange linkage shaft that aligns with the slot in the lever **(see illustration)**. If the mark isn't visible, make your own with a sharp punch, then remove the pinch bolt and pull the lever off the shaft.
27 To remove the gearchange linkage, check for the mark on the gearchange shaft that aligns with the slot in the lever **(see illustration)**. If the mark isn't visible, make your own with a sharp punch, then remove the pinch bolt and pull the lever off the shaft. Pull the linkage out of the bracket in the frame **(see illustration)**. Note the location of the circlip on the shaft. Clean the shaft and lubricate it with a smear of grease before reassembly **(see illustration)**.

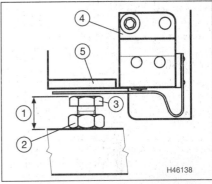

3.22b Adjusting the brake pedal stop

1 Stop bolt height
2 Lock nut
3 Stop bolt
4 Brake light switch
5 Brake pedal stop

3.26 Mark on shaft aligns with slot (arrowed) in lever

3.27a Mark on shaft aligns with slot (arrowed) in linkage lever

3.27b Removing the gearchange linkage

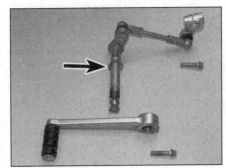

3.27c Gearchange linkage components – note the circlip (arrowed)

4.5 Undo the centre stand pivot bolts (arrowed)

4.6 Stand springs hook over lug (arrowed) on frame

4.12 Cover plate is secured by screws (arrowed)

4 Stands

1 R1200 GS, RT and ST models are fitted with a centrestand and a sidestand. R1200 S and R models are fitted with a sidestand only.
2 Lubricating the stand pivots is part of routine maintenance (see Chapter 1).
3 Make sure the stand springs are in good condition and capable of holding the stand up when not in use. A broken or weak spring is an obvious safety hazard – always renew a spring that is damaged or has sagged.

Centre stand

4 The centre stand is secured on the left and right-hand sides by counter-sunk bolts which screw into the pivot bushes in the rear sub-frame.
5 To remove the stand, ensure the machine is securely supported with an auxiliary stand, then counter-hold each bush with a spanner on the flats on the inner face of the bush and undo the bolts **(see illustration)**.
6 Unhook the stand springs from the lug on the frame and lift the stand off **(see illustration)**.
7 Inspect the stand, pivot holes and bushes for signs of wear and renew any components as necessary.
8 On installation, ensure that the pivot holes are clean and apply a smear of grease to the bushes.
9 Install the right-hand pivot bolt and tighten

it finger-tight, then install the stand springs, ensuring the ends are securely located.
10 Install the left-hand pivot bolt, then tighten both pivot bolts to the torque setting specified at the beginning of this Chapter.
11 Check the operation of the stand before riding the motorcycle.

Sidestand

12 Where fitted, undo the screws securing the sidestand switch cover plate and remove the plate **(see illustration)**.
13 Ensure the machine is securely supported on its centre stand or on an auxiliary stand, then unhook the stand springs **(see illustration)**.
14 Remove the circlip and washer securing the sidestand switch and displace the switch **(see illustration)**. Note how the switch locates against the peg on the stand bracket, and how the pin on the switch locates in the hole in the stand.
15 Unscrew the sidestand pivot bolt from the underside of the stand bracket and remove the stand. Remove the bush from the bracket if it is loose.
16 On installation, ensure that the pivot hole and bracket are clean and apply a smear of grease to the bush.
17 Clean the threads of the pivot bolt and apply a suitable non-permanent thread locking compound, then install the bolt and tighten it to the torque setting specified at the beginning of this Chapter.
18 Install the stand springs, ensuring the ends are securely located.
19 Install the sidestand switch and secure it with the washer and circlip (see Step 14).

20 If removed, install the switch cover plate.
21 Check the operation of the starter interlock system (see Chapter 1).
22 Check the operation of the stand before riding the motorcycle.

5 Handlebars and levers

Handlebars

Note 1: *The handlebars can be displaced without having to remove the lever or switch assemblies. In all cases, take care to avoid straining the handlebar wiring. Support or tie the handlebar assembly using rags to cushion it and anything it sits against. Also cover the master cylinder(s) with rag in case of leakage.*
Note 2: *The machines covered in this manual were available from new fitted with a range of optional electrical extras. When working on your machine, take care to ensure that all relevant electrical components are disconnected on disassembly and subsequently reconnected during the rebuild. Always take the precaution of disconnecting the battery negative (-ve) terminal before disconnecting an electrical wiring connector.*

R1200 GS

1 Remove the mirrors and the hand protectors (see Chapter 6). Disconnect the battery negative lead (see Chapter 7).
2 On machines with heated handlebar grips, trace the wiring from each grip and disconnect it at the connector – if required, remove the fuel tank to access the connector (see Chapter 3). Release the wiring from any clips or ties and feed it back to the handlebar, noting its routing.
3 Follow the procedure in Chapter 7 and displace the left and right-hand switch assemblies. There is no need to disconnect the wiring from its connectors, but free it from any ties on the handlebar.
4 Detach the throttle cable from the twistgrip pulley (see Chapter 3). On machines with unheated handlebar grips, slide the twistgrip off the handlebar.
5 Follow the procedure in Chapter 5 and displace the front brake master cylinder. There is no need to disconnect the brake hose.

4.13 Location of the side stand springs (arrowed)

4.14 Side stand switch is secured by circlip (arrowed)

5.8 Undo the bolts (arrowed) to remove the handlebar clamps – R1200 GS

5.10a Align the punch mark (arrowed) with the join in the clamp

Keep the reservoir upright to prevent fluid spillage and make sure no strain in placed on the hose.

6 Follow the procedure in Chapter 2, Section 24, and displace the clutch master cylinder. There is no need to disconnect the clutch hose. Keep the reservoir upright to prevent fluid spillage and make sure no strain in placed on the hose.

7 On machines with unheated handlebar grips, if required, pull the left-hand grip off the handlebar. Push a screwdriver between the grip and the bar and use spray lubricant to loosen the grip. If the grip has been bonded in place you may need to cut it free.

8 Loosen the bolts securing the handlebar clamps **(see illustration)**. Support the handlebars and remove the clamps, then lift the handlebars off.

9 On machines with heated handlebar grips, slide the twistgrip off the handlebar, taking care not to snag the wiring. Fold back the inner end of the left-hand grip and remove the screws securing it. Slide the grip off the handlebar, carefully pulling the wiring through as you do.

On machines with heated grips, before drawing the wiring through the handlebars, attach a piece of thin wire to the terminals on the end of the wiring and draw it into the handlebar, leaving the end exposed so it can be used to pull the wiring back through on installation.

10 Installation is the reverse of removal, noting the following:

● If applicable, install the heated handlebar grips before fitting the handlebars to the machine.

● Ensure that the handlebars are central in the clamps, and that the join in the left-hand clamp aligns with the punch mark on the handlebars **(see illustration)**.

● Tighten the clamp bolts to the torque setting specified at the beginning of this Chapter – tighten the front bolts first, then the rear bolts.

● Fit the front brake and clutch master cylinders so that the clamp mating surfaces align with the punch mark on the handlebar **(see illustration)**.

R1200 RT

Note: *Although not strictly necessary, before removing the handlebars it is recommended that the windshield is removed (see Chapter 6). This will improve access and prevent accidental damage should a tool slip.*

11 Disconnect the battery negative lead (see Chapter 7). Follow the procedure in Steps 2 to 7. Note how the wiring is clipped to the handlebars **(see illustration)**.

12 Undo the bolts securing the left and right-hand handlebars to the top yoke and lift them off **(see illustration)**. Note the O-rings fitted to the tops of the fork tubes and renew them if necessary on installation.

13 On machines fitted with heated handlebar grips, follow the procedure in Step 9 to remove them.

5.10b Align master cylinder clamp surfaces (arrowed) with punch mark

14 Do not attempt to remove the handlebar from its bracket. Individual components are not available – if the bar or bracket is damaged, fit a new assembly.

15 Installation is the reverse of removal, noting the points in Step 10 where applicable.

R1200 ST

16 Disconnect the battery negative lead (see Chapter 7). Remove the mirrors (see Chapter 6) then follow the procedure in Steps 2 to 7.

17 Working on one handlebar at a time, pull the E-clip off the handlebar locating pin, then loosen the handlebar clamp bolt and slide the handlebar down the fork tube until it is clear of the pin **(see illustration)**.

18 Note the position of the top of the fork tube in the top yoke, then loosen the fork clamp bolt in the top yoke and pull the tube down into the slider until there is enough

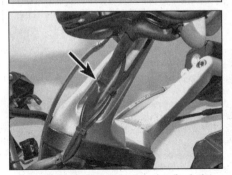

5.11 Note the location (arrowed) of the wiring clip – R1200 RT

5.12 Location of the handlebar mounting bolts (arrowed) – R1200 RT

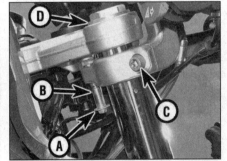

5.17 Location of the E-clip (A), handlebar locating pin (B), clamp bolt (C) and top of the fork tube (D) - R1200 ST

5.18a Loosen the fork clamp bolts (arrowed) . . .

5.18b . . . and slide the fork tube down

5.23 Location of the handlebar clamp bolts – R1200 S

room to slide the handlebar off the top **(see illustrations)**. Note that it may be necessary to loosen the air bleed screw in the centre of the fork top bolt to reduce pressure inside the fork leg **(see illustration 6.30)**.

19 On machines fitted with heated handlebar grips, follow the procedure in Step 9 to remove them.

20 Do not attempt to remove the handlebar from its bracket. Individual components are not available – if the bar or bracket is damaged, fit a new assembly.

21 Installation is the reverse of removal, noting the following:

● If applicable, install the heated handlebar grips before fitting the handlebars to the machine.
● Locate the handlebar on the fork tube, then pull the tube up into the top yoke. The tube should protrude 3 mm above the top of the yoke **(see illustration 5.17)**.

● Tighten the clamp bolts to the torque settings specified at the beginning of this Chapter.
● If loosened, don't forget to tighten the air bleed screw.
● If necessary, fit a new E-clip on the locating pin.
● Fit the front brake and clutch master cylinders so that the clamp mating surfaces align with the punch mark on the handlebar.

R1200 S

22 Disconnect the battery negative lead (see Chapter 7). Follow the procedure in Steps 2 to 7.

23 Undo the handlebar clamp bolts and remove them **(see illustration)**.

24 Pull the handlebar out of its bracket in the top fork yoke. Note the grooves in the bar for the location of the clamp bolts.

25 On machines fitted with heated handlebar

grips, follow the procedure in Step 9 to remove them.

26 Installation is the reverse of removal, noting the following:

● If applicable, install the heated handlebar grips before fitting the handlebars to the machine.
● Ensure that the grooves in the handlebars are aligned with the holes for the clamp bolts.
● Tighten the clamp bolts to the torque setting specified at the beginning of this Chapter – tighten the inner bolts first, then the outer bolts.
● Fit the front brake and clutch master cylinders so that the clamp mating surfaces align with the punch mark on the handlebar.

R1200 R

Note: *If the handlebars are being displaced to give access to the steering head, there is no need to detach the master cylinders, switch units, hoses or throttle cable – just follow Step 34.*

27 Disconnect the battery negative lead (see Chapter 7).

28 To remove components from the right-hand end of the handlebar, precede as follows: Remove the end-weight from the handlebar end **(see illustration)**. Remove the two screws from the front face of the switch and lift off the switch cover. Dislodge the wire connector(s) from their locations in the switch body and disconnect them **(see illustration)**.

29 Remove the two bolts from the master cylinder clamp and separate the clamp top half (complete with mirror) from the master cylinder and clamp lower half **(see illustration)**. At this point, you can either slacken off the clamp screw and slide the whole assembly off the handlebar end **(see illustration)** – there is just enough length in the throttle cable to do so – or you can remove the individual components as described in the next Step.

30 Remove the two screws from the front of the switch and free the switch unit from the handlebar **(see illustrations)**. Remove the screw from the throttle pulley rear cover and detach the cover **(see illustration)**. Unscrew the cable nut from the base of the switch, then disconnect the cable from the pulley. Slacken off the clamp screw and slide the grip and pulley assembly off the handlebar end.

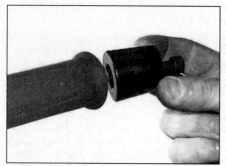

5.28a Remove the end-weight from the handlebar end

5.28b Disconnecting the switch wiring connectors

5.29a Detach the master cylinder clamp, complete with the mirror

5.29b Slacken the clamp screw to slide the assembly off the handlebar

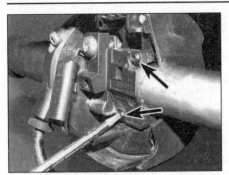

5.30a Remove the two screws
(arrowed) . . .

5.30b . . . to free the switch unit

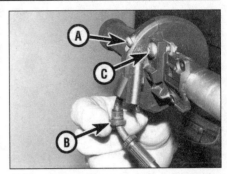

5.30c Cable pulley cover screw (A), cable
nut (B) and clamp screw (C)

5.31a Remove the clutch master cylinder
clamp bolts (arrowed) . . .

5.31b . . . and detach the lever and master
cylinder assembly

5.32a Switch cover is retained by two
screws

31 To remove components from the left-hand end of the handlebar, precede as follows: Remove the two bolts from the master cylinder clamp and separate the clamp top half (complete with mirror) from the master cylinder and clamp lower half – the assembly will still be linked to the switch unit by the wire harness **(see illustrations)**.

32 Remove the two screws from the front face of the switch and lift off the switch cover **(see illustration)**. Dislodge the wire connector(s) from their locations in the switch body and disconnect them **(see illustration)**. Remove the two screws from the switch and withdraw the switch unit from the handlebar **(see illustration)**.

33 Remove the end-weight from the handlebar end **(see illustration)**. Hold back the flange of the rubber grip to reveal the grip retaining screw at top and bottom; remove the screws and slide the grip off the handlebar end **(see illustration)**.

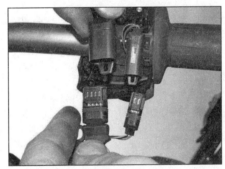

5.32b Disconnect the left switch wiring
connectors

5.32c Remove the two screws (arrowed)
to free the switch unit

34 Now remove the four handlebar clamp bolts, lift off the clamps and remove the handlebars from the top yoke.

35 Installation is the reverse of removal, noting the following:

● Position the handlebars on the top yoke so that their knurled sections align with the clamps, fit the clamp top halves and thread in the bolts making sure that the front bolt of each clamp is fully tightened first **(see**

5.33a Handlebar end-weight is retained by
a single screw . . .

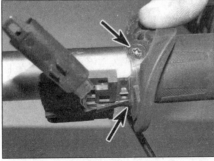

5.33b . . . and left grip by a screw top and
bottom (arrrowed)

5.35a Align the knurled sections in the
handlebar lower clamps

5.35b Tighten the clamp front bolts fully, then the rear . . .

5.35c . . . making sure punch mark aligns with slot at the rear

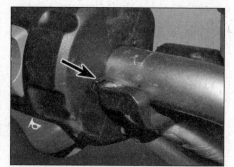

5.35d Align clamp surface with moulding (arrowed)

5.35e Ensure throttle pulley cover engages correctly at lower joint

5.35f Right switch unit moulding must align with punch mark

5.35g Brake master cylinder clamp correctly fitted with gap at the rear (arrowed)

illustrations). This will ensure that the gap is at the rear. Whilst doing this, align the punch mark on the handlebar with the clamp joint at the rear (see illustration).

● When installing the clutch master cylinder, align the rear surface of the clamp lower half with the moulded line of the left switch unit (see illustration). Tighten the clamp front bolt first, then the rear, so that the gap is at the rear (see illustration 5.31a).

● When installing the right-hand grip unit, build up the grip and throttle pulley and reconnect the cable, but don't tighten the clamp screw at this stage (see illustration). Install the end-weight. Install the switch unit and align its moulded line with the punch mark on the handlebar before tightening the clamp screw and installing the two small screws (see illustration). When installing the brake master cylinder, align the rear surface of the clamp lower half with the moulded line of the right switch unit and the punch mark. Tighten the clamp front bolt first, then the rear, so that the gap is at the rear (see illustration).

● Ensure the handlebar clamp bolts and end-weight bolts are tightened to the specified torque settings.

Levers

36 Follow the procedure in Chapter 2, Section 24, to remove and install the clutch lever.
37 Follow the procedure in Chapter 5, Section 5, to remove and install the front brake lever.

38 To adjust the lever span, refer to Chapter 1, Sections 3 and 4.

6 Front suspension

Fork leg
Fork removal

Note: *Unlike a conventional telescopic fork leg, the fork tube is not secured in the slider by the fork bushes or damper rod. When removing the fork leg, take care not to pull the tube out of the slider accidentally. If the tube and slider are separated, new oil seals must be fitted.*

1 Position the bike on its centre stand or support it securely on an auxiliary stand. Work can be made easier by raising the machine to

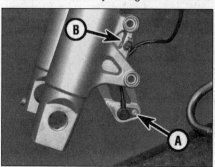

6.5a ABS sensor is secured by screw (A). Wiring is secured by clip at (B) . . .

a suitable working height on an hydraulic ramp or a suitable platform. Make sure the machine is secure and will not topple over.

2 Refer to the procedure in Chapter 6 and remove the fairing panels, according to your model, to gain access to the front suspension.

3 Remove the front wheel (see Chapter 5).
4 Remove the front mudguard (see Chapter 6).

5 On machines fitted with ABS, undo the screw securing the ABS sensor to the left-hand fork slider (see illustration). Release the sensor wiring from the clips on the slider and withdraw the sensor, noting how it fits (see illustrations). Secure the sensor clear of the fork legs.

6 On R1200 GS models, prise out the fork top cap, then counter-hold the fork top bolt and undo the nut securing the fork top stud in the

6.5b . . . and inside the fork slider at (C)

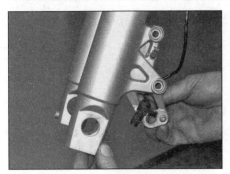

6.5c Withdraw the wiring carefully, noting it how it fits

6.6a Prise off the fork top cap

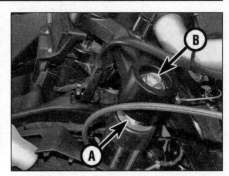

6.6b Counter-hold the fork top bolt (A) and undo the nut (B)

top yoke **(see illustrations)**. Loosen the clamp bolts in the fork bridge **(see illustration)**. Note the routing of all cables and wiring around the forks, then slide the fork leg down and out through the fork bridge **(see illustration)**.

7 On R1200 RT models, first displace the handlebars (see Section 5). Note that it is not necessary to remove any of the handlebar components. Keep the front brake and clutch master cylinders upright to prevent fluid spillage and make sure no strain in placed on the hoses and wiring. Counter-hold the fork top bolt and undo the nut securing the fork top stud in the top yoke **(see illustration 6.6b)**. Loosen the bolts securing the fork slider to the bridge, then support the fork leg and remove the bolts. Note the routing of all cables and wiring around the forks, then lower the fork leg down and out of the top yoke.

8 On R1200 ST models, first displace the handlebars (see Section 5). Note that it is not necessary to remove any of the handlebar components. Keep the front brake and clutch master cylinders upright to prevent fluid spillage and make sure no strain in placed on the hoses and wiring. Loosen the clamp bolts in the fork bridge **(see illustration 6.6c)**. Note the routing of all cables and wiring around the forks, then slide the fork leg down and out through the fork bridge **(see illustration 6.6d)**.

9 On R1200 S models, loosen the clamp bolts in the fork top yoke, then prise out the circlip from the top of the fork tube **(see illustration)**. Loosen the clamp bolts in the fork bridge **(see illustration 6.6c)**. Note the routing of all

6.6c Loosen the clamp bolts (arrowed) in the fork bridge

cables and wiring around the forks, then slide the fork leg down and out through the fork bridge **(see illustration 6.6d)**.

10 On R1200 R models, prise out the fork top cap, then counterhold the fork top bolt and undo the nut securing the fork top stud in the top yoke **(see illustrations 6.35c and b)**. Remove all four bolts from the fork bridge **(see illustration 6.34a)**, then slide each fork leg down and clear of the fork bridge.

Fork overhaul

11 If fitted, lift off the protective sleeve **(see illustration)**.

12 Inspect the area above the dust seal on the fork slider for signs of oil leakage, then carefully lever up the dust seal using a flat-bladed screwdriver and inspect the area above the oil seal **(see illustration)**. If leakage is evident, new seals must be fitted.

6.6d Slide the fork leg down through the fork bridge

13 Check the fork tube for score marks, scratches, flaking of the chrome finish and excessive or abnormal wear. Any damage to the surface of the tube will wear the seals, so the tube must be renewed. Look for dents in the tube and renew both fork tubes if any are found.

14 If the fork tube is thought to be bent, check it for runout using V-blocks and a dial gauge (see Step 19).

15 If the fork bushes are thought to be worn, have the fork legs inspected by a BMW dealer. The bushes are located inside the slider and require special equipment for removal and installation. If, when the fork oil is drained (see Step 16), it contains metallic particles, wear has been taking place on the bushes. Remove the oil seal and washer (see Step 18), then slide the tube into the slider and check for play between the two components. If there

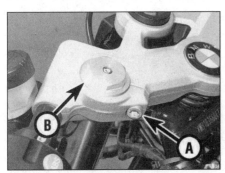

6.9 Top yoke clamp bolt (A) and circlip (B) – R1200 S

6.11 Remove the protective sleeve from the top of the fork tube

6.12 Check for oil leaks below underneath the dust seal

6.16a Undo the air bleed screw . . .

6.16b . . . and slide off the dust seal

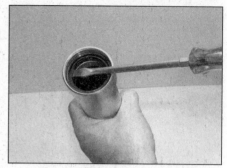

6.19 Lever the oil seal out carefully

is any play, either the bushes or the tube itself are worn.

16 To renew the oil seal, first undo the air bleed screw, noting the sealing O-ring, then slide off the dust seal **(see illustrations)**. Note that on R1200 ST and S models, the air bleed screw is located in the centre of the fork top bolt.

17 Support the fork leg upright and withdraw the tube from the slider, being prepared to catch any residual oil as the tube and slider are separated. Invert the slider over a suitable container and drain out all the oil.

Note: Do not loosen the bolt in the bottom of the slider – it is not a drain plug.

18 Note the location of the oil seal retaining clip, then prise the clip out carefully.

19 Carefully lever out the oil seal using a large flat-bladed screwdriver, taking care not to damage the rim of the slider **(see illustration)**.

Note which way up the seal is fitted. Note the location of the washer above the top fork bush.

20 Before reassembling the fork leg, check the fork tube for runout using V-blocks and a dial gauge **(see illustration)**. If the amount of runout exceeds the service limit specified, the tube should be renewed.

 Warning: If either fork tube is bent, it should not be straightened; replace both fork tubes with new ones.

21 Refill the slider with the specified type and amount of oil **(see illustration)**.

22 Insert the tube fully into the slider.

23 If removed, install the washer, then lubricate the new oil seal with a smear of fork oil and slide it over the tube with the small recess facing up. Tap the seal into place using a suitable piece of tubing or drift **(see**

illustration). Take care not to scratch the fork tube – make sure that the fork tube is pushed fully into the slider so that any accidental scratching is confined to the area above the oil seal.

24 When the seal is correctly seated, the groove for the retaining clip will be visible above the seal. Install the clip, making sure it is correctly located in its groove **(see illustrations)**.

25 Lubricate the lips of the new dust seal then slide it down the fork tube and press it into position **(see illustration 6.16b)**.

26 Fit a new O-ring onto the air bleed screw and install the screw loosely **(see illustration 6.16a)**.

27 If fitted, install the protective sleeve **(see illustration 6.11)**.

Fork installation

28 On R1200 GS and RT models, slide the fork leg up through the fork bridge, making sure all cables, hoses and wiring are correctly routed. When the slider is correctly seated in the fork bridge, tighten the clamp bolts to hold the slider in position **(see illustration)**. If removed, install the other fork leg, then install the axle to ensure both legs are correctly aligned **(see illustration)**. When the alignment has been checked, tighten the fork bridge clamp bolts to the torque setting specified at the beginning of this Chapter.

29 Push the tube up as far as it will go into the top yoke, then tighten the air bleed screw **(see illustration)**. Apply a suitable non-permanent thread-locking compound to the fork top

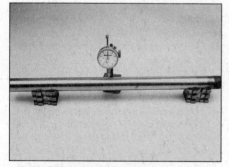

6.20 Check the fork tube runout using V-blocks and a dial gauge

6.21 Refill the slider with the specified type and amount of oil

6.23 Install the new seal carefully to avoid damage

6.24a Install the retaining clip . . .

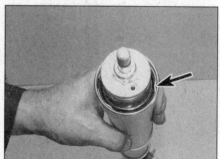

6.24b . . . ensuring it is correctly seated in its groove (arrowed)

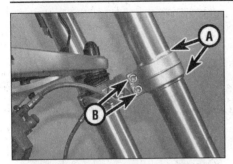

6.28a Ensure that the leg is correctly positioned in the bridge (A), then tighten the clamp bolts (B)

6.28b Install the axle to ensure fork alignment

6.29a Tighten the air bleed screw . . .

6.29b . . . then install the nut

6.31 Location of the air bleed screw (arrowed) - R1200 ST

6.33 Location of the air bleed screw (arrowed) - R1200 S

stud, then install the nut (see illustration). Counter-hold the fork top bolt and tighten the nut to the specified torque setting. Install the fork top cap. Install the remaining components in the reverse order of removal.

30 On R1200 ST models, slide the fork leg up through the fork bridge and install the handlebar on the tube. Make sure all cables, hoses and wiring are correctly routed. When the slider is correctly seated in the fork bridge, tighten the clamp bolts to hold the slider in position (see illustration 6.28a). If removed, install the other fork leg, then install the axle to ensure both legs are correctly aligned (see illustration 6.28b). When the alignment has been checked, tighten the fork bridge clamp bolts to the torque setting specified at the beginning of this Chapter.

31 Pull the tube up into the top yoke. The tube should protrude 3 mm above the top of the yoke (see illustration 5.17). Tighten the clamp bolt

in the top yoke to the torque setting specified at the beginning of this Chapter, then tighten the air bleed screw (see illustration). Install the handlebars and the remaining components in the reverse order of removal.

32 On R1200 S models, slide the fork leg up through the fork bridge, making sure all cables, hoses and wiring are correctly routed. When the slider is correctly seated in the fork bridge, tighten the clamp bolts to hold the slider in position (see illustration 6.28a). If removed, install the other fork leg, then install the axle to ensure both legs are correctly aligned (see illustration 6.28b). When the alignment has been checked, tighten the fork bridge clamp bolts to the torque setting specified at the beginning of this Chapter.

33 Pull the tube up through the top yoke until the circlip groove is visible and install the circlip, then push the tube back down to seat the circlip against the top of the yoke. Tighten

the clamp bolt in the top yoke to the torque setting specified at the beginning of this Chapter, then tighten the air bleed screw (see illustration). Install the remaining components in the reverse order of removal.

34 On R1200 R models, slide each fork leg up into the top yoke and fit the four fork bridge bolts (see illustration). Push the fork tube up as far as it will go into the top yoke, then tighten the air bleed screw (see illustration). Note that the bleed screw is tricky to access due to limited space between it and the top yoke. We found that this could be overcome by marking the fork tube position whilst held in the top yoke using tape wrapped around the tube at the joint with the dust seal; the fork bridge bolts were then slackened off to drop the fork leg 10 mm or so below the fork bridge, and with the edge of the tape still aligned with the dust seal the air bleed screw was tightened (see illustration).

6.34a On R1200 R install the fork bridge bolts . . .

6.34b . . . and push the fork tube up into the top yoke

6.34c Tightening the air bleed screw

6.35a Fit a new nut on the top bolt stud . . .

6.35b . . . then counterhold the fork top bolt and tighten the nut

6.35c Press the top cap into the yoke

35 Fit a new nut on the fork top bolt stud **(see illustration)**. Counterhold the hex of the top bolt and tighten the nut to the specified torque setting **(see illustration)**. Press the top cap into place **(see illustration)**. Install the wheel axle to ensure both fork legs are correctly aligned **(see illustration 6.28b)**. The distance between the inner faces of the forks should be 170 ± 0.5 mm; release the axle clamp bolt in the right fork and adjust the position until the setting is correct, then tighten the bolt. Now tighen the fork bridge bolts to the specified torque setting, then install the remaining components in the reverse order of removal.

Shock absorber

Shock removal

Note: *On machines equipped with electronic suspension adjustment (ESA), the operation of the ESA should be checked with both shocks in place on the bike (see Section 9).*

36 Position the bike on its centre stand or support it securely on an auxiliary stand. Work can be made easier by raising the machine to a suitable working height on an hydraulic ramp or a suitable platform.

37 If the front wheel is off the ground, place a block of wood under it to prevent it from dropping when the shock absorber lower bolt is removed. If the weight of the machine is on the front wheel, place a jack or block of wood under the engine to take the weight. It is essential that no loading is placed on the shock absorber. Make sure the motorcycle is secure and will not topple over.

38 Refer to the procedure in Chapter 6 and remove the fairing panels, according to your model, to gain access to the front suspension. Remove the fuel tank (see Chapter 3). On 1200 R models remove the oil cooler shroud (see Chapter 2).

39 On machines equipped with electronic suspension adjustment (ESA), trace the wiring from the damping adjustment motor on the shock absorber to the connector and disconnect it. Free the wiring from any ties securing it to the front sub-frame.

40 Undo the bolt securing the lower end of the shock absorber and remove it **(see illustration)**. Note that the bolt will have been thread-locked in place; use heat if necessary to help break the seal.

41 Counter-hold the stud on the top of the shock using an Allen key and loosen the nut **(see illustration)**. Support the shock absorber, then remove the nut and washer and withdraw the shock absorber from its upper mounting **(see illustrations)**.

6.40 Bolt (arrowed) secures lower end of the front shock absorber

6.41a Counter-hold the stud (arrowed) and loosen the nut

6.41b Remove the nut and washer . . .

6.41c . . . and withdraw the shock from its upper mounting (arrowed)

6.42 Remove the bushes and spacer

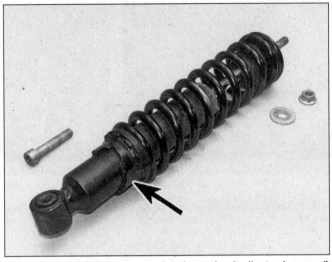

6.43 Where applicable, ensure that the preload adjuster (arrowed) is free to turn

42 Remove the upper and lower bushes and the spacer from the upper shock absorber mounting **(see illustration)**.

Shock inspection

43 Inspect the shock absorber for obvious physical damage. Check the spring for looseness, cracks or signs of fatigue and, where applicable, check that the spring pre-load adjuster is clean and free to turn **(see illustration)**.
44 Inspect the damper rod for signs of bending, pitting and oil leakage.
45 Inspect the pivot hardware at the top and bottom of the shock for wear or damage.
46 Apart from the shock mounting components, individual component parts for the front shock absorber are not available. The entire unit must be renewed if it is worn or damaged although it may be worth first seeking advice from a suspension specialist.

Shock installation

47 Installation is the reverse of removal, noting the following:
● Renew the upper mounting bushes if they are damaged or fatigued.

● Lubricate the shoulder of the lower mounting bolt with a smear of grease.
● Apply a suitable non-permanent thread-locking compound to the mounting bolt and nut.
● Tighten the upper and lower mountings to the torque settings specified at the beginning of this Chapter.
● On machines equipped with ESA, reconnect the wiring connector and secure the wiring to the sub-frame. Do this with the forks extended to avoid strain on the wiring when the machine is in use.

Telelever arm

Arm removal

Special tool: A ball joint splitter is necessary for this procedure **(see illustration 6.51b)**.
Note: The fork bridge is part of the front brake system, linking the hose from the handlebar master cylinder with the hoses to the brake calipers. If, during this procedure, the brake hoses are disconnected, the system will have to be topped-up and bled after reassembly to ensure that no air is trapped in the system (see Chapter 5). On machines fitted with ABS, the system must be serviced by a BMW dealer

using a BMW diagnostic tester afterwards to restore brake operation.
48 Follow the procedures above and remove both fork legs.
49 To avoid disconnecting the brake system, the lower ball joint must be split and the fork bridge separated from the Telelever arm as follows. If the bridge is to be left in place on the arm, proceed to Step 49.
50 On R1200S and R models, if the fork bridge is to be separated from the Telelever arm, remove the steering damper (see Section 8). Otherwise the damper can be left in place.
51 Prise the cap off the top of the ball joint. Using a hot air gun, heat the ball joint retaining nut to approximately 120°C, then counter-hold the stud on the top of the ball joint using an Allen key and undo the nut **(see illustration)**. Displace the boot on the ball joint and use a ball joint splitter to separate the Telelever arm from the fork bridge **(see illustration)**. Secure the fork bridge to the machine with a cable tie to avoid straining the brake hose. Now go to Step 53.

> **HAYNES HINT** Heating the nut softens the threadlock and will make it easier to undo. This will work on the particular threadlock that BMW use on assembly, however if the nut has since been tightened using a different type of threadlock, heat may actually make it more difficult to remove. If this is the case, allow the parts to cool and try again.

52 Follow the procedure in Chapter 5, Section 9, and separate the brake hoses from the fork bridge.
53 Follow the procedure in Steps 39 to 42 and remove the shock absorber.
54 Prise off the covers on both ends of the Telelever pivot shaft, noting the location of the

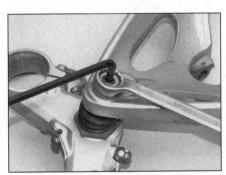

6.51a Counter-hold the stud and undo the ball joint nut

6.51b Separate the arm from the fork bridge using a ball joint splitter

6.54a Prise off the covers on both ends of the Telelever pivot shaft

6.54b Counter-hold the head of the pivot shaft . . .

6.54c . . . and undo the bolt

O-rings **(see illustration)**. Counter-hold the head of the pivot shaft and undo the bolt on the right-hand side **(see illustrations)**.

55 Support the Telelever arm and withdraw the pivot shaft, then lift the Telelever arm off **(see illustrations)**.

Arm inspection

56 Thoroughly clean all the components, removing all traces of dirt, corrosion and grease. Inspect all components closely, looking for obvious signs of wear such as heavy scoring and cracks or distortion due to accident damage. Any damaged or worn component must be renewed.

57 Slide the pivot shaft through the bearings and check that there is no resistance due to distortion of the Telelever arm. If there is, first ensure that the pivot shaft is straight by checking for runout using V-blocks and a dial gauge **(see illustration 6.20)**. If the shaft is straight, then the arm itself could be bent – have it checked by a BMW dealer.

58 There are two bearings fitted in each side of the arm – the outer bearing is a sealed caged ball bearing and the inner bearing is a needle roller bearing with a sleeve **(see illustrations)**. Press the sleeves out, noting which side they fit, and clean off the old grease. Refer to *Tools and Workshop Tips* in the *Reference* section and inspect the bearings and sleeves for wear or damage. If the bearings do not turn smoothly or if there is excessive freeplay, they must be renewed.

59 Inspect the ball joint on the fork bridge for signs of wear or damage. There should be no noticeable play in the joint, but it should move freely with no signs of roughness or notchiness. Note that on R1200 S and R models, if the fork bridge has not been separated from the Telelever arm, the steering damper must be removed to check the ball joint (see Section 8). If any wear or damage is evident, the joint must be renewed as follows.

60 If not already done, follow the procedure in Step 51 and separate the Telelever arm from the fork bridge. Note that the brake hoses must be disconnected from the bridge if the ball joint is going to be renewed (see Chapter 5, Section 9).

61 Clamp the fork bridge in a soft-jawed vice. Using a hot air gun, heat the bridge around the ball joint to approximately 120°C, then unscrew the ball joint (see *Haynes Hint*).

62 Smear the threads of the new joint with molybdenum grease, then install it and tighten it to the torque setting specified at the beginning of this Chapter.

63 Fit the Telelever arm onto the fork bridge. Apply a suitable non-permanent thread locking compound to the ball joint stud threads and install the nut. Counter-hold the stud using an Allen key and tighten the nut to the specified torque setting.

Arm installation

64 Lubricate the bearings with fresh grease and install the bearing sleeves **(see illustration 6.58b)**. Lubricate the pivot shaft with a smear of grease.

65 Fit the Telelever arm onto its engine mountings and install the pivot shaft from the left-hand side **(see illustrations 6.55b and a)**. Install the bolt on the right-hand side, then counter-hold the pivot shaft and tighten the bolt to the initial torque setting specified at the beginning of this Chapter. Now tighten the bolt to the final torque setting specified.

66 If necessary, fit new O-rings onto the pivot shaft covers, then press the covers into place **(see illustration 6.54a)**.

67 Install the shock absorber (see Step 47).

68 If not already done, install the fork bridge (see Step 63). If necessary, follow the procedure in Chapter 5 to reconnect the brake hoses.

69 If removed, install the steering damper (see Section 8).

70 Press the cap onto the top of the ball joint.

71 Install the fork legs (see Steps 28 to 35).

6.55a Withdraw the pivot shaft . . .

6.55b . . . then lift the Telelever arm off

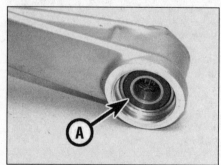

6.58a Outer sealed caged ball bearing (A) . . .

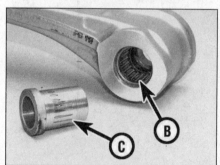

6.58b . . . and inner needle roller bearing (B) and bearing sleeve (C)

7 Steering head bearing or ball joint

1 The steering turns on a bearing (GS, RT and R models) or ball joint (ST and S models) in the top yoke, and a ball joint then links the

front of the Telelever arm to the fork bridge. These will wear during normal use, and may cause steering wobble – a condition that is potentially dangerous.

Check

2 Position the bike on its centre stand or support it securely on an auxiliary stand. Raise the front wheel off the ground either by having an assistant push down on the rear, or by placing a support under the engine.

3 Point the front wheel straight ahead, then slowly turn the handlebars from side to side. Any roughness in the bearings will be felt and the bars will not move smoothly and freely. If it is thought that the bearings are worn or damaged it will be necessary to partially disassemble the steering and suspension components for further investigation.

4 To check the ball joint on the Telelever arm, follow the procedure in Section 6 and remove both fork legs. The fork bridge should move freely without any sign of roughness or play in the joint. Note that on R1200 S and R models, the steering damper must be removed to check the ball joint (see Section 8). Check that the boot shows no signs of deterioration and is free from cracks and splits. To renew the ball joint, follow the procedure in Section 6, Steps 60 to 63.

5 To check the steering head bearing or ball joint, position the bike on its centre stand or support it securely on an auxiliary stand. Make sure the machine is secure and will not topple over.

6 Refer to the procedure in Chapter 6 and remove the fairing panels, according to your model, to gain access to the front suspension.

7 Remove the fuel tank (see Chapter 3).

8 On R1200 GS, RT, ST and R models, follow the procedure in Section 5 and displace the handlebars. Note that it is not necessary to remove any of the handlebar components. Keep the front brake and clutch master cylinders upright to prevent fluid spillage and make sure no strain in placed on the hoses and wiring.

9 On R1200 GS, RT, S and R models, follow the procedure in Section 6 and release the fork tubes from the top yoke. Pull the tubes down into the sliders until they are clear of the top yoke. Note that it may be necessary to loosen the air bleed screws in the fork top bolts to reduce pressure inside the fork legs.

10 The top yoke should turn freely on its bearing or ball joint without any sign of roughness or play. To renew the bearing or ball joint, proceed as follows.

Removal and installation – R1200 GS, RT and R

11 If not already done, refer to the procedure in Chapter 6 and remove the fairing panels to gain access to the front suspension.

12 Remove the fuel tank on all models (see Chapter 3). On R1200 R models remove the windshield (if fitted), followed by the headlamp and its mounting bracket.

13 Follow the procedure in Section 5 and displace the handlebars. Note that it is not necessary to remove any of the handlebar components. Keep the front brake and clutch master cylinders upright to prevent fluid spillage and make sure no strain in placed on the hoses and wiring.

14 Follow the procedure in Section 6 and release the fork tubes from the top yoke. Pull the tubes down into the sliders until they are clear of the top yoke. Note that it may be necessary to loosen the air bleed screws in the fork top bolts to reduce pressure inside the fork legs.

15 Undo the screws securing the ignition switch wiring connector cover and lift the cover off, then disconnect the wiring connectors **(see illustrations)**.

16 Remove the steering head cap **(see illustration)**.

17 Counter-hold the stud on the top of the steering head using an Allen key and undo the nut on the underside of the steering head **(see illustration)**. Lift off the top yoke.

18 It is advisable to remove the ignition switch (see Chapter 7). If left in place, take

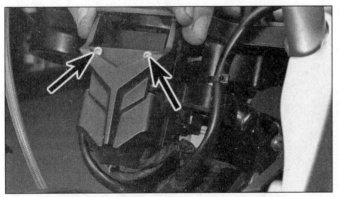

7.15a Cover is secured by two screws (arrowed)

7.15b Disconnect the ignition switch and immobiliser wiring connectors (arrowed)

7.16 Remove the steering head cap

7.17 Location of the nut (arrowed) on the underside of the steering head

extreme care to protect the ignition switch/steering lock when using heat or force on the top yoke.

19 Note the location of the circlip or retaining clip securing the bearing in the top yoke, then prise it out **(see illustration)**.

20 The bearing must be driven out of the top yoke from the underside. Support the top yoke on blocks of wood with sufficient clearance to

allow the bearing to come out. Use a hot air gun to heat the top yoke bearing housing, then drive the bearing and stud out with a suitably sized socket.

21 Support the edges of the bearing and drive the stud out, taking care not to damage the stud threads.

22 The fork top studs locate in bushes in the top yoke **(see illustration 7.19)**. If the bearing

is being renewed, it is good practice to renew the bushes also. Remove the circlip from the top of each bush, then turn the yoke over and press the bushes out from the underside of the yoke. Install the new bushes from the top using a drawbolt set-up (see *Tools and Workshop Tips* in the Reference section). Secure the bushes with new circlips.

23 Press the stud into the new steering head bearing.

24 The new bearing must be driven into the top yoke from the top. Support the top yoke on blocks of wood with sufficient clearance to allow the bearing/stud assembly to be fully installed. Use a hot air gun to heat the top yoke bearing housing, then drive the bearing in. Ensure that the socket or driver bears only on the bearing's outer race.

25 Secure the bearing with the circlip or retaining clip, making sure it seats properly in its groove.

26 Install the ignition switch (see Chapter 7).

27 Ensure that the threads of the stud are clean, then apply a suitable non-permanent thread-locking compound. Install the yoke onto the steering head and tighten the nut finger-tight. Counter-hold the stud using an Allen key and tighten the nut to the torque setting specified at the beginning of this Chapter. Fit the steering head cap **(see illustration 7.16)**.

28 Install the remaining components in the reverse order of removal.

Removal and installation – R1200 ST and S

29 If not already done, refer to the procedure in Chapter 6 and remove the fairing panels to gain access to the front suspension.

30 Remove the fuel tank (see Chapter 3).

31 On R1200 S models, follow the procedure in Section 5 and displace the handlebars. Note that it is not necessary to remove any of the handlebar components. Keep the front brake and clutch master cylinders upright to prevent fluid spillage and make sure no strain in placed on the hoses and wiring. On R1200 ST models, follow the procedure in Section 5 and slide the handlebars down the fork tubes until they are clear of the handlebar locating pins.

32 Follow the procedure in Section 6 and release the fork tubes from the top yoke. Pull the tubes down into the sliders until they are clear of the top yoke. Note that it may be necessary to loosen the air bleed screws in the fork top bolts to reduce pressure inside the fork legs.

33 Undo the screws securing the ignition switch wiring connector cover and lift the cover off, then disconnect the wiring connectors **(see illustrations 7.15a and b)**. Position any wiring clear of the underside of the top yoke.

34 Remove the steering head cap or prise the BMW badge off the top of the fork yoke to avoid getting it damaged **(see illustration 7.16)**.

35 Using a hot air gun, heat the ball joint retaining nut to approximately 120°C, then counter-hold the stud on the ball joint using

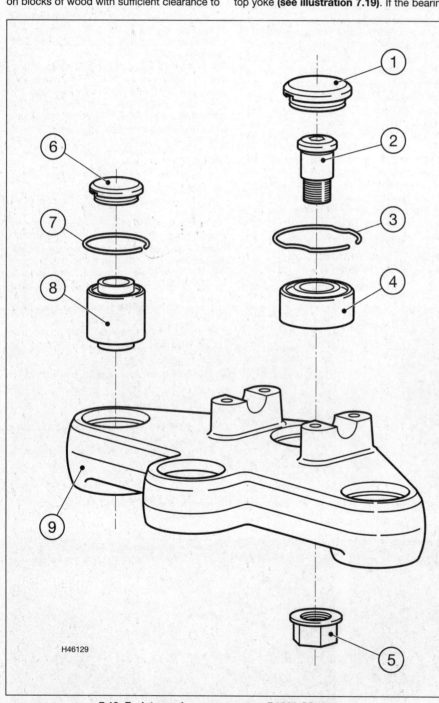

H46129

7.19 Fork top yoke components – R1200 GS shown

1	Steering head cap	4	Bearing	7	Circlip
2	Stud	5	Nut	8	Bush
3	Circlip or retaining clip	6	Fork top cap	9	Top yoke

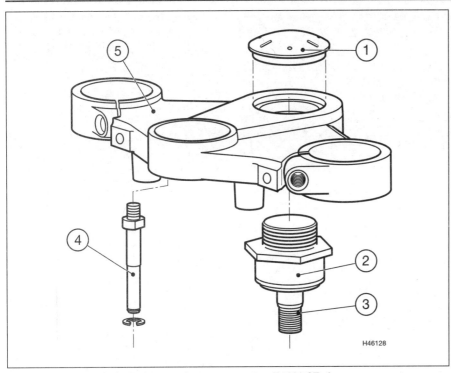

7.35 Fork top yoke components – R1200 ST shown

1 Steering head cap	3 Ball joint stud	5 Top yoke
2 Ball joint	4 Handlebar locating pin	

an Allen key and undo the nut. Lift off the top yoke **(see illustration)**.
36 Remove the ignition switch (see Chapter 7).
37 In order for the ball joint to be unscrewed from the top yoke, the yoke must be held securely in a vice and heated to approximately 120°C. BMW provide special tools to hold the yoke (Part Nos. 31 5 741 and 31 5 743). If the tools are not available, great care must be taken to avoid damaging the top yoke.
38 Using a hot air gun, heat the bridge around the ball joint to approximately 120°C, then unscrew the ball joint **(see illustration 7.35)**.
39 Smear the threads of the new joint with

molybdenum grease, then install it and tighten it to the torque setting specified at the beginning of this Chapter.
40 Install the ignition switch (see Chapter 7).
41 Ensure that the threads of the stud are clean, then apply a suitable non-permanent thread-locking compound. Install the yoke onto the steering head and tighten the nut finger-tight. Counter-hold the stud using an Allen key and tighten the nut to the torque setting specified at the beginning of this Chapter. Fit the steering head cap or badge.
42 Install the remaining components in the reverse order of removal.

8 Steering damper

Check

1 A steering damper is fitted as standard to the R1200 S and R. Follow the procedure in Chapter 6 and remove the fairing left-hand side panel.
2 Support the bike securely on an auxiliary stand with the front wheel off the ground, then turn the forks from lock to lock and check that there is no freeplay between the damper unit and its mountings **(see illustration)**.
3 If any freeplay is evident, check that the mounting bolts and the rose joint locknut are tightened securely **(see illustration)**. Note that the nut for the front mounting is on the underside of the fork bridge. If the mountings are tight, then either the rose joint itself is worn, or the bushes in the body mounting are worn. The bushes are available separately, but the rose joint is integral with the damper and so a new steering damper will have to be fitted.
4 Check that the damper rod moves smoothly in and out of the damper body with no signs of roughness or binding **(see illustration 8.3)**.
5 Check the rod for pitting and corrosion, and around each end of the damper body for signs of fluid leakage. Renew the damper if any of the above are evident.

Removal and installation

6 Counter-hold the hex on the front mounting and undo the nut, then separate the damper rod from the fork bridge. Undo the damper mounting bolt and lift the damper off, noting the location of the bushes.
7 Installation is the reverse of removal. Ensure that the mountings are tightened to the torque setting specified at the beginning of this Chapter. With the front wheel off the ground, check that the forks turn smoothly from lock to lock.

8.2 Steering damper is secured to the fork bridge (A) and the Telelever arm (B)

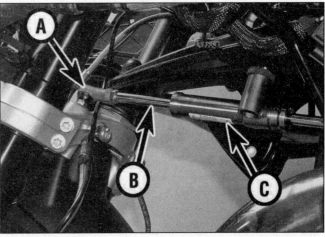

8.3 Steering damper rose joint (A), damper rod (B) and body (C)

9.4 Spring preload adjuster knob is secured by screw (arrowed) - R1200 RT

9.5 Spring preload adjuster knob is secured by screw (arrowed) - R1200 ST

9.6 Spring preload adjuster knob screw (A) and starter relay tab (B) – R1200 R

9 Rear shock absorber

Removal

Note: *On models equipped with electronic suspension adjustment (ESA), the operation of the ESA should be checked with the shock absorber on the bike (see Steps 15 to 27).*

1 Remove the seat (see Chapter 6).

2 Remove the exhaust silencer (see Chapter 3).

3 Remove the rear wheel (see Chapter 5). Place a support under the swingarm to prevent it dropping when the shock is removed.

4 On R1200 RT models, undo the two screws securing the lower section of the

rear mudguard and lift the mudguard off. On machines equipped with electronic suspension adjustment (ESA), unclip the cable from the mudguard. On machines equipped with manually adjusted spring preload, undo the screw securing the adjuster knob **(see illustration)**. On ESA-equipped machines, undo the two screws securing the suspension adjustment units, then disconnect the wiring connectors from the units. Ensure that the wiring is free from any clips or ties.

5 On R1200 ST models, undo the two screws securing the lower section of the rear mudguard and lift the mudguard off. On machines equipped with electronic suspension adjustment (ESA), unclip the cable from the mudguard. On machines equipped with manually adjusted spring preload, remove the left-hand seat cowling panel (see Chapter 6),

then undo the screw securing the adjuster knob **(see illustration)**. On ESA-equipped machines, disconnect the wiring connectors from the suspension adjustment units. Ensure that the wiring is free from any clips or ties.

6 On R1200 R models equipped with ESA, disconnect the three wiring connectors and any cable-ties securing the ESA wiring to the frame. On models with manually adjusted spring preload, undo the screw securing the adjuster knob, then pull the starter relay off its tab **(see illustration)**.

7 On all models, place a support (a block of wood or an axle stand is ideal) underneath the final drive unit to prevent the swingarm dropping when the lower shock absorber bolt is removed **(see illustration)**. Do not place the support under the rear brake disc.

8 Undo the bolt securing the lower end of the shock absorber to the swingarm **(see illustration)** – note that you may need to apply heat to the mounting point to assist bolt removal. On R1200 S models, note the location of the spacer in the lower mounting and remove it.

9 Undo the nut on the upper mounting bolt, then support the shock and withdraw the bolt **(see illustrations)**. Lift the shock out **(see illustration)**. On ESA-equipped machines, note the routing of the wiring.

Inspection

10 Inspect the shock absorber for obvious physical damage and the coil spring for

9.7 Place a support (arrowed) underneath the swingarm

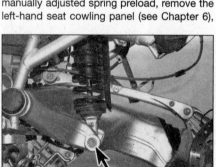

9.8 Bolt (arrowed) secures lower end of the shock absorber

9.9a Undo the nut on the upper mounting bolt . . .

9.9b . . . then support the shock and withdraw the bolt . . .

9.9c . . . and lift the shock absorber out

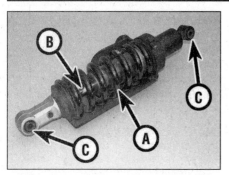
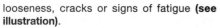

9.10 Inspect the rear shock spring (A), damper rod (B) and mounting bushes (C)

9.11 Spring pre-load adjuster. Note the calibrations (arrowed)

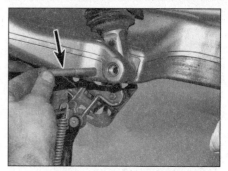

9.14 Apply a smear of grease to the shoulder (arrowed) of each mounting bolt

looseness, cracks or signs of fatigue (see illustration).

11 Inspect the damper rod for signs of pitting and oil leakage. Check the operation of the spring pre-load adjuster (see illustration). Where fitted, check the remote spring pre-load adjuster hose for fatigue and signs of leakage at the unions.

12 Inspect the pivot bushes at the top and bottom of the shock for wear or damage.

13 Individual components for the rear shock absorber are not available. The entire unit must be replaced with a new one if it is worn or damaged.

Installation

14 Installation is the reverse of removal, noting the following.
● Lubricate the shoulders of the mounting bolts with a smear of grease (see illustration).
● On R1200 S models, don't forget to fit the spacer in the shock lower mounting.
● Apply a suitable non-permanent thread-locking compound to the mounting bolts.
● Tighten the nuts and bolts to the torque settings specified at the beginning of this Chapter.
● On ESA-equipped machines, ensure that the wiring connectors are clean and secure. Renew any cable ties as noted on removal.
● Adjust the suspension as required (see Section 10).

Check – electronic suspension adjustment (ESA)

R1200 R, ST and RT models

15 To check that the ESA is changing the damping, sit on the bike with the stands up. Turn the ignition ON and use the ESA button to select the COMF (comfortable damping) setting (see Section 10, Step 18). Turn the ignition OFF.

16 Move your weight forwards in the seat and start a 'rocking' effect in the suspension, then turn the ignition ON – as the ESA re-adjusts, there should be a noticeable increase in the suspension damping. Turn the ignition OFF.

17 If no change is noted in the damping, have the system checked by a BMW dealer using the BMW diagnostic tester.

18 To check that the ESA is changing the spring pre-load, first remove the bodywork as necessary on your bike to access the rear shock absorber (see Chapter 6).

19 Sit on the bike with the stands up. Turn the ignition ON and use the ESA button to select a new pre-load setting (see Section 10, Step 18). Turn the ignition OFF. Depending upon whether the ESA has increased or decreased the pre-load, there should have been a noticeable rise or fall at the rear of the machine.

20 Measure the distance between the top of the spring and the main body of the shock – note that the sleeve inside the top of the spring is part of the adjusting mechanism (see illustration 9.24).

21 With the preload on its softest setting (helmet symbol – rider only) there should be zero clearance. With the preload on its middle

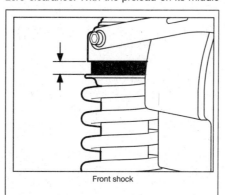
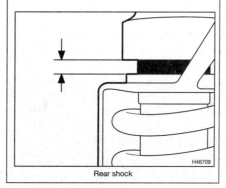

9.24 ESA shock preload measurement points

setting (helmet and bag symbols – rider with luggage) there should be 4 to 6 mm clearance. With the preload on its hardest setting (two helmet symbols – rider, passenger and luggage) there should be 9 to 10 mm clearance.

R1200 GS models

22 Refer to Steps 15 to 17 above to check the damping function.

23 To check the spring preload function, sit on the bike with the stands up and start the engine. Press the ESA button, then press and hold it down until the 'one helmet' symbol appears on the display. Note any change in the preload, then select the off-road preload setting 'large mountain' symbol. You should notice the suspension rise considerably.

24 If there is no real difference in ride height, measure the distance between the top of the spring and the main body of the shock – note that the sleeve inside the top of the spring is part of the adjusting mechanism (see illustration). This distance should be 11 to 13 mm on the front shock and 9 to 10 mm on the rear in the severe off-road 'large mountain' preload position.

25 The distance can be checked in other preload positions:

Symbol	Front shock	Rear shock
One helmet	0 mm	0 mm
One helmet and bag	0 mm	4 to 6 mm
Two helmets	0 mm	9 to 10 mm
Small mountain (light off-road riding)	5 to 7 mm	4 to 6 mm
Large mountain (severe off-road riding)	11 to 13 mm	9 to 10 mm

26 If the check and measurements do not give the results as described, it is likely the shock is defective and must be renewed, although it is advisable to have this confirmed by a BMW dealer. No individual components are available.

All models

27 If the check and measurements do not give the results as described, it is likely the

shock is defective and must be renewed, although it is advisable to have this confirmed by a BMW dealer. No individual components are available.

10 Suspension adjustments

R1200 GS

1 Position the bike on its centre stand or support it securely on an auxiliary stand.

Front shock absorber

2 The front shock is adjustable for spring pre-load. Adjustment is made using a suitable C-spanner (one is provided in the toolkit) to turn the spring seat on the base of the shock absorber **(see illustration)**.

3 There are nine settings. Position 1 is the softest setting, position 9 is the hardest. Align the setting required with the adjustment stopper. On 2004 to 2007 models, BMW recommend position 3 for road use, position 5 for gravel tracks and with load, and position 9 for off-road riding. On models from 2008, BMW recommend position 2 for road use, position 3 for gravel tracks and with load, and position 5 for off-road riding.

Rear shock absorber

4 The rear shock absorber is adjustable for spring pre-load and damping.

5 Spring pre-load adjustment is made by turning the adjuster knob on the shock **(see illustration)**. BMW recommend the following settings. For rider-only use, turn the knob fully anti-clockwise (LOW arrow) , then turn it 10 clicks clockwise. For rider and passenger with luggage, or off-road riding, turn the knob fully clockwise (HIGH arrow).

6 If further adjustments are required, turn the knob anti-clockwise (LOW arrow) to reduce preload, and clockwise (HIGH arrow) to increase preload.

10.2 Adjusting the front shock spring preload - R1200 GS

7 Suspension damping must be set-up to suit spring pre-load. An increase in pre-load requires firmer damping, a reduction in pre-load requires softer damping. Adjustment is made by turning the adjuster screw on the lower end of the shock **(see illustration)**.

8 For rider-only use, turn the screw fully clockwise (H arrow) , then turn it 1 1/2 turns anti-clockwise (S arrow). If further adjustments are required, turn the screw clockwise (H arrow) for harder damping and anti-clockwise (S arrow) for softer damping.

Front and rear shock absorbers – electronic suspension adjustment (ESA)

9 A combination of spring pre-load and damping options can be selected using the ESA button on the left-hand switch assembly. Both shock absorbers are adjustable simultaneously by the ESA system – there is no provision for adjusting the shocks individually or manually.

10 Turn the ignition ON and press the ESA button briefly to display the current setting. The selected options are displayed at the bottom of the multi-function display on the instrument cluster – damping on the left and spring pre-load on the right.

11 To change the damping setting, press the button briefly to scroll through each option

in turn. Scroll down these settings – COMF (comfortable damping), NORM (normal damping) and SPORT (sporty damping). On Adventure models you can also select off-road riding ESA settings, SOFT, NORMAL and HARD. Stop pressing the button when the desired setting is displayed. The damping can be adjusted while the motorcycle is being ridden.

12 To change the pre-load setting, press the button and hold it down until the display changes to scroll through each option in turn – helmet symbol (rider only), helmet and bag symbols (rider with luggage); two helmet symbols (rider, passenger and luggage); off-road settings are small mountain for light off-road riding and large mountain for severe off-road riding. Stop pressing the button when the desired setting is displayed. Wait until adjustment is complete and the display stops flashing before riding the motorcycle. The pre-load cannot be adjusted while the motorcycle is being ridden.

R1200 RT, ST and R

13 Position the bike on its centre stand or support it securely on an auxiliary stand. On machines with manually adjustable suspension, only the rear shock absorber is adjustable.

Rear shock absorber – manual adjustment

14 The rear shock absorber is adjustable for spring pre-load and damping.

15 Spring pre-load adjustment is made by turning the remotely mounted adjuster knob **(see illustrations 9.4, 9.5 or 9.6)**. BMW recommend the STD setting on the scale for rider-only use.

16 If further adjustments are required, turn the knob anti-clockwise (LOW arrow) to reduce preload, and clockwise (HIGH arrow) to increase preload.

17 Suspension damping must be set-up to suit spring pre-load. An increase in pre-load requires firmer damping, a reduction in

10.5 Rear shock spring preload adjuster knob - R1200 GS

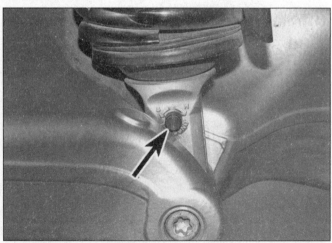

10.7 Suspension damping adjuster screw (arrowed) - R1200 GS

10.17 Suspension damping adjuster screw (arrowed) - R1200 ST

10.25a Rear shock spring preload adjuster (arrowed) - R1200 S standard shock

pre-load requires softer damping. Adjustment is made by turning the adjuster screw on the lower end of the shock (see illustration).

18 For rider-only use, first turn the screw fully clockwise (H arrow). On R1200 RT models, then turn the screw 3/4 turn anti-clockwise (S arrow). On R1200 ST models, then turn the screw one turn anti-clockwise (S arrow). On R1200 R models, then turn the screw one and a half turns anti-clockwise (S arrow). If further adjustments are required, turn the screw clockwise (H arrow) for harder damping and anti-clockwise (S arrow) for softer damping.

Front and rear shock absorbers – electronic suspension adjustment (ESA)

19 The front shock absorber is adjustable for damping only, the rear shock is adjustable for spring pre-load and damping. A combination of spring pre-load and damping options can be selected using the ESA button on the left-hand switch assembly. Both shock absorbers are adjustable simultaneously by the ESA system – there is no provision for adjusting the shocks individually.

20 Turn the ignition ON and press the ESA button briefly to display the current setting. The selected options are displayed at the bottom of the multi-function display on the instrument cluster – damping on the left and spring pre-load on the right.

21 To change the damping setting, press the button briefly to scroll through each option in turn – COMF (comfortable damping), NORM (normal damping) and SPORT (sporty damping). Stop pressing the button when the desired setting is displayed. The damping can be adjusted while the motorcycle is being ridden.

22 To change the pre-load setting, press the button and hold it down until the display changes to scroll through each option in turn – helmet symbol (rider only), helmet and bag symbols (rider with luggage) and two helmet symbols (rider, passenger and luggage). Stop pressing the button when the desired setting is displayed. The pre-load cannot be adjusted while the motorcycle is being ridden.

R1200 S

23 Support the bike securely on an auxiliary stand. The standard front shock absorber is not adjustable.

Standard rear shock absorber

24 The rear shock absorber is adjustable for spring pre-load and damping.

25 Spring pre-load adjustment is made using a suitable C-spanner (provided in the toolkit) to turn the spring seat on the top of the shock

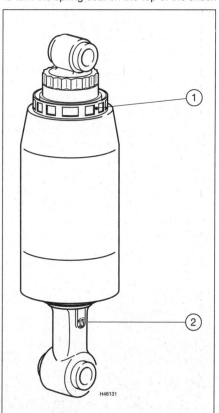

10.25b Standard rear shock absorber – R1200 S models

1 Spring seat
2 Damping adjuster screw

absorber (see illustrations). For rider-only use, BMW recommend position 2.

26 If further adjustments are required, turn the knob anti-clockwise to reduce preload, and clockwise to increase preload.

27 Suspension damping must be set-up to suit spring pre-load. An increase in pre-load requires firmer damping, a reduction in pre-load requires softer damping. Adjustment is made by turning the adjuster screw on the lower end of the shock (see illustration 10.21b).

28 For rider-only use, turn the screw fully clockwise (H arrow) , then turn it 3/4 turn anti-clockwise (S arrow). If further adjustments are required, turn the screw clockwise (H arrow) for harder damping and anti-clockwise (S arrow) for softer damping.

Sports front shock absorber

29 The sports front shock absorber is adjustable for spring pre-load and damping.

30 Spring pre-load adjustment is made using two suitable C-spanners (provided in the toolkit) to adjust the length of the spring. For rider-only use, with no load on the front wheel, the spring length should be set to 184 mm.

31 To set the spring length, hold the (lower) adjuster ring and turn the (upper) lock ring anti-clockwise to free the two rings. Now turn the adjuster ring until the spring measures the specified length. Hold the adjuster ring and turn the lock ring clockwise until the rings are locked together.

32 If further adjustments are required, free the rings and turn the adjuster ring anti-clockwise to reduce preload, and clockwise to increase preload. Don't forget to lock the rings together when adjustment has been completed.

33 Suspension damping must be set-up to suit spring pre-load. An increase in pre-load requires firmer damping, a reduction in pre-load requires softer damping. Adjustment is made by turning the adjuster ring on the lower end of the shock.

34 For rider-only use, turn the ring fully clockwise, then turn it 16 clicks anti-clockwise. If further adjustments are required, turn the ring anti-clockwise for harder damping and clockwise for softer damping.

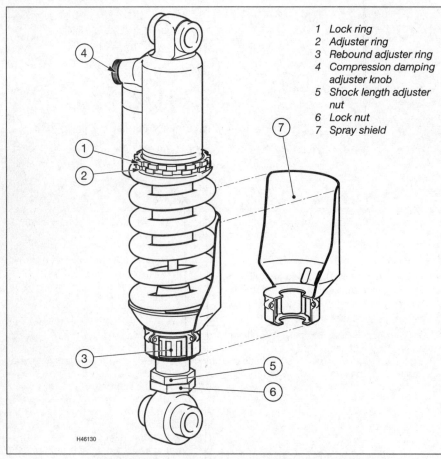

1 Lock ring
2 Adjuster ring
3 Rebound adjuster ring
4 Compression damping adjuster knob
5 Shock length adjuster nut
6 Lock nut
7 Spray shield

H46130

10.35 Sports rear shock absorber – R1200 S models

Sports rear shock absorber

35 The sports rear shock absorber is adjustable for spring pre-load, rebound and compression damping **(see illustration)**. The length of the shock is also adjustable. Note that suspension damping must be set-up to suit spring pre-load. An increase in pre-load requires firmer damping, a reduction in pre-load requires softer damping.

36 Spring pre-load adjustment is made using two suitable C-spanners (provided in the toolkit) to adjust the length of the spring. For rider-only use, with no load on the rear wheel, the spring length should be set to 158 mm.

37 Follow the procedure in Steps 26 to 28 to adjust the spring pre-load.

38 Rebound damping adjustment is made by turning the adjuster ring on the lower end of the shock.

39 Follow the procedure in Steps 29 and 30 to adjust rebound damping.

40 Compression damping adjustment is made by turning the adjuster knob on the top of the outside reservoir.

41 For rider-only use, turn the knob fully clockwise, then turn it 14 clicks anti-clockwise. If further adjustments are required, turn the knob clockwise (H arrow) for harder damping and anti-clockwise (S arrow) for softer damping.

42 To adjust the length of the rear shock, first remove the rear wheel (see Chapter 5). **Note:** *As standard, the adjustment is in its lowest position.*

43 Loosen the screws securing the spray shield.

44 Hold the (upper) adjuster nut and turn the (lower) lock nut clockwise to free the two nuts.

45 To increase the length of the shock, turn the adjuster nut anti-clockwise. To reduce the length of the shock, turn the adjuster nut clockwise. Once the shock is at the required length, hold the adjuster nut and turn the lock nut anti-clockwise until the nuts are locked together.

46 Don't forget to tighten the screws securing the spray shield when adjustment is complete.

11 Swingarm and driveshaft

Removal

Special tool: *A slide-hammer is necessary for this procedure (see illustration 11.16).*

1 The swingarm, drive shaft and final drive unit can be removed as an assembly. If the final drive unit has already been removed, ignore the steps which do not apply.

2 Position the bike on its centre stand or support it securely on an auxiliary stand.

3 Remove the seat (see Chapter 6).

4 On R1200 RT models, remove the fairing side panels (see Chapter 6) and the left and right-hand footrest mounting brackets (see Section 3).

5 Remove the exhaust silencer (see Chapter 3).

6 Remove the rear wheel (see Chapter 5).

7 Lift out the document tray, where fitted **(see illustration)**. Undo the screws securing the rear brake hose guide and lift the guide off the Paralever arm **(see illustrations)**. On models with ABS, trace the wiring from the rear wheel speed sensor to the wiring connector

11.7a Lift out the document tray

11.7b Undo the screws (arrowed)

11.7c ... and lift off the brake hose guide

11.7d Disconnect the rear ABS sensor wiring connector

11.8 Displace the rear brake calliper

11.9 Cut the cable tie on the driveshaft boot

11.11a Undo the nuts (arrowed) . . .

11.11b . . . then withdraw the front bolt . . .

11.11c . . . and the rear bolt . . .

and disconnect it (see illustration). Note the location of the cable ties securing the wiring to the frame, then cut the ties and secure the wiring next to the final drive unit, well clear of the rear sub-frame.

8 Displace the rear brake caliper (see Chapter 5), then secure the caliper to the rear sub-frame (see illustrations). Note that it is not necessary to disconnect the brake hose from the caliper.

9 Cut the cable tie securing the driveshaft boot to the rear of the gearbox (see illustration).

10 Remove the rear shock absorber (see Section 9). Place a support (a block of wood or an axle stand is ideal) underneath the final drive unit.

11 Counter-hold the bolts and undo the nuts securing the Paralever arm to the swingarm (front) and final drive unit (rear) (see

11.11d . . . and lift the Paralever arm off

illustration). Withdraw the bolts and lift the Paralever arm off, noting the location of the insulating washer (see illustrations).

12 Remove the support underneath the final

11.11e Note the location of the insulating washer

drive unit, then carefully tilt the housing back, displacing the coupling boot, to expose the rear driveshaft coupling (see illustrations). Note how the splined end of the bevel gear

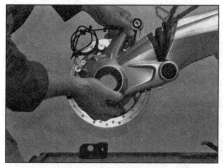

11.12a Remove the support and tilt the drive housing back . . .

11.12b . . . to displace the coupling boot (arrowed) . . .

11.12c . . . and expose the driveshaft coupling (arrowed)

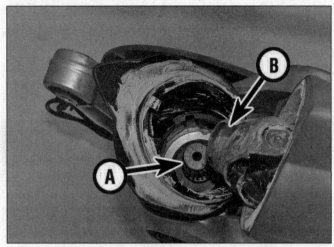

11.12d Note how the splined end of the bevel gear (A) locates inside the driveshaft coupling (B)

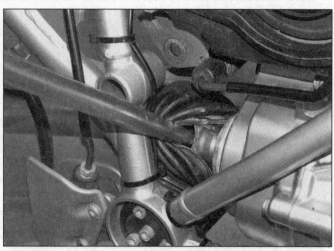

11.13a Lever the front driveshaft coupling off the gearbox output shaft . . .

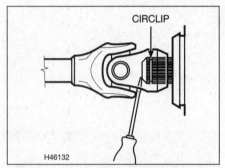

11.13b . . . by releasing the internal circlip (arrowed) from the groove in the output shaft

11.14 Undo the screws (arrowed) on the right-hand swingarm bearing pin

11.15a Prise the cover off the left-hand bearing pin . . .

in the final drive housing locates inside the driveshaft coupling (see illustration).
13 A circlip inside the front driveshaft coupling secures the coupling to the gearbox output shaft. To separate the driveshaft from the gearbox, first pull the driveshaft boot away from the gearbox. Insert a suitable bar or strong screwdriver between the two halves of the front driveshaft coupling so that it bears on the end of the gearbox output shaft, then prise the coupling off the gearbox shaft (see illustrations).

14 Undo the screws on the right-hand swingarm bearing pin (see illustration).
15 Prise the cover off the left-hand bearing pin (see illustration). Loosen the pin locknut, then unscrew the pin (see illustrations).

11.15b . . . then loosen the locknut (arrowed) . . .

11.15c . . . and unscrew the pin

11.16a Using a slide hammer . . .

11.16b . . . draw the right-hand bearing pin out

11.17 Lift the swingarm assembly off

16 Support the swingarm assembly. Using a slide-hammer or similar tool, threaded into the centre hole in the right-hand bearing pin, draw the pin out **(see illustrations)**.
17 Lift the swingarm assembly off **(see illustration)**.
18 If required for inspection, lift off the coupling boot and withdraw the driveshaft

from the swingarm, noting which way round it fits **(see illustrations)**.
19 If required, follow the procedure in Section 12 and separate the final drive unit from the swingarm.

Inspection
20 Remove the driveshaft boot from the

swingarm **(see illustration)**. Check the condition of the boot and renew it if it is cracked or split.
21 Clean all the components thoroughly, removing all traces of dirt, corrosion and grease.
22 Inspect the components closely for signs of wear or accident damage. Any damaged or worn components must be renewed.

11.18a Lift off the coupling boot . . .

11.18b . . . and withdraw the driveshaft

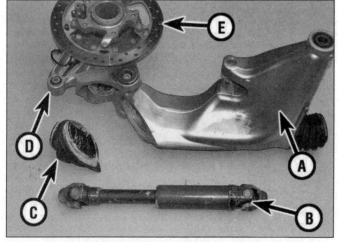

11.18c Swingarm assembly components. Swingarm (A), driveshaft (B), coupling boot (C), final drive unit (D) and rear brake disc (E)

11.20 Location of the driveshaft boot

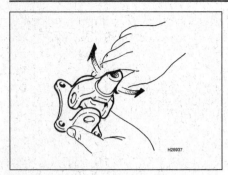

11.23 Check for any signs of freeplay or roughness in the universal joints

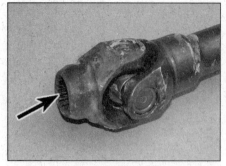

11.24 Inspect the splines (arrowed) inside the driveshaft couplings

11.25a Check the condition of the swingarm bearings . . .

23 Check the driveshaft coupling universal joints for wear. The joints should move smoothly and freely with no sign of roughness and there should be no play between the halves of the coupling **(see illustration)**. If wear is evident, a new driveshaft must be fitted – individual components are not available..

24 Inspect the splines for wear **(see illustration)**. The driveshaft couplings should be a sliding fit on the splined end of the bevel gear and on the gearbox output shaft. If there is excessive clearance at either end of the shaft the worn components must be renewed. To renew the gearbox output shaft, refer to Chapter 2, Section 30. Disassembling the final drive unit to renew the bevel gear is a task requiring special tools that must be undertaken by a BMW dealer.

25 Inspect the swingarm bearings and the surface of the bearing pins **(see illustrations)**. Refer to *Tools and Workshop Tips* in the *Reference* section for details of bearing inspection and renewal.

26 Inspect the bush in the front end of the Paralever arm. If the bush has deteriorated it should be renewed. Use a drawbolt arrangement to press the old bush out and the new bush in (see *Tools and Workshop Tips* in the *Reference* section).

Installation

27 Lubricate the gearbox output shaft splines with molybdenum disulphide grease. Push the driveshaft onto the output shaft until the circlip inside the front driveshaft coupling is felt to snap in its groove in the output shaft

(see illustrations). Make sure the driveshaft is secure on the output shaft.

28 Lubricate both ends of the driveshaft boot with silicone grease and install the boot on the swingarm **(see illustration 11.20)**.

29 Lubricate the right-hand bearing pin with a smear of grease, then slide the swingarm over the driveshaft and press the pin into place to secure it **(see illustrations)**.

30 Back-off the locknut on the left-hand bearing pin, lubricate the pin and install it finger-tight **(see illustration)**. Place a support underneath the swingarm.

31 Tighten the three outer screws securing the right-hand bearing pin to the torque setting specified at the beginning of this Chapter **(see illustration 11.14)**

32 Tighten the left-hand bearing pin to

11.25b . . . and the surface of the bearing pins (arrowed)

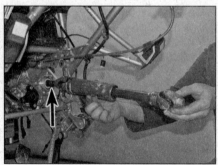

11.27a Push the driveshaft onto the gearbox output shaft (arrowed) . . .

11.27b . . . until it is held by the circlip inside the front coupling (arrowed)

11.29a Slide the swingarm over the driveshaft . . .

11.29b . . . and secure it with the right-hand bearing pin

11.30 Install the left-hand bearing pin finger-tight

11.32a Tighten the left-hand bearing pin to the specified torque . . .

11.32b . . . then mark its position (arrowed)

the specified torque setting, then mark the position of the pin with a dab of paint **(see illustrations)**. Tighten the locknut to the specified torque setting. Check that the bearing pin is still in the same position and check that the swingarm moves freely up and down **(see illustrations)**.

33 Install the rear shock absorber (see Section 9).

34 Ensure that the driveshaft boot is located fully around the end of the gearbox and secure it with a new cable tie **(see illustration 11.9)**.

35 If removed, install the final drive unit (see Section 12).

36 Fit the insulating washer onto the front end of the Paralever arm and position the arm inside the bracket on the rear sub-frame. Secure the arm with the bolt **(see illustrations 11.11e and b)**.

37 Lubricate the end of the coupling boot with silicone grease, then lift the final drive unit and engage the splined end of the bevel gear inside the driveshaft coupling **(see illustration)**. Ensure that the lip of the boot locates correctly inside the end of the swingarm and secure the final drive unit to the Paralever arm with the bolt **(see illustrations)**.

38 Apply a suitable non-permanent thread locking compound to the nuts and install the washers and nuts on the bolts securing the Paralever arm **(see illustration 11.11a)**.

11.32c Tighten the locknut to the specified torque . . .

Counter-hold the bolts and tighten the nuts to the specified torque settings.

39 Install the remaining components in the reverse order of removal.

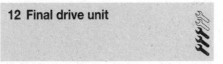

12 Final drive unit

Note: *This procedure covers removal and installation of the final drive unit. Further dismantling and set-up of the final drive unit requires special tools and is beyond the scope*

11.32d . . . and check that the swingarm moves freely up and down

of this manual. If the final drive unit is thought to be faulty have it checked by a BMW dealer.

Removal

1 Position the bike on its centre stand or support it securely on an auxiliary stand.

2 Remove the exhaust silencer (see Chapter 3).

3 Remove the rear wheel (see Chapter 5).

4 On R1200 RT models, remove the right-hand footrest mounting bracket (see Section 3).

5 Remove the seat (see Chapter 6), then lift out the document tray, where fitted **(see illustration 11.7a)**. Undo the screws securing

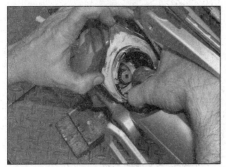

11.37a Engage the splined end of the bevel gear inside the driveshaft coupling

11.37b Locate the lip of the coupling boot inside the swingarm . . .

11.37c . . . and secure the final drive unit to the Paralever arm with the bolt

12.7 Undo the nut and washer (arrowed)

12.9a Prise off the cover . . .

12.9b . . . then counter-hold the pivot sleeve and undo the pivot bolt

the rear brake hose guide and lift the guide off the Paralever arm **(see illustration 11.7b and c)**. Trace the wiring from the rear wheel speed sensor to the wiring connector and disconnect it **(see illustration 11.7d)**. Note the location of the cable ties securing the wiring to the frame, then cut the ties and secure the wiring next to the final drive unit, well clear of the rear sub-frame.

6 Displace the rear brake caliper (see Chapter 5), then secure the caliper to the rear sub-frame **(see illustration 11.8)**. Note that it is not necessary to disconnect the brake hose from the caliper.

7 Undo the nut and remove the washer on the bolt securing the Paralever arm to the final drive unit **(see illustration)**.

8 Support the drive housing and withdraw the bolt, then carefully tilt the housing back, displacing the coupling boot **(see illustrations 11.37c and b)**. Support drive housing on a block of wood. Note how the splined end of the bevel gear in the final drive housing locates inside the driveshaft coupling **(see illustration 11.12d)**. Ease the coupling boot off the drive housing, noting which way round it fits **(see illustration 11.12b)**.

9 Prise the cover off the right-hand pivot sleeve on the drive housing, then counter-hold the pivot sleeve and undo the pivot bolt **(see illustrations)**.

10 Withdraw the pivot bolt **(see illustration)**.

11 Support the drive housing and pull out

the left-hand pivot pin, noting the location of the seal, then use a suitable drift to drive the right-hand pivot sleeve out **(see illustrations)**. Lift the drive housing off, noting the location of the spacer on the inside of the right-hand bearing housing **(see illustration)**.

Inspection

12 Clean the drive housing thoroughly, removing all traces of dirt and corrosion. Check for any evidence of oil leakage, particularly behind the brake disc flange and around the bevel gear shaft **(see illustration)**. Renewal of the drive housing seals must be undertaken by a BMW dealer.

13 Inspect the bearing surfaces of the pivot

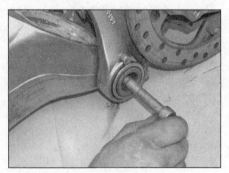

12.10 Withdraw the pivot bolt

12.11a Pull out the left-hand pivot pin, noting the seal (arrowed)

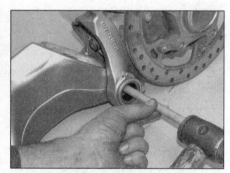

12.11b Use a suitable drift . . .

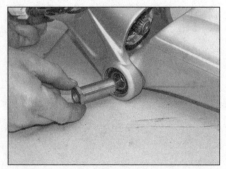

12.11c . . . to drive out the right-hand pivot sleeve

12.11d Note the spacer on the inside of the right-hand bearing housing

12.12 Check for oil leakage around the brake disc flange (arrowed)

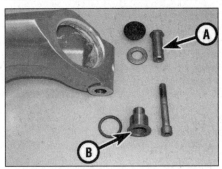

12.13a Inspect the bearing surfaces of the pivot sleeve (A) and the pivot pin (B)

12.13b Left-hand side needle roller bearing (arrowed)

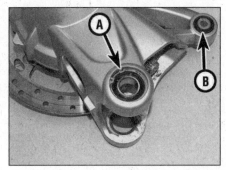

12.13c Sealed ball bearing is secured by circlip (A). Note location of bush (B)

sleeve and the pivot pin (see illustration). If they are worn, pitted or scored, renew them. Inspect the corresponding bearings in the drive housing – a needle roller bearing is fitted in the left-hand side and a sealed ball bearing is in the right-hand side (see illustrations). Note that the ball bearing is secured by a circlip. Refer to *Tools and Workshop Tips* in the *Reference* section for details of bearing inspection and renewal.

14 Inspect the bush in the top of the drive housing (see illustration 12.13c). If the bush has deteriorated it should be renewed. Use a drawbolt arrangement to press the old bush out and the new bush in (see *Tools and Workshop Tips* in the *Reference* section).

Installation

15 Press the spacer into the inside of the right-hand bearing housing (see illustration 12.11d).
16 Lubricate the splined end of the bevel gear with molybdenum disulphide grease.
17 Lubricate the pivot sleeve and the pivot pin with a smear of grease. Fit a new seal to the pivot pin.
18 Lubricate both ends of the coupling boot with silicone grease and install the boot on the drive housing (see illustration).

19 Support the drive housing in position and press the pivot sleeve in from the right-hand side and the pivot pin in from the left-hand side (see illustrations).
20 Install the pivot bolt (see illustration). Counter-hold the pivot sleeve and tighten the pivot bolt to the torque setting specified at the beginning of this Chapter (see illustration 12.9b).
21 Lift the final drive unit and engage the splined end of the bevel gear inside the driveshaft coupling (see illustration 11.37a). Ensure that the lip of the coupling boot locates

12.18 Lubricate the coupling boot with silicone grease before installation

correctly inside the end of the swingarm and insert the bolt to secure the final drive unit to the Paralever arm (see illustrations 11.37b and c).
22 Apply a suitable non-permanent thread locking compound to the nut and install the washer and nut on the bolt (see illustration 12.7). Counter-hold the bolt and tighten the nut to the specified torque setting.
23 Install the cover on the right-hand pivot sleeve (see illustration).
24 Install the remaining components in the reverse order of removal.

12.19a Press the pivot sleeve in from the right-hand side . . .

12.19b . . . and the pivot pin in from the left-hand side

12.20 Install the pivot bolt

12.23 Press the cover into the right-hand pivot sleeve

Notes

Chapter 5
Brakes, wheels and tyres

Contents

Degrees of difficulty

Easy, suitable for novice with little experience 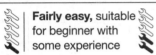	**Fairly easy,** suitable for beginner with some experience	**Fairly difficult,** suitable for competent DIY mechanic	**Difficult,** suitable for experienced DIY mechanic	**Very difficult,** suitable for expert DIY or professional

Specifications

Front brake

Brake fluid type	DOT 4
Brake pad friction material thickness (min)	1.0 mm
Disc thickness	
Standard	4.5 mm
Service limit	4.0 mm
Disc diameter	
R1200 RT, ST, S and R	320 mm
R1200 GS	305 mm
Runout (service limit)	0.1 mm
Caliper piston diameter	
Large	36 mm
Small	32 mm
Master cylinder piston diameter	16 mm
ABS sensor air gap	0.2 to 0.7 mm
ABS sensor ring no. of teeth	
Models with ABS I system	100
Models with ABS II system	48

Rear brake

Brake fluid type	DOT 4
Brake pad friction material thickness (min)	1.0 mm
Disc thickness	
Standard	5.0 mm
Service limit	4.5 mm
Disc diameter	265 mm
Runout (service limit)	0.6 mm
Caliper piston diameter	28 mm
Master cylinder piston diameter	
Non-ABS equipped	13 mm
ABS equipped	14.29 mm
ABS sensor air gap	0.2 to 0.7 mm
ABS sensor ring no. of teeth	
Models with ABS I system	78
Models with ABS II system	48

Wheels

Maximum wheel runout (axial and radial)
    Cast wheels (front and rear) . . . . 1.5 mm
    Spoke wheels (front and rear). . . . . 1.7 mm

Tyres

Tyre pressures . . . . *see Pre-ride checks*

Tyre sizes*	Front	Rear
R1200 GS.	110/80 H19 TL	150/70 H17 TL
R1200 RT, ST, S and R	120/70 ZR 17	180/55 ZR 17

*Also refer to your owners handbook or the tyre information label under the bike's seat.

Torque settings

Brake hose union bolts. . . . . 24 Nm
Brake pipe nuts . . . . 18 Nm
Front axle bolt . . . . 50 Nm
Front axle clamp bolt . . . . 19 Nm
Front brake caliper bleed valve
    R1200 GS, S, RT . . . . 10 Nm
    R1200 ST . . . . 5 Nm
    R1200 R . . . . 8 Nm
Front brake caliper mounting bolts . . . . 30 Nm
Front brake caliper pad pin . . . . 7 Nm
Front brake disc bolts – 2004 to Jul 2007 models
    Initial setting . . . . 12 Nm
    Final setting . . . . 24 Nm
Front brake disc bolts – models from Aug 2007 . . . . 19 Nm
Rear brake caliper bleed valve. . . . . 5 Nm
Rear brake caliper mounting bolts . . . . 24 Nm
Rear brake disc bolts
    Initial setting . . . . 12 Nm
    Final setting . . . . 30 Nm
Rear brake master cylinder mounting bolts
    R1200 GS, ST, S and R . . . . 8 Nm
    R1200 RT . . . . 6 Nm
Rear wheel bolts. . . . . 60 Nm
Wheel speed sensor screws. . . . . 4 Nm

1 General information

All models covered in this manual are fitted with wheels designed for tubeless tyres only. On RT, ST, S and R models, the wheels are cast alloy. GS and Adventure models have wire spoked wheels, with an option of cast wheels on the standard GS. The design of the wire spoked wheel used is somewhat unusual, the spokes being attached to the rim outside of the tyre's sealing area, thus permitting the use of tubeless tyres.

Both front and rear brakes are hydraulically operated disc brakes. On all models, the front brake calipers have four opposed pistons each, and the rear brake has two pistons in a sliding caliper.

Where fitted, the anti-lock braking system (ABS) prevents the wheels from locking-up under hard braking. A general description of the system is given in Section 16. However, it should be noted that any work on an ABS equipped bike, other than checking and renewing the brake pads, must be undertaken by a BMW dealer with the diagnostic tester required to confirm that the system is operating correctly afterwards.

 Warning: Any attempt to work on the ABS, or individual components of the system, without the use of the BMW diagnostic tester, will result in brake system failure.
Caution: Disc brake components rarely require disassembly. Do not disassemble components unless absolutely necessary. The dust created by the brake system may contain asbestos, which is harmful to your health. Never blow it out with compressed air and don't inhale any of it. An approved filtering mask should be worn when working on the brakes. Do not use solvents for cleaning brake system components.

Solvents will cause the seals to swell and distort. Use only clean brake fluid or dedicated brake system cleaner. Use care when working with brake fluid as it can injure your eyes and will damage painted surfaces and plastic parts.

2 Brake pad renewal

 Warning: The dust created by the brake system may contain asbestos, which is harmful to your health. Never blow it out with compressed air and don't inhale any of it. An approved filtering mask should be worn when working on the brakes.

Front brake pads

1 On the R1200 GS, RT, ST and S caliper pull out the R-clip and unscrew the pad pin,

2.1a Pull out the R-clip . . .

2.1b . . . and unscrew the pad pin . . .

2.1c . . . then lift off the pad spring

then lift off the pad spring, noting how it fits **(see illustrations)**. Withdraw the pads from the caliper, noting the location of the anti-chatter shim on the back of each pad **(see illustration)**.

2 On the R1200 R type caliper, remove the two screws to free the pad spring **(see illustration)**. Withdraw the R-clip from the pad pin, then push the pin out from the inner side of the caliper **(see illustration)**. Remove the pads from the caliper **(see illustration)**.

Caution: Do not operate the front brake lever whilst the pads are out of the caliper.

3 Inspect the surface of each pad for contamination and check that the friction material has not worn down to the bottom of the wear indicator grooves (refer to Chapter 1, Section 4 for details) or to the absolute minimum given in the specifications of this chapter.

4 If any pad is worn, fouled with oil or grease, or heavily scored or damaged, all the pads must be renewed as a set. Note that it is not possible to degrease the friction material – if the pads are contaminated in any way they must be renewed.

5 If the pads are in good condition clean them carefully, using a fine wire brush which is completely free of oil and grease to remove all traces of road dirt and corrosion. Use a pointed instrument to dig out any embedded particles of foreign matter. Ensure that the anti-chatter shims are a firm fit on the back of the pads.

6 Check the condition of the brake disc (see Section 4).

7 Remove all traces of corrosion from the pad pin. Inspect the pin for signs of wear and renew it if necessary. Renew the R-clip if it is corroded or sprained.

8 If you are installing new pads, follow the procedure in Section 3 and displace the caliper, then clean around the exposed section of each piston inside the caliper to remove any dirt or debris that could damage the piston seals **(see illustration)**. Now push the pistons back into the caliper to create room for the new pads – use a piece of wood as leverage, or install the old pads and use a metal bar or a screwdriver inserted between them. Do not lever against the brake disc. Do not push the pistons back further than is necessary to install

2.1d Pull out the pads. Note the location of the anti-chatter shims on the back

2.2b Pull the R-clip out, then push out the pad pin . . .

the pads, otherwise a system fault could be registered on ABS-equipped machines. BMW provide a service tool for this purpose (Part Nos. 34 1 531 and 34 1 532).

9 Smear the backs of the pads and the shank of the pad pin with copper-based grease,

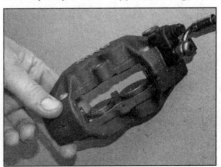

2.8 Clean the inside of the caliper, especially around the pistons

2.2a Caliper pad spring is held by two screws (arrowed)

2.2c . . . and lift out the pads

making sure that none gets on the front or sides of the pads.

10 If displaced, install the caliper (see Section 3), then insert the pads into the caliper so that the friction material faces the disc **(see illustration)**.

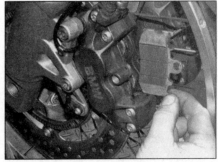

2.10 Ensure the friction material on the pads faces the disc

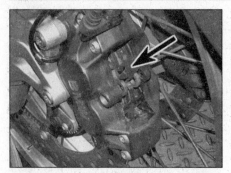

2.11 Ensure the pad spring (arrowed) is fitted correctly

2.12a Position the clip hole (arrowed) correctly when fitting the pad pin

2.12b Pads correctly installed and R-pin (arrowed) in place

2.16a Pull out the R-clip . . .

2.16b . . . and drive out the pad pin

2.17 Pull out the pads

11 On the R1200 GS, RT, ST and S caliper, install the pad spring, ensuring it is the right way round (see illustration). Insert the pad pin so that it passes through both pads and over the top of the spring, then tighten the pin to the specified torque setting (see illustration 2.1b). Secure the pad pin with the R-clip.

12 On the R1200 R caliper, insert the pad pin from the outside of the caliper, rotated so that its hole is accessible, and pass it through both pads and into the caliper bore on the inner side (see illustration). Insert the R-clip through the hole in the pin (see illustration).

13 Operate the brake lever several times to bring the pads back into contact with the discs.

14 Check the operation of the front brake before riding the motorcycle.

Rear brake pads

15 On R1200 GS models, remove the rear spray guard (see Chapter 6).

16 Pull out the R-clip, then use a suitable punch to drive the pad pin out (see illustrations).

17 Withdraw the pads from the caliper (see illustration). Note: *Do not operate the brake pedal while the pads are out of the caliper.*

18 Inspect the surface of each pad for contamination and check that the friction material has not worn down to the wear limit hole described in Chapter 1, Section 4 (see illustration). If required, measure the

thickness of the friction material and compare with the limit given in the specifications at the beginning of this chapter.

19 Follow Steps 4 to 7 to assess the condition of the pads and to check the disc, pad pin and R-clip. Note the spring clip on the pad pin and ensure that it is secure (see illustration 2.18). There are no anti-chatter shims fitted to the rear brake pads.

20 If you are installing new pads, follow the procedure in Section 6 and displace the caliper, then clean around the exposed section of both pistons to remove any dirt or debris that could damage the piston seals. Note the location of the pad spring inside the caliper (see illustration).

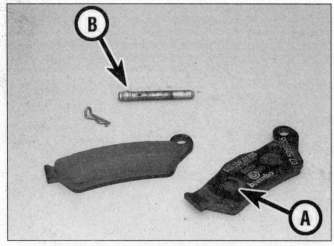

2.18 Location of the wear limit hole (A) in the back of the brake pad. Note the spring clip (B) on the pad pin

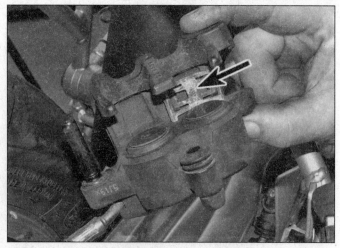

2.20 Location of the pad spring (arrowed) inside the rear brake caliper

2.22a Locate end (A) of pad against caliper bracket (B)

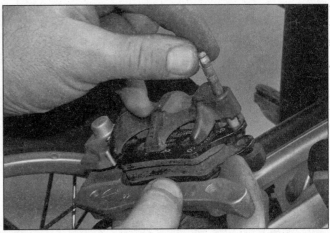

2.22b Ensure the pad pin passes through the holes in both pads

Now push the pistons back into the caliper to create room for the new pads – use a piece of wood as leverage, or install the old pads and use a metal bar or a screwdriver inserted between them. Do not lever against the brake disc. Do not push the pistons back further than is necessary to install the pads. BMW provide a service tool for this purpose (Part Nos. 34 1 531 and 34 1 536).

21 Smear the backs of the pads and the shank of the pad pin with copper-based grease, making sure that none gets on the front or sides of the pads.

22 If the caliper has been displaced, the pads can be installed before fitting the caliper onto the bike. Ensure that the pad spring is in position, then insert the pads so that the flat ends are pressed firmly against the caliper bracket and the friction material on both pads faces the disc **(see illustration)**. Press the pads against the pad spring and insert the pad pin **(see illustration)**. Install the caliper (see Section 6).

23 If the caliper has not been removed, insert the pads into the caliper so that the friction

material faces the disc **(see illustration 2.17)**. Ensure that both pads are pressed firmly against the caliper bracket, then align the holes in the pads with the holes in the caliper and insert the pad pin.

24 Use a suitable punch to drive the pad pin in so that the spring clip engages in the caliper **(see illustration)**.

25 Secure the pad pin with the R-clip **(see illustration)**.

26 On R1200 GS models, install the rear spray guard (see Chapter 6).

27 Operate the brake pedal several times to bring the pads into contact with the disc. Check the operation of the brakes before riding the motorcycle.

3 Front brake calipers

⚠️ *Warning: If a caliper indicates the need for an overhaul (usually due to leaking fluid or sticky operation),*

all old brake fluid should be flushed from the system. Also, the dust created by the brake system may contain asbestos, which is harmful to your health. Never blow it out with compressed air and don't inhale any of it. An approved filtering mask should be worn when working on the brakes. Do not use petroleum-based solvents for cleaning brake system components – they will cause the seals to swell and distort. Use only clean brake fluid or dedicated brake system cleaner. Use care when working with brake fluid as it can injure your eyes and will damage painted surfaces and plastic parts

⚠️ *Warning: On a machine equipped with ABS, the calipers can be displaced for cleaning, but do not disconnect the brake hoses unless a BMW diagnostic tester is available to check the operation of the system afterwards.*

Removal

1 It is only necessary to disconnect the

2.24 Drive the pad pin in until the spring clip engages

2.25 Note the location of the R-clip (arrowed)

3.4a Note the alignment of the union (arrowed) with the caliper

3.4b Sealing washers are fitted to both sides of the banjo union

3.6a Undo the bolts (arrowed) . . .

3.6b . . . and slide the caliper off the disc

brake hose if the caliper is being removed completely or overhauled. The brake hose can remain attached if you are just displacing the caliper for wheel removal, pad renewal or cleaning.

2 If poor brake action is the result of a sticking piston, or if a piston seal has failed and brake fluid is leaking from the caliper, the caliper must be overhauled. This procedure must be undertaken by a BMW dealer.

3 Remove the brake pads (see Section 2).

4 Cover the area around the end of the brake hose with clean rag to catch fluid spills. Note the alignment of the brake hose banjo union with the brake caliper, then undo union bolt and separate the hose from the caliper (see illustration). Note the sealing washers fitted to both sides of the banjo union (see illustration).

5 Plug the hose end or wrap a plastic bag tightly around it to minimise fluid loss and prevent dirt entering the system. Note: Do not operate the brake lever while the brake hose is

disconnected. Discard the sealing washers as new ones must be used on installation. Plug the caliper to avoid fluid spillage.

6 Undo the caliper mounting bolts and slide the caliper off the disc (see illustrations).

Installation

7 Ensure that the pistons are pushed back into the caliper to create room for the pads (see Section 2).

8 Slide the caliper onto the brake disc and install the mounting bolts, then tighten the bolts to the torque setting specified at the beginning of this Chapter (see illustrations 3.6b and a).

9 Connect the brake hose to the caliper, using new sealing washers on each side of the banjo union. Align the union as noted on removal (see illustration 3.4a). Tighten the union bolt to the torque setting specified at the beginning of this Chapter.

10 Install the brake pads (see Section 2).

11 Top-up the master cylinder reservoir

with DOT 4 brake fluid (see Pre-ride checks) and bleed the brake system as described in Section 10.

12 Check for leaks and thoroughly test the operation of the brakes before riding the motorcycle.

4 Front brake discs

Inspection

1 Inspect the surface of the disc for score marks and other damage. Light scratches are normal after use and won't affect brake operation, but deep grooves and heavy score marks will reduce braking efficiency and accelerate pad wear. If a disc is badly grooved it must be machined or renewed.

2 The disc must not be machined or allowed to wear down to a thickness less than the service limit as listed in this Chapter's Specifications and as marked on the disc itself. The thickness of the disc can be checked with a micrometer (see illustration). If the thickness of the disc is less than the service limit, it must be renewed.

3 To check disc runout, support the bike upright so that the front wheel is raised off the ground. Mount a dial gauge to the fork slider, with the plunger on the gauge touching the surface of the disc about 10 mm (1/2 in) from the outer edge (see illustration). Rotate the wheel and watch the gauge needle. Compare the reading with the limit listed in the Specifications at the beginning of this Chapter. If the runout is greater than the service limit, check the wheel bearings for play (see Chapter 1). If the bearings are worn, renew them (see Section 14) and repeat this check. If the disc runout is still excessive, a new one will have to be fitted.

Removal

4 Remove the wheel (see Section 12).

Caution: Do not lay the wheel down and allow it to rest on the disc – the disc could become warped. Set the wheel on wood blocks so the disc doesn't support the weight of the wheel.

5 Mark the relationship of the disc to the wheel, so it can be installed in the same position, and mark the disc itself to indicate left-or right-hand side, and which is the outer face. Undo the disc retaining bolts, loosening them a little at a time in a criss-cross pattern to avoid distorting the disc (see illustration).

6 On 2004 to Jul 2007 models, remove the bolts, sleeves and washers, noting their order of fitting (see illustration). Note that on 2006 and 2007 models, rubberised washers are fitted on each side of the disc to minimise brake squeal, which if required can be fitted to earlier machines. From Aug 2007 simply remove the disc retaining bolts; noting that the rivets remain in place on the disc.

7 Lift off the disc, and on early models note the presence of any washers fitted behind it.

4.2 Measuring the thickness of the disc with a micrometer

4.3 Set-up for checking brake disc runout with a dial gauge

4.5 Loosen the disc retaining bolts (arrowed) in a criss-cross pattern to avoid distorting the disc

4.6a Note the order of the sleeve and washers on the disc retaining bolts

On ABS models, if working on the left side disc, note the location of the sernor ring **(see illustration)**.

Installation

8 Before installing the disc, make sure there is no dirt or corrosion where the disc seats. If the disc does not sit flat when it is bolted down, it will appear to be warped when checked or when the brake is used.

9 Clean the threads of the disc retaining bolts and ensure that the threads in the bolt holes are clean.

10 Where applicable, lay the ABS sensor ring in place on the wheel. On early models, lay the disc on the wheel, aligning the previously made matchmarks if installing the original discs. Return any washers to their previous positions where fitted between the wheel and disc. Note that the minimum thickness markings on the disc should face outwards. On later models, lay the disc on the wheel, aligning the previously made matchmarks if installing the original discs, noting that the side with the beaded edge to the rivet centres must face outwards **(see illustration)**.

11 Clean up the threads of the disc mounting bolts and apply a suitable non-permanent locking compound to their threads before installing the bolts. Note that the bolts are micro-encapsulated with locking compound when new and BMW advise that new bolts are fitted.

12 Tighten the bolts evenly and a little at a time in a criss-cross pattern, to the initial torque setting specified at the beginning of this Chapter, then tighten them to the final torque setting.

13 Clean the disc using acetone or brake system cleaner. If a new brake disc has been installed, remove any protective coating from its working surfaces.

14 Install the wheel (see Section 12).

15 Operate the brake lever several times to bring the pads into contact with the disc. Check the operation of the brakes carefully before riding the bike.

5 Front brake master cylinder

⚠️ *Warning: On a machine equipped with ABS, do not disconnect the brake hoses unless a BMW diagnostic tester is available to check the operation of the system afterwards.*

Brake lever

Note: *On machines fitted with ABS, BMW advise that, after refitting the brake lever, the operation of the brake is checked by a BMW dealer before the bike is ridden.*

1 If the handlebar lever feels stiff, check the lever and the lever bracket for damage.

4.6b Location of the ABS sensor ring (arrowed)

2 Turn the lever span adjuster to its lowest setting (see Chapter 1). On R1200 ST, S and R models, undo the lever pivot bolt locknut on the underside of the lever, then withdraw the pivot bolt and lift the lever off **(see illustration)**. Note how the pushrod on the lever passes through rubber boot to locate on the master cylinder piston. On R1200 GS models, it is first necessary to remove the hand protector (see Chapter 6) and the upper half of the lever mounting bracket to access the pivot bolt, then follow the procedure above. On R1200 RT models, first remove the lower cover from the handlebar assembly, then undo the lever pivot bolt and lift the lever off **(see illustration)**. Note the location of the two lever return springs.

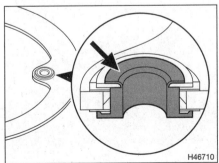

4.10 Disc must be installed with the beaded edge (arrowed) facing outwards

5.2a Location of the brake lever pivot bolt (arrowed) – R1200 GS shown

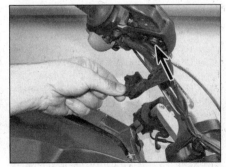

5.2b Location of the brake lever pivot bolt (arrowed) – R1200 RT

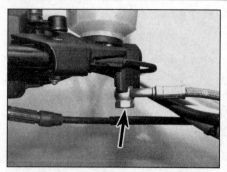

5.10 Location of the brake hose banjo bolt (arrowed) on the master cylinder

5.11a Undo the handlebar clamp screws . . .

5.11b . . . and remove the clamp and master cylinder

3 Clean the contact surfaces of the lever, bracket and pivot bolt. If they are in good condition, lubricate the components with dry film lubricant prior to assembly.

4 If, after cleaning and lubricating the lever, the lever action is still stiff, the master cylinder will have to be removed from the machine and checked.

Master cylinder

Note: *If the master cylinder is just being displaced and not completely removed from the motorcycle it is not necessary to disconnect the brake hose. Secure the master cylinder to the machine with a cable tie to avoid straining the hose and keep the reservoir upright to prevent air entering the system.*

5 If there is evidence of air in the system (spongy feel to the lever), bleed the system (see Section 10).

6 If brake fluid is leaking from the master cylinder on R1200 RT models, have the master cylinder overhauled by a BMW dealer. On all other models, a new master cylinder must be fitted – seal kits are not available (see *Warning* at the beginning of this Section).

7 To remove the master cylinder on R1200 GS, ST and R models, first remove the right-hand mirror (see Chapter 6). On GS models also remove the hand protector.

8 On all models, refer to the procedure in Chapter 7 and displace the brake light switch from the underside of the master cylinder.

9 On R1200 RT models, undo the screws securing the switch unit to the back of the master cylinder and displace the unit (see Chapter 7).

10 Undo the brake hose banjo bolt and separate the hose from the master cylinder, noting its alignment **(see illustration)**. Be prepared to catch any residual fluid in the union. **Note:** *To prevent damage to the paint from spilled brake fluid, always cover the fuel tank and bodywork when working on the master cylinder.* Discard the sealing washers as new ones must be used. Wrap a clean plastic bag over the end of the hose to prevent dirt entering the system and secure the hose in an upright position to minimise fluid loss.

Caution: Do not operate the brake lever while the hose is disconnected.

11 Support the master cylinder, then undo the handlebar clamp screws and remove the clamp **(see illustrations)**. Note the alignment of the master cylinder with the handlebar, then lift the master cylinder off.

12 On R1200 RT models, undo the screws securing the reservoir cover and lift off the cover and diaphragm (see *Pre-ride checks*).

13 On all other models, press the locking tabs in and unscrew the cap, then remove the diaphragm plate and diaphragm (see *Pre-ride checks*).

14 Empty the brake fluid into a suitable container.

15 To check the action of the master cylinder piston, temporarily install the reservoir cover or cap. Wrap some clean rag over the open end of the master cylinder hose union and operate the lever. If the lever sticks, or the action is stiff, there is a fault with the master cylinder piston. On R1200 RT models, have the master cylinder overhauled by a BMW dealer. On all other models, a new master cylinder must be fitted – seal kits are not available.

Caution: Do not, under any circumstances, use a petroleum-based solvent to clean the master cylinder.

Installation

16 Installation is the reverse of removal, noting the following:

● Align the master cylinder as noted on removal and tighten the handlebar clamp screws securely.

● Align the brake hose with the master cylinder and fit new sealing washers on both sides of the banjo union.

● Tighten the union bolt to the torque setting specified at the beginning of this Chapter.

● Fill the fluid reservoir with new DOT 4 fluid (see *Pre-ride checks*). Bleed the air from the brake system (see Section 10).

● Check the operation of the brake before riding the motorcycle.

6 Rear brake caliper

Warning: If a caliper indicates the need for an overhaul (usually due to leaking fluid or sticky operation), all old brake fluid should be flushed from the system. Also, the dust created by the brake system may contain asbestos, which is harmful to your health. Never blow it out with compressed air and don't inhale any of it. An approved filtering mask should be worn when working on the brakes. Do not use petroleum-based solvents for cleaning brake system components – they will cause the seals to swell and distort. Use only clean brake fluid or dedicated brake system cleaner. Use care when working with brake fluid as it can injure your eyes and will damage painted surfaces and plastic parts

Warning: On a machine equipped with ABS, the caliper can be displaced for cleaning, but do not disconnect the brake hose unless a BMW diagnostic tester is available to check the operation of the system afterwards.

Removal

1 On R1200 GS models, remove the rear spray guard (see Chapter 6).

2 If required, undo the screws securing the rear brake hose guide and lift the guide off the Paralever arm (see Chapter 4, Section 11). On machines equipped with ABS, unclip the ABS sensor wiring from the brake hose **(see illustration)**.

3 It is not necessary to remove the brake pads if the caliper is just being displaced – otherwise, remove the pads.

4 If poor brake action is the result of a sticking piston, or if a piston seal has failed and brake

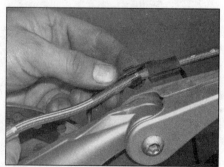

6.2 Unclip the ABS sensor wiring from the brake hose

6.6 Note the alignment of the union (arrowed) with the caliper

6.8a Undo the caliper mounting bolts (arrowed) . . .

6.8b . . . and slide the caliper off the disc

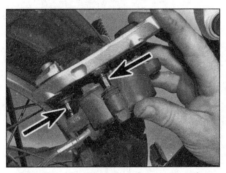

6.9a Rear brake caliper locates on the slider pins

6.9b Draw the caliper off the bracket

fluid is leaking from the caliper, the caliper must be overhauled. This procedure must be undertaken by a BMW dealer.

5 The brake hose can remain attached if you are just displacing the caliper for pad renewal or cleaning. If the caliper is being removed completely or overhauled, disconnect the brake hose as follows.

6 Cover the area around the end of the brake hose with clean rag to catch fluid spills. Note the alignment of the brake hose banjo union with the brake caliper, then undo union bolt and separate the hose from the caliper **(see illustration)**. Note the sealing washers fitted to both sides of the banjo union.

7 Plug the hose end or wrap a plastic bag tightly around it to minimise fluid loss and prevent dirt entering the system. **Note:** *Do not operate the brake pedal while the brake hose is disconnected.* Discard the sealing washers as new ones must be used on installation. Plug the caliper to avoid fluid spillage.

8 Undo the caliper mounting bolts and slide the caliper off the disc **(see illustrations)**.

9 Note how the caliper locates on the slider pins on the caliper bracket, then draw the caliper off the bracket **(see illustrations)**.

Installation

10 Ensure that the slider pins are clean and free from corrosion, then lubricate the pins with a smear of silicone grease. If the brake pads have been removed, check that the pad spring is correctly located inside the caliper. Slide the caliper onto the bracket.

11 If removed, install the brake pads (see Section 2).

7.5 Brake disc (A) is mounted on the final drive unit flange (B)

12 Slide the caliper onto the brake disc and install the mounting bolts, then tighten the bolts to the torque setting specified at the beginning of this Chapter **(see illustrations 6.8b and a)**.

13 Connect the brake hose to the caliper, using new sealing washers on each side of the banjo union. Align the union as noted on removal **(see illustration 6.6)**. Tighten the union bolt to the torque setting specified at the beginning of this Chapter.

14 Top-up the master cylinder reservoir with DOT 4 brake fluid (see *Pre-ride checks*) and bleed the brake system as described in Section 10.

15 If applicable, clip the ABS sensor wiring from the brake hose. Install the brake hose guide on the Paralever arm (see Chapter 4, Section 11).

16 On R1200 GS models, install the rear spray guard (see Chapter 6).

7.6 Access to the disc retaining bolts is only available one at a time (arrowed)

17 Check that there are no leaks and thoroughly test the operation of the brake before riding the motorcycle.

7 Rear brake disc

Inspection

1 Refer to the procedure in Section 4 to check the condition of the disc. When checking disc runout, mount the dial gauge on the swingarm. If runout is greater than the service limit, either the disc is warped or the final drive unit bearings are worn. If the bearings need attention, have the machine checked a BMW dealer.

Removal

2 Displace the rear brake caliper (see Section 6).

3 On R1200 GS, RT and ST models, remove the exhaust silencer (see Chapter 3).

4 Remove the rear wheel (see Section 13).

5 The brake disc is mounted on the external flange of the final drive unit **(see illustration)**. Mark the relationship of the disc to the flange, so it can be installed in the same position, and mark the disc itself to indicate which is the outer face.

6 Undo the disc retaining bolts, loosening them a little at a time in a criss-cross pattern to avoid distorting the disc – note that the disc must be rotated each time to make each bolt accessible in turn **(see illustration)**.

7 Lift off the disc, manoeuvring it off the final drive unit flange.

Installation

8 Before installing the disc, make sure there is no dirt or corrosion where the disc seats. If the disc does not sit flat when it is bolted down, it will appear to be warped when checked or when the brake is used.

9 Clean the threads of the disc retaining bolts and ensure that the threads in the bolt holes are clean.

10 Position the disc on the final drive flange – if the original disc is being installed, align the previously applied matchmarks.

11 Apply a suitable non-permanent thread locking compound to the bolts and install the bolts finger-tight.

12 Tighten the bolts evenly and a little at a time in a criss-cross pattern, to the initial torque setting specified at the beginning of this Chapter, then tighten them to the final torque setting – note that the disc must be rotated each time to make each bolt accessible in turn **(see illustration 7.6)**.

13 Clean the disc using acetone or brake system cleaner. If a new brake disc has been installed, remove any protective coating from its working surfaces.

14 Install the remaining components in the reverse order of removal.

15 Operate the brake pedal several times to bring the pads into contact with the disc. Check the operation of the brakes carefully before riding the bike.

8 Rear brake master cylinder

![warning symbol] **Warning: On a machine equipped with ABS, do not disconnect the brake hoses unless a BMW diagnostic tester is available to check the operation of the system afterwards.**

1 If there is evidence of air in the brake system (spongy feel to the pedal), bleed the system (see Section 10).

2 If brake fluid is leaking from the master cylinder, a new master cylinder must be fitted – seal kits are not available.

Removal

Note 1: *If the master cylinder is just being displaced and not completely removed from*

8.5a Remove the heel plate . . .

8.3a Location of the rear brake fluid reservoir – R1200 GS

8.3c Location of the rear brake fluid reservoir – R1200 S

8.3b Location of the rear brake fluid reservoir – R1200 ST

8.3d Location of the rear brake fluid reservoir (arrowed) – R1200 RT (R similar)

the motorcycle it is not necessary to drain the fluid reservoir or disconnect the reservoir hose from the master cylinder. Keep the reservoir upright to prevent air entering the system. However, note that the on machines where a rigid brake pipe is connected to the master cylinder, movement of the master cylinder is limited – take care not to damage or bend the brake pipe.

Note 2: *To prevent damage to the paint from spilled brake fluid, always cover any painted parts when working on the master cylinder.*

3 On R1200 GS, ST and S models, the brake fluid reservoir is located on the right-hand side of the machine **(see illustrations)**. On R1200 ST models, remove the right-hand seat cowling to access the reservoir (see Chapter 6). On R1200 RT and R models, the brake fluid reservoir is located underneath the rider's seat **(see illustration)**. Follow the procedure in Chapter 6 to remove the seat.

4 Release the reservoir from its clip on the frame, then remove the reservoir cover and diaphragm (see *Pre-ride checks*) and empty the brake fluid into a suitable container. Temporarily install the diaphragm and reservoir cover.

5 On R1200 GS, ST and R models, undo the screws securing the heel plate and lift it off **(see illustrations)**. Follow the procedure in Chapter 4, Section 3, and disconnect the master cylinder pushrod from the brake pedal. Undo the hose clamp securing the reservoir hose to the elbow on the master cylinder and lift the reservoir off **(see illustration)**. Undo the brake pipe nut and separate the pipe from the master cylinder **(see illustration 8.5c)**. Be prepared to catch any residual fluid remaining in the pipe. Wrap a clean plastic bag over the end of the pipe to prevent dirt entering the system and to minimise fluid spillage.

6 On R1200 RT models, the rear brake

8.5b . . . to access the rear brake master cylinder

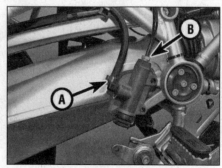

8.5c Reservoir hose is secured by clamp (A). Brake pipe is secured by nut (B)

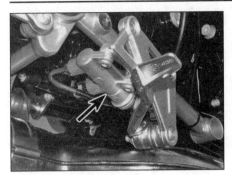

8.7a Location of rear brake master cylinder (arrowed) – R1200 S

8.7b Reservoir hose is secured by clamp (A). Brake pipe is secured by nut (B)

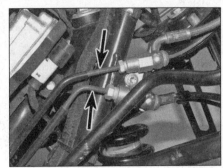

9.2 Rigid brake pipes (arrowed) connect to flexible hoses

master cylinder is mounted on the back of the right-hand footrest bracket. Follow the procedure in Chapter 4, Section 3, to remove the bracket. Undo the hose clamp securing the reservoir hose to the elbow on the master cylinder and lift the reservoir off. Undo the brake pipe nut and separate the pipe from the master cylinder. Be prepared to catch any residual fluid in the pipe. **Note:** *To prevent damage to the paint from spilled brake fluid, always cover any painted parts when working on the master cylinder.* Wrap a clean plastic bag over the end of the pipe to prevent dirt entering the system and to minimise fluid spillage.

7 On R1200 S models, the rear brake master cylinder is mounted on the back of the right-hand footrest bracket **(see illustration)**. Follow the procedure in Chapter 4, Section 3, and disconnect the master cylinder pushrod from the brake pedal. Undo the hose clamp securing the reservoir hose to the elbow on the master cylinder and lift the reservoir off **(see illustration)**. Undo the brake pipe nut and separate the pipe from the master cylinder **(see illustration 8.7b)**. Be prepared to catch any residual fluid in the pipe. **Note:** *To prevent damage to the paint from spilled brake fluid, always cover any painted parts when working on the master cylinder.* Wrap a clean plastic bag over the end of the pipe to prevent dirt entering the system and to minimise fluid spillage. Note that on machines not equipped with ABS, a flexible brake hose is fitted instead of a rigid brake pipe. Undo the hose banjo union bolt and separate the hose

from the master cylinder, noting its alignment. Note the sealing washers fitted on both sides of the banjo union and discard them as new ones must be used. Undo the master cylinder mounting bolts and lift the master cylinder off.

Installation

8 Installation is the reverse of removal, noting the following:

● Tighten the master cylinder mounting bolts to the torque setting specified at the beginning of this Chapter.
● Fit new sealing washers on both sides of the banjo union.
● Tighten the brake pipe nut/union bolt to the specified torque.
● Tighten the fluid reservoir hose clamp securely.
● Check the brake pedal stop clearance (see Chapter 4, Section 3).
● Fill the reservoir with new DOT 4 fluid (see *Pre-ride checks*). Bleed the air from the brake system (see Section 10).
● Check the operation of the brakes before riding the motorcycle.

9 Brake hoses, pipes and unions

Warning: On a machine equipped with ABS, do not disconnect the brake hoses or pipes unless a BMW diagnostic tester is available to check the operation of the system afterwards.

Inspection

1 Brake hose condition should be checked regularly as described in Chapter 1.
2 On machines equipped with ABS, rigid brake pipes connect the pressure modulator to the flexible brake hoses from the master cylinders and calipers. Remove the fuel tank (see Chapter 3) to inspect the rigid brake pipes and the pipe unions **(see illustration)**. Check that there is no sign of corrosion or fluid leakage.

Renewal

Note: *Do not operate the brake lever or pedal while a brake hose is disconnected.*
3 Before loosening a hose or pipe connection, cover the surrounding area with plenty of rags to soak up any spilled brake fluid and prevent damage to painted parts.
4 The brake hoses have banjo unions on each end and the brake pipes have union nuts or spring clip connectors **(see illustrations)**.
5 To renew a brake hose, note the alignment of the banjo unions, then undo the union bolts. Note the sealing washers fitted on both sides of the banjo union and discard them as new ones must be used. Make careful note of the exact routing of the hose and the position of all retaining clips.
6 Position the new hose exactly as noted on removal, making sure it isn't twisted or strained. Fit new sealing washers on both sides of the banjo unions and tighten the union bolts finger-tight. Make sure the hose is routed clear of all moving components, then

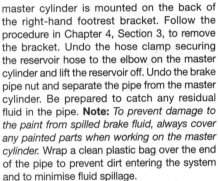

9.4a Brake hose banjo union on front fork bridge

9.4b Brake pipe union nut (arrowed)

9.4c Brake pipe spring clip connector on ABS modulator (arrowed)

tighten the banjo bolts to the torque setting specified at the beginning of this Chapter. Secure the hose with any clips or ties.

7 To renew a brake pipe, undo the nut or withdraw the clip, as applicable, then pull the pipe out from its union **(see illustrations)**. Where the end of the pipe is secured by a nut, the pipe is flared and the nut is retained on the pipe; where the pipe is retained by a spring clip, note the seal on the pipe. Make careful note of the exact routing of the pipe and the position of all retaining clips.

8 Position the new pipe exactly as noted on removal – a new union nut and/or seal, as applicable, will be fitted onto the pipe. Tighten the nut(s) to the torque setting specified at the beginning of this Chapter. Where a seal is fitted, push the end of the pipe into the union and secure it with the spring clip.

9 Top-up the appropriate fluid reservoir with new DOT 4 brake fluid and use the brake bleeding procedure to flush the old brake fluid from the system (see Section 10).

⚠ **Warning: On machines fitted with ABS, once the brake pipes have been reconnected, the system must be topped-up and bled by a BMW dealer using a BMW diagnostic tester. This is essential to restore brake operation.**

10 Check the operation of the brakes before riding the motorcycle.

10 Brake fluid change and system bleeding

Brake fluid change

1 The brake fluid should be changed at the prescribed service interval. On machines fitted with ABS it is not possible to change the fluid without the use of a diagnostic tester – the procedure **must** be undertaken by a BMW dealer.

⚠ **Warning: Any attempt to drain and refill the ABS in the conventional way will result in air trapped in the system and brake system failure.**

2 To change the brake fluid on a non-ABS equipped machine you will need some new DOT 4 brake fluid, a length of clear vinyl or plastic hose, a suitable tool for siphoning the fluid out of the fluid reservoir, a container

9.7a Withdraw the spring clip . . .

partially filled with clean brake fluid and large enough to take all the old fluid when it is flushed out of the system, some rags and a spanner to fit the brake caliper bleed valve.

3 Cover the fuel tank and other painted components to prevent damage in the event that brake fluid is spilled.

4 Pull the dust cap off the bleed valve **(see illustration)**. Attach one end of the clear hose to the bleed valve and submerge the other end in the clean brake fluid in the container **(see illustration)**. **Note:** *To avoid damaging the bleed valve during the procedure, loosen it and then tighten it temporarily with a ring spanner before attaching the hose. With the hose attached, the valve can then be opened and closed with an open-ended spanner.*

5 Remove the reservoir cap or cover, diaphragm plate (if fitted) and diaphragm (see *Pre-ride checks*). Siphon the old fluid out of the reservoir, then fill it with new brake fluid.

6 Carefully pump the brake lever or pedal three or four times and hold it in (front) or down (rear) while opening the caliper bleed valve. When the valve is opened, brake fluid will flow out of the caliper into the hose, and the lever will move toward the handlebar, or the pedal will move down.

7 Retighten the bleed valve, then release the brake lever or pedal gradually. Keep the reservoir topped-up with new fluid above the MIN level at all times or air may enter the system and greatly increase the length of the task – air in the system will be indicated by air bubbles in the fluid leaving the caliper. Repeat the process until new fluid can be seen emerging from the bleed valve.

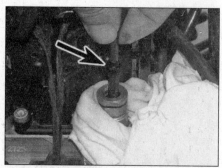
9.7b . . . then pull the pipe out from the union. Note the seal (arrowed)

> **HAYNES HiNT**
> *Old brake fluid is invariably much darker in colour than new fluid, making it easy to see when all old fluid has been expelled from the system.*

8 Disconnect the hose, then tighten the bleed valve to the specified torque setting and install the dust cap.

9 Top-up the reservoir, install the diaphragm, diaphragm plate (if fitted) and cap or cover. Wipe up any spilled brake fluid.

10 Check that there are no fluid leaks and test the operation of the brakes thoroughly before riding the motorcycle.

Brake bleeding - non ABS models

⚠ **Warning: The BMW ABS cannot be bled in the conventional way. The procedure must be undertaken by a BMW dealer using the BMW diagnostic tester. If the bleed valves or any of the brake system connections are loosened on a machine equipped with ABS, air will become trapped in the system resulting in brake failure.**

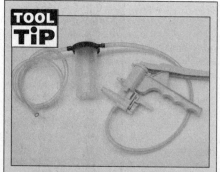

> **TOOL TiP**
>
> *In its simplest form, the brake bleeding equipment described in Step 12 will be required. A quicker alternative would be a 'one-man' brake bleeding kit consisting of a non-return valve in the pipe which prevents air being drawn back into the caliper. If, however, either set-up fails to bleed the brake effectively use a vacuum-type brake bleeding tool as shown here.*

10.4a Caliper bleed valve dust cap (arrowed) – rear brake shown

10.4b Set-up for changing the brake fluid and bleeding the brakes

11 Bleeding the brakes is simply the process of removing all the air bubbles from the brake system – the hoses, calipers and master cylinders. Bleeding is necessary whenever a brake system connection is loosened, when a component or hose is renewed. Leaks in the system may also allow air to enter, but leaking brake fluid will reveal their presence and warn you of the need for repair.

12 To bleed the brakes, you will need some new DOT 4 brake fluid, a length of clear vinyl or plastic hose, a small container partially filled with clean brake fluid, some rags and a spanner to fit the brake caliper bleed valves.

13 Cover the fuel tank and other painted components to prevent damage in the event that brake fluid is spilled.

14 BMW advise that bleeding the brakes is more effective if the pads are removed, and the pistons pushed back into the calipers and held in this position, thus reducing the fluid volume in the system. The service tool for the front brake is Part Nos. 34 1 531 and 34 1 532. The service tool for the rear brake is Part Nos. 34 1 531 and 34 1 536. Follow the procedure in Section 2 to remove the brake pads.

15 Remove the reservoir cover, diaphragm plate (where fitted) and diaphragm (see *Pre-ride checks*). Slowly pump the brake lever or pedal a few times, until no air bubbles can be seen floating up from the holes in the bottom of the reservoir. Doing this bleeds the air from the master cylinder end of the line. Loosely refit the reservoir cover.

16 Pull the dust cap off the bleed valve **(see illustrations 10.4a)**. Attach one end of the clear hose to the bleed valve and submerge the other end in the brake fluid in the container **(see illustration 10.4b)**. Remove the reservoir cap or cover and check the fluid level. Do not allow the fluid level to drop below the MIN level during the bleeding process otherwise air may enter the system.

17 Carefully pump the brake lever or pedal three or four times and hold it in (front) or down (rear) while opening the caliper bleed valve. When the valve is opened, brake fluid will flow out of the caliper into the hose and the lever will move toward the handlebar or the pedal will move down. Air in the system will be seen as a stream of bubbles in the fluid leaving the caliper.

18 Retighten the bleed valve, then release the brake lever or pedal gradually. Repeat the process until no air bubbles are visible in the brake fluid leaving the caliper and the lever or pedal is firm when applied. On completion, disconnect the hose, then tighten the bleed valve to the specified torque setting and install the dust cap.

19 Check the brake fluid level and top-up if necessary, then install the diaphragm, diaphragm plate (where fitted) and cap or cover. Wipe up any spilled brake fluid and check that there are no fluid leaks.

20 If the service tools were used to displace the caliper pistons, remove them and install the brake pads (see Section 2). Don't forget to check the brake fluid level and top-up if necessary.

21 Check that there are no fluid leaks and test the operation of the brakes thoroughly before riding the motorcycle.

> **HAYNES HiNT** *If it is not possible to produce a firm feel to the lever or pedal, the brake fluid may be aerated. Let the new fluid in the system stabilise for a few hours and then repeat the procedure to ensure any tiny air bubbles have settled out.*

11 Wheel runout and alignment

Wheel runout

1 In order to carry out a proper inspection of the wheels, it is necessary to support the bike upright so that the wheel being inspected is raised off the ground. Position the motorcycle on its centre stand or an auxiliary stand.

2 Clean the wheels thoroughly to remove mud and dirt that may interfere with the inspection procedure or mask defects. Make a general check of the wheels (see Chapter 1, Section 15) and tyres (see *Pre-ride checks*).

3 Attach a dial gauge to the fork or the swingarm and position its tip against the side of the rim. Spin the wheel slowly and check the axial (side-to-side) runout of the rim **(see illustration)**.

4 In order to accurately check radial (out-of-round) runout with the dial gauge, the wheel will have to be removed from the machine, and the tyre from the wheel. With the axle clamped in a vice and the dial gauge positioned on the top of the rim, the wheel can be rotated to check the runout **(see illustration 11.3)**.

5 An easier, though slightly less accurate, method is to attach a stiff wire pointer to the fork or the swingarm and position the end a fraction of an inch from the wheel (where the wheel and tyre join). If the wheel is true, the distance from the pointer to the rim will be constant as the wheel is rotated. **Note:** *If wheel runout is excessive, check the wheel bearings (front wheel) or final drive unit bearings (rear wheel) very carefully before renewing the wheel.*

Wheel alignment

6 Misalignment of the wheels can cause

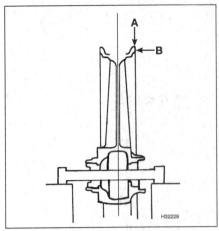

11.3 Check for radial (out-of-round) runout at point A, and axial (side-to-side) runout at point B

serious handling problems. Due to the BMW's solid engine and running gear construction, the normal problem areas for wheel misalignment (distorted frame or cocked rear wheel) do not apply. If the wheels are out of alignment, this could be due to worn or damaged Telelever components at the front, or worn swingarm bearings at the rear. If accident damage has occurred, the machine should be taken to a BMW dealer for a thorough check of the structural components.

7 To check wheel alignment you will need an assistant, a length of string or a perfectly straight length of wood or metal bar, and a ruler. A plumb bob or spirit level will also be required.

8 Support the bike in an upright position, either on its centre stand or on an auxiliary stand. Measure the width of both tyres at their widest points. Subtract the smaller measurement from the larger measurement, then divide the difference by two. The result is the amount of offset that should exist between the front and rear tyres on both sides.

9 If a string is used, have your assistant hold one end of it about halfway between the floor and the rear axle, touching the rear sidewall of the rear tyre.

10 Run the other end of the string forward and pull it tight so that it is roughly parallel to the floor. Slowly bring the string into contact with the front sidewall of the rear tyre, then turn the front wheel until it is parallel with the string **(see illustration)**. Measure the distance from the front tyre sidewall to the string.

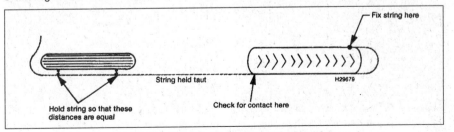

11.10 Checking the wheel alignment with string

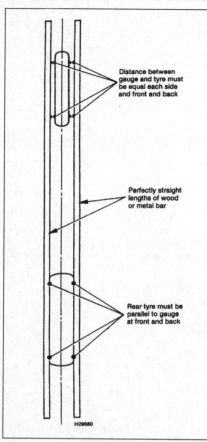

11.13 Checking the wheel alignment with a straight-edge

11 Repeat the procedure on the other side of the motorcycle.

12 The distance from the front tyre sidewall to the string should be the same on both sides of the bike and equal to the tyre width offset. If the measurement differs, the wheels are out of alignment by this amount.

13 As previously mentioned, a perfectly straight length of wood or metal bar may be substituted for the string **(see illustration)**. The procedure is the same.

14 If the wheels are out of alignment, and the fault cannot be traced to the Telelever or swingarm assemblies, the bike should be taken to a BMW dealer for verification of your findings using a track alignment gauge.

15 If the front-to-back alignment is correct, the wheels still may be out of alignment vertically.

16 Using a plumb bob or spirit level, check the rear wheel to make sure it is vertical. To do this with the plumb bob, hold the string against the tyre upper sidewall and allow the weight to settle just off the floor. When the string touches both the upper and lower tyre sidewalls and is perfectly straight, the wheel is vertical. If necessary, place thin spacers under one leg of the stand until the wheel is vertical. Using a spirit level, the level should be held against the upper and lower tyre sidewalls.

17 Once the rear wheel is vertical, check the front wheel in the same manner. If the front wheel is not perfectly vertical, the frame and/or major suspension components are bent.

12 Front wheel

Removal

1 Position the bike on its centre stand or support it securely on an auxiliary stand so that the front wheel is off the ground. Always make sure the motorcycle is properly supported.

2 On R1200 RT, ST and S models, remove the front section of the front mudguard (see Chapter 6).

3 Displace the front brake calipers (see Section 3). There is no need to disconnect the hoses from the calipers. Support the calipers with a piece of wire or cable tie so that no strain is placed on the brake hoses. **Note:** *Do not operate the front brake lever with the wheel removed.*

4 Loosen the axle clamp bolt on the bottom of the right-hand fork slider **(see illustration)**.

5 Locate a suitable hex drive tool in the head of the axle and unscrew the axle from the left-hand fork slider, then support the wheel and withdraw the axle **(see illustrations)**.

6 Note the location of the spacer on the left-hand side of the wheel, then withdraw the wheel and remove the spacer for safekeeping **(see illustration)**. On ABS equipped machines, take care not to damage the ABS sensor located on the left-hand fork slider **(see illustration)**.

Caution: Don't lay the wheel down and allow it to rest on either brake disc – the

12.4 Location of the axle clamp bolt (arrowed)

12.5a Use a hex-head tool to loosen the axle . . .

12.5b . . . then pull the axle out

12.6a Note the location of the spacer (arrowed) . . .

12.6b . . . and remove it for safekeeping

12.6c Take care not to damage the ABS sensor (arrowed)

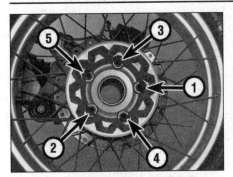

13.4a Loosen the rear wheel bolts
evenly . . .

13.4b . . . then withdraw the bolts –
R1200 GS shown

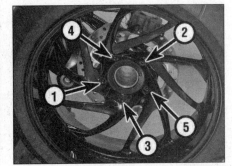

13.4c Loosen the rear wheel bolts
evenly . . .

13.4d . . . then withdraw the bolts –
R1200 S shown

13.5a Lift the wheel off the flange –
R1200 GS shown

13.5b Lift the wheel off the flange –
R1200 S shown

*disc could become warped. Set the wheel
on wood blocks so the tyre supports the
weight of the wheel.*
7 Check the axle for straightness by rolling it
on a flat surface such as a piece of plate glass
(first wipe off all old grease and remove any
corrosion using wire wool). If the equipment
is available, check the axle runout using
V-blocks and a dial gauge.
8 Check the condition of the wheel bearings
(see Section 14).

Installation

9 Lubricate the axle and the inside of the left-
hand hub seal with a smear of grease, then install
the spacer into the seal **(see illustration 12.6b)**.
10 Manoeuvre the wheel into position, then
insert the axle from the right-hand side, making
sure that the spacer remains in place. Screw
the axle into the left-hand fork slider finger-
tight. On ABS equipped machines, take care
not to damage the ABS sensor located on the
left-hand fork slider **(see illustration 12.6c)**.
11 Temporarily take the bike off its stand and
compress the front suspension several times
to align the wheel and fork legs.
12 Tighten the axle to the torque setting
specified at the beginning of this Chapter, then
tighten the axle clamp bolt to the specified
torque.
13 Install the front brake calipers (see Section 3).
14 On R1200 RT, ST and S models, install
the front section of the front mudguard (see
Chapter 6).
15 Check for correct operation of the front
brake before riding the motorcycle.

13 Rear wheel

Removal

1 Position the bike on its centre stand or
support it securely on an auxiliary stand so that
the rear wheel is off the ground. Always make
sure the motorcycle is properly supported.
2 On R1200 GS models, remove the rear
spray guard (see Chapter 6).
3 On R1200 RT, ST and R models, remove
the exhaust silencer (see Chapter 3).
4 Loosen the bolts securing the wheel to the
flange on the final drive unit evenly in a criss-
cross pattern, then support the wheel and
withdraw the bolts **(see illustrations)**.
5 Lift the wheel off the flange **(see illustrations)**.

Installation

6 Make sure the contact faces between the
wheel hub and the final drive flange are clean.
7 Clean the threads of the wheel bolts and
the bolt holes in the flange.
8 Lift the wheel onto the flange, making sure it
engages correctly, and install the bolts finger-
tight.
9 Tighten the bolts evenly in a criss-cross
pattern to the torque setting specified at the
beginning of this Chapter **(see illustrations
13.4a and c)**.
10 On R1200 RT, ST and R models, install the
exhaust silencer (see Chapter 3).
11 On R1200 GS models, install the rear
spray guard (see Chapter 6).

14 Wheel bearings

Front wheel bearings

Note: *Always renew the wheel bearings in
pairs, never individually. Avoid using a high
pressure cleaner on the wheel bearing area.*

Check and removal

1 Remove the wheel (see Section 12).
2 Set the wheel on wood blocks so the tyre
supports the weight of the wheel.
3 Prise out the seals on both sides of the wheel
hub using a flat-bladed screwdriver – use a piece
of wood or thick card to protect the edge of the
bearing housing **(see illustration)**. Discard the
seals as new ones must be used.
4 Refer to *Tools and Workshop Tips* in the

14.3 Prise the old seals out carefully

14.4 Check the bearings as described

14.5a Driving out the wheel bearings

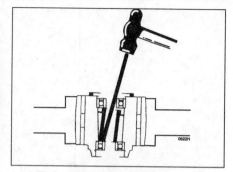

14.5b Locate the drift against the inner edge of the lower bearing

Reference section and inspect the bearings for wear or damage. If the bearings do not turn smoothly or if there is freeplay between the races, they must be renewed (see illustration).

5 To remove the bearings, heat the wheel hub around the bearing housing to 100°C and use a metal rod (preferably a brass drift) inserted through the centre of the upper bearing, to tap evenly around the inner race of the lower bearing to drive it from the hub (see illustrations). The bearing spacer will also come out. Note which way round the bearing is fitted.

6 Turn the wheel over so that the remaining

14.7 Driving a bearing in using a suitably-sized socket

bearing faces down. Drive the bearing out using the same technique as above, heating the hub again if necessary.

Installation

7 Thoroughly clean the hub and bearing housings. Heat the left-hand bearing housing to 100°C and install the new bearing with the marked or sealed side facing outwards. Use the old bearing, a bearing driver or a socket large enough to contact the outer race of the bearing to drive it in until it's completely seated (see illustration).

8 Turn the wheel over and install the bearing spacer, then drive the right-hand bearing into place as described above.

9 Lubricate the new seals a smear of grease, then press them into the hub (see illustration). Ensure that the seals are level with the edge of the hub by tapping them with a flat piece of wood (see illustration).

10 Clean any grease off the brake discs using acetone or brake system cleaner, then install the wheel (see Section 12).

11 On ABS equipped machines, use a feeler gauge to check the air gap between the tip of the speed sensor and the sensor ring (see illustrations 12.6c and 4.6b). Compare the result with the specification at the beginning

of this Chapter. If the bearings have not been fitted correctly, the gap will be outside the specification, resulting either in damage to the sensor or ABS malfunction. If necessary, check the fitment of the bearings.

Rear wheel bearings

12 The rear wheel bearings are part of the final drive unit. If the unit is thought to be faulty have it checked by a BMW dealer – dismantling and set-up of the final drive requires special tools and is beyond the scope of this manual. To remove the final drive unit follow the procedure in Chapter 4.

15 Tyres – general information

General information

1 The wheels fitted to all models are designed to take tubeless tyres only.
2 Refer to the *Pre-ride checks* for details of tyre maintenance.

Fitting new tyres

3 When selecting new tyres, refer to the tyre sizes given at the beginning of this chapter, the tyre options listed in rider's handbook and

14.9a Install the seals carefully . . .

14.9b . . . and ensure they are level with the edge of the hub

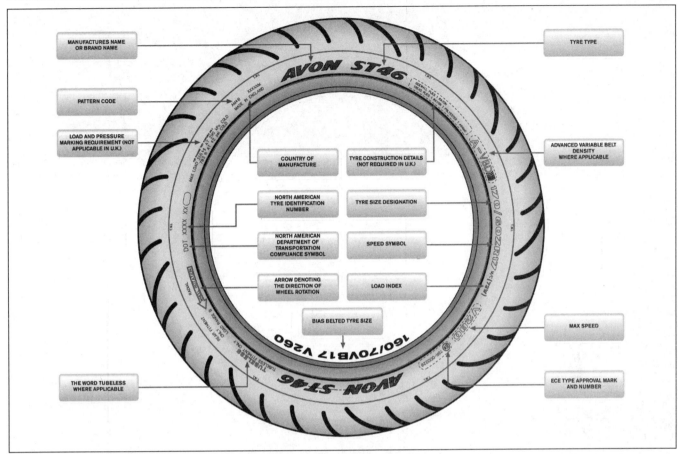

15.3 Common tyre sidewall markings

the tyre information label under the bike's seat. Ensure that the front and rear tyre types are compatible, and that they are of the correct size and speed rating **(see illustration)**. If necessary, seek advice from a BMW dealer or tyre fitting specialist.

4 It is recommended that tyres are fitted by a motorcycle tyre specialist rather than attempted in the home workshop. The force required to break the seal between the wheel rim and tyre bead is substantial, and is usually beyond the capabilities of an individual working with normal tyre levers. Additionally, the specialist will be able to balance the wheels after tyre fitting.

5 Note that punctured tubeless tyres can in some cases be repaired. BMW recommend that such repairs are assessed and carried out professionally.

16 ABS – general information

System type

1 Models from 2004 to 2006 are fitted with BMW's generation I ABS system. This electro-hydraulic servo assisted ABS system reduces the force required at the lever by up to 35%.

Models from 2007-on have the non-servo ABS generation II system.

2 All models have partially integral brakes, i.e. operation of the front brake lever applies both front brakes and the rear brake, whereas operation of the rear brake pedal applies only the rear brake.

3 The ABS features an adaptive brake force distribution system that changes the proportions of front to rear brake power according to load on the wheel, thus ensuring good stability.

4 The system also takes into account the additional loading of luggage and/or passenger.

5 The ABS prevents the wheels from locking-up under hard braking or on uneven road surfaces. A sensor on each wheel transmits wheel speed information to the ABS control unit. If the control unit senses that a wheel is about to lock, the pressure modulator releases brake pressure momentarily to that wheel, preventing a skid.

⚠ *Warning: If there is a fault with the ABS, extreme care must be taken when riding the motorcycle, and it should be taken immediately to a BMW dealer for analysis. If the servo-assistance is not working there will be a marked reduction in braking efficiency, requiring more physical effort to apply the brakes and greater anticipation of braking needs.*

System operation – 2004 to 2006 models

6 The ABS is self-checking. A self-diagnosis and pull-away test are performed every time the machine is started and ridden. However, self-diagnosis will not take place if either brake is already applied, as when starting on a gradient. For this reason, BMW suggest you first engage a gear to steady the bike, then switch the ignition on and wait for the self-diagnosis is complete.

7 When the ignition is switched on, the general warning light comes on and the ABS warning light flashes 4 times a second – this means the self-diagnosis is performing. When self-diagnosis is complete, the general warning light extinguishes and the ABS warning light flashes once per second. You can now select neutral and apply the brakes as required.

8 When the engine is started and the bike moves off, the ABS performs a pull-away test. If the test is successful, the ABS warning light extinguishes. If the warning light continues to flash once per second, the pull-away self-test was not completed. Stop the machine and switch the engine off. Carry-out the starting procedure once again.

9 If there is a fault with the ABS, the warning light will continue to flash and/or the general warning light will come on. Depending on the fault, the ABS function may not be available, resulting in a reduced braking efficiency (see accompanying table).

10 The ABS control unit stores faults in its memory which can be read and cleared using the BMW diagnostic tester. The tester connects into a diagnostic plug on the machine **(see illustrations)**. Interrogation of the ABS must be carried out by a BMW dealer who can then rectify the faults and clear the fault codes from the control unit memory.

11 If using an ABS equipped R1200 GS or Adventure model off-road, it may be desirable to ride without the ABS functioning. To deactivate the system, turn the ignition off, hold down the ABS button on the left-hand handlebar switch housing, then turn the ignition on and release the ABS button. The ABS light will illuminate to remind the rider that ABS is not functioning. To reactivate the system, stop the bike and switch the ignition off and on again.

12 To deactivate the system on an

16.10a Location of the plug for the ABS diagnostic tester (arrowed) – R1200 RT shown

16.10b Diagnostic plug is located underneath the seat cowling on R1200 GS models (arrowed)

ABS equipped R1200S, bring the motorcycle to a stop or switch the ignition on, then hold down the ABS button. When the ABS light illuminates, release the button. The ABS is now deactivated and the

ABS light will remain on as a reminder to the rider that the ABS is not functioning. To reactive the system, bring the motorcycle to a stop, then hold down the ABS button - the warning light will go out and the ABS will be active.

ABS faults	
General warning light red	Defective brake switch which could result in a delayed braking response
ABS warning light flashes once per second	Pull-away test not completed. The ABS function is not available and the wheels could lock when the brakes are applied hard or in an emergency.
ABS warning light flashes four times per second	Self-diagnosis not completed. The ABS function is not available and the wheels could lock when the brakes are applied hard or in an emergency.
General warning light red/ABS warning light on	ABS warnings not available due to a defect in the control unit.
General warning light red/ABS warning light flashes once per second	ABS is unavailable in at least one brake circuit
General warning light red/ABS warning light flashes four times per second	ABS is not functioning and the wheels could lock when the brakes are applied hard or in an emergency.
General warning light flashes red once per second/ABS warning light flashes once per second	Brake fluid level too low. Note this applies to the fluid in the circuit between the modulator and the caliper and cannot be determined from the level in the fluid reservoirs. Check for fluid leaks. This warning can also be triggered by badly worn brake pads. Do not continue riding the motorcycle.
General warning light flashes red four times per second/ABS warning light flashes four times per second	At least two faults have been detected in the brake system. Do not continue riding the motorcycle.

System operation – 2007-on models

13 A pull-away self diagnosis test of the system is completed as the motorcycle moves forwards. If all is well, the ABS warning light, or in some markets the 'brake faillure' warning light, should extinguish. This light will flash if the ABS system hasn't completed its pull-away test and will stay illuminated if there is a fault in the ABS system. In both situations, ABS will not be available.

14 On GS models it is possible to cancel the ABS function. With the motorcycle at a standstill and the ignition on, press the ASC/ABS button until the warning light changes status (it will alternate between the ASC symbol and ABS symbol). Now press the button again until the ABS light stays on. The light will remain on as a reminder to the rider that ABS is turned off. To reactivate ABS, again press the ASC/ABS until the warning

light shows the ABS symbol, then press and hold the button until the light goes out.

15 If a fault is registered by the ABS system, the warning light will remain on. Faults can only be downloaded using the BMW diagnostic tester.

Wheel speed sensors – all models

Front wheel

16 The front wheel sensor is located on the left-hand fork slider and the sensor ring is on the left-hand side of the wheel hub **(see illustrations 12.6c and 4.6b)**. The air gap between the tip of the sensor and the ring is critical for the ABS to function correctly, although no provision is made for adjusting the gap. Use a feeler gauge to check the gap and compare the result with the specification at the beginning of this Chapter. If the gap is

outside the specification, first check that the sensor is fitted securely and that the sensor ring is not damaged, then check that the front wheel is fitted correctly and check the wheel bearings for wear (see Section 14).

17 Ensure that the sensor and sensor ring are clean and free from obstructions. If the sensor ring is damaged, follow the procedure in Section 4 to remove the left-hand brake disc and renew the ring. To renew the sensor, refer to Chapter 4, Section 6, to remove the sensor from the left-hand front fork slider, noting how the sensor wire is clipped to the brake hose **(see illustrations)**. Remove the fuel tank (see Chapter 3) and disconnect the wire at the connector.

18 Installation is the reverse of removal. Don't forget that any fault code arising from the sensor/sensor ring damage will have to be cleared from the control unit memory using the BMW diagnostic tester.

16.17a Note the clips (arrowed) . . .

16.17b . . . and routing of the ABS sensor wire

Rear wheel

19 The rear wheel sensor is located in the top of the final drive unit housing, behind the drive flange **(see illustration)**. The sensor ring is an integral part of the gear assembly inside the housing.

20 To renew the sensor, refer to Chapter 4, Section 11, to trace the sensor wire to the connector under the seat and disconnect it. Remove the rear wheel (see Section 13). Undo the screw securing the sensor and draw the sensor out from the housing, noting the location of the sealing O-ring, and on later models the centering ring. Release the wire from any clips.

16.19 Location of the rear wheel speed sensor

21 Installation is the reverse of removal. Ensure that a new O-ring is fitted to the sensor. Don't forget that any fault code arising from a sensor fault will have to be cleared from the control unit memory using the BMW diagnostic tester.

ABS control unit and pressure modulator

22 The integral control unit and modulator is located under the fuel tank **(see illustrations)**. Remove the fuel tank for access (see Chapter 3). Work on these components is outside of the scope of this manual. If a problem is indicated, all that can be done is to check that the wiring connections to the unit are secure, clean and undamaged.

23 Refer to Chapter 2, Section 4, for details of removing the modulator.

17 ASC (Automatic Stability Control) system

1 ASC is a traction control system which compares the speed of both wheels and via calculation determines the amount of rear wheel slip. If the parameters are exceeded, engine torque is reduced via the engine management unit. The system is entirely automatic in operation, but can be deactivated by the rider if required.

2 An ASC button on the left handlebar switch enables the system to be deactivated when the motorcycle is in motion; the ASC warning light in the instruments will remain on to show that ASC is turned off. To reactivate the system, press the ASC button and release it within 3 seconds – the warning light should go out to indicate that ASC is turned on. Alternatively the system will reactivate when the ignition is next turned off and then on again. Note that on GS models, the ABS and ASC button is combined; press the button until the S symbol warning light appears, then press the button and release within 2 seconds to deactivate ASC – the warning light should remain on.

3 In normal use the ASC warning light will be off. Slow flashing of the warning light indicates that the system's self-diagnosis cycle has not yet completed. Quick flashing of the light occurs if ASC is in use, i.e. if the system has detected a traction problem and is reducing rear wheel torque to compensate. If the warning light comes on, and the system hasn't been deactivated by the rider, a fault is indicated in the ASC system and ASC is not working – is this instance the fault must be investigated by a BMW dealer.

16.22a Location of the ABS control unit and modulator – R1200 GS

16.22b Location of the ABS control unit and modulator – R1200 S

16.22c Location of ABS control unit and modulator – R1200 R

18 RDC (Tyre Pressure Control) system

1 Sensors in the wheels relay tyre pressure values to the instrument display via a wireless link to the RDC control unit. The system is activated by scrolling down through the display functions using the BC button on the right handlebar switch. RDC denotes the tyre pressure settings, with that for the front tyre on the left and rear tyre on the right – pressures are in Bars. Note that the pressure information is only transmitted at road speeds above 19 mph (30 kmh). The RDC control unit is located inside the rear bodywork **(see illustration)**.

2 If the tyre pressure is close to the edge of the permitted range the warning triangle above the LCD display will illuminate yellow. If the pressure goes outside of the range the light changes to red. Note that the sensors transmit tyre temperature as well as pressure

18.1 RDC unit can be accessed by removing the passenger seat on the R1200 RT

to the control unit. The pressure settings are based on a reference temperature of 20°C and the control unit ensures that the pressure displayed is 'temperature compensated' to take into account tyre temperature outside of this figure.

3 The sensors are located inside the wheel rim and are part of the tyre valve. Fitting a

18.3 Sticker on wheel rim indicates the presence of the sensor

new sensor, requires the new sensor to be registered with the control unit using the BMW diagnostic tester. A sticker on the wheel rim marks the position of the sensor **(see illustration)**. Be sure to advise the dealer or tyre fitter that pressure sensors are fitted as damage could be caused to the sensor if care is not taken in this area.

Chapter 6
Bodywork

Contents

Degrees of difficulty

Easy, suitable for novice with little experience	Fairly easy, suitable for beginner with some experience	Fairly difficult, suitable for competent DIY mechanic	Difficult, suitable for experienced DIY mechanic	Very difficult, suitable for expert DIY or professional

Specifications

Torque settings

Fuel tank filler cap assembly screws	
R1200 GS and ST	5 Nm
R1200 S	2 Nm
R1200 R	3.5 Nm
Handlebar end-weight bolt	
GS and ST	21 Nm
S, RT and R	19 Nm
Luggage rack bolts	
R1200 GS, RT and R	8 Nm
R1200 ST	11 Nm
Rear brake caliper/spray guard bracket mounting bolt	24 Nm
Spray guard mounting bolts	8 Nm
Sump guard front 6 mm mounting bolt	8 Nm
Sump guard front 8 mm mounting bolt	19 Nm
Windshield screws – R1200 R	2.4 Nm

1 General information

This Chapter covers the procedures necessary to remove and install the bodywork. Since many service and repair operations on these motorcycles require the removal of the body parts, the procedures are grouped here and referred to from other Chapters.

In the case of damage to the body parts, it is usually necessary to remove the broken component and replace it with a new (or used) one. There are however some shops that specialise in 'plastic welding', so it may be worthwhile seeking the advice of one of these specialists before consigning an expensive component to the bin. Alternatively some of the DIY bodywork repair kits are ideal for small repairs.

When attempting to remove any body panel, first study it closely, noting any fasteners and associated fittings, to be sure of returning everything to its correct place on installation. In some cases the aid of an assistant will be required when removing panels, to help avoid the risk of damage to paintwork. Once the evident fasteners have been removed, try to withdraw the panel as described but DO NOT FORCE IT – if it will not release, check that all fasteners have been removed and try again. Where a panel engages another by means of tabs, be careful not to break the tab or its mating slot or to damage the paintwork. Remember that a few moments of patience at this stage will save you a lot of money in replacing broken fairing panels!

When installing a body panel, first study it closely, noting any fasteners and associated fittings removed with it, to be sure of returning everything to its correct place. Check that all fasteners are in good condition, including all trim nuts or clips and damping/rubber mounts; any of these must be replaced if faulty before the panel is reassembled. Check also that all mounting brackets are straight and repair or replace them if necessary before attempting to install the panel. Where assistance was required to remove a panel, make sure your assistant is on hand to install it.

Tighten the fasteners securely, but be careful not to overtighten any of them or the panel may break (not always immediately) due to the uneven stress.

2 R1200 GS models

Seats

1 Insert the ignition key into the seat lock located on the left-hand side. Turn the key clockwise while pressing down on the front of the passenger's seat to unlock it, then lift the front of the seat **(see illustration)**. Note how the hooks on the underside of the seat engage in the top of the luggage carrier **(see illustration)**.

2 To remove the rider's seat, turn the key anticlockwise while pressing down on the rear of the rider's seat to unlock it, then lift the rear of the seat **(see illustration)**. Draw the seat back and lift it off – note how the two bars on the underside of the seat rest in the supports on the frame **(see illustration)**.

3 Install the seats in the reverse order of removal. Check the operation of the seat catch mechanism **(see illustration)**. Ensure the rider's seat is located on the supports and press it down until the catch is heard to click. Engage the hooks on the underside of the passenger's seat with the carrier and press the seat down until the catch is heard to click.

Luggage rack and carrier

4 Remove the seats (see above).
5 Undo the bolts securing the luggage rack and lift it off, noting the arrangement of

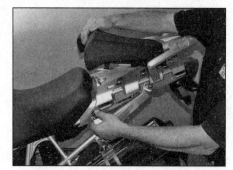

2.1a Lift the passenger's seat from the front

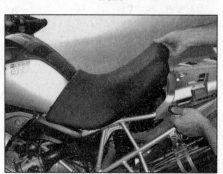

2.2a Lift the rider's seat from the rear

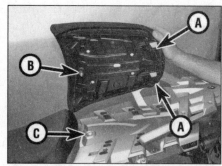

2.1b Note how the hooks (A) locate, and how the lock pin (B) locates in the catch (C)

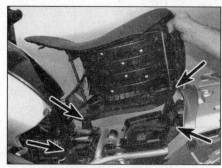

2.2b Note how the bars on the underside of the seat rest in the supports on the frame (arrowed)

washers and spacers on the centre rear bolt **(see illustrations)**.
6 Lift off the spacers **(see illustrations)**.

7 Undo the screws securing the carrier and lift it off **(see illustration)**.
8 Installation is the reverse of removal. Don't

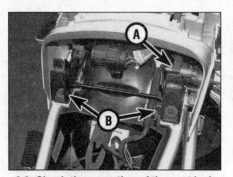

2.3 Check the operation of the seat lock (A) and catch mechanism (B)

2.5a Rack is secured by three bolts (arrowed)

2.5b Note the arrangement of the washers and spacers

2.6a Remove the spacer at the rear . . .

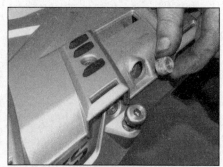

2.6b . . . and one from the left and right-hand side

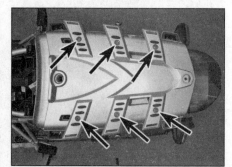

2.7 Carrier is secured by six screws (arrowed)

2.9 Spray guard is secured by three bolts (arrowed)

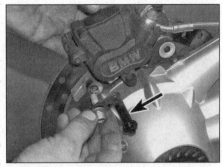

2.10 Undo the caliper mounting bolt to remove the spray guard bracket (arrowed)

2.14a Screw on the underside of the mudguard . . .

2.14b . . . secures the rear wheel sensor wiring connector

2.15 Screw (arrowed) secures starter relay

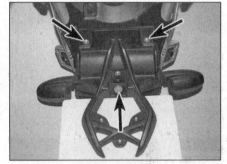

2.16a Tail light/number plate bracket assembly is secured by three screws (arrowed)

forget to fit the spacers before installing the luggage rack. Clean the threads of the luggage rack bolts and apply a suitable non-permanent thread locking compound. Tighten the bolts to the torque setting specified at the beginning of this Chapter.

Spray guard

9 Undo the bolts securing the spray guard and lift it off (see illustration).
10 Note the location of the bracket which is retained by one of the rear brake caliper mounting bolts. If required, undo the mounting bolt and remove the bracket (see illustration).
11 Installation is the reverse of removal. Clean the threads of the spray guard bolts and apply a suitable non-permanent thread

locking compound. Tighten the bolts to the torque settings specified at the beginning of this Chapter.

Rear mudguard

12 Remove the seats and the spray guard (see above).
13 Where fitted, lift out the document tray.
14 On machines equipped with ABS, displace the rear wheel sensor wiring connector (see illustrations).
15 Undo the screw and displace the starter relay (see illustration).
16 Undo the screws securing the tail light/number plate bracket assembly and displace the assembly (see illustration). Disconnect the light unit wiring connector, then unclip the

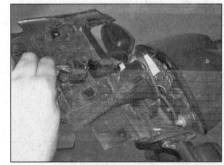

2.16b Disconnect the wiring connector . . .

body of the connector from the mudguard and lift the tail light/number plate bracket off (see illustrations).

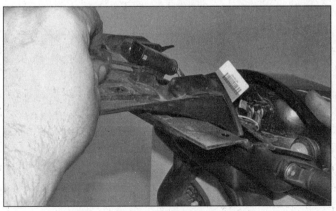

2.16c . . . then unclip the connector . . .

2.16d . . . and lift the tail light/number plate bracket assembly off

2.17a Undo the screws (arrowed) on the underside . . .

2.17b . . . and the screws (arrowed) on the top of the mudguard

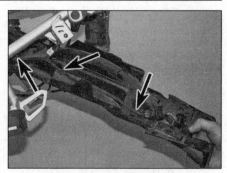

2.18a Release the wiring clips (arrowed) . . .

17 Undo the screws securing the underside and top of the mudguard (see illustrations).
18 Draw the mudguard down and to the rear and unclip the wiring and any electrical components attached to the mudguard, then lift the mudguard off (see illustrations).
19 Installation is the reverse of removal. Don't forget to secure the wiring before securing the mudguard to the rear sub-frame. Check the operation of the lights before riding the motorcycle.

Side covers and side panels

20 Ease the side cover off, noting how the two pegs on the back of the cover locate in grommets (see illustrations).
21 To ease installation, apply a small amount of dry film lubricant to the grommets before pressing the cover on.
22 The side panel is secured by three turnbuckles – twist these 90° to release them, then pull the panel back carefully to release the peg from the grommet on the oil cooler bracket (see illustrations). Note how the top edge of the side panel locates on tabs on the adjacent panel (see illustration).
23 Installation is the reverse of removal. Check the condition of the U-clips securing

2.18b . . . and any electrical components from the mudguard – diagnostic tester socket shown

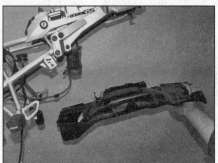

2.18c Lift the mudguard off

2.20a Pull the side cover off . . .

2.20b . . . noting the grommets (arrowed) in the frame

2.22a Two turnbuckles (arrowed) are located on the outside of the side panel . . .

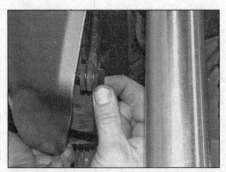

2.22b . . . and one on the inside at the front

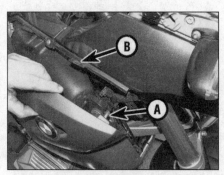

2.22c Note the location of the peg (A). Panel is secured by tabs (B)

2.23 Check the condition of the fixings (arrowed) on the frame

2.25a Undo the screws (arrowed) . . .

2.25b . . . noting the location of the washers (arrowed)

2.25c Lower the panel to release the tab

2.27 Undo the screw (arrowed) on the left and right-hand side

2.28 Remove the filler cap assembly . . .

2.29 . . . then lift off the fuel tank top panel

the turnbuckles and renew them if they are sprained **(see illustration)**. Ensure that the top edge of the panel is correctly located on the tabs before pressing the peg into the grommet. Twist the turnbuckles 90° to secure them.

Fuel tank panels

Side panels

24 Remove the rider's seat and the main side panel (see above).
25 Undo the screws securing the side panel to the tank, noting the location of the washers, then draw the panel down to release the tab on the top edge and lift it off **(see illustrations)**. Installation is the reverse of removal.

Top panel

26 Remove both tank side panels (see above).
27 Undo the screws securing the front edges of the top panel **(see illustration)**.
28 Undo the screws securing the fuel tank filler cap assembly and lift it off **(see illustration)**.
29 Lift off the top panel **(see illustration)**. Temporarily install the filler cap assembly.
30 Installation is the reverse of removal. Tighten the filler cap assembly screws evenly to the torque setting specified at the beginning of this Chapter.

Front mudguards

Upper mudguard

31 Remove both main side panels (see above).
32 Undo the screws securing the rear edges of the mudguard to the front edges of the fuel tank top panel **(see illustration 2.27)**. Note how the rear edges of the mudguard fit underneath the front edges of the top panel **(see illustration)**.
33 Undo the screws securing the mudguard to the oil cooler bracket **(see illustration)**.
34 Unclip the trim panel from both sides of the mudguard, then draw the mudguard

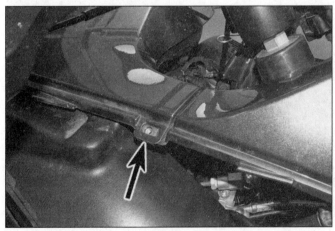

2.32 Note the alignment (arrowed) of the mudguard and tank top panel

2.33 Mudguard is secured by screws (arrowed) on both sides

2.34a Unclip the trim panel . . .

2.34b . . . and release the mudguard from the tab on both sides . . .

2.34c . . . then lift the mudguard off

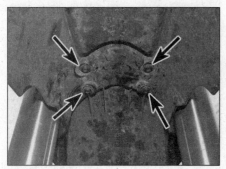

2.37a Mudguard is secured to fork bridge by four screws (arrowed)

2.37b Draw the mudguard forwards to remove it

2.39 Take care not to lose the nuts on the inside of the windshield

forward to release it from the tabs on the headlight brackets and lift the mudguard off **(see illustrations)**.

35 Installation is the reverse of removal. Ensure that the mudguard is correctly aligned and the trim panel clipped in position before installing the fixing screws.

Lower mudguard

36 Remove the front wheel (see Chapter 5).
37 Undo the screws on the underside of the mudguard securing it to the front fork bridge, then draw the mudguard forwards and off the bike. **(see illustrations)**.

38 Installation is the reverse of removal.

Windshield

39 Undo the screws securing the windshield to the front bracket, taking care to secure the nuts on the inside of the windshield **(see illustration)**.

40 Counter-hold the locknut on the end of the adjuster knob thread and unscrew the adjuster, then unscrew the adjuster out from the threaded sleeve – take care to remove the locknut and inner and outer sleeves with the adjuster knob **(see illustration)**.

41 Lift the windshield off. Note the position of the angled mounting stubs which locate on the metal bracket and remove them for safekeeping **(see illustrations)**. Remove the plastic sleeves from the windshield and note

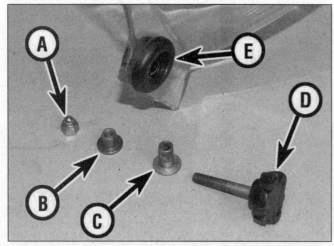

2.40 Components of the windshield adjuster – locknut (A), threaded sleeve (B), outer sleeve (C), knob (D) and latching plates (E)

2.41a Note the location of the mounting stubs . . .

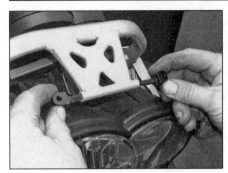

2.41b . . . then pull them out of the bracket

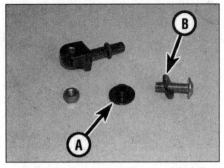

2.41c Note the plastic sleeve (A) and washer (B) on both mounting screws

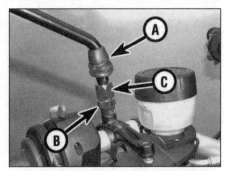

2.45 Peel back the boot (A), counter-hold the bracket (B) and unscrew the nut (C) . . .

2.46 . . . then pull the mirror out from the bracket

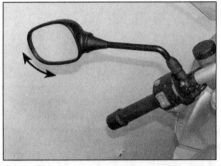

2.47 Make final adjustments by tilting the mirror head

2.48 Undo the screw (arrowed)

the location of the washers on the windshield screws (see illustration).

42 Unless they are damaged, the two-piece latching plates that fit through from either side of the windshield and clip together should be left in position – trying to prise them apart may result in damage.

43 Installation is the reverse of removal. Ensure that the stubs are installed the correct way round in the metal bracket, angled upwards with the recess for the nuts at the back (see illustration 2.41a). Don't forget to fit the plastic sleeves and washers onto the mounting screws, and apply a suitable non-permanent thread locking compound to the screws. Take care not to over-tighten the screws.

Mirrors

44 The mirror stems are secured in the left and right-hand handlebar brackets by gland nuts.

45 To remove the mirror, first peel back the boot covering the gland nut, then counter-hold the bracket and unscrew the nut (see illustration).

46 Pull the mirror stem out of the handle-bar bracket and lift off the nut (see illustration).

47 Installation is the reverse of removal. Hold the mirror in the desired position and tighten the gland nut and refit the boot. Final adjustment can be made by tilting the mirror head (see illustration).

Hand protectors

48 Undo the screw securing the hand protector bracket to the handlebar bracket (see illustration).

49 Unscrew the handlebar end-weight bolt, then withdraw the bolt and collar (see illustrations).

50 Lift off the hand protector and pull the end-weight out from the handlebar (see illustration).

51 Installation is the reverse of removal. Ensure that the cables, hoses and wiring are correctly routed inside the hand protector, as appropriate. Apply a suitable non-permanent thread locking compound to the end-weight bolt and tighten it to the specified torque setting.

2.49a Unscrew the end weight bolt . . .

2.49b . . . then withdraw the bolt and collar

2.50 Remove the hand protector and end weight

2.52 Undo the bolt (arrowed) on the left and right-hand side

2.53 Remove the nuts and bolts from the lower mounting brackets

Crash bars

52 Undo the bolts securing the crash bar to the upper crankcase (see illustration).
53 Counter-hold the nuts and undo the bolts securing the crash bar to the brackets on the lower crankcase, then withdraw the bolts (see illustration).
54 Undo the bolts securing the crash bar directly to the lower crankcase and withdraw the bolts (see illustration).

55 Ease the rear ends of the crash bar out from the sockets in the lower frame rails and over the exhaust pipes, then manoeuvre the crash bar off. If required, undo the bolts securing the brackets to the crankcase and remove the brackets, noting how they fit.
56 Installation is the reverse of removal. Tighten all the bolts finger-tight and ensure that the crash bar is correctly aligned, then tighten the bolts securely.

Sump guard

57 Loosen the bolts and nuts securing the sump guard to the crankcase (see illustration). Support the sump guard, then remove the fixings and lift the sump guard off (see illustration).
58 If required, unscrew the mountings from the bottom of the crankcase (see illustration). On later models (from May 2007) note that there are two rubber mountings at the rear and a mounting bracket at the front; the mounting bracket is secured by a through bolt and nut to the sump.
59 Installation is the reverse of removal.

3 R1200 RT models

Seats

1 Insert the ignition key into the seat lock located below the tail light. Turn the key anti-

2.54 Undo the bolts securing the crash bar to the crankcase

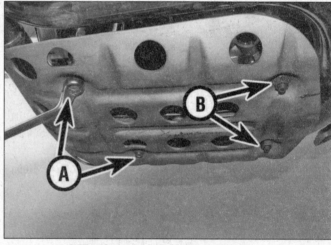

2.57a Undo the bolts (A) and nuts (B) . . .

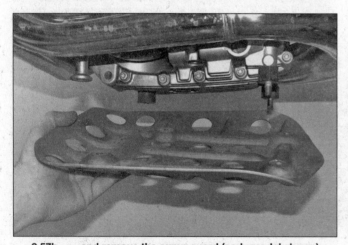

2.57b . . . and remove the sump guard (early model shown)

2.58 Unscrew the mountings (arrowed) from the crankcase (early model shown)

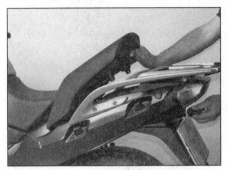

3.1 Unlock the passenger's seat and lift it from the rear

3.2 Lift the rider's seat from the rear

3.3a Position the front mounting bar (arrowed) in the appropriate holder

3.3b High (A) and low (B) positions for the front bar

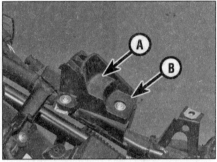

3.3c High (A) and low (B) positions on the frame brackets for the seat supports

3.3d Location of the frame brackets (arrowed)

clockwise while pressing down on the rear of the passenger's seat to unlock it. Lift the rear of the seat (see illustration). On models with heated seats, disconnect the seat wiring connector. Pull the seat backwards and off.

2 To remove the rider's seat, first remove the passenger's seat. On models with heated seats, disconnect the seat wiring connector. Lift the rear of the seat and pull it backwards and off (see illustration).

3 The height of the rider's seat is adjustable.

To adjust the height, position the front mounting bar in the appropriate holder (see illustration). With the bar in the low position, the supports on the rear underside of the seat should locate in the forward mounting position on the frame brackets (see illustrations).

4 Install the seats in the reverse order of removal. Check the operation of the seat catch mechanism (see illustration). Ensure the rider's seat is fully located on the frame brackets, then push the passenger's seat into

position and press it down until the catch is heard to click.

Luggage rack

5 Remove the passenger's seat (see above).
6 Remove the tail light unit (see Chapter 7).
7 Undo the bolts securing the rear underside of the luggage rack to the rear sub-frame – note that the bolts are located up inside the frame (see illustration).

3.4 Check the operation of the seat catch mechanism (arrowed)

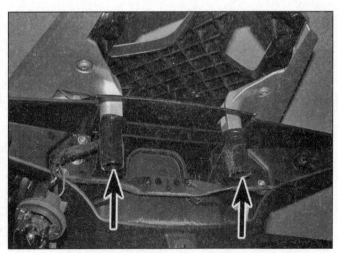

3.7 Location of the rear luggage rack bolts (arrowed)

3.8 Undo the bolts (arrowed) on the left and right-hand sides

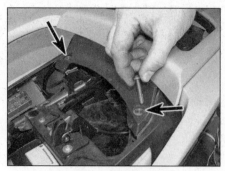

3.9a Undo the bolts (arrowed) . . .

3.9b . . . and lift the luggage rack off

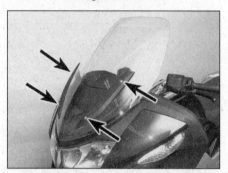

3.11a Undo the screws (arrowed) . . .

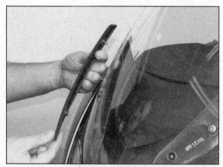

3.11b . . . and lift the windshield trim panels off

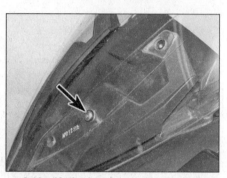

3.12a Undo the screw on both sides (arrowed) . . .

3.12b . . . and remove the screws and washers

8 Undo the bolts securing both sides of the luggage rack to the sub-frame **(see illustration)**.

9 Undo the bolts securing the top of the luggage rack and lift the rack off **(see illustrations)**.

10 Installation is the reverse of removal. Clean the threads of the luggage rack bolts and apply a suitable non-permanent thread locking compound. Tighten the bolts to the torque setting specified at the beginning of this Chapter. Check the operation of the lights before riding the motorcycle.

Windshield

11 Undo the screws securing the windshield trim panels and lift the panels off **(see illustrations)**.

12 Undo the screws securing the windshield and remove the screws and washers **(see illustrations)**.

13 Lift off the windshield and lift the inner panel off the windshield brackets **(see illustrations)**.

14 To remove the windshield brackets, carefully prise the E-clips off the pivot pins, noting which way round the pins are fitted

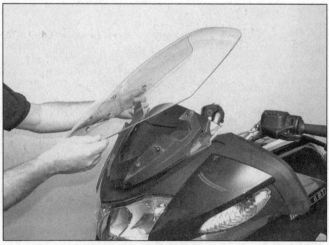

3.13a Lift off the windshield . . .

3.13b . . . and the inner panel

3.14a Prise off the E-clips . . .

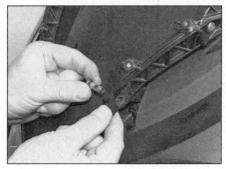

3.14b . . . then press out the pins . . .

3.14c . . . and lift the brackets off

(see illustration). Press the pins out and lift the brackets off **(see illustrations).**

15 To gain access to the motor that raises and lowers the windshield, follow the procedure in Steps 33 to 38 and remove the fairing headlight panel.

16 Installation is the reverse of removal. Ensure that the brackets are fitted the right way round. Press the upper pivot pins in from the outside and the lower pins in from the inside **(see illustration).** If the E-clips are strained or corroded replace them with new ones. Ensure the washers are fitted on the windshield screws and take care not to over-tighten the screws. Check the operation of the windshield motor.

Mirrors

17 The left and right-hand mirror assemblies are a push fit on three pegs on the back of the fairing headlight panel. Ease the assembly off carefully to avoid damage **(see illustration).** If required, the mirror glass can be purchased as a separate item. Use a large flat-bladed screwdriver as a lever to ease the glass and its plastic backing out of the assembly – place

a thick piece of card between the lever and mirror housing to prevent damage.

18 To ease installation, apply a small amount of dry film lubricant to the pegs before pressing the mirror assembly on **(see illustration).**

Fairing panels

Note: *The machines covered in this manual were available from new fitted with a range of optional electrical extras. When working on your machine, take care to ensure that all relevant*

3.16 Ensure the pins are inserted correctly (arrowed)

electrical components are disconnected on disassembly and subsequently reconnected during the rebuild. Always take the precaution of disconnecting the battery negative (-ve) terminal before disconnecting an electrical wiring connector.

Upper side panels

19 Both panels are secured by four screws **(see illustration).**

20 Undo the screws on the inside front edge of the panel, then undo the screw next to the steering head and the screw on the rear

3.17 Ease the mirror unit off carefully

3.18 Use dry film lubricant on the pegs to ease installation (arrowed)

3.19 Both upper side panels are secured by four screws on panel inner edges (arrowed)

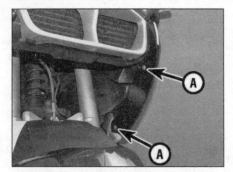

3.20a Undo the screws (A) on the inside front edge . . .

3.20b . . . the screw (B) next to the steering head . . .

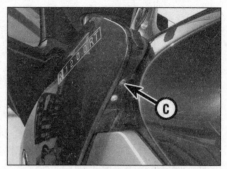

3.20c . . . and the screw (C) on the rear edge of the panel

edge of the panel **(see illustration)**. Ease the panel off carefully and disconnect any wiring connectors for equipment housed in the panel, then lift the panel off **(see illustrations)**.

21 Installation is the reverse of removal. Ensure that the U-clips are secure on the mounting points **(see illustration)**. Don't forget to connect the wiring for equipment housed in the panel before installing the panel.

Main side panels

22 Remove the seats (see above).
23 Remove the upper side panels as required (see above).
24 Undo the screws securing the fuel tank centre panel and lift the panel off **(see illustrations)**.

3.20d Disconnect any wiring connectors . . .

3.20e . . . then lift the panel off

25 To remove the fairing left-hand panel, undo the screws located above and below the exhaust header pipe and the screws

securing the panel to the footrest bracket **(see illustrations)**.
26 Undo the screws on the front and back of

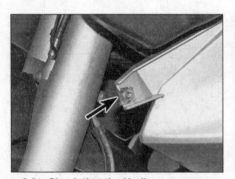

3.21 Check that the U-clips are secure

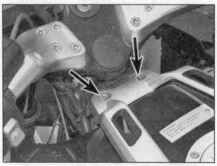

3.24a Undo the screws at the front (arrowed) . . .

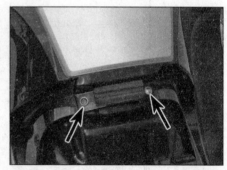

3.24b . . . and at the rear of the tank centre panel (arrowed) . . .

3.24c . . . then lift the panel off

3.25a Undo the screws at the front (arrowed) . . .

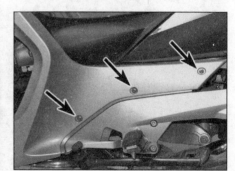

3.25b . . . and at the rear of the fairing panel (arrowed)

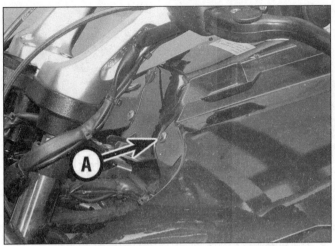

3.26a Undo the screws on the front (A) (arrowed) . . .

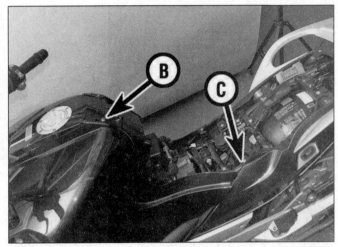

3.26b . . . and back (B) of the fuel tank and on the top edge (C) of the panel

the fuel tank and the screw on the top edge of the panel **(see illustrations)**.

27 Support the panel and undo the quick-release catch, then lift the panel off **(see illustrations)**.

28 To remove the fairing right-hand panel, first undo the screws securing the storage compartment lid and lift the lid off **(see illustrations)**.

29 Undo the screws securing the top of the panel to the storage compartment **(see illustration)**.

30 Now follow Steps 25 to 27 and lift the panel off.

31 The main side panels are constructed from three sections **(see illustration)**. If required, undo the screws securing the sections together and separate them carefully.

32 Installation is the reverse of removal. Ensure that the U-clips are secure on the mounting points **(see illustration)**. Don't forget to connect the wiring for equipment housed in the panel before installing the panel. Ensure the panel is correctly aligned with its mounting points and adjacent panels before tightening the mounting screws. When installing the right-hand panel, check the operation of the storage compartment lid catch before

3.27a Undo the quick-release catch . . .

3.27b . . . and lift the panel off

3.28a Undo the screws (arrowed) on the right-hand side . . .

3.28b . . . and lift off the storage compartment lid

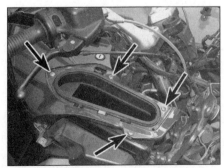

3.29 Panel is secured to the storage compartment by four screws (arrowed)

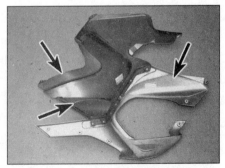

3.31 The main side panels are constructed from three sections (arrowed)

3.32 Check that the U-clips are secure (arrowed)

3.34a Undo the screws (arrowed) . . .

3.34b . . . and lift off the trim panel

3.35a Undo the screws (arrowed) on the left and right-hand sides . . .

installing the upper side panel. Renew the quick-release catches if they are too worn to grip in their locations (see illustration 3.27a).

Headlight panel

33 Remove the windshield and windshield brackets, mirrors and fairing upper side panels (see above).

34 Undo the screws on both sides and lift off the left and right-hand trim panels (see illustrations).

35 Undo the screws on the left and right-hand side of the cockpit trim panel (see illustration). Undo the screws on the forward edge of the trim panel, then lift the panel off (see illustrations).

36 Displace the turn signal bulbholders (see Chapter 7).

37 Undo the screws securing the left and right-hand sides of the headlight panel,

3.35b . . . and on the forward edge of the cockpit trim panel (arrowed) . . .

3.35c . . . then lift the trim panel off

noting the location of the washers (see illustrations).

38 Draw the headlight panel forwards, noting how the windshield pivot arms locate through the slots in the panel, and disconnect

the wiring connector, then lift the panel off (see illustrations). Note the location of the grommets on the fairing bracket and renew them if they are damaged or deteriorated (see illustration).

3.37a Undo the screws at the front (arrowed) . . .

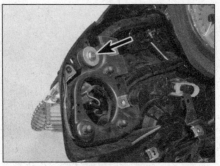

3.37b . . . and at the rear of the headlight panel (arrowed) . . .

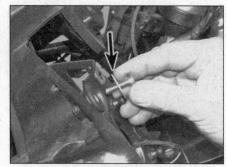

3.37c . . . noting the location of the washers (arrowed)

3.38a Disconnect the wiring connector . . .

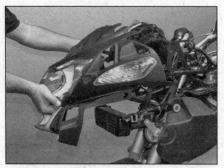

3.38b . . . and lift the headlight panel off

3.38c Check the condition of the mounting grommets (arrowed)

3.40 Seat cowling panels are removed separately

3.43 Undo the screw (arrowed) on the lower edge of the cowling panel

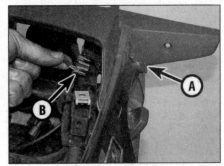

3.44 Disconnect the accessory socket (A) wiring connector (B)

39 Installation is the reverse of removal. To ease installation, apply a small amount of dry film lubricant to the grommets before pressing the panel on. Align the windshield pivot arms correctly. Ensure that the headlight wiring connector is secure and press the pegs on the rear of the panel into the grommets on the mounting bracket before installing the screws and washers. Check the operation of the lights before riding the motorcycle.

Seat cowling

40 The left and right-hand cowling panels are remove separately **(see illustration)**.
41 Remove the seats and luggage rack (see above).

43 To remove the left-hand cowling panel, first undo the screw securing the main side panel below the exhaust header pipe and the screws securing the side panel to the footrest bracket **(see illustrations 3.25a and b)**. Ease the rear section of the main side panel back to access the screw on the lower edge of the cowling panel and undo the screw **(see illustration)**. Alternatively, remove the main side panel to access the cowling panel screw (see above).
44 Where fitted, disconnect the wiring connector for the accessory socket **(see illustration)**.
45 Undo the screws securing the cowling panel and lift it off **(see illustrations)**. The cowling panel locates over the mounting

points for the panniers – if required, undo the screws securing the pannier bracket and remove the bracket **(see illustration)**.
46 Follow the same procedure to remove the right-hand cowling panel.
47 Installation is the reverse of removal.

Tail light and number plate bracket

48 Remove both seat cowling panels (see above).
49 Release the seat catch mechanism outer cable from the cable stop, then detach the inner cable end from the catch **(see illustrations)**.
50 Undo the screws securing the bracket to

3.45a Undo the screw (arrowed) on the underside . . .

3.45b . . . and in the centre of the panel (arrowed) . . .

3.45c . . . then lift the cowling panel off

3.45d Pannier bracket is secured by two screws (arrowed)

3.49a Release the outer cable from the cable stop . . .

3.49b . . . then detach the inner cable end from the catch

3.50a Number plate bracket is secured by screw (arrowed) on both sides . . .

3.50b . . . and four screws (arrowed) at the rear

3.50c Feed the tail light and turn signal bulbholders through the bracket . . .

3.50d . . . and lift the bracket off

3.54 Rear mudguard is secured to upper rear sub-frame by four screws (arrowed)

3.56a Undo the screws (arrowed) on both sides . . .

the rear sub-frame **(see illustrations)**. Ease the bracket rearwards, taking care to feed the tail light and turn signal bulbholders through the bracket, then lift the bracket off **(see illustrations)**.

51 Installation is the reverse of removal. Check the operation of the seat catch before installing the passenger's seat.

Rear mudguard

52 Remove both seat cowling panels and the tail light and number plate bracket (see above).

53 A number of electrical components are mounted on the top of the mudguard, including the starter relay and ABS diagnostic plug unit, and where applicable, the anti-theft alarm and ambient air temperature sensor. Also note that the connectors for the heated seats and electronic suspension adjustment are clipped to the mudguard. Check that all

the components and connectors are free from the mudguard before proceeding.

54 Undo the screws securing the front lower edge of the mudguard, then undo the screws securing the mudguard to the upper rear sub-frame cross-members and lift the mudguard off **(see illustration)**.

55 Installation is the reverse of removal. Check that all the wiring connectors are secure before installing the seat cowling panels.

Front mudguard

56 To remove the front section of the mudguard, undo the screws on both sides, then draw the front section forwards and unclip it from the main mudguard **(see illustrations)**.

57 Installation is the reverse of removal. Ensure that the clip in the centre of the mudguard is correctly located before installing the screws.

58 To remove the main section of the

mudguard, first remove the front section and the front wheel (see Chapter 5).

59 Undo the screws on the underside of the mudguard securing it to the front fork bridge, then undo the screws securing the mudguard to the front fork sliders and draw the mudguard forwards and off the bike.

60 Installation is the reverse of removal.

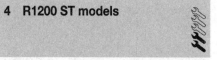

4 R1200 ST models

Seats

1 Insert the ignition key into the seat lock located behind the passenger's seat. Turn the key clockwise while pressing down on the rear of the passenger's seat to unlock it, then lift the rear of the seat and pull it backwards and off **(see illustration)**.

3.56b . . . then draw the front section forwards

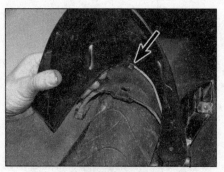

3.56c Note the location of the clip (arrowed)

4.1 Unlock the passenger's seat and lift it from the rear

4.2 Lift the rider's seat from the rear

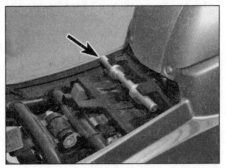

4.3a Locate the bar (arrowed) in the low or high position . . .

4.3b . . . and adjust the support accordingly

2 To remove the rider's seat, first remove the passenger's seat. Lift the rear of the rider's seat and pull it backwards and off **(see illustration)**.

3 The height of the rider's seat is adjustable. To adjust the height, position the front mounting bar in the appropriate holder **(see illustration)**. With the bar in the low position, the support in the centre underside of the seat should also be in the low position. If the front mounting bar is in the high position, turn the support around to the high position also **(see illustration)**. Note that there are two mounting positions on the rear brackets on the underside of the seat to correspond with the high or low seat setting **(see illustration)**.

4 Install the seats in the reverse order of removal. Check the operation of the seat catch mechanism. Ensure the rider's seat is fully located on its brackets, then push the passenger's seat into position so that the

hooks on the underside locate underneath the rider's seat **(see illustration)**. Press the passenger's seat down until the catch is heard to click.

Side covers

5 Undo the screw on the bottom edge of the side cover, then ease the cover off, noting how the two pegs on the back of the cover locate in grommets **(see illustrations)**.

6 To ease installation, apply a small amount of dry film lubricant to the grommets before pressing the cover on. Tighten the screw securely

Fairing side panels

7 Remove the seats and both side covers (see above).

8 Undo the screws securing the upper and lower edges of the side panel **(see illustration)**.

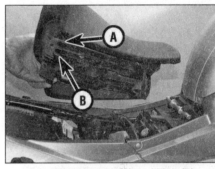

4.3c Note the low (A) and high (B) mounting positions on the rear brackets

9 Undo the screw on the inside front of the side panel, securing the panel to the oil cooler bracket **(see illustration)**.

10 Undo the screws securing the side panel to the fairing front panel **(see illustration)**.

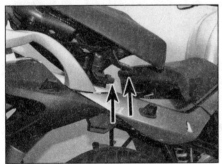

4.4 Hooks (arrowed) locate underneath the rider's seat

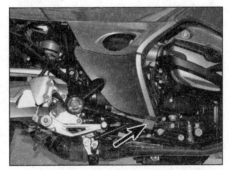

4.5a Undo the screw (arrowed)

4.5b Note the location of the grommets (arrowed)

4.8 Undo the side panel screws (arrowed)

4.9 Location of the screw (arrowed) on the inside front of the side panel

4.10 Screws (arrowed) secure the side panel to the fairing front panel

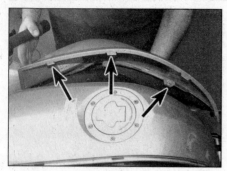

4.11a Lift the panel to release the tabs (arrowed) . . .

4.11b . . . then lift the panel off

4.17a Undo the screws (arrowed) . . .

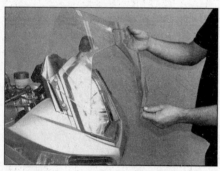

4.17b . . . and lift the windshield off

4.18a Undo the screw (arrowed) . . .

4.18b . . . and lift the bracket cover off

11 Carefully lift the side panel to release the tabs on the top edge from the slots in the fuel tank centre panel, then lift the side panel off **(see illustrations)**.

12 Installation is the reverse of removal. Ensure that the U-clips are secure on the mounting points. Ensure the panel is correctly aligned with its mounting points and adjacent panels before tightening the mounting screws.

Fuel tank centre panel

13 Remove both fairing side panels (see above).

14 Undo the screws securing the fuel tank filler cap assembly and lift it off **(see illustration 2.28)**.

15 Lift off the centre panel. Temporarily install the filler cap assembly.

16 Installation is the reverse of removal. Tighten the filler cap assembly screws evenly to the torque setting specified at the beginning of this Chapter.

Windshield

17 Undo the screws securing the windshield to the brackets and lift it off **(see illustrations)**.

18 If required, undo the screws securing the bracket covers and lift the covers off **(see illustrations)**.

19 The bracket sliding mechanism is attached to the main headlight/oil cooler bracket **(see illustration)**. If the sliding mechanism is faulty, remove the fairing front panel (see below) to access the mechanism spring tensioners **(see illustration)**.

20 Installation is the reverse of removal.

Cockpit trim panels

Note: *The machines covered in this manual were available from new fitted with a range of optional electrical extras. When working on your machine, take care to ensure that all relevant electrical components are disconnected on disassembly and subsequently reconnected during the rebuild. Always take the precaution of disconnecting the battery negative (-ve) terminal before disconnecting an electrical wiring connector.*

21 Remove both fairing side panels (see above).

22 Remove the windshield and the windshield bracket covers (see above).

23 To remove the right-hand trim panel, first undo the screws securing the panel to the fairing front panel **(see illustration)**. Ease the

4.19a The bracket sliding mechanism is located behind the fairing front panel

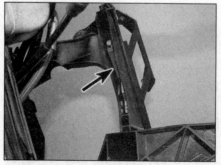

4.19b Location of the spring tensioners (arrowed)

4.23a Undo the screws (arrowed) . . .

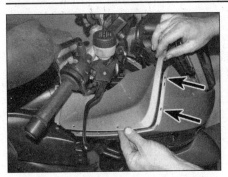

4.23b . . . then release the tabs from the slots (arrowed) . . .

4.23c . . . and lift the trim panel off

4.28a Undo the screws (arrowed) on the left and right-hand sides . . .

4.28b . . . then draw the front panel off

4.32a Undo the screw (arrowed) at the front . . .

4.32b . . . and on the underside of the seat cowling

trim panel up to release the tabs from the slots in the edge of the front panel and lift the trim panel off (see illustrations).

24 Follow the same procedure to remove the left-hand trim panel.

25 Installation is the reverse of removal.

Fairing front panel

26 Remove both cockpit trim panels (see above).

27 Remove the left and right-hand front turn signal bulb holders (see Chapter 7).

28 Undo the screws securing both sides of the front panel to the main headlight/oil cooler bracket, then draw the front panel off (see illustrations).

29 Installation is the reverse of removal. Don't

forget to install the turn signal bulb holders before installing the cockpit trim panels.

Seat cowling

30 The left and right-hand cowling panels are removed separately.

31 Remove the seats (see above).

32 To remove the right-hand cowling panel, undo the screw securing the rear edge of the fairing side panel to the cowling panel and the screw securing the underside of the cowling panel (see illustrations).

33 Ease the panel over the pannier bracket and release the tab from the underside of the passenger grab handle, then draw the panel back and off (see illustrations).

34 Follow the same procedure to remove the left-hand cowling panel.

35 Installation is the reverse of removal. Ensure that the tab on the front edge of the cowling panel is fitted behind the rear edge of the fairing side panel, and the tab at the rear edge of the cowling panel is fitted in the slot on the underside of the passenger grab handle.

Passenger grab handle and luggage rack

36 Remove the seats and both seat cowling panels (see above).

37 Remove the tail light unit (see Chapter 7).

38 Undo the nut securing the rear underside of the luggage rack to the rear sub-frame (see illustration).

39 Undo the screws securing the sides and

4.33a Release the tab (arrowed) from the grab handle . . .

4.33b . . . then lift the cowling panel off

4.38 Undo the nut on the underside of the luggage rack

4.39a Undo the screws on the left and right-hand sides (arrowed) . . .

4.39b . . . and the screws on the top (arrowed) . . .

4.39c . . . then lift the luggage rack off

the top of the luggage rack and lift the rack off **(see illustrations)**.

40 Installation is the reverse of removal. Clean the threads of the luggage rack screws and apply a suitable non-permanent thread locking compound. Tighten the screws to the torque setting specified at the beginning of this Chapter. Check the operation of the lights before riding the motorcycle.

Tail light side panel assembly

41 Remove the passenger grab handle and luggage rack (see above).
42 Remove the rear turn signal units (see Chapter 7).
43 Undo the screw on the underside of the tail light housing and the screws on the top edge of the number plate bracket **(see illustrations)**.

44 Undo the screws securing the assembly to the rear sub-frame **(see illustration)**. Ease the assembly rearwards, taking care to feed the tail light bulbholder and turn signal wiring through the assembly, then lift the assembly off **(see illustration)**. If required, mark the signal wiring to aid installation.
45 The tail light side panel assembly locates over the mounting points for the panniers – if required, undo the screws securing the pannier brackets and remove the brackets **(see illustration)**.
46 A handle for lifting the bike onto the centre stand is located on the left-hand side of the rear sub-frame – if required, undo the mounting screws and remove the handle **(see illustration)**.
47 Installation is the reverse of removal. Take care not to damage the turn signal wiring when feeding it through the bracket

Front mudguard

48 To remove the front section of the mudguard, undo the screws on both sides, then draw the front section forwards and unclip it from the main mudguard **(see illustration 3.56a, b and c)**.
49 Installation is the reverse of removal. Ensure that the clip in the centre of the mudguard is correctly located before installing the screws.
50 To remove the main section of the mudguard, first remove the front section and the front wheel (see Chapter 5).
51 Undo the screws on the underside of the mudguard securing it to the front fork bridge, then undo the screws securing the mudguard to the front fork sliders and draw the mudguard forwards and off the bike.
52 Installation is the reverse of removal.

4.43a Undo the screw on the underside of the light housing (arrowed) . . .

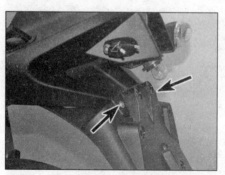

4.43b . . . and the two screws on the top of the number plate bracket

4.44a Undo the four screws (arrowed) . . .

4.44b . . . and ease the side panel assembly off

4.45 Undo the screws (arrowed) to remove the pannier bracket

4.46 Undo the screws (arrowed) to remove the lifting handle

Mirrors

53 The mirror stems are secured in the left and right-hand handlebar brackets by gland nuts.

54 To remove the mirror, first peel back the boot covering the gland nut, then counter-hold the bracket and unscrew the nut **(see illustration 2.45).**

55 Pull the mirror stem out of the handlebar bracket and lift off the nut **(see illustration 2.46).**

56 Installation is the reverse of removal. Hold the mirror in the desired position and tighten the gland nut and refit the boot. Final adjustment can be made by tilting the mirror head **(see illustration 2.47).**

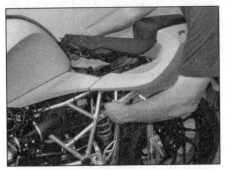

5.1 Unlock the rider's seat and lift it from the front

| 5 | R1200 S models |

Seats

1 Insert the ignition key into the seat lock located below the seat cowling. Turn the key clockwise while pressing down on the front of the rider's seat to unlock it, then lift the front of the seat and lift it off **(see illustration).**

2 To remove the passenger's seat, first remove the rider's seat. Pull the catch loop and lift the seat forwards **(see illustration).** Note the location of the passenger's seat lock **(see illustration).**

3 Install the seats in the reverse order of removal. Make sure that the catch loop is accessible, then push the passenger's seat back so that the pegs on the frame locate on the underside of the seat correctly and the catch is heard to click **(see illustration).** Ensure the back of the rider's seat is fully located on its brackets **(see illustration 5.3).** Push the front of the seat down until the catch is heard to click.

Fairing and fuel tank side panels

4 Remove the rider's seat (see above).

5 Undo the screws securing the front top edge of the panel **(see illustration).**

6 Undo the screw on the front underside of the panel and the screws on the rear top edge **(see illustrations).**

7 Carefully ease the edge of the panel away

5.2a Pull the catch loop to unlock the passenger's seat

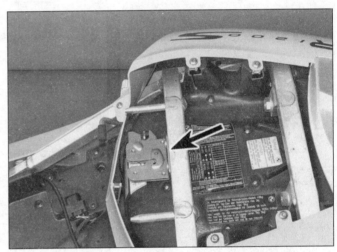

5.2b Location of passenger's seat lock (arrowed)

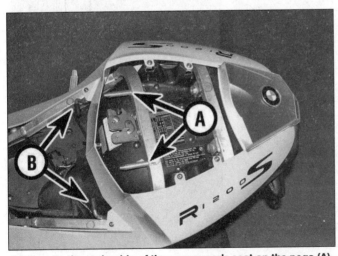

5.3 Locate the underside of the passenger's seat on the pegs (A). Note the brackets for the rider's seat (B)

5.5 Screws (arrowed) secure the front top edge of the panel

5.6a Undo the screw on the front underside of the panel . . .

5.6b . . . and the screws on the rear top edge

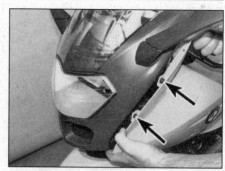

5.7 Note the location of the pins (arrowed) on the edge of the panel

from the front panel, noting how it is retained by the two pins **(see illustration)**.

8 Lift the panel to disengage the tabs from the edge of the tank centre panel, then carefully ease the tab on the back edge out

from behind the seat cowling and lift the panel off **(see illustrations)**.

9 If required, undo the screws securing the side covers to the side panels **(see illustration)**.

10 Installation is the reverse of removal. Take care to ensure all the tabs are correctly positioned before installing the screws **(see illustration)**.

Fuel tank centre panel

11 Remove both fairing and fuel tank side panels (see above).

12 Undo the screws securing the fuel tank filler cap assembly and lift it off **(see illustration)**.

13 Lift off the centre panel **(see illustration)**. Temporarily install the filler cap assembly.

14 Installation is the reverse of removal. Tighten the filler cap assembly screws evenly to the torque setting specified at the beginning of this Chapter.

Mirrors

15 If required, the mirror glass can be purchased separately from the mirror

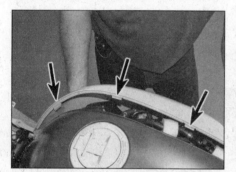

5.8a Lift the panel to release the tabs (arrowed) along the top edge

5.8b Release the tab (arrowed) from the seat cowling . . .

5.8c . . . then lift the panel off

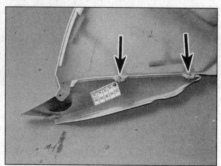

5.9 Undo the screws to separate the panels (arrowed)

5.10 Take great care when aligning the tab (arrowed) with the seat cowling

5.12a Undo the screws (arrowed) . . .

5.12b . . . and remove the filler cap assembly

5.13 Lift off the tank centre panel

5.16 Disconnect the wiring connector

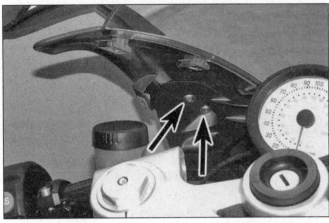

5.17a Loosen the mirror/turn signal unit mounting screws (arrowed)

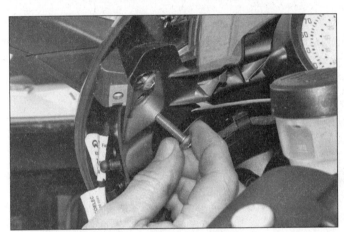

5.17b Withdraw the screws . . .

5.17c . . . and lift the mirror/turn signal unit off

assembly. Use a large flat-bladed screwdriver as a lever to ease the glass and its plastic backing out of the assembly – place a thick piece of card between the lever and outer edge of the mirror housing to prevent damage. Ease the retaining clip off the centre stub with the tip of the screwdriver. To fit the new mirror glass, check that the clip is in place on the back of the glass, then press the glass into the housing,

applying pressure to the centre of the glass.

16 Remove the left or right-hand fairing and fuel tank side panel as applicable (see above). Disconnect the turn signal wiring connector **(see illustration)**.

17 Loosen the screws securing the mirror/ turn signal assembly, then support it, remove the screws and lift the assembly off **(see illustrations)**.

18 Installation is the reverse of removal. Check the operation of the turn signals before riding the motorcycle.

Fairing front panel

19 Remove both mirrors and both fairing/fuel tank side panels (see above).

20 Ease the edges of the panel away from the pegs on the mounting bracket, then draw the panel off **(see illustrations)**.

5.20a Ease the panel forwards to release the pegs . . .

5.20b . . . then lift the panel off

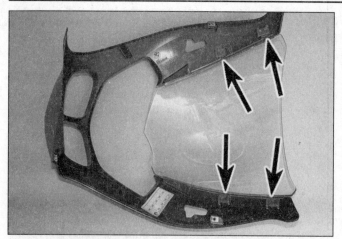

5.21a Pull off the clips to remove the windshield . . .

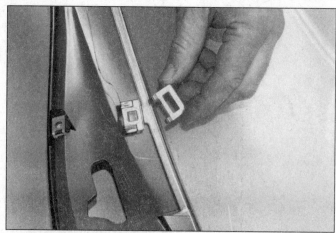

5.21b . . . noting how they locate onto the brackets

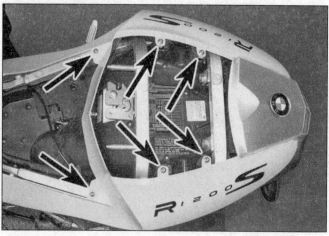

5.26 Undo the screws (arrowed) securing both sides of the seat cowling

5.27 Ease the sides of the cowling back and off the pegs (arrowed)

21 If required, pull off the clips securing the windshield and lift the windshield out of the panel **(see illustrations)**. **Note:** *If required, the windshield can be removed without removing the front panel from the machine.*

22 Installation is the reverse of removal. To ease installation, apply a small amount of dry film lubricant to the grommets on the inside of the panel before pressing them onto the pegs.

Seat cowling

23 The left and right-hand cowling panels are removed as a unit.

24 Remove the seats (see above).

25 Undo the screws securing the front edges of the cowling to the rear edges of the fairing and fuel tank side panels **(see illustration 5.6b)**.

26 Undo the screws securing both sides of the cowling to the under-seat panel **(see illustration)**.

27 Draw the cowling back and release the left and right-hand rear edges from the pegs on the sides of the tail light unit **(see illustration)**.

28 Ease the cowling off **(see illustration)**. Note the location of the grommets in the brackets on the inside of the cowling **(see illustration)**.

29 If required, release the clips and separate the halves of the seat cowling **(see illustration)**.

5.28a Lift the seat cowling off

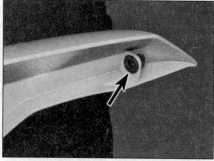

5.28b Note the location of the grommets (arrowed)

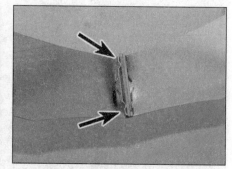

5.29 The two halves of the cowling are secured by clips (arrowed)

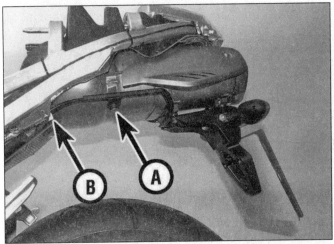

5.32 Disconnect the wiring connector (B) and undo the screw (A)

5.33 Number plate bracket is secured by four screws (arrowed)

30 Installation is the reverse of removal. Ensure that the grommets are located over the pegs. To ease installation, apply a small amount of dry film lubricant to the grommets before pressing the pegs in. Ensure that the front edges of the cowling are located on the inside of the rear edges of the fairing and fuel tank side panels (see illustration 5.10).

5.35a Undo the screws (arrowed) on both sides . . .

Number plate bracket

31 Remove the seat cowling (see above).
32 Disconnect the wiring connector for the rear turn signals/number plate light assembly and undo the screw securing the wiring guide to the underside of the exhaust silencer (see illustration).
33 Undo the screws securing the number plate bracket to the underside of the silencer and lift the bracket off (see illustration).
34 Installation is the reverse of removal. Check the operation of the lights before riding the motorcycle.

Front mudguard

35 To remove the front section of the mudguard, undo the screws on both sides, then draw the front section forwards and unclip it from the main mudguard (see illustrations).
36 Installation is the reverse of removal. Ensure that the clip in the centre of the

mudguard is correctly located before installing the screws.
37 To remove the main section of the mudguard, first remove the front section and the front wheel (see Chapter 5).
38 Undo the screws on the underside of the mudguard securing it to the front fork bridge, then undo the screws securing the mudguard to the front fork sliders and draw the mudguard forwards and off the bike.
39 Installation is the reverse of removal.

6 R1200 R models

Seat

1 Insert the ignition key into the seat lock located under the tail light. Turn the key clockwise in the lock, lift up the rear of the seat and pull it backwards and off.

5.35b . . . then draw the front section forwards

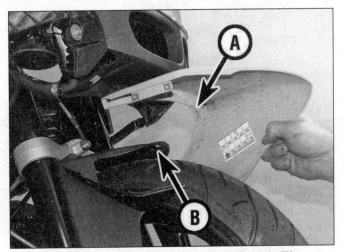

5.35c Note how the clip (A) locates in the hole (B)

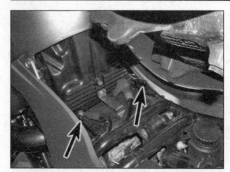

6.2 Mounting holes in seat engage the hooks (arrowed)

6.5a Side cover is retained by two screws (arrowed) . . .

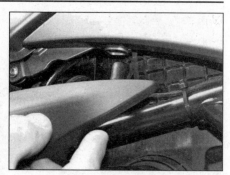

6.5b . . . and a peg

6.6 Side panel screws (arrrowed) on left side

6.7 Three screws retain centre rear body panel

Side panels and rear bodywork

4 Remove the seat as described in Step 1.
5 The small black side cover must be removed before the main side panel can be detached. Remove the two screws and pull the side cover downwards to disengage its peg from the side panel **(see illustrations)**.
6 The side panel is retained by four screws **(see illustration)**.
7 The centre rear bodypanel is retained by three screws **(see illustration)**.
8 Remove the rear turn signal light (see Chapter 7).
9 From the inside of the bodywork, push out the plastic access cover to gain access to the hidden panel screw **(see illustration)**. The other panel screws are on the top and front edges **(see illustration)**.
10 Installation is the reverse of removal. Check the operation of the turn signals afterwards.

2 Install the seat in the reverse order of removal. Ensure that the two prongs on the frame engage the holes in the seat underside **(see illustration)**.

3 Firmly press down on the seat at the rear until you hear it click into place and check that the seat is secure.

Front mudguard

11 Remove the front wheel (see Chapter 5).
12 Undo the two screws on the underside of the mudguard securing it to the fork bridge and the two screws from each side which also retain the air deflectors **(see illustrations)**, then draw it forwards and off the bike **(see illustration)**.
13 Installation is the reverse of removal, noting that the slot in the base of the air deflector

6.9a Push out access cover from inside . . .

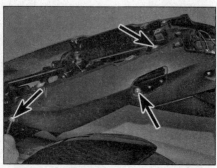

6.9b . . . and release the three screws (arrowed)

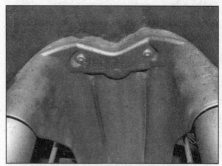

6.12a Two screws retain underside of mudguard to fork bridge

6.12b Air deflectors are retained by two screws

6.12c Removing the front mudguard

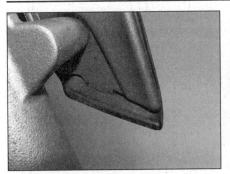

6.13 Make sure tab engages the slot in deflector

6.16a Free the E-clip to release the seat cable

6.16b Cut the cable-tie as shown . . .

must engage the tab on the mudguard (see illustration).

Rear mudguard

14 Remove the seat (see Step 1), side panels and all items of rear bodywork (see Steps 5 to 9).

15 Remove the tail light unit (see Chapter 7).

16 Release the E-clip, then free the seat cable from its latch (see illustration). Remove the four screws to free the licence plate bracket, noting that you'll need to cut the wire cable-ties (see illustrations).

17 If the machine is equipped with ESA, remove the two screws, one on each side of the ESA holder and release the plug.

18 Free the starter relay from its tab and the rear brake fluid reservoir from its cut-out in the mudguard (see illustrations).

19 Disconnect the diagnostic plug and bulbholder from their locations on the mudguard; the alarm connector is grouped with them, but not fixed to the mudguard (see illustration).

6.16c . . . then remove the licence plate bracket (two bolts on left side arrowed)

6.18a Pull the starter relay off its tab . . .

6.18b . . . and ease the rear brake fluid reservoir out of its location in the mudguard

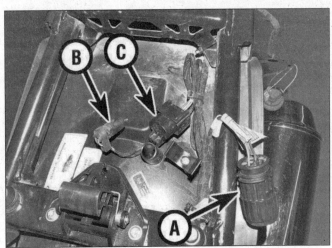

6.19 Diagnostic plug (A) and bulbholder (B) freed from their locations. Alarm connector (C)

6.21a Mudguard is retained by three screws at the front . . .

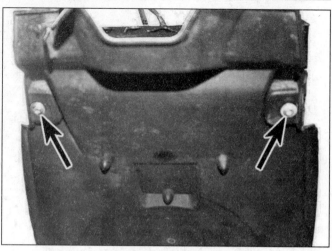

6.21b . . . and two screws at the rear (arrowed)

20 Cut any cable-ties which secure the wiring to the mudguard. Those securing wiring to the frame can remain in place.

6.22a Seat cable correctly installed in the latch and bracket

21 All components should now be free of the rear mudguard. Remove the five screws located on the underside and ease the mudguard downwards to remove it from the rear frame (see illustrations).

22 Installation is the reverse of removal, noting the following:

● Wash all road dirt from the underside of the rear mudguard and the licence plate bracket.

● Locate the seat cable trunnion in the latch and the outer cable in the bracket; fit the E-clip to secure it (see illustration).

● Check the function of all electrical equipment afterwards and ensure the wiring is correctly secured with new cable-ties (see illustration).

Windshield (optional)

23 Remove the two screws which retain the windshield bracket to the top yoke (see illustration). Disengage the lower bracket from the hook above the headlight and manoeuvre it free (see illustration).

24 Installation is the reverse of removal.

Mirrors

25 To remove the mirror, first peel back the boot covering the gland nut, then unscrew the nut and thread the mirror out of the master cylinder clamp.

26 Slacken the top nut to adjust the angle of the mirror stalk – note that it has a left-hand thread.

6.22b Secure the wiring to the mudguard with new cable-ties (arrowed)

6.23a Windshield bracket is retained by two screws to top yoke (arrowed) . . .

6.23b . . . and by a hook above the headlight

Chapter 7
Electrical system

Contents

Degrees of difficulty

Easy, suitable for novice with little experience

Fairly easy, suitable for beginner with some experience

Fairly difficult, suitable for competent DIY mechanic

Difficult, suitable for experienced DIY mechanic

Very difficult, suitable for expert DIY or professional

Specifications

On-board accessory socket

Current rating
  R1200 RT . . . . 10 A
  All other models . . . . 5 A

Alternator

Type . . . . Three-phase AC with integral regulator/rectifier
Maximum output
  R1200GS 2004 to 2007, R1200 S 600W
  R1200GS 2008-on, all GS Adv, R1200 RT, ST and R. 720W

Battery

R1200 GS, ST, S and R . . . . 12 V, 14 Ah
R1200 RT . . . . 12 V, 19 Ah

Bulbs

Headlight
  R1200 GS, RT and S
    High beam . . . . 55W H7 halogen
    Low beam . . . . 55W H7 halogen
  R1200 ST
    High beam . . . . 55W H4 halogen
    Low beam . . . . 55W H4 halogen
  R1200 R
    High beam . . . . 55 W H11 halogen
    Low beam . . . . 55 W H11 halogen
Side light 5W
Brake/tail light
  R1200 GS, ST and R 21/5W
  R1200 RT 21W
  R1200 S and later GS . . . . LED
Turn signal lights
  R1200 GS, S and R . . . . 10W (LEDs on later GS)
  R1200 RT 21W
  R1200 ST
    Front 21W
    Rear 10W
Instrument lighting and warning lights . . . . LED
Fog light – R1200 GS Adventure . . . . 55W H11 halogen

Fuse

Fog light (R1200 GS Adventure) . . . . 7.5A x 2

Torque settings

Alternator mounting bolts . . . . 18 Nm
Ignition switch and steering lock . . . . 20 Nm
Engine oil pressure switch . . . . 30 Nm
Engine oil temperature sensor . . . . 30 Nm
Headlight shell screws – R1200 R . . . . 8 Nm
Starter motor cover bolt . . . . 7 Nm
Starter motor terminal nut . . . . 10 Nm
Starter motor mounting bolts . . . . 19 Nm

1 General information

General information

All models covered in this manual have a 12-volt electrical system charged by a three-phase alternator. The alternator has integral regulator and rectifier units.

The regulator maintains the charging system output within the specified range to prevent overcharging, and the rectifier converts the ac (alternating current) output of the alternator to dc (direct current) to power the lights and other components and to charge the battery. The alternator is mounted centrally on top of the engine unit and is driven by belt off a pulley on the front end of the crankshaft.

The starter motor is mounted on the lower left-hand side of the engine. The starting system includes the starter motor, solenoid, starter relay and switches. If the engine kill switch is in the RUN position and the ignition (main) switch is ON, the starter relay allows the starter motor to operate only if the transmission is in neutral or, if the transmission is in gear, with the clutch lever pulled into the handlebar and the side stand up.

CAN-bus technology

All models covered in this manual utilise Controlled Area Network (CAN)-bus technology to create an electronic information network between the control units, sensors and power-consuming components. This allows rapid and reliable data transfer around the network. It also allows comprehensive diagnosis of the entire system from one central point.

To reduce the amount of wiring in the network, all the components are designed to communicate via one or two wires. These wires are known as a 'data bus'. Each control unit (engine control unit, central electronics unit, instruments cluster and, where fitted, ABS control unit and anti-theft system control unit) has an integral transceiver which sends and receives data 'packets' along the bus. As the data packets travel between the units, each one examines the information and either acts upon it or ignores it, depending upon its relevance.

No fuses are fitted in the network – in the event of a short-circuit or component fault, the affected part of the network is isolated and switched off, leaving the rest of the network intact.

Note: *Keep in mind that electrical parts, once purchased, cannot be returned. To avoid unnecessary expense, make very sure the faulty component has been positively identified before buying a replacement part.*

2 Electrical system fault finding

⚠️ *Warning: Make sure that the ignition (main) switch is OFF and that the battery is disconnected before any electrical components are disconnected. Failure to do so will result in fault codes being recorded in the associated system and the need to have these erased using the BMW diagnostic tester. Depending upon the system concerned, the bike's performance may be affected.*

Fault finding

1 In the absence of test data, traditional probing with a multimeter should be avoided unless a specific result, as detailed in the text, is sought. The central electronics unit and the engine control unit are extremely sensitive to interference, and for the most part system checks should be confined to continuity tests

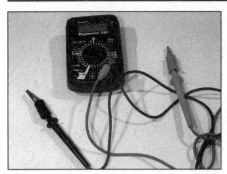

2.8 A digital multimeter is ideal for all electrical tests

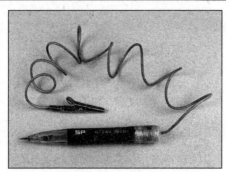

2.11 A simple test light can be used for voltage checks

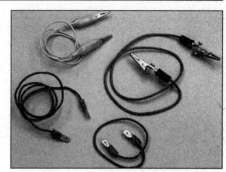

2.17 A selection of insulated jumper wires

of relevant sections of the wiring loom with the ignition (main) switch OFF.

2 When testing for power supply to a component, always ensure that the multimeter is securely connected to the relevant wiring terminals before turning the ignition (main) switch ON. It should be noted that in some cases, a test with the power ON may result in a fault being recorded by the ECU.

3 If at all possible, have the machine checked by a BMW dealer – recorded faults can then be analysed using the BMW diagnostic tester and remedial action taken. Fault codes should be erased from the ECU when the repair has been completed.

4 Note that once a new component has been installed it will be necessary to re-instate the system programme using the diagnostic tester.

Simple wiring checks

5 Electrical problems often stem from simple causes, such as loose or corroded connections. Study the appropriate wiring diagram at the end of this Chapter to get a complete picture of what makes up that individual circuit.

6 Faults can often be tracked down by noting if other components related to that circuit are operating properly or not. If several components or circuits fail at one time, it may be that the fault lies in the earth (ground) connection, as several circuits are routed through the same earth connection.

7 Always check the condition of the wires and connections in the problem circuit. Intermittent failures can be especially frustrating, since you can't always duplicate the failure when it's convenient to test. In such situations, a good practice is to clean all connections in the affected circuit, whether or not they appear to be good. All of the connections and wires should also be wiggled to check for looseness which can cause intermittent failure.

Continuity checks

8 Continuity checks can be made with a multimeter **(see illustration)**. These testers are self-powered by a battery, therefore the checks are made with the ignition OFF. As a safety precaution, disconnect the battery negative (-) lead before making continuity

checks, particularly if the ignition switch is being checked.

9 If using a multimeter, select the appropriate ohms scale and check that the meter reads infinity (∞). Touch the meter probes together and check that the meter reads zero; where necessary adjust the meter so that it reads zero. Make the test across the terminals described. After using the meter always switch if off to conserve its battery.

10 Reconnect the machine's battery, noting the procedure in Section 3.

Voltage checks

Note the possible results of making voltage checks in Step 2.

11 A voltage check can determine whether current is reaching a component. Tests can be made with a multimeter set to the dc volts scale or a test light **(see illustration)**.

12 Check that the multimeter leads are inserted in the correct terminals on the meter, red to positive (+) and black to negative (-). Incorrect connections could damage the meter.

13 The meter (set the dc volts scale) should always be connected in parallel (across the load). Connecting it in series will not harm the meter, but the result will not be meaningful.

14 Voltage checks are made with the ignition ON. Connect the meter's red lead to the power supply wire and the negative lead to a good earth or directly to the battery's negative terminal.

Earth (ground) checks

15 Earth (ground) connections are made either directly to the engine or by a separate wire into the brown wired earth circuit of the wire harness; internal earth circuit connections are represented by DIN symbols 31I, 31II and 31III on the *Wiring Diagrams*.

16 Corrosion is often the cause of a poor earth connection. If total electrical failure is experienced, check the security of the main earth lead from the negative (-) terminal of the battery and also the earth lead connections on the cylinders and crankcase (see Chapter 2, Section 4). If corroded, dismantle the connection and clean all surfaces back to bare metal.

17 To check the earth on a component, use an insulated jumper wire **(see illustration)**

to temporarily bypass its earth connection. Connect one end of the jumper wire between the earth terminal or metal body of the component and the other end to the motorcycle's engine or sub-frame.

18 If the circuit works with the jumper wire installed, the original earth circuit is faulty. Check the wiring for open-circuits or poor connections.

3 Battery

Caution: Be extremely careful when handling or working around the battery. The electrolyte is very caustic and an explosive gas (hydrogen) is given off when the battery is charging.

Removal and installation

Note: *Disconnecting the battery leads deletes all memorised settings (e.g. throttle position sensor). Loss of this information could temporarily upset the running of the engine. Make sure the procedure in Step 11 is carried out before starting the engine.*

1 Ensure that the ignition is OFF. Remove the rider's seat (see Chapter 6).

2 On R1200 ST models, lift off the battery cover/seat height adjuster **(see illustration)**.

3 On R1200 S models, displace the BMW diagnostic connector.

4 On all models, unscrew the negative (-ve) terminal bolt and disconnect the lead from the

3.2 Lift off the battery cover – R1200 ST

3.4 Disconnect the battery negative (-ve) lead first

3.5a Undo the screw . . .

3.5b . . . and unhook the battery strap

3.6 Remove the document holder – R1200 GS

3.7 Note which way round the battery is fitted

3.14 The BMW battery charger connected to the on-board power socket

battery **(see illustration)**. Next displace the cover from the positive battery terminal and unscrew the positive (+ve) terminal bolt and disconnect the lead.

5 Undo the screw securing the battery strap, then unhook the lower end of the strap and lift it out **(see illustrations)**.

6 On R1200 GS models, undo the screw securing the document holder and remove the holder **(see illustration)**.

7 Lift out the battery, noting which way round it is installed **(see illustration)**.

8 On installation, ensure that the battery terminals and lead ends are clean. Install the battery so that the positive (+ve) and negative (-ve) terminals align with the appropriate leads.

9 Reconnect the leads, connecting the positive (+ve) terminal first. Don't forget to install the cover over the positive (+ve) terminal. Secure the battery with its strap.

> **HAYNES HINT** *Battery corrosion can be kept to a minimum by applying a layer of petroleum jelly to the terminals after the leads have been connected.*

10 Install the remaining components in the reverse order of removal.

11 Switch the ignition ON. Fully open and close the throttle a couple of times – this allows the engine control unit to register the throttle butterfly positions via the sensor.

12 Reset the clock (see Section 13).

Charging

13 All models are fitted with a sealed MF (maintenance free) battery. All that should be done is to check that the terminals are clean and tight and that the casing is neither damaged nor leaking. **Note:** *Do not attempt to remove the battery caps to check the electrolyte level or battery specific gravity. Removal will damage the caps, resulting in electrolyte leakage and battery damage.*

14 If the machine is not in regular use, remove the battery and give it a refresher charge every four weeks as described below. Note that the battery can be charged on the machine via the on-board power socket and dedicated BMW battery charger **(see illustration)**.

Caution: Be extremely careful when handling or working around the battery. The electrolyte is very caustic and an explosive gas (hydrogen) is given off when the battery is charging.

15 Whatever charger is used, ensure that it is suitable for charging a 12V battery.

16 Remove the battery (see above), then check that the charger is switched off before connecting the positive (+ve) lead on the charger to the positive (+ve) terminal on the battery, and the negative (-ve) charger lead to the negative (-ve) battery terminal. Turn the charger on.

17 BMW do not specify a recommended charging rate, although the battery will be marked with a regular charge rate, plus a quick charge rate which can be used in emergencies for a short time. As a guide, a

discharged battery should be charged at a low rate (approx. 1.5 amps) for 10 hours. Exceeding this figure can cause the battery to overheat, buckling the plates and rendering it useless.

18 Few owners will have access to an expensive current controlled charger, so if a normal domestic charger is used check that after a possible initial peak, the charge rate falls to a safe level **(see illustration)**. If the battery becomes hot during charging **STOP**. Further charging will cause damage.

19 Let the battery settle for 30 minutes after charging, then measure the voltage across its terminals with a multimeter set to the dc volts scale – meter positive prove to battery positive terminal and meter negative prove to battery negative terminal. The battery

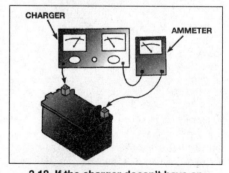

3.18 If the charger doesn't have an ammeter built-in, connect one in series as shown. DO NOT connect the ammeter between the battery terminals or it will be ruined

4.2a Unclip the holder . . .

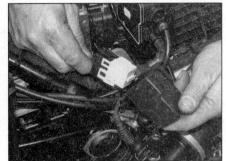

4.2b . . . and withdraw the fog light relay

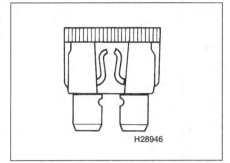

4.9 A blown fuse is easily identified by a break in the element

should indicate 12.8 volts or more when fully charged.

20 If the recharged battery discharges rapidly if left disconnected it is likely that an internal short caused by physical damage or sulphation has occurred. A new battery will be required. A good battery will tend to lose its charge at about 1% per day. If the battery discharges while the machine is in regular use, either the battery is faulty or the charging system is defective. Refer to Section 27 for details of the charging system output test.

4 Fog light relay and fuses

1 On R1200 GS Adventure models equipped with fog lights, a relay and fusebox are located behind the ECU. To access the relay and fuses, follow the procedure in Chapter 3, Section 14, and displace the ECU.

Relay check and renewal

2 Unclip the relay holder, then unclip the base of the holder and withdraw the relay and its socket **(see illustrations)**. Pull the relay out from the socket.

3 Referring to the appropriate wiring diagram at the end of this Chapter, test the relay as follows. Set a multimeter to the ohms x 1 scale, or use a continuity tester, and connect it across Nos. 1 and 2 terminals of the connector face (symbols 3 and 5 on relay). There should be no continuity (infinite resistance).

4 Using a fully-charged 12 volt battery and two insulated jumper wires, connect the positive (+ve) battery terminal to the No. 5 terminal of the connector face, and the negative (-ve) battery terminal to the No. 3 terminal (symbols 2 and 1 respectively on relay). The multimeter should now read zero ohms (continuity).

5 If the test results are not as described, the relay is faulty and must be renewed.

6 Installation is the reverse of removal. Ensure that the terminals inside the socket are clean and that the relay is a secure fit.

Fuse check and renewal

7 The fuses are located in the base of the relay socket (see above).

8 The fuses can be checked visually. Use a

pair of needle-nose pliers to pull them out.
9 A blown fuse is easily identified by a break in the element **(see illustration)**. Each fuse is clearly marked with its rating and must only be replaced by a fuse of the same rating (see Specifications at the beginning of this Chapter).

⚠ **Warning: Never put in a fuse of a higher rating or bridge the terminals with any other substitute, however temporary it may be. Serious damage may be done to the circuit, or a fire may start.**

10 If a fuse blows, be sure to check the wiring circuit very carefully for evidence of a short-circuit. Look for bare wires and chafed, melted or burned insulation. If the fuse is replaced before the cause is located, the new fuse will blow immediately.

11 Occasionally a fuse will blow or cause an open-circuit for no obvious reason. Corrosion of the fuse ends and fusebox terminals may occur and cause poor fuse contact. If this happens, remove the corrosion with a small knife or emery paper, then spray the fuse end and terminals with electrical contact cleaner.

12 Installation is the reverse of removal.

5 Lighting system check

Note 1: *All models will display a warning on the instrument cluster in the event of a bulb failure. For details see Steps 21 to 30.*

Note 2: *If the ignition is switched ON for any checks, remember to switch it OFF again before proceeding further or removing any electrical component from the system.*

1 The battery provides power for operation of the headlight, tail light, brake light, turn signals and instrument cluster lights. If none of the lights operate, always check battery condition before proceeding (see Section 3).

2 When checking for a blown filament in a bulb, it is advisable to back up a visual check with a continuity test of the filament as it is not always apparent that the filament is broken. When checking continuity, remember that on tail light and turn signal bulbs it is often the metal body of the bulb that is the earth (ground).

Headlight

3 If the headlight fails to work, check the bulb and bulb terminals first (see Section 6). Next disconnect the headlight wiring connector and check for battery voltage on the supply side of the wiring connector with a test light or multimeter as follows. Refer to *Wiring Diagrams* at the end of this Chapter, then connect the negative probe of the multimeter to earth (ground) and the positive probe to either the high or low beam connector terminal as appropriate. Turn the ignition switch ON and select either high or low beam at the handlebar switch while conducting this test.

4 If no voltage is indicated, check the wiring between the connector and the central electronics unit. Also check the wiring for the dimmer switch and the ignition switch, then check the switches themselves (see Sections 22 and 23).

5 If voltage is indicated, check for continuity between the brown wire connector terminal and earth (ground). If there is no continuity, check the earth (ground) circuit for an open or poor connection.

Sidelight

6 If the sidelight fails to work, check the bulb and the bulb terminals first (see Section 6). Next disconnect the sidelight wiring connector and check for battery voltage on the supply side of the wiring connector with a test light or multimeter as follows. Refer to *Wiring Diagrams* at the end of this Chapter, then connect the negative probe of the multimeter to earth (ground) and the positive probe to the sidelight connector terminal. Turn the ignition switch ON.

7 If no voltage is indicated, check the wiring between the connector and the central electronics unit. Also check the wiring for the ignition switch, then check the switch itself (see Section 22).

8 If voltage is indicated, check for continuity between the brown wire connector terminal and earth (ground). If there is no continuity, check the earth (ground) circuit for an open or poor connection.

Tail light

Note: *If a tail light bulb of bulb filament fails, the brake light is illuminated at reduced* *voltage to compensate. However, the bulb failure warning will remain on in the instrument cluster multifunction display until a new bulb has been fitted (see Steps 21 to 30).*

9 If the tail light fails to work on R1200 GS (2004 to 2007), RT and ST models, check the bulb and the bulb terminals first (see Section 8). Next disconnect the brake/tail light wiring connector and check for battery voltage on the tail light supply side of the connector with a test light or multimeter as follows. Refer to *Wiring Diagrams* at the end of this Chapter, then connect the negative probe of the multimeter to earth (ground) and the positive probe to the tail light connector terminal. Turn the ignition switch ON.

10 If no voltage is indicated, check the wiring between the connector and the central electronics unit. Also check the wiring for the ignition switch, then check the switch itself (see Section 22).

11 If voltage is indicated, check for continuity between the brown wire connector terminal and earth (ground). If there is no continuity, check the earth (ground) circuit for an open or poor connection.

12 On R1200 S and later GS models, the tail light consists of a number of LEDs in a sealed unit. When a single LED fails it cannot be renewed, however the failure of one LED will not affect the function of the others. If the tail light fails to work completely, follow Steps 6 to 8. When sufficient LEDs have failed so as to impair the safe operation of the motorcycle, renew the tail light unit.

Brake light

13 If the brake light fails to work on R1200 GS (2004 to 2007), RT and ST models, check the bulb and the bulb terminals first (see Section 8). Note that on R1200 RT models, tail light and brake light functions are performed by the same bulbs – the bulb burns brighter when the brakes are applied as opposed to when the lights are illuminated.

14 Next disconnect the brake/tail light wiring connector and check for battery voltage on the brake light supply side of the connector with a test light or multimeter as follows. Refer to *Wiring Diagrams* at the end of this Chapter, then connect the negative probe of the multimeter to earth (ground) and the positive probe to the brake light connector terminal. Turn the ignition switch ON and apply the brake lever or pedal.

15 If no voltage is indicated, check the wiring between the brake light and the central electronics unit, and check the brake light switches (see Section 11).

16 If voltage is indicated, check for continuity between the brown wire connector terminal and earth (ground). If there is no continuity, check the earth (ground) circuit for an open or poor connection.

Turn signal lights

17 If one light fails to work, check the bulb and the bulb terminals (see Section

10). Next disconnect the turn signal wiring connector and check for battery voltage on the supply side of the connector with a test light or multimeter as follows. Refer to *Wiring Diagrams* at the end of this Chapter, then connect the negative probe of the multimeter to earth (ground) and the positive probe to the signal connector terminal. Turn the ignition switch ON and select the appropriate signal (left or right) with the turn signal switch.

18 If no voltage is indicated, check the wiring between the turn signal and the central electronics unit, and check the turn signal switch (see Section 23).

19 If voltage is indicated, check for continuity between the brown wire connector terminal and earth (ground). If there is no continuity, check the earth (ground) circuit for an open or poor connection.

Instrument and warning lights

20 The instrument cluster is a sealed unit. In the event of a light failure, have the instrument cluster checked by a BMW dealer.

Defective bulb warnings

21 In the event of a bulb failure, a warning appears on the instrument cluster multifunction display (see details for individual models below). Once the fault has been corrected, the warning will be cancelled, but a fault code will be stored in either the ABS or central electronics unit which should be erased using the BMW diagnostic tester.

R1200 GS and ST

22 If a headlight, sidelight or turn signal bulb fails, the defective bulb symbol with an arrow pointing forwards appears on the multifunction display.

23 If a tail light or brake light bulb fails, the general warning light illuminates yellow and the defective bulb symbol with an arrow pointing rearwards appears on the multifunction display.

24 If a combination of the above faults occurs, the general warning light illuminates yellow and the defective bulb symbol with an arrow pointing forwards and rearwards appears on the multifunction display.

R1200 RT

25 If a headlight, sidelight or front turn signal bulb fails, the defective bulb symbol with

an arrow pointing forwards appears on the multifunction display.

26 If a tail light, brake light or rear turn signal bulb fails, the general warning light illuminates yellow and the defective bulb symbol with an arrow pointing rearwards appears on the multifunction display.

27 If a combination of the above faults occurs, the general warning light illuminates yellow and the defective bulb symbol with an arrow pointing forwards and rearwards appears on the multifunction display.

R1200 S

28 If a headlight, sidelight or turn signal bulb fails, the LAMPF warning appears on the multifunction display.

29 If a tail light or brake light LED fails, the general warning light illuminates yellow and the LAMPR warning appears on the multifunction display.

30 If a combination of the above faults occurs, the general warning light illuminates yellow and the LAMPS warning appears on the multifunction display.

R1200 R

31 If a bulb fails, the general warning light triangle will illuminate yellow and LAMP will appear on the multifunction display.

6 Headlight and sidelight bulbs

Note: The headlight bulb is of the quartz-halogen type. Do not touch the bulb glass as skin acids will shorten the bulb's service life. If the bulb is accidentally touched, it should be wiped carefully when cold with a rag soaked in methylated spirit and dried before fitting.

⚠ *Warning: Allow the bulb time to cool before removing it if the headlight has just been on.*

R1200 GS
Headlight

1 To remove the high beam bulb, first turn the handlebars to full lock on the right-hand side.
2 Unscrew the bulb cover anti-clockwise, then pull off the wiring connector **(see illustrations)**.
3 Release the bulb retaining clip, noting how it

6.2a Unscrew the bulb cover . . .

6.2b . . . and pull off the wiring connector

6.3a Release the bulb retaining clip . . .

6.3b . . . and withdraw the bulb

6.4 Tab (arrowed) on high beam bulb should face down

fits, and withdraw the bulb **(see illustrations).**
4 Install the new bulb, bearing in mind the **Note** above. Make sure the bulb locates correctly with the tab facing down **(see illustration).**
5 Secure the bulb with the clip and reconnect the wiring connector.
6 Install the bulb cover, turning it clockwise, so that the TOP lettering is uppermost **(see illustration 6.2a).**
7 Check the operation of the headlight.
8 To remove the low beam bulb, first turn the handlebars to full lock on the left-hand side.
9 Follow the procedure in Steps 2 and 3 to remove the bulb.
10 Install the new bulb, bearing in mind the **Note** above. Make sure the bulb locates correctly with the tab facing up **(see illustration).**
11 Follow the procedure in Steps 5 and 7, then check the operation of the headlight.

Sidelight

12 To remove the sidelight bulb, first turn the handlebars to full lock on the right-hand side.
13 The sidelight bulbholder is located on the lower left-hand side of the headlight unit.
14 Pull the bulbholder out, then carefully pull the bulb out of the bulbholder **(see illustration).**
15 Fit the new bulb and check the operation of the sidelight, then install the bulbholder in the back of the headlight unit.

R1200 RT

Headlight

16 If required, to gain access to the headlight bulbs, remove the left or right-hand fairing upper side panels as appropriate (see Chapter 6, Section 3).
17 To remove the right-hand low beam bulb, unscrew the bulb cover anti-clockwise, then pull off the wiring connector **(see illustrations).**
18 Release the bulb retaining clip, noting how it fits, and withdraw the bulb.
19 Install the new bulb, bearing in mind the **Note** above. Make sure the bulb locates correctly with the tab facing up.

6.10 Tab (arrowed) on low beam bulb should face up

20 Secure the bulb with the clip and reconnect the wiring connector.
21 Install the bulb cover, turning it clockwise.
22 Check the operation of the headlight.
23 To remove and install the left-hand low beam bulb and the central high beam bulb, follow the procedure in Steps 17 to 22 **(see illustration).**

Sidelight

24 To remove the sidelight bulbs, first remove the left or right-hand mirror and fairing trim panel as appropriate. The sidelight bulbholder is accessible through the opening behind the trim panel.
25 Turn the bulbholder anti-clockwise and withdraw it from the headlight unit, then

6.14 Pull the sidelight bulbholder (arrowed) out from the back of the headlight unit

6.17a Unscrew the bulb cover . . .

6.17b . . . and pull off the wiring connector

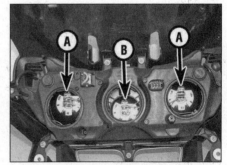

6.23 Location of low beam bulbs (A) and high beam bulb (B)

6.25a Turn the sidelight bulbholder anti-clockwise . . .

6.25b . . . and withdraw it from the headlight unit . . .

6.25c . . . then carefully pull the capless bulb out

carefully pull the bulb out of the bulbholder **(see illustrations)**. The bulb is of the capless type.

26 Fit the new bulb and check the operation of the sidelight, then install the bulbholder in the back of the headlight unit.

6.28a Remove the cover . . .

6.28b . . . then pull off the wiring connector

6.29a Release both ends (arrowed) of the bulb retaining clip . . .

6.29b . . . and withdraw the bulb. Note the position of the widest tab (arrowed)

6.34 Pull the capless bulb out carefully

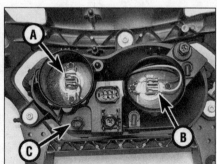

6.36 Location of the high beam (A), low beam (B) and sidelight (C) bulbs – R1200 S

R1200 ST

Headlight

27 To remove the upper or lower headlight bulbs, first turn the handlebars to full lock on the left-hand side.
28 Pull the tab to remove the cover, then pull off the wiring connector **(see illustrations)**.
29 Release the bulb retaining clip, noting how it fits, and withdraw the bulb **(see illustrations)**.
30 Install the new bulb, bearing in mind the **Note** above. Make sure the bulb locates correctly with the widest tab facing up **(see illustration 6.29b)**.
31 Secure the bulb with the clip and reconnect the wiring connector. Install the bulb cover.
32 Check the operation of the headlight.

Sidelight

33 To remove the sidelight bulb, first remove the cover for the lower headlight bulb.
34 Pull the bulbholder out, then carefully pull the bulb out of the bulbholder **(see illustration)**. The bulb is of the capless type.
35 Fit the new bulb and check the operation of the sidelight, then install the bulbholder and fit the cover.

R1200 S

Headlight

36 To remove the high beam bulb, pull the tab to remove the cover, then pull off the wiring connector **(see illustration)**.
37 Release the bulb retaining clip, noting how it fits, and withdraw the bulb **(see illustration)**.

6.37 Withdraw the high beam bulb. Note the position of the tab (arrowed)

6.42 Installation of the low beam bulb. Note the position of the tab (arrowed)

6.45a Pull out the bulbholder (arrowed) . . .

6.45b . . . then pull the capless bulb out carefully

38 Install the new bulb, bearing in mind the **Note** above. Make sure the bulb locates correctly with the tab facing down **(see illustration 6.37)**.
39 Secure the bulb with the clip and reconnect the wiring connector. Install the bulb cover.
40 Check the operation of the headlight.
41 To remove the low beam bulb, follow the procedure in Steps 36 and 37.
42 Install the new bulb, bearing in mind the **Note** above. Make sure the bulb locates correctly with the tab facing up **(see illustration)**.
43 Follow the procedure in Step 39, then check the operation of the headlight.

Sidelight

44 The sidelight bulbholder is located on the lower left-hand side of the headlight unit **(see illustration 6.36)**.

45 Pull the bulbholder out, then carefully pull the bulb out of the bulbholder **(see illustrations)**. The bulb is of the capless type.
46 Fit the new bulb and check the operation of the sidelight, then install the bulbholder in the back of the headlight unit.

R1200 R

Headlight and sidelight

47 Remove the single screw from the base of the shell and ease the rim off its locating lugs at the top **(see illustration)**. Now remove the single screw from the top of the shell and withdraw the lens and reflector unit **(see illustration)**. Support the unit and disconnect the wire connectors from the Hi and Lo beam bulbholders and the sidelight bulbholder.

48 Twist the Hi and Lo beam bulbholders to free them from the reflector unit **(see illustration)**. The sidelight bulbholder is a push fit in the reflector unit and its capless bulb is a push fit in the holder **(see illustration)**.
49 Install the new bulb, bearing in mind the **Note** above. Refit the reflector unit and rim, noting that the lugs at the top of the rim must engage the cut-outs in the shell **(see illustration)**.
50 Check the operation of the headlight bulbs and sidelight bulb.

7 Headlight unit

Note: *An improperly adjusted headlight may cause problems for oncoming traffic or provide poor, unsafe illumination of the road ahead. Before adjusting the headlight aim, be sure to consult with local traffic laws and regulations – for UK models refer to MOT Test Checks in the Reference section.*

R1200 GS

Removal

1 Remove the windshield (see Chapter 6, Section 2).
2 Undo the left and right-hand bolts securing

6.47a Headlight rim is retained by single screw (arrowed)

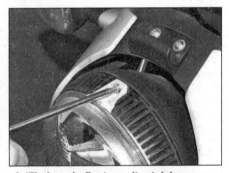

6.47b Lens/reflector unit retaining screw

6.48a Twist the headlight bulbs to release them from the reflector

6.48b Sidelight bulb is a push fit in its holder

6.49 Rim lugs locate cut-outs in headlight shell (arrowed)

7.2 Headlight unit is secured by a bolt (arrowed) on both sides

7.3a Lift the headlight unit off the pegs (arrowed) . . .

7.3b . . . then disconnect the wiring for the instrument cluster . . .

7.3c . . . and for the headlight unit (arrowed)

7.5a Pull off the clips securing the instrument cluster . . .

7.5b . . . and separate the instruments from the headlight unit

the headlight unit/instrument cluster assembly to the mounting bracket (see illustration).

3 Lift the headlight unit off the pegs on the mounting bracket, then disconnect the wiring connectors for the instrument cluster and headlight unit (see illustrations).

4 Pull the sidelight bulbholder out from the back of the unit (see illustration 6.14).

5 Lift the headlight unit/instrument cluster assembly off. If required, pull off the clips securing the instrument cluster and separate the instruments from the headlight unit (see illustrations).

Installation

6 Installation is the reverse of removal. Make sure all the wiring is correctly connected and secured. Check the operation of the headlight and sidelight.

7 Check the headlight aim as follows.

Adjustment

8 The headlight beam can be adjusted both horizontally and vertically. Before making any adjustment, check that the tyre pressures are correct and the suspension is adjusted as required. Make any adjustments to the headlight aim with the machine on level ground, with the fuel tank half full and with an assistant sitting on the seat. If the bike is usually ridden with a passenger on the back, have a second assistant to do this. See **Note** above.

9 Vertical adjustment is made by turning the adjuster on the back of the headlight unit between the two lights (see illustration). Ensure that the heavy load lever is in the normal position (straight out), then turn the adjuster to achieve the desired setting.

10 If a heavy load is being carried, the headlight beam can be temporarily lowered

without altering the standard setting by pressing the heavy load lever into the 'down' position. Don't forget to reset the lever for normal riding.

11 Horizontal adjustment is made by turning the adjuster on the top right-hand corner of the headlight unit (see illustration).

R1200 RT

Removal

12 Follow the procedure in Chapter 6, Sec-tion 3, to remove the fairing headlight panel.

13 Undo the screws securing the headlight unit in the fairing panel and lift the unit out.

Installation

14 Installation is the reverse of removal. Make sure all the wiring is correctly connected and secured. Check the operation of the headlight and sidelight.

15 Check the headlight aim as follows.

Adjustment

16 The headlight beam can be adjusted both horizontally and vertically. Before making any adjustment, check that the tyre pressures are correct and the suspension is adjusted as required. Make any adjustments to the headlight aim with the machine on level ground, with the fuel tank half full and with an assistant sitting on the seat. If the bike is usually ridden with a passenger on the back, have a second assistant to do this. See **Note** above.

17 If required, remove the fairing side panels to access the headlight adjusters (see Chapter 6, Section 3).

7.9 Vertical headlight beam adjuster (A) and heavy load lever (B) – R1200 GS

7.11 Horizontal headlight beam adjuster (arrowed)

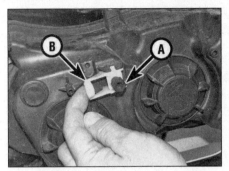

7.18 **Vertical headlight beam adjuster (A) and heavy load lever (B) – R1200 RT**

7.20 **Horizontal headlight beam adjuster (arrowed)**

7.22 **Headlight unit wiring connector (arrowed)**

18 Vertical adjustment is made by turning the adjuster on the back of the headlight unit between the left-hand and centre lights (**see illustration**). Ensure that the heavy load lever is in the normal position (to the left), then turn the adjuster to achieve the desired setting.

19 If a heavy load is being carried, the headlight beam can be temporarily lowered without altering the standard setting by pulling the heavy load lever into the 'straight out' position. Don't forget to reset the lever for normal riding.

20 Horizontal adjustment is made by turning the adjuster on the lower right-hand side of the headlight unit (**see illustration**).

R1200 ST

Removal

21 Remove the fairing front panel (see Chapter 6, Section 4).

22 Disconnect the headlight unit wiring connector (**see illustration**).

23 Undo the left and right-hand screws securing the rear of the unit to the mounting bracket, then support the unit and undo the screws at the front (**see illustrations**).

24 Lift the headlight unit off (**see illustration**). If required, undo the screws securing the headlight surround and lift it off (**see illustration**).

7.23a **Headlight unit is secured by a screw (arrowed) on both sides at the back . . .**

7.23b **. . . and two screws (arrowed) at the front**

Installation

25 Installation is the reverse of removal. Make sure all the wiring is correctly connected and secured. Check the operation of the headlight and sidelight.

26 Check the headlight aim as follows.

Adjustment

27 The headlight beam can be adjusted both horizontally and vertically. Before making any adjustment, check that the tyre pressures are correct and the suspension is adjusted as required. Make any adjustments to the headlight aim with the machine on level ground, with the fuel tank half full and with an assistant

sitting on the seat. If the bike is usually ridden with a passenger on the back, have a second assistant to do this. See **Note** above.

28 Vertical adjustment is made by turning the adjuster on the back left-hand side of the headlight unit (**see illustration 7.24b**). Ensure that the heavy load lever is in the normal position (straight out), then turn the adjuster to achieve the desired setting.

29 If a heavy load is being carried, the headlight beam can be temporarily lowered without altering the standard setting by pressing the heavy load lever into the 'up' position. Don't forget to reset the lever for normal riding.

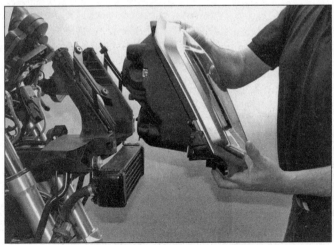

7.24a **Lift the headlight unit off – R1200 ST**

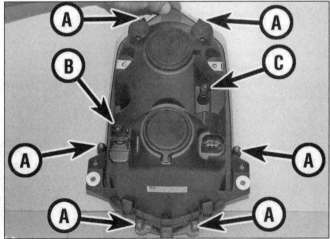

7.24b **Screws (A) secure headlight surround. Note vertical adjuster (B) and horizontal adjuster (C)**

7.33 Disconnect the headlight unit wiring connectors – R1200 S

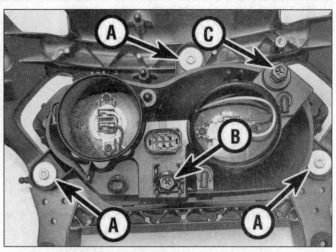

7.34 Headlight unit mounting bolts (A). Note the vertical beam adjuster (B) and horizontal beam adjuster (C)

30 Horizontal adjustment is made by turning the adjuster on the right-hand side of the headlight unit **(see illustration 7.24b)**.

R1200 S

Removal

31 Remove the fairing front panel (see Chapter 6, Section 5).
32 Remove the instrument cluster (see Section 12).
33 Disconnect the headlight unit wiring connectors **(see illustration)**.
34 Loosen the bolts securing the rear of the unit to the mounting bracket, then support the unit and remove the bolts **(see illustration)**.
35 Lift the headlight unit off.

Installation

36 Installation is the reverse of removal. Make sure all the wiring is correctly connected and secured. Check the operation of the headlight and sidelight.
37 Check the headlight aim as follows.

Adjustment

38 The headlight beam can be adjusted both horizontally and vertically. Before making any adjustment, check that the tyre pressures are correct and the suspension is adjusted as required. Make any adjustments to the

headlight aim with the machine on level ground, with the fuel tank half full and with an assistant sitting on the seat. If the bike is usually ridden with a passenger on the back, have a second assistant to do this. See **Note** above.
39 Vertical adjustment is made by turning the adjuster on the back of the headlight unit between the two lights **(see illustration 7.34)**. Ensure that the heavy load lever is in the normal position (straight out), then turn the adjuster to achieve the desired setting.
40 If a heavy load is being carried, the headlight beam can be temporarily lowered without altering the standard setting by pressing the heavy load lever into the 'down' position. Don't forget to reset the lever for normal riding.
41 Horizontal adjustment is made by turning the adjuster on the top right-hand side of the headlight unit **(see illustration 7.34)**.

R1200 R

Removal

42 Disconnect the wiring plug from the back of the shell **(see illustration)**.
43 Remove the screw from each side of the headlight unit to release it from the mounting brackets **(see illustration)**; make a note of how the washers fit into place.

Installation

44 Installation is the reverse of removal, noting that the beam height will have to be set as described below. Make sure all the wiring is correctly connected and secured. Check the operation of the headlight and sidelight. Check the headlight beam as follows.

Adjustment

45 The headlight beam can be adjusted horizontally and vertically. Before making any adjustment, check that the tyre pressures are correct and the suspension is adjusted as required. Make any adjustments to the headlight aim with the machine on level ground, with the fuel tank half full and with an assistant sitting on the seat. If the bike is usually ridden with a passenger on the back, have a second assistant to do this. See **Note** at the beginning of this section.
46 Slightly slacken the screws on the left and right-hand side of the headlight **(see illustration 7.43)**.
47 To adjust the vertical beam apply sufficient pressure to the headlight to overcome any resistance and adjust the beam by tilting the headlight housing.
48 To adjust the horizontal beam pivot the headlight housing within the mounting screw slots.
49 Tighten the shell retaining screws to the torque setting specified at the beginning of this chapter, being careful not to disturb the beam height setting.

7.42 Disconnect wiring plug (arrowed) from the back of the shell

7.43 Headlight shell is retained by a screw on each side. Slotted mounting enables beam height adjustment

8 Brake/tail light bulb

R1200 GS

Note: *The tail light on 2008-on GS models uses LEDs – see Step 15.*

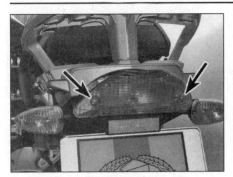

8.1a Undo the screws (arrowed) . . .

8.1b . . . and lift off the tail light lens –
R1200 GS

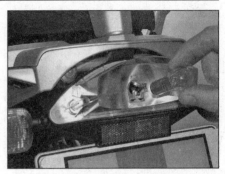

8.2 Push the bulb in and twist it
anti-clockwise to release it

1 Undo the screws securing the tail light lens and remove the lens **(see illustrations)**.
2 Gently push the bulb into the holder and twist it anti-clockwise to release it **(see illustration)**.
3 Check the socket terminals for corrosion and clean them if necessary. Line up the pins of the new bulb with the slots in the socket, then push the bulb in and turn it clockwise until it locks into place. **Note:** *The pins on the bulb are offset so it can only be installed one way. It is a good idea to use a paper towel or dry cloth when handling the new bulb to prevent injury if the bulb should break and to increase bulb life.*
4 Fit the tail light lens and tighten the screws, taking care not to overtighten them and damage the lens.
5 Check the operation of the brake/tail light.

R1200 RT

6 Undo the screws securing the tail light/turn

signal assembly and displace the assembly **(see illustrations)**.
7 Turn the bulbholder anti-clockwise and withdraw it from the assembly, then gently push the bulb into the holder and twist it anti-clockwise to remove it.
8 Check the socket terminals and install the new bulb as described in Step 3.
9 Installation is the reverse of removal. Check the operation of the brake/tail light and rear turn signals.

R1200 ST

10 Remove the passenger's seat (see Chapter 6).
11 Undo the screws securing the tail light unit and displace the unit **(see illustrations)**.
12 Turn the bulbholder anti-clockwise and withdraw it from the tail light, then gently

push the bulb into the holder and twist it anti-clockwise to remove it **(see illustration)**.
13 Check the socket terminals and install the new bulb as described in Step 3.
14 Installation is the reverse of removal. Check the operation of the brake/tail light.

R1200 S

15 The tail light consists of a number of LEDs in a sealed unit. When a single LED fails it cannot be renewed, however the failure of one LED will not affect the function of the others. If the tail light fails to work completely, refer to Section 5 to check the circuit. When sufficient LEDs have failed so as to impair the safe operation of the motorcycle, renew the tail light unit (see Section 9).

R1200 R

16 Remove the seat and the centre rear body panel **(see illustration)**.

8.6a Undo the screw (arrowed) on both
sides . . .

8.6b . . . and displace the tail light
assembly – R1200 RT

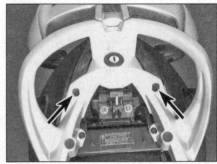

8.11a Undo the screws securing the tail
light (arrowed) . . .

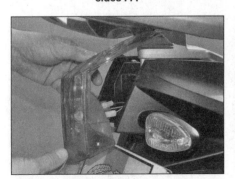

8.11b . . . and draw the unit off – R1200 ST

8.12 Remove the bulbholder as described

8.16 Centre rear body panel is retained by
three screws

8.17 Remove screw to free tail light unit

8.18 Twist bulbholder to free it from tail light

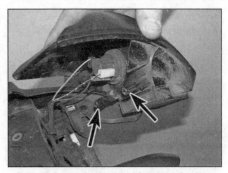

8.20 Engage guide pins (arrowed) when installing the tail light

17 Undo the single screw from the top of the unit **(see illustration)**. Pull the unit gently rearwards to ease the guide pins from their mounting holes.
18 Twist the bulbholder anti-clockwise to free it from the tail light unit **(see illustration)**. Push the bulb into the holder and twist it anticlockwise to remove it.
19 Check the socket terminals and install the new bulb as described in Step 3.
20 Installation is the reverse of removal **(see illustration)**. Check the operation of the brake/tail light.

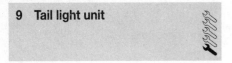

9 Tail light unit

R1200 GS

1 Follow the procedure in Chapter 6, Section 2, and remove the tail light/number plate bracket.
2 Undo the nuts securing the tail light unit and remove it. Note the arrangement of the washers and grommets on the number plate bracket.
3 Installation is the reverse of removal. Check the operation of the brake/tail light.

R1200 RT

4 Follow the procedure in Section 8 and displace the tail light/turn signal assembly **(see illustrations 8.6a and b)**.
5 Turn the tail light and turn signal bulbholders anti-clockwise and withdraw them from the assembly **(see illustration)**.
6 To remove the tail light/number plate bracket, refer to Chapter 6, Section 3.
7 Installation is the reverse of removal. Check the operation of the brake/tail light and turn signals.

R1200 ST

8 Follow the procedure in Section 8 to remove and install the tail light unit.

R1200 S

9 Follow the procedure in Chapter 6, Section 5, and remove the seat cowling.
10 Undo the screws securing the tail light unit and draw it back to release the pegs on

the underside of the unit from the brackets on the edge of the underseat panel **(see illustrations)**.
11 Disconnect the wiring connector from the unit and lift it off **(see illustration)**.
12 Installation is the reverse of removal. Check the operation of the brake/tail light.

R1200 R

13 Follow the procedure in Section 8 to remove and install the tail light unit.

10 Turn signals

1 Most turn signal problems are the result of a burned out bulb or corroded socket. This is especially true when the turn signals function properly in one direction, but fail to flash in

9.5 Remove the bulbholders from the tail light/turn signal assembly – R1200 RT

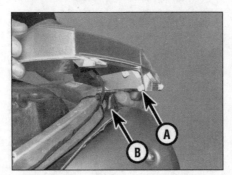

9.10b ... then draw the unit back to release peg (A) from bracket (B) on both sides

the other direction. Check the bulbs and the sockets as follows.

> **HAYNES HiNT** *If the socket contacts are dirty or corroded, scrape them clean and spray with electrical contact cleaner before a new bulb is installed.*

R1200 GS 2004 to 2007, R1200 R

Note: *The turn signals on 2008-on GS models are one-piece units which use LEDs.*

2 To remove a turn signal bulb, undo the screw securing the turn signal lens and remove the lens, noting how the tab locates **(see illustrations)**.
3 Push the bulb into the holder and twist it anti-clockwise to remove it **(see illustration)**.

9.10a Undo the screws (arrowed) ...

9.11 Disconnect the wiring connector from the tail light unit

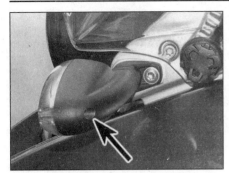

10.2a Undo the screw (arrowed) at the back of the unit . . .

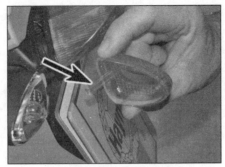

10.2b . . . and lift off the lens. Note how the tab (arrowed) locates

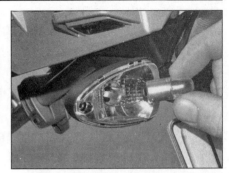

10.3 Push the bulb in and twist it anti-clockwise to remove it

10.8 Note how the tabs (arrowed) secure the signal body on the bracket

10.9 Feed the wiring through the body of the turn signal

10.10 Feed the wiring through the turn signal bracket

4 Check the socket and terminal for corrosion and clean them if necessary. Line up the pins of the new bulb with the slots in the socket, then push the bulb in and turn it clockwise until it locks into place.

5 Locate the tab on the lens on the inner side of the signal body and tighten the screw, taking care not to overtighten it and damage the lens.

6 Check the operation of the turn signals.

7 To remove the turn signal unit, first remove the bulb (see above).

8 Pull out the reflector, noting how the tabs secure the signal body on the bracket (see illustration).

9 Disconnect the wiring from the back of the reflector and feed the wiring through the body (see illustration).

10 If required, undo the screw securing the bracket, then feed the wiring through the bracket and draw the bracket off (see

illustration). Take care not to damage the wiring.

11 Installation is the reverse of removal. Check the operation of the turn signals.

R1200 RT
Front

12 Remove the appropriate mirror (see Chapter 6, Section 3).

13 Turn the turn signal bulbholder anti-clockwise and withdraw it from the back of the fairing, then gently push the bulb into the holder and twist it anti-clockwise to remove it (see illustrations).

14 Check the socket and terminal and install the new bulb as described in Step 4.

15 Installation is the reverse of removal. Check the operation of the turn signals.

16 To remove the turn signal unit, first follow the procedure in Chapter 6 and remove the fairing headlight panel.

17 Undo the screws securing the signal unit in the back of the panel and lift the unit out (see illustration).

18 Installation is the reverse of removal. Check the operation of the turn signals.

Rear

19 Undo the screws securing the tail light/turn signal assembly and displace the assembly (see illustrations 8.6a and b).

20 Turn the bulbholder anti-clockwise and withdraw it from the assembly, then gently push the bulb into the holder and twist it anti-clockwise to remove it (see illustration 9.5).

21 Check the socket and terminal and install the new bulb as described in Step 4.

22 Installation is the reverse of removal. Check the operation of the turn signals.

23 To remove the tail light/turn signal assembly, follow the procedure in Section 9.

10.13a Remove the bulbholder from the back of the fairing . . .

10.13b . . . push the bulb in and twist it anti-clockwise to remove it

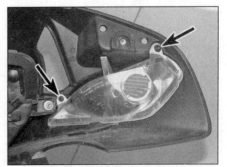

10.17 Front turn signal unit is secured by screws (arrowed)

10.24a Undo the screw (arrowed) and withdraw the turn signal unit

10.24b Removing the turn signal bulbholder from inside the front fairing

10.25 Push the bulb in and twist it anti-clockwise to remove it

R1200 ST

Front

24 Undo the screw securing the turn signal unit and displace the unit from the fairing front panel **(see illustration)**. Note that if the cockpit trim panels have been removed, the turn signal bulbholders can be removed from inside the front fairing **(see illustration)**.

25 If the turn signal unit has been displaced, turn the bulbholder anti-clockwise and withdraw it from the unit, then gently push the bulb into the holder and twist it anti-clockwise to remove it **(see illustration)**.

26 Check the socket and terminal and install the new bulb as described in Step 4.

27 Installation is the reverse of removal. Check the operation of the turn signals.

Rear

28 Undo the screw securing the turn signal lens and remove the lens, noting how the tab locates **(see illustrations 10.2a and b)**.

29 Push the bulb into the holder and twist it anti-clockwise to remove it **(see illustration 10.3)**.

30 Check the socket and terminal and install the new bulb as described in Step 4.

31 Installation is the reverse of removal. Check the operation of the turn signals.

32 To remove the turn signal unit, follow the procedure in Steps 7 to 10.

R1200 S

Front

33 Undo the screw securing the turn signal unit and displace the unit, noting how the tab locates **(see illustrations)**.

10.33a Undo the screw (arrowed) . . .

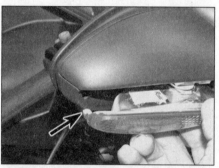

10.33b . . . and displace the unit. Note how the tab (arrowed) locates

10.34a Pull the bulbholder out . . .

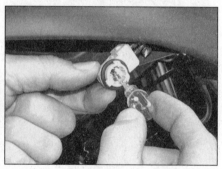

10.34b . . . then pull the capless bulb out carefully

34 Pull the bulbholder out of the unit, noting the location of the O-ring, then pull the bulb out of the bulbholder **(see illustrations)**. Note that the bulb is of the capless type.

35 Check the socket inside the bulbholder for corrosion and clean it if necessary.

36 Installation is the reverse of removal. Locate the tab on the turn signal unit on the outer edge of the mirror body and tighten the screw, taking care not to overtighten it and damage the lens.

Rear

37 Follow the procedure in Steps 28 to 32.

11 Brake light switches

Circuit check

1 Before checking any electrical circuit, check the bulb (see Section 8) on GS, RT and ST models, or LED circuit on S models (see Section 5).

2 The front brake light switch is located on the underside of the handlebar lever **(see illustration)**. The rear brake light switch is located adjacent to the rear brake pedal **(see illustration)**.

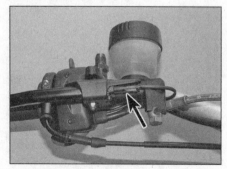

11.2a Location of the front brake light switch (arrowed)

11.2b Location of the rear brake light switch (arrowed) – R1200 GS shown

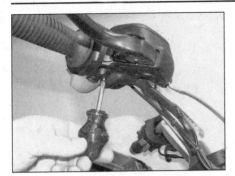

11.5a Undo the screws . . .

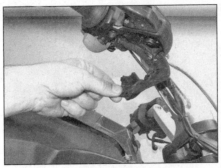

11.5b . . . and lift off the lower cover

11.6a Disconnect the wiring connector . . .

3 Disconnect the wiring connector from the switch or trace the wiring from the switch and disconnect it at the connector. Note that on R1200 RT models, it will be necessary to remove the fuel tank to access the wiring connector (see Chapter 3). Using a multimeter or test light connected to a good earth (ground), check for voltage on the supply side of the brake light switch wiring connector with the ignition switch ON. If no voltage is indicated, check the wire between the switch and the central electronics unit (see *Wiring Diagrams* at the end of this Chapter).

4 If voltage is indicated, check for continuity between the terminals on the switch side of the wiring connector – first with the lever or pedal at rest, then with the lever or pedal applied. There should be continuity with the lever pulled in or pedal depressed. If the switch doesn't behave as described, displace it and check its operation as described below.

Renewal

Front brake lever switch

5 On R1200 RT models, undo the screws securing the lower switch unit cover and remove the cover **(see illustrations)**. Undo the screw securing the switch and displace the switch. Check that the switch contact plate is free to move – if it is stuck or dirty, clean it carefully with suitable solvent and lubricate the switch electric contact cleaner. Check the switch for continuity as described in Step 4. If the switch is proved to be faulty, renew it. Trace the wiring back to the connector and release it from any clips or ties. Installation is the reverse of removal. Check the operation of the brake light.

6 On all other models, disconnect the wiring connector from the switch, then undo the screw securing the switch to the underside of the handlebar lever and lift the switch off **(see illustrations)**. Note that on R1200 GS models, it is first necessary to remove the hand protector (see Chapter 6). Check that the switch contact plate is free to move – if it is stuck or dirty, clean it carefully with suitable solvent and lubricate the switch electric contact cleaner. Check the operation of the switch as described in Step 4. If the switch is proved to be faulty, renew it.

7 Installation is the reverse of removal. Check

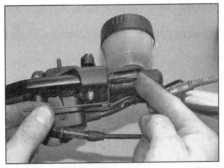

11.6b . . . then undo the screw securing the switch . . .

the operation of the brake light as follows. There should be approximately 5 mm of movement in the brake lever before the brake light illuminates. To adjust the setting, loosen the screw securing the switch and move the switch in or out of the handlebar bracket until the desired setting is achieved. Tighten the screw.

Rear brake pedal switch

8 Trace the wiring from the switch and disconnect it at the connector. Release the wiring from any clips or ties.

9 Pull off the switch cover, then undo the screw securing the switch to its bracket and lift the switch off **(see illustrations)**.

10 Check that the switch contact plate is free to move – if it is stuck or dirty, clean it carefully with suitable solvent and lubricate the switch with electrical contact cleaner. Check the operation of the switch as described in Step 4. If the switch is proved to be faulty, renew it.

11.9a Pull off the switch cover . . .

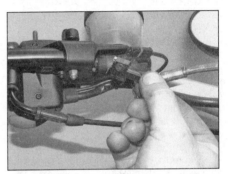

11.6c . . . and lift the switch off

11 Installation is the reverse of removal. Check the operation of the brake light and ensure that the brake pedal stop is set at the correct height (see Chapter 4, Section 3).

12 Instrument cluster

Note 1: *The instrument cluster is a sealed unit. In the event of an instrument failure, have the instrument cluster checked by a BMW dealer.*
Note 2: *If replacing the instruments on a machine equipped with the on-board computer, the BMW diagnostic tester must be used to register the new instrument cluster with the central electronics unit and transfer the mileage and service data. On no account should the instrument wiring be disconnected without first turning the ignition OFF and disconnecting the battery.*

11.9b . . . then undo the screw (arrowed) securing the switch

12.5a Pull off the upper clips (arrowed) . . .

12.5b . . . and lower clip (arrowed) securing the instrument cluster

12.5c Disconnect the wiring connector (arrowed) . . .

R1200 GS

1 Follow the procedure in Section 7 and remove the headlight unit/instrument cluster assembly, then separate the instrument cluster from the headlight unit (see illustrations 7.5a and b).

2 Note the location of the grommets on the mounting bracket and renew them if they are damaged of deteriorated.

3 Installation is the reverse of removal. Make sure the wiring is correctly connected and secured. Check the operation of the instrument cluster.

R1200 RT

4 Follow the procedure in Chapter 6, Section 3, and remove the fairing headlight panel.

5 Pull off the clips securing the instrument cluster, then disconnect the instruments wiring connector and lift the cluster off (see illustrations). If required, lift off the instrument cluster surround.

6 Note the location of the grommets on the mounting bracket and renew them if they are damaged of deteriorated.

7 Installation is the reverse of removal. Make sure the wiring is correctly connected and secured. Check the operation of the instrument cluster.

R1200 ST

8 Follow the procedure in Section 7 and remove the headlight unit.

9 Disconnect the instrument cluster wiring connector (see illustration).

10 Pull off the clips securing the instrument cluster and lift the cluster off (see illustration).

11 Note the location of the grommets on the mounting bracket and renew them if they are damaged of deteriorated.

12 Installation is the reverse of removal. Make sure the wiring is correctly connected and secured. Check the operation of the instrument cluster.

R1200 S

13 Follow the procedure in Chapter 6, Section 5, and remove the windshield – note that it is not necessary to remove the fairing front panel.

14 Undo the screw securing the instrument cluster bracket, then pull the instrument cluster off the mounting pegs (see illustrations).

15 Disconnect the instrument cluster wiring connector and lift the cluster off (see illustration).

16 If required, pull off the clips securing the

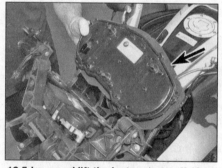

12.5d . . . and lift the instruments off. Note the surround (arrowed)

12.9 Disconnect the wiring connector – R1200 ST

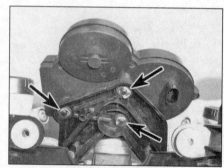

12.10 Location of the clips (arrowed) securing the instrument cluster

12.14a Undo the screw (arrowed) . . .

12.14b . . . then pull the instrument cluster off the pegs (arrowed) . . .

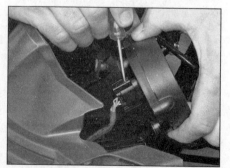

12.15 . . . and disconnect the wiring connector

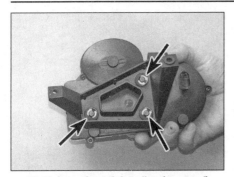

12.16 Location of the clips (arrowed) securing the instrument cluster

12.20 Unclip the instrument lower cover

12.21a Remove the three E-clips (arrowed) . . .

12.21b . . . and disconnect the wiring connector

instrument cluster to the bracket and lift the bracket off **(see illustration)**.

17 Note the location of the grommets on the mounting bracket and renew them if they are damaged of deteriorated.

18 Installation is the reverse of removal. Make sure the wiring is correctly connected and secured. Check the operation of the instrument cluster.

R1200 R

19 Remove the windshield if fitted (see Chapter 6, Section 6).

20 The lower cover is a clip-fit on the instrument mounting bracket. Pull it off its tabs at the sides and bottom to release it **(see illustration)**.

21 Remove the three E-clips securing the

instrument cluster to the mounting bracket, disconnect the wiring connector and lift the instruments off **(see illustrations)**.

22 Note the location of the grommets on the mounting bracket and renew them if they are deteriorated.

23 Installation is the reverse of removal. Check that the lower tabs are felt to 'click' into place. Check the operation of the instrument cluster.

13 Clock

1 Whenever the battery or the instrument cluster has been disconnected, the clock will require resetting as follows.

2 On R1200 GS, ST, S and R models, the clock reset button is between the speedometer and the multi-function display on the instrument cluster **(see illustration)**. On R1200 RT models, the clock reset button is on the right-hand side of the instrument cluster, next to the rev counter.

3 Switch the ignition ON and hold the reset button down for more that 2 seconds – the hours reading on the multi-function display will start to flash. Release the reset button.

4 Press the button briefly to scroll through each hour in turn. When the correct hour is displayed, hold the button down for more that 2 seconds – the minutes reading will start to flash. Release the reset button.

5 Press the button briefly to scroll through each minute in turn. When the correct minute is displayed, hold the button down for more that 2 seconds to confirm the setting.

14 Windshield motor

1 R1200 RT models are equipped with an electric motor for windshield height adjustment. The motor is controlled by a switch on the left-hand handlebar.

2 To access the windshield motor, first follow the procedure in Chapter 6, Section 3, and remove the fairing headlight panel.

3 Remove the instrument cluster (see Section 12).

4 Disconnect the motor wiring connector **(see illustration)**.

5 Undo the screws securing the motor to the support bracket and lift the motor off, noting how the drive shaft locates in the actuator coupling.

6 If required, remove the clips securing the raising arms to both ends of the actuator shaft and pull the arms off.

7 The windshield motor is a sealed unit. If it appears to be faulty, refer to *Wiring Diagrams* at the end of this Chapter and check the wiring between the connector and the central electronics unit. Also check the wiring

13.2 Location of the clock reset button – R1200 S shown

14.4 Disconnect the motor wiring connector

15.1 Location of the rear wheel speed sensor

16.2 Location of the oil pressure switch

between the handlebar switch and the central electronics unit. If the wiring is good, the motor is probably faulty – have it tested by a BMW dealer.

8 Installation is the reverse of removal. Make sure all the wiring is correctly connected and secured. Check the operation of the windshield motor.

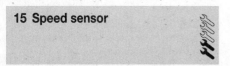

15 Speed sensor

1 The speedometer is activated by a speed sensor located in the top of the final drive unit housing, behind the drive flange (see illustration). The sensor ring is an integral part of the gear assembly inside the housing. Note that on ABS models, this sensor also supplies wheel speed information to the ABS control unit.

2 To access the sensor, first remove the rear wheel (see Chapter 5, Section 13).

3 To renew the sensor, refer to illustration 11.7d in Chapter 4 and trace the sensor wire to the connector under the seat and disconnect it.

4 Undo the screw securing the sensor and draw the sensor out from the housing, noting the location of the sealing O-ring. Release the wire from any clips.

5 Installation is the reverse of removal. Ensure that a new O-ring is fitted to the sensor. Don't forget that any fault code arising from a sensor fault will have to be cleared from the control unit memory using the BMW diagnostic tester.

16 Oil pressure switch

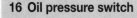

Check

1 The oil pressure warning light should come on together with a red general warning light when the ignition (main) switch is first turned ON – this is part of the electronic 'self-checking' system and serves as a check that

the warning indicators are working. If the oil pressure light comes on whilst the engine is running, low oil pressure is indicated – stop the engine immediately and check the engine oil level (see *Pre-ride checks*).

2 If the oil level is correct, check the switch wiring connector and the wiring for damage between the switch and the engine control unit (see *Wiring Diagrams* at the end of this Chapter). The switch is located in the left-hand side of the crankcase below the cylinder (see illustration). Refer to Chapter 6 to remove any bodywork as necessary to inspect the wiring and refer to Chapter 3 to remove the fuel tank.

3 If the wiring is good, carry out an oil pressure check (see Chapter 2, Section 3). Note: *Some machines are fitted with an oil level warning sender. If an engine oil warning cannot be traced to a faulty pressure switch or low oil pressure, check the operation of the oil level sender (see Section 17).*

4 If the oil pressure warning light does not come on when the ignition is turned on, check the switch as follows.

5 Disconnect the wiring connector. Use an insulated jumper wire to connect the terminal inside the connector to earth (ground) on the crankcase. Switch the ignition ON and check that the warning light comes on. If the light comes on, the switch is defective and must be renewed.

6 If the light still does not come on, check for voltage at the wire terminal. If there is no voltage, check for a break the wire between the switch and the ECU.

Renewal

7 On R1200 RT models, if not already done, remove the fairing left-hand side panel (see Chapter 6).

8 Detach the wiring connector and unscrew the oil pressure switch from the crankcase. Be prepared to catch any residual oil from the switch location.

9 Before installing the new switch, apply a suitable sealant to the upper portion of the switch threads, leaving the lower 3 to 4 mm of thread clean. Wipe the threads in the crankcase clean, then install the switch and tighten it to the torque setting specified at the beginning of this Chapter. Ensure that the wiring connector is secure.

10 Run the engine and check that the switch operates correctly.

11 Install the remaining components in the reverse order of removal.

17 Oil level warning sender

1 When fitted, the oil level warning sender is located in the right-hand side of the crankcase below the cylinder.

2 If the sender is thought to be faulty, check the sender wiring connector and the wiring for damage between the sender and the engine control unit (see *Wiring Diagrams* at the end of this Chapter). Refer to Chapter 6 to remove any bodywork as necessary to inspect the wiring and refer to Chapter 3 to remove the fuel tank.

3 If the wiring is good, check the operation of the sender as follows. Note: *No specifications are available for the sender. If, after testing, it is thought to be faulty, have its condition confirmed by a BMW dealer.*

4 Trace the wiring from the sender and disconnect it at the connector. Free the wiring from any clips or ties.

5 Undo the screws securing the sender in the crankcase and withdraw the sender carefully to avoid damaging the float assembly. Note the location of the sealing O-ring.

6 Check that the float is free to move up and down. If required, prise off the E-clip and remove the float, noting which way round it is fitted, then clean the components in suitable solvent. Install the float and secure it with a new E-clip.

7 Using a multimeter set to the ohms x 100 scale, test for resistance between the terminals on the sender side of the wiring connector with the float in both the high and low positions. If there is no difference in the results (from high to low positions) it is likely that the sender is faulty and a new one must be fitted.

8 Installation is the reverse of removal. Fit a new O-ring and tighten the screws securely. Ensure that the wiring connector is secure.

18 Ambient air temperature sensor

1 An ambient air temperature sensor is fitted to models with the on-board computer. When the air temperature drops below 3°C the ice warning symbol appears on the instrument cluster multi-function display.

2 No specifications are available for testing the sensor. However, before condemning it, remove the appropriate body panels and inspect the wiring connector and wiring for damage.

18.3 Location of the ambient air temperature sensor – R1200 RT shown

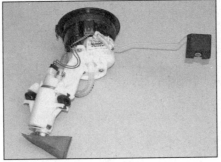

19.4 Fuel level sensor float in the tank full position

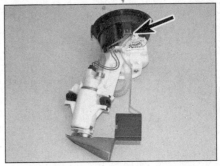

19.5 Fuel level sensor float in the tank empty position. Note the wiring connector (arrowed)

3 On R1200 RT models, the air temperature sensor is located on the rear mudguard (see illustration). Follow the procedure in Chapter 6 and remove the right-hand seat cowling to access the sensor and its wiring connector.

4 On R1200 ST models, the air temperature sensor is located in the fairing front panel behind the air intake grille. Before removing the fairing panel, disconnect the sensor wiring connector.

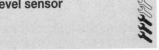

19 Fuel level sensor

⚠️ **Warning: Petrol (gasoline) is extremely flammable, so take extra precautions when you work on any part of the fuel system. Don't smoke or allow open flames or bare light bulbs near the work area, and don't work in a garage where a natural gas-type appliance is present. If you spill any fuel on your skin, rinse it off immediately with soap and water. When you perform any kind of work on the fuel system, wear safety glasses and have a fire extinguisher suitable for a class B type fire (flammable liquids) on hand.**

1 The fuel tank contains a lever-type level sensor and a low level warning sender. The sensor monitors the amount of fuel in the tank and relays that information to the gauge on the instrument cluster multi-function display. The sender illuminates a yellow general warning light and a flashing fuel reserve symbol when the fuel content in the tank reaches the reserve capacity of 4 litres.

2 No specifications are available for testing the level sensor or the low level warning sender. However, if the sensor is thought to be faulty, a general check of its function can be made as follows.

3 Follow the procedure in Chapter 3 and remove the fuel pump assembly from the tank.

4 Referring to the appropriate wiring diagram at the end of this Chapter, identify the level sensor wire terminals in the connector on the top of the pump assembly. Connect the probes of a multimeter set to the ohms x 100

scale to the sensor terminals and measure the resistance with the float in the tank full (up) position (see illustration).

5 Now move the float slowly to the tank empty (down) position (see illustration). If the sensor is working correctly, the meter should show a progressive change in the resistance.

6 If there is no difference in the results it is likely that the level sensor is faulty and a new one must be fitted. Disconnect the sensor wiring connector, then unclip the sensor from the pump assembly. Installation is the reverse of removal.

7 If the level sensor is good, check the wiring between the fuel tank and the central electronics unit (see *Wiring Diagrams* at the end of the Chapter).

20 Clutch switch

Check

1 The clutch switch is mounted on the underside of the handlebar lever. The switch is part of the safety circuit which allows the starter motor to operate only if the transmission is in neutral or, if the transmission is in gear, with the clutch lever pulled into the handlebar and the side stand up. To check the safety circuit, follow the procedure in Steps 7 to 11. **Note:** *To start the engine with the transmission in gear, switch the ignition ON before pulling the*

clutch lever in, otherwise the starting system will not be enabled.

2 To check the operation of the switch, disconnect the wiring connector from the switch or trace the wiring from the switch and disconnect it at the connector. Note that on R1200 RT models, it will be necessary to remove the fuel tank to access the wiring connector (see Chapter 3).

3 Using a multimeter or test light, check for continuity between the terminals on the switch side of the wiring connector – first with the lever at rest, then with the lever pulled in. There should be continuity with the lever in one position only. If the switch doesn't behave as described, displace it and check its operation as described below.

Renewal

4 On R1200 RT models, undo the screws securing the lower switch unit cover and remove the cover (see illustrations). Undo the screw securing the switch and displace the switch. Check that the switch contact plate is free to move – if it is stuck or dirty, clean it carefully with suitable solvent and lubricate the switch electric contact cleaner. Check the switch for continuity as described in Step 3. If the switch is proved to be faulty, renew it. Trace the wiring back to the connector and release it from any clips or ties. Installation is the reverse of removal.

5 On all other models, disconnect the wiring connector from the switch, then undo the screw securing the switch to the underside of the handlebar lever and lift the switch off

20.4a Undo the screws . . .

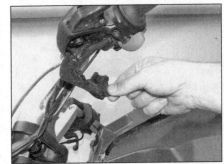

20.4b . . . and lift off the lower cover

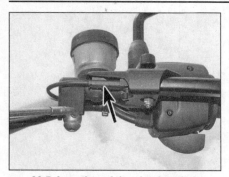

20.5 Location of the clutch switch (arrowed) – R1200 GS shown

(see illustration). Note that on R1200 GS models, it is first necessary to remove the hand protector (see Chapter 6). Check that the switch contact plate is free to move – if it is stuck or dirty, clean it carefully with suitable solvent and lubricate the switch electric contact cleaner. Check the operation of the switch as described in Step 3. If the switch is proved to be faulty, renew it.

6 Installation is the reverse of removal. Check the operation of the clutch switch as follows. There should be between 5 and 9 mm of movement in the clutch lever before the switching point is reached and pressure builds up in the lever. To adjust the setting, loosen the screw securing the switch and move the switch in or out of the handlebar bracket until the desired setting is achieved. Tighten the screw.

Safety circuit check

7 Ensure that the kill switch is OFF, the side stand is UP and the transmission is in neutral. Turn the ignition ON – neutral light N should illuminate on the instrument cluster multi-function display.
8 Select a gear – neutral light should go OFF.
9 Press the starter button – starter should not operate.
10 Extend the side stand DOWN, pull in the clutch lever and press the starter button – starter should not operate.
11 Retract the side stand UP and, with the clutch lever still pulled in, press the starter button – starter should operate.

21 Side stand switch

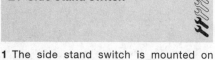

1 The side stand switch is mounted on the side stand pivot (see illustration). The switch is part of the safety circuit which allows the starter motor to operate only if the transmission is in neutral or, if the transmission is in gear, with the clutch lever pulled into the handlebar and the side stand up.
2 To check the operation of the switch, support the machine on its centre stand or on an auxiliary stand. Trace the wiring back from the switch to its connector and disconnect it – refer to Chapter 6 to remove any bodywork as necessary.

21.1 Location of the side stand switch (arrowed)

3 Referring to the appropriate wiring diagram at the end of this Chapter, use a multimeter or continuity tester to check for continuity between the wire terminals on the switch side of the connector, first with the stand up and then with the stand down.
4 If the switch does not perform as illustrated in the wiring diagram a new one must be fitted. Follow the procedure in Chapter 4, Section 4, to install a new switch.
5 If the switch is good, check the wiring between the connector and the ECU.
6 If required, follow the procedure in Section 20, Steps 7 to 11, to check the operation of the safety circuit.

22 Ignition switch

General

1 Two ignition keys are supplied with each new machine. The keys are security coded and contain an integral transponder. When a key is inserted into the ignition switch the security code is transmitted to the immobiliser and the immobiliser is deactivated. Only the keys supplied with the machine will deactivate the immobiliser.
2 The keys should not be kept together – apart from the obvious risk of loosing both keys, the spare key may interfere with the enabling signal for starting and the EWS immobiliser warning will appear on the instrument cluster multi-function display.

22.6a Screws (arrowed) secure the ignition switch cover

3 If a key is lost, or if a key loses its security code, a replacement can only be obtained from a BMW dealer. For security, the new key and the remaining original key can be re-coded by the dealer.

Switch check

4 Disconnect the battery negative (-ve) lead (see Section 3).
5 Remove the fuel tank (see Chapter 3) and any fairing panels as necessary to access the front of the steering head (see Chapter 6).
6 Undo the screws securing the ignition switch wiring connector cover and lift the cover off, then disconnect the connector from the base of the ignition (main) switch (see illustrations).
7 Using an ohmmeter or a continuity tester, check the continuity of the connector terminal pairs according to the ignition switch table – see the relevant wiring diagram at the end of this Chapter. Continuity should exist when the switch connections are joined by a bar in the table.
8 If the switch fails any of the tests, renew it.
Note: *If a new switch is being fitted, the BMW diagnostic tester must be used to register the new unit with the central electronics unit.*

Removal

9 Follow the procedure in Chapter 4, Section 7, and remove the fork top yoke.
10 Special security bolts are used to mount the ignition switch/steering lock assembly on the underside of the top yoke. Drill the heads off the bolts and draw the assembly off. Use a stud extractor to unscrew the remains of the security bolts (see *Tools and Workshop Tips* in the *Reference* section).

Installation

11 Install the switch/lock assembly onto the fork bridge and secure it with new security bolts. Note that these bolts are micro-encapsulated and require a service tool (No. 51 0 531) to engage their heads; tighten the bolts to the torque setting specified at the beginning of this Chapter.
12 Follow the procedure in Chapter 4, Section 7, and install the fork top yoke. Make sure wiring for the ignition switch and the immobiliser is securely connected and check the operation of the ignition switch.

22.6b Ignition (main) switch (A) and ignition immobiliser (B)

23.5a Undo the screws (arrowed) on the right-hand switch unit . . .

23.5b . . . and ease the front half off

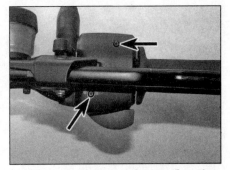

23.5c Undo the screws (arrowed) on the left-hand switch unit . . .

23 Handlebar switches

1 Generally speaking, the switches are reliable and trouble-free. Most problems, when they do occur, are caused by dirty or corroded contacts, but wear and breakage of internal parts is a possibility that should not be overlooked. If breakage does occur, the entire switch and related wiring harness will have to be renewed, since individual parts are not available.

2 The switches can be checked for continuity using an ohmmeter or a continuity test light.

3 On R1200 RT models, first remove the fuel tank (see Chapter 3). Trace the wiring harness of the switch in question back to its connector and disconnect it.

4 On R1200 GS models, first remove the hand protectors (see Chapter 6).

5 On R1200 GS, ST, S and R models, undo the screws securing the front half of the switch unit and ease it off **(see illustrations)**. Undo the screw securing the switch wiring connector, then disconnect the connector **(see illustration)**.

6 On all models, referring to the appropriate wiring diagram at the end of this Chapter, check for continuity between the terminals on the switch side of the connectors with the switch in various positions e.g. switch off – no continuity, switch on – continuity.

7 The switch units are sealed – if the continuity check indicates a problem exists, follow the procedure below to remove the switch and fit a new one.

Removal and installation

R1200 RT

8 Remove the fuel tank (see Chapter 3). Trace the wiring harness of the switch in question back to its connector and disconnect it, then work back along the harness, freeing it from all the relevant clips and ties, whilst noting its correct routing **(see illustration)**.

9 If an additional switch unit for optional electrical equipment – radio controls and electronic suspension adjustment (ESA) – is

23.5d . . . and ease the front half off

fitted to the left-hand handlebar unit, first undo the screw securing the additional switch and unclip it from its mounting, then undo the screws on the underside securing the mounting and lift it off.

10 To remove either the left or right-hand

23.8 Note how the wiring is secured to the handlebars (arrowed) – R1200 RT

23.11b . . . and on the back of the unit . . .

23.5e Wiring connector (A) is secured by screw (B)

switch unit, undo the screws securing the lower cover and remove it **(see illustrations 20.4a and b)**.

11 Undo the screws on the front and back of the switch unit and draw the unit off **(see illustrations)**.

23.11a Undo the screw on the front . . .

23.11c . . . then draw the switch unit off

23.14 Disconnect the heated handlebar grips connector

23.15a Undo the large screw . . .

24 Horn

1 The horn is located at the front of the machine, either on the front sub-frame, below the steering head or on the fairing bracket **(see illustrations)**. On R1200 R models it is mounted to the right-hand side of the front sub-frame. Refer to Chapter 6 to remove any bodywork as necessary to access the horn.
2 Unplug the wiring connector from the horn **(see illustration)**. Using a fully charged 12 volt battery and two insulated jumper wires, apply voltage directly to the terminals on the horn.
3 If the horn sounds, check the switch (see Section 23) and the wiring between the switch, the central electronics unit and the horn (see *Wiring Diagrams* at the end of this Chapter).
4 Check for continuity between the brown wire connector terminal and earth (ground). If there is no continuity, check the earth (ground) circuit for an open or poor connection.
5 If the horn doesn't sound, renew it.
6 If not already done, unplug the wiring connector from the horn, then unscrew the nut securing the horn and remove it from the bike.
7 Installation is the reverse of removal. Check the operation of the horn.

23.15b . . . and the two small screws (arrowed) . . .

23.15c . . . then lift the switch unit off

12 Installation is the reverse of removal. Ensure that the wiring is correctly routed and secured by any clips and ties, and that the connector is secure. Check the operation of the switch unit.

24.1a Horn located on front sub-frame – R1200 GS

R1200 GS, ST, S and R

13 On R1200 GS models, first remove the hand protectors (see Chapter 6).
14 To remove either the left or right-hand switch unit, undo the screws securing the front half of the unit and ease it off **(see illustrations 23.5a, b, c and d)**. Undo the screw securing the switch wiring connector **(see illustration 23.5e)**, then disconnect the connector for the switch and, where fitted, the heated handlebar grips **(see illustration)**.
15 Undo the screws securing the switch unit to the handlebar bracket and lift the unit off **(see illustrations)**.
16 Installation is the reverse of removal. Ensure that the wiring connectors are secure. Check the operation of the switch unit.

25 Starter relay

1 If the starter circuit is faulty, first check that the battery is fully charged. Check that the engine kill switch is in the run (centre) position, that the side stand is up, and that the transmission is in neutral. If the starter motor still fails to operate, turn the ignition OFF and disconnect the battery negative (-ve) lead (see Section 3).
2 The starter relay is located under the seat. On R1200 GS models, unclip the relay from its socket **(see illustration)**. On R1200 RT and ST models the relay is located inside a cover next to the plug for the BMW diagnostic tool. Undo the screws securing the cover, then

24.1b Horn located below the steering head – R1200 RT

24.1c Horn located on front fairing bracket (arrowed) – R1200 ST and S

24.2 Location of the horn wiring connector (arrowed)

25.2a Location of starter relay (arrowed) – R1200 GS

25.2b Undo the screws (arrowed) . . .

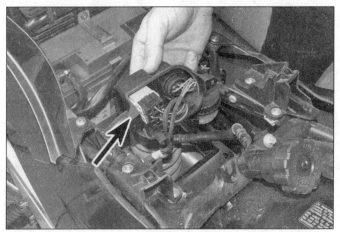

25.2c . . . to access the starter relay (arrowed) – R1200 RT

25.2d Unclip the box lid . . .

draw the relay out and unclip it from its socket **(see illustrations)**. On R1200 S models, the relay is housed inside a box clipped to the left-hand side of the frame. Unclip the box from the frame bracket, then open the box and ease the relay out **(see illustrations)**. Unclip the relay from its socket **(see illustration)**. On R1200 R models, the relay is mounted to the rear mudguard by a tab **(see illustration)**.

3 Set a multimeter to the ohms x 1 scale, or use a continuity tester, and connect it across the relay's No. 30 and No. 87 terminals (relay

holder terminals 6 and 2). There should be no continuity (infinite resistance).

4 Using a fully-charged 12 volt battery and two insulated jumper wires, connect the positive (+ve) battery terminal to the relay No. 85 terminal (holder terminal 4), and the negative (-ve) battery terminal to the relay No. 86 terminal (holder terminal 8). The multimeter should now read zero ohms (continuity).

5 If the test results are not as described, the relay is faulty and must be renewed.

6 Before installing the relay, refer to the

25.2e . . . then unclip the relay . . .

25.2f . . . and ease it out – R1200 S

25.2g Unclip the relay from its socket

25.2h R1200 R starter relay mounts on tab fixed to rear mudguard

26.4a Undo the screw (arrowed) . . .

26.4b . . . then manoeuvre the starter motor cover out

26.4c Note the peg (arrowed) on the cover that locates in a hole in the engine casing

appropriate wiring diagram at the end of this Chapter and check the holder wiring and wiring connections as follows.

7 Connect the meter positive (+ve) lead to terminal 87 (holder terminal No. 2) and connect the meter negative (-ve) lead to a good earth. There should be battery voltage. Now connect the meter positive (+ve) lead to terminal 86 (holder terminal No. 8) and the negative (-ve) lead to terminal 85 (holder terminal No. 4). Turn the ignition (main) switch ON and check for battery voltage when the starter button is pressed. Finally, check for continuity between terminal 30 (holder terminal No. 6) and the black wiring connector on the starter motor solenoid

8 If the relay and its wiring are good, check the other components in the starter circuit (clutch switch, side stand switch, starter switch and kill switch) as described in the relevant

sections of this Chapter. If all components are good, check the wiring between the various components in the starter circuit (see *Wiring Diagrams* at the end of this Chapter).

9 Check the wiring and wiring connector for the gear position sensor (see Chapter 3, Section 15).

10 If all components in the starter circuit are proved good, the fault could be due to a sticking or damaged starter motor solenoid (see Section 26).

26 Starter motor and solenoid

Removal

1 The starter motor is located on the lower left-hand side of the engine.

2 On R1200 RT models, remove the fairing left-hand main side panel (see Chapter 6) and the left-hand footrest bracket (see Chapter 4) to access the starter motor.

3 On all models, disconnect the battery negative (-ve) lead (see Section 3).

4 Where fitted, undo the screw securing the starter motor cover and lift the cover off, noting how it fits **(see illustrations)**.

5 Undo the terminal nut (covered with a cap on some models) and disconnect the battery lead from the starter solenoid, then disconnect the wiring connector and lift off the solenoid cover **(see illustrations)**.

6 Undo the bolts securing the starter motor and solenoid assembly and lift it off, noting how the starter gear engages with the clutch ring gear **(see illustrations)**.

7 Inspect the starter gear and the clutch ring gear for worn or damaged teeth. If the starter gear is worn a new starter motor will have to be fitted – no individual components are available for the starter motor or solenoid. If the clutch ring gear is worn or damaged, refer to Chapter 2, Section 23, to remove the clutch.

8 If necessary, have the operation of the starter motor and solenoid checked by a BMW dealer.

Installation

9 Installation is the reverse of removal. Tighten the mounting bolts and the starter motor terminal nut to the torque settings specified at the beginning of this Chapter. Ensure that solenoid wiring connector is secure. Where

26.5a Undo the terminal nut securing the battery lead . . .

26.5b . . . then disconnect the wiring connector . . .

26.5c . . . and lift the solenoid cover off

26.6a Starter motor is secured by two bolts (arrowed)

26.6b Note how the starter gear engages with the clutch ring gear (arrowed)

fitted, tighten the cover bolt to the specified torque setting.
10 Check the operation of the starter motor.

27 Charging system check

1 Accurate assessment of alternator output should be undertaken by a BMW dealer. However, a charging voltage output test can be undertaken as follows.
2 Make sure that the battery is fully charged (see Section 3).
3 Start the engine and run it at a fast idle. Using a multimeter set to the 0 to 20 volts DC scale, connect the positive (+ve) meter lead to the battery positive (+ve) terminal and the negative (-ve) lead to the negative (-ve) terminal. The meter should indicate 13 to 15 volts.
4 Now select high beam – the voltage may drop momentarily, but should then return to the original indicated 13 to 15 volts.
5 If the output test indicates a voltage either lower or higher than the suggested range, it is likely that the alternator or its inbuilt voltage regulator is faulty – have the charging system checked by a BMW dealer.
6 Refer to Section 28 for details of alternator removal and installation.

28 Alternator

1 Refer to Section 27 to check the alternator output. If the alternator is faulty, a new one must be fitted – no replacement parts are available.

Removal

2 The alternator is located on the top of the crankcase between the left and right-hand struts of the front sub-frame **(see illustration)**.
3 Disconnect the battery negative (-ve) lead (see Section 3).
4 Remove the left and right-hand fairing side panels (see Chapter 6) and the fuel tank (see Chapter 3).
5 Remove front suspension shock absorber (see Chapter 4, Section 6).
6 Remove the alternator drive belt (see Chapter 1, Section 13).
7 Undo the screws securing the alternator drive belt top cover and remove the cover **(see illustration)**.
8 Disconnect the wiring connector from the alternator, then remove the cover and undo the terminal nut to disconnect the lead from the alternator **(see illustrations)**.
9 Undo the two bolts securing the alternator on the left-hand side **(see illustrations)**.
10 Undo the bolt securing the alternator on the right-hand side **(see illustrations)**.
11 Manoeuvre the alternator off towards the front of the machine.

28.2 Location of the alternator on top of the crankcase

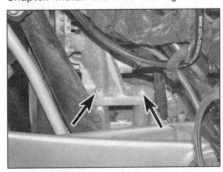
28.8a Disconnect the wiring connector (arrowed) . . .

Installation

12 Installation is the reverse of removal. Tighten the mounting bolts to the torque setting specified at the beginning of this Chapter. Install the lead and tighten the

28.9a Undo the two bolts (arrowed) . . .

28.10a Undo the single bolt (arrowed) . . .

28.7 Alternator drive belt top cover is secured by two screws (arrowed)

28.8b . . . and the lead from the alternator terminal (arrowed)

terminal nut securely, then fit the cover. Ensure that the wiring connector is secure.
13 Follow the procedure in Chapter 1, Section 13, to install the drive belt and cover.
14 Install the remaining components in the reverse order of removal.

28.9b . . . on the left-hand side

28.10b . . . on the right-hand side

29 Wiring diagrams

1 The wiring diagrams for each model are presented as separate circuits e.g. *Starting and charging, Lighting systems* etc.

2 Connector plug terminal number details are given to aid testing and terminal identification. For the engine control unit and central electronics unit the terminal numbers are represented in squares or circles to differentiate between the two connectors on the unit **(see illustration)**. Study the wiring diagram and the two connectors on the unit to determine the identity of the connector. The engine control unit on all models has two connectors. The central electronics unit has two connectors on RT and RS models, but just a single connector on GS and S models.

3 The control units are drawn with a solid black outline where the unit connections are complete within that circuit. Where a hatched outline is used, their connections are shown on different circuits and thus the unit is not shown complete in any one circuit.

4 Wires can be identified by their colour and wire thickness details, expressed in millimetres.

5 Internal connections within the wiring harness are respresented by full points with a DIN symbol alongisde, e.g. 31 denoting the earth (ground) circuit.

6 Engine cylinders are referred to as cyl 1 for the left-hand cylinder and cyl 2 for the right-hand cylinder.

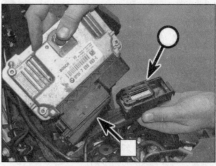

29.2 Terminal numbers are shown in circles or squares to identify the appropriate connector

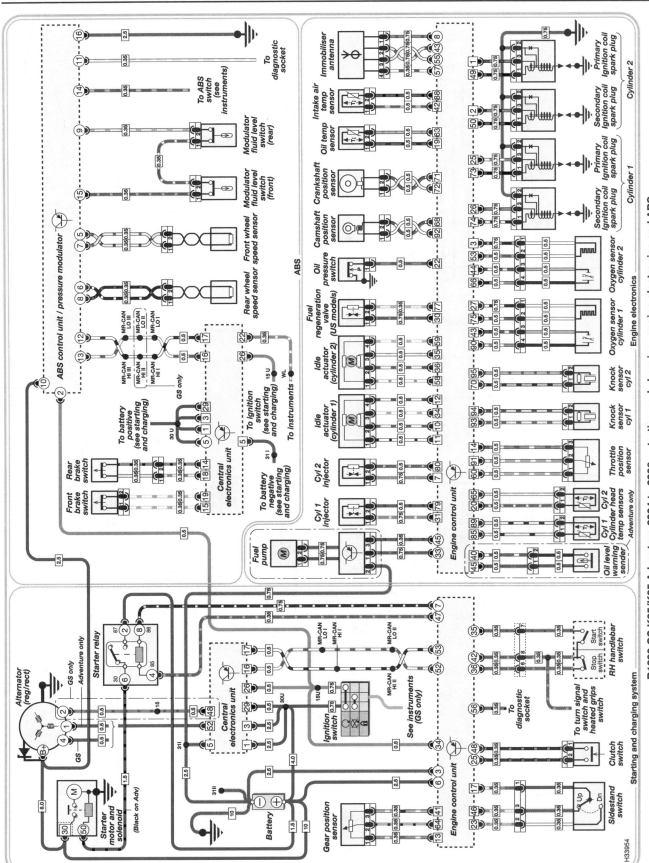

R1200 GS K25/K25 Adventure 2004 to 2006 - starting and charging, engine electronics and ABS

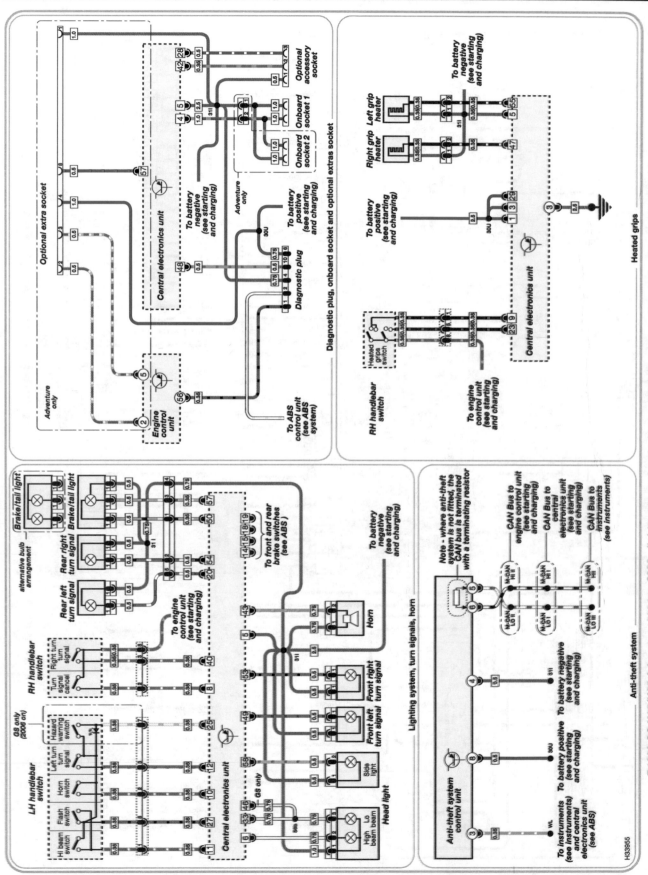

Diagnostic plug, onboard socket and optional extras socket

Heated grips

Lighting system, turn signals, horn

Anti-theft system

R1200 GS K25/K25 Adventure 2004 to 2006 - lighting, turn signals, horn, anti-theft system, diagnostic plug and heated grips

H33955

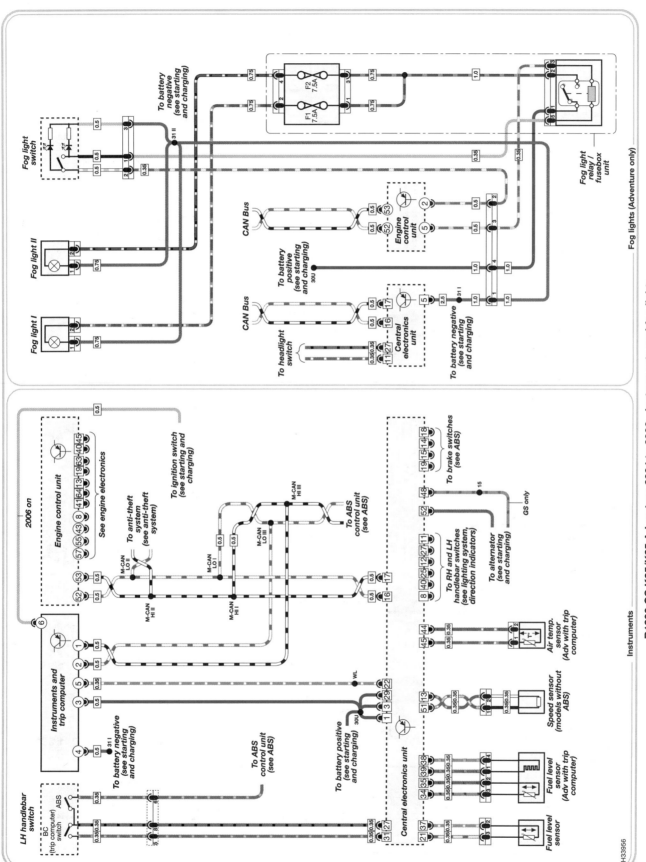

Fog lights (Adventure only)

Instruments

R1200 GS K25/K25 Adventure 2004 to 2006 - instruments and fog lights

H33956

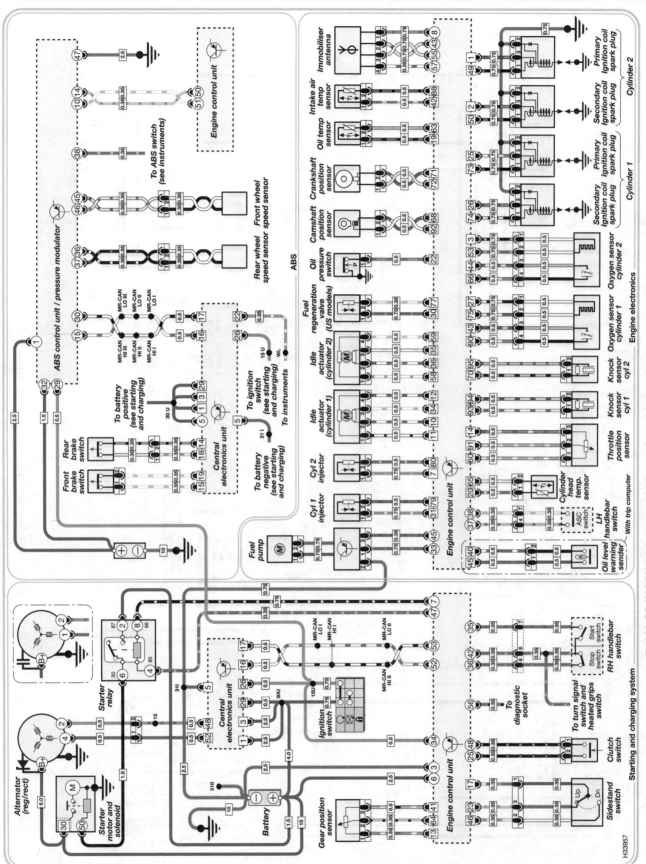

R1200 GS K25/K25 Adventure 2007 - starting and charging, engine electronics and ABS

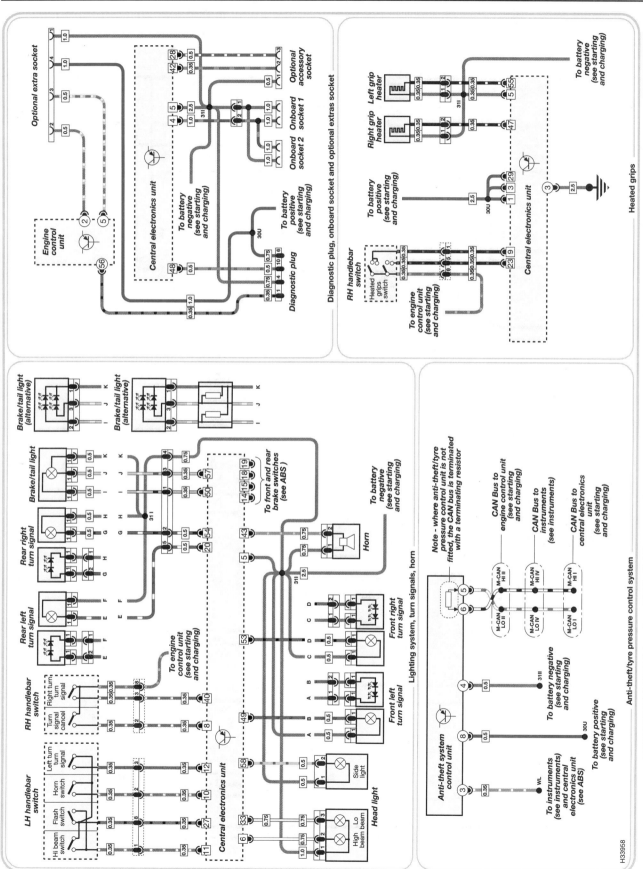

Diagnostic plug, onboard socket and optional extras socket

Heated grips

Lighting system, turn signals, horn

Anti-theft/tyre pressure control system

R1200 GS K25/K25 Adventure 2007 – lighting, turn signals, horn, anti-theft system, diagnostic plug and heated grips

H33958

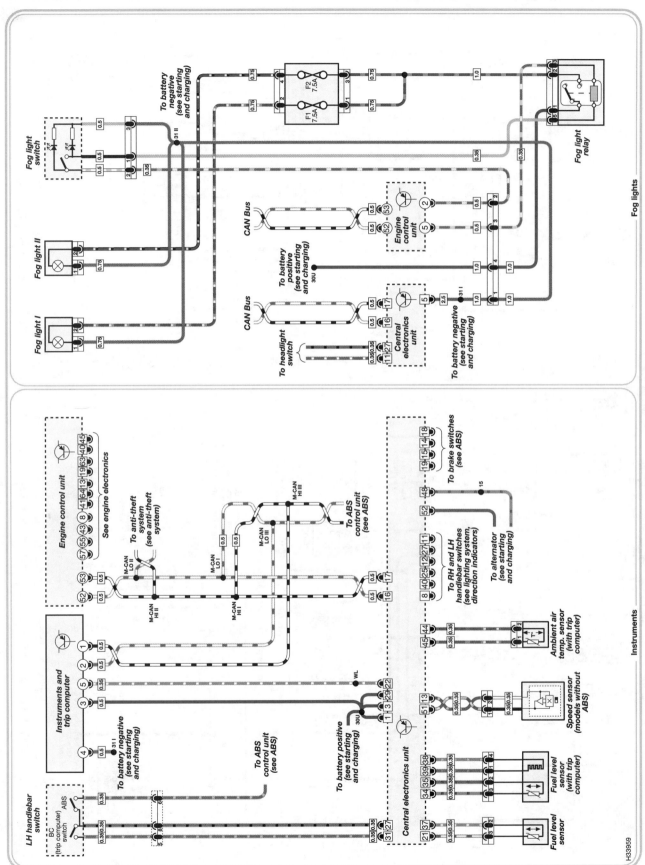

Fog lights

Instruments

R1200 GS K25/K25 Adventure 2007 - instruments and fog lights

H33959

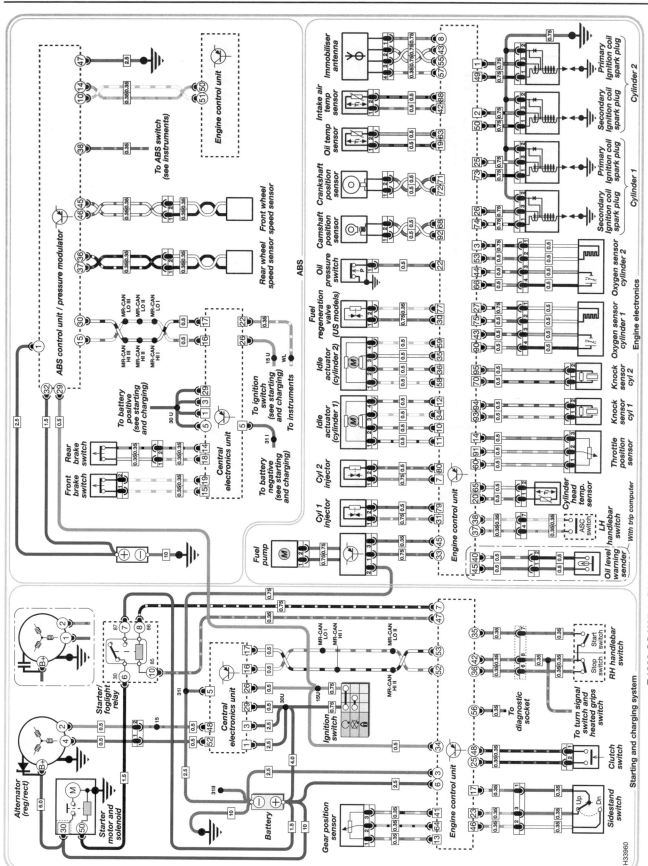

R1200 GS K25 11/K25 12 Adventure 2008 on - starting and charging, engine electronics and ABS

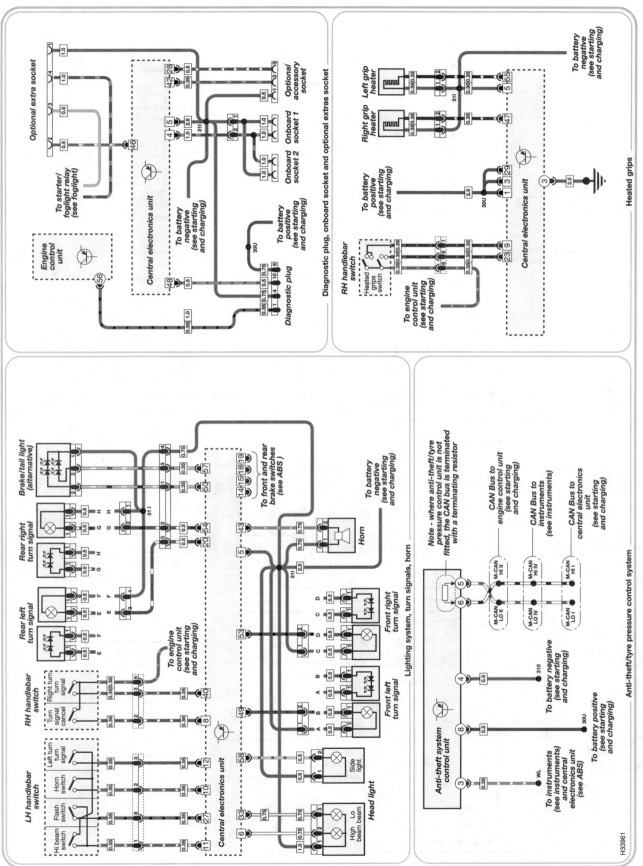

Diagnostic plug, onboard socket and optional extras socket

Heated grips

Lighting system, turn signals, horn

Anti-theft/tyre pressure control system

R1200 GS K25 11/K25 12 Adventure 2008 on – lighting, turn signals, horn, anti-theft system, diagnostic plug and heated grips

H33961

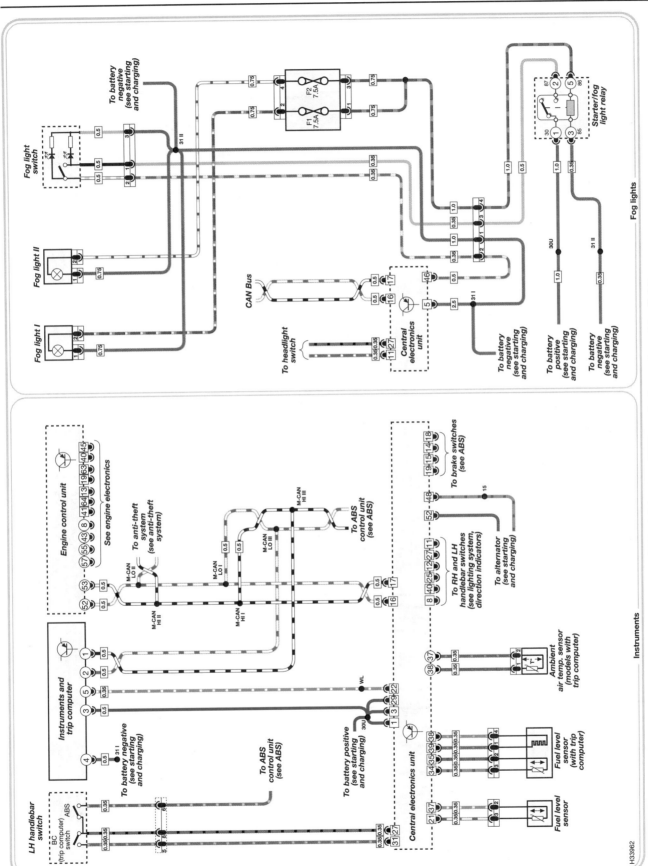

R1200 GS K25 11/K25 12 Adventure 2008 on – instruments and fog lights

Fog lights

Instruments

H33962

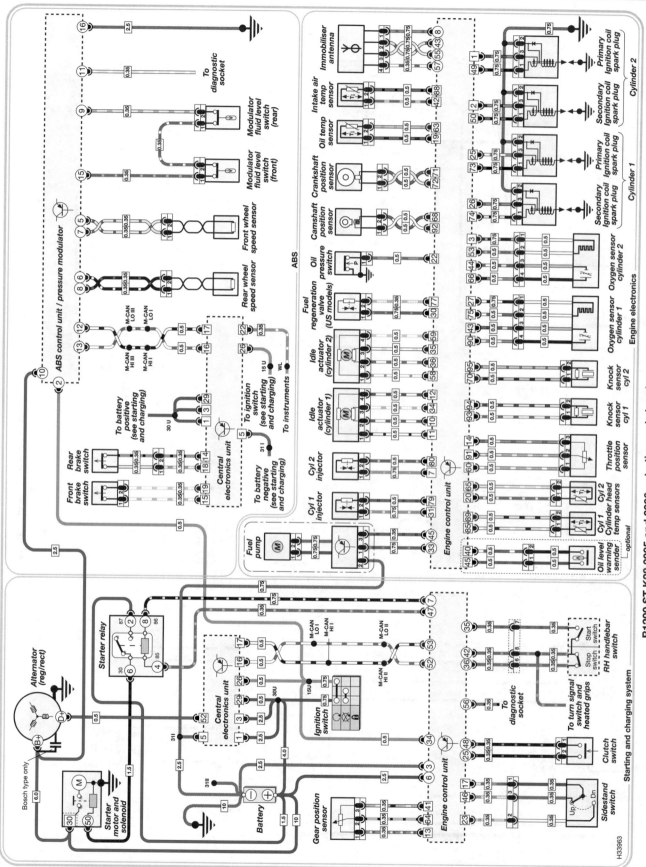

R1200 ST K28 2005 and 2006 – starting and charging, engine electronics and ABS

H33963

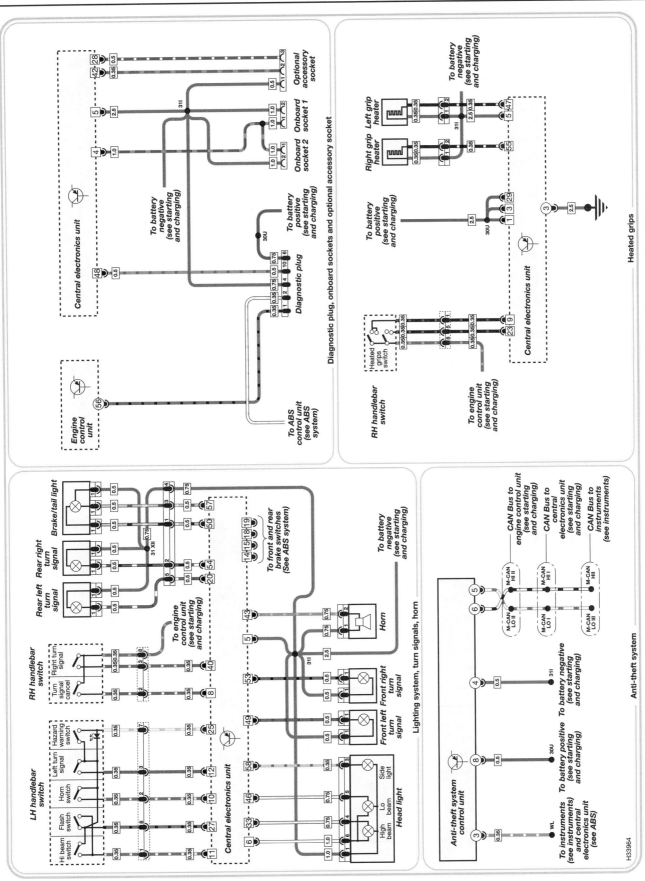

Diagnostic plug, onboard sockets and optional accessory socket

Heated grips

Lighting system, turn signals, horn

Anti-theft system

R1200 ST K28 2005 and 2006 - lighting, turn signals, horn, anti-theft system, diagnostic plug and heated grips

H33964

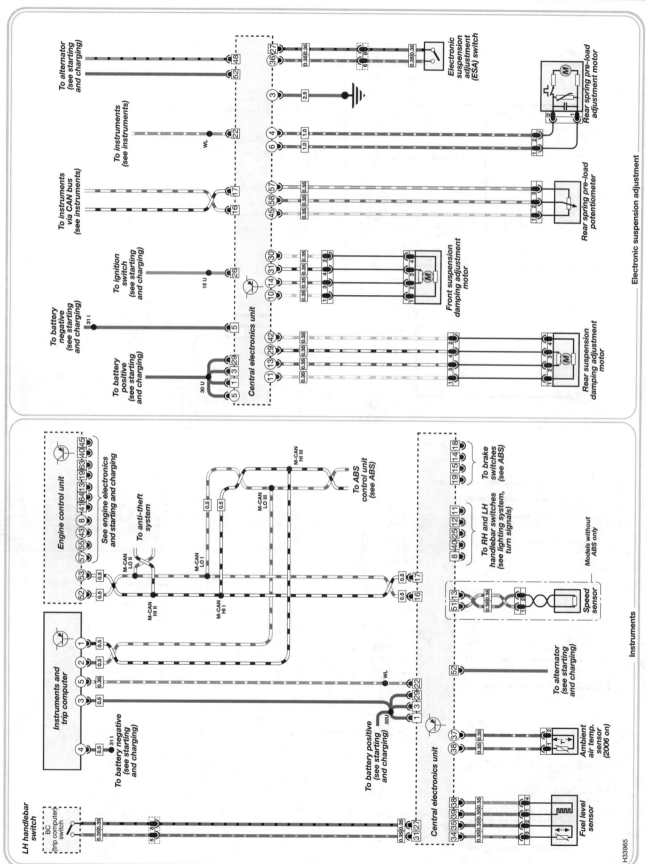

R1200 ST K28 2005 and 2006 - instruments and ESA

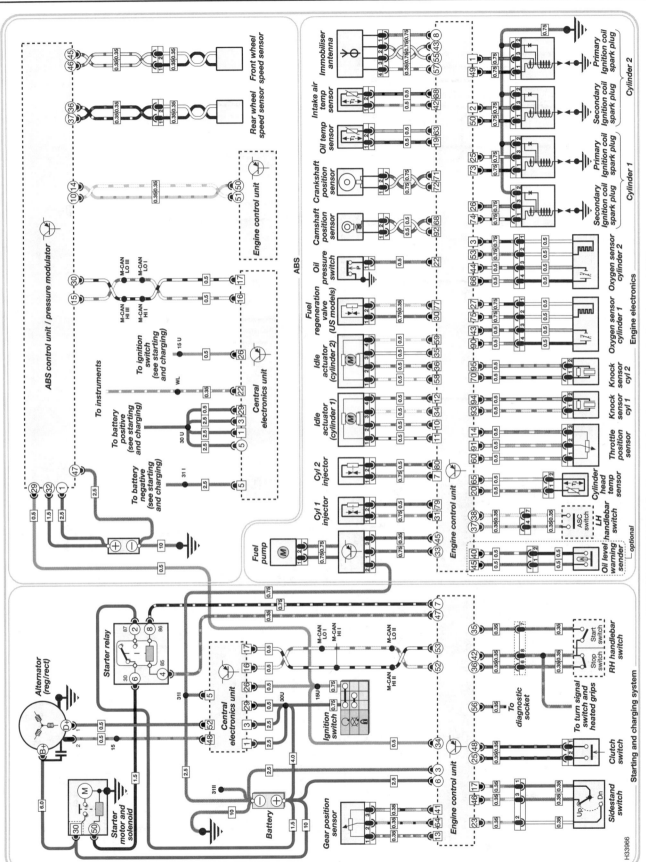

R1200 ST K28 2007 - starting and charging, engine electronics and ABS

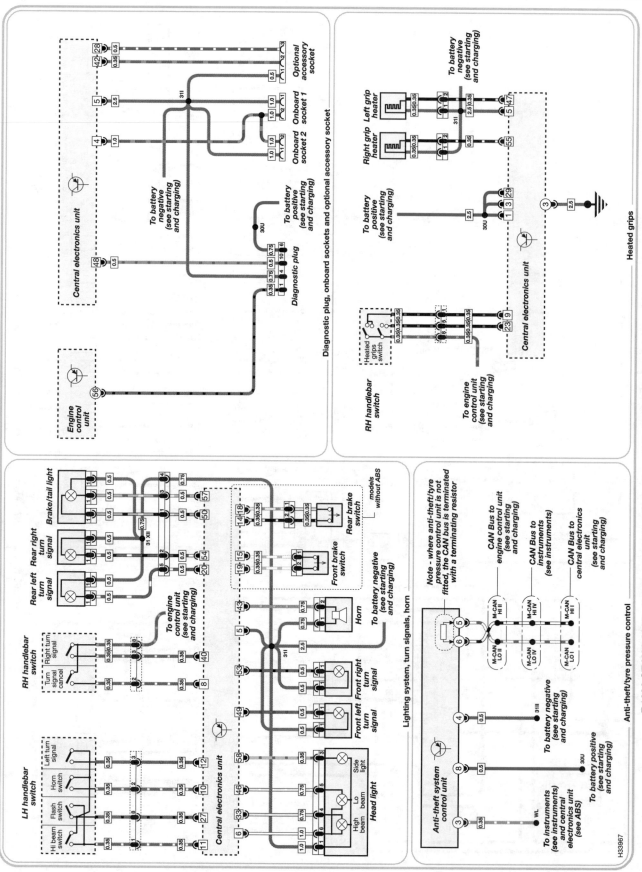

Diagnostic plug, onboard sockets and optional accessory socket

Heated grips

Lighting system, turn signals, horn

Anti-theft/tyre pressure control

R1200 ST K28 2007 - lighting, turn signals, horn, anti-theft system, diagnostic plug and heated grips

H33967

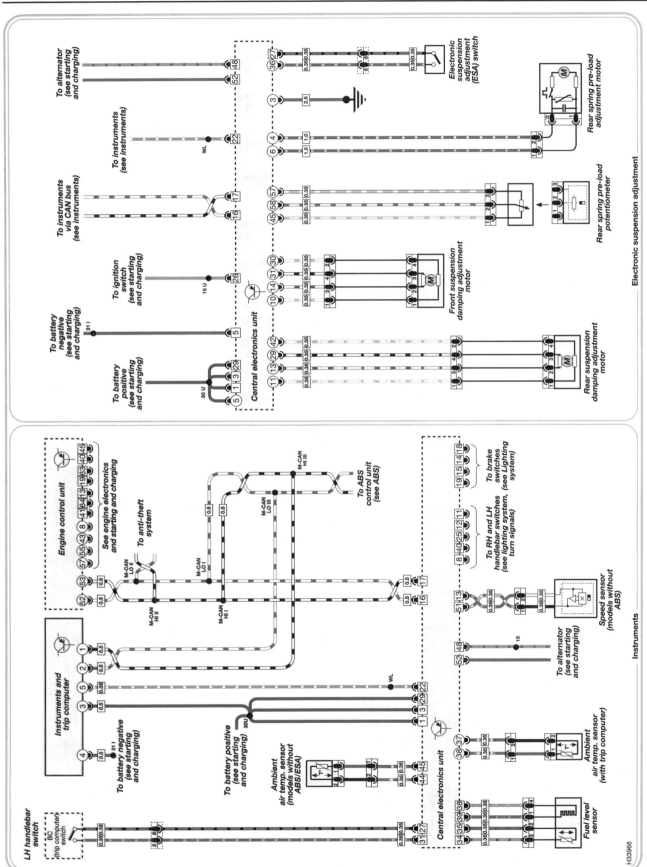

R1200 ST K28 2007 - instruments and ESA

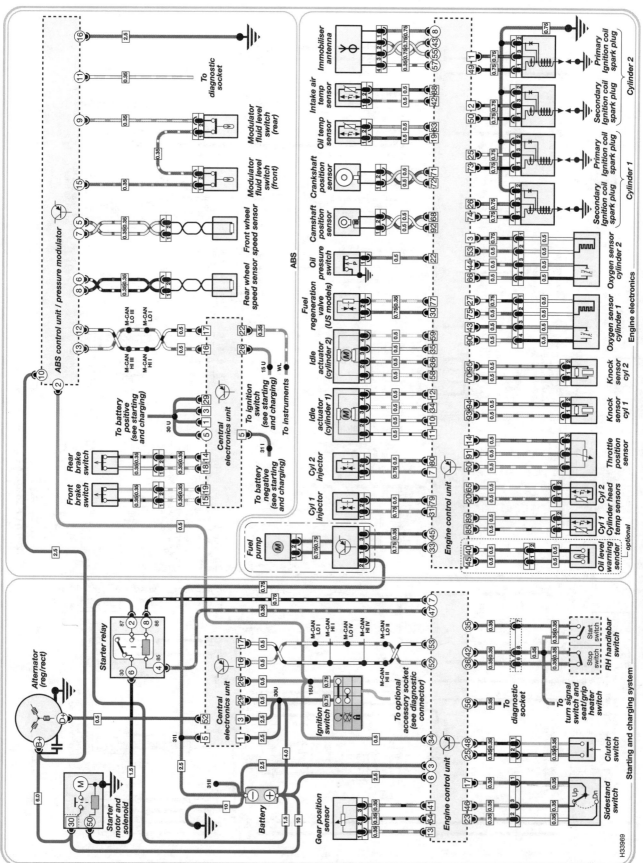

R1200 RT K26 2005 and 2006 - starting and charging systems, engine electronics and ABS

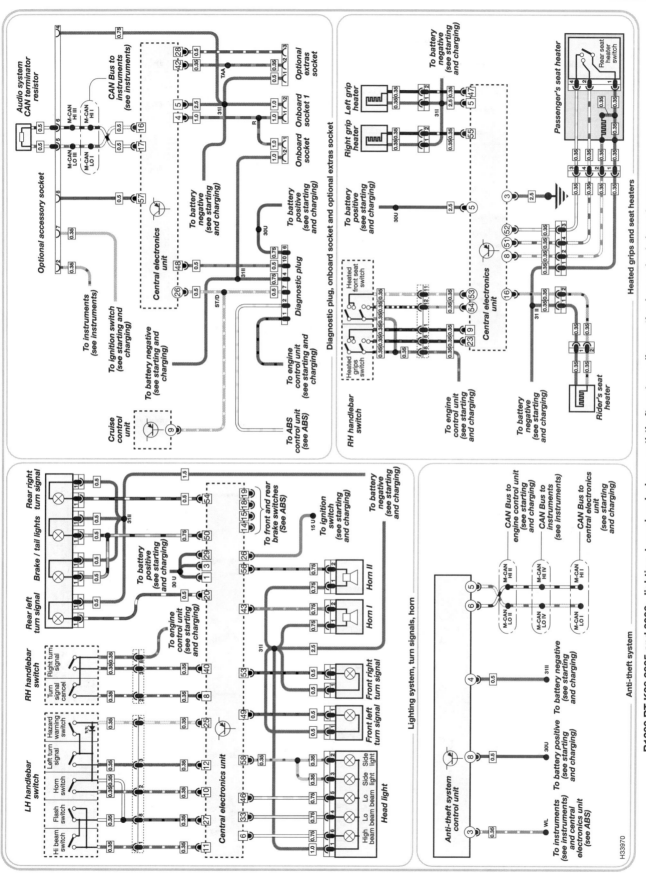

R1200 RT K26 2005 and 2006 - lighting, turn signals, horn, anti-theft system, diagnostic plug and grip/seat heaters

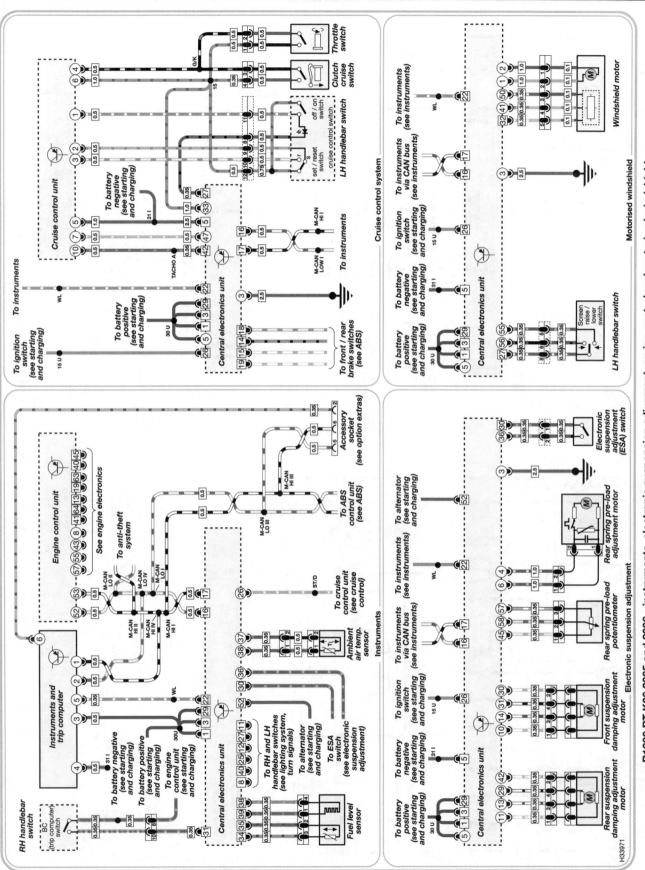

R1200 RT K26 2005 and 2006 - instruments, electronic suspension adjustment, cruise control and motorised windshield

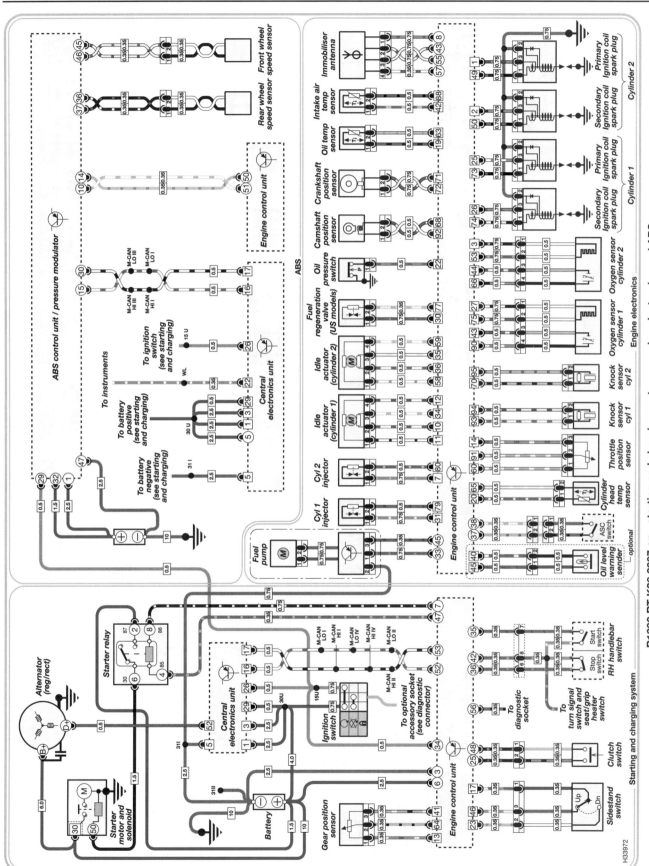

R1200 RT K26 2007 on - starting and charging systems, engine electronics and ABS

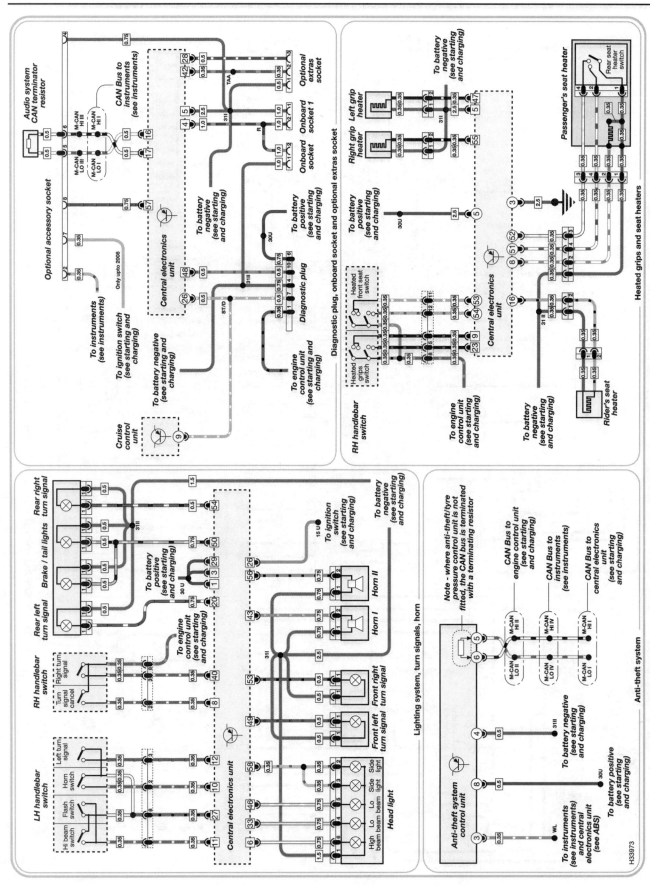

Heated grips and seat heaters

R1200 RT K26 2007 on – lighting, turn signals, horn, anti-theft system, diagnostic plug and grip/seat heaters

Lighting system, turn signals, horn

Anti-theft system

H33973

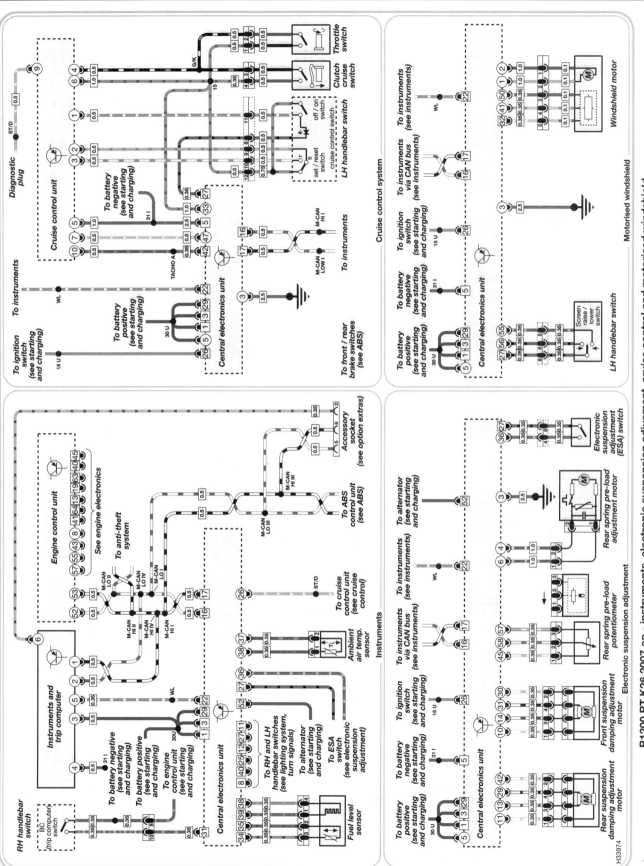

R1200 RT K26 2007 on - instruments, electronic suspension adjusment, cruise control and motorised windshield

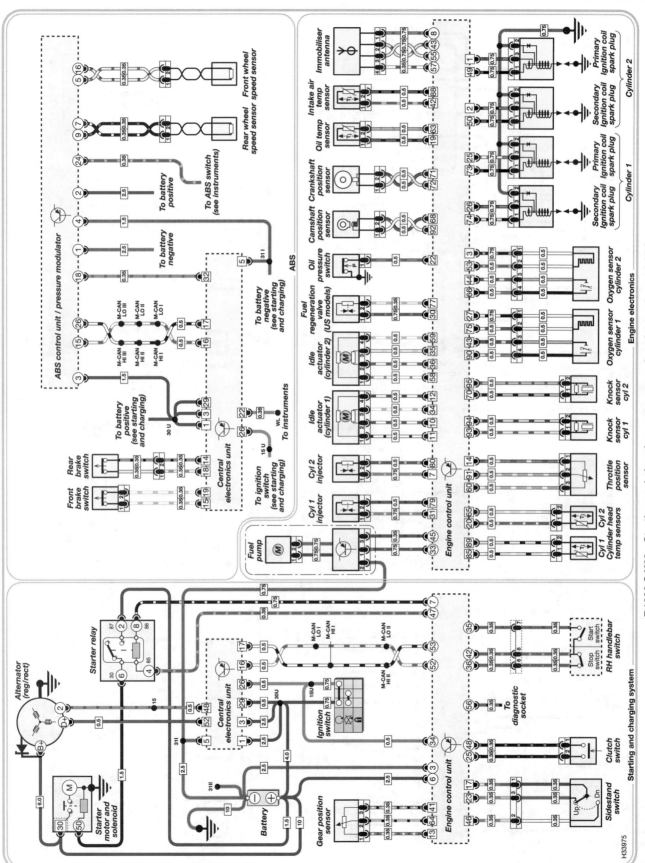

R1200 S K29 - Starting and charging systems, engine electronics and ABS

H33975

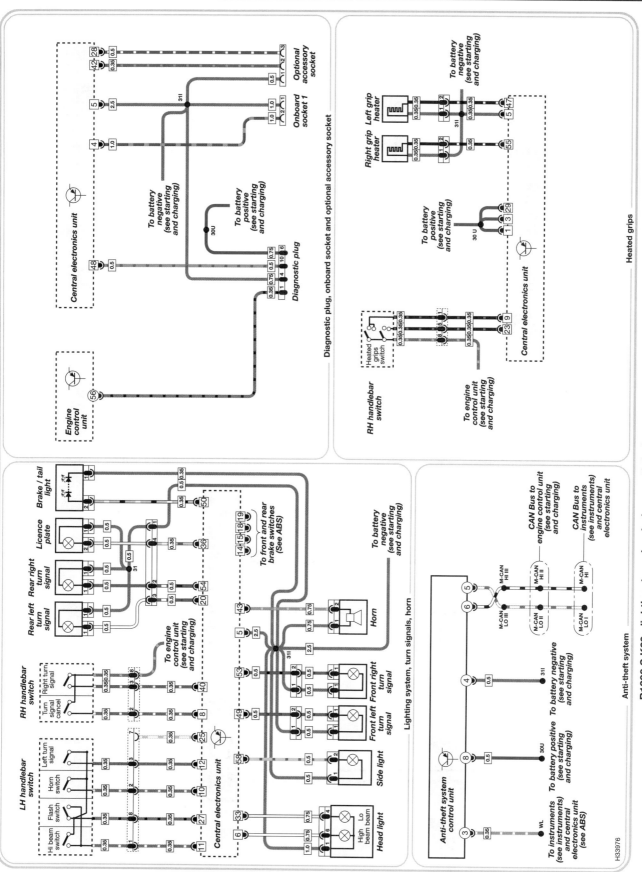

Diagnostic plug, onboard socket and optional accessory socket

Heated grips

Lighting system, turn signals, horn

Anti-theft system

R1200 S K29 - lighting, turn signals, horn, anti-theft system, diagnostic plug and heated grips

H33976

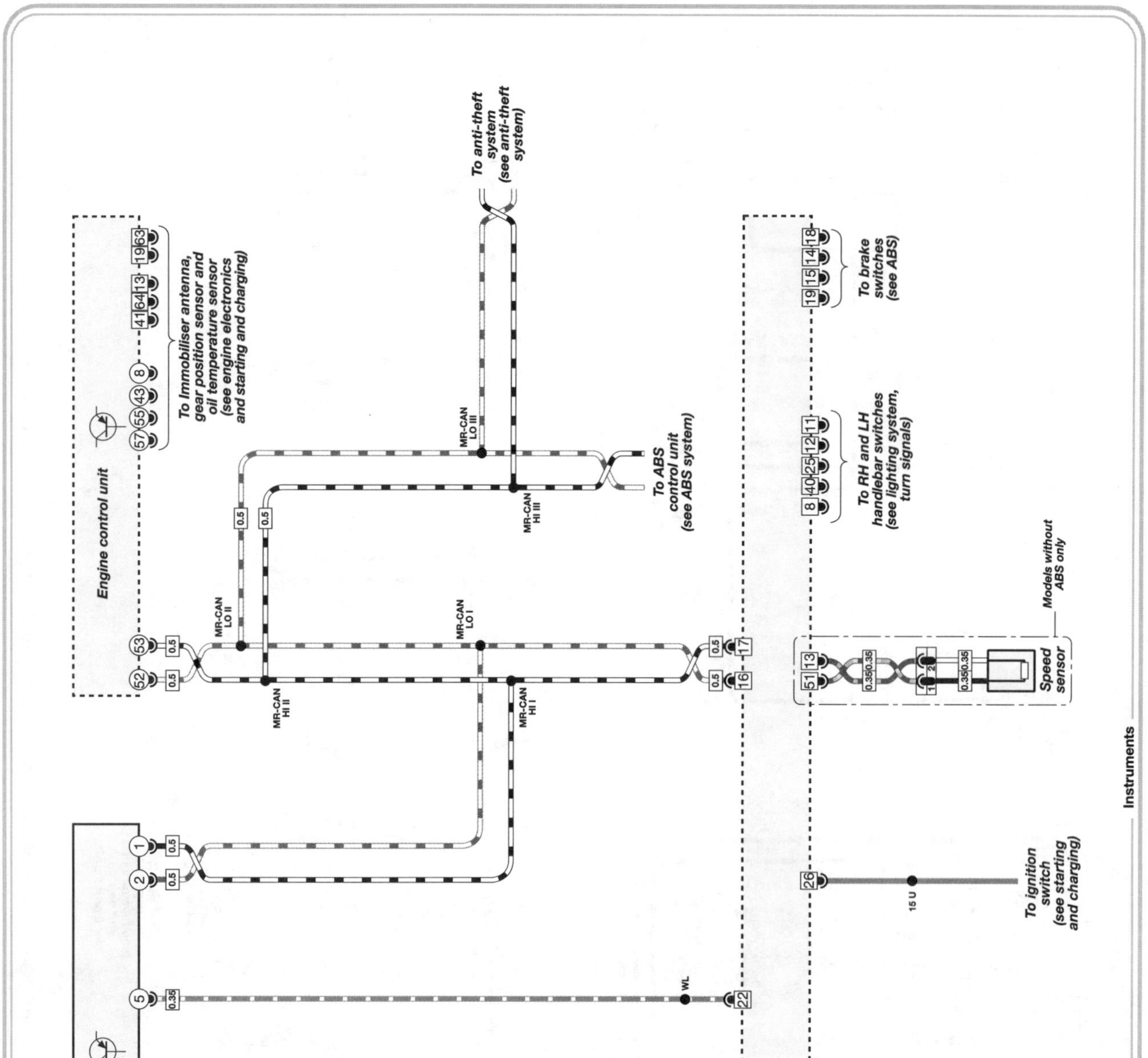

Engine control unit
57 55 43 8
41 64 13 19 63
52 53
To Immobiliser antenna, gear position sensor and oil temperature sensor (see engine electronics and starting and charging)
To anti-theft system (see anti-theft system)
MR-CAN LO III
MR-CAN HI III
To ABS control unit (see ABS system)
MR-CAN LO II
MR-CAN HI II
MR-CAN LO I
MR-CAN HI I
0.5
0.35
Instruments and trip computer
1 2 5 3 4
31 I
To battery negative (see starting and charging)
WL
30 U
15 U
To battery positive (see starting and charging)
To ABS control unit (see ABS)
LH handlebar switch
BC (trip computer) switch
ABS
Central electronics unit
17 16
8 40 25 12 11
19 15 14 18
To brake switches (see ABS)
To RH and LH handlebar switches (see lighting system, turn signals)
51 13
Speed sensor
Models without ABS only
26
To ignition switch (see starting and charging)
22
29 3 1
52
To alternator (see starting and charging)
31 27
21 37
Fuel level sensor
Instruments
H33977

R1200 S K29 - instruments

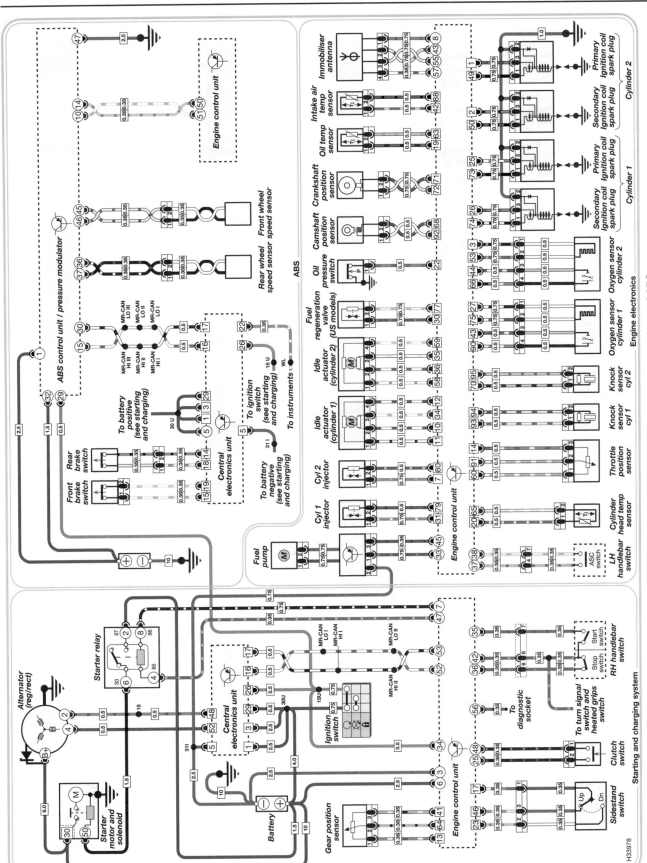

R1200 R K27 - starting and charging, engine electronics and ABS

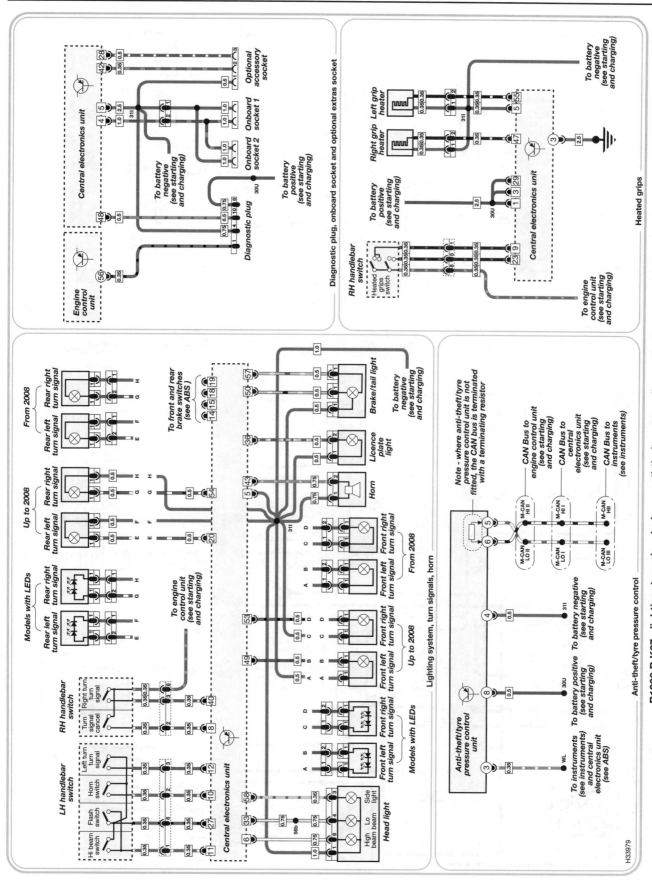

R1200 R K27 - lighting, turn signals, horn, anti-theft system, diagnostic plug and heated grips

H33979

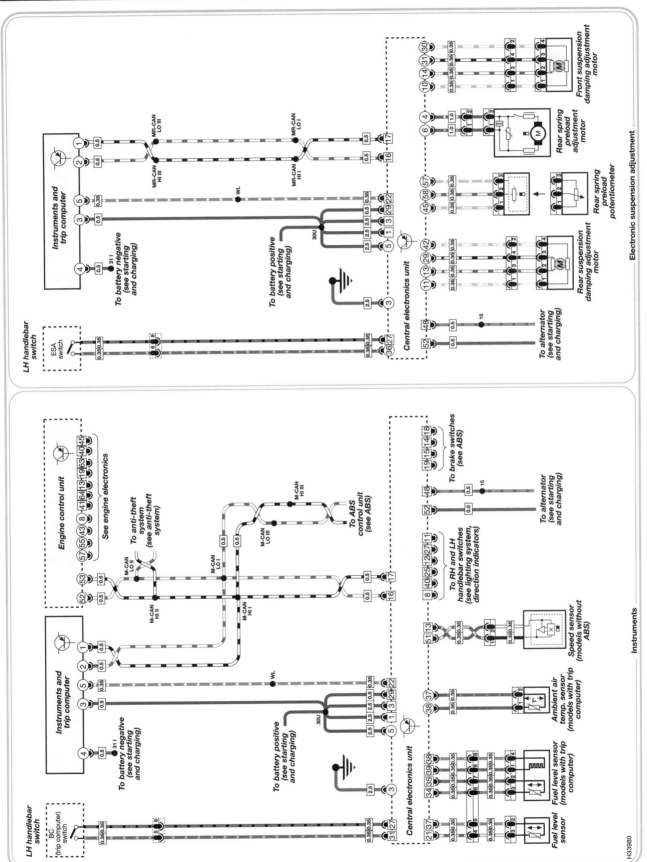

Electronic suspension adjustment

Instruments

R1200 R K27 - instruments and electronic suspension adjustment

H33980

Notes

Reference

Tools and Workshop Tips REF•2

- Building up a tool kit and equipping your workshop ● Using tools ● Understanding bearing, seal, fastener and chain sizes and markings ● Repair techniques

Security REF•20

- Locks and chains ● U-locks ● Disc locks ● Alarms and immobilisers ● Security marking systems ● Tips on how to prevent bike theft

Lubricants and fluids REF•23

- Engine oils ● Transmission (gear) oils ● Coolant/anti-freeze ● Fork oils and suspension fluids ● Brake/clutch fluids ● Spray lubes, degreasers and solvents

Conversion Factors REF•26

$$34 \text{ Nm} \times 0.738$$
$$= 25 \text{ lbf ft}$$

- Formulae for conversion of the metric (SI) units used throughout the manual into Imperial measures

MOT Test Checks REF•27

- A guide to the UK MOT test ● Which items are tested ● How to prepare your motorcycle for the test and perform a pre-test check

Storage REF•32

- How to prepare your motorcycle for going into storage and protect essential systems ● How to get the motorcycle back on the road

Fault Finding REF•35

- Common faults and their likely causes ● How to check engine cylinder compression ● How to make electrical tests and use test meters

Technical Terms Explained REF•43

- Component names, technical terms and common abbreviations explained

Index REF•47

Buying tools

A toolkit is a fundamental requirement for servicing and repairing a motorcycle. Although there will be an initial expense in building up enough tools for servicing, this will soon be offset by the savings made by doing the job yourself. As experience and confidence grow, additional tools can be added to enable the repair and overhaul of the motorcycle. Many of the specialist tools are expensive and not often used so it may be preferable to hire them, or for a group of friends or motorcycle club to join in the purchase.

As a rule, it is better to buy more expensive, good quality tools. Cheaper tools are likely to wear out faster and need to be renewed more often, nullifying the original saving.

> **Warning: To avoid the risk of a poor quality tool breaking in use, causing injury or damage to the component being worked on, always aim to purchase tools which meet the relevant national safety standards.**

The following lists of tools do not represent the manufacturer's service tools, but serve as a guide to help the owner decide which tools are needed for this level of work. In addition, items such as an electric drill, hacksaw, files, soldering iron and a workbench equipped with a vice, may be needed. Although not classed as tools, a selection of bolts, screws, nuts, washers and pieces of tubing always come in useful.

For more information about tools, refer to the Haynes *Motorcycle Workshop Practice Techbook* (Bk. No. 3470).

Manufacturer's service tools

Inevitably certain tasks require the use of a service tool. Where possible an alternative tool or method of approach is recommended, but sometimes there is no option if personal injury or damage to the component is to be avoided. Where required, service tools are referred to in the relevant procedure.

Service tools can usually only be purchased from a motorcycle dealer and are identified by a part number. Some of the commonly-used tools, such as rotor pullers, are available in aftermarket form from mail-order motorcycle tool and accessory suppliers.

Maintenance and minor repair tools

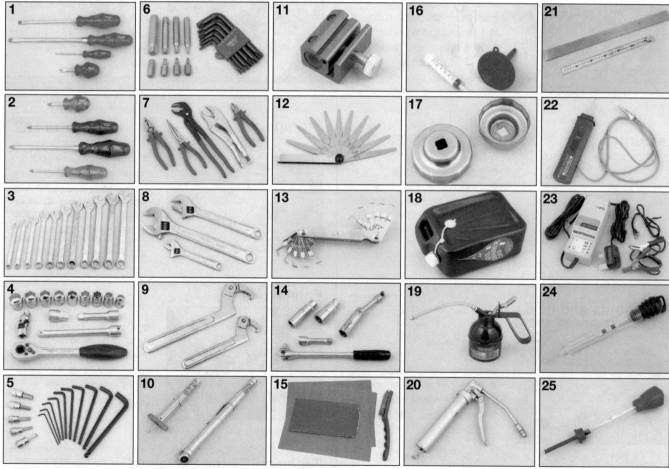

1 Set of flat-bladed screwdrivers
2 Set of Phillips head screwdrivers
3 Combination open-end and ring spanners
4 Socket set (3/8 inch or 1/2 inch drive)
5 Set of Allen keys or bits

6 Set of Torx keys or bits
7 Pliers, cutters and self-locking grips (Mole grips)
8 Adjustable spanners
9 C-spanners
10 Tread depth gauge and tyre pressure gauge

11 Cable oiler clamp
12 Feeler gauges
13 Spark plug gap measuring tool
14 Spark plug spanner or deep plug sockets
15 Wire brush and emery paper

16 Calibrated syringe, measuring vessel and funnel
17 Oil filter adapters
18 Oil drainer can or tray
19 Pump type oil can
20 Grease gun

21 Straight-edge and steel rule
22 Continuity tester
23 Battery charger
24 Hydrometer (for battery specific gravity check)
25 Anti-freeze tester (for liquid-cooled engines)

Repair and overhaul tools

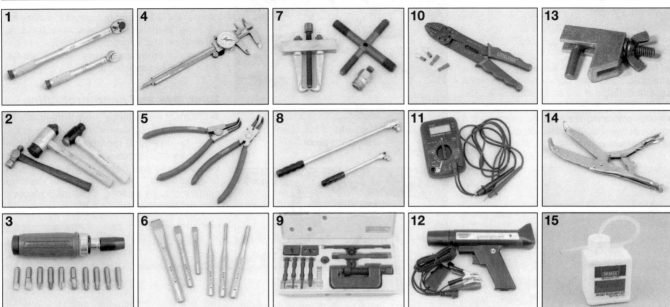

1 Torque wrench
   (small and mid-ranges)
2 Conventional, plastic or
   soft-faced hammers
3 Impact driver set

4 Vernier gauge
5 Circlip pliers (internal and
   external, or combination)
6 Set of cold chisels
   and punches

7 Selection of pullers
8 Breaker bars
9 Chain breaking/
   riveting tool set

10 Wire stripper and
    crimper tool
11 Multimeter (measures
    amps, volts and ohms)
12 Stroboscope (for
    dynamic timing checks)

13 Hose clamp
    (wingnut type shown)
14 Clutch holding tool
15 One-man brake/clutch
    bleeder kit

Specialist tools

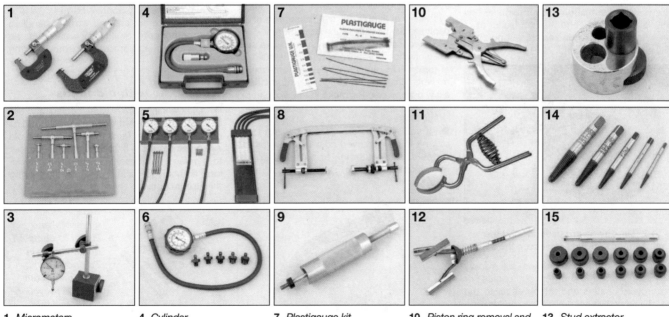

1 Micrometers
   (external type)
2 Telescoping gauges
3 Dial gauge

4 Cylinder
   compression gauge
5 Vacuum gauges (left) or
   manometer (right)
6 Oil pressure gauge

7 Plastigauge kit
8 Valve spring compressor
   (4-stroke engines)
9 Piston pin drawbolt tool

10 Piston ring removal and
    installation tool
11 Piston ring clamp
12 Cylinder bore hone
    (stone type shown)

13 Stud extractor
14 Screw extractor set
15 Bearing driver set

1 Workshop equipment and facilities

The workbench

● Work is made much easier by raising the bike up on a ramp - components are much more accessible if raised to waist level. The hydraulic or pneumatic types seen in the dealer's workshop are a sound investment if you undertake a lot of repairs or overhauls **(see illustration 1.1)**.

1.1 Hydraulic motorcycle ramp

● If raised off ground level, the bike must be supported on the ramp to avoid it falling. Most ramps incorporate a front wheel locating clamp which can be adjusted to suit different diameter wheels. When tightening the clamp, take care not to mark the wheel rim or damage the tyre - use wood blocks on each side to prevent this.
● Secure the bike to the ramp using tie-downs **(see illustration 1.2)**. If the bike has only a sidestand, and hence leans at a dangerous angle when raised, support the bike on an auxiliary stand.

1.2 Tie-downs are used around the passenger footrests to secure the bike

● Auxiliary (paddock) stands are widely available from mail order companies or motorcycle dealers and attach either to the wheel axle or swingarm pivot **(see illustration 1.3)**. If the motorcycle has a centrestand, you can support it under the crankcase to prevent it toppling whilst either wheel is removed **(see illustration 1.4)**.

1.3 This auxiliary stand attaches to the swingarm pivot

1.4 Always use a block of wood between the engine and jack head when supporting the engine in this way

Fumes and fire

● Refer to the Safety first! page at the beginning of the manual for full details. Make sure your workshop is equipped with a fire extinguisher suitable for fuel-related fires (Class B fire - flammable liquids) - it is not sufficient to have a water-filled extinguisher.
● Always ensure adequate ventilation is available. Unless an exhaust gas extraction system is available for use, ensure that the engine is run outside of the workshop.
● If working on the fuel system, make sure the workshop is ventilated to avoid a build-up of fumes. This applies equally to fume build-up when charging a battery. Do not smoke or allow anyone else to smoke in the workshop.

Fluids

● If you need to drain fuel from the tank, store it in an approved container marked as suitable for the storage of petrol (gasoline) **(see illustration 1.5)**. Do not store fuel in glass jars or bottles.

1.5 Use an approved can only for storing petrol (gasoline)

● Use proprietary engine degreasers or solvents which have a high flash-point, such as paraffin (kerosene), for cleaning off oil, grease and dirt - never use petrol (gasoline) for cleaning. Wear rubber gloves when handling solvent and engine degreaser. The fumes from certain solvents can be dangerous - always work in a well-ventilated area.

Dust, eye and hand protection

● Protect your lungs from inhalation of dust particles by wearing a filtering mask over the nose and mouth. Many frictional materials still contain asbestos which is dangerous to your health. Protect your eyes from spouts of liquid and sprung components by wearing a pair of protective goggles **(see illustration 1.6)**.

1.6 A fire extinguisher, goggles, mask and protective gloves should be at hand in the workshop

● Protect your hands from contact with solvents, fuel and oils by wearing rubber gloves. Alternatively apply a barrier cream to your hands before starting work. If handling hot components or fluids, wear suitable gloves to protect your hands from scalding and burns.

What to do with old fluids

● Old cleaning solvent, fuel, coolant and oils should not be poured down domestic drains or onto the ground. Package the fluid up in old oil containers, label it accordingly, and take it to a garage or disposal facility. Contact your local authority for location of such sites or ring the oil care hotline.

OIL CARE
FOLLOW THE CODE
OIL BANK LINE
0800 66 33 66
www.oilbankline.org.uk

Note: It is antisocial and illegal to dump oil down the drain. To find the location of your local oil recycling bank, call this number free.

In the USA, note that any oil supplier must accept used oil for recycling.

2 Fasteners -
screws, bolts and nuts

Fastener types and applications

Bolts and screws

● Fastener head types are either of hexagonal, Torx or splined design, with internal and external versions of each type **(see illustrations 2.1 and 2.2)**; splined head fasteners are not in common use on motorcycles. The conventional slotted or Phillips head design is used for certain screws. Bolt or screw length is always measured from the underside of the head to the end of the item **(see illustration 2.11)**.

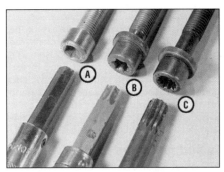

2.1 Internal hexagon/Allen (A), Torx (B) and splined (C) fasteners, with corresponding bits

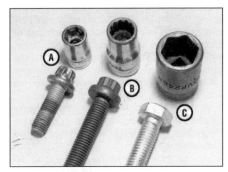

2.2 External Torx (A), splined (B) and hexagon (C) fasteners, with corresponding sockets

● Certain fasteners on the motorcycle have a tensile marking on their heads, the higher the marking the stronger the fastener. High tensile fasteners generally carry a 10 or higher marking. Never replace a high tensile fastener with one of a lower tensile strength.

Washers (see illustration 2.3)

● Plain washers are used between a fastener head and a component to prevent damage to the component or to spread the load when torque is applied. Plain washers can also be used as spacers or shims in certain assemblies. Copper or aluminium plain washers are often used as sealing washers on drain plugs.

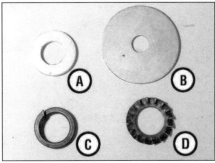

2.3 Plain washer (A), penny washer (B), spring washer (C) and serrated washer (D)

● The split-ring spring washer works by applying axial tension between the fastener head and component. If flattened, it is fatigued and must be renewed. If a plain (flat) washer is used on the fastener, position the spring washer between the fastener and the plain washer.
● Serrated star type washers dig into the fastener and component faces, preventing loosening. They are often used on electrical earth (ground) connections to the frame.
● Cone type washers (sometimes called Belleville) are conical and when tightened apply axial tension between the fastener head and component. They must be installed with the dished side against the component and often carry an OUTSIDE marking on their outer face. If flattened, they are fatigued and must be renewed.
● Tab washers are used to lock plain nuts or bolts on a shaft. A portion of the tab washer is bent up hard against one flat of the nut or bolt to prevent it loosening. Due to the tab washer being deformed in use, a new tab washer should be used every time it is disturbed.
● Wave washers are used to take up endfloat on a shaft. They provide light springing and prevent excessive side-to-side play of a component. Can be found on rocker arm shafts.

Nuts and split pins

● Conventional plain nuts are usually six-sided **(see illustration 2.4)**. They are sized by thread diameter and pitch. High tensile nuts carry a number on one end to denote their tensile strength.

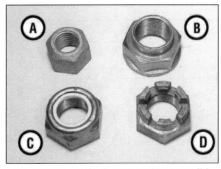

2.4 Plain nut (A), shouldered locknut (B), nylon insert nut (C) and castellated nut (D)

● Self-locking nuts either have a nylon insert, or two spring metal tabs, or a shoulder which is staked into a groove in the shaft - their advantage over conventional plain nuts is a resistance to loosening due to vibration. The nylon insert type can be used a number of times, but must be renewed when the friction of the nylon insert is reduced, ie when the nut spins freely on the shaft. The spring tab type can be reused unless the tabs are damaged. The shouldered type must be renewed every time it is disturbed.
● Split pins (cotter pins) are used to lock a castellated nut to a shaft or to prevent slackening of a plain nut. Common applications are wheel axles and brake torque arms. Because the split pin arms are deformed to lock around the nut a new split pin must always be used on installation - always fit the correct size split pin which will fit snugly in the shaft hole. Make sure the split pin arms are correctly located around the nut **(see illustrations 2.5 and 2.6)**.

2.5 Bend split pin (cotter pin) arms as shown (arrows) to secure a castellated nut

2.6 Bend split pin (cotter pin) arms as shown to secure a plain nut

Caution: If the castellated nut slots do not align with the shaft hole after tightening to the torque setting, tighten the nut until the next slot aligns with the hole - never slacken the nut to align its slot.

● R-pins (shaped like the letter R), or slip pins as they are sometimes called, are sprung and can be reused if they are otherwise in good condition. Always install R-pins with their closed end facing forwards **(see illustration 2.7)**.

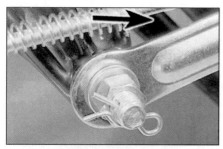

**2.7 Correct fitting of R-pin.
Arrow indicates forward direction**

Circlips (see illustration 2.8)

● Circlips (sometimes called snap-rings) are used to retain components on a shaft or in a housing and have corresponding external or internal ears to permit removal. Parallel-sided (machined) circlips can be installed either way round in their groove, whereas stamped circlips (which have a chamfered edge on one face) must be installed with the chamfer facing away from the direction of thrust load **(see illustration 2.9)**.

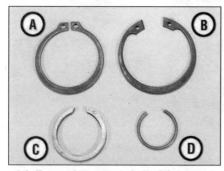

2.8 External stamped circlip (A), internal stamped circlip (B), machined circlip (C) and wire circlip (D)

● Always use circlip pliers to remove and install circlips; expand or compress them just enough to remove them. After installation, rotate the circlip in its groove to ensure it is securely seated. If installing a circlip on a splined shaft, always align its opening with a shaft channel to ensure the circlip ends are well supported and unlikely to catch **(see illustration 2.10)**.

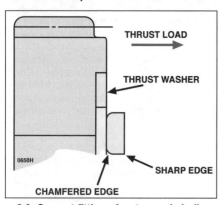

2.9 Correct fitting of a stamped circlip

THRUST LOAD

THRUST WASHER

SHARP EDGE

CHAMFERED EDGE

0650H

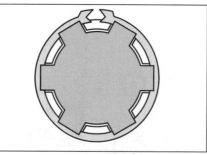

**2.10 Align circlip opening
with shaft channel**

● Circlips can wear due to the thrust of components and become loose in their grooves, with the subsequent danger of becoming dislodged in operation. For this reason, renewal is advised every time a circlip is disturbed.

● Wire circlips are commonly used as piston pin retaining clips. If a removal tang is provided, long-nosed pliers can be used to dislodge them, otherwise careful use of a small flat-bladed screwdriver is necessary. Wire circlips should be renewed every time they are disturbed.

Thread diameter and pitch

● Diameter of a male thread (screw, bolt or stud) is the outside diameter of the threaded portion **(see illustration 2.11)**. Most motorcycle manufacturers use the ISO (International Standards Organisation) metric system expressed in millimetres, eg M6 refers to a 6 mm diameter thread. Sizing is the same for nuts, except that the thread diameter is measured across the valleys of the nut.

● Pitch is the distance between the peaks of the thread **(see illustration 2.11)**. It is expressed in millimetres, thus a common bolt size may be expressed as 6.0 x 1.0 mm (6 mm thread diameter and 1 mm pitch). Generally pitch increases in proportion to thread diameter, although there are always exceptions.

● Thread diameter and pitch are related for conventional fastener applications and the accompanying table can be used as a guide. Additionally, the AF (Across Flats), spanner or socket size dimension of the bolt or nut **(see illustration 2.11)** is linked to thread and pitch specification. Thread pitch can be measured with a thread gauge **(see illustration 2.12)**.

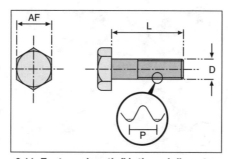

2.11 Fastener length (L), thread diameter (D), thread pitch (P) and head size (AF)

**2.12 Using a thread gauge
to measure pitch**

AF size	Thread diameter x pitch (mm)
8 mm	M5 x 0.8
8 mm	M6 x 1.0
10 mm	M6 x 1.0
12 mm	M8 x 1.25
14 mm	M10 x 1.25
17 mm	M12 x 1.25

● The threads of most fasteners are of the right-hand type, ie they are turned clockwise to tighten and anti-clockwise to loosen. The reverse situation applies to left-hand thread fasteners, which are turned anti-clockwise to tighten and clockwise to loosen. Left-hand threads are used where rotation of a component might loosen a conventional right-hand thread fastener.

Seized fasteners

● Corrosion of external fasteners due to water or reaction between two dissimilar metals can occur over a period of time. It will build up sooner in wet conditions or in countries where salt is used on the roads during the winter. If a fastener is severely corroded it is likely that normal methods of removal will fail and result in its head being ruined. When you attempt removal, the fastener thread should be heard to crack free and unscrew easily - if it doesn't, stop there before damaging something.

● A smart tap on the head of the fastener will often succeed in breaking free corrosion which has occurred in the threads **(see illustration 2.13)**.

● An aerosol penetrating fluid (such as WD-40) applied the night beforehand may work its way down into the thread and ease removal. Depending on the location, you may be able to make up a Plasticine well around the fastener head and fill it with penetrating fluid.

2.13 A sharp tap on the head of a fastener will often break free a corroded thread

● If you are working on an engine internal component, corrosion will most likely not be a problem due to the well lubricated environment. However, components can be very tight and an impact driver is a useful tool in freeing them (see illustration 2.14).

2.14 Using an impact driver to free a fastener

● Where corrosion has occurred between dissimilar metals (eg steel and aluminium alloy), the application of heat to the fastener head will create a disproportionate expansion rate between the two metals and break the seizure caused by the corrosion. Whether heat can be applied depends on the location of the fastener - any surrounding components likely to be damaged must first be removed (see illustration 2.15). Heat can be applied using a paint stripper heat gun or clothes iron, or by immersing the component in boiling water - wear protective gloves to prevent scalding or burns to the hands.

2.15 Using heat to free a seized fastener

● As a last resort, it is possible to use a hammer and cold chisel to work the fastener head unscrewed (see illustration 2.16). This will damage the fastener, but more importantly extreme care must be taken not to damage the surrounding component.

> *Caution: Remember that the component being secured is generally of more value than the bolt, nut or screw - when the fastener is freed, do not unscrew it with force, instead work the fastener back and forth when resistance is felt to prevent thread damage.*

2.16 Using a hammer and chisel to free a seized fastener

Broken fasteners and damaged heads

● If the shank of a broken bolt or screw is accessible you can grip it with self-locking grips. The knurled wheel type stud extractor tool or self-gripping stud puller tool is particularly useful for removing the long studs which screw into the cylinder mouth surface of the crankcase or bolts and screws from which the head has broken off (see illustration 2.17). Studs can also be removed by locking two nuts together on the threaded end of the stud and using a spanner on the lower nut (see illustration 2.18).

2.17 Using a stud extractor tool to remove a broken crankcase stud

2.18 Two nuts can be locked together to unscrew a stud from a component

● A bolt or screw which has broken off below or level with the casing must be extracted using a screw extractor set. Centre punch the fastener to centralise the drill bit, then drill a hole in the fastener (see illustration 2.19). Select a drill bit which is approximately half to three-quarters the

2.19 When using a screw extractor, first drill a hole in the fastener . . .

diameter of the fastener and drill to a depth which will accommodate the extractor. Use the largest size extractor possible, but avoid leaving too small a wall thickness otherwise the extractor will merely force the fastener walls outwards wedging it in the casing thread.

● If a spiral type extractor is used, thread it anti-clockwise into the fastener. As it is screwed in, it will grip the fastener and unscrew it from the casing (see illustration 2.20).

2.20 . . . then thread the extractor anti-clockwise into the fastener

● If a taper type extractor is used, tap it into the fastener so that it is firmly wedged in place. Unscrew the extractor (anti-clockwise) to draw the fastener out.

> ⚠ *Warning: Stud extractors are very hard and may break off in the fastener if care is not taken - ask an engineer about spark erosion if this happens.*

● Alternatively, the broken bolt/screw can be drilled out and the hole retapped for an oversize bolt/screw or a diamond-section thread insert. It is essential that the drilling is carried out squarely and to the correct depth, otherwise the casing may be ruined - if in doubt, entrust the work to an engineer.

● Bolts and nuts with rounded corners cause the correct size spanner or socket to slip when force is applied. Of the types of spanner/socket available always use a six-point type rather than an eight or twelve-point type - better grip

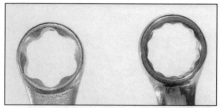

2.21 Comparison of surface drive ring spanner (left) with 12-point type (right)

is obtained. Surface drive spanners grip the middle of the hex flats, rather than the corners, and are thus good in cases of damaged heads **(see illustration 2.21)**.

● Slotted-head or Phillips-head screws are often damaged by the use of the wrong size screwdriver. Allen-head and Torx-head screws are much less likely to sustain damage. If enough of the screw head is exposed you can use a hacksaw to cut a slot in its head and then use a conventional flat-bladed screwdriver to remove it. Alternatively use a hammer and cold chisel to tap the head of the fastener around to slacken it. Always replace damaged fasteners with new ones, preferably Torx or Allen-head type.

HAYNES HiNT

A dab of valve grinding compound between the screw head and screw-driver tip will often give a good grip.

Thread repair

● Threads (particularly those in aluminium alloy components) can be damaged by overtightening, being assembled with dirt in the threads, or from a component working loose and vibrating. Eventually the thread will fail completely, and it will be impossible to tighten the fastener.

● If a thread is damaged or clogged with old locking compound it can be renovated with a thread repair tool (thread chaser) **(see illustrations 2.22 and 2.23)**; special thread

2.22 A thread repair tool being used to correct an internal thread

2.23 A thread repair tool being used to correct an external thread

chasers are available for spark plug hole threads. The tool will not cut a new thread, but clean and true the original thread. Make sure that you use the correct diameter and pitch tool. Similarly, external threads can be cleaned up with a die or a thread restorer file **(see illustration 2.24)**.

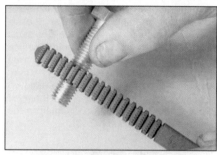

2.24 Using a thread restorer file

● It is possible to drill out the old thread and retap the component to the next thread size. This will work where there is enough surrounding material and a new bolt or screw can be obtained. Sometimes, however, this is not possible - such as where the bolt/screw passes through another component which must also be suitably modified, also in cases where a spark plug or oil drain plug cannot be obtained in a larger diameter thread size.

● The diamond-section thread insert (often known by its popular trade name of Heli-Coil) is a simple and effective method of renewing the thread and retaining the original size. A kit can be purchased which contains the tap, insert and installing tool **(see illustration 2.25)**. Drill out the damaged thread with the size drill specified **(see illustration 2.26)**. Carefully retap the thread **(see illustration 2.27)**. Install the

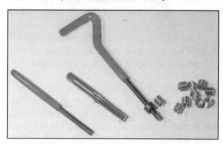

2.25 Obtain a thread insert kit to suit the thread diameter and pitch required

2.26 To install a thread insert, first drill out the original thread . . .

2.27 . . . tap a new thread . . .

2.28 . . . fit insert on the installing tool . . .

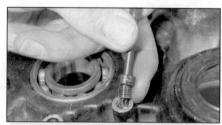

2.29 . . . and thread into the component . . .

2.30 . . . break off the tang when complete

insert on the installing tool and thread it slowly into place using a light downward pressure **(see illustrations 2.28 and 2.29)**. When positioned between a 1/4 and 1/2 turn below the surface withdraw the installing tool and use the break-off tool to press down on the tang, breaking it off **(see illustration 2.30)**.

● There are epoxy thread repair kits on the market which can rebuild stripped internal threads, although this repair should not be used on high load-bearing components.

Thread locking and sealing compounds

● Locking compounds are used in locations where the fastener is prone to loosening due to vibration or on important safety-related items which might cause loss of control of the motorcycle if they fail. It is also used where important fasteners cannot be secured by other means such as lockwashers or split pins.

● Before applying locking compound, make sure that the threads (internal and external) are clean and dry with all old compound removed. Select a compound to suit the component being secured - a non-permanent general locking and sealing type is suitable for most applications, but a high strength type is needed for permanent fixing of studs in castings. Apply a drop or two of the compound to the first few threads of the fastener, then thread it into place and tighten to the specified torque. Do not apply excessive thread locking compound otherwise the thread may be damaged on subsequent removal.

● Certain fasteners are impregnated with a dry film type coating of locking compound on their threads. Always renew this type of fastener if disturbed.

● Anti-seize compounds, such as copper-based greases, can be applied to protect threads from seizure due to extreme heat and corrosion. A common instance is spark plug threads and exhaust system fasteners.

3 Measuring tools and gauges

Feeler gauges

● Feeler gauges (or blades) are used for measuring small gaps and clearances **(see illustration 3.1)**. They can also be used to measure endfloat (sideplay) of a component on a shaft where access is not possible with a dial gauge.

● Feeler gauge sets should be treated with care and not bent or damaged. They are etched with their size on one face. Keep them clean and very lightly oiled to prevent corrosion build-up.

3.1 Feeler gauges are used for measuring small gaps and clearances - thickness is marked on one face of gauge

● When measuring a clearance, select a gauge which is a light sliding fit between the two components. You may need to use two gauges together to measure the clearance accurately.

Micrometers

● A micrometer is a precision tool capable of measuring to 0.01 or 0.001 of a millimetre. It should always be stored in its case and not in the general toolbox. It must be kept clean and never dropped, otherwise its frame or measuring anvils could be distorted resulting in inaccurate readings.

● External micrometers are used for measuring outside diameters of components and have many more applications than internal micrometers. Micrometers are available in different size ranges, eg 0 to 25 mm, 25 to 50 mm, and upwards in 25 mm steps; some large micrometers have interchangeable anvils to allow a range of measurements to be taken. Generally the largest precision measurement you are likely to take on a motorcycle is the piston diameter.

● Internal micrometers (or bore micrometers) are used for measuring inside diameters, such as valve guides and cylinder bores. Telescoping gauges and small hole gauges are used in conjunction with an external micro-meter, whereas the more expensive internal micrometers have their own measuring device.

External micrometer

Note: *The conventional analogue type instrument is described. Although much easier to read, digital micrometers are considerably more expensive.*

● Always check the calibration of the micrometer before use. With the anvils closed (0 to 25 mm type) or set over a test gauge (for

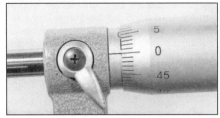

3.2 Check micrometer calibration before use

the larger types) the scale should read zero **(see illustration 3.2)**; make sure that the anvils (and test piece) are clean first. Any discrepancy can be adjusted by referring to the instructions supplied with the tool. Remember that the micrometer is a precision measuring tool - don't force the anvils closed, use the ratchet (4) on the end of the micrometer to close it. In this way, a measured force is always applied.

● To use, first make sure that the item being measured is clean. Place the anvil of the micrometer (1) against the item and use the thimble (2) to bring the spindle (3) lightly into contact with the other side of the item **(see illustration 3.3)**. Don't tighten the thimble down because this will damage the micrometer - instead use the ratchet (4) on the end of the micrometer. The ratchet mechanism applies a measured force preventing damage to the instrument.

● The micrometer is read by referring to the linear scale on the sleeve and the annular scale on the thimble. Read off the sleeve first to obtain the base measurement, then add the fine measurement from the thimble to obtain the overall reading. The linear scale on the sleeve represents the measuring range of the micrometer (eg 0 to 25 mm). The annular scale

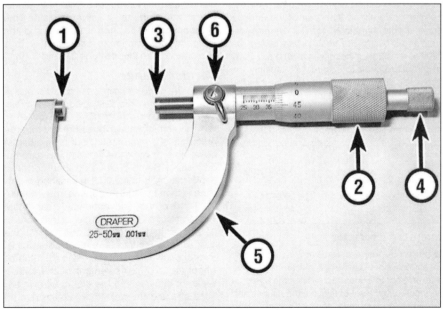

3.3 Micrometer component parts

1 Anvil	3 Spindle	5 Frame
2 Thimble	4 Ratchet	6 Locking lever

on the thimble will be in graduations of 0.01 mm (or as marked on the frame) - one full revolution of the thimble will move 0.5 mm on the linear scale. Take the reading where the datum line on the sleeve intersects the thimble's scale. Always position the eye directly above the scale otherwise an inaccurate reading will result.

In the example shown the item measures 2.95 mm **(see illustration 3.4)**:

Linear scale	2.00 mm
Linear scale	0.50 mm
Annular scale	0.45 mm
Total figure	**2.95 mm**

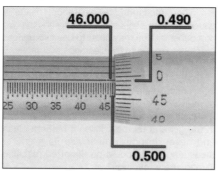

3.5 Micrometer reading of 46.99 mm on linear and annular scales . . .

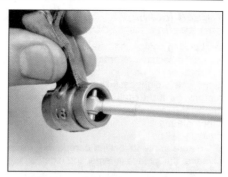

3.7 Expand the telescoping gauge in the bore, lock its position . . .

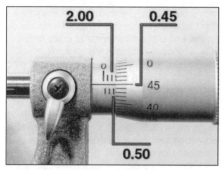

3.4 Micrometer reading of 2.95 mm

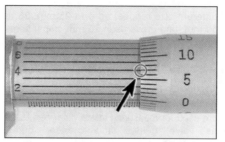

3.6 . . . and 0.004 mm on vernier scale

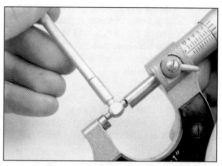

3.8 . . . then measure the gauge with a micrometer

Most micrometers have a locking lever (6) on the frame to hold the setting in place, allowing the item to be removed from the micrometer.
● Some micrometers have a vernier scale on their sleeve, providing an even finer measurement to be taken, in 0.001 increments of a millimetre. Take the sleeve and thimble measurement as described above, then check which graduation on the vernier scale aligns with that of the annular scale on the thimble **Note:** *The eye must be perpendicular to the scale when taking the vernier reading - if necessary rotate the body of the micrometer to ensure this.* Multiply the vernier scale figure by 0.001 and add it to the base and fine measurement figures.

In the example shown the item measures 46.994 mm **(see illustrations 3.5 and 3.6)**:

Linear scale (base)	46.000 mm
Linear scale (base)	00.500 mm
Annular scale (fine)	00.490 mm
Vernier scale	00.004 mm
Total figure	**46.994 mm**

Internal micrometer

● Internal micrometers are available for measuring bore diameters, but are expensive and unlikely to be available for home use. It is suggested that a set of telescoping gauges and small hole gauges, both of which must be used with an external micrometer, will suffice for taking internal measurements on a motorcycle.
● Telescoping gauges can be used to

measure internal diameters of components. Select a gauge with the correct size range, make sure its ends are clean and insert it into the bore. Expand the gauge, then lock its position and withdraw it from the bore **(see illustration 3.7)**. Measure across the gauge ends with a micrometer **(see illustration 3.8)**.
● Very small diameter bores (such as valve guides) are measured with a small hole gauge. Once adjusted to a slip-fit inside the component, its position is locked and the gauge withdrawn for measurement with a micrometer **(see illustrations 3.9 and 3.10)**.

Vernier caliper

Note: *The conventional linear and dial gauge type instruments are described. Digital types are easier to read, but are far more expensive.*
● The vernier caliper does not provide the precision of a micrometer, but is versatile in being able to measure internal and external diameters. Some types also incorporate a depth gauge. It is ideal for measuring clutch plate friction material and spring free lengths.
● To use the conventional linear scale vernier, slacken off the vernier clamp screws (1) and set its jaws over (2), or inside (3), the item to be measured **(see illustration 3.11)**. Slide the jaw into contact, using the thumb-wheel (4) for fine movement of the sliding scale (5) then tighten the clamp screws (1). Read off the main scale (6) where the zero on the sliding scale (5) intersects it, taking the whole number to the left of the zero; this provides the base measurement. View along the sliding scale and select the division which

3.9 Expand the small hole gauge in the bore, lock its position . . .

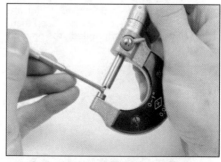

3.10 . . . then measure the gauge with a micrometer

lines up exactly with any of the divisions on the main scale, noting that the divisions usually represents 0.02 of a millimetre. Add this fine measurement to the base measurement to obtain the total reading.

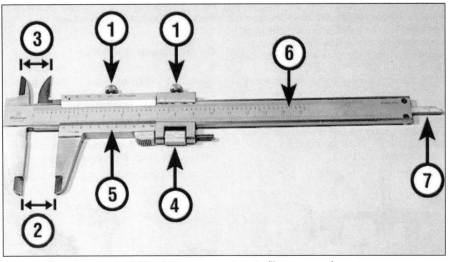

3.11 Vernier component parts (linear gauge)

1 Clamp screws	3 Internal jaws	5 Sliding scale	7 Depth gauge
2 External jaws	4 Thumbwheel	6 Main scale	

In the example shown the item measures 55.92 mm (see illustration 3.12):

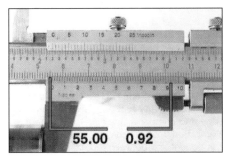

3.12 Vernier gauge reading of 55.92 mm

Base measurement	55.00 mm
Fine measurement	00.92 mm
Total figure	**55.92 mm**

● Some vernier calipers are equipped with a dial gauge for fine measurement. Before use, check that the jaws are clean, then close them fully and check that the dial gauge reads zero. If necessary adjust the gauge ring accordingly. Slacken the vernier clamp screw (1) and set its jaws over (2), or inside (3), the item to be measured (see illustration 3.13). Slide the jaws into contact, using the thumbwheel (4) for fine movement. Read off the main scale (5) where the edge of the sliding scale (6) intersects it, taking the whole number to the left of the zero; this provides the base measurement. Read off the needle position on the dial gauge (7) scale to provide the fine measurement; each division represents 0.05 of a millimetre. Add this fine measurement to the base measurement to obtain the total reading.

In the example shown the item measures 55.95 mm (see illustration 3.14):

Base measurement	55.00 mm
Fine measurement	00.95 mm
Total figure	**55.95 mm**

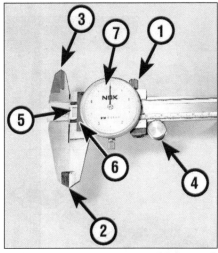

3.13 Vernier component parts (dial gauge)

1 Clamp screw	5 Main scale
2 External jaws	6 Sliding scale
3 Internal jaws	7 Dial gauge
4 Thumbwheel	

3.14 Vernier gauge reading of 55.95 mm

Plastigauge

● Plastigauge is a plastic material which can be compressed between two surfaces to measure the oil clearance between them. The width of the compressed Plastigauge is measured against a calibrated scale to determine the clearance.

● Common uses of Plastigauge are for measuring the clearance between crankshaft journal and main bearing inserts, between crankshaft journal and big-end bearing inserts, and between camshaft and bearing surfaces. The following example describes big-end oil clearance measurement.

● Handle the Plastigauge material carefully to prevent distortion. Using a sharp knife, cut a length which corresponds with the width of the bearing being measured and place it carefully across the journal so that it is parallel with the shaft (see illustration 3.15). Carefully install both bearing shells and the connecting rod. Without rotating the rod on the journal tighten its bolts or nuts (as applicable) to the specified torque. The connecting rod and bearings are then disassembled and the crushed Plastigauge examined.

3.15 Plastigauge placed across shaft journal

● Using the scale provided in the Plastigauge kit, measure the width of the material to determine the oil clearance (see illustration 3.16). Always remove all traces of Plastigauge after use using your fingernails.

Caution: Arriving at the correct clearance demands that the assembly is torqued correctly, according to the settings and sequence (where applicable) provided by the motorcycle manufacturer.

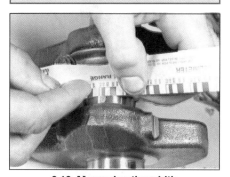

**3.16 Measuring the width
of the crushed Plastigauge**

Dial gauge or DTI (Dial Test Indicator)

● A dial gauge can be used to accurately measure small amounts of movement. Typical uses are measuring shaft runout or shaft endfloat (sideplay) and setting piston position for ignition timing on two-strokes. A dial gauge set usually comes with a range of different probes and adapters and mounting equipment.
● The gauge needle must point to zero when at rest. Rotate the ring around its periphery to zero the gauge.
● Check that the gauge is capable of reading the extent of movement in the work. Most gauges have a small dial set in the face which records whole millimetres of movement as well as the fine scale around the face periphery which is calibrated in 0.01 mm divisions. Read off the small dial first to obtain the base measurement, then add the measurement from the fine scale to obtain the total reading.

In the example shown the gauge reads 1.48 mm (see illustration 3.17):

Base measurement	1.00 mm
Fine measurement	0.48 mm
Total figure	**1.48 mm**

3.17 Dial gauge reading of 1.48 mm

● If measuring shaft runout, the shaft must be supported in vee-blocks and the gauge mounted on a stand perpendicular to the shaft. Rest the tip of the gauge against the centre of the shaft and rotate the shaft slowly whilst watching the gauge reading (see illustration 3.18). Take several measurements along the length of the shaft and record the

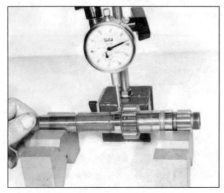

3.18 Using a dial gauge to measure shaft runout

maximum gauge reading as the amount of runout in the shaft. **Note:** *The reading obtained will be total runout at that point - some manufacturers specify that the runout figure is halved to compare with their specified runout limit.*
● Endfloat (sideplay) measurement requires that the gauge is mounted securely to the surrounding component with its probe touching the end of the shaft. Using hand pressure, push and pull on the shaft noting the maximum endfloat recorded on the gauge (see illustration 3.19).

3.19 Using a dial gauge to measure shaft endfloat

● A dial gauge with suitable adapters can be used to determine piston position BTDC on two-stroke engines for the purposes of ignition timing. The gauge, adapter and suitable length probe are installed in the place of the spark plug and the gauge zeroed at TDC. If the piston position is specified as 1.14 mm BTDC, rotate the engine back to 2.00 mm BTDC, then slowly forwards to 1.14 mm BTDC.

Cylinder compression gauges

● A compression gauge is used for measuring cylinder compression. Either the rubber-cone type or the threaded adapter type can be used. The latter is preferred to ensure a perfect seal against the cylinder head. A 0 to 300 psi (0 to 20 Bar) type gauge (for petrol/gasoline engines) will be suitable for motorcycles.
● The spark plug is removed and the gauge either held hard against the cylinder head (cone type) or the gauge adapter screwed into the cylinder head (threaded type) (see illustration 3.20). Cylinder compression is measured with the engine turning over, but not running - carry out the compression test as described in

3.20 Using a rubber-cone type cylinder compression gauge

Fault Finding Equipment. The gauge will hold the reading until manually released.

Oil pressure gauge

● An oil pressure gauge is used for measuring engine oil pressure. Most gauges come with a set of adapters to fit the thread of the take-off point (see illustration 3.21). If the take-off point specified by the motorcycle manufacturer is an external oil pipe union, make sure that the specified replacement union is used to prevent oil starvation.

3.21 Oil pressure gauge and take-off point adapter (arrow)

● Oil pressure is measured with the engine running (at a specific rpm) and often the manufacturer will specify pressure limits for a cold and hot engine.

Straight-edge and surface plate

● If checking the gasket face of a component for warpage, place a steel rule or precision straight-edge across the gasket face and measure any gap between the straight-edge and component with feeler gauges (see illustration 3.22). Check diagonally across the component and between mounting holes (see illustration 3.23).

3.22 Use a straight-edge and feeler gauges to check for warpage

3.23 Check for warpage in these directions

● Checking individual components for warpage, such as clutch plain (metal) plates, requires a perfectly flat plate or piece or plate glass and feeler gauges.

4 Torque and leverage

What is torque?

● Torque describes the twisting force about a shaft. The amount of torque applied is determined by the distance from the centre of the shaft to the end of the lever and the amount of force being applied to the end of the lever; distance multiplied by force equals torque.

● The manufacturer applies a measured torque to a bolt or nut to ensure that it will not slacken in use and to hold two components securely together without movement in the joint. The actual torque setting depends on the thread size, bolt or nut material and the composition of the components being held.

● Too little torque may cause the fastener to loosen due to vibration, whereas too much torque will distort the joint faces of the component or cause the fastener to shear off. Always stick to the specified torque setting.

Using a torque wrench

● Check the calibration of the torque wrench and make sure it has a suitable range for the job. Torque wrenches are available in Nm (Newton-metres), kgf m (kilograms-force metre), lbf ft (pounds-feet), lbf in (inch-pounds). Do not confuse lbf ft with lbf in.

● Adjust the tool to the desired torque on the scale (see illustration 4.1). If your torque wrench is not calibrated in the units specified, carefully convert the figure (see Conversion Factors). A manufacturer sometimes gives a torque setting as a range (8 to 10 Nm) rather than a single figure - in this case set the tool midway between the two settings. The same torque may be expressed as 9 Nm ± 1 Nm. Some torque wrenches have a method of locking the setting so that it isn't inadvertently altered during use.

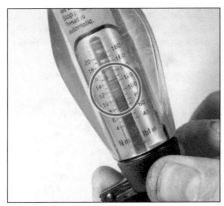

4.1 Set the torque wrench index mark to the setting required, in this case 12 Nm

● Install the bolts/nuts in their correct location and secure them lightly. Their threads must be clean and free of any old locking compound. Unless specified the threads and flange should be dry - oiled threads are necessary in certain circumstances and the manufacturer will take this into account in the specified torque figure. Similarly, the manufacturer may also specify the application of thread-locking compound.

● Tighten the fasteners in the specified sequence until the torque wrench clicks, indicating that the torque setting has been reached. Apply the torque again to double-check the setting. Where different thread diameter fasteners secure the component, as a rule tighten the larger diameter ones first.

● When the torque wrench has been finished with, release the lock (where applicable) and fully back off its setting to zero - do not leave the torque wrench tensioned. Also, do not use a torque wrench for slackening a fastener.

Angle-tightening

● Manufacturers often specify a figure in degrees for final tightening of a fastener. This usually follows tightening to a specific torque setting.

● A degree disc can be set and attached to the socket (see illustration 4.2) or a protractor can be used to mark the angle of movement on the bolt/nut head and the surrounding casting (see illustration 4.3).

4.2 Angle tightening can be accomplished with a torque-angle gauge . . .

4.3 . . . or by marking the angle on the surrounding component

Loosening sequences

● Where more than one bolt/nut secures a component, loosen each fastener evenly a little at a time. In this way, not all the stress of the joint is held by one fastener and the components are not likely to distort.

● If a tightening sequence is provided, work in the REVERSE of this, but if not, work from the outside in, in a criss-cross sequence (see illustration 4.4).

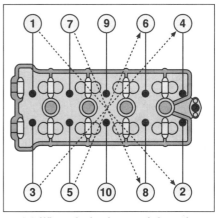

4.4 When slackening, work from the outside inwards

Tightening sequences

● If a component is held by more than one fastener it is important that the retaining bolts/nuts are tightened evenly to prevent uneven stress build-up and distortion of sealing faces. This is especially important on high-compression joints such as the cylinder head.

● A sequence is usually provided by the manufacturer, either in a diagram or actually marked in the casting. If not, always start in the centre and work outwards in a criss-cross pattern (see illustration 4.5). Start off by securing all bolts/nuts finger-tight, then set the torque wrench and tighten each fastener by a small amount in sequence until the final torque is reached. By following this practice,

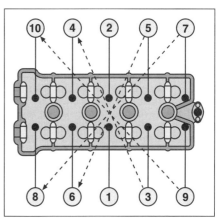

4.5 When tightening, work from the inside outwards

the joint will be held evenly and will not be distorted. Important joints, such as the cylinder head and big-end fasteners often have two- or three-stage torque settings.

Applying leverage

● Use tools at the correct angle. Position a socket wrench or spanner on the bolt/nut so that you pull it towards you when loosening. If this can't be done, push the spanner without curling your fingers around it **(see illustration 4.6)** - the spanner may slip or the fastener loosen suddenly, resulting in your fingers being crushed against a component.

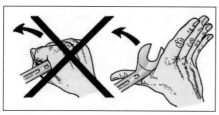

4.6 If you can't pull on the spanner to loosen a fastener, push with your hand open

● Additional leverage is gained by extending the length of the lever. The best way to do this is to use a breaker bar instead of the regular length tool, or to slip a length of tubing over the end of the spanner or socket wrench.
● If additional leverage will not work, the fastener head is either damaged or firmly corroded in place (see *Fasteners*).

5 Bearings

Bearing removal and installation

Drivers and sockets

● Before removing a bearing, always inspect the casing to see which way it must be driven out - some casings will have retaining plates or a cast step. Also check for any identifying markings on the bearing and if installed to a certain depth, measure this at this stage. Some roller bearings are sealed on one side - take note of the original fitted position.
● Bearings can be driven out of a casing using a bearing driver tool (with the correct size head) or a socket of the correct diameter. Select the driver head or socket so that it contacts the outer race of the bearing, not the balls/rollers or inner race. Always support the casing around the bearing housing with wood blocks, otherwise there is a risk of fracture. The bearing is driven out with a few blows on the driver or socket from a heavy mallet. Unless access is severely restricted (as with wheel bearings), a pin-punch is not recommended unless it is moved around the bearing to keep it square in its housing.

● The same equipment can be used to install bearings. Make sure the bearing housing is supported on wood blocks and line up the bearing in its housing. Fit the bearing as noted on removal - generally they are installed with their marked side facing outwards. Tap the bearing squarely into its housing using a driver or socket which bears only on the bearing's outer race - contact with the bearing balls/rollers or inner race will destroy it **(see illustrations 5.1 and 5.2)**.
● Check that the bearing inner race and balls/rollers rotate freely.

5.1 Using a bearing driver against the bearing's outer race

5.2 Using a large socket against the bearing's outer race

Pullers and slide-hammers

● Where a bearing is pressed on a shaft a puller will be required to extract it **(see illustration 5.3)**. Make sure that the puller clamp or legs fit securely behind the bearing and are unlikely to slip out. If pulling a bearing

5.3 This bearing puller clamps behind the bearing and pressure is applied to the shaft end to draw the bearing off

off a gear shaft for example, you may have to locate the puller behind a gear pinion if there is no access to the race and draw the gear pinion off the shaft as well **(see illustration 5.4)**.

> **Caution: Ensure that the puller's centre bolt locates securely against the end of the shaft and will not slip when pressure is applied. Also ensure that puller does not damage the shaft end.**

5.4 Where no access is available to the rear of the bearing, it is sometimes possible to draw off the adjacent component

● Operate the puller so that its centre bolt exerts pressure on the shaft end and draws the bearing off the shaft.
● When installing the bearing on the shaft, tap only on the bearing's inner race - contact with the balls/rollers or outer race with destroy the bearing. Use a socket or length of tubing as a drift which fits over the shaft end **(see illustration 5.5)**.

5.5 When installing a bearing on a shaft use a piece of tubing which bears only on the bearing's inner race

● Where a bearing locates in a blind hole in a casing, it cannot be driven or pulled out as described above. A slide-hammer with knife-edged bearing puller attachment will be required. The puller attachment passes through the bearing and when tightened expands to fit firmly behind the bearing **(see illustration 5.6)**. By operating the slide-hammer part of the tool the bearing is jarred out of its housing **(see illustration 5.7)**.
● It is possible, if the bearing is of reasonable weight, for it to drop out of its housing if the casing is heated as described opposite. If this

5.6 Expand the bearing puller so that it locks behind the bearing . . .

5.7 . . . attach the slide hammer to the bearing puller

method is attempted, first prepare a work surface which will enable the casing to be tapped face down to help dislodge the bearing - a wood surface is ideal since it will not damage the casing's gasket surface. Wearing protective gloves, tap the heated casing several times against the work surface to dislodge the bearing under its own weight **(see illustration 5.8)**.

5.8 Tapping a casing face down on wood blocks can often dislodge a bearing

● Bearings can be installed in blind holes using the driver or socket method described above.

Drawbolts

● Where a bearing or bush is set in the eye of a component, such as a suspension linkage arm or connecting rod small-end, removal by drift may damage the component. Furthermore, a rubber bushing in a shock absorber eye cannot successfully be driven out of position. If access is available to a engineering press, the task is straightforward. If not, a drawbolt can be fabricated to extract the bearing or bush.

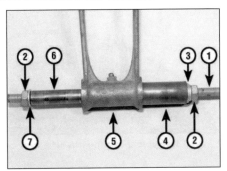

5.9 Drawbolt component parts assembled on a suspension arm

1   Bolt or length of threaded bar
2   Nuts
3   Washer (external diameter greater than tubing internal diameter)
4   Tubing (internal diameter sufficient to accommodate bearing)
5   Suspension arm with bearing
6   Tubing (external diameter slightly smaller than bearing)
7   Washer (external diameter slightly smaller than bearing)

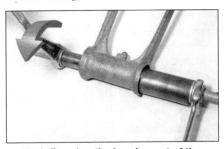

5.10 Drawing the bearing out of the suspension arm

● To extract the bearing/bush you will need a long bolt with nut (or piece of threaded bar with two nuts), a piece of tubing which has an internal diameter larger than the bearing/bush, another piece of tubing which has an external diameter slightly smaller than the bearing/bush, and a selection of washers **(see illustrations 5.9 and 5.10)**. Note that the pieces of tubing must be of the same length, or longer, than the bearing/bush.
● The same kit (without the pieces of tubing) can be used to draw the new bearing/bush back into place **(see illustration 5.11)**.

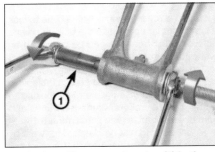

5.11 Installing a new bearing (1) in the suspension arm

Temperature change

● If the bearing's outer race is a tight fit in the casing, the aluminium casing can be heated to release its grip on the bearing. Aluminium will expand at a greater rate than the steel bearing outer race. There are several ways to do this, but avoid any localised extreme heat (such as a blow torch) - aluminium alloy has a low melting point.
● Approved methods of heating a casing are using a domestic oven (heated to 100°C) or immersing the casing in boiling water **(see illustration 5.12)**. Low temperature range localised heat sources such as a paint stripper heat gun or clothes iron can also be used **(see illustration 5.13)**. Alternatively, soak a rag in boiling water, wring it out and wrap it around the bearing housing.

> ⚠️ **Warning: All of these methods require care in use to prevent scalding and burns to the hands. Wear protective gloves when handling hot components.**

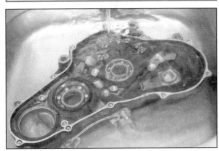

5.12 A casing can be immersed in a sink of boiling water to aid bearing removal

5.13 Using a localised heat source to aid bearing removal

● If heating the whole casing note that plastic components, such as the neutral switch, may suffer - remove them beforehand.
● After heating, remove the bearing as described above. You may find that the expansion is sufficient for the bearing to fall out of the casing under its own weight or with a light tap on the driver or socket.
● If necessary, the casing can be heated to aid bearing installation, and this is sometimes the recommended procedure if the motorcycle manufacturer has designed the housing and bearing fit with this intention.

● Installation of bearings can be eased by placing them in a freezer the night before installation. The steel bearing will contract slightly, allowing easy insertion in its housing. This is often useful when installing steering head outer races in the frame.

Bearing types and markings

● Plain shell bearings, ball bearings, needle roller bearings and tapered roller bearings will all be found on motorcycles (see illustrations 5.14 and 5.15). The ball and roller types are usually caged between an inner and outer race, but uncaged variations may be found.

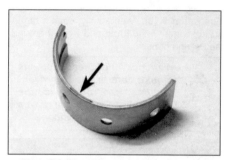

5.14 Shell bearings are either plain or grooved. They are usually identified by colour code (arrow)

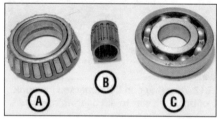

5.15 Tapered roller bearing (A), needle roller bearing (B) and ball journal bearing (C)

● Shell bearings (often called inserts) are usually found at the crankshaft main and connecting rod big-end where they are good at coping with high loads. They are made of a phosphor-bronze material and are impregnated with self-lubricating properties.

● Ball bearings and needle roller bearings consist of a steel inner and outer race with the balls or rollers between the races. They require constant lubrication by oil or grease and are good at coping with axial loads. Taper roller bearings consist of rollers set in a tapered cage set on the inner race; the outer race is separate. They are good at coping with axial loads and prevent movement along the shaft - a typical application is in the steering head.

● Bearing manufacturers produce bearings to ISO size standards and stamp one face of the bearing to indicate its internal and external diameter, load capacity and type (see illustration 5.16).

● Metal bushes are usually of phosphor-bronze material. Rubber bushes are used in suspension mounting eyes. Fibre bushes have also been used in suspension pivots.

5.16 Typical bearing marking

Bearing fault finding

● If a bearing outer race has spun in its housing, the housing material will be damaged. You can use a bearing locking compound to bond the outer race in place if damage is not too severe.

● Shell bearings will fail due to damage of their working surface, as a result of lack of lubrication, corrosion or abrasive particles in the oil (see illustration 5.17). Small particles of dirt in the oil may embed in the bearing material whereas larger particles will score the bearing and shaft journal. If a number of short journeys are made, insufficient heat will be generated to drive off condensation which has built up on the bearings.

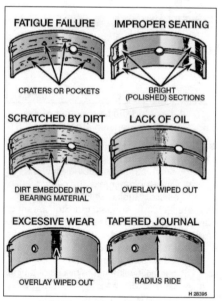

5.17 Typical bearing failures

● Ball and roller bearings will fail due to lack of lubrication or damage to the balls or rollers. Tapered-roller bearings can be damaged by overloading them. Unless the bearing is sealed on both sides, wash it in paraffin (kerosene) to remove all old grease then allow it to dry. Make a visual inspection looking to dented balls or rollers, damaged cages and worn or pitted races (see illustration 5.18).

● A ball bearing can be checked for wear by listening to it when spun. Apply a film of light oil to the bearing and hold it close to the ear - hold the outer race with one hand and spin the inner

5.18 Example of ball journal bearing with damaged balls and cages

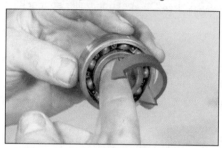

5.19 Hold outer race and listen to inner race when spun

race with the other hand (see illustration 5.19). The bearing should be almost silent when spun; if it grates or rattles it is worn.

6 Oil seals

Oil seal removal and installation

● Oil seals should be renewed every time a component is dismantled. This is because the seal lips will become set to the sealing surface and will not necessarily reseal.

● Oil seals can be prised out of position using a large flat-bladed screwdriver (see illustration 6.1). In the case of crankcase seals, check first that the seal is not lipped on the inside, preventing its removal with the crankcases joined.

6.1 Prise out oil seals with a large flat-bladed screwdriver

● New seals are usually installed with their marked face (containing the seal reference code) outwards and the spring side towards the fluid being retained. In certain cases, such as a two-stroke engine crankshaft seal, a double lipped seal may be used due to there being fluid or gas on each side of the joint.

● Use a bearing driver or socket which bears only on the outer hard edge of the seal to install it in the casing - tapping on the inner edge will damage the sealing lip.

Oil seal types and markings

● Oil seals are usually of the single-lipped type. Double-lipped seals are found where a liquid or gas is on both sides of the joint.
● Oil seals can harden and lose their sealing ability if the motorcycle has been in storage for a long period - renewal is the only solution.
● Oil seal manufacturers also conform to the ISO markings for seal size - these are moulded into the outer face of the seal **(see illustration 6.2)**.

6.2 These oil seal markings indicate inside diameter, outside diameter and seal thickness

7 Gaskets and sealants

Types of gasket and sealant

● Gaskets are used to seal the mating surfaces between components and keep lubricants, fluids, vacuum or pressure contained within the assembly. Aluminium gaskets are sometimes found at the cylinder joints, but most gaskets are paper-based. If the mating surfaces of the components being joined are undamaged the gasket can be installed dry, although a dab of sealant or grease will be useful to hold it in place during assembly.
● RTV (Room Temperature Vulcanising) silicone rubber sealants cure when exposed to moisture in the atmosphere. These sealants are good at filling pits or irregular gasket faces, but will tend to be forced out of the joint under very high torque. They can be used to replace a paper gasket, but first make sure that the width of the paper gasket is not essential to the shimming of internal components. RTV sealants should not be used on components containing petrol (gasoline).
● Non-hardening, semi-hardening and hard setting liquid gasket compounds can be used with a gasket or between a metal-to-metal joint. Select the sealant to suit the application: universal non-hardening sealant can be used on virtually all joints; semi-hardening on joint faces which are rough or damaged; hard setting sealant on joints which require a permanent bond and are subjected to high temperature and pressure. **Note:** *Check first if the paper gasket has a bead of sealant*

impregnated in its surface before applying additional sealant.
● When choosing a sealant, make sure it is suitable for the application, particularly if being applied in a high-temperature area or in the vicinity of fuel. Certain manufacturers produce sealants in either clear, silver or black colours to match the finish of the engine. This has a particular application on motorcycles where much of the engine is exposed.
● Do not over-apply sealant. That which is squeezed out on the outside of the joint can be wiped off, whereas an excess of sealant on the inside can break off and clog oilways.

Breaking a sealed joint

● Age, heat, pressure and the use of hard setting sealant can cause two components to stick together so tightly that they are difficult to separate using finger pressure alone. Do not resort to using levers unless there is a pry point provided for this purpose **(see illustration 7.1)** or else the gasket surfaces will be damaged.
● Use a soft-faced hammer **(see illustration 7.2)** or a wood block and conventional hammer to strike the component near the mating surface. Avoid hammering against cast extremities since they may break off. If this method fails, try using a wood wedge between the two components.

Caution: If the joint will not separate, double-check that you have removed all the fasteners.

7.1 If a pry point is provided, apply gently pressure with a flat-bladed screwdriver

7.2 Tap around the joint with a soft-faced mallet if necessary - don't strike cooling fins

Removal of old gasket and sealant

● Paper gaskets will most likely come away complete, leaving only a few traces stuck on

Most components have one or two hollow locating dowels between the two gasket faces. If a dowel cannot be removed, do not resort to gripping it with pliers - it will almost certainly be distorted. Install a close-fitting socket or Phillips screwdriver into the dowel and then grip the outer edge of the dowel to free it.

the sealing faces of the components. It is imperative that all traces are removed to ensure correct sealing of the new gasket.
● Very carefully scrape all traces of gasket away making sure that the sealing surfaces are not gouged or scored by the scraper **(see illustrations 7.3, 7.4 and 7.5)**. Stubborn deposits can be removed by spraying with an aerosol gasket remover. Final preparation of

7.3 Paper gaskets can be scraped off with a gasket scraper tool . . .

7.4 . . . a knife blade . . .

7.5 . . . or a household scraper

7.6 Fine abrasive paper is wrapped around a flat file to clean up the gasket face

7.7 A kitchen scourer can be used on stubborn deposits

the gasket surface can be made with very fine abrasive paper or a plastic kitchen scourer (see illustrations 7.6 and 7.7).

● Old sealant can be scraped or peeled off components, depending on the type originally used. Note that gasket removal compounds are available to avoid scraping the components clean; make sure the gasket remover suits the type of sealant used.

8 Chains

Breaking and joining final drive chains

● Drive chains for all but small bikes are continuous and do not have a clip-type connecting link. The chain must be broken using a chain breaker tool and the new chain securely riveted together using a new soft rivet-type link. Never use a clip-type connecting link instead of a rivet-type link, except in an emergency. Various chain breaking and riveting tools are available, either as separate tools or combined as illustrated in the accompanying photographs - read the instructions supplied with the tool carefully.

> ⚠ Warning: The need to rivet the new link pins correctly cannot be overstressed - loss of control of the motorcycle is very likely to result if the chain breaks in use.

● Rotate the chain and look for the soft link. The soft link pins look like they have been

8.1 Tighten the chain breaker to push the pin out of the link . . .

8.2 . . . withdraw the pin, remove the tool . . .

8.3 . . . and separate the chain link

deeply centre-punched instead of peened over like all the other pins (see illustration 8.9) and its sideplate may be a different colour. Position the soft link midway between the sprockets and assemble the chain breaker tool over one of the soft link pins (see illustration 8.1). Operate the tool to push the pin out through the chain (see illustration 8.2). On an O-ring chain, remove the O-rings (see illustration 8.3). Carry out the same procedure on the other soft link pin.

> Caution: Certain soft link pins (particularly on the larger chains) may require their ends to be filed or ground off before they can be pressed out using the tool.

● Check that you have the correct size and strength (standard or heavy duty) new soft link - do not reuse the old link. Look for the size marking on the chain sideplates (see illustration 8.10).
● Position the chain ends so that they are engaged over the rear sprocket. On an O-ring

8.4 Insert the new soft link, with O-rings, through the chain ends . . .

8.5 . . . install the O-rings over the pin ends . . .

8.6 . . . followed by the sideplate

chain, install a new O-ring over each pin of the link and insert the link through the two chain ends (see illustration 8.4). Install a new O-ring over the end of each pin, followed by the sideplate (with the chain manufacturer's marking facing outwards) (see illustrations 8.5 and 8.6). On an unsealed chain, insert the link through the two chain ends, then install the sideplate with the chain manufacturer's marking facing outwards.
● Note that it may not be possible to install the sideplate using finger pressure alone. If using a joining tool, assemble it so that the plates of the tool clamp the link and press the sideplate over the pins (see illustration 8.7). Otherwise, use two small sockets placed over

8.7 Push the sideplate into position using a clamp

8.8 Assemble the chain riveting tool over one pin at a time and tighten it fully

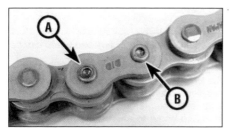

8.9 Pin end correctly riveted (A), pin end unriveted (B)

the rivet ends and two pieces of the wood between a G-clamp. Operate the clamp to press the sideplate over the pins.

● Assemble the joining tool over one pin (following the maker's instructions) and tighten the tool down to spread the pin end securely **(see illustrations 8.8 and 8.9)**. Do the same on the other pin.

> ⚠ **Warning: Check that the pin ends are secure and that there is no danger of the sideplate coming loose. If the pin ends are cracked the soft link must be renewed.**

Final drive chain sizing

● Chains are sized using a three digit number, followed by a suffix to denote the chain type **(see illustration 8.10)**. Chain type is either standard or heavy duty (thicker sideplates), and also unsealed or O-ring/X-ring type.

● The first digit of the number relates to the pitch of the chain, ie the distance from the centre of one pin to the centre of the next pin **(see illustration 8.11)**. Pitch is expressed in eighths of an inch, as follows:

8.10 Typical chain size and type marking

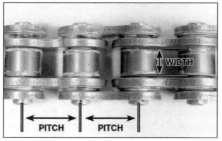

8.11 Chain dimensions

| Sizes commencing with a 4 (eg 428) have a pitch of 1/2 inch (12.7 mm) |
| Sizes commencing with a 5 (eg 520) have a pitch of 5/8 inch (15.9 mm) |
| Sizes commencing with a 6 (eg 630) have a pitch of 3/4 inch (19.1 mm) |

● The second and third digits of the chain size relate to the width of the rollers, again in imperial units, eg the 525 shown has 5/16 inch (7.94 mm) rollers **(see illustration 8.11)**.

9 Hoses

Clamping to prevent flow

● Small-bore flexible hoses can be clamped to prevent fluid flow whilst a component is worked on. Whichever method is used, ensure that the hose material is not permanently distorted or damaged by the clamp.

a) A brake hose clamp available from auto accessory shops **(see illustration 9.1)**.
b) A wingnut type hose clamp **(see illustration 9.2)**.

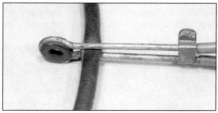

9.1 Hoses can be clamped with an automotive brake hose clamp . . .

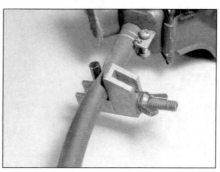

9.2 . . . a wingnut type hose clamp . . .

c) Two sockets placed each side of the hose and held with straight-jawed self-locking grips **(see illustration 9.3)**.
d) Thick card each side of the hose held between straight-jawed self-locking grips **(see illustration 9.4)**.

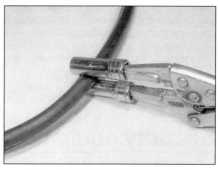

9.3 . . . two sockets and a pair of self-locking grips . . .

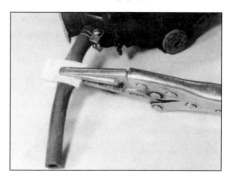

9.4 . . . or thick card and self-locking grips

Freeing and fitting hoses

● Always make sure the hose clamp is moved well clear of the hose end. Grip the hose with your hand and rotate it whilst pulling it off the union. If the hose has hardened due to age and will not move, slit it with a sharp knife and peel its ends off the union **(see illustration 9.5)**.

● Resist the temptation to use grease or soap on the unions to aid installation; although it helps the hose slip over the union it will equally aid the escape of fluid from the joint. It is preferable to soften the hose ends in hot water and wet the inside surface of the hose with water or a fluid which will evaporate.

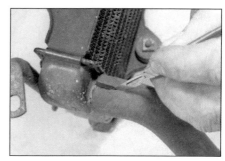

9.5 Cutting a coolant hose free with a sharp knife

Introduction

In less time than it takes to read this introduction, a thief could steal your motorcycle. Returning only to find your bike has gone is one of the worst feelings in the world. Even if the motorcycle is insured against theft, once you've got over the initial shock, you will have the inconvenience of dealing with the police and your insurance company.

The motorcycle is an easy target for the professional thief and the joyrider alike and

the official figures on motorcycle theft make for depressing reading; on average a motorcycle is stolen every 16 minutes in the UK!

Motorcycle thefts fall into two categories, those stolen 'to order' and those taken by opportunists. The thief stealing to order will be on the look out for a specific make and model and will go to extraordinary lengths to obtain that motorcycle. The opportunist thief on the other hand will look for easy targets which can be stolen with the minimum of effort and risk.

Whilst it is never going to be possible to make your machine 100% secure, it is estimated that around half of all stolen motorcycles are taken by opportunist thieves. Remember that the opportunist thief is always on the look out for the easy option: if there are two similar motorcycles parked side-by-side, they will target the one with the lowest level of security. By taking a few precautions, you can reduce the chances of your motorcycle being stolen.

Security equipment

There are many specialised motorcycle security devices available and the following text summarises their applications and their good and bad points.

Once you have decided on the type of security equipment which best suits your needs, we recommended that you read one of the many equipment tests regularly carried

Ensure the lock and chain you buy is of good quality and long enough to shackle your bike to a solid object

out by the motorcycle press. These tests compare the products from all the major manufacturers and give impartial ratings on their effectiveness, value-for-money and ease of use.

No one item of security equipment can provide complete protection. It is highly recommended that two or more of the items described below are combined to increase the security of your motorcycle (a lock and chain plus an alarm system is just about ideal). The more security measures fitted to the bike, the less likely it is to be stolen.

Lock and chain

Pros: *Very flexible to use; can be used to secure the motorcycle to almost any immovable object. On some locks and chains, the lock can be used on its own as a disc lock (see below).*

Cons: *Can be very heavy and awkward to carry on the motorcycle, although some types*

will be supplied with a carry bag which can be strapped to the pillion seat.

● Heavy-duty chains and locks are an excellent security measure **(see illustration 1)**. Whenever the motorcycle is parked, use the lock and chain to secure the machine to a solid, immovable object such as a post or railings. This will prevent the machine from being ridden away or being lifted into the back of a van.

● When fitting the chain, always ensure the chain is routed around the motorcycle frame or swingarm **(see illustrations 2 and 3)**. Never merely pass the chain around one of the wheel rims; a thief may unbolt the wheel and lift the rest of the machine into a van, leaving you with just the wheel! Try to avoid having excess chain free, thus making it difficult to use cutting tools, and keep the chain and lock off the ground to prevent thieves attacking it with a cold chisel. Position the lock so that its lock barrel is facing downwards; this will make it harder for the thief to attack the lock mechanism.

Pass the chain through the bike's frame, rather than just through a wheel . . .

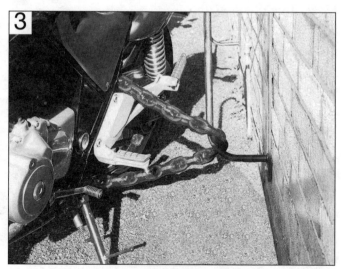

. . . and loop it around a solid object

U-locks

Pros: *Highly effective deterrent which can be used to secure the bike to a post or railings. Most U-locks come with a carrier which allows the lock to be easily carried on the bike.*

Cons: *Not as flexible to use as a lock and chain.*

● These are solid locks which are similar in use to a lock and chain. U-locks are lighter than a lock and chain but not so flexible to use. The length and shape of the lock shackle limit the objects to which the bike can be secured **(see illustration 4)**.

Disc locks

Pros: *Small, light and very easy to carry; most can be stored underneath the seat.*

Cons: *Does not prevent the motorcycle being lifted into a van. Can be very embarrassing if you*

U-locks can be used to secure the bike to a solid object – ensure you purchase one which is long enough

forget to remove the lock before attempting to ride off!

● Disc locks are designed to be attached to the front brake disc. The lock passes through one of the holes in the disc and prevents the wheel rotating by jamming against the fork/brake caliper **(see illustration 5)**. Some are equipped with an alarm siren which sounds if the disc lock is moved; this not only acts as a theft deterrent but also as a handy reminder if you try to move the bike with the lock still fitted.

● Combining the disc lock with a length of cable which can be looped around a post or railings provides an additional measure of security **(see illustration 6)**.

Alarms and immobilisers

Pros: *Once installed it is completely hassle-free to use. If the system is 'Thatcham' or 'Sold Secure-approved', insurance companies may give you a discount.*

Cons: *Can be expensive to buy and complex to install. No system will prevent the motorcycle from being lifted into a van and taken away.*

● Electronic alarms and immobilisers are available to suit a variety of budgets. There are three different types of system available: pure alarms, pure immobilisers, and the more expensive systems which are combined alarm/immobilisers **(see illustration 7)**.
● An alarm system is designed to emit an audible warning if the motorcycle is being tampered with.
● An immobiliser prevents the motorcycle being started and ridden away by disabling its electrical systems.
● When purchasing an alarm/immobiliser system, check the cost of installing the system unless you are able to do it yourself. If the motorcycle is not used regularly, another consideration is the current drain of the system. All alarm/immobiliser systems are powered by the motorcycle's battery; purchasing a system with a very low current drain could prevent the battery losing its charge whilst the motorcycle is not being used.

A typical disc lock attached through one of the holes in the disc

A disc lock combined with a security cable provides additional protection

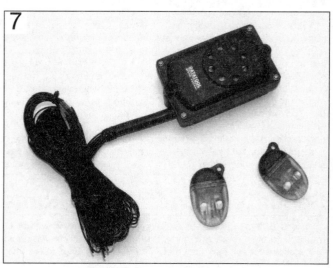

A typical alarm/immobiliser system

Indelible markings can be applied to most areas of the bike – always apply the manufacturer's sticker to warn off thieves

Chemically-etched code numbers can be applied to main body panels . . .

. . . again, always ensure that the kit manufacturer's sticker is applied in a prominent position

Security marking kits

Pros: *Very cheap and effective deterrent. Many insurance companies will give you a discount on your insurance premium if a recognised security marking kit is used on your motorcycle.*

Cons: *Does not prevent the motorcycle being stolen by joyriders.*

● There are many different types of security marking kits available. The idea is to mark as many parts of the motorcycle as possible with a unique security number **(see illustrations 8, 9 and 10)**. A form will be included with the kit to register your personal details and those of the motorcycle with the kit manufacturer. This register is made available to the police to help them trace the rightful owner of any motorcycle or components which they recover should all other forms of identification have been removed. Always apply the warning stickers provided with the kit to deter thieves.

Ground anchors, wheel clamps and security posts

Pros: *An excellent form of security which will deter all but the most determined of thieves.*

Cons: *Awkward to install and can be expensive.*

● Whilst the motorcycle is at home, it is a good idea to attach it securely to the floor or a solid wall, even if it is kept in a securely locked garage. Various types of ground anchors, security posts and wheel clamps are available for this purpose **(see illustration 11)**. These security devices are either bolted to a solid concrete or brick structure or can be cemented into the ground.

Permanent ground anchors provide an excellent level of security when the bike is at home

Security at home

A high percentage of motorcycle thefts are from the owner's home. Here are some things to consider whenever your motorcycle is at home:

✔ Where possible, always keep the motorcycle in a securely locked garage. Never rely solely on the standard lock on the garage door, these are usual hopelessly inadequate. Fit an additional locking mechanism to the door and consider having the garage alarmed. A security light, activated by a movement sensor, is also a good investment.

✔ Always secure the motorcycle to the ground or a wall, even if it is inside a securely locked garage.
✔ Do not regularly leave the motorcycle outside your home, try to keep it out of sight wherever possible. If a garage is not available, fit a motorcycle cover over the bike to disguise its true identity.
✔ It is not uncommon for thieves to follow a motorcyclist home to find out where the bike is kept. They will then return at a later date. Be aware of this whenever you are returning

home on your motorcycle. If you suspect you are being followed, do not return home, instead ride to a garage or shop and stop as a precaution.
✔ When selling a motorcycle, do not provide your home address or the location where the bike is normally kept. Arrange to meet the buyer at a location away from your home. Thieves have been known to pose as potential buyers to find out where motorcycles are kept and then return later to steal them.

Security away from the home

As well as fitting security equipment to your motorcycle here are a few general rules to follow whenever you park your motorcycle.
✔ Park in a busy, public place.
✔ Use car parks which incorporate security features, such as CCTV.

✔ At night, park in a well-lit area, preferably directly underneath a street light.
✔ Engage the steering lock.
✔ Secure the motorcycle to a solid, immovable object such as a post or railings with an additional lock. If this is not possible,

secure the bike to a friend's motorcycle. Some public parking places provide security loops for motorcycles.
✔ Never leave your helmet or luggage attached to the motorcycle. Take them with you at all times.

Lubricants and fluids

A wide range of lubricants, fluids and cleaning agents is available for motor-cycles. This is a guide as to what is available, its applications and properties.

Four-stroke engine oil

● Engine oil is without doubt the most important component of any four-stroke engine. Modern motorcycle engines place a lot of demands on their oil and choosing the right type is essential. Using an unsuitable oil will lead to an increased rate of engine wear and could result in serious engine damage. Before purchasing oil, always check the recommended oil specification given by the manufacturer. The manufacturer will state a recommended 'type or classification' and also a specific 'viscosity' range for engine oil.

● The oil 'type or classification' is identified by its API (American Petroleum Institute) rating. The API rating will be in the form of two letters, e.g. SG. The S identifies the oil as being suitable for use in a petrol (gasoline) engine (S stands for spark ignition) and the second letter, ranging from A to J, identifies the oil's performance rating. The later this letter, the higher the specification of the oil; for example API SG oil exceeds the requirements of API SF oil. **Note:** *On some oils there may also be a second rating consisting of another two letters, the first letter being C, e.g. API SF/CD. This rating indicates the oil is also suitable for use in a diesel engines (the C stands for compression ignition) and is thus of no relevance for motorcycle use.*

● The 'viscosity' of the oil is identified by its SAE (Society of Automotive Engineers) rating. All modern engines require multigrade oils and the SAE rating will consist of two numbers, the first followed by a W, e.g. 10W/40. The first number indicates the viscosity rating of the oil at low temperatures (W stands for winter – tested at –20°C) and the second number represents the viscosity of the oil at high temperatures (tested at 100°C). The lower the number, the thinner the oil. For example an oil with an SAE 10W/40 rating will give better cold starting and running than an SAE 15W/40 oil.

● As well as ensuring the 'type' and 'viscosity' of the oil match the recommendations, another consideration to make when buying engine oil is whether to purchase a standard mineral-based oil, a semi-synthetic oil (also known as a synthetic blend or synthetic-based oil) or a fully-synthetic oil. Although all oils will have a similar rating and viscosity, their cost will vary considerably; mineral-based oils are the cheapest, the fully-synthetic oils the most expensive with the semi-synthetic oils falling somewhere in-between. This decision is very much up to the owner, but it should be noted that modern synthetic oils have far better lubricating and cleaning qualities than traditional mineral-based oils and tend to retain these properties for far longer. Bearing in mind the operating conditions inside a modern, high-revving motorcycle engine it is highly recommended that a fully synthetic oil is used. The extra expense at each service could save you money in the long term by preventing premature engine wear.

● As a final note always ensure that the oil is specifically designed for use in motorcycle engines. Engine oils designed primarily for use in car engines sometimes contain additives or friction modifiers which could cause clutch slip on a motorcycle fitted with a wet-clutch.

Two-stroke engine oil

● Modern two-stroke engines, with their high power outputs, place high demands on their oil. If engine seizure is to be avoided it is essential that a high-quality oil is used. Two-stroke oils differ hugely from four-stroke oils. The oil lubricates only the crankshaft and piston(s) (the transmission has its own lubricating oil) and is used on a total-loss basis where it is burnt completely during the combustion process.

● The Japanese have recently introduced a classification system for two-stroke oils, the JASO rating. This rating is in the form of two letters, either FA, FB or FC – FA is the lowest classification and FC the highest. Ensure the oil being used meets or exceeds the recommended rating specified by the manufacturer.

● As well as ensuring the oil rating matches the recommendation, another consideration to make when buying engine oil is whether to purchase a standard mineral-based oil, a semi-synthetic oil (also known as a synthetic blend or synthetic-based oil) or a fully-synthetic oil. The cost of each type of oil varies considerably; mineral-based oils are the cheapest, the fully-synthetic oils the most expensive with the semi-synthetic oils falling somewhere in-between. This decision is very much up to the owner, but it should be noted that modern synthetic oils have far better lubricating properties and burn cleaner than traditional mineral-based oils. It is therefore recommended that a fully synthetic oil is used. The extra expense could save you money in the long term by preventing premature engine wear, engine performance will be improved, carbon deposits and exhaust smoke will be reduced.

● Always ensure that the oil is specifically designed for use in an injector system. Many high quality two-stroke oils are designed for competition use and need to be pre-mixed with fuel. These oils are of a much higher viscosity and are not designed to flow through the injector pumps used on road-going two-stroke motorcycles.

Transmission (gear) oil

● On a two-stroke engine, the transmission and clutch are lubricated by their own separate oil bath which must be changed in accordance with the Maintenance Schedule.
● Although the engine and transmission units of most four-strokes use a common lubrication supply, there are some exceptions where the engine and gearbox have separate oil reservoirs and a dry clutch is used.
● Motorcycle manufacturers will either recommend a monograde transmission oil or a four-stroke multigrade engine oil to lubricate the transmission.
● Transmission oils, or gear oils as they are often called, are designed specifically for use in transmission systems. The viscosity of these oils is represented by an SAE number, but the scale of measurement applied is different to that used to grade engine oils. As a rough guide a SAE90 gear oil will be of the same viscosity as an SAE50 engine oil.

Shaft drive oil

● On models equipped with shaft final drive, the shaft drive gears are will have their own oil supply. The manufacturer will state a recommended 'type or classification' and also a specific 'viscosity' range in the same manner as for four-stroke engine oil.
● Gear oil classification is given by the number which follows the API GL (GL standing for gear lubricant) rating, the higher the number, the higher the specification of the oil, e.g. API GL5 oil is a higher specification than API GL4 oil. Ensure the oil meets or

exceeds the classification specified and is of the correct viscosity. The viscosity of gear oils is also represented by an SAE number but the scale of measurement used is different to that used to grade engine oils. As a rough guide an SAE90 gear oil will be of the same viscosity as an SAE50 engine oil.
● If the use of an EP (Extreme Pressure) gear oil is specified, ensure the oil purchased is suitable.

Fork oil and suspension fluid

● Conventional telescopic front forks are hydraulic and require fork oil to work. To ensure the forks function correctly, the fork oil must be changed in accordance with the Maintenance Schedule.
● Fork oil is available in a variety of viscosities, identified by their SAE rating; fork oil ratings vary from light (SAE 5) to heavy (SAE 30). When purchasing fork oil, ensure the viscosity rating matches that specified by the manufacturer.
● Some lubricant manufacturers also produce a range of high-quality suspension fluids which are very similar to fork oil but are designed mainly for competition use. These fluids may have a different viscosity rating system which is not to be confused with the SAE rating of normal fork oil. Refer to the manufacturer's instructions if in any doubt.

Brake and clutch fluid

● All disc brake systems and some clutch systems are hydraulically operated. To ensure correct operation, the hydraulic fluid must be changed in accordance with the Maintenance Schedule.
● Brake and clutch fluid is classified by its DOT rating with most motorcycle manufacturers specifying DOT 3 or 4 fluid. Both fluid types are glycol-based and can be mixed together without adverse effect; DOT 4 fluid exceeds the requirements of DOT 3

fluid. Although it is safe to use DOT 4 fluid in a system designed for use with DOT 3 fluid, never use DOT 3 fluid in a system which specifies the use of DOT 4 as this will adversely affect the system's performance. The type required for the system will be marked on the fluid reservoir cap.
● Some manufacturers also produce a DOT 5 hydraulic fluid. DOT 5 hydraulic fluid is silicone-based and is not compatible with the glycol-based DOT 3 and 4 fluids. Never mix DOT 5 fluid with DOT 3 or 4 fluid as this will seriously affect the performance of the hydraulic system.

Coolant/antifreeze

● When purchasing coolant/antifreeze, always ensure it is suitable for use in an aluminium engine and contains corrosion inhibitors to prevent possible blockages of the internal coolant passages of the system. As a general rule, most coolants are designed to be used neat and should not be diluted whereas antifreeze can be mixed with distilled water to provide a coolant solution of the required strength. Refer to the manufacturer's instructions on the bottle.
● Ensure the coolant is changed in accordance with the Maintenance Schedule.

Chain lube

● Chain lube is an aerosol-type spray lubricant specifically designed for use on motorcycle final drive chains. Chain lube has two functions, to minimise friction between the final drive chain and sprockets and to prevent corrosion of the chain. Regular use of a good-quality chain lube will extend the life of the drive chain and sprockets and thus maximise the power being transmitted from the transmission to the rear wheel.
● When using chain lube, always allow some time for the solvents in the lube to evaporate before riding the motorcycle. This will minimise the amount of lube which will

'fling' off from the chain when the motorcycle is used. If the motorcycle is equipped with an 'O-ring' chain, ensure the chain lube is labelled as being suitable for use on 'O-ring' chains.

Degreasers and solvents

● There are many different types of solvents and degreasers available to remove the grime and grease which accumulate around the motorcycle during normal use. Degreasers and solvents are usually available as an aerosol-type spray or as a liquid which you apply with a brush. Always closely follow the manufacturer's instructions and wear eye protection during use. Be aware that many solvents are flammable and may give off noxious fumes; take adequate precautions when using them (see Safety First!).
● For general cleaning, use one of the many solvents or degreasers available from most motorcycle accessory shops. These solvents are usually applied then left for a certain time before being washed off with water.

Brake cleaner is a solvent specifically designed to remove all traces of oil, grease and dust from braking system components. Brake cleaner is designed to evaporate quickly and leaves behind no residue.

Carburettor cleaner is an aerosol-type solvent specifically designed to clear carburettor blockages and break down the hard deposits and gum often found inside carburettors during overhaul.

Contact cleaner is an aerosol-type solvent designed for cleaning electrical components. The cleaner will remove all traces of oil and dirt from components such as switch contacts or fouled spark plugs and then dry, leaving behind no residue.

Gasket remover is an aerosol-type solvent designed for removing stubborn gaskets from engine components during overhaul. Gasket remover will minimise the amount of scraping required to remove the gasket and therefore reduce the risk of damage to the mating surface.

Spray lubricants

● Aerosol-based spray lubricants are widely available and are excellent for lubricating lever pivots and exposed cables and switches. Try to use a lubricant which is of the dry-film type as the fluid evaporates, leaving behind a dry-film of lubricant. Lubricants which leave behind an oily residue will attract dust and dirt which will increase the rate of wear of the cable/lever.

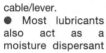

● Most lubricants also act as a moisture dispersant and a penetrating fluid. This means they can also be used to 'dry out' electrical components such as wiring connectors or switches as well as helping to free seized fasteners.

Greases

● Grease is used to lubricate many of the pivot-points. A good-quality multi-purpose grease is suitable for most applications but some manufacturers will specify the use of specialist greases for use on components such as swingarm and suspension linkage bushes. These specialist greases can be purchased from most motorcycle (or car) accessory shops; commonly specified types include molybdenum disulphide grease, lithium-based grease, graphite-based grease, silicone-based grease and high-temperature copper-based grease.

Gasket sealing compounds

● Gasket sealing compounds can be used in conjunction with gaskets, to improve their sealing capabilities, or on their own to seal metal-to-metal joints. Depending on their type, sealing compounds either set hard or stay relatively soft and pliable.

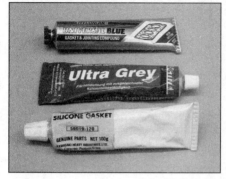

● When purchasing a gasket sealing compound, ensure that it is designed specifically for use on an internal combustion engine. General multi-purpose sealants available from DIY stores may appear visibly similar but they are not designed to withstand the extreme heat or contact with fuel and oil encountered when used on an engine (see 'Tools and Workshop Tips' for further information).

Thread locking compound

● Thread locking compounds are used to secure certain threaded fasteners in position to prevent them from loosening due to vibration. Thread locking compounds can be purchased from most motorcycle (and car) accessory shops. Ensure the threads of the both components are completely clean and dry before sparingly applying the locking compound (see 'Tools and Workshop Tips' for further information).

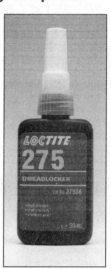

Fuel additives

● Fuel additives which protect and clean the fuel system components are widely available. These additives are designed to remove all traces of deposits that build up on the carburettors/injectors and prevent wear, helping the fuel system to operate more efficiently. If a fuel additive is being used, check that it is suitable for use with your motorcycle, especially if your motorcycle is equipped with a catalytic converter.

● Octane boosters are also available. These additives are designed to improve the performance of highly-tuned engines being run on normal pump-fuel and are of no real use on standard motorcycles.

Conversion factors

Length (distance)
Inches (in)	x 25.4	= Millimetres (mm)	x 0.0394	= Inches (in)
Feet (ft)	x 0.305	= Metres (m)	x 3.281	= Feet (ft)
Miles	x 1.609	= Kilometres (km)	x 0.621	= Miles

Volume (capacity)
Cubic inches (cu in; in³)	x 16.387	= Cubic centimetres (cc; cm³)	x 0.061	= Cubic inches (cu in; in³)
Imperial pints (Imp pt)	x 0.568	= Litres (l)	x 1.76	= Imperial pints (Imp pt)
Imperial quarts (Imp qt)	x 1.137	= Litres (l)	x 0.88	= Imperial quarts (Imp qt)
Imperial quarts (Imp qt)	x 1.201	= US quarts (US qt)	x 0.833	= Imperial quarts (Imp qt)
US quarts (US qt)	x 0.946	= Litres (l)	x 1.057	= US quarts (US qt)
Imperial gallons (Imp gal)	x 4.546	= Litres (l)	x 0.22	= Imperial gallons (Imp gal)
Imperial gallons (Imp gal)	x 1.201	= US gallons (US gal)	x 0.833	= Imperial gallons (Imp gal)
US gallons (US gal)	x 3.785	= Litres (l)	x 0.264	= US gallons (US gal)

Mass (weight)
Ounces (oz)	x 28.35	= Grams (g)	x 0.035	= Ounces (oz)
Pounds (lb)	x 0.454	= Kilograms (kg)	x 2.205	= Pounds (lb)

Force
Ounces-force (ozf; oz)	x 0.278	= Newtons (N)	x 3.6	= Ounces-force (ozf; oz)
Pounds-force (lbf; lb)	x 4.448	= Newtons (N)	x 0.225	= Pounds-force (lbf; lb)
Newtons (N)	x 0.1	= Kilograms-force (kgf; kg)	x 9.81	= Newtons (N)

Pressure
Pounds-force per square inch (psi; lbf/in²; lb/in²)	x 0.070	= Kilograms-force per square centimetre (kgf/cm²; kg/cm²)	x 14.223	= Pounds-force per square inch (psi; lbf/in²; lb/in²)
Pounds-force per square inch (psi; lbf/in²; lb/in²)	x 0.068	= Atmospheres (atm)	x 14.696	= Pounds-force per square inch (psi; lbf/in²; lb/in²)
Pounds-force per square inch (psi; lbf/in²; lb/in²)	x 0.069	= Bars	x 14.5	= Pounds-force per square inch (psi; lbf/in²; lb/in²)
Pounds-force per square inch (psi; lbf/in²; lb/in²)	x 6.895	= Kilopascals (kPa)	x 0.145	= Pounds-force per square inch (psi; lbf/in²; lb/in²)
Kilopascals (kPa)	x 0.01	= Kilograms-force per square centimetre (kgf/cm²; kg/cm²)	x 98.1	= Kilopascals (kPa)
Millibar (mbar)	x 100	= Pascals (Pa)	x 0.01	= Millibar (mbar)
Millibar (mbar)	x 0.0145	= Pounds-force per square inch (psi; lbf/in²; lb/in²)	x 68.947	= Millibar (mbar)
Millibar (mbar)	x 0.75	= Millimetres of mercury (mmHg)	x 1.333	= Millibar (mbar)
Millibar (mbar)	x 0.401	= Inches of water (inH₂O)	x 2.491	= Millibar (mbar)
Millimetres of mercury (mmHg)	x 0.535	= Inches of water (inH₂O)	x 1.868	= Millimetres of mercury (mmHg)
Inches of water (inH₂O)	x 0.036	= Pounds-force per square inch (psi; lbf/in²; lb/in²)	x 27.68	= Inches of water (inH₂O)

Torque (moment of force)
Pounds-force inches (lbf in; lb in)	x 1.152	= Kilograms-force centimetre (kgf cm; kg cm)	x 0.868	= Pounds-force inches (lbf in; lb in)
Pounds-force inches (lbf in; lb in)	x 0.113	= Newton metres (Nm)	x 8.85	= Pounds-force inches (lbf in; lb in)
Pounds-force inches (lbf in; lb in)	x 0.083	= Pounds-force feet (lbf ft; lb ft)	x 12	= Pounds-force inches (lbf in; lb in)
Pounds-force feet (lbf ft; lb ft)	x 0.138	= Kilograms-force metres (kgf m; kg m)	x 7.233	= Pounds-force feet (lbf ft; lb ft)
Pounds-force feet (lbf ft; lb ft)	x 1.356	= Newton metres (Nm)	x 0.738	= Pounds-force feet (lbf ft; lb ft)
Newton metres (Nm)	x 0.102	= Kilograms-force metres (kgf m; kg m)	x 9.804	= Newton metres (Nm)

Power
Horsepower (hp)	x 745.7	= Watts (W)	x 0.0013	= Horsepower (hp)

Velocity (speed)
Miles per hour (miles/hr; mph)	x 1.609	= Kilometres per hour (km/hr; kph)	x 0.621	= Miles per hour (miles/hr; mph)

Fuel consumption*
Miles per gallon (mpg)	x 0.354	= Kilometres per litre (km/l)	x 2.825	= Miles per gallon (mpg)

Temperature
Degrees Fahrenheit = (°C x 1.8) + 32

Degrees Celsius (Degrees Centigrade; °C) = (°F - 32) x 0.56

It is common practice to convert from miles per gallon (mpg) to litres/100 kilometres (l/100km), where mpg x l/100 km = 282

About the MOT Test

In the UK, all vehicles more than three years old are subject to an annual test to ensure that they meet minimum safety requirements. A current test certificate must be issued before a machine can be used on public roads, and is required before a road fund licence can be issued. Riding without a current test certificate will also invalidate your insurance.

For most owners, the MOT test is an annual cause for anxiety, and this is largely due to owners not being sure what needs to be checked prior to submitting the motorcycle for testing. The simple answer is that a fully roadworthy motorcycle will have no difficulty in passing the test.

This is a guide to getting your motorcycle through the MOT test. Obviously it will not be possible to examine the motorcycle to the same standard as the professional MOT tester, particularly in view of the equipment required for some of the checks. However, working through the following procedures will enable you to identify any problem areas before submitting the motorcycle for the test.

It has only been possible to summarise the test requirements here, based on the regulations in force at the time of printing. Test standards are becoming increasingly stringent, although there are some exemptions for older vehicles. More information about the MOT test can be obtained from the TSO publications, *How Safe is your Motorcycle* and *The MOT Inspection Manual for Motorcycle Testing*.

Many of the checks require that one of the wheels is raised off the ground. If the motorcycle doesn't have a centre stand, note that an auxiliary stand will be required. Additionally, the help of an assistant may prove useful.

Certain exceptions apply to machines under 50 cc, machines without a lighting system, and Classic bikes - if in doubt about any of the requirements listed below seek confirmation from an MOT tester prior to submitting the motorcycle for the test.

Check that the frame number is clearly visible.

Electrical System

Lights, turn signals, horn and reflector

✔ With the ignition on, check the operation of the following electrical components. **Note:** *The electrical components on certain small-capacity machines are powered by the generator, requiring that the engine is run for this check.*

a) *Headlight and tail light. Check that both illuminate in the low and high beam switch positions.*
b) *Position lights. Check that the front position light (or sidelight) and tail light illuminate in this switch position.*
c) *Turn signals. Check that all flash at the correct rate, and that the warning light(s) function correctly. Check that the turn signal switch works correctly.*
d) *Hazard warning system (where fitted). Check that all four turn signals flash in this switch position.*
e) *Brake stop light. Check that the light comes on when the front and rear brakes are independently applied. Models first used on or after 1st April 1986 must have a brake light switch on each brake.*
f) *Horn. Check that the sound is continuous and of reasonable volume.*

✔ Check that there is a red reflector on the rear of the machine, either mounted separately or as part of the tail light lens.
✔ Check the condition of the headlight, tail light and turn signal lenses.

Headlight beam height

✔ The MOT tester will perform a headlight beam height check using specialised beam setting equipment **(see illustration 1)**. This equipment will not be available to the home mechanic, but if you suspect that the headlight is incorrectly set or may have been maladjusted in the past, you can perform a rough test as follows.
✔ Position the bike in a straight line facing a brick wall. The bike must be off its stand, upright and with a rider seated. Measure the height from the ground to the centre of the headlight and mark a horizontal line on the wall at this height. Position the motorcycle 3.8 metres from the wall and draw a vertical

Headlight beam height checking equipment

line up the wall central to the centreline of the motorcycle. Switch to dipped beam and check that the beam pattern falls slightly lower than the horizontal line and to the left of the vertical line **(see illustration 2)**.

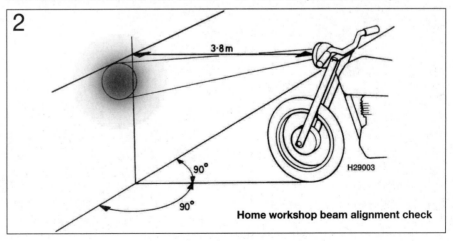

3·8 m

90°

90°

H29003

Home workshop beam alignment check

Exhaust System and Final Drive

Exhaust

✔ Check that the exhaust mountings are secure and that the system does not foul any of the rear suspension components.
✔ Start the motorcycle. When the revs are increased, check that the exhaust is neither holed nor leaking from any of its joints. On a linked system, check that the collector box is not leaking due to corrosion.

✔ Note that the exhaust decibel level ("loudness" of the exhaust) is assessed at the discretion of the tester. If the motorcycle was first used on or after 1st January 1985 the silencer must carry the BSAU 193 stamp, or a marking relating to its make and model, or be of OE (original equipment) manufacture. If the silencer is marked NOT FOR ROAD USE, RACING USE ONLY or similar, it will fail the MOT.

Final drive

✔ On chain or belt drive machines, check that the chain/belt is in good condition and does not have excessive slack. Also check that the sprocket is securely mounted on the rear wheel hub. Check that the chain/belt guard is in place.
✔ On shaft drive bikes, check for oil leaking from the drive unit and fouling the rear tyre.

Steering and Suspension

Steering

✔ With the front wheel raised off the ground, rotate the steering from lock to lock. The handlebar or switches must not contact the fuel tank or be close enough to trap the rider's hand. Problems can be caused by damaged lock stops on the lower yoke and frame, or by the fitting of non-standard handlebars.
✔ When performing the lock to lock check, also ensure that the steering moves freely without drag or notchiness. Steering movement can be impaired by poorly routed cables, or by overtight head bearings or worn bearings. The tester will perform a check of the steering head bearing lower race by mounting the front wheel on a surface plate, then performing a lock to

lock check with the weight of the machine on the lower bearing (see illustration 3).
✔ Grasp the fork sliders (lower legs) and attempt to push and pull on the forks (see

Front wheel mounted on a surface plate for steering head bearing lower race check

illustration 4). Any play in the steering head bearings will be felt. Note that in extreme cases, wear of the front fork bushes can be misinterpreted for head bearing play.
✔ Check that the handlebars are securely mounted.
✔ Check that the handlebar grip rubbers are secure. They should by bonded to the bar left end and to the throttle cable pulley on the right end.

Front suspension

✔ With the motorcycle off the stand, hold the front brake on and pump the front forks up and down (see illustration 5). Check that they are adequately damped.

Checking the steering head bearings for freeplay

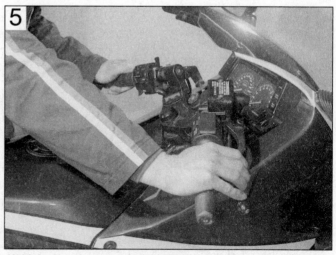

Hold the front brake on and pump the front forks up and down to check operation

Inspect the area around the fork dust seal for oil leakage (arrow)

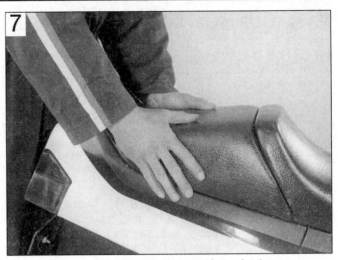

Bounce the rear of the motorcycle to check rear suspension operation

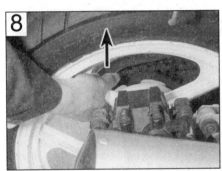

Checking for rear suspension linkage play

✔ Inspect the area above and around the front fork oil seals **(see illustration 6)**. There should be no sign of oil on the fork tube (stanchion) nor leaking down the slider (lower

leg). On models so equipped, check that there is no oil leaking from the anti-dive units.
✔ On models with swingarm front suspension, check that there is no freeplay in the linkage when moved from side to side.

Rear suspension

✔ With the motorcycle off the stand and an assistant supporting the motorcycle by its handlebars, bounce the rear suspension **(see illustration 7)**. Check that the suspension components do not foul on any of the cycle parts and check that the shock absorber(s) provide adequate damping.
✔ Visually inspect the shock absorber(s) and

check that there is no sign of oil leakage from its damper. This is somewhat restricted on certain single shock models due to the location of the shock absorber.
✔ With the rear wheel raised off the ground, grasp the wheel at the highest point and attempt to pull it up **(see illustration 8)**. Any play in the swingarm pivot or suspension linkage bearings will be felt as movement. **Note:** *Do not confuse play with actual suspension movement.* Failure to lubricate suspension linkage bearings can lead to bearing failure **(see illustration 9)**.
✔ With the rear wheel raised off the ground, grasp the swingarm ends and attempt to move the swingarm from side to side and forwards and backwards - any play indicates wear of the swingarm pivot bearings **(see illustration 10)**.

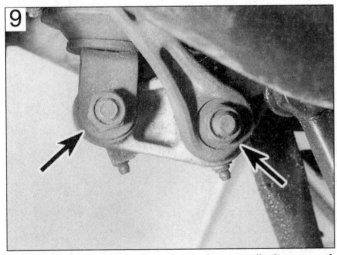

Worn suspension linkage pivots (arrows) are usually the cause of play in the rear suspension

Grasp the swingarm at the ends to check for play in its pivot bearings

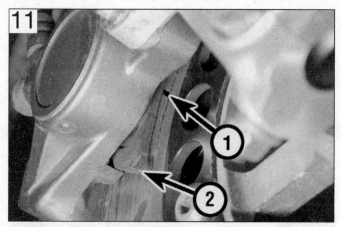

Brake pad wear can usually be viewed without removing the caliper. Most pads have wear indicator grooves (1) and some also have indicator tangs (2)

On drum brakes, check the angle of the operating lever with the brake fully applied. Most drum brakes have a wear indicator pointer and scale.

Brakes, Wheels and Tyres

Brakes

✔ With the wheel raised off the ground, apply the brake then free it off, and check that the wheel is about to revolve freely without brake drag.

✔ On disc brakes, examine the disc itself. Check that it is securely mounted and not cracked.

✔ On disc brakes, view the pad material through the caliper mouth and check that the pads are not worn down beyond the limit **(see illustration 11)**.

✔ On drum brakes, check that when the brake is applied the angle between the operating lever and cable or rod is not too great **(see illustration 12)**. Check also that the operating lever doesn't foul any other components.

✔ On disc brakes, examine the flexible hoses from top to bottom. Have an assistant hold the brake on so that the fluid in the hose is under pressure, and check that there is no sign of fluid leakage, bulges or cracking. If there are any metal brake pipes or unions, check that these are free from corrosion and damage. Where a brake-linked anti-dive system is fitted, check the hoses to the anti-dive in a similar manner.

✔ Check that the rear brake torque arm is secure and that its fasteners are secured by self-locking nuts or castellated nuts with split-pins or R-pins **(see illustration 13)**.

✔ On models with ABS, check that the self-check warning light in the instrument panel works.

✔ The MOT tester will perform a test of the motorcycle's braking efficiency based on a calculation of rider and motorcycle weight. Although this cannot be carried out at home, you can at least ensure that the braking systems are properly maintained. For hydraulic disc brakes, check the fluid level, lever/pedal feel (bleed of air if its spongy) and pad material. For drum brakes, check adjustment, cable or rod operation and shoe lining thickness.

Wheels and tyres

✔ Check the wheel condition. Cast wheels should be free from cracks and if of the built-up design, all fasteners should be secure. Spoked wheels should be checked for broken, corroded, loose or bent spokes.

✔ With the wheel raised off the ground, spin the wheel and visually check that the tyre and wheel run true. Check that the tyre does not foul the suspension or mudguards.

✔ With the wheel raised off the ground, grasp the wheel and attempt to move it about the axle (spindle) **(see illustration 14)**. Any play felt here indicates wheel bearing failure.

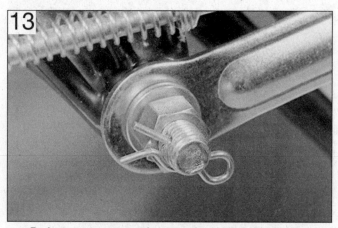

Brake torque arm must be properly secured at both ends

Check for wheel bearing play by trying to move the wheel about the axle (spindle)

Checking the tyre tread depth

Tyre direction of rotation arrow can be found on tyre sidewall

Castellated type wheel axle (spindle) nut must be secured by a split pin or R-pin

Two straightedges are used to check wheel alignment

✔ Check the tyre tread depth, tread condition and sidewall condition (see illustration 15).

✔ Check the tyre type. Front and rear tyre types must be compatible and be suitable for road use. Tyres marked NOT FOR ROAD USE, COMPETITION USE ONLY or similar, will fail the MOT.

✔ If the tyre sidewall carries a direction of rotation arrow, this must be pointing in the direction of normal wheel rotation (see illustration 16).

✔ Check that the wheel axle (spindle) nuts (where applicable) are properly secured. A self-locking nut or castellated nut with a split-pin or R-pin can be used (see illustration 17).

✔ Wheel alignment is checked with the motorcycle off the stand and a rider seated. With the front wheel pointing straight ahead, two perfectly straight lengths of metal or wood and placed against the sidewalls of both tyres (see illustration 18). The gap each side of the front tyre must be equidistant on both sides. Incorrect wheel alignment may be due to a cocked rear wheel (often as the result of poor chain adjustment) or in extreme cases, a bent frame.

General checks and condition

✔ Check the security of all major fasteners, bodypanels, seat, fairings (where fitted) and mudguards.

✔ Check that the rider and pillion footrests, handlebar levers and brake pedal are securely mounted.

✔ Check for corrosion on the frame or any load-bearing components. If severe, this may affect the structure, particularly under stress.

Sidecars

A motorcycle fitted with a sidecar requires additional checks relating to the stability of the machine and security of attachment and swivel joints, plus specific wheel alignment (toe-in) requirements. Additionally, tyre and lighting requirements differ from conventional motorcycle use. Owners are advised to check MOT test requirements with an official test centre.

Preparing for storage

Before you start

If repairs or an overhaul is needed, see that this is carried out now rather than left until you want to ride the bike again.

Give the bike a good wash and scrub all dirt from its underside. Make sure the bike dries completely before preparing for storage.

Engine

● Remove the spark plug(s) and lubricate the cylinder bores with approximately a teaspoon of motor oil using a spout-type oil can **(see illustration 1)**. Reinstall the spark plug(s). Crank the engine over a couple of times to coat the piston rings and bores with oil. If the bike has a kickstart, use this to turn the engine over. If not, flick the kill switch to the OFF position and crank the engine over on the starter **(see illustration 2)**. If the nature on the ignition system prevents the starter operating with the kill switch in the OFF position,

remove the spark plugs and fit them back in their caps; ensure that the plugs are earthed (grounded) against the cylinder head when the starter is operated **(see illustration 3)**.

⚠ **Warning: It is important that the plugs are earthed (grounded) away from the spark plug holes otherwise there is a risk of atomised fuel from the cylinders igniting.**

> **HAYNES HINT** *On a single cylinder four-stroke engine, you can seal the combustion chamber completely by positioning the piston at TDC on the compression stroke.*

● Drain the carburettor(s) otherwise there is a risk of jets becoming blocked by gum deposits from the fuel **(see illustration 4)**.

● If the bike is going into long-term storage, consider adding a fuel stabiliser to the fuel in the tank. If the tank is drained completely, corrosion of its internal surfaces may occur if left unprotected for a long period. The tank can be treated with a rust preventative especially for this purpose. Alternatively, remove the tank and pour half a litre of motor oil into it, install the filler cap and shake the tank to coat its internals with oil before draining off the excess. The same effect can also be achieved by spraying WD40 or a similar water-dispersant around the inside of the tank via its flexible nozzle.

● Make sure the cooling system contains the correct mix of antifreeze. Antifreeze also contains important corrosion inhibitors.

● The air intakes and exhaust can be sealed off by covering or plugging the openings. Ensure that you do not seal in any condensation; run the engine until it is hot,

Squirt a drop of motor oil into each cylinder

Flick the kill switch to OFF . . .

. . . and ensure that the metal bodies of the plugs (arrows) are earthed against the cylinder head

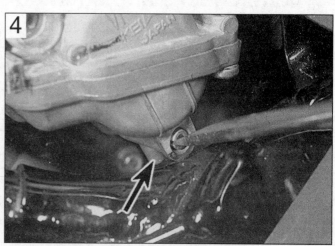

Connect a hose to the carburettor float chamber drain stub (arrow) and unscrew the drain screw

1 Engine doesn't start or is difficult to start (continued)

Rough idle

- [ ] Ignition malfunction (Chapter 3).
- [ ] Throttles not synchronised – adjust throttle synchronisation (Chapter 1).
- [ ] Injector malfunction (Chapter 3).
- [ ] Fuel contaminated. The fuel can be contaminated with either dirt or water, or can change chemically if the machine has been stored for many months without running. Drain the tank and fuel hoses (Chapter 3).
- [ ] Intake air leak. Check for loose throttle body-to-intake manifold and air duct connections, loose or missing vacuum gauge caps, or loose injectors (Chapter 3).
- [ ] Air filter clogged – renew the filter element (Chapter 1).

2 Poor running at low speeds

Spark weak

- [ ] Battery voltage low – check and recharge battery (Chapter 7).
- [ ] Spark plugs dirty, defective or worn out. Locate reason for fouled plugs using spark plug condition chart at the end of this manual and follow the plug maintenance procedures (Chapter 1).
- [ ] Incorrect spark plugs. Wrong type, heat range or cap configuration. Check and install correct plugs (Chapter 1).
- [ ] HT coil not making good contact over spark plug.
- [ ] HT coil or HT wiring defective (Chapter 3).
- [ ] Engine control unit (ECU) or ignition system component faulty (Chapter 3). Refer to a BMW dealer equipped with the diagnostic tester.

Fuel/air mixture incorrect

- [ ] Air filter clogged, poorly sealed or missing (Chapter 1).
- [ ] Air intake duct blocked or disconnected (Chapter 1).
- [ ] Intake air leak. Check for loose throttle body-to-intake manifold and air duct connections, loose or missing vacuum take-off caps, or loose injectors (see Chapter 3).
- [ ] Fuel pump failure or filter blocked (Chapter 3).
- [ ] Fuel tank breather hose obstructed.
- [ ] Injector clogged. Dirt, water or other contaminants can clog the injectors. Clean the injectors (Chapter 3) and renew the fuel filter (Chapter 1).

Compression low

- [ ] Spark plugs loose. Remove the plugs and inspect their threads. Reinstall and tighten to the specified torque (Chapter 1).
- [ ] Cylinder head not sufficiently tightened down. If the cylinder head is suspected of being loose, then there's a chance that the gasket and head are damaged if the problem has persisted for any length of time. The head nuts should be tightened to the specified torque in the correct sequence (Chapter 2).
- [ ] Improper valve clearance. This means that the valve is not closing completely and compression pressure is leaking past the valve. Check and adjust the valve clearances (Chapter 1).
- [ ] Cylinder and/or piston worn. Excessive wear will cause compression pressure to leak past the rings. This is usually accompanied by worn rings as well. A top-end overhaul is necessary (Chapter 2).
- [ ] Piston rings worn, weak, broken, or sticking. Broken or sticking piston rings usually indicate a lubrication or mixture problem that causes excess carbon deposits or seizures to form on the pistons and rings. Top-end overhaul is necessary (Chapter 2).
- [ ] Piston ring-to-groove clearance excessive. This is caused by excessive wear of the piston ring lands. Piston renewal is necessary (Chapter 2).
- [ ] Cylinder head gasket damaged. If the head is allowed to become loose, or if excessive carbon build-up on the piston crown and combustion chamber causes extremely high compression, the head gasket may leak. A new gasket is necessary (Chapter 2).
- [ ] Cylinder head warped. This is caused by overheating or improperly tightened head nuts. Machine shop resurfacing or head renewal is necessary (Chapter 2).
- [ ] Valve spring broken or weak. Caused by component failure or wear, the springs must be renewed (Chapter 2).
- [ ] Valve not seating properly. This is caused by a bent valve (from over-revving or improper valve adjustment), burned valve or seat or an accumulation of carbon deposits on the seat. The valves must be cleaned and/or renewed and the seats serviced (Chapter 2).

Poor acceleration

- [ ] Timing not advancing. Refer to a BMW dealer equipped with the diagnostic tester.
- [ ] Throttle bodies not synchronised (Chapter 1).
- [ ] Engine oil viscosity too high. Using a heavier oil than that recommended in Pre-ride checks can damage the oil pump or lubrication system and cause drag on the engine.
- [ ] Brakes dragging. Usually caused by debris which has entered the brake piston seals, or from a warped disc or bent axle (Chapter 5).

3 Poor running or no power at high speed

Firing incorrect

- [ ] Air filter clogged – renew the filter element (Chapter 1).
- [ ] Spark plugs dirty, defective or worn out. Locate reason for fouled plugs using spark plug condition chart at the end of this manual and follow the plug maintenance procedures (Chapter 1).
- [ ] Incorrect spark plugs. Wrong type, heat range or cap configuration. Check and install correct plugs (Chapter 1).
- [ ] HT coil not in good contact over spark plug.
- [ ] HT coil or HT wiring defective (Chapter 3).
- [ ] Engine control unit (ECU) or ignition system component faulty (Chapter 3). Refer to a BMW dealer equipped with the diagnostic tester.

Fuel/air mixture incorrect

- [ ] Air filter clogged, poorly sealed or missing (Chapter 1).
- [ ] Air intake duct blocked or disconnected (Chapter 1).
- [ ] Intake air leak. Check for loose throttle body-to-intake manifold and air duct connections, loose or missing vacuum take-off caps, or loose injectors (see Chapter 3).
- [ ] Fuel pump failure or filter blocked (Chapter 3).
- [ ] Fuel tank breather hose obstructed.
- [ ] Injector clogged. Dirt, water or other contaminants can clog the injectors. Clean the injectors (Chapter 3) and renew the fuel filter (Chapter 1).

Compression low

- [ ] Spark plugs loose. Remove the plugs and inspect their threads. Reinstall and tighten to the specified torque (Chapter 1).
- [ ] Cylinder head not sufficiently tightened down. If the cylinder head is suspected of being loose, then there's a chance that the gasket and head are damaged if the problem has persisted for any length of time. The head nuts should be tightened to the specified torque in the correct sequence (Chapter 2).
- [ ] Improper valve clearance. This means that the valve is not closing completely and compression pressure is leaking past the valve. Check and adjust the valve clearances (Chapter 1).
- [ ] Cylinder and/or piston worn. Excessive wear will cause compression pressure to leak past the rings. This is usually accompanied by worn rings as well. A top-end overhaul is necessary (Chapter 2).
- [ ] Piston rings worn, weak, broken, or sticking. Broken or sticking piston rings usually indicate a lubrication or mixture problem that causes excess carbon deposits or seizures to form on the pistons and rings. Top-end overhaul is necessary (Chapter 2).
- [ ] Piston ring-to-groove clearance excessive. This is caused by excessive wear of the piston ring lands. Piston renewal is necessary (Chapter 2).

- [ ] Cylinder head gasket damaged. If the head is allowed to become loose, or if excessive carbon build-up on the piston crown and combustion chamber causes extremely high compression, the head gasket may leak. A new gasket is necessary (Chapter 2).
- [ ] Cylinder head warped. This is caused by overheating or improperly tightened head nuts. Machine shop resurfacing or head renewal is necessary (Chapter 2).
- [ ] Valve spring broken or weak. Caused by component failure or wear, the springs must be renewed (Chapter 2).
- [ ] Valve not seating properly. This is caused by a bent valve (from over-revving or improper valve adjustment), burned valve or seat or an accumulation of carbon deposits on the seat. The valves must be cleaned and/or renewed and the seats serviced (Chapter 2).

Knocking or pinking

- [ ] Incorrect or poor quality fuel. Old or improper grades of fuel can cause detonation. This causes the piston to rattle, thus the knocking or pinking sound. Drain old fuel and refill with the recommended fuel grade.
- [ ] Knock sensors incorrectly fitted or defective (Chapter 2).
- [ ] Carbon build-up in combustion chamber. Use of a fuel additive that will dissolve the adhesive bonding the carbon particles to the crown and chamber is the easiest way to remove the build-up. Otherwise, the cylinder heads will have to be removed and decarbonised (Chapter 2).
- [ ] Spark plug heat range incorrect. Uncontrolled detonation indicates the plug heat range is too hot. The plug in effect becomes a glow plug, raising cylinder temperatures. Install the specified plugs (Chapter 1).
- [ ] Improper air/fuel mixture. This will cause the cylinder to run hot, which leads to detonation. Refer to a BMW dealer equipped with the diagnostic tester.

Miscellaneous causes

- [ ] Faulty or incorrectly installed side stand switch causing the safety interlock circuit to cut ignition. Check the installation and function of the switch, and its wiring and connectors (see Chapter 7).
- [ ] Throttle body valve doesn't open fully. Adjust the throttle cable freeplay and throttle body synchronisation (Chapter 1).
- [ ] Clutch slipping. May be caused by loose or worn clutch components. Refer to Chapter 2 for clutch overhaul procedures.
- [ ] Timing not advancing – refer to a BMW dealer equipped with the diagnostic tester.
- [ ] Engine oil viscosity too high. Using a heavier oil than the one recommended in Pre-ride checks can damage the oil pump or lubrication system and cause drag on the engine.
- [ ] Brakes dragging. Usually caused by debris which has entered the brake piston seals, or from a warped disc or bent axle (Chapter 5).

4 Overheating

Engine overheats

- [ ] Oil cooling circuit defective. Check the oil cooler, hoses, thermostat and the oil pump (see Chapter 2).

Firing incorrect

- [ ] Spark plugs dirty, defective or worn out. Locate reason for fouled plugs using spark plug condition chart at the end of this manual and follow the plug maintenance procedures (Chapter 1).
- [ ] Incorrect spark plugs. Wrong type, heat range or cap configuration. Check and install correct plugs (Chapter 1).
- [ ] Engine control unit (ECU) or ignition system component faulty (Chapter 3). Refer to a BMW dealer equipped with the diagnostic tester.
- [ ] Ignition HT coils defective (Chapter 3).

Fuel/air mixture incorrect

- [ ] Air filter clogged, poorly sealed or missing (Chapter 1).
- [ ] Air intake duct blocked or disconnected (Chapter 1).
- [ ] Intake air leak. Check for loose throttle body-to-intake manifold and air duct connections, loose or missing vacuum take-off caps, or loose injectors (see Chapter 3).
- [ ] Fuel pump failure or filter blocked (Chapter 3).
- [ ] Fuel tank breather hose obstructed.
- [ ] Injector clogged. Dirt, water or other contaminants can clog the injectors. Clean the injectors (Chapter 3) and renew the fuel filter (Chapter 1).

Compression too high

- [ ] Carbon build-up in combustion chamber. Use of a fuel additive that will dissolve the adhesive bonding the carbon particles to the piston crown and chamber is the easiest way to remove the build-up. Otherwise, the cylinder heads will have to be removed and decarbonised (Chapter 2).
- [ ] Improperly machined head surface or installation of incorrect gasket during engine assembly.

Engine load excessive

- [ ] Clutch slipping. Can be caused by damaged, loose or worn clutch components. Refer to Chapter 2 for overhaul procedures.
- [ ] Engine oil level too high. The addition of too much oil will cause pressurisation of the crankcase and inefficient engine operation. Drain to proper level (Chapter 1 and *Pre-ride checks*).
- [ ] Engine oil viscosity too high. Using a heavier oil than the one recommended in *Pre-ride checks* can damage the oil pump or lubrication system as well as cause drag on the engine.
- [ ] Brakes dragging. Usually caused by debris which has entered the brake piston seals, or from a warped disc or bent axle (Chapter 5).

Lubrication inadequate

- [ ] Engine oil level too low. Friction caused by intermittent lack of lubrication or from oil that is overworked can cause overheating. The oil provides a definite cooling function in the engine. Check the oil level (*Pre-ride checks*).
- [ ] Poor quality engine oil or incorrect viscosity or type. Oil is rated not only according to viscosity but also according to type. Some oils are not rated high enough for use in this engine. Check the Specifications (*Pre-ride checks*) and drain and refill with the correct oil if necessary (Chapter 1).

Miscellaneous causes

- [ ] Modification to exhaust system. Most aftermarket exhaust systems cause the engine to run leaner, which make them run hotter.

5 Clutch problems

Clutch slipping

- [ ] Clutch friction plate worn (Chapter 2).
- [ ] Clutch diaphragm spring broken or weak (Chapter 2).
- [ ] Clutch release mechanism faulty (Chapter 2).
- [ ] Clutch contaminated with oil. Renew the crankshaft and gearbox input shaft oil seals (see Chapter 2).

Clutch not disengaging completely (drag)

- [ ] Clutch release mechanism faulty (Chapter 2). This will cause clutch drag, which in turn will cause the machine to creep.
- [ ] Clutch pressure plate warped or damaged (Chapter 2).
- [ ] Clutch diaphragm spring broken or weak (Chapter 2).

6 Gearchange problems

Doesn't go into gear or lever doesn't return

☐ Clutch not disengaging – check the clutch release mechanism (Chapter 2).
☐ Selector fork(s) bent or seized - overhaul the gearchange mechanism (Chapter 2).
☐ Gear(s) stuck on shaft. Most often caused by a lack of lubrication or excessive wear in transmission bearings and bushings. Overhaul the gearbox (Chapter 2).
☐ Selector drum binding. Caused by lubrication failure or excessive wear. Renew the drum and bearing (Chapter 2).
☐ Gearchange lever return spring weak or broken (Chapter 2).
☐ Gearchange lever broken. Splines stripped out of lever or shaft, caused by allowing the lever to get loose. Renew necessary parts (Chapter 2).
☐ Stopper arm broken or worn. Poor gear engagement and rotary movement of selector drum results. Renew the arm (Chapter 2).
☐ Stopper arm spring broken. Allows arm to float, causing sporadic shift operation. Renew spring (Chapter 2).

Jumps out of gear

☐ Selector fork(s) worn – overhaul the transmission (Chapter 2).
☐ Gear groove(s) worn – overhaul the transmission (Chapter 2).
☐ Gear dogs or dog slots worn or damaged. The gears should be inspected and renewed. No attempt should be made to service the worn parts.

Overshifts

☐ Stopper arm spring weak or broken (Chapter 2).
☐ Gearchange shaft return spring post broken or distorted (Chapter 2).

7 Abnormal engine noise

Knocking or pinking

☐ Incorrect or poor quality fuel. Old or improper grades of fuel can cause detonation. This causes the piston to rattle, thus the knocking or pinking sound. Drain old fuel and refill with the recommended fuel grade.
☐ Knock sensors incorrectly fitted or defective (Chapter 2).
☐ Carbon build-up in combustion chamber. Use of a fuel additive that will dissolve the adhesive bonding the carbon particles to the crown and chamber is the easiest way to remove the build-up. Otherwise, the cylinder heads will have to be removed and decarbonised (Chapter 2).
☐ Spark plug heat range incorrect. Uncontrolled detonation indicates the plug heat range is too hot. The plug in effect becomes a glow plug, raising cylinder temperatures. Install the specified plugs (Chapter 1).
☐ Improper air/fuel mixture. This will cause the cylinder to run hot, which leads to detonation. Refer to a BMW dealer equipped with the diagnostic tester.

Piston slap or rattling

☐ Cylinder-to-piston clearance excessive, caused by wear or improper assembly (Chapter 2).
☐ Connecting rod bent. Caused by over-revving, trying to start a badly flooded engine or from ingesting a foreign object into the combustion chamber (Chapter 2).

☐ Piston pin or piston pin bore worn or seized from wear or lack of lubrication (Chapter 2).
☐ Piston rings worn, broken or sticking in their grooves (Chapter 2).
☐ Piston seizure damage. Usually from lack of lubrication or overheating. Renew the pistons and cylinders, as necessary (Chapter 2).
☐ Connecting rod small-end or big-end bearing clearance excessive. Caused by excessive wear or lack of lubrication (Chapter 2).

Valve noise

☐ Incorrect valve clearances (Chapter 1).
☐ Valve spring broken or weak (Chapter 2).
☐ Camshafts or auxiliary shaft worn, or their bearing surfaces worn (Chapter 2).

Other noise

☐ Cylinder head gasket leaking (Chapter 2).
☐ Exhaust pipe leaking at cylinder head connection. Caused by improper fit of pipe(s) or loose exhaust flange. All exhaust fasteners should be tightened evenly and carefully (Chapter 3).
☐ Crankshaft runout excessive. Caused by a bent crankshaft (from over-revving) or damage from an upper cylinder component failure (Chapter 2).
☐ Crankshaft main bearings worn (Chapter 2).
☐ Cam chain tensioner defective (Chapter 2).
☐ Cam chain, sprockets or guides worn (Chapter 2).

8 Abnormal driveline noise

Clutch noise

☐ Loose or damaged clutch components (Chapter 2).

Gearbox noise

☐ Bearings worn. Also includes the possibility that the shafts are worn (Chapter 2).
☐ Gears worn or chipped (Chapter 2).
☐ Metal chips jammed in gear teeth. Probably pieces from a broken gear or selector mechanism that were picked up by the gears. This will cause early bearing failure (Chapter 2).
☐ Gearbox oil level too low. Causes a howl from gearbox (Chapter 1).

Final drive noise

☐ Final drive oil level low, worn or damaged gears or final drive bearings. Refer to a BMW dealer.
☐ Driveshaft splines or universal joint worn (Chapter 4).

9 Abnormal frame and suspension noise

Front end noise

- ☐ Telelever ball joint loose or worn (Chapter 4).
- ☐ Telelever mountings loose or bearings worn (Chapter 4).
- ☐ Worn fork slider bushes (Chapter 4).
- ☐ Steering head bearing worn or damaged – clicks when braking (Chapter 4).
- ☐ Fork bridge or top yoke loose – ensure that all bolts are tight (Chapter 4).
- ☐ Fork tube bent – possibility if machine has crashed. Renew both fork tubes (Chapter 4).
- ☐ Front axle or axle clamp bolt loose. Tighten to the specified torque settings (Chapter 5).
- ☐ Loose or worn wheel bearings (Chapter 5).
- ☐ Shock absorber faulty (see below).

Rear end noise

- ☐ Swingarm mountings loose or bearings worn (Chapter 4).
- ☐ Final drive unit mountings loose or bearings worn (Chapter 4).

- ☐ Paralever arm mountings loose (Chapter 4).
- ☐ Shock absorber faulty (see below).

Shock absorber noise

- ☐ Loose or worn mounting bolts, or worn bushes (Chapter 4).
- ☐ Fluid level low due to leak caused by defective seal (Chapter 4).
- ☐ Defective shock absorber with internal damage (Chapter 4).
- ☐ Bent damper rod or damaged shock body (Chapter 4).

Brake noise

- ☐ Squeal caused by dust on brake pads – usually found in combination with glazed pads (Chapter 5).
- ☐ Contamination of brake pads – oil or brake fluid causing brake to chatter or squeal (Chapter 5).
- ☐ Pads glazed caused by excessive heat from prolonged use or from contamination (Chapter 5).
- ☐ Disc warped – can cause a chattering, clicking or intermittent squeal, usually accompanied by a pulsating lever and uneven braking (Chapter 5).

10 Oil pressure warning light comes on

Engine lubrication system

- ☐ Engine oil level low. Inspect for leak or other problem causing low oil level and top-up with recommended oil (Pre-ride checks).
- ☐ Engine oil viscosity too low. Very old, thin oil or an improper weight of oil used in the engine. Drain and refill with specified oil (Chapter 1).
- ☐ Engine oil pump defective, blocked oil strainer gauze or failed relief valve. Carry out an oil pressure check (Chapter 2).

- ☐ Camshafts, auxiliary shaft or crankshaft bearings worn, causing drop in oil pressure (Chapter 2).

Electrical system

- ☐ Oil pressure switch defective – check the switch (Chapter 7).
- ☐ Oil pressure warning light circuit defective. Check for pinched, shorted, disconnected or damaged wiring (Chapter 7).

11 Excessive exhaust smoke

White smoke

- ☐ Piston oil ring worn or broken, causing oil from the crankcase to be pulled past the piston into the combustion chamber. Renew the rings (Chapter 2).
- ☐ Cylinders worn or scored, caused by overheating or oil starvation. Measure cylinder diameter and renew if necessary (Chapter 2).
- ☐ Valve oil seals damaged or worn – renew oil seals (Chapter 2).
- ☐ Valve guides worn – complete valve job required (Chapter 2).
- ☐ Engine oil level too high, which causes the oil to be forced past the rings. Drain oil to the proper level (Chapter 1 and Pre-ride checks).
- ☐ Head gasket broken between oil return and cylinder. Causes oil to be pulled into the combustion chamber. Renew the head gasket and check the head for warpage (Chapter 2).
- ☐ Abnormal crankcase pressurisation, which forces oil past the

rings. Damaged or dirty vent valve or clogged breather hose is usually the cause (Chapter 2).

Black smoke

- ☐ Air filter clogged – renew the filter element (Chapter 1).
- ☐ Engine control unit (ECU) defective. Refer to a BMW dealer equipped with the diagnostic tester.

Brown smoke

- ☐ Fuel filter clogged - renew the fuel filter (Chapter 3).
- ☐ Fuel flow insufficient. Have a BMW dealer perform a fuel pressure check.
- ☐ Intake air leak. Check for loose throttle body-to-intake manifold and air duct connections, loose or missing vacuum take-off caps, or loose injectors (Chapter 3).
- ☐ Air filter poorly sealed or not installed (Chapter 1).

12 Poor handling or stability

Handlebars hard to turn

- [ ] Steering head bearing defective (Chapter 4).
- [ ] Front tyre air pressure too low (*Pre-ride checks*).

Handlebar shakes or vibrates excessively

- [ ] Tyres worn or out of balance. Inspect for wear (*Pre-ride checks*). Have a tyre specialist balance the wheels.
- [ ] Swingarm or Telelever bearings worn (Chapter 4).
- [ ] Wheel rim(s) warped or damaged – check wheel runout (Chapter 5).
- [ ] Wheel bearings worn (Chapters 1 and 5).
- [ ] Handlebar mounting bolts loose (Chapter 4).
- [ ] Fork bridge or top yoke bolts loose (Chapter 4).

Handlebar pulls to one side

- [ ] Wheels out of alignment (Chapter 5).
- [ ] Front or rear suspension components worn or damaged caused by accident. Have the machine checked thoroughly by a BMW dealer or frame specialist.
- [ ] Fork tube bent – renew both fork tubes (Chapter 4).

Poor shock absorbing qualities

- [ ] Incorrect adjustment of suspension (Chapter 4).
- [ ] Tyre pressures incorrect (*Pre-ride checks*).
- [ ] Front or rear shock absorber damage (Chapter 4).

13 Braking problems

Brakes are spongy, don't hold

- [ ] Air in brake line. Caused by inattention to master cylinder fluid level or by leakage. Locate problem and bleed brakes (Chapter 5).
- [ ] Brake fluid leak.
- [ ] Brake fluid deteriorated through age or contaminated. Change brake fluid (Chapter 5).
- [ ] Master cylinder internal parts worn or damaged causing fluid to bypass. Overhaul master cylinder (Chapter 5).
- [ ] Pads or disc worn (Chapter 5).
- [ ] Brake pads contaminated with oil, grease or brake fluid. Renew pads and clean disc thoroughly with brake cleaner (Chapter 5).
- [ ] Disc warped (Chapter 5).
- [ ] ABS system faulty (Chapter 5).

Brake lever or pedal pulsates

- [ ] Disc warped (Chapter 5).
- [ ] Axle bent (Chapter 5).
- [ ] Brake caliper mounting bolts loose (Chapter 5).

- [ ] Rear brake caliper sliders damaged or sticking, causing caliper to bind. Clean and lubricate the sliders (Chapter 5).
- [ ] Wheel warped or otherwise damaged (Chapter 5).
- [ ] Wheel bearings (front) or final drive bearings (rear) damaged or worn (Chapters 1 and 5).
- [ ] ABS system faulty (Chapter 5).

Brakes drag

- [ ] Master cylinder piston seized (Chapter 5).
- [ ] Lever balky or stuck (Chapter 1).
- [ ] Rear brake caliper binds – caused by inadequate lubrication or damage to caliper slider pins (Chapter 5).
- [ ] Brake caliper piston seized in bore (Chapter 5).
- [ ] Brake pad damaged. Pad material separated from backing plate, usually caused by faulty manufacturing process or from contact with chemicals. Renew pads (Chapter 5).
- [ ] Pads improperly installed (Chapter 5).

14 Electrical problems

Battery dead or weak

- [ ] Battery faulty due to lack of maintenance or internal damage (Chapter 7).
- [ ] Battery leads making poor contact (Chapter 7).
- [ ] Load excessive. Caused by addition of high wattage lights or other electrical accessories.
- [ ] Ignition (main) switch defective. Switch either earths (grounds) internally or fails to shut off system (Chapter 7).
- [ ] Charging system defective (Chapter 7).
- [ ] Wiring faulty. Wiring earthed (grounded) or connections loose in ignition, charging or lighting circuits (Chapter 7).

Battery overcharged

- [ ] Alternator defective. Overcharging is noticed when battery gets excessively warm (Chapter 7).
- [ ] Battery has internal fault (Chapter 7).
- [ ] Battery amperage too low, wrong type or size. Install manufacturer's specified amp-hour battery to handle charging load (Chapter 7).

A

ABS (Anti-lock braking system) A system, usually electronically controlled, that senses incipient wheel lockup during braking and relieves hydraulic pressure at wheel which is about to skid.

Aftermarket Components suitable for the motorcycle, but not produced by the motorcycle manufacturer.

Allen key A hexagonal wrench which fits into a recessed hexagonal hole.

Alternating current (ac) Current produced by an alternator. Requires converting to direct current by a rectifier for charging purposes.

Alternator Converts mechanical energy from the engine into electrical energy to charge the battery and power the electrical system.

Ampere (amp) A unit of measurement for the flow of electrical current. Current = Volts ÷ Ohms.

Ampere-hour (Ah) Measure of battery capacity.

Angle-tightening A torque expressed in degrees. Often follows a conventional tightening torque for cylinder head or main bearing fasteners **(see illustration)**.

Angle-tightening cylinder head bolts

Antifreeze A substance (usually ethylene glycol) mixed with water, and added to the cooling system, to prevent freezing of the coolant in winter. Antifreeze also contains chemicals to inhibit corrosion and the formation of rust and other deposits that would tend to clog the radiator and coolant passages and reduce cooling efficiency.

Anti-dive System attached to the fork lower leg (slider) to prevent fork dive when braking hard.

Anti-seize compound A coating that reduces the risk of seizing on fasteners that are subjected to high temperatures, such as exhaust clamp bolts and nuts.

API American Petroleum Institute. A quality standard for 4-stroke motor oils.

Asbestos A natural fibrous mineral with great heat resistance, commonly used in the composition of brake friction materials. Asbestos is a health hazard and the dust created by brake systems should never be inhaled or ingested.

ATF Automatic Transmission Fluid. Often used in front forks.

ATU Automatic Timing Unit. Mechanical device for advancing the ignition timing on early engines.

ATV All Terrain Vehicle. Often called a Quad.

Axial play Side-to-side movement.

Axle A shaft on which a wheel revolves. Also known as a spindle.

B

Backlash The amount of movement between meshed components when one component is held still. Usually applies to gear teeth.

Ball bearing A bearing consisting of a hardened inner and outer race with hardened steel balls between the two races.

Bearings Used between two working surfaces to prevent wear of the components and a build-up of heat. Four types of bearing are commonly used on motorcycles: plain shell bearings, ball bearings, tapered roller bearings and needle roller bearings.

Bevel gears Used to turn the drive through 90°. Typical applications are shaft final drive and camshaft drive **(see illustration)**.

Bevel gears are used to turn the drive through 90°

BHP Brake Horsepower. The British measurement for engine power output. Power output is now usually expressed in kilowatts (kW).

Bias-belted tyre Similar construction to radial tyre, but with outer belt running at an angle to the wheel rim.

Big-end bearing The bearing in the end of the connecting rod that's attached to the crankshaft.

Bleeding The process of removing air from an hydraulic system via a bleed nipple or bleed screw.

Bottom-end A description of an engine's crankcase components and all components contained there-in.

BTDC Before Top Dead Centre in terms of piston position. Ignition timing is often expressed in terms of degrees or millimetres BTDC.

Bush A cylindrical metal or rubber component used between two moving parts.

Burr Rough edge left on a component after machining or as a result of excessive wear.

C

Cam chain The chain which takes drive from the crankshaft to the camshaft(s).

Canister The main component in an evaporative emission control system (California market only); contains activated charcoal granules to trap vapours from the fuel system rather than allowing them to vent to the atmosphere.

Castellated Resembling the parapets along the top of a castle wall. For example, a castellated wheel axle or spindle nut.

Catalytic converter A device in the exhaust system of some machines which converts certain pollutants in the exhaust gases into less harmful substances.

Charging system Description of the components which charge the battery, ie the alternator, rectifer and regulator.

Circlip A ring-shaped clip used to prevent endwise movement of cylindrical parts and shafts. An internal circlip is installed in a groove in a housing; an external circlip fits into a groove on the outside of a cylindrical piece such as a shaft. Also known as a snap-ring.

Clearance The amount of space between two parts. For example, between a piston and a cylinder, between a bearing and a journal, etc.

Coil spring A spiral of elastic steel found in various sizes throughout a vehicle, for example as a springing medium in the suspension and in the valve train.

Compression Reduction in volume, and increase in pressure and temperature, of a gas, caused by squeezing it into a smaller space.

Compression damping Controls the speed the suspension compresses when hitting a bump.

Compression ratio The relationship between cylinder volume when the piston is at top dead centre and cylinder volume when the piston is at bottom dead centre.

Continuity The uninterrupted path in the flow of electricity. Little or no measurable resistance.

Continuity tester Self-powered bleeper or test light which indicates continuity.

Cp Candlepower. Bulb rating commonly found on US motorcycles.

Crossply tyre Tyre plies arranged in a criss-cross pattern. Usually four or six plies used, hence 4PR or 6PR in tyre size codes.

Cush drive Rubber damper segments fitted between the rear wheel and final drive sprocket to absorb transmission shocks **(see illustration)**.

Cush drive rubbers dampen out transmission shocks

D

Degree disc Calibrated disc for measuring piston position. Expressed in degrees.

Dial gauge Clock-type gauge with adapters for measuring runout and piston position. Expressed in mm or inches.

Diaphragm The rubber membrane in a master cylinder or carburettor which seals the upper chamber.

Diaphragm spring A single sprung plate often used in clutches.

Direct current (dc) Current produced by a dc generator.

Decarbonisation The process of removing carbon deposits - typically from the combustion chamber, valves and exhaust port/system.
Detonation Destructive and damaging explosion of fuel/air mixture in combustion chamber instead of controlled burning.
Diode An electrical valve which only allows current to flow in one direction. Commonly used in rectifiers and starter interlock systems.
Disc valve (or rotary valve) A induction system used on some two-stroke engines.
Double-overhead camshaft (DOHC) An engine that uses two overhead camshafts, one for the intake valves and one for the exhaust valves.
Drivebelt A toothed belt used to transmit drive to the rear wheel on some motorcycles. A drivebelt has also been used to drive the camshafts. Drivebelts are usually made of Kevlar.
Driveshaft Any shaft used to transmit motion. Commonly used when referring to the final driveshaft on shaft drive motorcycles.

E

Earth return The return path of an electrical circuit, utilising the motorcycle's frame.
ECU (Electronic Control Unit) A computer which controls (for instance) an ignition system, or an anti-lock braking system.
EGO Exhaust Gas Oxygen sensor. Sometimes called a Lambda sensor.
Electrolyte The fluid in a lead-acid battery.
EMS (Engine Management System) A computer controlled system which manages the fuel injection and the ignition systems in an integrated fashion.
Endfloat The amount of lengthways movement between two parts. As applied to a crankshaft, the distance that the crankshaft can move side-to-side in the crankcase.
Endless chain A chain having no joining link. Common use for cam chains and final drive chains.
EP (Extreme Pressure) Oil type used in locations where high loads are applied, such as between gear teeth.
Evaporative emission control system Describes a charcoal filled canister which stores fuel vapours from the tank rather than allowing them to vent to the atmosphere. Usually only fitted to California models and referred to as an EVAP system.
Expansion chamber Section of two-stroke engine exhaust system so designed to improve engine efficiency and boost power.

F

Feeler blade or gauge A thin strip or blade of hardened steel, ground to an exact thickness, used to check or measure clearances between parts.
Final drive Description of the drive from the transmission to the rear wheel. Usually by chain or shaft, but sometimes by belt.
Firing order The order in which the engine cylinders fire, or deliver their power strokes, beginning with the number one cylinder.
Flooding Term used to describe a high fuel level in the carburettor float chambers, leading to fuel overflow. Also refers to excess fuel in the combustion chamber due to incorrect starting technique.

Free length The no-load state of a component when measured. Clutch, valve and fork spring lengths are measured at rest, without any preload.
Freeplay The amount of travel before any action takes place. The looseness in a linkage, or an assembly of parts, between the initial application of force and actual movement. For example, the distance the rear brake pedal moves before the rear brake is actuated.
Fuel injection The fuel/air mixture is metered electronically and directed into the engine intake ports (indirect injection) or into the cylinders (direct injection). Sensors supply information on engine speed and conditions.
Fuel/air mixture The charge of fuel and air going into the engine. See **Stoichiometric ratio**.
Fuse An electrical device which protects a circuit against accidental overload. The typical fuse contains a soft piece of metal which is calibrated to melt at a predetermined current flow (expressed as amps) and break the circuit.

G

Gap The distance the spark must travel in jumping from the centre electrode to the side electrode in a spark plug. Also refers to the distance between the ignition rotor and the pickup coil in an electronic ignition system.
Gasket Any thin, soft material - usually cork, cardboard, asbestos or soft metal - installed between two metal surfaces to ensure a good seal. For instance, the cylinder head gasket seals the joint between the block and the cylinder head.
Gauge An instrument panel display used to monitor engine conditions. A gauge with a movable pointer on a dial or a fixed scale is an analogue gauge. A gauge with a numerical readout is called a digital gauge.
Gear ratios The drive ratio of a pair of gears in a gearbox, calculated on their number of teeth.
Glaze-busting see **Honing**
Grinding Process for renovating the valve face and valve seat contact area in the cylinder head.
Gudgeon pin The shaft which connects the connecting rod small-end with the piston. Often called a piston pin or wrist pin.

H

Helical gears Gear teeth are slightly curved and produce less gear noise that straight-cut gears. Often used for primary drives.

Installing a Helicoil thread insert in a cylinder head

Helicoil A thread insert repair system. Commonly used as a repair for stripped spark plug threads **(see illustration)**.
Honing A process used to break down the glaze on a cylinder bore (also called glaze-busting). Can also be carried out to roughen a rebored cylinder to aid ring bedding-in.
HT (High Tension) Description of the electrical circuit from the secondary winding of the ignition coil to the spark plug.
Hydraulic A liquid filled system used to transmit pressure from one component to another. Common uses on motorcycles are brakes and clutches.
Hydrometer An instrument for measuring the specific gravity of a lead-acid battery.
Hygroscopic Water absorbing. In motorcycle applications, braking efficiency will be reduced if DOT 3 or 4 hydraulic fluid absorbs water from the air - care must be taken to keep new brake fluid in tightly sealed containers.

I

lbf ft Pounds-force feet. An imperial unit of torque. Sometimes written as ft-lbs.
lbf in Pound-force inch. An imperial unit of torque, applied to components where a very low torque is required. Sometimes written as in-lbs.
IC Abbreviation for Integrated Circuit.
Ignition advance Means of increasing the timing of the spark at higher engine speeds. Done by mechanical means (ATU) on early engines or electronically by the ignition control unit on later engines.
Ignition timing The moment at which the spark plug fires, expressed in the number of crankshaft degrees before the piston reaches the top of its stroke, or in the number of millimetres before the piston reaches the top of its stroke.
Infinity (∞) Description of an open-circuit electrical state, where no continuity exists.
Inverted forks (upside down forks) The sliders or lower legs are held in the yokes and the fork tubes or stanchions are connected to the wheel axle (spindle). Less unsprung weight and stiffer construction than conventional forks.

J

JASO Quality standard for 2-stroke oils.
Joule The unit of electrical energy.
Journal The bearing surface of a shaft.

K

Kickstart Mechanical means of turning the engine over for starting purposes. Only usually fitted to mopeds, small capacity motorcycles and off-road motorcycles.
Kill switch Handebar-mounted switch for emergency ignition cut-out. Cuts the ignition circuit on all models, and additionally prevent starter motor operation on others.
km Symbol for kilometre.
kmh Abbreviation for kilometres per hour.

L

Lambda (λ) sensor A sensor fitted in the exhaust system to measure the exhaust gas oxygen content (excess air factor).

Lapping see **Grinding**.

LCD Abbreviation for Liquid Crystal Display.

LED Abbreviation for Light Emitting Diode.

Liner A steel cylinder liner inserted in a aluminium alloy cylinder block.

Locknut A nut used to lock an adjustment nut, or other threaded component, in place.

Lockstops The lugs on the lower triple clamp (yoke) which abut those on the frame, preventing handlebar-to-fuel tank contact.

Lockwasher A form of washer designed to prevent an attaching nut from working loose.

LT Low Tension Description of the electrical circuit from the power supply to the primary winding of the ignition coil.

M

Main bearings The bearings between the crankshaft and crankcase.

Maintenance-free (MF) battery A sealed battery which cannot be topped up.

Manometer Mercury-filled calibrated tubes used to measure intake tract vacuum. Used to synchronise carburettors on multi-cylinder engines.

Micrometer A precision measuring instrument that measures component outside diameters **(see illustration)**.

Tappet shims are measured with a micrometer

MON (Motor Octane Number) A measure of a fuel's resistance to knock.

Monograde oil An oil with a single viscosity, eg SAE80W.

Monoshock A single suspension unit linking the swingarm or suspension linkage to the frame.

mph Abbreviation for miles per hour.

Multigrade oil Having a wide viscosity range (eg 10W40). The W stands for Winter, thus the viscosity ranges from SAE10 when cold to SAE40 when hot.

Multimeter An electrical test instrument with the capability to measure voltage, current and resistance. Some meters also incorporate a continuity tester and buzzer.

N

Needle roller bearing Inner race of caged needle rollers and hardened outer race. Examples of uncaged needle rollers can be found on some engines. Commonly used in rear suspension applications and in two-stroke engines.

Nm Newton metres.

NOx Oxides of Nitrogen. A common toxic pollutant emitted by petrol engines at higher temperatures.

O

Octane The measure of a fuel's resistance to knock.

OE (Original Equipment) Relates to components fitted to a motorcycle as standard or replacement parts supplied by the motorcycle manufacturer.

Ohm The unit of electrical resistance. Ohms = Volts ÷ Current.

Ohmmeter An instrument for measuring electrical resistance.

Oil cooler System for diverting engine oil outside of the engine to a radiator for cooling purposes.

Oil injection A system of two-stroke engine lubrication where oil is pump-fed to the engine in accordance with throttle position.

Open-circuit An electrical condition where there is a break in the flow of electricity - no continuity (high resistance).

O-ring A type of sealing ring made of a special rubber-like material; in use, the O-ring is compressed into a groove to provide the sealing action.

Oversize (OS) Term used for piston and ring size options fitted to a rebored cylinder.

Overhead cam (sohc) engine An engine with single camshaft located on top of the cylinder head.

Overhead valve (ohv) engine An engine with the valves located in the cylinder head, but with the camshaft located in the engine block or crankcase.

Oxygen sensor A device installed in the exhaust system which senses the oxygen content in the exhaust and converts this information into an electric current. Also called a Lambda sensor.

P

Plastigauge A thin strip of plastic thread, available in different sizes, used for measuring clearances. For example, a strip of Plastigauge is laid across a bearing journal. The parts are assembled and dismantled; the width of the crushed strip indicates the clearance between journal and bearing.

Polarity Either negative or positive earth (ground), determined by which battery lead is connected to the frame (earth return). Modern motorcycles are usually negative earth.

Pre-ignition A situation where the fuel/air mixture ignites before the spark plug fires. Often due to a hot spot in the combustion chamber caused by carbon build-up. Engine has a tendency to 'run-on'.

Pre-load (suspension) The amount a spring is compressed when in the unloaded state. Preload can be applied by gas, spacer or mechanical adjuster.

Premix The method of engine lubrication on older two-stroke engines. Engine oil is mixed with the petrol in the fuel tank in a specific ratio. The fuel/oil mix is sometimes referred to as "petroil".

Primary drive Description of the drive from the crankshaft to the clutch. Usually by gear or chain.

PS Pfedestärke - a German interpretation of BHP.

PSI Pounds-force per square inch. Imperial measurement of tyre pressure and cylinder pressure measurement.

PTFE Polytetrafluoroethylene. A low friction substance.

Pulse secondary air injection system A process of promoting the burning of excess fuel present in the exhaust gases by routing fresh air into the exhaust ports.

Q

Quartz halogen bulb Tungsten filament surrounded by a halogen gas. Typically used for the headlight **(see illustration)**.

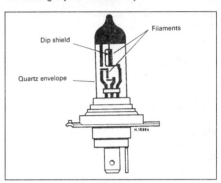

Quartz halogen headlight bulb construction

R

Rack-and-pinion A pinion gear on the end of a shaft that mates with a rack (think of a geared wheel opened up and laid flat). Sometimes used in clutch operating systems.

Radial play Up and down movement about a shaft.

Radial ply tyres Tyre plies run across the tyre (from bead to bead) and around the circumference of the tyre. Less resistant to tread distortion than other tyre types.

Radiator A liquid-to-air heat transfer device designed to reduce the temperature of the coolant in a liquid cooled engine.

Rake A feature of steering geometry - the angle of the steering head in relation to the vertical **(see illustration)**.

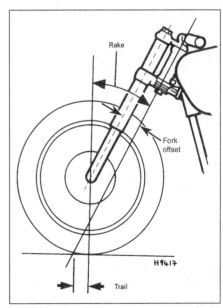

Steering geometry

Rebore Providing a new working surface to the cylinder bore by boring out the old surface. Necessitates the use of oversize piston and rings.

Rebound damping A means of controlling the oscillation of a suspension unit spring after it has been compressed. Resists the spring's natural tendency to bounce back after being compressed.

Rectifier Device for converting the ac output of an alternator into dc for battery charging.

Reed valve An induction system commonly used on two-stroke engines.

Regulator Device for maintaining the charging voltage from the generator or alternator within a specified range.

Relay A electrical device used to switch heavy current on and off by using a low current auxiliary circuit.

Resistance Measured in ohms. An electrical component's ability to pass electrical current.

RON (Research Octane Number) A measure of a fuel's resistance to knock.

rpm revolutions per minute.

Runout The amount of wobble (in-and-out movement) of a wheel or shaft as it's rotated. The amount a shaft rotates 'out-of-true'. The out-of-round condition of a rotating part.

S

SAE (Society of Automotive Engineers) A standard for the viscosity of a fluid.

Sealant A liquid or paste used to prevent leakage at a joint. Sometimes used in conjunction with a gasket.

Service limit Term for the point where a component is no longer useable and must be renewed.

Shaft drive A method of transmitting drive from the transmission to the rear wheel.

Shell bearings Plain bearings consisting of two shell halves. Most often used as big-end and main bearings in a four-stroke engine. Often called bearing inserts.

Shim Thin spacer, commonly used to adjust the clearance or relative positions between two parts. For example, shims inserted into or under tappets or followers to control valve clearances. Clearance is adjusted by changing the thickness of the shim.

Short-circuit An electrical condition where current shorts to earth (ground) bypassing the circuit components.

Skimming Process to correct warpage or repair a damaged surface, eg on brake discs or drums.

Slide-hammer A special puller that screws into or hooks onto a component such as a shaft or bearing; a heavy sliding handle on the shaft bottoms against the end of the shaft to knock the component free.

Small-end bearing The bearing in the upper end of the connecting rod at its joint with the gudgeon pin.

Spalling Damage to camshaft lobes or bearing journals shown as pitting of the working surface.

Specific gravity (SG) The state of charge of the electrolyte in a lead-acid battery. A measure of the electrolyte's density compared with water.

Straight-cut gears Common type gear used on gearbox shafts and for oil pump and water pump drives.

Stanchion The inner sliding part of the front forks, held by the yokes. Often called a fork tube.

Stoichiometric ratio The optimum chemical air/fuel ratio for a petrol engine, said to be 14.7 parts of air to 1 part of fuel.

Sulphuric acid The liquid (electrolyte) used in a lead-acid battery. Poisonous and extremely corrosive.

Surface grinding (lapping) Process to correct a warped gasket face, commonly used on cylinder heads.

T

Tapered-roller bearing Tapered inner race of caged needle rollers and separate tapered outer race. Examples of taper roller bearings can be found on steering heads.

Tappet A cylindrical component which transmits motion from the cam to the valve stem, either directly or via a pushrod and rocker arm. Also called a cam follower.

TCS Traction Control System. An electronically-controlled system which senses wheel spin and reduces engine speed accordingly.

TDC Top Dead Centre denotes that the piston is at its highest point in the cylinder.

Thread-locking compound Solution applied to fastener threads to prevent slackening. Select type to suit application.

Thrust washer A washer positioned between two moving components on a shaft. For example, between gear pinions on gearshaft.

Timing chain See **Cam Chain**.

Timing light Stroboscopic lamp for carrying out ignition timing checks with the engine running.

Top-end A description of an engine's cylinder block, head and valve gear components.

Torque Turning or twisting force about a shaft.

Torque setting A prescribed tightness specified by the motorcycle manufacturer to ensure that the bolt or nut is secured correctly. Undertightening can result in the bolt or nut coming loose or a surface not being sealed. Overtightening can result in stripped threads, distortion or damage to the component being retained.

Torx key A six-point wrench.

Tracer A stripe of a second colour applied to a wire insulator to distinguish that wire from another one with the same colour insulator. For example, Br/W is often used to denote a brown insulator with a white tracer.

Trail A feature of steering geometry. Distance from the steering head axis to the tyre's central contact point.

Triple clamps The cast components which extend from the steering head and support the fork stanchions or tubes. Often called fork yokes.

Turbocharger A centrifugal device, driven by exhaust gases, that pressurises the intake air. Normally used to increase the power output from a given engine displacement.

TWI Abbreviation for Tyre Wear Indicator. Indicates the location of the tread depth indicator bars on tyres.

U

Universal joint or U-joint (UJ) A double-pivoted connection for transmitting power from a driving to a driven shaft through an angle. Typically found in shaft drive assemblies.

Unsprung weight Anything not supported by the bike's suspension (ie the wheel, tyres, brakes, final drive and bottom (moving) part of the suspension).

V

Vacuum gauges Clock-type gauges for measuring intake tract vacuum. Used for carburettor synchronisation on multi-cylinder engines.

Valve A device through which the flow of liquid, gas or vacuum may be stopped, started or regulated by a moveable part that opens, shuts or partially obstructs one or more ports or passageways. The intake and exhaust valves in the cylinder head are of the poppet type.

Valve clearance The clearance between the valve tip (the end of the valve stem) and the rocker arm or tappet/follower. The valve clearance is measured when the valve is closed. The correct clearance is important - if too small the valve won't close fully and will burn out, whereas if too large noisy operation will result.

Valve lift The amount a valve is lifted off its seat by the camshaft lobe.

Valve timing The exact setting for the opening and closing of the valves in relation to piston position.

Vernier caliper A precision measuring instrument that measures inside and outside dimensions. Not quite as accurate as a micrometer, but more convenient.

VIN Vehicle Identification Number. Term for the bike's engine and frame numbers.

Viscosity The thickness of a liquid or its resistance to flow.

Volt A unit for expressing electrical "pressure" in a circuit. Volts = current x ohms.

W

Water pump A mechanically-driven device for moving coolant around the engine.

Watt A unit for expressing electrical power. Watts = volts x current.

Wear limit see **Service limit**

Wet liner A liquid-cooled engine design where the pistons run in liners which are directly surrounded by coolant **(see illustration)**.

Wet liner arrangement

Wheelbase Distance from the centre of the front wheel to the centre of the rear wheel.

Wiring harness or loom Describes the electrical wires running the length of the motorcycle and enclosed in tape or plastic sheathing. Wiring coming off the main harness is usually referred to as a sub harness.

Woodruff key A key of semi-circular or square section used to locate a gear to a shaft. Often used to locate the alternator rotor on the crankshaft.

Wrist pin Another name for gudgeon or piston pin.

Note: *References throughout this index are in the form - "Chapter number" • "Page number"*

Note: *References throughout this index are in the form - "Chapter number" • "Page number"*

Note: *References throughout this index are in the form - "Chapter number" • "Page number"*

Haynes Motorcycle Manuals – The Complete List

Title	Book No
APRILIA RS50 (99 - 06) & RS125 (93 - 06)	4298
Aprilia RSV1000 Mille (98 - 03)	♦ 4255
Aprilia SR50	4755
BMW 2-valve Twins (70 - 96)	♦ 0249
BMW F650	♦ 4761
BMW K100 & 75 2-valve Models (83 - 96)	♦ 1373
BMW R850, 1100 & 1150 4-valve Twins (93 - 04)	♦ 3466
BMW R1200 (04 - 06)	♦ 4598
BSA Bantam (48 - 71)	0117
BSA Unit Singles (58 - 72)	0127
BSA Pre-unit Singles (54 - 61)	0326
BSA A7 & A10 Twins (47 - 62)	0121
BSA A50 & A65 Twins (62 - 73)	0155
Chinese Scooters	4768
DUCATI 600, 620, 750 and 900 2-valve V-Twins (91 - 05)	♦ 3290
Ducati MK III & Desmo Singles (69 - 76)	◊ 0445
Ducati 748, 916 & 996 4-valve V-Twins (94 - 01)	♦ 3756
GILERA Runner, DNA, Ice & SKP/Stalker (97 - 07)	4163
HARLEY-DAVIDSON Sportsters (70 - 08)	♦ 2534
Harley-Davidson Shovelhead and Evolution Big Twins (70 - 99)	♦ 2536
Harley-Davidson Twin Cam 88 (99 - 03)	♦ 2478
HONDA NB, ND, NP & NS50 Melody (81 - 85)	◊ 0622
Honda NE/NB50 Vision & SA50 Vision Met-in (85 - 95)	◊ 1278
Honda MB, MBX, MT & MTX50 (80 - 93)	0731
Honda C50, C70 & C90 (67 - 03)	0324
Honda XR80/100R & CRF80/100F (85 - 04)	2218
Honda XL/XR 80, 100, 125, 185 & 200 2-valve Models (78 - 87)	0566
Honda H100 & H100S Singles (80 - 92)	◊ 0734
Honda CB/CD125T & CM125C Twins (77 - 88)	◊ 0571
Honda CG125 (76 - 07)	◊ 0433
Honda NS125 (86 - 93)	◊ 3056
Honda CBR125R (04 - 07)	4620
Honda MBX/MTX125 & MTX200 (83 - 93)	◊ 1132
Honda CD/CM185 200T & CM250C 2-valve Twins (77 - 85)	0572
Honda XL/XR 250 & 500 (78 - 84)	0567
Honda XR250L, XR250R & XR400R (86 - 03)	2219
Honda CB250 & CB400N Super Dreams (78 - 84)	◊ 0540
Honda CR Motocross Bikes (86 - 01)	2222
Honda CRF250 & CRF450 (02 - 06)	2630
Honda CB400RR Fours (88 - 99)	◊ ♦ 3552
Honda VFR400 (NC30) & RVF400 (NC35) V-Fours (89 - 98)	◊ ♦ 3496
Honda CB500 (93 - 02) & CBF500 03 - 08	◊ 3753
Honda CB400 & CB550 Fours (73 - 77)	0262
Honda CX/GL500 & 650 V-Twins (78 - 86)	0442
Honda CBX550 Four (82 - 86)	◊ 0940
Honda XL600R & XR600R (83 - 08)	♦ 2183
Honda XL600/650V Transalp & XRV750 Africa Twin (87 to 07)	♦ 3919
Honda CBR600F1 & 1000F Fours (87 - 96)	♦ 1730
Honda CBR600F2 & F3 Fours (91 - 98)	♦ 2070
Honda CBR600F4 (99 - 06)	♦ 3911
Honda CB600F Hornet & CBF600 (98 - 06)	◊ ♦ 3915
Honda CBR600RR (03 - 06)	♦ 4590
Honda CB650 sohc Fours (78 - 84)	0665
Honda NTV600 Revere, NTV650 and NT650V Deauville (88 - 05)	◊ 3243
Honda Shadow VT600 & 750 (USA) (88 - 03)	2312
Honda CB750 sohc Four (69 - 79)	0131
Honda V45/65 Sabre & Magna (82 - 88)	0820
Honda VFR750 & 700 V-Fours (86 - 97)	♦ 2101
Honda VFR800 V-Fours (97 - 01)	♦ 3703
Honda VFR800 V-Tec V-Fours (02 - 05)	♦ 4196
Honda CB750 & CB900 dohc Fours (78 - 84)	0535
Honda VTR1000 (FireStorm, Super Hawk) & XL1000V (Varadero) (97 - 08)	♦ 3744
Honda CBR900RR FireBlade (92 - 99)	♦ 2161
Honda CBR900RR FireBlade (00 - 03)	♦ 4060
Honda CBR1000RR Fireblade (04 - 07)	♦ 4604
Honda CBR1100XX Super Blackbird (97 - 07)	♦ 3901
Honda ST1100 Pan European V-Fours (90 - 02)	♦ 3384
Honda Shadow VT1100 (USA) (85 - 98)	2313
Honda GL1000 Gold Wing (75 - 79)	0309

Title	Book No
Honda GL1100 Gold Wing (79 - 81)	0669
Honda Gold Wing 1200 (USA) (84 - 87)	2199
Honda Gold Wing 1500 (USA) (88 - 00)	2225
KAWASAKI AE/AR 50 & 80 (81 - 95)	1007
Kawasaki KC, KE & KH100 (75 - 99)	1371
Kawasaki KMX125 & 200 (86 - 02)	◊ 3046
Kawasaki 250, 350 & 400 Triples (72 - 79)	0134
Kawasaki 400 & 440 Twins (74 - 81)	0281
Kawasaki 400, 500 & 550 Fours (79 - 91)	0910
Kawasaki EN450 & 500 Twins (Ltd/Vulcan) (85 - 07)	2053
Kawasaki EX500 (GPZ500S) & ER500 (ER-5) (87 - 08)	♦ 2052
Kawasaki ZX600 (ZZ-R600 & Ninja ZX-6) (90 - 06)	♦ 2146
Kawasaki ZX-6R Ninja Fours (95 - 02)	♦ 3541
Kawasaki ZX-6R (03 - 06)	♦ 4742
Kawasaki ZX600 (GPZ600R, GPX600R, Ninja 600R & RX) & ZX750 (GPX750R, Ninja 750R)	♦ 1780
Kawasaki 650 Four (76 - 78)	0373
Kawasaki Vulcan 700/750 & 800 (85 - 04)	2457
Kawasaki 750 Air-cooled Fours (80 - 91)	0574
Kawasaki ZR550 & 750 Zephyr Fours (90 - 97)	♦ 3382
Kawasaki Z750 & Z1000 (03 - 08)	♦ 4762
Kawasaki ZX750 (Ninja ZX-7 & ZXR750) Fours (89 - 96)	♦ 2054
Kawasaki Ninja ZX-7R & ZX-9R (94 - 04)	♦ 3721
Kawasaki 900 & 1000 Fours (73 - 77)	0222
Kawasaki ZX900, 1000 & 1100 Liquid-cooled Fours (83 - 97)	♦ 1681
KTM EXC Enduro & SX Motocross (00 - 07)	♦ 4629
MOTO GUZZI 750, 850 & 1000 V-Twins (74 - 78)	0339
MZ ETZ Models (81 - 95)	◊ 1680
NORTON 500, 600, 650 & 750 Twins (57 - 70)	0187
Norton Commando (68 - 77)	0125
PEUGEOT Speedfight, Trekker & Vivacity Scooters (96 - 08)	◊ 3920
PIAGGIO (Vespa) Scooters (91 - 06)	◊ 3492
SUZUKI GT, ZR & TS50 (77 - 90)	0799
Suzuki TS50X (84 - 00)	◊ 1599
Suzuki 100, 125, 185 & 250 Air-cooled Trail bikes (79 - 89)	0797
Suzuki GP100 & 125 Singles (78 - 93)	◊ 0576
Suzuki GS, GN, GZ & DR125 Singles (82 - 05)	◊ 0888
Suzuki 250 & 350 Twins (68 - 78)	0120
Suzuki GT250X7, GT200X5 & SB200 Twins (78 - 83)	◊ 0469
Suzuki GS/GSX250, 400 & 450 Twins (79 - 85)	0736
Suzuki GS500 Twin (89 - 06)	♦ 3238
Suzuki GS550 (77 - 82) & GS750 Fours (76 - 79)	0363
Suzuki GS/GSX550 4-valve Fours (83 - 88)	1133
Suzuki SV650 & SV650S (99 - 08)	♦ 3912
Suzuki GSX-R600 & 750 (96 - 00)	♦ 3553
Suzuki GSX-R600 (01 - 03), GSX-R750 (00 - 03) & GSX-R1000 (01 - 02)	♦ 3986
Suzuki GSX-R600/750 (04 - 05) & GSX-R1000 (03 - 06)	♦ 4382
Suzuki GSF600, 650 & 1200 Bandit Fours (95 - 06)	♦ 3367
Suzuki Intruder, Marauder, Volusia & Boulevard (85 - 06)	♦ 2618
Suzuki GS850 Fours (78 - 88)	0536
Suzuki GS1000 Four (77 - 79)	0484
Suzuki GSX-R750, GSX-R1100 (85 - 92), GSX600F, GSX750F, GSX1100F (Katana) Fours	♦ 2055
Suzuki GSX600/750F & GSX750 (98 - 02)	♦ 3987
Suzuki GS/GSX1000, 1100 & 1150 4-valve Fours (79 - 88)	0737
Suzuki TL1000S/R & DL1000 V-Strom (97 - 04)	♦ 4083
Suzuki GSF650/1250 (05 - 09)	♦ 4798
Suzuki GSX1300R Hayabusa (99 - 04)	♦ 4184
Suzuki GSX1400 (02 - 07)	♦ 4758
TRIUMPH Tiger Cub & Terrier (52 - 68)	0414
Triumph 350 & 500 Unit Twins (58 - 73)	0137
Triumph Pre-Unit Twins (47 - 62)	0251
Triumph 650 & 750 2-valve Unit Twins (63 - 83)	0122
Triumph Trident & BSA Rocket 3 (69 - 75)	0136
Triumph Bonneville (01 - 07)	♦ 4364
Triumph Daytona, Speed Triple, Sprint & Tiger (97 - 05)	♦ 3755
Triumph Triples and Fours (carburettor engines) (91 - 04)	♦ 2162
VESPA P/PX125, 150 & 200 Scooters (78 - 06)	0707
Vespa Scooters (59 - 78)	0126
YAMAHA DT50 & 80 Trail Bikes (78 - 95)	◊ 0800
Yamaha T50 & 80 Townmate (83 - 95)	◊ 1247

Title	Book No
Yamaha YB100 Singles (73 - 91)	◊ 0474
Yamaha RS/RXS100 & 125 Singles (74 - 95)	0331
Yamaha RD & DT125LC (82 - 95)	◊ 0887
Yamaha TZR125 (87 - 93) & DT125R (88 - 07)	◊ 1655
Yamaha TY50, 80, 125 & 175 (74 - 84)	◊ 0464
Yamaha XT & SR125 (82 - 03)	◊ 1021
Yamaha YBR125	4797
Yamaha Trail Bikes (81 - 00)	2350
Yamaha 2-stroke Motocross Bikes 1986 - 2006	2662
Yamaha YZ & WR 4-stroke Motocross Bikes (98 - 08)	2689
Yamaha 250 & 350 Twins (70 - 79)	0040
Yamaha XS250, 360 & 400 sohc Twins (75 - 84)	0378
Yamaha RD250 & 350LC Twins (80 - 82)	0803
Yamaha RD350 YPVS Twins (83 - 95)	1158
Yamaha RD400 Twin (75 - 79)	0333
Yamaha XT, TT & SR500 Singles (75 - 83)	0342
Yamaha XZ550 Vision V-Twins (82 - 85)	0821
Yamaha FJ, FZ, XJ & YX600 Radian (84 - 92)	2100
Yamaha XJ600S (Diversion, Seca II) & XJ600N Fours (92 - 03)	♦ 2145
Yamaha YZF600R Thundercat & FZS600 Fazer (96 - 03)	♦ 3702
Yamaha FZ-6 Fazer (04 - 07)	♦ 4751
Yamaha YZF-R6 (99 - 02)	♦ 3900
Yamaha YZF-R6 (03 - 05)	♦ 4601
Yamaha 650 Twins (70 - 83)	0341
Yamaha XJ650 & 750 Fours (80 - 84)	0738
Yamaha XS750 & 850 Triples (76 - 85)	0340
Yamaha TDM850, TRX850 & XTZ750 (89 - 99)	◊ ♦ 3540
Yamaha YZF750R & YZF1000R Thunderace (93 - 00)	♦ 3720
Yamaha FZR600, 750 & 1000 Fours (87 - 96)	♦ 2056
Yamaha XV (Virago) V-Twins (81 - 03)	♦ 0802
Yamaha XVS650 & 1100 Drag Star/V-Star (97 - 05)	♦ 4195
Yamaha XJ900F Fours (83 - 94)	♦ 3239
Yamaha XJ900S Diversion (94 - 01)	♦ 3739
Yamaha YZF-R1 (98 - 03)	♦ 3754
Yamaha YZF-R1 (04 - 06)	♦ 4605
Yamaha FZS1000 Fazer (01 - 05)	♦ 4287
Yamaha FJ1100 & 1200 Fours (84 - 96)	♦ 2057
Yamaha XJR1200 & 1300 (95 - 06)	♦ 3981
Yamaha V-Max (85 - 03)	♦ 4072

ATVs

Title	Book No
Honda ATC70, 90, 110, 185 & 200 (71 - 85)	0565
Honda Rancher, Recon & TRX250EX ATVs	2553
Honda TRX300 Shaft Drive ATVs (88 - 00)	2125
Honda Foreman (95 - 07)	2465
Honda TRX300EX, TRX400EX & TRX450R/ER ATVs (93 - 06)	2318
Kawasaki Bayou 220/250/300 & Prairie 300 ATVs (86 - 03)	2351
Polaris ATVs (85 - 97)	2302
Polaris ATVs (98 - 06)	2508
Yamaha YFS200 Blaster ATV (88 - 06)	2317
Yamaha YFB250 Timberwolf ATVs (92 - 00)	2217
Yamaha YFM350 & YFM400 (ER and Big Bear) ATVs (87 - 03)	2126
Yamaha Banshee and Warrior ATVs (87 - 03)	2314
Yamaha Kodiak and Grizzly ATVs (93 - 05)	2567
ATV Basics	10450

TECHBOOK SERIES

Title	Book No
Twist and Go (automatic transmission) Scooters Service and Repair Manual	4082
Motorcycle Basics TechBook (2nd Edition)	3515
Motorcycle Electrical TechBook (3rd Edition)	3471
Motorcycle Fuel Systems TechBook	3514
Motorcycle Maintenance TechBook	4071
Motorcycle Modifying	4272
Motorcycle Workshop Practice TechBook (2nd Edition)	3470

◊ = not available in the USA   ♦ = Superbike

The manuals on this page are available through good motorcycle dealers and accessory shops.
In case of difficulty, contact: **Haynes Publishing**
(UK) **+44 1963 442030**   (USA) **+1 805 498 6703**
(SV) **+46 18 124016**
(Australia/New Zealand) **+61 3 9763 8100**

MCL24.08/09

Preserving Our Motoring Heritage

<
The Model J Duesenberg
Derham Tourster.
Only eight of these
magnificent cars were
ever built – this is the
only example to be found
outside the United States
of America

Almost every car you've ever loved, loathed or desired is gathered under one roof at the Haynes Motor Museum. Over 300 immaculately presented cars and motorbikes represent every aspect of our motoring heritage, from elegant reminders of bygone days, such as the superb Model J Duesenberg to curiosities like the bug-eyed BMW Isetta. There are also many old friends and flames. Perhaps you remember the 1959 Ford Popular that you did your courting in? The magnificent 'Red Collection' is a spectacle of classic sports cars including AC, Alfa Romeo, Austin Healey, Ferrari, Lamborghini, Maserati, MG, Riley, Porsche and Triumph.

A Perfect Day Out

Each and every vehicle at the Haynes Motor Museum has played its part in the history and culture of Motoring. Today, they make a wonderful spectacle and a great day out for all the family. Bring the kids, bring Mum and Dad, but above all bring your camera to capture those golden memories for ever. You will also find an impressive array of motoring memorabilia, a comfortable 70 seat video cinema and one of the most extensive transport book shops in Britain. The Pit Stop Cafe serves everything from a cup of tea to wholesome, home-made meals or, if you prefer, you can enjoy the large picnic area nestled in the beautiful rural surroundings of Somerset.

John Haynes O.B.E.,
Founder and
Chairman of the
museum at the wheel
of a Haynes Light 12.

>

<
The 1936 490cc
sohc-engined
International
Norton – well known
for its racing success

The Museum is situated on the A359 Yeovil to Frome road at Sparkford, just off the A303 in Somerset. It is about 40 miles south of Bristol, and 25 minutes drive from the M5 intersection at Taunton.
Open 9.30am - 5.30pm (10.00am - 4.00pm Winter) 7 days a week, *except Christmas Day, Boxing Day and New Years Day*
Special rates available for schools, coach parties and outings Charitable Trust No. 292048